A VIETNAM PRESENCE:

MENNONITES IN VIETNAM
DURING THE AMERICAN WAR

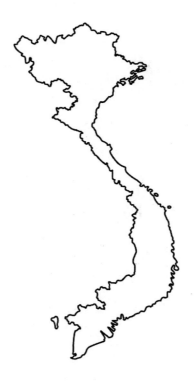

Luke S. Martin

A VIETNAM PRESENCE:
MENNONITES IN VIETNAM DURING THE AMERICAN WAR

by Luke S. Martin

Library of Congress Number: 2016914162
International Standard Book Number: 978-1-60126-509-8

Masthof Press
219 Mill Road
Morgantown, PA 19543-9516
www.masthof.com

DEDICATION

In recognition of my father, Daniel Hoover Martin,
who modeled a life of Christian integrity.

Blessed are the peacemakers,
for they will be called children of God.

-JESUS

TABLE OF CONTENTS

Foreword vii

Preface viii

Further Introduction x

AVP Maps for Vietnam xi

Acronyms xiv

BOOK ONE
Engagement, 1954-1963

CHAPTER 1 | Missionaries Arrive..3

CHAPTER 2 | Mennonite Entry Into Vietnam..6

CHAPTER 3 | MCC Looks for a Niche..15

CHAPTER 4 | Vision and Role of Orie O. Miller..24

CHAPTER 5 | Religious Milieu in Vietnam...31

CHAPTER 6 | Medical Program at Ban Me Thuot 34

CHAPTER 7 | Other Developments 1956-1959...41

CHAPTER 8 | Material Aid..50

CHAPTER 9 | MCC Student Activities..56

CHAPTER 10 | The Missionaries' First Six Months...62

CHAPTER 11 | Getting a Feel for Vietnam 70

CHAPTER 12 | Preparation for Ministry 78

CHAPTER 13 | Month of Decision—June 1959...84

CHAPTER 14 | Beginning the Mission Witness...93

CHAPTER 15 | MCC Works with the Evangelical Church 105

CHAPTER 16 | Incident at Ban Me Thuot 113

CHAPTER 17 | Turbulence 1963 128

BOOK TWO
Partnership, 1964-1970

CHAPTER 18 | US Expands Military Actions 1964 142

CHAPTER 19 | New Programs..154

CHAPTER 20 | Church Growth..165

CHAPTER 21 | MCC Responds to Widening War...187

CHAPTER 22 | Public Statements Against the War 197

CHAPTER 23 | VNCS Era Begins 1966..205

CHAPTER 24 | Witness in Time of Political Uncertainty 224

CHAPTER 25 | VNCS Caring Amid Challenges and Controversy 242

CHAPTER 26 | VNCS 1967—A Pivotal Year 252

CHAPTER 27 | Work and Witness While the War Grinds On 280

CHAPTER 28 | Tet Mau Than 1968 307

CHAPTER 29 | Post-Tet Developments 335

CHAPTER 30 | Post Hostilities Planning 349

CHAPTER 31 | Vietnamization Tested..372

BOOK THREE
Transition, 1971-1975

CHAPTER 32 | Elusive Peace 390

CHAPTER 33 | Transitions 416

CHAPTER 34 | New Direction 1973 442

CHAPTER 35 | Peace and Reconciliation 461

CHAPTER 36 | The Revolution Succeeds..486

CHAPTER 37 | A New Day 517

Afterword...538

Brief Vietnam Time Line..544

Glossary of Vietnamese Words 545

Persons Who Served with Mennonite Central Committee 549

Persons Who Served with Eastern Mennonite Board of
  Missions & Charities..552

VNCS Expatriate Personnel 1966-1975 553

Annotated Bibliography of Further Readings 555

Photo Credits..559

Index...564

FOREWORD

During the 1960s and 1970s the small Southeast Asian country of Vietnam was the focal point of much world-wide attention. Locally the struggle involved the principal world powers of Asia, Europe and North America, particularly the United States and its allies and the Soviet Union and its allies.

In the midst of the struggle on the ground in South Vietnam there was a small North American Christian group representing the Eastern Mennonite Board of Missions and Charities (now Eastern Mennonite Missions) who dared to establish a Vietnamese Mennonite Church. Living through violent conflict and its aftermath, the church has today become a network of thriving congregations.

This volume records this remarkable story of a developing church. Although billed as a memoir, *A Vietnam Presence* is also a reliable history. It also includes an account of the work of a partner service group, the Mennonite Central Committee (MCC). The earlier established MCC provided an entrée for the launching of a mission program.

The author of this significant study story lived most of this story. He provides us with a wise, trustworthy and understated account. Luke Martin read widely in letters, diaries, reports, and published material while writing and digging deeply into his own memory as well as that of his colleagues. He hopes this work will encourage further exploration of Christian witness and service, especially by Vietnamese writers and others who examine such topics as relationships with other Protestant and Roman Catholic churches as well as Buddhist and other local religions.

Readers will be inspired by this contemporary mission story. They will discover the profound commitments of missionaries, how they engaged Vietnamese people, and communicated the realities of living in a war zone to their North American friends and sponsors. None caught their significance for the world-wide Christian movement better than William T. Snyder, then Executive Secretary of Mennonite Central Committee. In 1968 he observed that "there were no clearer peace positions being taken by Mennonites at home and abroad than that made by this small group of Eastern Mennonite Board of Missions people."

Indeed there are few mission stories that provide such graphic detail on living through a war that ended in the transition to the new revolutionary government. This volume is a reminder to not forget the past but to also pray for the growing Christian movement in Vietnam.

-John A. Lapp,
Executive Secretary Emeritus of Mennonite Central Committee,
co-editor of the Mennonite World Conference *Global Mennonite History* series

PREFACE

For many years I considered sketching the work of the Eastern Mennonite Board of Missions and Charities (EMBMC) in Vietnam. After coordinating a study in the late seventies on the Vietnam ministries of EMBMC, Mennonite Central Committee (MCC), and the MCC Peace Section from 1954 to 1975, friends suggested I prepare a readable story for the general public. There were other things to do at that time. However, after the release of James Klassen's book about his MCC experiences, *Jimshoes in Vietnam,* an MCC colleague sent me the following note:

"I hope someone writes about the history of the Mennonite mission in Viet Nam as well. I think there is much there which we all need to remember. Much work was done in a very difficult situation, and the story should be an encouragement to young people who need to be pushed a little in the direction of service. Luke, why don't you write a book?"

Rather than toss that note in the wastebasket, I posted it on my bulletin board, and kept it for a few decades while I gave priority to other things.

Around 2006 I interviewed James Stauffer and wrote the story of his and Arlene's going to Vietnam. Only after I terminated my employment was I able to seriously research the Vietnam story in the archives of Eastern Mennonite Missions. When I invited historian John A. Lapp to critique my writing, he said I should also tell the Mennonite Central Committee story. I hesitated because of the enormity of the task, yet soon realized that I could not tell the EMBMC story without telling some of the preceding MCC story for MCC was involved in Vietnam three years before the first Mennonite missionaries arrived. This meant spending considerable time in the MCC files. Still, my primary interest is to tell the story of the missionaries in their attempts to share the gospel and establish a church.

Besides the archival records, I had access to personal letters sent from Vietnam to my parents along with a monthly newsletter prepared by the missionaries. Personal letters from James Stauffer, James Metzler, Paul and Esther Bucher, and journal entries from Paul Bucher and Margaret Metzler were very helpful. Stauffer's letters from 1957 to 1975 were particularly important. Paul Longacre who served with MCC also helpfully provided letters. I viewed official mission board minutes at the Lancaster Mennonite Historical Society as well as prayer letters and feature articles.

Most of the Mennonite personnel who served in Vietnam are still with us today, so I had the opportunity to corroborate certain bits of information. However, I have chosen to rely primarily on written records—not interviews—believing that from these we can get a more reliable sense of the setting in which we worked a half-century ago. Regrettably I have not been able to read all the reports, personal letters and diaries of those who served with EMBMC and MCC.

I did not set out to write a definitive history of Mennonite missions in Vietnam. I wanted to focus more specifically on how Mennonite personnel in Vietnam carried out their ministries within the context of the American War. Mennonite missionaries, heirs of the Anabaptist Christians committed to a biblical pacifism, viewed the Vietnam landscape quite differently from many other American Christians in Vietnam. While we held an aversion to standard communist political structures, we could not view "the other side" as the enemy.

Who is my audience? Our children and the coming generation; I want our children to understand why we went to Vietnam, what we did and why we did it. I am writing for historians and missiologists; I want them to reflect on and critique the validity of what we did in Vietnam. I also want those who served with the American armed forces to read this story. Given the strong emotions generated by the Vietnam conflict, this story has ongoing relevance especially now when we are remembering events of fifty years ago.

My intention was to tell the story in an academic format that would satisfy the needs of those who want to probe deeper. However my editor, Glenn Knight, convinced me that it must be written as a memoir. At the same time the Mennonite story in Vietnam began—after the signing of the Geneva Accords—I was beginning a life-transforming international experience in post-war Europe with the Mennonite Central Committee. Besides the invaluable insight and guidance of my editor, I want to acknowledge the helpful critique and encouragement of my Vietnam colleague Donald Sensenig and of John A. Lapp, MCC Executive Secretary Emeritus. Rachel Metzler, my son Steven Martin, and my wife Mary Kauffman Martin proofread the manuscript. I thank Mary for her patience and support through this entire undertaking.

As I began writing, concerned that the resulting manuscript might be too voluminous, I asked an editor friend how long a book should be. "The subject will tell you how long the book should be," she replied. A few of my Vietnamese friends who have difficulty distinguishing when to use *very* or *too* would say, "Your book is *too* long!" Rather than shortening the work or publishing multiple volumes, I chose to divide the work into three *books*. While the story is continuous, some readers may want to read the story as three separate volumes. Readers who want to research this story further will find information about sources and notes at the end of this book.

I title the first book *Engagement*, the story of how American Mennonites went to Vietnam and became involved with the Vietnamese peoples, both the dominant ethnic *Kinh* and the minority ethnic people in the Central Highlands of Vietnam around Ban Me Thuot. This was also the time when the United States of America chose to become deeply involved in the political and military life of southern Vietnam.

The second book, *Partnership,* describes the era when the United States made a fateful choice to pursue its objectives militarily and blundered into an inferno from which deliverance seemed impossible. During this time Mennonite missionaries and MCC personnel worked closely with the people of Vietnam and the community Mennonite church took shape.

The third book is the story of *Transition* when the Mennonite Mission encouraged the maturing church to greater independence. This was the era when the United States sought to extricate its military forces from Vietnam while continuing to exercise political influence. This period ended in a radical change with the triumph of the revolutionary forces.

Storytellers do not live in a vacuum. I have chosen to tell the story from the perspective of a Christian living within a community committed to the way of peace when the society around us was being torn about by conflicting loyalties. Rather than trying to ignore these realities, we chose rather to live within this struggle. Readers will easily identify a whole range of issues, problems and questions that we encountered in Vietnam which can become grist for discussion groups. Even though the Vietnam era had its special characteristics, many observations and learnings can be immensely useful in reflecting on our own time in the early twenty-first century. The heart of the story I tell is the experience of American Mennonites seeking to live out Jesus Christ's gospel of peace in Vietnam when the United States of America engaged in a military conflict in which three million Vietnamese were killed.

-L.S.M.
October 2016

FURTHER INTRODUCTION

A few explanations should be given about terms. I am not fully consistent in the spelling of names. Although Vietnamese is a monosyllabic language, I use *Vietnam* rather than *Viet Nam*. But I have chosen to use *Ban Me Thuot* rather than *Banmethuot*. Today maps show it as *Buon Ma Thuot*. One of the larger minority ethnic groups is the Rhade people. There are various ways this is written: *Raday, E-de, Ra-de* and several other ways. *Saigon* is occasionally written as *Sai Gon,* but even Vietnamese generally write this as one word.

When writing Vietnamese names, the family name comes first, and the given name last, as in Nguyen Van Hai. But he is referred to as Mr. Hai, not Mr. Nguyen. Readers will recognize a duplication of names among the missionaries; there were two *Metzler* families, two *Jameses* and two *Lukes.* Although today's name of the mission agency is *Eastern Mennonite Missions,* I use *Eastern Mennonite Board of Missions and Charities, (EMBMC),* the name used before 1993.

Written Vietnamese has tonal markings which are used sparingly in this book. Interested persons can find the tonal and vowel markings for the Vietnamese names and words used in the Glossary. Readers should note that there are two *d*s in the Vietnamese alphabet—the *Đ/đ* which is similar to the English *d,* and the *D/d* which, along with *Gi/gi,* has the *ze* sound in the northern accent and the *ye* sound in the south. Thus the name *Dung* is pronounced *zoom* or *yoom.*

VIETNAM TODAY

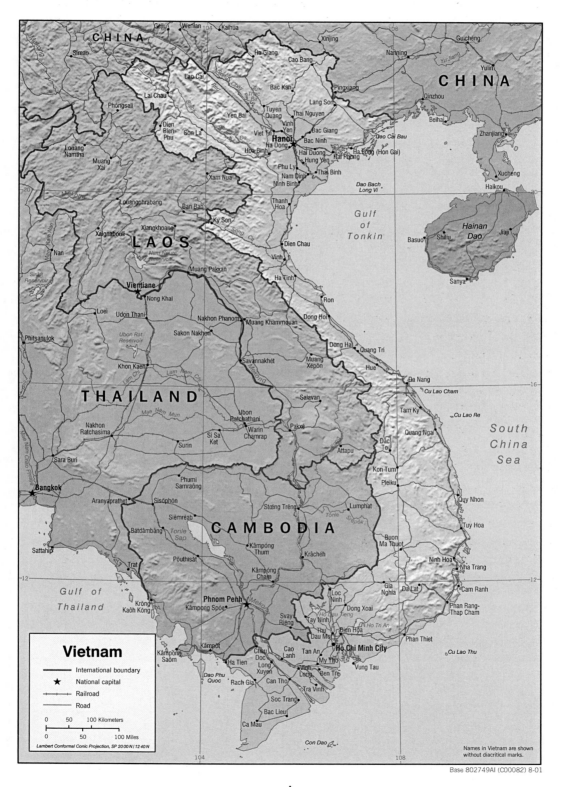

Names in Vietnam are shown without diacritical marks.

Base 802749AI (C00082) 8-01

MCC (VNCS) AND EMBMC PERSONNEL
PLACEMENTS IN REPUBLIC OF VIETNAM

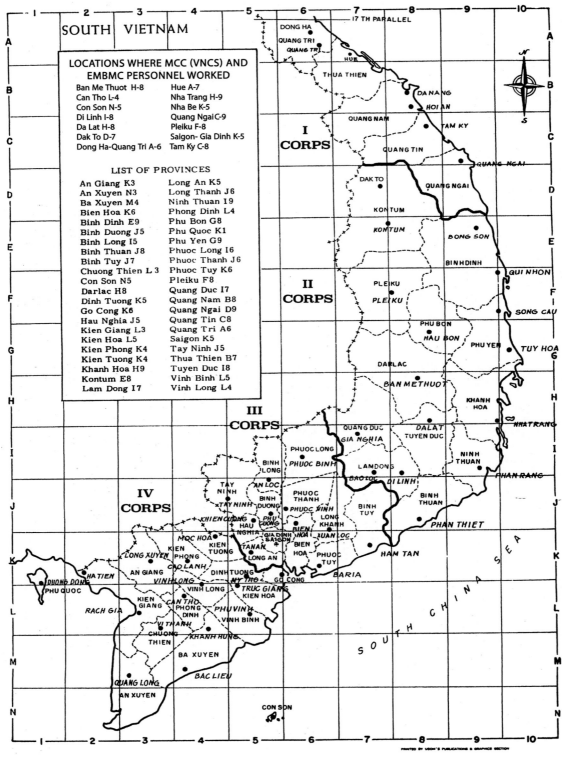

SOUTH VIETNAM

LOCATIONS WHERE MCC (VNCS) AND EMBMC PERSONNEL WORKED

Ban Me Thuot H-8	Hue A-7
Can Tho L-4	Nha Trang H-9
Con Son N-5	Nha Be K-5
Di Linh I-8	Quang Ngai C-9
Da Lat H-8	Pleiku F-8
Dak To D-7	Saigon- Gia Dinh K-5
Dong Ha-Quang Tri A-6	Tam Ky C-8

LIST OF PROVINCES

An Giang K3	Long An K5
An Xuyen N3	Long Thanh J6
Ba Xuyen M4	Ninh Thuan I9
Bien Hoa K6	Phong Dinh L4
Binh Dinh E9	Phu Bon G8
Binh Duong J5	Phu Quoc K1
Binh Long I5	Phu Yen G9
Binh Thuan J8	Phuoc Long I6
Binh Tuy J7	Phuoc Thanh J6
Chuong Thien L 3	Phuoc Tuy K6
Con Son N5	Pleiku F8
Darlac H8	Quang Duc I7
Dinh Tuong K5	Quang Nam B8
Go Cong K6	Quang Ngai D9
Hau Nghia J5	Quang Tin C8
Kien Giang L3	Quang Tri A6
Kien Hoa L5	Saigon K5
Kien Phong K4	Tay Ninh J5
Kien Tuong K4	Thua Thien B7
Khanh Hoa H9	Tuyen Duc I8
Kontum E8	Vinh Binh L5
Lam Dong I7	Vinh Long L4

SAIGON – GIA DINH AREA

M = Market

ACRONYMS

AFSC	American Friends Service Committee
ALM	American Leprosy Mission
ARVN	Army of the Republic of Vietnam (South)
ACS	Asian Christian Service
CIA	Central Intelligence Agency (United States)
C&MA	Christian & Missionary Alliance
CVA	Council of Voluntary Agencies
CWS	Church World Service
COR	Committee of Responsibility
CORDS	Civil Operations & Revolutionary Development Support
CRS	Catholic Relief Services
CYSS	Christian Youth for Social Service
DMZ	Demilitarized Zone
DRV	Democratic Republic of Vietnam (North)
EACC	East Asia Christian Council
EAP	MCC Educational Assistance Program
ECVN	Evangelical Church of Vietnam
EMBMC	Eastern Mennonite Board of Missions and Charities
EMC	Eastern Mennonite College (University)
FCA	MCC Family Child Assistance Program
FOA	Foreign Operations Administration
FOR	Fellowship of Reconciliation
GOV	Government of Vietnam (South)
IPC	International Protestant Church
IRC	International Rescue Committee
IVS	International Voluntary Services
JAC	Joint Administrative Council (Mission and Church)
JUSPAO	Joint United States Public Affairs Office
LWR	Lutheran World Relief
MAAG	Military Advisory Assistance Group (United States)
MAC-V	Military Assistance Command, Vietnam (United States)
MBMC	Mennonite Board of Missions and Charities
MCC	Mennonite Central Committee
MEDA	Mennonite Economic Development Associates
MILPHAP	Military Provincial Health Assistance Program
NAE	National Association of Evangelicals (United States)
NVN	North Vietnam
NLF	National Liberation Front
NGO	Non-governmental Organization

OCO	Office of Civil Operations (United States)
PAVN	People's Army of Vietnam (North Vietnam)
PMSI	South Indochinese Mountainous Country
PRG	Provisional Revolutionary Government
RVN	Republic of Vietnam (South)
SBC	Southern Baptist Convention
SIL	Summer Institute of Linguistics
STEM	Special Technical and Economic Mission (US)
UBCV	United Buddhist Church of Vietnam
USAID	United States Agency for International Assistance
USOM	United States Operations Mission
UXO	Unexploded Ordnance
VMM	Vietnam Mennonite Mission
VNCS	Vietnam Christian Service
WEC	Worldwide Evangelization Crusade
WRC	World Relief Commission
WCC	World Council of Churches
YMCA	Young Men's Christian Association
YSS	(Buddhist) Youth for Social Service

BOOK ONE

ENGAGEMENT
1954-1963

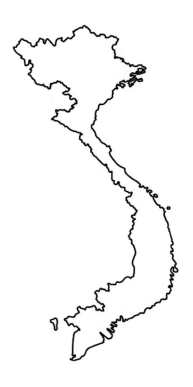

MISSIONARIES ARRIVE

Chapter 1

The French freighter SS *Sindh* waited in the Saigon River downstream from the "Pearl of the Orient" until high tide so the ship could navigate above the rocky shelf to dock at the Saigon waterfront. Arlene and James Stauffer were anxious to begin their new life in Saigon, a sprawling city with around three million people.

Their journey across the Pacific Ocean on the SS *Mandeville* to Manila and Hong Kong took several weeks. But they had actually begun their journey to Vietnam several years before.

James grew up in the Shenandoah Valley of Virginia, the son of Mennonite bishop J. L. Stauffer who served fifteen years as president of Eastern Mennonite College (EMC, now Eastern Mennonite University), Harrisonburg, Virginia. James graduated from EMC in the spring of 1953 when he and Arlene Krupp, an EMC student from Souderton, Pennsylvania, announced their engagement. Arlene had already experienced a call to missionary service at the age of fourteen.

A year earlier Arlene and James both attended what was called the Brunk Revivals, an evangelistic and spiritual renewal ministry led by George R. Brunk, Jr., and his brother Lawrence. After hearing a stirring sermon under the canvas tent, both Arlene and James went forward together to receive the promise of the presence and power of God's Holy Spirit received through faith. James described this as a turning point in his spiritual pilgrimage.

After World War II ended in 1945, there was a blossoming of interest in missionary work within Mennonite churches. Most of their young men drafted during the war registered as conscientious objectors to war and were assigned to civilian service far from home. This nudged many Mennonites from their insular communities and enabled them to see opportunities to share the gospel message of Jesus Christ in new areas, both nationally and internationally. The war had stimulated the American economy, and churches now had additional finances to implement this mission vision.

In 1948 the United States became embroiled in a military conflict on the Korean Peninsula. With Mennonite young men continuing to be drafted, the church encouraged both women and men to enter Christian voluntary service, and hundreds of youth gave up to two years or more to various ministries in the United States and overseas.

EMC fostered students' involvement in local mission opportunities and preparation for longer term missions. While a student, James served as assistant to the pastor of a newly established congregation in Harrisonburg. After graduation he accepted an invitation to pastor the Sonnenberg Mennonite Church in Kidron, Ohio, and was ordained in November 1953.

The following June, Arlene and James married and moved to Apple Creek, Ohio. That summer they attended a missionary conference at Laurelville Mennonite Church in western Pennsylvania featuring J. Oswald Smith, the well-known evangelist and pastor of the People's Church in Toronto, Canada. This, James said, was the culmination of their call to missionary service.

Eastern Mennonite Board of Missions and Charities (EMBMC, now Eastern Mennonite Missions), the missionary organization of Lancaster Mennonite Conference in Lancaster, Pennsylvania, was contemplating missionary work in Indonesia and Vietnam. In the fall of 1955 Paul N. Kraybill, the EMBMC assistant secretary, invited James and Arlene to participate in that vision. After months of prayerful consideration, they indicated their willingness to go to Vietnam. In preparation for language study, they took a six-week linguistics course at the Summer Institute of Linguistics in Toronto the summer of 1956.

When the Stauffers wrote to Delbert Wiens, the Mennonite Central Committee (MCC) representative in Saigon, asking how to prepare for their Vietnam assignment, Wiens said it was most important to bring "an open mind."

"Especially difficult for Mennonite missionaries will be the nationalism here," Wiens wrote. "Any hint of even suspected non-conformism here is immediately checked. Anything less than unswerving devotion to the full party line is immediately labeled 'pro-communism.'"

Referring to the "one Protestant church," Wiens continued, "The local church has already had a good deal of trouble with having been charged as being pro-communist. I think that you are going to have trouble getting the visa. I have evidence that the government does not want missionaries to come, but doesn't know how to refuse because of all the American Aid that comes here." Yet Wiens concluded, "I suppose you will be able to get your visa to come. And then you can work things out."

Wiens wondered whether he would ever see Mennonite missionaries in Vietnam. When meeting earlier with South Vietnam's President Ngo Dinh Diem to request permission to do medical work, the president quizzed Wiens about the Mennonites. Wiens noted that Mennonites were non-resistant pacifists who eschewed military service. Wiens sensed that the president did not appreciate this stance, and feared Mennonites might be considered *persona non grata* in Vietnam.

The Stauffers were appointed for missionary service at the EMBMC bimonthly board meeting September 11. At the November board meeting at the Hammer Creek Mennonite Church near Lititz, Pennsylvania, James spoke about the "open doors" in Southeast Asia. In the next few months he and Arlene visited many congregations sharing their vision for missionary work. While they tried to learn about the country, at that time there were few English language materials about Vietnam or its people. Arlene and James left the United States by ship from San Francisco on April 22, 1957.

The March 1957 issue of *Missionary Messenger*, EMBMC's monthly magazine, printed an article James had written, "The Challenge of Viet-Nam." He said Southeast Asia was a "battle-ground" between the various forces of nationalism, communism and Christianity. Noting that South Vietnam might still come under communist political control, he wrote: "We thank the Lord that one little country . . . has withstood the siege of communism and today is a free democratic nation open to the Gospel." However, the real reason for going to Vietnam was "not simply to defend Christianity against communism," James wrote, but because "the love of Christ constrains us."

Saigon was embroiled in its typical heat and humidity as the ship docked in downtown Saigon on Thursday afternoon, May 30, 1957. Wiens and Carl Hurst, MCC material aid worker, met the Stauffers at the dock, and took them to the MCC house in the northern Saigon suburb of Phu Nhuan.

Within a week of their arrival, Wiens introduced James and Arlene to D. Ivory Jeffrey and Jack Revelle, missionary field administrators for the Christian and Missionary Alliance (C&MA).

In his June 5 letter to Kraybill and Orie O. Miller, EMBMC secretary, James indicated a special liking for Jeffrey and wrote, "I don't think that we will have any difficulty working with them."

Miller wanted to combine evangelism with educational and service ministries. Articulating Miller's vision, the Stauffers told the C&MA administrators about Mennonite interest in establishing schools. James reported that the missionaries would like to see a Christian high school. "Their other main concern was that we would establish an indigenous local church," financially self-supporting. "This, of course, is our conviction and aim," James wrote.

By the end of June, James and Arlene had begun studying the Vietnamese language—ten hours of instruction weekly. Their teacher was Dao Van Hoa, a twenty-three-year-old Christian man from the Evangelical Church of Vietnam (ECVN) whose brother was a pastor in central Vietnam.

In a late August letter to the Salunga, Pennsylvania, EMBMC headquarters, James said he and Arlene had an opportunity to travel to Da Lat and Nha Trang where they met other Alliance missionaries. He reported that D. I. and Ruth Goforth Jeffrey had invited Arlene and him "to take charge of an evangelistic service" each Tuesday evening at a new youth center the Jeffreys had opened.

In early November, James wrote to Kraybill: "Arlene and I are both well and happy in our work here." They and some MCC personnel had just returned home from the annual ECVN conference where the Evangelical Church expressed a desire to open a medical clinic and asked MCC to staff the clinic with a doctor and nurses.

The Stauffer couple had just learned that Everett and Margaret Metzler left New York October 19 by ship to France; from Marseilles they would board the SS *Cambodge* which was scheduled to arrive in Saigon on November 18.

MENNONITE ENTRY INTO VIETNAM

Chapter 2

Nearly three years before the Mennonite missionaries went to Vietnam, the Mennonite Central Committee (MCC) entered Vietnam with its mission to assist needy persons "in the name of Christ."

The Mennonite Central Committee was formed in July 1920 as a cooperative program among three North American denominations—the Mennonite Church, the General Conference Mennonite Church, and the Mennonite Brethren Church—to give famine relief aid in Russia. MCC worked with the American Relief Administration, administered by Herbert Hoover, which had received an appropriation from the U.S. Congress. From 1920 to 1923 MCC contributed over $1,250,000 in food, clothing and medical supplies plus twenty-five tractor and plow outfits.

During the thirties the Mennonite Central Committee assisted thousands of refugees from the Russian revolution to resettle in North, Central and South America. MCC came of age during and following World War II with extensive relief programs in Western Europe. During the forties MCC administered smaller programs in Paraguay, the Middle East, China, and Indonesia. In addition to the three larger North American groups mentioned above, other smaller Mennonite, Amish and Brethren in Christ groups in Canada and the United States worked together under its motto, "In the Name of Christ." Later MCC became involved in relief and self-help projects in Taiwan (1948) and South Korea (1950).

Vietnam came into greater American consciousness during the waning years of the French colonial presence in Indochina. Vietnam was invaded and occupied by Japan in 1940. After the Japanese surrender to Allied forces, Ho Chi Minh on September 2, 1945, declared independence from France and the formation of the Democratic Republic of Vietnam (DRV). China and the Soviet Union recognized the DRV. France's refusal to cede control of its colonies led to the French Indochina War. The United States, while advocating independence to former colonies, agreed in May 1950 to support France in Indochina in exchange for French support of U.S. European policies. In August President Harry S. Truman sent a U.S. Military Assistance Advisory Group (MAAG) of thirty-five men to Vietnam. After Dwight D. Eisenhower was inaugurated president in 1953, his Secretary of State, John Foster Dulles, ignored France's colonial legacy and increased military aid in what he saw as a "free world" fight against an international Communism.

In March 1950 the MCC Executive Committee met with representatives of Mennonite mission agencies to discuss ministry coordination "in light of the developing world situation since World War II." Ernest E. Miller, Orie Miller's brother, on leave as president of Goshen College in Indiana, was appointed as Far-East Area Commissioner-Director from mid-June until mid-August the following year.

Emperor Bao Dai had abdicated to the Viet Minh forces under Ho Chi Minh in August 1945, but the French persuaded the former emperor to return in 1949 as Head of State of the anti-communist faction that controlled the urban areas. Many people fled the countryside for the cities, and Hanoi's mayor in 1950 requested relief assistance. Ernest Miller visited Vietnam in October, first making contact with the Christian and Missionary Alliance (C&MA) missionaries in Saigon, H. Curwen Smith and E. Franklin Irwin. He then traveled to Hanoi and called on the mayor, and met with representatives of the Economic Cooperation Administration (ECA), an American agency formed in 1948 under the Marshall Plan to provide assistance to European countries, including France, and to woo people away from Soviet communist influence. ECA was giving medical assistance in the Hanoi area, and urgently needed more personnel. ECA also proposed constructing housing for refugees.

Due to declining financial contributions, the MCC Executive Committee declined in October 1950 to endorse a proposal to assign a three-member team to Vietnam. Military action in the Hanoi area soon made such a project impossible. However, by year's end MCC considered working in the Saigon area if ECA provided program funds. In early 1951 MCC worked out a plan with the Washington ECA office to send a team of twenty Pax men, young conscientious objectors to war, who would serve in relief work and housing construction two or three years in lieu of military service, but this plan was rejected by the French Indochinese government.

Ernest Miller returned to Saigon in May to review these developments. The ECA staff were supportive, but Indochina officials demurred; an official said it would be difficult "to raise a big Nationalist army with a group of Pacifists operating a relief center!" Miller learned that this position was prompted by French officials who were optimistic about military success and did not want to see such a large group of foreign personnel in Indochina. In contrast, Miller recognized the bankruptcy of French policies; he understood that the Vietnamese people supported the Viet Minh whom he said were "the only leaders tough enough to drive the French out."

The French Indochina War dragged on. Unwilling to recognize a communist state in Southeast Asia, the United States eventually provided French military forces with most of the war materiel, but did not send combat personnel nor fighter bomber support. With the French control slipping, major world powers agreed in early 1954 to hold a conference on Indochina. Shortly after the Far Eastern Conference convened late April in Geneva, the French suffered a humiliating defeat by the Viet Minh forces at Dien Bien Phu, the remote post in northwest Vietnam that France had vowed to hold at all costs. With its collapse the French public support also crumbled—a harbinger of the American experience two decades later.

The Geneva Accords, signed on July 21, 1954, established a provisional military demarcation line at the seventeenth parallel, with the French Union forces in the south and the People's Army of Vietnam in the north. During the time of the regrouping of military forces, civilians residing in either zone were permitted to move to the other zone—even helped if they chose to move. The agreement called for national elections within two years to form an independent united Vietnam. The armed forces were permitted to replace military equipment but not to increase their military capabilities.

Already in early 1954 MCC anticipated a program of relief assistance to Vietnam. William T. Snyder, MCC's assistant executive secretary, was in contact with government officials in Washington, and on June 23 Snyder reported to Orie Miller, MCC's executive secretary, that U.S. officials in Saigon "definitely want voluntary agencies" to help meet anticipated relief needs.

Delbert Wiens had begun work at the MCC headquarters in Akron, Pennsylvania, late 1953—a voluntary service assignment in lieu of military service. Miller soon identified Wiens as an ideal candidate to head up a new venture in Vietnam. A native of Oklahoma who moved with his Mennonite Brethren family to Reedley, California, he had attended Tabor College in Hillsboro, Kansas, two years and graduated from Fresno State College in 1953. Wiens accompanied Miller and Snyder to New York City to meet C&MA mission leaders to elicit their support and cooperation.

The same day the Geneva Accords were signed, U.S. Foreign Operations Administration (FOR) officials assured MCC that voluntary agencies would "be welcome and needed in Vietnam" since it was expected that some residents of North Vietnam would move south. Twenty-three-year-old Wiens was instructed to fly to Vietnam. Orie Miller, on an extensive administrative deputation schedule, had plans to travel to both Hanoi and Saigon on this his first visit to Vietnam. Delayed in Indonesia, he dropped Hanoi from his itinerary. Miller met Wiens at Saigon's airport on August 16 and introduced him to Smith and other C&MA missionaries. The Smiths arranged for Wiens to stay for a time at their home.

When Miller returned to Akron September 5, he reported that a Vietnamese official in Saigon emphasized the importance of MCC involvement, even without large quantities of aid "since Vietnam needs visible signs of foreign interest and concern." Political support was more important than material assistance.

Before leaving Saigon, Miller penned a memorandum outlining his vision for the Vietnam program.

MEMO OF UNDERSTANDING
Vietnam Unit
8/16/54

Orie Miller will recommend and arrange for initial team of four single workers (3 men, 1 woman) for Saigon Refugee and Relief Services, and under Delbert Wiens leadership.

Wiens (with Curwen Smith counsel) will arrange suitable Unit housing and transportation facilities and within STEM and Vietnam Government agencies' suggestion develop a consistently MCC pattern of service—submitting its essence and basic budget requirements by cable or otherwise for approval.

STEM was the Special Technical and Economic Mission which operated under FOA; STEM became United States Operations Mission (USOM) a few months later. FOA eventually became U.S. Agency for International Development.

After leaving Vietnam, Miller cabled the home office proposing that three personnel already in Asia transfer to Vietnam: Mrs. Eva Harshbarger and Adam Ewert from Korea, and Roy Eby from Taiwan. They agreed, and within a few months MCC had a team of four persons in Vietnam.

In early September J. N. Byler, MCC Director of Relief, informed Wiens of the availability of U.S. government surplus food commodities such as powdered milk, butter, and cheese, as well as clothing, canned meat, and wheat from MCC's own sources.

The U.S. government's surplus food had just become available under the Agricultural Trade Development Assistance Act, known as Public Law 480, signed by President Eisenhower in early July. The purpose of the legislation, the President said, was to "lay the basis for a permanent expansion of our exports of agricultural products with lasting benefits to ourselves and peoples of other lands." PL-480 commodities would become a factor in the Vietnamese economy for the next two decades.

Miller's desire to "develop a consistently MCC pattern of service" anticipated providing emergency relief to persons moving from the communist Democratic Republic of Vietnam to the southern State of Vietnam. Considering what MCC was doing in other countries, he likely also envisioned medical and community development programs. Most certainly he could not have foreseen that MCC would continue working in Vietnam into the twenty-first century.

On September 3, two and a half weeks after arriving, Wiens sent his first report to Byler. He described the hordes of people from northern Vietnam flying south or ferried by the French navy to the south seaport of Cape St. Jacques (Vung Tau). Already 200,000 had arrived in what would become more than 900,000 persons. They were "hauled" in army trucks to temporary camps where each refugee was given twelve piasters—the equivalent of thirty-four cents. Wiens reported that ninety percent of these displaced persons were Catholics.

The government in the south was unprepared for this influx of refugees. Ngo Dinh Diem had just returned to Saigon in late June, and assumed the post of Prime Minister on July 7. As an example of the chaos, Wiens noted that the directorship of the government refugee program changed hands several times within the previous two weeks. With the U.S. Foreign Operations Administration providing the local government with money and supplies, the Catholic priests who accompanied their people to the south assumed the responsibility of resettling their people.

Ten days after Wiens' arrival, J. Lawrence Burkholder, a veteran Mennonite relief worker who had earlier served in China with Church World Service (CWS), came to Saigon on a CWS assignment to evaluate relief needs. The two worked together during Burkholder's one-month stay. Wiens was grateful for Burkholder's experienced perspective. Since the American National Catholic Welfare Conference—soon to be called Catholic Relief Services—was making plans to resettle the Catholic communities, Burkholder and Wiens proposed to governmental officials a plan to secure land where some non-Catholic persons could resettle. Wiens and Burkholder also flew to Hanoi, but got no further than the airport, and met no official persons.

Wiens' report must have given gray hairs to Willis F. Detweiler, MCC's Assistant Treasurer. Even though Miller had recommended that Detweiler send Wiens $1,000 U.S., he had only sent $750 because MCC's cash reserves were low. Wiens had to pay an entrance tax of $185 when he entered the country and a similar deposit so he would have funds to leave the country! He had purchased a motorbike. Room and board and transportation were eating up his funds. In his unique humor, Wiens projected program expenses at $1,000,000!

In an "interim report" prepared for Byler September 15, Wiens reported that FOA was "going all out" to assist voluntary agencies, offering them office space. Wiens shared his "immature impression" that some agencies were relying entirely on FOA—"get surplus commodities from the government and ship them at government expense. Store it in a government-provided warehouse, and direct operations from an office provided by our government. And then, in some cases, they even turn it over to the Vietnamese government for distribution. Why not let the government take it over all the way?" he asked. While not opposed to receiving office space nor free shipping, Wiens was grateful that some relief aid came from Mennonite sources "to make it distinctively a Mennonite contribution."

In late September Byler informed Wiens that the Advisory Committee on Voluntary Foreign Aid of the United States Government had signed an agreement with Vietnam's government regarding relief shipments; voluntary agencies needed to work out individual agreements with the Vietnamese government.

The MCC Executive Committee met at the Hotel Atlantic in Chicago on September 23. Present were C. N. Hostetter, Jr., H. A. Fast, Orie O. Miller, J. J. Thiessen, H. S. Bender, William T. Snyder, and P. C. Hiebert. Also in attendance were MCC staff J. N. Byler, Elmer Ediger, Willis Detweiler, and Albert Gaeddert. Orie Miller's "Memo of Understanding" and recommendations were approved "with the provision that the total relief budget not be increased thereby."

Wiens' September 28 report described the refugee resettlement in various parts of the country. He was appalled with the inability of the C&MA and the local Evangelical Church of Vietnam (ECVN) to assist the evangelical Christians who came south. He described the missionaries as friendly, but they "never had the social outlook." He said they feel they have finished their responsibility when people "are saved and have gotten some instruction on how to study the Bible." Wiens frequently recalled that, when visiting the C&MA office in New York before leaving for Vietnam, an administrator had slowly and deliberately said: "We do not engage in institutional work because we have discovered that the cost per soul in institutional work is greater than the cost per soul in direct evangelism."

Although C&MA administrators viewed the ecumenical service agency Church World Service as motivated by "modernist" theological views, Wiens expressed optimism that "having CWS and MCC here will educate them." He was pleased that, with encouragement from C&MA mission chairman Rev. D. Ivory Jeffrey and French Protestant chaplain and pastor, Rev. Bertrand DeLuze, the ECVN pastors had formed a relief committee, something one pastor told Wiens they had wanted to do for twenty years.

One missionary impressed Wiens positively; he described Gordon Smith as enlightened, "the most intelligent missionary that I have seen out here." Still Wiens recognized Smith as "an opportunist" who did not relate well with his mission agency. At a time when C&MA did not even support the establishment of a leprosarium to care for victims of leprosy at Ban Me Thuot, Smith had independently raised funds to do this. Wiens said that Smith was "most anxious" to have MCC come to that area to work among the minority peoples.

After Burkholder returned to the United States, Director of Relief Byler wrote to Wiens: "J. Lawrence Burkholder has informed me of the tendencies of the missionaries in Indo-China. It will be necessary for us as a relief organization to work with them as best we can. We must accept them as they are and try and adapt our own program as best we can."

While the majority Vietnamese population, the ethnic *Kinh*, primarily populated the lower elevations, some fifty different ethnic minority peoples lived in the mountainous highlands. The French colonial government in 1950 formed a political unit in the central highlands from Kontum south to below Ban Me Thuot and east to include Da Lat which was called *Pays Montagnard du Sud* (PMS), the South Mountainous Country, under the authority of Vietnamese Emperor Bao Dai, whom the French installed as nominal chief of state in 1949 as an alternative to Ho Chi Minh's Democratic Republic of Vietnam. There were some thirty different ethnic groups in this area. During the fifties C&MA still maintained two field administrations in Vietnam, each reporting directly to the New York office. The Tribes Mission worked in the PMS area among the ethnic minorities; the Vietnam Mission worked primarily among the Kinh.

Wiens reported that the government was resettling 30,000 to 50,000 refugees in the PMS area, mostly Kinh but some minorities from the north as well. Working in this area seemed attractive to Wiens who saw "unlimited opportunities" for medical work and community development projects.

"By the time we will have seen the end of the immediate need of feeding and putting the people on the land, we will have had time to assess the area and type of work that would best answer the needs of the people," Wiens wrote, suggesting MCC could provide agriculturists, medical personnel and social workers. In a meeting of voluntary agency people, already including Catholic Relief Services (CRS), International Rescue Committee (IRC) and CARE, Wiens proposed that MCC work in the PMS area. STEM's director of Community Development Division supported this.

Earlier Byler telegrammed Wiens that MCC was ready to ship ten tons of light clothing and up to fifty tons of canned meat and government surplus food as soon as Wiens requested it. Now Wiens asked MCC to send canned pork, blankets, cotton and woolen cloth, men's clothing and coats, netting to protect against malarial mosquitoes, and soap. Church World Service was securing agricultural tools and would provide some of these to MCC.

In an early October letter to Detweiler, Wiens suggested that Detweiler's assistant John Lerch persuade MCC to approve the purchase of golf clubs for recreation on a course near Saigon! This precipitated a cautionary reply from Relief Director Byler. Byler was not laughing as he in all seriousness wrote, "As far as I know MCC has as yet not furnished golf equipment for foreign workers. It would be my personal opinion that it would be unwise for MCC to comply with this request. I am quite sure that our constituency would not feel that this is an item of absolute necessity." Amused, Wiens responded to Byler: "Oh, yes, those golf clubs. . . . I meant that as sort of a mild joke for the benefit of John Lerch. I had no intention of using MCC money for them. I wasn't quite sure from your replies whether you took me seriously or not."

Byler informed Wiens that MCC had requested 20,000 gift packages from a U.S. government surplus food commodities program called Operation Reindeer. Each fourteen-pound package contained five pounds of rice, one pound cooking oil, and two pounds each of beans, butter, cheese, and shortening. In his response, Wiens suggested that the dairy items like milk, butter, and cheese should not be sent; these foods made many Vietnamese ill since they were used to a low protein diet. If large amounts of the U.S. surplus dairy products had to be discarded, Wiens wrote cynically, "at least it is a bit of a load off [U.S. Agricultural Secretary Ezra] Benson's shoulders." Wiens suggested that the quantity of rice be increased since five pounds was "too little even to provide a meal for larger families!"

Wiens hoped to soon meet with Mr. Doi, the refugee commissioner, and then travel to Da Lat to choose a distribution center. "I will be glad when we can begin," he wrote. "It is frustrating to wait and lonely to be alone."

Wiens informed Byler that Mr. Doi was asking for large quantities of cooking oil, black cotton cloth, soap, agricultural tools and money. Doi was not enthusiastic about the "Reindeer" packages, especially the butter and cheese. However, since the butter was packed in a metal container, Wiens said the tin itself would be valuable!

The Vietnamese did indeed find ways to use these commodities. In later years many anecdotes circulated about how these smelly dairy products were used, including the story of a farmer who found that cheese worked fine as a lubricant for the wheels of his ox cart!

In the country only two months, Wiens observed that there was "not much chance of outright starvation" among the refugees, and suggested that MCC consider community development projects as MCC was doing in other countries. Looking at Da Lat and Ban Me Thuot as possible places to work, Wiens wrote that it was difficult to develop concrete plans "when I learn one thing one day and unlearn it the next."

After staying two months with the Curwen and Sheila Smith family, Wiens looked for other housing. His interpreter checked hotel rooms which were often booked a month in advance. After checking twenty hotels, the interpreter found only two vacant rooms in such poor hotels that did not even have electricity. He eventually rented a room from a Frenchman, M. Sauvage. Wiens also began studying French, the language spoken by many Vietnamese officials, and hired a Mr. Phan as interpreter.

Wiens was pleased with interagency cooperation. Catholic Relief Services director Monsignor Joseph Harnett coordinated a six-month joint material aid order of surplus American foods for the various agencies.

William Snyder in a late October letter proposed to Wiens a possible placement of ten to twenty young men on a two-year assignment, working with FOA to use heavy equipment to clear land and help construct houses for resettling refugees. MCC was significantly involved in relief and reconstruction in Europe following World War II, and developed the Pax program in 1951 for American conscientious objectors to war required to perform two years of civilian work in lieu of military service. By 1955 more than one hundred men were serving overseas in this program—most of them constructing refugee housing in Germany. Others were involved in agricultural and community development programs in Greece, Algeria and other countries, building roads in Peru and Paraguay, and giving assistance to refugees in Jordan and Korea. Since the men had to solicit funds for their own personal support, fielding a Pax team was not a huge drain on the MCC budget.

Were a Vietnam assignment to materialize, Snyder assumed that MCC would administer the program, but would want FOA to provide the transportation, program support and basic maintenance costs. The STEM officials told Wiens he would first have to get approval from the Vietnamese government; many officials responded well to the proposal. Not everyone was enthusiastic about such a project, however. Wiens in November reported to Snyder that the missionaries were laughing at the idea of American young men coming to Vietnam to build simple straw huts for the displaced persons!

Prime Minister Ngo Dinh Diem was in office just over three months when in mid-September he faced a hostile armed forces chief of staff and a coalition of armed units of two religious sects—Cao Dai and Hoa Hao—and the Binh Xuyen pirate units which controlled the underworld activities in Saigon and the Chinese twin city of Cholon. All were working to oust the Prime Minister.

Wiens mused about how seriously to take all the rumors. In letters to the MCC home office late October, he wrote: "If it seemed likely that the Viet Minh would take over in two years, a program may be set up on a more temporary basis. . . . I think the best thing to do is to ignore politics, but to be realistic enough to do the kind of things which would justify themselves over a two-year span. If the Commies don't take over then, this type of program would probably need little modification to become something of long-range importance."

In early November Wiens had made a three-day trip to central Vietnam, from Quang Tri—just south of the seventeenth parallel demarcation line—south through Hue and Da Nang to Hoi An; he observed that the immediate needs of these refugees were already being met. "The officials are spending money like salesmen on an unlimited expense account," he wrote. "Nor is it used wisely. But things are being done.

Delbert Wiens waiting for ferry to cross a river.

Settlements are under construction for most of the people and several thousand are already self-sufficient enough to be taken off the subsistence allowance."

In mid-November President Eisenhower dispatched to Saigon General J. Lawton Collins, the former Army Chief of Staff, amid concerns that Diem's government would collapse. Given the rank of ambassador, Gen. Collins began coordinating and directing U.S. activities in Vietnam. The Special Technical and Economic Mission (STEM) now became the United States Operations Mission (USOM), representing greater American commitment to South Vietnam. "The political situation does not seem to be improving," Wiens wrote Akron on November 25. "Almost everyone is pessimistic," not expecting the Diem government to survive six months.

Although Catholic institutions were already active in Da Lat, CARE and Catholic Relief Services agreed that MCC could also distribute relief supplies there, so Wiens made arrangements with the government's social welfare regional director. Adam Ewert arrived in early November from Korea, and Roy Eby from Taiwan a week or so later, followed by Eva Harshbarger.

CRS had already received shipments of powdered milk. The agency requested 2,400 tons of supplies per month—milk, cheese, butter, cooking oil and flour—to feed 300,000 families. The United Nations Children's Fund (UNICEF) and the Australian Red Cross had brought in cloth and soap. With MCC's first shipment of supplies soon to arrive, Wiens asked Mr. Doi for a jeep and trailer for transportation, but the refugee chief complained that even he did not have sufficient transportation.

With transportation a serious problem, newly-arrived Ewert in his first activity report said they "remain alert for some good horses to rustle some dark night!" Considering how they might distribute 20,000 "Reindeer" packages that MCC had requested, Eby figured it would require 5,000 trips by motorcycle to deliver them to the refugees!

Eby in his November report described his transfer from Taiwan: "Hongkong was a pleasant experience with the milkshakes, cokes, hamburgers & anything else one could want to buy; all that and with the citizens speaking English. . . . Then came Saigon and again I couldn't read or understand a word, not knowing French or Vietnamese. But that problem has become almost nil. Armed with an English-French dictionary, gesturing of hands, holding up fingers, shaking the head, etc., one finds it no task at all to swing a big deal like buying a banana on the street!"

In her November report Harshbarger told how she, on arrival, stayed in Wiens' rented space in Saigon one night since Wiens was not able to find her a room. His French landlord, M. Sauvage, was upset thinking that his house was being used as a hotel, so the next night she rented a room in Hotel Majestique, one of Saigon's top hotels. But even this best-in-the-city hotel had no hot water! The following day Harshbarger flew to Da Lat where she stayed in a hotel until they were able to find suitable housing. She used her "school-girl French" to get around. Eby was able to speak a bit of Mandarin Chinese with the owner of a Chinese-run hotel where he and Ewert stayed.

The next Sunday these newly-arrived MCC personnel in Da Lat attended the English-language worship service at the Christian and Missionary Alliance center with its boarding school for missionary children, a clinic, a Bible school for Christian workers, and a school for the ethnic minorities.

By early December—one hundred days after Wiens arrived in Vietnam—the MCC team in Da Lat was prepared to begin distributing food commodities to needy persons.

It was reported at MCC's annual meeting in December 1954 that "considerable" material aid shipments were sent to Vietnam. "Until or unless political circumstances should prevent" these efforts, refugee and relief services would continue, Orie Miller wrote in his unique syntax. "Vietnam represents one of today's world's most tragic situations, a needy land and people indeed and of possible strategic missions outreach opportunities as well."

MCC LOOKS FOR A NICHE

Chapter 3

In early December 1954 Delbert Wiens sent correspondence to the Akron, Pennsylvania, MCC headquarters office on letterhead stationery: Mennonite Central Committee, Agency for Relief and Other Christian Services. The office was located at 181 Rue Catinat, Saigon. MCC was in business.

South Vietnam politics were quite chaotic. U.S. General J. Lawton Collins, head of the U.S. Operations Mission (USOM) with ambassadorial rank, had just come to Vietnam in mid-November with the task of assessing the political situation and charting a future policy for President Eisenhower. While privately agreeing with the French that President Ngo Dinh Diem was incapable of leading the government, he publically proclaimed that he had come to aid the Government of Diem.

Wiens tried to make sense of these developments. In a December letter to J. N. Byler, MCC Director of Relief, he said the General's task was to determine whether Vietnam was "worth saving." If it was, the United States would "throw everything into the country short of troops. If not, the U.S. will go along pretty much as it has and hope to hide from the Communists that we have given up." Most international journalists had already conceded that South Vietnam was not a viable state; Wiens thought them "unduly pessimistic." Yet he recommended that MCC defer any project requiring expensive capital outlay.

Before William Snyder, MCC's Assistant Executive Secretary, saw Wiens' letter, he asked Wiens to hold off any major projects. Snyder had read a *New York Times* article stating that Gen. Collins had no better than one in ten chances of preventing southern Vietnam from coming under Communist control.

Distribution plans were in place when MCC's first shipment of beef, soap and clothing arrived in November. To transport the supplies from the warehouse near the Saigon River docks to Da Lat, 300 kilometers northeast of Saigon, the government loaned two old vehicles—a four-ton French truck and a Dodge Power Wagon. In December they began their distributions in Da Lat from a house arranged by Alliance missionary Herbert Jackson. MCC later rented a house at Villa Vieux Moulan, Cite Bellevue.

Though Vietnam is a tropical country, average December low nighttime temperatures in the mile-high city (1,475m) are 14°C/57°F. After distributing clothing, Eby said he "saw one kid wearing underwear several sizes too large over the top of all his other clothes, and an old woman wearing a flannel nightgown overtop of her dress and coat, and other funny arrangements." American aid made some sewing machines available, and the MCCers hoped that some people could use the machines to alter the clothing. Wiens saw irony in the material aid pouring into Vietnam, much of it of dubious value to the refugees.

Wiens had problems distributing "Poinsettia" food packages from Operation Reindeer. When a rail shipment to Phan Ri did not arrive in time for a scheduled distribution, he left the distribution in charge of officials he did not trust, and asked the pastor of the Evangelical Church in Phan Thiet to report any "shady dealings." Wiens later learned that some goods ended up in the markets—uncertain whether it was sold by recipients or officials. Some refugees tried to wash their clothes with cheese, thinking it was soap. Eby considered these packages a U.S. propaganda ploy to get rid of surplus food, and questioned whether MCC should have agreed to participate in this distribution.

After completing the initial material aid distributions, there was still a supply of beef, soap and clothes. Wiens learned that some Evangelical Christians were "as poor as anyone" and asked the Relief and Welfare Committee of the Evangelical Church to prepare a distribution plan and he would allocate some beef, soap, and cheese to needy families. In a letter to Byler early February, he reasoned that since the Catholic Relief Services was providing "staggering" amounts of material aid to priests for distribution, it would be appropriate to help the Protestants "but with a little closer control."

Wiens reported to Byler in mid-March 1955 that 12,000 persons had benefitted from the initial MCC shipment of clothes (162 bales/7330 kilograms) and soap (1830 kilograms) distributed within the Pays Montagnard du Sud area. Some surplus American cheese, 220 cartons of MCC beef and 159 cartons of soap were also distributed through the Church's Relief and Welfare Committee to various locations. The Committee's secretary and chairman sent a letter of thanks to the "Reverend" Wiens. Some canned beef and soap were sent to the Ban Me Thuot Leprosarium and to the Church's orphanage at Nha Trang. This orphanage, the vision of Pastor Le Van Thai, President of the Evangelical Church, had just opened in September 1953. Twenty-seven of the initial thirty-eight children were children of pastors killed during the French-Indochina War.

Wiens also received letters of thanks from several pastors. One came from the pastor of the church in Ben Tre, eighty-six kilometers south of Saigon. Another came from Tay Ninh, nearly 100 kilometers west of Saigon. In an April 5 letter to Akron, Wiens admitted the Evangelical Christians followed the same pattern they had complained about, distributing almost exclusively to Evangelical Christians although he insisted supplies be given to all within a community on the basis of need. "I am somewhat dubious about giving through the local church. But sometimes it is just about the only thing to do," he wrote.

In a late March letter to Byler, Wiens spoke of plans to investigate relief needs along the central Vietnam coast after the last elements of the Viet Minh forces left in May for North Vietnam. Pondering, Wiens wrote, "I wish MCC had lots of money and I could try to get relief to North [Vietnam]. That part of the country has never grown enough rice to support its population. And now thousands of farmers have come South, the war has disrupted the agriculture, and much rice that is left is being sent to China. One Communist official has predicted that they would have two million deaths by starvation this year. Rice is smuggled across the buffer zone around the 17th parallel."

How to get relief assistance to North Vietnam was also on the minds of others. In an August letter to Wiens, Byler referred to correspondence from theologian John Howard Yoder, then in graduate studies, proposing that MCC assist people in North Vietnam. Byler did not see how this could be done, and asked Wiens for any suggestions. Aware that the French Protestant relief agency, CIMADE, was giving relief assistance to both sides in the military conflict in Algeria, Yoder insisted that this should also be done in Vietnam.

With so much U.S. food aid flowing into the country, there appeared little need for continued large-scale material aid distributions. In early February Wiens proposed that MCC place community development teams in poor villages. He cited an area near the coastal town of Phan Thiet that needed development in the fields of irrigation, animal husbandry, education, and health, and prepared a draft budget for this.

Three months after J. Lawrence Burkholder completed his investigative assignment for Church World Service in late September 1954, Rev. Robert P. Kellerman arrived for a six-month assignment. Kellerman developed plans to establish Da Hoa village for non-Catholics at Kilometer 158, southwest of Bao Loc and Djiring, located on Highway #20 between Saigon and Da Lat. Kellerman envisioned having Eby and Ewert assist in its development. Here they might gain experience for a possible MCC community development project.

Snyder affirmed Wiens' proposal for a community development project and authorized Wiens to begin discussions on a contractual relationship with U.S. Operations Mission (USOM) on the condition that the MCC team would have complete freedom to develop their program. Snyder proposed in February that MCC might reassign two Pax men from Korea to work with Ewert.

Wiens had already discussed community development teams with USOM, and was told to contact the Government's Minister of Social Action. When he reported back to USOM that the Minister was enthusiastic about the proposal, he learned that it needed presidential approval. So on March 18 Wiens met with President Ngo Dinh Diem, presenting a written proposal with further explanations. Wiens told Snyder that the President expressed interest but would have to discuss it first with USOM!

A crisis within the MCC Korea team brought the issue of cooperation with governmental agencies to the fore. In a March letter, Snyder reported that two Pax men in Korea had just resigned, returned to the States, and applied for I-A-O draft classification (non-combatant military service), greatly disturbing MCC administrators and the men's families. The men claimed that MCC Korea did not have clear program objectives. They also objected to MCC's ties to the United Nations Korean Reconstruction Agency, the Republic of Korea, and related agencies. Snyder was informed that a couple men in Vietnam had similar concerns, a clear reference to Roy Eby and Adam Ewert who had just transferred from Taiwan and Korea. Snyder instructed Wiens "to lay on the line whatever misgivings you or others have with respect to our co-operation with FOA. . . . MCC is not interested in pursuing a course that will not have the moral and spiritual support of the workers who must carry on the task."

While neither man opposed cooperating with governmental agencies per se, they said MCC needed clear objectives to determine whether any proposed cooperative programs fit those objectives. Wiens proposed that MCC consider starting some community development program independently if a USOM-supported project was not soon forthcoming.

Orie Miller, MCC's Executive Secretary, replied to Wiens early April, saying that MCC personnel in nearly every country since 1945 had to deal with the issue of relationships and find appropriate responses. "MCC needs to remain sensitive and careful in this whole area and . . . will continue to need the counsel and conscience and help and constructive suggestion of every worker," Miller wrote. He encouraged Wiens to develop an autonomous program and submit a minimal six-month budget proposal, suggesting that USOM might even grant financial support without a contractual arrangement.

Miller also affirmed Wiens' leadership. "From every judgment I can form from your letters and reports, we feel that you are headed right in developing the MCC program and service there. . . . You can be assured of our full confidence in your future judgments and conclusions as they develop and of our readiness to give you every help and support possible."

In May Wiens reported that he received authorization from the Vietnamese government to work with USOM in fielding a community team. This came from the Administrator General of Foreign Aid who held a cabinet-like position. The letter was approved by President Diem himself. It read:

In answer to your letter dated 27th April 1955, I have the honor to inform you that the Government of Vietnam will be glad to receive the assistance that you intend to bring to this country in the field of Health and Social work, in liaison with corresponding organizations of USOM in Saigon and according to the project you have communicated to me.

I will take the opportunity to request you kindly to transmit to the "MENNONITE CENTRAL COMMITTEE" our grateful sentiments for all that has been done in Viet Nam under the auspices of this Committee.

Please receive, Dear Mr. D. L. Wiens, the assurance of my high consideration.

/signed/ DINH QUANG CHIEU

A program with USOM never developed.

By this time Wiens was also wearing another hat. When Rev. Kellerman completed his Church World Service assignment in May, Wiens began overseeing the programs CWS had begun. In early June Wiens summarized the CWS tasks left to him. One item was the 5,000 hoes that CWS had ordered from a local foundry. The Church social welfare committee worked with the Ministry of Agriculture officials in distributing most of them, and Wiens was giving the remaining hoes to farmers in Da Hoa village. CWS agreed to provide some of Wiens' overhead expenses, and donated their Jeep Station Wagon to MCC. (This vehicle was still being used for Mennonite programs twenty years later.)

The CWS relationship to MCC was positive and enabled Wiens to do things he otherwise would not have been able to do. When Diem on April 28 ordered his armed forces to crush the Binh Xuyen mafia units, the ensuing battle devastated some of the poorer sections of Saigon and the twin Chinatown city of Cho Lon. Five hundred civilians died, and thousands of homes were destroyed. Although MCC goods in the warehouse near the docks were lost, Wiens used CWS funds to purchase rice and 50,000 yards of cloth to supplement a large quantity of rice from Catholic Relief Services to distribute to the victims.

Kellerman visited the MCC Akron headquarters on his return to the States. He and Snyder discussed the relationship of CWS and MCC to the Christian and Missionary Alliance and the Evangelical Church. Writing to Wiens, Snyder commented on the perceived jockeying by the World Council of Churches and the U.S.-based National Association of Evangelicals for a relationship with the Evangelical Church. Le Van Thai, the Church president, had told Kellerman that their church people owe allegiance and feel the warmest spiritual tie to C&MA and the NAE, and yet sensing "the need to identify with a larger world body."

"The strong interest the Vietnamese church has shown in Mennonite Central Committee and CWS expressions of Christian concern through relief places a heavy responsibility on us that we do not misuse the confidence placed in us," Snyder wrote. He emphasized "the importance of our own MCC statesmanship if the best interest of the National Church is to be served." Wiens responded that he "kept out of their struggles" of when and with whom to affiliate. Were he to become involved, he wrote, he would recommend to Church leaders "that they enter as much as possible into the world activities of both organizations without officially joining either." In this Wiens reflected the stance of major North American Mennonite denominations that had joined neither the World Council of Churches nor the fledgling World Evangelical Fellowship. This neutral stance enabled Mennonites in later years to build relationships with many agencies in Vietnam.

Kellerman informed Snyder that 150 people were already living at the CWS-sponsored Da Hoa village, and that it could go as high as a thousand people. Plans were in place to build a community center, clinic, school and Protestant church—though the village was not just for Protestants. Kellerman proposed that MCC might consider a medical project, so Snyder asked Wiens to visualize fielding a mobile clinic similar to what MCC was doing in Taiwan.

Eby, who had worked with the MCC medical team in Taiwan, had already prodded Wiens to consider medical work. Eby spoke with the USOM Health and Sanitation director, and both Eby and Wiens met with Dr. Le Du, the acting director of the Ministry of Health, who had a Master's degree from Johns Hopkins University. In a May letter to Byler, Eby documented a critical shortage of doctors in Vietnam. Vietnam had only one doctor per 35,000 people, and most doctors were in Saigon or other cities. Eby made a strong case for fielding a medical team, perhaps providing personnel to an unstaffed provincial clinic. The two men had already visited two such clinics. With French doctors leaving the country, three provinces had no doctors at all. USOM and Health Ministry officials were enthusiastic about MCC recruiting a medical team, and promised to provide equipment and medicines. Wiens suggested that an independent clinic would be more expensive to set up, although more effective. "If MCC wanted to turn a doctoring project over into a mission," Wiens noted parenthetically, it would not be advisable to work in a government clinic.

Akron was recruiting medical personnel. Byler reported that Dr. Willard Krabill would be able to come to Vietnam by November, and that Juliette Sebus from the Netherlands would likely be one of the two nurses MCC was recruiting.

In early August Wiens reported the work he and Eby were doing in researching possible medical projects. Although Ministry of Health favored having volunteer doctors help staff an established hospital, he and Eby preferred having MCC develop its own program. Eby went to Ban Me Thuot to discuss this idea with the government health director of the central highlands area.

In this letter to Byler, Wiens mentioned the dicey security in Saigon. Several American cars had recently been bombed. "Nearly every night there are bombs thrown right in Saigon," Wiens wrote. "Not a pleasant situation. . . . I get a funny feeling when I regularly check the car for a plastic bomb before getting in if I have had to park it on a dark street in the evening. There are lots of nasty little saboteurs running around in this country. And they do not love Americans. I'm somewhat fatalistic and don't worry for myself, but I'd hate to have anything happen to the others or even to me. I don't think this should stop us, but it's something to think on."

Akron administrators also had another concern—the high expenses of the Vietnam program. A June letter from the treasurer's office noted that the cost of room and board for personnel in

Vietnam was five times higher than the cost of volunteers at the Akron headquarters, and Wiens was asked to check his figures. Wiens replied that his monthly costs for room and board were around $200 U.S. while many persons in Vietnam were paying twice that for room alone.

Wiens in early August asked Byler to send canned beef. In mid-April Wiens had gone to Laos to check out reports of famine. At that time MCC had no available resources. Now Church World Service had sent $4,000 to buy needed rice. When Wiens asked the Lao government to transport the rice from Vietnam, officials agreed only on the condition that they would be solely in charge of the rice distribution. Viewing the officials as "completely corrupt," Wiens took the money to Laos and arranged to smuggle rice across the Mekong River from Thailand; although illegal, Wiens said the government "smiles on" this due to the food crisis. Wiens got his French Protestant army chaplain friend, Rev. DeLuze, to arrange for the French army to ship the canned beef to be distributed with the rice.

With humor Wiens wrote in the colloquial Pennsylvania language he had picked up during his time at Akron: "But that means that our meat is all. So please also send another load of beef if you have it. As you can see, business is picking up."

As it turned out, the beef shipment to Laos arrived late, so Eby went later to coordinate that distribution. Ewert was sick the whole month with infectious hepatitis, first in the hospital in Da Lat, and later in the Saigon Adventist hospital near the MCC unit house.

While Wiens was in Laos mid-August, Eby wrote to Byler, delighted to hear that his Goshen College friend Krabill was coming to Vietnam. He related what he had learned on his visit to Ban Me Thuot where he had spoken with the director of the C&MA Leprosarium. They had a long-term lease on the land, and expressed interest in having MCC develop a medical program. Their medical director, Dr. J. M. Webber, had left for health reasons. If approved by the Health Ministry, it would be eligible to receive USOM aid. Eby hoped Dr. Krabill would soon arrive.

In June and July there had been an exchange of public statements between North and South Vietnam. Prime Minister Pham Van Dong asked that preparations be made for 1956 elections to reunify the country. Prime Minister Ngo Dinh Diem dismissed the request, noting that South Vietnam had not signed the Geneva Accords and, furthermore, argued that there could not be fair democratic elections.

In an August 23 letter to Snyder, Wiens wrote:

> Things are quiet politically now, but sometimes I am pretty pessimistic. The Diem government still hasn't been able to get out of the city offices, and increasing numbers of able Vietnamese are easing out of responsible positions since they say it is impossible to work with Diem. He trusts nobody except his brothers and this is a bad situation. But all is not lost, and we might as well go ahead as if we'll be here for quite a while yet. The French troops are leaving. The French civilians are pouring out. Within a year there may be only about 2,000 civilians left, according to a Frenchman friend. This is bad since it will throw the economy completely out of whack. There could easily be hard times coming.

In October Wiens expressed hesitancy about any "contractual relationship" with USOM in a community development project. Snyder agreed, telling Wiens not to pursue this. Although the MCC Ban Me Thuot medical team later developed some health and sanitation programs, MCC initiated no stand-alone developmental programs until the Vietnam Christian Service era ten years later.

Grace and Willard Krabill flew into Saigon on October 18. A few days later, on October 23, Diem deposed the Emperor Bao Dai in a rigged referendum and proclaimed the Republic of Vietnam with himself as President—also serving as prime minister and defense minister as well.

When Dr. Krabill sent an eight-page report in mid-November to Miller, Snyder and Byler, the Krabills had already "weathered the listlessness and bouts of diarrhea which seem to be the lot of most Westerners," met with Ministry of Health officials, traveled to and spoken with health officials in Da Lat, Pleiku and Ban Me Thuot, and enjoyed "the extreme friendliness of the Christian & Missionary Alliance missionaries." Krabill then laid out three options for developing a medical program: work with a government hospital, work with the C&MA Leprosarium in Ban Me Thuot, or start a separate program.

In his report, Krabill said Ministry of Health officials were interested in having him and the two nurses work in the Pleiku government hospital. Krabill, however, was apprehensive about whether he could work satisfactorily under a military doctor, a political appointee. In Vietnam, Krabill wrote, "there is no clear distinction between the civil government and the military. The military is the government, and vice versa." Krabill wrote, "In all our attempts to explain why our MCC medical team must remain aloof from the military, I am not sure we got our point across. On one occasion we were told, 'but in this country [the] civil and military [are] all the same.'"

Krabill found the option of working with the Ban Me Thuot Leprosarium an "interesting possibility." Established in 1951, it was now treating 200 persons. Since Alliance missions' policy did not embrace social and medical institutional work, the C&MA was in the process of turning the leprosarium over to the supervision of the American Leprosy Mission (ALM). C&MA's Asia area secretary, Louis L. King, was visiting their missionaries at the time of Krabill's visit to Ban Me Thuot, and he invited Krabill to work there—even to direct the program—on a temporary or long-term basis.

Krabill saw advantages to this offer. The MCC medical team could begin working immediately. They would be relatively free from government control and have minimum costs. Were MCC to work here, Krabill envisioned the development of a mobile clinic to serve the general medical needs of the surrounding ethnic minority community. Working there would also enable personnel to gain experience, and "would keep alive a regular MCC program here until such time as it may be more feasible to develop an independent Mennonite program."

A third option—develop an independent medical program—would be an "opportunity to give a clear Mennonite witness, and freedom to operate a program in accordance with our spiritual and medical ideals," Krabill wrote. Furthermore, it could become "a possible forerunner of a long range Mennonite witness in this country." He continued:

> Before leaving the United States, I was told that Viet Nam is a country where a Mennonite type of witness is sorely needed, and with that I now concur. It was further suggested that if a medical program developed here satisfactorily, one of the Mennonite mission boards (e.g. Elkhart) might be interested in taking over our work as a new mission outreach such as happened with MCC projects in Puerto Rico, Ethiopia, and Formosa. If such an interest exists, or can be anticipated, then an independent project should be developed here as soon as possible. Any work we would do in a government hospital set-up would contribute little or nothing to the development of a long range Mennonite witness in this country, especially with the current nationalistic trend.

Krabill cautioned, however, that it would be quite expensive for MCC to develop an independent medical project, partly due to the poor monetary exchange rate. There was also the question of political security.

Krabill asked the Akron administrators for advice. Since there was "unofficial interest" of some leaders of the Mennonite Board of Missions and Charities in Elkhart, Indiana, for developing a Vietnam program, he suggested that Akron also consult them. In 1950 and 1951 Ernest E. Miller had indicated an "opportunity for mission work in Indochina," and expressed the view that the Christian and Missionary Alliance would "welcome a group like the Mennonites coming in and sharing responsibility if it were done above-board and in a cooperative fashion."

While Krabill waited for a response, he said that he and Grace would stay at the home of the vacationing director of the leprosarium, help the nurses, study tropical medicine, and "learn a little French."

Five months later on April 8, 1956, Krabill wrote Byler, saying: "I will take charge of the medical work here [at the leprosarium] tomorrow on the basis of an understanding reached with the Executive Committee of C&MA's Tribes Mission on April 5, 1956."

Why did it take so long to sort out the pros and cons of these three options and come to a decision?

After receiving Krabill's November 12 report, Akron administrators on November 29 cabled that they favored Krabill's assignment to the Ban Me Thuot Leprosarium until future program opportunities became clearer. Orie O. Miller followed this with a December 2 letter to Wiens and Krabill: "In any new country we find that MCC can find itself best and get going the quickest by staying in neighborly . . . and brotherly relationships with the evangelical missionary and church forces resident—this rather than a lone tie-up with government without regard to these evangelical interests."

Miller said they were budgeting for a Vietnam program and that they had already appointed two nurses for Vietnam. Miller, who was planning a visit to Vietnam late May, acknowledged that there was . . .

> future Mennonite Vietnam mission interest. . . . Both of you will know how this MCC mission interest and planning developed in other parts as for instance Puerto Rico, Ethiopia, Formosa, Espelkamp, Germany, etc., and one can assume the same eager interest within our constituency regarding Vietnam. . . . The locating of any MCC project should however at this time not be contingent at all on such future development. Most likely, any mission project to Vietnam should begin in Saigon itself and then after a good acquaintanceship with the country and other Christian interests concerned, develop further outreach strategy.

Before the Akron administrators cabled their preference for the leprosarium, Krabill and Wiens had conversations with the Ministry of Health about a possible placement of a MCC medical team at the government hospital in Pleiku, also located in an ethnic minority area 200 kilometers north of Ban Me Thuot. This seemed attractive as a possible base from which MCC might later establish an independent medical program in the district town of An Khe, ninety kilometers east of Pleiku, which had no medical facilities. Krabill and Wiens wanted the Akron administrators to be aware of this possibility before fully committing to the leprosarium.

In early January 1956 Krabill and Wiens were surprised to receive a letter from Byler mentioning "a very interesting discussion" he and Miller had with C&MA administrators in New York. Without giving any indication why they no longer supported their earlier recommendation for Krabill to go to Ban Me Thuot, Byler now wrote: "It is our feeling that you should move ahead and work temporarily at Pleiku . . . [and] plan to locate permanently in An Khe."

Still checking out the feasibility of working at the Pleiku provincial hospital, Wiens and Krabill learned that the medical director did not want an American doctor there. So the Health Minister Dr. Khai suggested it might be better for Krabill to go to the Ban Me Thuot Leprosarium!

Krabill and Wiens asked the Akron administrators for more details of their meeting with the C&MA leaders. Byler said that there was little to report—quite an understatement! Byler indicated that Alliance leaders looked forward to Krabill giving medical service. However, hearing that Eastern Mennonite Board of Missions and Charities intended to send missionaries to Vietnam, they were concerned that Mennonites would assign personnel to areas where they were already working.

Krabill liked the set-up at the leprosarium. On March 10 he wrote to T. Grady Mangham, Chairman of the Tribes of Viet Nam Mission, accepting their invitation to work at Ban Me Thuot, "anticipating a happy association" with Mangham and other Alliance personnel. In addition to locating the new medical program at the leprosarium, MCC planned to operate a mobile clinic in the area. MCC would provide additional staff housing and outpatient and ward facilities for non-leprous patients. Krabill's address would be *Leprosarie de Mission Evangelique, PMS, Banmethuot, Viet Nam.*

MCC would have a good experience working in Ban Me Thuot. But the Alliance reluctance to manage institutional ministries would cause frequent interruptions and endless frustration. Had MCC gone to An Khe, they would have been neighbors to the American First Cavalry Division which located there in 1965.

VISION AND ROLE OF ORIE O. MILLER

Chapter 4

Orie O. Miller took Mennonite Central Committee to Vietnam in 1954. It was also Orie O. Miller's vision that led the Eastern Mennonite Board of Missions and Charities (EM-BMC) into Vietnam a few years later. For several decades Orie Miller served as the Executive Secretary of MCC—1935 to 1958. He was also the Secretary of EMBMC.

Orie was born into an Indiana farm family in 1892, the oldest son of a Mennonite church leader. After graduating from Goshen College, in 1915 he married the daughter of a shoe manufacturer in the small town of Akron in Lancaster County, Pennsylvania, and accepted his father-in-law's offer of employment there. He believed he would eventually be called to serve the church as an ordained minister.

In January 1919 Orie was invited to a meeting of the Mennonite Relief Commission for War Sufferers, organized in 1917 by Mennonite church leaders in Elkhart, Indiana. The Commission had decided to support the American Friends Service Committee and the American Committee for Armenian and Syrian Relief, caring for victims of genocide and deportations. Orie was asked to go with other volunteers to Syria. By this time he and Elta had a young daughter, so leaving home for fifteen months was not easy. In the Middle East Orie's administrative skills were recognized, and Orie himself gradually began to realize that he would fulfill his life calling as a lay church leader.

On Miller's return journey in March 1920 he and a colleague met a commission of Russian Mennonites in Basel, Switzerland, which reported the suffering of their people in Russia. After arriving home Miller prodded the Relief Commission for War Sufferers to respond to these needs. Already in late 1919 the Commission had decided to send a unit to southern Russia. Believing that someone with experience should head up this unit, Orie was asked to consider this.

Since other North American Mennonite groups were interested in supporting Russian relief work, representatives of these groups met on July 27, 1920, to see how they could work together. Orie volunteered to go to Russia if they could work together and select two others to go with him. Out of this meeting came the formation of Mennonite Central Committee (MCC). Again leaving his family and business in October, he spent seven months in this assignment.

Orie's leadership with MCC spanned several decades. He served as Assistant to the Secretary, 1921-1935; Executive Secretary and Treasurer, 1935-1958; Associate Executive Secretary, 1958-1963; and then Executive Secretary Emeritus until his death in 1977. Orie continued with the shoe company when he became MCC's Executive Secretary, and worked from his home office. Thus Akron, Pennsylvania, became the international headquarters of Mennonite Central Committee. Although Orie became synonymous with MCC, he was involved with many other organizations as well. His leadership roles within Lancaster Mennonite Conference are of special importance to our story.

Orie's unique view of the world was gradually but cautiously welcomed by the Lancaster area Mennonites. Although one of the more conservative conferences within the Mennonite Church, Lancaster Mennonite Conference also embraced a missionary vision. The denominational mission agency was Mennonite Board of Missions and Charities (MBMC). Several regional conferences formed their own mission and service organizations, among them Lancaster Mennonite Conference which organized Eastern Mennonite Board of Missions and Charities in 1914. (The name was changed to Eastern Mennonite Missions in 1993.)

To further encourage mission interest, in 1924 Orie became the founding editor of *Missionary Messenger*, EMBMC's mission quarterly. Within a year he was elected to the Board and also elected vice-president.

The foreign mission work of the Mennonite Church, first begun in India, remained the responsibility of Mennonite Board of Missions and Charities. (This agency is now Mennonite Mission Network of Mennonite Church USA.) By the late 1920s there was, however, interest within Lancaster Conference for involvement in an overseas mission. In 1930 the Board of Bishops unanimously requested that EMBMC establish a mission in Africa.

With his overseas experience, Orie had a significant role in implementing this. In December 1933 he traveled to east Africa with one of the designated missionaries, choosing an area in Tanganyika (Tanzania) at the southern end of Lake Victoria. With his administrative acumen, he prepared a constitution and mission structure that served the mission a full generation until the Tanganyika Mennonite Conference was organized.

When the EMBMC Secretary died in 1935, Orie accepted this position, and served until 1958. By that date EMBMC had also sent missionaries to Honduras, Ethiopia, Luxembourg, Somalia, Israel, France—and now Vietnam.

Active in relief work, MCC was able to respond rather quickly to international crisis issues, and often created development programs to address longer-term needs within the countries it served. As MCC concluded ministries within a given country, various Mennonite mission agencies sometimes assumed these programs and expanded their work into preaching, teaching and church-planting ministries. Through his MCC contacts in Indonesia, Orie had projected a mission program for Sumatra.

Orie introduced Southeast Asia to EMBMC in 1955. The minutes of the EMBMC Board of March 10, 1955, read: "Brother Miller . . . pointed out on the map the various Mennonite mission enterprises throughout the world, noting the fruitful ministry which has been established. He further referred to two areas in Southeast Asia, namely Viet Nam and the island of Sumatra in Indonesia, both of which represent very needy places and where there is a great opportunity for missionary service. There has never been an American Mennonite missionary in this southeast Asia area."

The Eastern Mennonite Board in May approved opening a mission program in Sumatra, authorizing sending missionary personnel there by late 1956.

Miller had a close relationship with J. D. Graber (1900-1978), General Secretary of the Mennonite Board of Missions and Charities. In an October 20, 1955, letter to Graber, Orie wrote, "Reference your Board's interest in finding a new mission field, . . . why not consider Vietnam?" Orie suggested that Vietnam might be a good place for both mission boards to work together. Each would support their individual ministries, but the two might work together in institutional programs like a school or hospital. He said he had "the feeling that Vietnam would remain open" for mission opportunities, and that they could enter with "quite a large-sized group and a variety of skills and gifts in its workers." He noted that EMBMC had approved a mission to Sumatra.

"In total Southeast Asia strategy, however, Vietnam should have the immediate preference and should also prove more promptly fruitful in church building results," he wrote. "As intimated, I believe that our Eastern Board would be open to entry into Vietnam too and also to a strategy for association with Elkhart in such entry, and I feel also that MCC is already preparing a good approach thereto and as has been MCC's role and opportunity in other fields in the past."

In this conversation we observe not only Orie's unique writing style, but an assumption that Mennonites would begin missionary work in Vietnam. Noting that the population of Sumatra was largely Islamic, Orie believed that evangelism within Vietnam could perhaps be more "fruitful" than in Indonesia.

MBMC was already administering a program in Israel with EMBMC support. Orie saw some variation of this model as the way for both the denominational and regional mission agencies to work together in Vietnam.

Having heard Ernest Miller's reports a few years earlier, J. D. Graber was already considering possible mission work in Vietnam.

The MCC Executive Committee at their December 16-17, 1955, meeting adopted a minute welcoming a Mennonite mission agency to Vietnam. The EMBMC Executive Committee picked up this discussion again late December. The minutes of the January 4, 1956, Board meeting read: "Orie O. Miller reported on the open door and challenging opportunity in Viet Nam where . . . there is prospect of a good response. In light of previous board action approving entry into Sumatra (at which time the door was not open in Viet Nam) the board authorized entry into Viet Nam first instead of Sumatra if the way continues to be clear in that direction and if Brother Miller's proposed MCC trip to that area continues to confirm this leading."

What transpired in the previous eight months—between the May 11, 1955, Eastern Board action to send missionaries to Sumatra because "the door was not open in Vietnam" and now in January when it is considered timely to send missionary personnel?

There was still serious reservation in early 1955 about whether the government of Ngo Dinh Diem would survive. But Prime Minister Diem not only crushed his local armed opposition in May, in June and July he stated he would refuse to allow elections to unify the country. And he used an October referendum in the South to depose Emperor Bao Dai and proclaimed the Republic of South Vietnam with himself as President. It was looking more like an independent South Vietnam might survive.

On January 6, 1956, two days after the EMBMC Board gave tentative approval to sending missionaries to Vietnam, Miller and J. N. Byler, the MCC Relief Administrator, met in New York with Christian and Missionary Alliance Administrators. In a March 19 follow-up letter to Dr. Alfred Snead, Miller described the various countries where Eastern Mennonite Board of Missions and Charities was working internationally, and indicated that both EMBMC and MBMC were interested in placing missionary personnel in the former Indo-China area and anticipated good relationships with "other evangelical agencies in the field."

Amos S. Horst, a friend on the Lancaster Conference Bishops' Foreign Missions Committee, asked Miller in May how two Mennonite mission agencies would work together in Vietnam. Noting that four Mennonite mission agencies began missionary ministries in Japan after World

War II, Miller said it was now equally "strategic" for multiple agencies to engage in missionary work in Vietnam, working in different locations. "The Vietnamese are still largely a pagan animist people," he wrote, "and one can look for them to respond to the Gospel more quickly and readily than from work in Islamic areas. For this reason, it would be my own conviction that we should send our mission workers to Vietnam and then plan to enter Padang, Sumatra, as soon . . . as workers and resources would seem to permit."

It seems perplexing that Miller described the Vietnamese as "still largely a pagan animist people." This characterized the ethnic minorities in the central highlands where Grace and Willard Krabill were now beginning their work—rather than the dominant Vietnamese people who emphasized ancestral veneration. Miller made no mention of the pervasive Buddhist influence in Vietnamese life.

In late May and early June, Orie traveled to Vietnam, visiting Ban Me Thuot, Da Lat, and Saigon. MCC doctor Willard Krabill was now serving as medical director at the C&MA Leprosarium. J. D. Graber followed Miller in visiting Vietnam in July. Graber sent a letter to Miller August 10, expressing hope that MBMC could enter Vietnam. He noted that Miller was proposing that EMBMC work in Saigon, and he believed that MBMC "should establish a medical service in some needy area . . . and then attach other general missionaries."

Graber had spoken with D. I. Jeffrey, Alliance Field Chairman, and with T. Grady Mangham, Jr., the chair of the Tribes Mission among the minorities in Ban Me Thuot, and they both welcomed Mennonite missionaries. Graber's visit coincided with the annual conference of the Evangelical Church in Vietnam (ECVN) in Tourane (Da Nang) where he was invited to speak. His meeting with the ECVN president Rev. Le Van Thai and other church leaders "was most cordial." Rev. Thai told Graber that they had been asking Rev. Jeffrey for years to invite some other mission agency into Vietnam, and "now they feel that our coming is an answer to their prayer and desire."

Graber was enthusiastic about Mennonite Board of Missions beginning missionary activity in Vietnam, and wrote that he hoped that Willard and Grace Krabill would continue with MBMC in Vietnam after completing their three-year MCC assignment. He saw no particular administrative problem in two mission agencies working cooperatively in different geographical areas.

Miller responded to Graber's letter on August 21, reporting that James and Arlene Stauffer were being recruited to lead the missionary team in Vietnam. Miller made plans to meet with Graber to discuss a mission partnership.

In a memo to the EMBMC Executive Committee on August 17, Miller proposed that EMBMC begin working in Saigon, and that Mennonite Board of Missions and Charities be invited to cooperate with Eastern Board. He also recommended that James and Arlene Stauffer be appointed as the first missionaries. Following the September 6 Executive Committee Meeting, the Board in its bi-monthly session on September 11 approved these recommendations.

In correspondence with Frank Epp in June 1968—more than a decade later—Miller told of visiting West Sumatra in 1956 with a Javanese Mennonite church leader. "We were struck with the spiritual need in this area, but also with the very apparent difficulties for Christian mission," he wrote. "Our Board had one such in Somalia by then, and we were really looking for something more akin to what we had experienced in Tanzania. Also on the 1956 visit to Saigon,

South Vietnam, I was impressed that South Vietnam was as needy, but probably more promising than Sumatra. With these two alternatives then on my return home in the fall of 1956, our Board decided on Saigon."

The speed in which Eastern Mennonite Board of Missions and Charities turned its focus from Indonesia to Vietnam and its unilateral action in placing personnel there surprised and disappointed Graber, who felt that the Eastern Board had unfairly seized an opportunity that Mennonite Board of Missions was planning to pursue. Graber immediately sent a letter to Miller September 15 to "express a concern." He wrote: "Although we have not named Viet Nam in our minutes, this country has been in our planning for several years. When we read the Eastern Board minute laying down plans for a fairly extensive mission program in Sumatra we assumed that you would not be entering still another country in eastern Asia so soon and thus our interest in possibilities in a country like Viet Nam continued to develop."

Graber reported that the MBMC Executive Committee "feels strongly" they should not give the impression that two agencies within the Mennonite Church are competing with each other or duplicating ministries. Therefore, their Committee members were not authorizing his proposed MBMC "medical-evangelistic approach in Vietnam." They asked that representatives of the two Boards meet to discuss coordination of missionary activities.

The Mennonite Board of Missions and Charities, the denominational agency, clearly viewed the regional mission agency as upsetting the equilibrium within the Mennonite Church in carrying out international mission ministries. The Eastern Board, with a mandate from Lancaster Mennonite Conference, one of the denomination's regional conferences, had begun work in Africa (Tanzania) in 1933. It followed with mission programs to other countries in east Africa, to Europe and to Central America. Other regional conferences ventured into overseas missions, but on a smaller scale—Virginia Mennonite Conference to Sicily, Italy (1949) and Jamaica (1955), and Franconia Mennonite Conference to Cuba (1954). Mennonite Board of Missions was seen as the "General" Mission Board of the Mennonite Church. With its entry into Asia it appeared that the Eastern Board was now operating as another "general board."

Graber noted that MBMC "had acquiesced to the Eastern Board" in placing missionary personnel in Ethiopia in 1948 when the Mennonite Relief Committee was discontinuing its Ethiopian programs "in order to maintain the unity of Church approach in East Africa" since EMBMC was already working in nearby Tanganyika (Tanzania). Graber did not want to divide areas of the world geographically between administrative spheres of the two boards, but said "we dare not compete or duplicate without doing harm to the missionary interest and confidence of our constituencies."

On October 3 Graber informed MBMC Board members and staff that he had spoken with Miller and was proposing that members of both Boards meet to clarify relationships. This meeting, he wrote, would discuss not only the dynamics of the beginning of missionary work in Vietnam, but also "the total problem of cooperation and coordination between our two Boards. We feel here that such a full-fledged discussion is perhaps overdue and since the Eastern Board is more and more operating as a general board for the entire Church and since they are entering mission fields also in all parts of the world, it becomes very necessary that we have an understanding with each other as to how we represent our Church in this total world-wide outreach program."

Miller was not waiting, even as the anticipated MBMC mission partnership was now in question. On October 3 he wrote to C&MA Field Administrator Rev. D. I. Jeffrey, reporting that the Stauffers were coming to Vietnam "with a deep sense of call to missionary service there." He also sent a letter to ECVN President Rev. Thai, introducing James and Arlene, saying that Thai would certainly "appreciate having this couple added to the evangelical missionary group in Saigon." Miller said that they would be "sensitive in every way to the interests and concerns" of the Evangelical Church.

On November 16 and 17 members and staff personnel of the two Boards met at the Atlantic Hotel in Chicago. On November 20 Graber wrote to Miller, quoting from MBMC Executive Committee minutes: "Following a review of the discussion with the Eastern Mennonite Board of Missions and Charities Executive Committee, the General Board Executive Committee instructed its secretary to discontinue further exploration of Viet Nam as a field in which the General Board should work." Graber continued:

> Naturally we have relinquished our interest in the field of Viet Nam with some hesitation after having made the investigation and developed a considerable interest and even thought in terms of program. It was the clear consensus of our Committee, however, that it would be better to acquiesce to the program of the Eastern Board in Viet Nam and channel our resources and interest into other fields. Our Executive Committee feels very strongly that for both Boards to enter into the same field, even if one were in the Tribes and the other in the Coastal areas, would be a source of confusion and probable misunderstanding among our common constituency. We wish you the Lord's blessing as you develop the program in Viet Nam and trust that through your efforts a great many people will come to know of the blessed Gospel of salvation through Christ Jesus.

Graber's disappointment was made easier by new opportunities in Ghana. Graber invited Dr. Krabill to consider a medical missionary assignment there. Krabill expressed regret that MBMC would not be working in Vietnam. He said it would have been possible for the two agencies to work together if the field administration had been closely integrated, but this possibility was now compromised by "the way in which the Eastern Board . . . forged ahead very independently." In reflection, however, Krabill said they were not bitter about this, especially since MBMC now had "an even greater opportunity" for a ministry in Ghana.

Orie replied to Graber in early December: "We do regret the chain of circumstances regarding Vietnam missions' entry that led your Committee finally to conclude as you did, but do appreciate this gracious attitude and your Committee's good wishes. My own personal regrets for my own fault in this were given you . . . last week. . . . All of us certainly share with you and your Committee the desire to continue working in good relationship and in Christian mutual planning in the spirit and attitude that should become Christian folks as closely allied and in common purpose as we are."

Orie's vision for a large multi-agency Mennonite ministry in Vietnam was now gone, and the Eastern Board proceeded on its own. However, political and military developments within the next decade would place Vietnam in the consciousness of the entire North American Mennonite church.

Miller did not give up his dream; writing to Krabill mid-December, Miller expressed hope that other Mennonite mission agencies would become involved in Vietnam, Cambodia and Laos.

With regards to Mennonite Central Committee, Miller said "We will want to continue closely connected with service needs and interests in Indo-China."

It is significant to note here that Miller was now anticipating that MCC would continue working in Vietnam indefinitely even if other Mennonite mission agencies developed programs, rather than phase out as MCC had done previously in some countries.

In a July 1958 article in the *Missionary Messenger* when he retired as the EMBMC Secretary, Orie O. Miller reflects on his involvement with the Eastern Board, noting the fast expansion of overseas missionary activity from 1946 on. He "thrills" at the reality of 1,800 new believers from six countries where the Eastern Board was working, and rejoices at their eagerness to continue the mission of the church. He wanted to see the EMBMC constituency serve in the spirit of Jesus Christ and to partner in evangelism with the new churches.

In the May 1957 edition of *Missionary Messenger*, Paul N. Kraybill, who would follow Miller as Eastern Board Secretary, wrote about beginning the work in Vietnam:

It may seem presumptuous for a small mission board with a limited constituency to undertake a sixth foreign mission field, but on the other hand it would be a sinful act of disobedience if the Lord is calling us and we fail to heed. It does seem clear that in the years ahead there will be an increasing number of young folks available for foreign missionary service. . . . The resources of our people have not been diminished as a result of our present program. The increasing prosperity and rising level of living one sees everywhere in our brotherhood would urge us to increase our giving and sharing. Unless we are faithful disciples in faithfully carrying out an enlarging program of evangelism we can expect that worldliness and materialism will engulf us completely as it is already threatening to do.

So the time has come for the James Stauffers to leave as the first of what we trust will be a large group of young folks who will be ready to go to this country with the message of the Gospel. One looks forward eagerly to that day in the future when we can stretch our hands across the miles to greet and welcome a new sister church whom the Lord will be calling out from among those people.

The multifaceted Mennonite ministries in Vietnam are greatly indebted to the legacy of Orie O. Miller.

RELIGIOUS MILIEU IN VIETNAM

Chapter 5

Mennonite missionaries entering Vietnam in the fifties and sixties understood their call to teach, preach, and live the gospel, inviting people to faith in Jesus Christ and experience the joy of reconciliation with God and with others.

Though details are sketchy, the Gospel of Jesus Christ was introduced into Vietnam in the early sixteenth century. In 1550, and again in 1580, Portuguese Dominican priests from Malacca (Malaysia) went to Vietnam, and in 1583 four Franciscan priests and four lay brothers came from the Philippines. Two Jesuit missionaries came to central Vietnam in 1615.

Much of the Catholic missionary work during the first half of the seventeenth century was carried on by Jesuit missionaries from France. Most famous among them was Alexandre de Rhodes (1591-1660) who evangelized in central and northern Vietnam. Though expelled several times, as Christianity was a perceived threat to the emperor's status in the Confucian political structure, he kept going back until his final expulsion in 1645. His indefatigable ministry left a permanent mark on the Church. He prepared a *Cathechismus* and trained a team of lay catechists who taught new believers in the Christian faith. After his final expulsion he went to Rome where he successfully lobbied the Vatican to establish a church hierarchy for Vietnam. In *Cathechismus* de Rhodes Romanized the Vietnamese language—previously written in a variation of Chinese characters—which became the foundation of *quốc ngữ,* Vietnam's national language.

Catholic missionary work in the eighteenth and nineteenth centuries was highly successful, but was often accompanied by severe persecution. It is estimated that 30,000 Christians were martyred in the seventeenth and eighteenth centuries, and 100,000 more during the reign of three emperors from 1820 to 1885. This included several bishops, more than 200 priests, and a few hundred members of a women's order. Memories of these sufferings buttress the faith of Vietnamese Catholics today.

When Vietnam was partitioned by the 1954 Geneva Accords, more than 700,000 Catholics came south, raising the Catholic population in the South to 1,100,000, approximately fifteen percent of the total population. Around 830,500 Catholics remained in the North.

The Vietnamese people, *Kính,* were an ethnic group in southern China that moved south over centuries. They lived under Chinese control for a millennium, and secured an independent state only in AD 939. They generally embraced the philosophies and religions of China—Confucianism, Taoism and Buddhism. Isolated from the *Kính* in the mountain areas were dozens of smaller animistic ethnic groups.

Confucianism, a comprehensive social, political, philosophical and quasi-religious system that was embraced by the ruling classes in China and other Asian countries, emphasized human morality and good deeds and articulated the responsibilities of each person and class within their families and communities.

The common people embraced Taoism (The Way) which included elements of animism.

Popular Taoism revered nature and the care of ancestral spirits. It emphasized compassion, moderation and humility. Taoist rituals were performed in village communal houses (đình).

The third of the Tam Giáo (Three Religions) inherited from the Chinese was Buddhism. The Theravada Buddhism of Thailand and Cambodia today more closely resembles the original way of the Gautama Buddha. When the religion spread from India into China, however, it evolved into Mahayana Buddhism which enables followers of the Buddha to trust in the merits of bodhisattvas—saints who have refrained from entering nirvana in order to help deliver others. Buddhism was able to incorporate cultic elements from Taoism and Confucianism such as ancestral veneration. Missionaries coming to Vietnam in the twentieth century learned that ancestral veneration was the pervasive orientation of the majority of the people, whether or not they claimed to be Buddhists.

The twentieth century saw the development of a Vietnamese reformed Buddhism known as Hòa Hảo Buddhism which began in 1939; it emphasized lay activity rather than temple worship. Another wholly indigenous Vietnamese religious movement began within the Mekong River delta in the 1920s. Borrowing from Buddhism and the older religious impulses with an infusion of Christianity and current philosophies, the syncretistic Cao Đài religion held Confucius, Gautama Buddha, Jesus Christ and other figures such as Joan of Arc, Victor Hugo and Sun Yat Sen as important deities. This movement spread very rapidly, but waned by mid-century.

There were a few Protestant chaplains in Vietnam during the French colonial era, and churches were established in Hai Phong and Hanoi in the last decade of the nineteenth century. (Nguyen Kim Son and Dang Ngoc Phuc describe this development.) Substantial church buildings in these cities did not survive subsequent wars. A church building in Saigon built in 1904 survives to this day. While some of these pastor-chaplains urged the French Protestants to engage in missionary work among the indigenous people, little was done. Kenneth Scott Latourette in The Great Century: A History of the Expansion of Christianity, notes that Vietnam was bypassed in the nineteenth century.

When the Christian and Missionary Alliance (C&MA) was formed in 1887, one of the main objectives was "to take the Gospel to the closed land of Indo-China." The C&MA Foreign Secretary visited Saigon as early as 1893. Several C&MA missionaries working near the border in south China during the last decade of the nineteenth century tried to enter Vietnam.

The French kept close watch over the various movements within the countries they administered as colonies from the 1880s on: Vietnam, Cambodia, and Laos. Three sections of Vietnam were administered separately: Tonkin, Annam, and Cochin-China—the northern, central and southern areas.

An 1884 treaty between the French government and the Annamese Empire, centered in Hue, restricted all missionary activity within the Empire to the Roman Catholic Church. But in 1911 the Alliance purchased a property in Tourane (Da Nang) from the British and Foreign Bible Society and began a witness. (The first chairman was Isaac L. Hess, an Alliance missionary from China who was a former member of a Mennonite congregation near Lancaster, Pennsylvania.) Four years later the French government decreed there should be no further missionary activity. When this ban was lifted in 1916, mission activity was still restricted to the northern and central port cities and to Cochin-China.

Although the Alliance had limited missionary personnel, they quickly placed missionaries in Hanoi and Hai Phong in the north and at Saigon, My Tho, and Can Tho in the south. Though there were only a few baptisms the first five years, the church later grew quite rapidly through the witness of committed Christians. Stories of church growth in these areas read like the *Acts of the Apostles* with many of the new believers filled with a missionary zeal. The Tourane church in Annam doubled its membership yearly for a number of years until there were more than a thousand members.

The Alliance emphasized self-supporting, self-governing, and self-propagating congregations. A training program was established in Tourane and the scriptures translated—a process completed in 1926. The Vietnam Alliance Mission in 1927 recognized the Church as a separate body from the Mission. It was later officially called *Hội Thánh Tin Lành Việt Nam* (Evangelical Church of Vietnam).

By the year 1935 there were sixty-three self-supporting congregations. By 1941, 121 congregations were self-supporting, three-fourth of the total 160 churches. Occupying Vietnam during World War II, the Japanese interned some missionaries. Christians suffered along with their neighbors during the French Indochina War (1945-54). With the partitioning of the country in 1954, forty congregations with only eleven pastors remained north of the seventeenth parallel in the Democratic Republic of Vietnam led by President Ho Chi Minh. There were 154 organized congregations in the South—seventy-six with self-supporting status. By 1955 the Evangelical Church of Vietnam had 30,000 baptized members with a total Christian community of 50,000. Twenty-seven missionaries were assisting the church.

In addition to the work among the dominant *Kinh* community, the Alliance engaged in missionary work among several of the ethnic peoples in the central highlands. In 1955 there were thirty-one foreign missionaries working with the C&MA Tribes Mission, several Vietnamese missionaries, and a growing number of trained ethnic leaders. Church membership was 3,183 within seventy-one organized congregations and ninety-one other preaching points.

The Seventh Day Adventist Church began missionary activity in Vietnam in 1929, but by mid-century remained a fairly small church compared to the Evangelical Church of Vietnam.

MEDICAL PROGRAM AT BAN ME THUOT

Chapter 6

By the spring of 1956, a year and a half after MCC first came to Vietnam, a medical program was taking shape at the leprosarium located by the Rhade ethnic minority village of Buon Ea Ana—sixteen kilometers from Ban Me Thuot, the highland city of 12,000.

Delbert Wiens continued as director of the MCC programs. Adam Ewert was extending his term. Roy Eby completed his term in February and worked for a few months with a government resettlement project at Cai San in the Mekong delta maintaining tractors sent in to plow fallow land.

Wiens rented a three-bedroom apartment in early February to better accommodate the comings and goings of the MCC personnel. Eva Harshbarger closed the household in Da Lat and came to Saigon where she helped distribute MCC canned meat to local charitable institutions. She left in June.

A key member of the MCC team was Nguyen Van Ninh, a twenty-five-year-old refugee from the North whom Wiens hired the previous year. Ninh would continue working with the Mennonites for the next twenty years.

Knowing he would be leaving in just over a year, Wiens suggested that the home office might want to recruit personnel to handle administrative tasks who also might contemplate future mission work, including a witness to the Evangelical Church which, he said, had "a very one-sided orientation and needs an unobtrusive witness to the other aspects of Christianity."

Grace and Willard Krabill began studying the language of the Rhade minority group. Needing additional facilities at the leprosarium, Wiens' friend, French Chaplain Bertrand DeLuze, facilitated a donation from the departing French armed forces of three barracks, two large water tanks, mosquito nets and sheets. Adam Ewert assembled the old barracks on the leprosarium grounds. By summer's end there was a clinic building, warehouse, and living quarters for additional personnel. The two nurses, Juliette Sebus and Margaret Janzen, arrived in April and assisted Ewert in construction. Dr. Krabill observed that they were "ready for any task" and would make a positive spiritual contribution to unit life.

Writing to Byler, Krabill expressed optimism that MCC personnel would demonstrate to the young Tribes Church "the implications of discipleship, of Christian love, of Christian service." He also hoped they would "stimulate the C&MA toward a more sensitive social conscience" and become more accepting; he had heard some Alliance missionaries negatively refer to some Mennonites as theological "modernists."

The draft agreement between MCC and the Tribes Mission included the following points: Dr. Krabill would direct the medical department. MCC would finance any expansion of work to non-leprous patients. A mobile clinic was anticipated. MCC was not considering any missionary activities, and all spiritual ministries connected with the medical work would be under the Tribes Mission and Church.

Krabill and T. Grady Mangham, Jr., signed the draft agreement. It was accepted at the May C&MA Missionary Conference in Da Lat and sent to their New York office for approval.

Orie Miller came to Vietnam in late May for ten days—his second visit. After visiting Ban Me Thuot with Wiens, he flew to Da Lat while Wiens took a taxi to Saigon. He later described his unforgettable brush with death: "On the way down, the driver went too fast around a corner and we went down a bank and turned over a time or two. It was dark and I was pinned under by my leg, but a Vietnamese yanked me out. And for 125 kilometers into Saigon, we rode on the back of an empty truck. I still have a lump and a couple of not-yet-healed sores."

Miller was pleased with developments in Ban Me Thuot and approved adding additional facilities, but recognized the need to clarify long-term relationships with the C&MA New York office. He recommended recruiting another doctor and other personnel, including logistics support in a Saigon office.

In early September Krabill admitted their first hospital inpatient and would soon use the operating room—initially to perform surgery on ulcerated feet of leprous patients.

MCC had not yet received official permission from the government for a medical program—though President Diem had indicated it would be forthcoming. More disconcerting was news that the New York Alliance mission administrators did not support the draft agreement. In their revised plan dated late August, they eliminated the agreement to expand the leprosarium to provide for non-leprous patients, even though MCC had agreed to provide these facilities. Further, they added a statement casting doubt on any long-term relationship with MCC: *"In any event, this agreement with MCC will automatically be terminated when Doctor Krabill is no longer Director of the Medical Department, subject to renewal if desired by both sides."*

These changes upset the MCC team. The April agreement had been affirmed by the C&MA Vietnam leadership in May. If the New York administrators did not like it, why had it taken until mid-August for them to respond? MCC had already purchased materials to build the inpatient ward. Ewert had staked out the proposed buildings that Miller had approved, and another Pax man was being recruited to help with the construction. Put simply, the Alliance administrators did not want to see an expansion of the current facilities for which they would be responsible at such a time MCC might leave. Although they ac-

Grace Krabill with children of leprous parents. Rear: C&MA nurse Olive Kingsbury.

cepted Dr. Krabill, they were also concerned that MCC might send personnel they would find unacceptable. This was the first of several frustrating stops and starts over the next few years.

The New York administrators did not scuttle the whole project. A clinic for non-leprous patients was approved. The planned mobile medical program was also not jeopardized. However, without an inpatient ward, MCC medical staff would be unable to provide nursing care or treatment for injured or seriously ill patients encountered by the mobile medical team. And they might lose the USOM-donated medical equipment if it were not put to good use.

Miller promised Wiens and Krabill that he would meet with Alliance administrators. In spite of the current problem, Miller said, "I deeply believe the Lord has led us as a people to Vietnam and is leading to MCC and missions participation there, and that He will also lead in all the necessary relationships and understanding with C&MA."

Krabill wrote to L. Louis King in early October, trying to make a convincing argument to reverse their position on hospital expansion. He said that ethnic minorities in the area were asking for improved medical services and the leprosarium staff supported this. He noted that Dr. J. M. Webber, who had left the leprosarium three years earlier, had also insisted that there be an inpatient ward for non-leprous patients.

Krabill argued that the leprosarium required the services of a doctor but without this proposed expansion there was insufficient work to justify recruiting a doctor. These expanded services were important for good relationships with USOM and especially with the Vietnamese government, for President Diem had visited the leprosarium. Krabill reminded King that MCC was financing the capital development. He questioned their stipulation that the agreement be terminated when he was no longer medical director. If the revised stipulations of the C&MA administrators prevailed, it would require a reappraisal of the MCC medical unit plans.

Miller reported that the American Leprosy Missions had assured him that ALM was interested in supporting the leprosy project if a good continuing medical program could be assured. Miller, an ALM board member, was hopeful that joint consultations between C&MA, ALM and MCC might lead to a satisfactory agreement.

On a deputation visit early 1956 King met Krabill and Wiens and explained to them that the Alliance found that institutional work "has no value for their missions except for building up good will." He said "to spend money for hospitals is to waste it—from the standpoint of effectiveness in saving souls." Whenever an inpatient hospital is established, he said, there is always the impetus to expand the program. This was especially true in Ban Me Thuot, King argued, where an eventual MCC termination "could leave them with a real white elephant."

Wiens said that their conversation with King was sincere, frank, and very friendly. "If one accepts their beginning premises about institutional work," he wrote, "then a case can be made for their position as Mr. King ably did."

Given King's position, Wiens had already cabled Akron that the construction program was being halted. Miller would have to resolve the issues with C&MA in New York.

Still anticipating that Mennonite Board of Missions and Charities would develop a program in Vietnam, Executive Secretary J. D. Graber had visited Vietnam in August. Miller and Graber met with Alliance executives in New York City October 24. Afterward Miller wrote King confirming their "understanding" that an expansion of medical facilities at the leprosarium would not constitute a problem. Miller pledged that MCC would clear with the New York office before assigning an additional doctor.

Miller minimized C&MA-MCC differences and told Wiens and Krabill to proceed with the building program. However, King was much more direct and specific when he wrote late October to Raymond Currier of the American Leprosy Missions:

> The position of the Christian and Missionary Alliance is that the present relationship of the MCC to our Banmethuot leprosarium is of a temporary nature inasmuch as we would much prefer a relationship with the American Leprosy Missions. Until such a time as this relationship can be established, however, we are quite willing to have the MCC continue their present medical ministries. The MCC has agreed to work under these conditions with the full understanding that no permanent facility is to be developed which might constitute a problem for The Christians and Missionary Alliance in any future relationship it might enter into with the American Leprosy Missions.

When Krabill saw King's letter to Currier, it seemed obvious that King had not changed his mind at all, and was uncertain whether they should continue construction of the needed facilities. While waiting for more clarity on these matters, Dr. Krabill continued his care of the leprosarium residents who had not had been treated by a doctor for several years. He and the nurses also saw patients in the mobile clinic they had begun. During the months of August and September they had treated 618 patients from thirty-five villages and preparations were underway to begin a regular mobile clinic schedule.

MCC hired Y'Dun Ksor and his wife, H'Chioh, to serve as interpreters. They were trained in some nursing and diagnostic skills which increased their effectiveness to the MCC team. Y'Dun, one of the best educated minority persons in the area, spoke English, French, Vietnamese and several ethnic minority languages and dialects. The MCC nurses, Juliette Sebus and Margaret Janzen, both spoke French which was useful in relating to government officials.

Amid conflicting signals from the MCC Akron office and C&MA's New York office, Miller in early December informed Krabill that, unless there were unforeseen developments, MCC could "move forward . . . in faith" in line with the C&MA's August revised plan. MCC was recruiting another doctor and would provide the needed financial support even though the relief department was urging budget reductions.

Beside the off-again on-again drama playing out between MCC and the Christian and Missionary Alliance, Wiens and Krabill were attempting to get the Vietnamese government to approve its medical program. Since entering Vietnam in 1954, MCC worked under a blanket authorization granted to voluntary agencies. Without a specific contract, there was concern that MCC might need to pay tariffs on imported medical supplies.

With Wiens' January 1955 request for a contract still pending, Wiens arranged to meet President Diem in May 1956. It is unclear why Wiens did not ask Krabill to accompany him, since the doctor would have had much more clout in convincing the President.

Three months later Ninh, the MCC interpreter, learned from one of Ngo Dinh Diem's secretaries that the President needed more time to consider this request because Mennonites did not "join their army" in the United States. The President had asked Wiens about Mennonites, and Wiens had briefly explained their history and theology, including non-participation in military service. "A good many of the religious sects here preach pacifism," Wiens wrote to Orie Miller. "I don't blame him for being worried about people that practice it."

In mid-September Dr. Krabill submitted an outline of the proposed MCC Medical Services Project to Dr. Duong Cam Chuong, the head of the regional medical programs. He explained that MCC, though not a mission organization, carried out this service "as an expression of our Christian faith" and concern for all people.

They would have a base treatment clinic at the leprosarium and hold a clinic twice weekly at the Evangelical Bible School in Ban Me Thuot. The mobile clinic would be outfitted on a four-wheel drive vehicle that would visit ten surrounding villages, five each week over two weeks, with the third week used for maintenance and restocking supplies. They would focus on special needs like sanitation, privy construction, water supply, vaccinations, and distribute food and clothing as needed. A third component would be simple inpatient facilities for those requiring constant nursing care.

Krabill was concerned about President Diem's delay in granting approval for the medical program. Krabill's August request to meet with the President was unanswered. Although the local health officials in October had given verbal approval to operate the mobile clinic on a tentative basis, the Minister of Health said the program would have to be put on hold until receiving approval from the President. But MCC continued the clinic, assuming they could temporarily operate under prior authorization given the C&MA infirmary to carry out work for the benefit of the local people.

In late 1956 Krabill and his wife spent nearly two months visiting the MCC medical programs in Indonesia and leprosaria in Malaya (Malaysia) and Thailand, gaining information helpful in developing the Vietnam program.

In April 1957 Mangham authorized MCC to proceed with plans to build an inpatient facility.

Alliance arranged for a service of dedication of the clinic facilities on Saturday, April 20, with many local ethnic minority persons as well as Vietnamese government officials attending. This also included a warehouse and a nursery for young children born to leprous patients.

That very same day President Ngo Dinh Diem signed an order authorizing MCC "to establish a consultation house and dispensary and a hospital. Having a feature of relief, these establishments will be built to give free services to the patients." The medical programs would be responsible to the Minister of Health. The document stipulated that "the MCC engage themselves not to incite or make propaganda for anything against the Vietnamese laws."

Building the inpatient ward hit another roadblock a few months later. Robert M.

Willard Krabill with interpreter Y'Dun Ksor.

Chrisman replaced King as Asia Secretary without being fully briefed. Now in September Chrisman notified their Vietnam administrator that MCC has not been authorized to establish the inpatient facility! Clearly frustrated, Krabill asked the Akron office, "Has there not been the tendency for MCC to 'gloss over' some very fundamental differences in approach between us and C&MA?" Failure to recognize these differences would "simply postpone the day of even greater frustration and disappointment."

Looking ahead, Krabill wrote, the team feels "that we should begin now to seriously seek out other medical service projects where MCC would be free to carry out its own objectives and ideals, and to gradually taper off the program here and make an exit as gracefully as possible."

Robert Miller, MCC's Director of Relief, acknowledged Krabill's concerns, saying the matter would "be cleared up soon" and MCC would have their inpatient facility. Miller said MCC hoped to stay in Ban Me Thuot a few years until the general medical program could be turned over to C&MA or some other group. Yet he gave approval for staff to look for an opportunity to develop a medical program in another needy area.

Responding, Krabill said he did not know the basis of MCC's hope to stay at Ban Me Thuot several more years. It was clear to the doctor that MCC was welcome only until the C&MA doctor arrived and completed her language study. Dr. Ardel Vietti was planning to arrive in January 1958.

Orie Miller had "a very satisfactory interview" with Alliance administrators in mid-November, receiving authorization to complete constructing inpatient facilities. But Chrisman's correspondence to the leprosarium administer was vague, so MCC was asked not to proceed! Only after Robert Miller phoned Chrisman were the Vietnam staff free to complete the construction and begin using the inpatient facility.

In a comprehensive medical report submitted in November 1957 to Dr. Chuong, the regional medical director, Krabill described MCC's two general clinics, one at the leprosarium for treatment of villagers from surrounding villages, the other at the Mission Evangelique, the C&MA Tribes Mission headquarters in Ban Me Thuot, and the Land Rover mobile clinic that served five villages. Beginning with 541 patient treatments given during the initial month of October 1956 to as many as 1,612 in May 1957, in thirteen months MCC's clinics had given 14,090 patient treatments. Donald Goering arrived in August as the second doctor.

The Alliance New York administrators were not pleased with the size of MCC's Ban Me Thuot team. In late 1955 King had invited Dr. Krabill to become medical director of the leprosarium, and now—two years later—nine staff members were there! Besides the doctors and two nurses, Juliette Sebus and Margaret Janzen, Duane Swartzendruber was general maintenance man, replacing Adam Ewert. Grace Krabill was secretary to the director, and Loua Goering the laboratory technician. Esther Lefever was the matron, and Harry served as unit leader in addition to his responsibilities with the mobile clinic.

When Chrisman and King visited Vietnam in late January 1958, they met with Dr. Krabill and the Tribes Mission Executive Committee. The two executives expressed support for an inpatient ward; Krabill said it "was all we could have hoped for." Learning that Evangelical Church leaders wanted to develop a cooperative medical program with MCC, King supported this as a valid Christian ministry that would not affect the Alliance focus to channel all of their available financial resources into direct evangelistic ministries.

Swartzendruber resumed construction, soon completing the twelve-bed hospital ward. But Krabill faced another unexpected challenge when the Ministry of Health informed him that MCC had not been authorized to operate a mobile clinic. The matter was resolved several weeks later in discussions with the Ministry of Health. The government was opposed in principle to mobile operations over which the government had no prior knowledge and over which it could exercise little control.

Krabill explained: "But when Dr. Khai realized that our clinic was scheduled long in advance, that only a limited number of villages were included, and that members of the government health services were welcome to accompany us from time to time, then Dr. Khai agreed our work could continue—provided we did not call it a mobile clinic. So, as of now, MCC no longer operates a mobile clinic in Viet Nam, but rather has a number of village dispensaries which it regularly visits. An interesting world, this."

A very interesting world indeed!

OTHER DEVELOPMENTS 1956-1959

Chapter 7

Although the Geneva Accords of July 1954 called for elections within two years to unify the country, the Republic of Vietnam's President Ngo Dinh Diem in Saigon refused Hanoi's request to organize an all-country election. He maintained that South Vietnam was not bound by the Accords because it had not signed them. Further, he declared that the North did not have sufficient freedom to guarantee fair elections. Hanoi lacked sufficient international support to force the issue, so July 1956 came and went without elections. Meanwhile Diem was consolidating his power in the South, but at the cost of internal support.

The Mennonite Central Committee was not motivated by political objectives in Vietnam. The Akron administrators, its personnel in the field, and the thousands of church members in its supporting constituency were concerned about ameliorating physical needs in the spirit of care exemplified by Jesus Christ as the MCC motto stated so succinctly, "In the name of Christ."

The Mennonites did not embrace an anti-communist agenda. At the same time, however, Mennonites did not accept the communist ideology of the Soviet Union or of the new People's Republic of China. Communism's atheistic ideology seemed quite incompatible with their understanding of the Christian faith. Furthermore, within many Mennonite communities in Canada and the United States were first and second generation refugees with shared memories of the tragedies their families suffered within Russia as they fled the Soviet revolution in the 1920s.

Harry and Esther (Peachey) Lefever came to Vietnam in August 1956 and were assigned to Ban Me Thuot. Harry served as unit leader and Esther as matron. Paxmen Carl Hurst and Duane Swartzendruber arrived from Europe in February 1957. Hurst stayed in Saigon to work with the material aid program since Wiens was near the end of his term. Robert Miller, Akron's Director of Relief, asked Krabill to become Vietnam director when Wiens terminated; he served effectively even though he had to travel frequently from his Ban Me Thuot base.

Krabill urged William T. Snyder, MCC's Assistant Executive Secretary, to request an appointment with President Diem during his May 1957 U.S. visit in order to further "good relations with the Diem government." The President's schedule was too full for such a meeting.

MCC personnel, like the Alliance missionaries, enjoyed working with the ethnic minorities. Rhade and Jarai were dominant groups in the Ban Me Thuot area. Although called "savages" by some people, Krabill experienced them as "extremely passive, peace-loving people."

In a May publicity piece, Harry Lefever described the communities:

> Scattered throughout the mountains of central Viet Nam are many man-made clearings upon which stand the long bamboo houses of the Rhade tribe. These thatched-roofed houses raised on stilts are always surrounded by the village cows, buffalos, and chickens, which keep the village grass lawn-like. Right next to the clearings rise the green, jagged branches of the king of the forest—the bamboo trees.... The nearby flowing stream adds beauty to the village scene, but it is more important to the villagers as their source of water and village bath. These villagers rise at the break of dawn to the chatter of the monkeys, to get at their work before the hot noon-day sun

chases them to shelter. Some of the men and women spend the day in the rice fields, the children carry water in gourds placed in a basket on their backs, the young girls winnow rice by tossing it into the wind from their large oval baskets, and then grind it with a Biblical-like mortar and pestle. Those who are not busy with these jobs, spend the hot days in their cool bamboo houses talking or sleeping.

Lefever told how the MCC mobile medical clinic came to one such village in April 1957 the day after a wind-swept fire devastated the village, destroying thirteen long houses, leaving 200 people homeless. The fire also burned rice granaries. MCC distributed blankets and clothes, but had no rice to give. The Raday Christian Church sent out a plea to donate rice, gourds, clothes and mats, and the following week the MCC vehicle was able to deliver rice, gourds, mats and building supplies, the first time this church had responded to such relief needs.

After James and Arlene Stauffer arrived in Saigon late May, Wiens wrote to the home office, "We enjoy having the missionaries with us, though I am afraid we are being rather hard on them." A flu epidemic had floored many people, including the MCC housekeeper cook, and Arlene volunteered to do "the rather difficult experience" of cooking in a Vietnamese kitchen. Orie Miller thanked Wiens for his support in procuring the visas for the Stauffers, and welcomed his help in securing visas for a second missionary couple, Everett and Margaret Metzler.

The summer of 1957 saw an unusual population explosion within the MCC Ban Me Thuot unit. Grace Krabill gave birth to Merrill Owen in June, and Esther Lefever gave birth to Kristina Joy in September. Dr. Donald and Loua Goering arrived in early August, and Loua gave birth to Donna Lou in October. Esther and Grace also made plans to teach a sewing class, and Harry taught English to interested students. The MCC team also began training village nurse aides.

In July Krabill received a request from the United States Operations Mission to have MCC supervise their medical assistance in several rural areas of central Vietnam. Anticipating Dr. Goering's arrival, Krabill tested the idea with Akron. Robert Miller initially expressed no objection if it would not "compromise any principles of faith and witness." But after conversation with Snyder and his father, Orie, he wrote that it would be better to enter into agreements with the Vietnamese Ministry of Health rather than with USOM.

Krabill also reported to Akron that the Evangelical Church had "indicated interest in a church-sponsored hospital." Although Krabill realized that ECVN leaders were not aware of the complexities of administering a medical program, he said an MCC expression of interest could hasten such a development.

Concluding his Vietnam assignment, Delbert Wiens left Vietnam on August 18. Now twenty-six years old, Wiens had enabled MCC to begin its ministries in Vietnam. In these three years Wiens wrote hundreds of letters and reports to MCC administrators, traveled throughout South Vietnam frequently to assess the needs and keep informed of new opportunities, and communicated with officials at all levels of the new Vietnamese government and with officials of the United States Operations Mission. He developed good ties with the Social Welfare Committee of the Evangelical Church and had good relations with Alliance missionaries.

New MCC personnel Glenn and Geneva Stoltzfus arrived in Saigon late September. In mid-November Everett and Margaret Metzler arrived in Saigon to join the Stauffers with Eastern Mennonite Board of Missions and Charities. The MCC personnel looked forward to partnering with them as they developed a mission program in Saigon.

At the request of a visiting professor, Richard W. Lindholm, Krabill prepared a paper in early 1958 about the work of the Protestant churches in Vietnam. Observing that the Indo-China War was followed by "the movement of over 800,000 refugees from the communist controlled north zone to the free zone of South Viet Nam," Krabill said this stirred North American Protestant churches to action. He noted how Church World Service and the Mennonite Central Committee came to Vietnam immediately after the Geneva Accords.

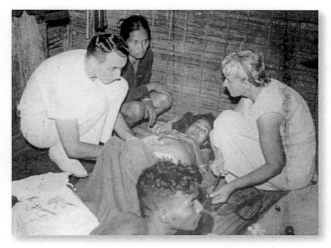

Dr. Goering and Margaret Janzen making a house call.

By this date the Evangelical Church of Vietnam had some 40,000 adherents in 180 congregations throughout the country with 280 pastors. Besides this, the evangelizing work of the Christian and Missionary Alliance and the Evangelical Church in Vietnam led to a Christian community of 3,000 among the ethnic minority peoples. Krabill noted the formation of a 1954 ad hoc social welfare committee in the Evangelical Church which then became part of the organizational structure of the church. The Alliance Mission, while not subsidizing pastors, assisted the church with special projects such as church buildings and parsonages, and responded to relief needs. Krabill said that C&MA leaders "played an important role in assisting and advising" MCC and Church World Service personnel.

"Certainly the Christian church has been one of the major bulwarks against the spread of totalitarian communism in Viet Nam," Krabill wrote, "and the C&MA with its extensive program is one of the major groups which . . . will continue to be a strengthening influence." He cited the contribution of "numerous Bible schools," several primary schools for ethnic minorities around Da Lat, a clinic at Da Lat, and the Ban Me Thuot Leprosarium which a government official had called "the foremost leprosy treatment center in Viet Nam."

While in a real sense Mennonite Central Committee was contributing to a "free-world" coalition headed by the United States with a desire to build and strengthen a non-communist country in Southeast Asia, and working alongside people from agencies dedicated to these political objectives, neither Dr. Krabill nor other MCC personnel viewed their service in Vietnam in political terms.

Krabill's concluding statements suggest a religious missionary motivation rather than a political rationale. The objectives of Protestant churches, he wrote, were "to serve the needs of a suffering people regardless of creed; to conduct a person-to-person ministry which will be of maximum benefit to the giver and the recipient of material aid; to strengthen the Vietnamese church for the tasks it faces, tasks made more strenuous by the difficult times just passed through; [and] to acquaint the Vietnamese people, with deeds as well as words, with the essence of the Christian gospel."

Nevertheless, in referring to the government appreciation for the Protestant relief work, Krabill was acknowledging their contribution to nation-building.

Willard Krabill's primary concern was to be a good physician. In February 1958 he wrote a publicity piece entitled "A Day with a Doctor." He told of waking at 6:00 a.m. to the whooping call of the gibbons and the songs of many birds. At 7:30 there was a Rhade language devotional service for all the staff who cared for the two hundred people in the leprosarium. At 8:00 they made the rounds in the forty-six bed dormitory ward. Patients came to the non-leprous clinic at 10:00. At 11:00 a.m. staff met in conference, followed by lunch and family devotions.

At 2:00 p.m. Krabill was back at the leprosarium, in the operating room, taking x-rays, consulting with nurses. Kraybill noted that a total of 450 leprosy patients receive treatment.

At 6:30 the whole MCC unit gathered for supper, followed by staff reviews and preparation for the next days. The day ended at 11:00 p.m.

Krabill concluded his article: "Today those of us connected with this ministry have reached 500 people who otherwise would have received no care at all. God alone knows the spiritual fruit which result from this day's activities."

Orie Miller made another administrative visit to Vietnam early June 1958, a few months after the death of his wife, Elta Wolf Miller, in mid-February.

After spending a few days in Ban Me Thuot, Miller observed that the hospital "begins to have and to look respectability," yet indicated that MCC was prepared to further upgrade the leprosarium facilities, and could provide a builder team and assign available medical personnel. The MCC Board approved his recommendation to appropriate $2,000 "toward capital facility upgrading" with the understanding that both the Alliance and the Leprosy Mission would each contribute a similar amount.

In Saigon, Miller met with an ethnic Chinese pastor and also with the Evangelical Church hospital committee and affirmed MCC's readiness to work with both groups in developing medical programs, indicating that a doctor was being recruited.

With Krabill terminating, Miller proposed an Executive Committee Administration to direct MCC programs, consisting of Stoltzfus as executive chairman, Donald Goering, and missionary James Stauffer. Miller reasoned that if both MCC and Eastern Mennonite Board of Missions and Charities were to work harmoniously together in Vietnam, there should be some official liaison. Paul Kraybill, however, questioned EMBMC involvement in MCC administration. Nevertheless, Stauffer did meet with MCC personnel regularly to review developments.

Clearing his desk two days before leaving Vietnam July 3, 1958, Willard Krabill reviewed the MCC

Dr. Krabill and Esther Lefever welcome Orie Miller to Ban Me Thuot.

programs. MCC would plan to end its official involvement in the Alliance medical program by mid-1959, but would consider longer service if requested. There was still uncertainty about the proposed medical program in Saigon, with both a Chinese evangelical congregation and the Evangelical Church seeking MCC medical personnel.

Krabill sensed that Mennonite-Alliance relationships were good. "Basic goodwill is present and strong" in MCC's relationship with the Evangelical Church, Krabill wrote, but "some repairs [are] needed."

Krabill's reference to "needed repairs" with the Evangelical Church stemmed from poor communication with the Evangelical Church President Le Van Thai at the time of Orie Miller's recent visit. Miller needed to shorten his original Vietnam schedule, and did not meet with Pastor Thai until the morning of his departure when he met with Alliance mission leaders and members of the Church's executive committee. Following his typical administrative pattern, Miller reported his findings and recommendations, then asked whether they had any questions. He addressed his comments primarily to C&MA leaders. Pastor Thai was hoping to discuss with Miller ways that the Mennonites might work with the Church, but instead heard Miller's conclusions without any prior conversations! Too late Krabill and Stauffer realized that Miller inadvertently snubbed the Church president. After Miller's presentation, Thai had only a short time to ask a few questions before Miller hurried off to the airport to catch his plane.

Aware that Pastor Thai was slighted, Krabill and Stauffer apologized, and insisted on the need to talk together. Thai invited them to meet with him and the Church executive committee in Nha Trang the following week. There Stauffer and Krabill were reminded of the importance of good communication with Church officials; Thai told them that government officials sometimes asked him about the Mennonites, and he was unable to give much information. Thai inferred that the Mennonites were able to work in Vietnam, thanks to the affirmation of the Evangelical Church. It was clear that Thai appreciated what the Mennonites contributed to their Church and to Vietnamese society and wanted to see them continue their work. Out of this meeting with Pastor Thai came a proposal for MCC and Vietnam Mennonite Mission leaders to have monthly meetings with Evangelical Church leaders.

A few weeks after the Krabill family left, Mrs. Goering was diagnosed with a serious illness and advised to transfer immediately to the States for treatment. The Goering family left on August 15. Thus within a few weeks MCC Vietnam went from having two doctors to having none at all.

Thanks to a delay in receiving visas for Indonesia, Dr. Clarence Rutt and his wife Helen, a nurse, were able to assist briefly at Ban Me Thuot. Arriving in country late August, they immediately went to the leprosarium. Dr. Rutt kept very busy, performing many surgeries. Swartzendruber observed that Dr. Rutt was eager "to try anything he had seen tried while in med school!"

Dr. Vietti, the Alliance doctor in language study, was deeply appreciative of their six weeks' service. After they left, she arranged to spend a day weekly at the leprosarium.

Nurse Juliette Sebus, having served two and one-half years, returned home in October, replaced by Elfrieda Neufeld. Lois Cressman served as matron for a few months, but transferred to Saigon when Ann Ewert arrived in November. Don Voth arrived in August.

Swartzendruber and Voth gave a glimpse of unit life in their October 1958 Unit Report. The men attended English language worship service twice that month at the "Grand Bungalow" compound of the U.S. Military Advisory Assistance Group in Ban Me Thuot. Alliance missionaries were in charge of planning these services which were attended by MAAG, C&MA, International Voluntary Service, and MCC personnel. One Sunday, when Stoltzfus and Ninh were up from Saigon, the MCC unit was in charge of the services. Voth preached the sermon, and the four Pax men—Duane Swartzendruber, Leland Good, Don Voth and newly-arrived Alan Hochstetler—provided the music.

In their October report Swartzendruber and Voth commented on political activity involving the local Rhade and Jarai minority people. President Diem had resettled tens of thousands of displaced Vietnamese *Kinh* from the North into this area. These new settlers were granted titles to fallow land that had been cultivated for generations by the minority people who never held legal titles to this common land. They practiced swidden agriculture, the traditional pattern which involved slashing and burning vegetation, farming the area for a few years before moving on to other areas before eventually returning.

Already in early 1955 a group of mostly Christian Rhade and Bahnar young people, upset with Vietnamese discrimination and violation of their land rights, formed *Le Front pour la Liberation des Montagnards*—the front for liberation of the mountain people. Early in 1958 this group merged with Jerai and other minorities in the Pleiku area further north to form the Bajaraka Movement which in July issued a notice to the United Nations and to the French and U.S. embassies, denouncing racial discrimination and requesting assistance to secure independence. After peaceful demonstrations in Ban Me Thuot and Pleiku in August and September calling for the return of their lands and self-government, the Diem government used military force to end the demonstrations and on September 15 arrested and imprisoned the leaders. Y'Nam, one of the leprosarium Rhade nurses, was interrogated by police and barely escaped being jailed.

When the twelve-bed inpatient hospital expansion was approved, Alan Hostetler as project foreman drew plans to Dr. Vietti's specifications. While still waiting on all the funds to come together to build the new wards, Stoltzfus on February 6, 1959, participated in the dedication of the clinic and hospital facilities completed months before which were now in full use. In his presentation speech, he gave the background of MCC's three and one-half years involvement and concluded by saying: "This building and this leprosarium are not located in Saigon or in Da Lat or even in Ban Me Thuot. They are not located along the main highways of Vietnam nor are they by an airport or river. The site for this leprosarium is in the center of the people who need medical care. It is a part of a Raday village. It was built and is operated to benefit the people of this area. It is your leprosarium. It is a privilege this morning to present this Christian hospital and clinic to you."

Leprosarium-Hospital at Ban Me Thuot.

Pastor Y'Ham, Secretary of the Tribes Church of Viet Nam, responded, thanking the MCC personnel. Addressing the assembled group, he said:

> As a representative of my own people, I must say something at this occasion about the dedication of this hospital.
>
> Seeing this new hospital that you are going to dedicate as God's work in this province of Darlak, for us, Raday and Vietnamese people, I realize your love and mercy for us who are miserable because of many kinds of diseases. . . . I see your love for God is revealed in your love for people. That's why you have built this hospital for our people in the name of Christ, who is our love and mercy. So you have obeyed Jesus' word: "Verily I say unto you, Inasmuch as ye have done it unto one of the least of these my brethren, ye have done it unto me" (Matt. 24:40) . . .
>
> Now, how about us, brothers and sisters, what do we think about this dedication? As for me, I think we must carefully listen and open our hearts so we could clearly see God loves us, He wants to cure our souls and our bodies. These MCC members are Christians [who] love God and obey what Jesus has said, "Be good to everyone, treat their souls and their bodies at the same time." . . . In this hospital they give out medicines to treat two kinds of diseases. They treat sins with Gospel and prayer. . . . They also then give medicine to the patients.

Two hundred and fifty Rhade people attended the dedication, coming from fourteen villages. The Rhade employees and the MCCers joined together in singing "Great is Thy Faithfulness" in the Rhade language.

Voth summarized the history of the MCC work in Ban Me Thuot. In an understatement he said "there were difficulties" in building the small hospital. Duane Swartzendruber drew up the plans in March 1957 and the foundation was laid on May 15. With help from Vietnamese carpenters and masons, the clinic began treating outpatients in August 1957. In November 1958 the inpatient ward was first used.

The new facility, Voth said, was a 30 x 6 meter wood frame structure divided into three sections with steel siding and asbestos sheet roof. The treatment section included a consulting room, a treatment room, a sterilizing room, and a store room. The one-room ward had thirteen beds. This section also included a large bath and a room for the on-call nurse. The third section was a large room providing housing for patients' families who came to care for them.

The pattern of holding clinics in outlying villages was changed, largely due to delays in building inpatient facilities and limited personnel. Nurses continued to visit a distant village, but clinics to several villages were discontinued because of an impassable river bridge.

Around thirty patients were treated daily in the clinic at the hospital, and the average ward population was nine patients. Clinic patients were expected to contribute two piasters and ward patients ten piasters daily ($.03 and $.15 U.S.). Local Christian nurses led devotional services in the ward each morning.

Margaret Janzen, the outpatient clinic nurse who planned to leave in June, described both the challenges and the joys of working at the hospital. She referred to Elfrieda's difficult task "trying to make nurses of native boys who can read and write but know almost no arithmetic . . . , who can't read a calendar, and who have various other gaps in their knowledge." The nurses were rarely free on Saturday afternoons, and worked part-time nearly every Sunday.

But Margaret was happy to work there. In a February 1959 report to Akron, she said: "I think any doctor and any nurse would be happy to work in circumstances where the need for service is so evident, and also where results of one's work are so evident. In my estimation the medical work among the tribespeople here is urgently needed, and it has been a very gratifying experience to have a part in it."

She continued: "Dr. Krabill worked hard to minimize all the petty difficulties there were at times in our relationship with C&MA and he laid a good foundation for our work here. At present again we have a staff here which has the confidence and respect of the missionaries here and we enjoy good working relationship."

The MCC team in the highlands in May 1959 was functioning smoothly, albeit without a regular doctor. Dr. Vietti was still studying the Vietnamese and Rhade languages, and then planned to visit leprosaria in South East Asia before becoming medical director of the leprosarium. Elfrieda would continue as the outpatient clinic nurse. Elnora Weaver, who arrived in Vietnam April 15, was the inpatient nurse. Dr. John Dick and his family were planning to come late summer. Don Voth served as unit leader with all sorts of duties. N. Robert Ziemer, Alliance director of the leprosarium, commended Voth for organizing a devotional service presenting the gospel to patients confined to the inpatient hospital unit. Ann Ewert managed the household. Alan Hochstetler was making progress in the hospital ward construction project. Leland Good had a variety of maintenance jobs and helped Hochstetler. Ziemer also praised Good and Hochstetler for grading the road with the tractor to permit easier travel from the leprosarium to town. Duane Swartzendruber was nearing the end of his term. Stoltzfus said that Duane was "one of the 'good things'" that had happened to the MCC unit. He had become fluent in the Rhade language and had many friends. His mechanical skills made him a valuable team member.

Life was not all work and no play. Good and Hochstetler had just purchased a used motorcycle to travel around. Good was itching to get wild game, and purchased Harry Lefever's shotgun. James Stauffer, who with Arlene had spent four days visiting Ban Me Thuot at the time

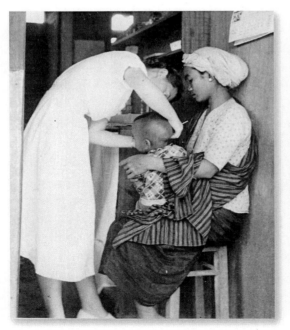

Elnora Weaver treating child at leprosarium.

Don Voth giving Lee Good a haircut.

of the February dedication service, wrote about going out one evening to look for the wild elephants that had ruined the banana groves in one village. Voth, he said, climbed a tree and saw one of the elephants amble away. Stauffer described a recent incident in another village where a tiger pounced on a man as he went to the toilet at night. The villagers heard his screams and ran out with lights—yelling and scaring the tiger from his dead body.

While MCC had made the decision to phase out of the Ban Me Thuot medical program, the future program direction was not yet clear. William T. Snyder, newly-named MCC Executive Secretary, and Paul N. Kraybill, newly-named Secretary of Eastern Mennonite Board of Missions and Charities—both of them protégés of Orie O. Miller—were both planning to visit Vietnam the end of May 1959. Stoltzfus suggested that May "could well prove to be a month of decision."

The Mennonites and the Alliance staff shared mutual appreciation. When William Snyder arrived in Vietnam late May, Dr. Vietti handed him a letter. It read:

Dear Mr. Snyder:

Since hearing of your intended visit we have been praying that you might be filled with His wisdom in your evaluation of the M.C.C. work here and in all of Viet Nam. Through unstinting activities of each of the M.C.C. personnel as well as through the abundant food, medicines, and equipment supplied by the home churches in America, the Banmethuot Leprosarium is accomplishing its purpose of Christian service to the community. Now may God guide you in future assistance so that the name of Christ may be glorified among the heathen.

The leprosarium staff wishes to assure you and our brethren in the Mennonite churches of our deep appreciation and thankfulness for the work accomplished and assistance given in so many ways. May God richly reward you with more of Himself and the fullness of His grace.

Sincerely for the Leprosarium Staff,
/s/ E. Ardel Vietti, M. D.

MATERIAL AID

Chapter 8

The Ban Me Thuot medical program became MCC's primary Vietnam work. However, as the only Protestant relief agency in Vietnam after Church World Service phased out in 1958, MCC continued to administer a modest program of material aid distribution from its Saigon base.

This assistance expressed international support for the Vietnamese people and—in a very real sense—symbolized support for the government in South Vietnam. Delbert Wiens tells of a Sunday evening reception in November 1956 when two Vietnamese officials said to him: "Really, we almost feel ashamed to receive help from America when other countries need it so much more. But we needed your help. It was the knowledge that we had friends helping us that make it possible for us to have hope and strength to build Viet Nam."

Although Mennonite Central Committee's mission was not political, Wiens recognized the political import of MCC's programs. During these years when MCC handled U.S. surplus food items, all packing lists, export declarations, and bills of lading required this printed statement: "United States law prohibits disposition of these commodities to the Soviet bloc, Communist China, North Korea, Macao, Hong Kong, or communist-controlled areas of Vietnam and Laos unless otherwise authorized by the United States." While this restriction concerned some MCC personnel, it was generally assumed not possible to distribute these goods to "communist controlled areas of Vietnam."

One of the unique commodities MCC distributed was canned meat, prepared by MCC's own portable canner that travels to North America communities where volunteers donate time and meats. In May and June 1956 MCC Vietnam distributed 300 cartons, twenty-four cans each, to hospitals, orphanages, refugee camps, refugee schools, and some to the Evangelical Social Welfare Committee to aid needy families. Some was retained to supplement the diets of leprosarium patients. A can of beef was given to each patient every three weeks.

Another special item were the Christmas Bundles prepared by North American families for children of various ages; each contained new clothing and hygienic items pinned inside a folded towel. In January 1957 MCC distributed 4,000 bundles. It was no problem that the shipment arrived too late to be given out by Christmas; the children would have new clothing for the more important Tet New Year that fell on January 31. The Ban Me Thuot team distributed 200 of these bundles to children four to sixteen years of age in five different villages through the mobile health clinic. Before the bundles were given out, their interpreter, Y-Dun Ksor, told the Christmas story to the children and their parents.

Children were delighted to receive these bundles. Wiens reminded the home office not to put blue jeans in bundles for children over eight years of age. It was "against the law to wear them," he wrote. Vietnam's First Lady, Madam Nhu, wanted to protect the country from a "cowboy" mentality.

MCC distributed forty tons of U.S. government surplus rice in hundred pound sacks in 1956. Nearly half of this went to the Ban Me Thuot Leprosarium; some was distributed through

50

the Church's welfare committee, and some given directly to the Church's orphanage in Nha Trang. In 1956 Wiens also arranged for the distribution of 158 tons of surplus food imported by Church World Service: rice, beans, dried milk and cheese. Much of this was distributed through the Church committee. By contrast, the Catholic Relief Services in 1956 disbursed 140,000 tons of surplus foods!

Shortly before Wiens terminated, he reflected on the changes he saw; people were "less poor" than when he arrived in 1954. The Evangelical Church pastors were among the "neediest groups," he observed, with large families, little support from their congregations, and church polity that prevented them from taking another job. Although the amount of commodities distributed through the Church's Social Welfare Committee was not large, Wiens believed it had some positive impact on the Vietnamese Church, "encouraging them to social action."

After Wiens left in August 1957, Carl Hurst, who had arrived in February, managed the material aid program from Saigon. Glenn Stoltzfus gradually took over these duties after he and Geneva arrived in August.

In mid-1957 Hurst cancelled an order of forty tons of broken rice which the U.S. government was offering. After Catholic Relief Services received a sample of this rice, the Vietnamese who examined it insisted that it was only fit to feed pigs! Distributing such rice would destroy the good will that had been built up by the assistance program, they said, and the communists would use this as proof that the Americans give only the junk they cannot use at home!

The 1957 typhoon season was exceptionally long with multiple tropical storms and typhoons. Typhoon Irma struck central Vietnam the second week in October, causing extensive flooding. MCC shipped relief supplies to Da Nang by boat and Lefever and Swartzendruber took additional goods by truck. Although the men were unable to personally distribute the aid because of the flooded conditions, they did meet with many Evangelical Church pastors.

MCC's Director of Relief, J. N. Byler, regularly requested evaluation of material aid supplies. In 1957 Esther and Harry Lefever encouraged Byler to send black poplin materials hemmed in fifty-inch squares that the ethnic minority women could use for wrap-around skirts—rather than North American women's clothing. Blankets and comforters were appreciated. Not all garments that found their way into the bales of clothing were appropriate. In a humorous letter from Glenn Stoltzfus to Akron, he wrote: "No snowsuits worn here for 25,000 years!"

Wiens, Krabill, and the Lefevers all noted that when distributions were made through the Church Relief Committee, the recipients were primarily Christians, even though physical need as the only criterion for distribution was thoroughly explained. Yet Church distributions could be more easily monitored than when goods were given through government channels.

When Hurst in September reported that some distributions of MCC beef were supervised by a "very conscientious man" from the Ministry of Social Action, Byler expressed concern about large food distribution programs, specifically that some of the MCC canned beef was being distributed by the government. Quoting from the MCC Handbook, Byler said relief assistance should be "properly supervised by American personnel and consistently administered in a Christian manner and as an evangelical witness to Christian love." While granting the freedom of MCC personnel to develop patterns of assistance appropriate to each country, he said MCC was not able to respond to great areas of need "where a government is responsible" but only to supplement larger distribution programs.

Byler urged Stoltzfus to follow careful distribution procedures. Smaller distributions would minimize waste and the temptation to sell the goods, Byler said. Periodic checkups should be made, including unannounced visits.

Byler's concern prompted changes in MCC's material aid program. In conversations with the Ministry of Social Action, MCC agreed to continue direct assistance to some institutions in the Saigon area but would not transfer commodities to the Ministry for distribution. The Church's Social Welfare Committee was also informed that MCC would terminate assistance to the poor families within the church, though they would still respond to emergency needs.

Saigon support staff Carl Hurst, Geneva and Glenn Stoltzfus.

Since the Church provided no budget to the relief committee, Stoltzfus continued the practice of giving small grants for the committee's overhead expenses. Later MCC administrators would insist that the Church cover overhead expenses, and emphasized the need to solicit contributions from the Church constituency to assist those in need.

The choir of the American Community Church, which Glenn and Geneva attended, sponsored a program at an orphanage in Saigon around Christmas 1957. Begun by a group of private Vietnamese philanthropic women more than twenty years earlier, Duc Anh Association now supported a thousand children in four facilities. Three hundred children, ages five to fifteen, came together to hear the Christmas story and receive gifts. Stoltzfus said this program "was a high spot in my month."

MCC was providing monthly assistance to nearly 1,500 children in eleven institutions. In addition to Duc Anh, there were several other orphanages or centers for children of poor parents—run by Catholics, Protestants or Buddhists. Food was also given to the Ban Me Thuot Leprosarium and another Chinese-run leprosarium, a government re-education center for prostitutes, a minority boarding school, and a center for the deaf. Krabill had written materials prepared in Vietnamese explaining MCC's history, its principles and philosophy, and its Christian motivation.

In early 1958 a special material aid distribution was made in the Cai San resettlement area in the Mekong delta 200 kilometers southwest of Saigon where 70,000 displaced people from the North resettled following the Geneva Accords. Fifty Evangelical Christian families were living by a canal. Along an adjacent canal Buddhist families had settled. As the settlers anticipated harvesting their first crop of rice, the rice fields dried too early and thousands of rats infested the area, completely destroying the crop within a few nights. After Glenn and Carl surveyed this area with Pastor Bang and with Tai, the Buddhist leader, in late January they distributed eight tons of rice, milk, flour, cornmeal, beef, cheese and soap to 170 families—1150 people. The rice was purchased locally.

In 1958 Stoltzfus developed what became a very successful project in the Saigon area— baking bread using U.S. surplus flour. The Duc Anh Orphanage provided a building and agreed to cover the daily operating costs to have the bakery built at their facilities. The bakery itself, which cost $1,000, was financed by Church World Service and the American Women's Association in Saigon. Since Catholic Relief Services was importing lots of U.S. surplus wheat flour, MCC made an agreement with CRS to secure 1,100 pounds of flour daily. Harry Lefever delivered the flour to the bakery which turned out 1,600 five hundred-gram loaves of bread each day to help feed 4,000 orphans and needy children in twenty-one institutions in the Saigon area. This program continued for many years.

In late May 1958 Glenn, Geneva and Ninh spent several days in Lam Dong province around Da Lat to learn about the Alliance programs among the Koho minority people, staying as guests in the homes of Alliance missionaries. In addition to these Alliance missionaries, sixteen Vietnamese couples from the Evangelical Church also worked among the ethnic minorities in several provinces. They met missionary Nguyen Van Tot in a minority village near Da Lat and in D'Ran village spoke with Pham Xuan Tin, the chairman of Vietnamese missionaries to the ethnic minorities. The missionaries were involved in evangelism, long-term and short-term Bible schools, day schools and translation work.

In a report to the home office, Stoltzfus commented on the political and social impact of the government's program of tribal resettlement. In order to isolate the ethnic minorities from communist forces operating in the jungle highlands, Diem's government was forcibly moving ethnic minority villages to lower areas, breaking cultural traditions and disrupting their familiar agricultural practices—leading to food shortages. The missionaries recognized that this resettlement created evangelistic opportunities for both the Evangelical and Catholic churches.

Duane Swartzendruber had supervised the material aid distribution in Ban Me Thuot after the Lefevers transferred to Saigon early 1958. Interpreters Y-Dun Ksor and H'Chioh helped coordinate a material aid distribution in May 1958 at a Rhade village only five kilometers from Ban Me Thuot "by elephant or motorbike," but thirty-five kilometers "by way of the only passable road."

Although fluent in the Rhade language, Swartzendruber on this day faced unanticipated cultural challenges. He learned that the pastor who requested the distribution intended to "teach an object lesson to the non-Christian members of the village that it pays to be a Christian!" After explaining to a well-to-do Christian villager that the distribution was only for poor people, Swartzendruber found it gratifying that Christians brought the poorest villagers for clothing and blankets, even bringing people in from the fields.

In July 1958 Stoltzfus arranged a CWS distribution of surplus foods at a poor area in central Vietnam that had just experienced crop failure. A few months later he again responded to a request to assist the victims of an October flood. By sea Stoltzfus shipped seven and a half tons of MCC canned beef—three hundred cartons—plus bedding, clothing, laundry soap, cheese, flour, milk, cornmeal, wheat and corn, a total of nearly eighty tons. After the commodities arrived and were warehoused in Da Nang, Stoltzfus, Ninh and Pastor Nguyen Thien Sy of the Church welfare committee flew there for a mid-November distribution. Twenty-two pastors met at the home of Huynh Kim Luyen, the superintendent of the Church's central district, to allocate the supplies which were distributed in thirty-some sites throughout the flooded area. Glenn and Ninh spent hours talking with these pastors, learning about the situation and needs of the Church and received assurance that the aid was useful and appreciated.

In late 1958 Le Van Thai, the President of the Evangelical Church, requested monthly material aid support for twenty-seven retired pastors, spouses and widows of pastors. Stoltzfus checked first with Akron and with the chairman of the C&MA Vietnam Mission who supported the proposal since it did not include active pastors. Months later when Robert Miller and William Snyder met with Alliance administrators in New York, the Alliance men said they had heard that MCC "was giving material aid and money to Vietnamese Christians" and that some of them wanted to become Mennonites! Miller explained that the assistance was requested by the Church!

Just before Christmas 1958 MCCers again distributed Christmas gifts at the Hoi Duc Anh orphanage. Now Esther Lefever was teaching a sewing class for the girls and Geneva was teaching English. On this day the children gave a performance and Margaret Metzler told the Christmas story in the Vietnamese language, the first time most of them heard the story. New Testaments were given to 240 of the children aged ten to sixteen. The children were delighted with the Christmas Bundles.

The president of Duc Anh Association, in her welcoming speech in English, said:

On behalf of the Administrative Committee of our Association and our orphans and unfortunate children, we have the honor of heartily thanking the Director for Social Welfare, all the members of the Mennonite Central Committee, Honorable Benefactors and all our distinguished guests for their very enhancing presence in this modest festival of our society, and showing thus their great care for our orphans and the unfortunate little children to whom they will, as they already have done, breathe warmer tenderness . . .

The . . . Mennonite Central Committee has enabled us to build up a baker's shop which can yield monthly 40,000 loaves of bread. The Duc Anh Association may take pride in the confidence

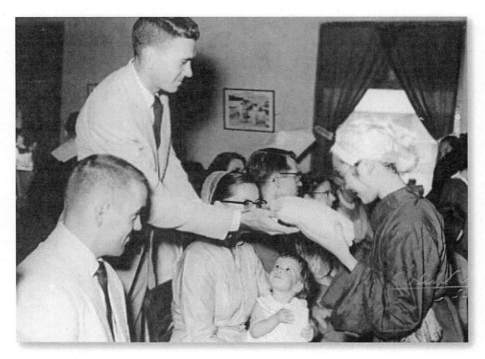

Harry Lefever giving a Christmas Bundle to a child at Duc Anh Orphanage.

that the Mennonite Central Committee has placed in us for the distribution of bread and the management of the baker's shop. Besides this the Mennonite Central Committee has given us monthly food supplies for more than a year.

Today the Mennonite Central Committee has offered us 600 Christmas bundles estimated at 180,000 VN piasters [over $1.500 US]. Last year it gave us 650 packages estimated at 160,000 piasters. Such gifts did and will come to fill our children's hearts with great joy . . .

The Director of this Mennonite Central Committee and his wife always think of our orphans and unfortunate children. They and their assistants feel merry to obey the orders of God to do good in this world. Especially Mrs. Stoltzfus has spared some time every week to teach English to our children whereas Mrs. Lefever deals with household art lessons on behalf of grown-up girls in our Society . . . .

To the Mennonite Central Committee, to all our Honorable Benefactors at home and abroad we express sincerely our heartfelt thanks.

In the 1958 Christmas season 1,419 of the available 3,500 Christmas Bundles were given to children of the Tin Lanh pastors' families—both ethnic minority and Vietnamese. Using special cash gifts, Stoltzfus supplemented these with Bibles, New Testaments and hymnbooks; a new hymnbook for the Evangelical Church had just come off the press. (Half a century later, some recipients shed tears as they related their memories of receiving these gifts as poor children.)

Other bundles were distributed to children at the Evangelical Church Orphanage in Nha Trang, and to poor ethnic minority children in the Da Lat area. Stoltzfus said this "continues to be a good way for Mennonites to share their concern and interest for needy children and orphans in Viet Nam."

Stoltzfus in mid-1959 proposed that 375 tons of U.S. surplus food commodities and 100 tons of MCC supplies be allocated for distribution in 1960 by the Church's Social Welfare Committee. While MCC would retain final review of distribution plans, Stoltzfus said the Committee was better equipped than the MCC staff to evaluate the validity of the many requests for assistance.

William Snyder, however, recommended a 30 percent reduction in material aid commodities. There would be no reductions to the Church's Nha Trang Orphanage or the Ban Me Thuot Leprosarium. He asked the MCC staff to closely monitor distributions. One way of doing this, Snyder said, was to implement "a can-for-can" distribution and exchange—requiring an empty can in exchange for a filled can—to prevent MCC beef from being sold on the open market!

MCC STUDENT ACTIVITIES

Chapter 9

Participation in student activities began quite naturally by MCC personnel in Saigon. Carl Hurst from Goshen, Indiana, was with MCC's European Pax program the summer of 1956, and transferred to Vietnam in February 1957 to assist with material aid and to manage the Saigon office until Glenn Stoltzfus arrived in September. Hurst was looking for other opportunities, and student ministries excited him. In September he began teaching English in classes sponsored by the Vietnamese-American Culture Association. He was also interested in providing consultative support to organize a local Young Men's Christian Association; Vietnam was the only Southeast Asian country without a YMCA.

Through participation in the Association of Voluntary Agencies in Saigon, Hurst met David and Pat Cole, representatives of the International Rescue Committee. IRC had facilitated student participation in international student work camps. With Pat Cole leaving, IRC was phasing out its Vietnam programs, and no other voluntary agency expressed interest in student work.

Willard Krabill spent a week with Carl and Glenn in Saigon late September 1957. In a letter to MCC's Relief Director Robert Miller, he proposed that MCC continue what had been done through IRC. If that program would be abandoned, it would require more effort to resurrect later. Krabill discussed this with Mennonite missionary James Stauffer—who had arrived in late May and was committed to two years of language study. (Krabill hoped that eventually a Bible study group would be formed where the missionaries could be fully involved.)

A one-page description gave the rationale for a student services program. Recognizing that university students would have a significant role in the country's future, the MCC team wanted to stimulate their spiritual and intellectual development. They wanted students to experience the thought and life of the Christian church and to interact with students of other countries, particularly Christian students. As Christians committed to the way of love in human relationships, they wanted "to confront each student with the claims of the Christian gospel."

Student services would include facilitating informal discussion groups, advisory support to the YMCA planning group, sponsoring work camps in Vietnam and expediting student participation in out-of-country work camps and seminars. Hurst had already begun meeting with the student discussion groups and helping organize work camps. By relating to the Young Men's Christian Association planning group, Krabill hoped their influence would help "keep the C in YMCA" as much as possible.

While building on the previous activities of the International Rescue Committee, Hurst and Stoltzfus had a different agenda. The statement read: "We plan to build these groups initially around a group already functioning including those students who have participated in work camps and seminars abroad. We hope to make our MCC house in Saigon an informal meeting place for students, for fellowship, and discussion. We also hope to build a small library of Christian literature (including books of Mennonite history and doctrine, and peace literature) at the MCC house."

By the end of October Hurst reported "the student work is now entirely in our hands." A work camp involving twenty-five to thirty students was being organized in "a needy center for children in the Saigon area" on Friday and Saturday, October 31 and November 1, where they would make a garden, and repair and paint the buildings. He later proclaimed this work camp "an enthusiastic success."

Robert Miller supported their vision. "I think your aims and goals in this work are clear and good," Miller wrote. "We want to help Christian students learn more about Christian faith and approach to life and also want to be a good influence and clear witness to non-Christian students."

With Glenn Stoltzfus taking charge of the Saigon office, Hurst was invited to transfer to Indonesia to handle material aid logistics for MCC and Church World Service. Harry Lefever was quite ready to transfer from Ban Me Thuot to Saigon to engage in student ministries should Hurst leave.

Lefever was already working with Hurst in planning a week-long work camp at Ban Me Thuot over the Christmas holidays. For a work project they planned to paint classrooms at a Rhade school. Here the students were able to complete the project and view the end results. Hurst and Lefever also chose this project to enable Vietnamese students to interact with the ethnic minority community. It took the twenty-five university and high school students eleven hours to travel from Saigon by bus because of two tire blowouts and engine trouble, "about par for the course," Hurst said. Hurst was pleased with the lectures and discussion groups which Lefever facilitated, though it was difficult at first to get students to participate in a format they were not familiar with. Several university students who had attended work camps in Japan and Hong Kong rated this camp as "the most enjoyable one they had yet attended."

In January 1958 Hurst helped organize a Saturday to Tuesday work camp with thirty Saigon students in Thu Duc, a district capital twenty kilometers east of Saigon. An amiable *bonze* (monk) invited the campers to stay in a local Buddhist pagoda. The project involved filling holes in a road leading up to a ferry crossing at a branch of the Saigon River. The community was very supportive. Fifty older students from a local school worked alongside the campers six hours in the hot sun, broken by a long rest and siesta over the noon hour. The camp rising time was 6:00 a.m., but the 4:00 a.m. gongs at the pagoda calling the devotees to meditation left the campers little choice but to get up with the monks. On the last day of the camp the district chief thanked the campers for the example they set for the community. In his report to Akron, Hurst wrote:

> We, as MCC, are of course also interested in the spiritual influence which we can have on the students. This task is a very delicate and difficult one because of the wide range of backgrounds which are represented. Out of the group of thirty students who attended the last camp there were perhaps six Catholics, ten Buddhists, and the remaining students from a religious vacuum. They may call themselves Buddhists and are probably influenced by Confucianism and ancestral worship, but they are in practice really nothing. As yet we have had no Protestant participants although we hope to have some in the future.
>
> The spiritual work must go slowly and cautiously. . . . We have instituted a few simple things. We have a simple singing grace and a short, silent meditation period before meals. Because of the shortness of a weekend camp, we must work on Sundays. However, anyone who wishes to attend church in the morning is free to do so and the Catholics in the group do this. The greatest influence has been and will continue to be our personal contacts with the students as we work and play together. Several of the students have shown some interest in knowing more about the Christian religion.

A few of these campers were studying English with Arlene and James Stauffer at the Saigon chapel led by D. I. and Ruth Jeffrey. However, Hurst said that most of the students expressed "little interest in religion." Yet, Hurst concluded, through God's help and the prayers of his people, "some good results may come out of this work."

Krabill was pleased with Hurst's organization of the work camps, but felt that Lefever would bring a "greater maturity" to the program. Hurst had initially planned for recreational square dancing at the Ban Me Thuot camp. Krabill and Lefever considered this unacceptable so it was scratched. Krabill also said Hurst had scheduled work on Sundays at the weekend camps which he considered unnecessary.

Krabill's comment on dancing may have reflected more a concern for what conservative Mennonites in the United States might say about MCC personnel organizing questionable social activities! But the regime of President Ngo Dinh Diem was also quite straight-laced. At the instigation of First Lady Madam Nhu, the later 1962 Law for the Protection of Morality made illegal a wide range of social activities, including dancing. Likewise the reluctance to see the campers do manual work on Sundays might have been more a reflection of Americans eschewing Sunday work than on anything inherent in Vietnamese agrarian society where market shops were open on Sundays and farmers worked seven days a week.

Harry and Esther Lefever transferred from Ban Me Thuot to Saigon early March 1958, and Harry and Carl worked together on student services until Carl left for Indonesia in late August.

The administrative secretary of East Asia Christian Council (EACC) came to Saigon in March with a proposal to sponsor an international work camp in Vietnam. Lefever wrote to the Church president, Le Van Thai, proposing the camp be held at the Church's Bible institute in Da Nang, performing some community work. Nothing came of this.

Lefever attended a two-week Quaker-sponsored seminar in Ubol, Thailand, late April which brought together persons from fifteen countries. Focusing on the post-colonial era, the seminar theme was "The Role and Contribution of the Young Citizen in a Changing Society." For Lefever a highlight was participating in a discussion group about the role of religion in society. Beside this Mennonite from Lancaster, Pennsylvania, the group included "a Catholic, a follower of Zoroastrianism, a Baptist, a Quaker, a Hindu, a Ceylonese and an American girl who didn't profess to follow any religion." With a vision for establishing a Christian student center in Saigon, Lefever visited the student hostel of the Student Christian Center in Bangkok.

One of the consultants at the seminar was Daw Mya Sein, a professor of history and political science at Rangoon University; she came to Saigon after the seminar and spoke one evening to fifteen students at the MCC house.

Other speakers Hurst and Lefever invited to speak at student discussion groups included David C. Cole, International Rescue Committee; MCC's Glenn Stoltzfus; a Mr. DeClerk from UNESCO; James B. Hendry, an economist with the Michigan State University advisory group; Jean Jacque Dunn and E. B. Brown, professors at the Saigon University; Truong Cong Cuu, a France-educated official with the Ministry of Education who later served as President of the National Assembly and Foreign Minister under President Diem (1963); and Joseph Buttinger, who worked with American Friends of Vietnam, and authored *The Smaller Dragon*, a political history of Vietnam. Although many of these persons were advocates of the government of Ngo Dinh Diem, they were invited as prominent personalities of that era.

Lefever and Stoltzfus prepared a list of books they wanted Akron to send for an MCC library. The list contained titles like *The Anabaptist Vision* (Harold S. Bender), *War, Peace and Nonresistance* (Guy F. Hershberger), *The Secret of Happiness* (Billy Graham), and *Customs and Cultures* (Eugene A. Nida). The books were to eventually go to a student center.

MCC was also preparing a brochure to be given to students describing MCC's history and Christian philosophy.

Lefever and Hurst interacted with fifty students, relating closely to twenty of them. None of these students were Protestant; they were Buddhist, Catholic or of no faith. Aware that students were sometimes accused of "working too closely with Americans," Lefever tried to minimize his leadership role. Hurst had been keenly aware of the need to be sensitive and transparent in relating to students, since the government was "very suspicious" of international groups associating with students who "might develop new ideas" which would undermine government propaganda. Yet when the student group in November drew up a constitution for a Youth Voluntary Workcamp and Seminar Association, Lefever reluctantly accepted the role of vice chairman.

Lefever identified only twelve Evangelical Church university students scattered around the city, having little contact with one another. Harry introduced two of these students and six high school students to the thirty-two-bed student hostel operated by the French Protestant Church. The number of Evangelical university students would rise sharply within a few years.

One of the Evangelical students asked Lefever to help organize and support a program of summer community service in 1958. Lefever proposed to Church President Thai that teams of Christian students would go into villages to engage in activities related to their fields of study. This might involve dispensing medicines, dentistry, recreation, singing, sanitation, and literacy classes. The teams would be supervised by a local Tin Lanh pastor, and might include direct evangelism. Even though MCC offered to provide two-month support, Thai did not respond to this proposal.

Lefever also wrote to Pastor Thai in July 1958 about the need for a Christian student center to provide a Christian atmosphere for the students, good study facilities and activities to supplement the academic courses—such as Bible studies, discussion groups, recreation, and English classes, and also provide opportunities for an evangelistic witness. Lefever hoped both MCC and the Vietnam Mennonite Mission would cooperate with the Evangelical Church in this.

Pastor Thai was very much interested in the formation of a student hostel. Robert Miller suggested that the Mennonite Mission, rather than MCC, should provide leadership. But Orie Miller said that a hostel for Evangelical Church students was a matter for their Church to respond to—Mennonites might give supportive counsel and perhaps a budget subsidy. James Stauffer pointed out that since the Mennonite Mission was committed to establishing churches, should the Mission work directly with Christian students it would undoubtedly be viewed as an attempt to win the students' loyalty to the Mennonite Church. The missionaries viewed this more problematically than did Church President Thai.

Nearing the end of their formal language studies, the Mennonite missionaries anticipated beginning an evangelistic ministry among students. Yet they encouraged MCC to continue student ministries. Robert Miller promised to support Lefever until the end of his term, but argued that the missionaries could make a better long-term contribution to student ministries. This lukewarm support was a great disappointment to Lefever.

In November the Asia Secretary of World Student Christian Federation came to Saigon to arrange for two Vietnamese students to attend an upcoming WSCF conference in Rangoon. Bob

Bates came at the invitation of the Evangelical Church's Scholarship Committee that had been formed to help select students to receive World Council of Churches scholarships to study in Vietnam. Bates was invited to preach at the large Saigon Evangelical Church on Tran Hung Dao Street and met with thirty Evangelical Church students at the French Protestant Church hostel.

Bates encouraged Lefever to further develop the hostel facilities at the French Protestant Church, something he was already planning to do. By the 1958 fall term nineteen of the thirty-four students residing at the hostel were Evangelical Christians. Lefever planned to provide students with MCC foods, and was helping set up a reading room. Nguyen Van Van of the Evangelical Church's scholarship committee was in charge of securing books for the library.

Bates tried to facilitate fellowship among Christian students and witness to other students. Understanding that the Evangelical Church might be hesitant to relate to the Federation because of its ecumenical character—related to WCC—he suggested they might prefer to associate with the more evangelical Inter-Varsity student organization. Harry and Esther attended the ten-day WSCF Conference in early 1959 in Rangoon. Two Evangelical students selected were unable to go because the government did not issue them passports.

Lefever continued to coordinate work camps. Everett Metzler spent ten days at the Hue camp which had forty-five students. Another camp at Go Vap, northeast of Saigon, assisted sixty-one families whose houses were destroyed by fire. Having experienced campers giving leadership, it was an excellent camp.

In February 1959 Church President Thai accepted an invitation from East Asia Christian Council to send a delegation to visit Burma and Thailand. The group leader was Pastor Doan Van Mieng—soon to replace Thai as Church President. Thai told Lefever that he "had consulted with the C&MA missionaries for advice regarding the team, and received a negative reply." Nevertheless the Church Executive Committee accepted the invitation. Lefever encouraged the EACC Administrative Secretary to make the delegation's visit a positive experience.

At a meeting of the MCC-VMM Coordination Committee early March 1959, Lefever reviewed eighteen months of student ministries. Seven work camps had been organized with two more planned. MCC also arranged for nine students to participate in work camps in Thailand, Japan and Ceylon.

At this meeting Stauffer observed that MCC staff relationships with ecumenical organizations tended to negatively influence C&MA and Evangelical perceptions of the Mennonite missionaries. Lefever noted that MCC had not sought out those relationships, but persons from these organizations had come to them. Stauffer said that MCC's relationship with Vietnam Mennonite Mission was generally positive, except that Tin Lanh Christians often viewed the missionaries as social workers rather than as evangelists or church planters.

David Adeney, representing Inter-Varsity Christian Fellowship, and Bob Bates of World Student Christian Federation both visited Vietnam in April—Adeney to speak at a Christian youth conference. By this time a student fellowship of Evangelical Christian students was meeting weekly on Sunday afternoons for Bible study and prayer.

MCC also contributed to the formation of a Vietnam chapter of the local Young Men's Christian Association. When a few young Vietnamese men who traveled overseas returned with an interest in forming a local YMCA in 1957, Hurst and some YMCA persons from the Philippines drew up a draft constitution which was submitted to President Diem's office for approval.

The officers included two or three men who claimed no religious faith and a Catholic who resigned due to Vietnamese Catholic leaders' opposition to the YMCA movement.

When M. G. Dharmaraj, the YMCA Southeast Asia Secretary, reviewed the proposed constitution, he insisted that the total Y leadership had to be Christian. This was now a challenge, since Catholics did not want to go against their church leaders, and the Protestants were not involved at all. Three of the young men promoting the YMCA were interested in considering the Christian faith but were not attracted to the Evangelical Church. They realized, Lefever explained, that if they become Protestant Christians "they have only the Evangelical Church with which to affiliate, which represents a lower social status, a less educated group, and a group very individualistic in the practice of their Christian faith, with very little emphasis on the social dimensions of Christianity. In their minds, the Seventh Day Adventist group represents a more intellectual approach to Christianity and for them has more attraction."

Lefever arranged for these young men to meet with ECVN President Thai and the members of the ECVN Scholarship Committee. At first President Thai showed little interest in the YMCA concept, but Lefever persuaded Thai in February 1959 to invite ten Evangelical Christian leaders to a meeting where there was rigorous discussion. Lefever learned that respected senior missionary D. I. Jeffrey, then on furlough, supported the Y movement.

When Dharmaraj visited Vietnam in early June, Alliance leaders were ready to lend support if the Y leaders were all Evangelical Christians. On June 9 a new board was chosen of lay and ordained leaders of the Evangelical Church. Dhamaraj expressed profound thanks to Lefever for his role in getting the Church to support the YMCA. William Snyder on his May-June visit promised to meet in New York with the Director of the International Committee of the YMCA in the USA to urge support for the Saigon YMCA.

Snyder praised Lefever for giving himself "unstintingly in working with students," but concluded that the student program was not top priority and would terminate. Snyder also said it would be "likely to cause awkward working relationships in Saigon with the [Mennonite] mission if we were to continue." The MCC Director would still correspond with Mennonite and affiliated colleges in North America on behalf of prospective Vietnamese students.

As an alternative to an MCC student program, Lefever proposed that MCC or the MCC Peace Section recruit a professor to teach at the Saigon or the Hue Universities for a year or two.

Three years later Samuel A. Yoder, Goshen College English professor, taught a year at Hue University. Located 1,100 kilometers north of Saigon, he was unable to relate to Saigon students, but he did interact with the Evangelical students who lived in a small student hostel in the home of C&MA missionaries Robert and Mildred Davis in Hue.

Within a year the Mennonite Mission would begin activities among high school and university students in Saigon, organizing English language classes and Vietnamese and English Bible study classes. One can only speculate whether the missionaries might have seen a church formed through continuing the relationships and programs nurtured by Hurst and Lefever.

In 1960 Paul and Maida (Mary) Contento would come to Saigon to formally organize a Vietnam chapter of Inter-Varsity Christian Fellowship. Evangelical Christian university graduates working with IVCF contributed greatly to strengthening the witness of the Evangelical Church in Vietnam. When the war intensified in the mid-sixties, these students organized the Christian Youth for Social Service which provided effective ministries to the victims of the conflict.

THE MISSIONARIES' FIRST SIX MONTHS

Chapter 10

In James Stauffer's first letter to his parents written Saturday, June 1, 1957—two days after they arrived—he described Saigon as an "interesting place." They were staying with MCC Director Delbert Wiens and his assistant, Carl Hurst, in the unit house located five kilometers from downtown in the Phu Nhuan District of Gia Dinh city, part of Saigon's metropolitan area northeast of the city limits. Wiens and Hurst made them feel at home. They had had a "good old fashioned hymn-sing" Friday evening, and all made plans to attend the English language worship service at the American Community Church on Sunday.

At this worship service James and Arlene met a "typical group of Americans" and learned that the Christian and Missionary Alliance was planning to assign a full-time missionary pastor to serve this group and the two thousand Americans in Saigon who Stauffer saw as "a real mission field in themselves."

Saigon's central Ben Thanh Market.

A few days later the Stauffers met C&MA mission leaders D. Ivory Jeffrey and Jack Revelle, who was replacing Jeffrey as field chairman. They sensed a "very fine spirit" in these two men. In a letter to the home office of Eastern Mennonite Board of Missions and Charities (EMBMC), Stauffer said that Jeffrey and Revelle wanted assurance that the Mennonites would establish a self-supporting indigenous church—something Stauffer could affirm. They did not want to see some new mission attracting persons away from the 20,000 member Evangelical Church of Vietnam (ECVN). "I don't think we will have any difficulty working with them," Stauffer wrote.

Since Eastern Mennonite Board was entering Vietnam in-

Inside Ben Thanh Market.

Cyclo taxi stand.

Street scene.

Saigon fast food.

dependently of the Alliance mission, the Stauffers sensed they were "being watched like a hawk." Before long a pastor who had left the Evangelical Church came to visit them. While they appreciated his interest and friendship, they were cautious about cooperating with him.

In a June 4 letter to MCC Administrator Robert Miller, Wiens reported that they enjoyed hosting the missionaries. Due to a flu epidemic their cook was off, so Arlene assumed the task of preparing food. In a letter home, James described helping Arlene prepare meals in the "rather primitive 'kitchen' with an abundance of flies, mosquitoes, dogs and a cat waiting to get in on the feed." James said Arlene's "somewhat Americanized meals have helped to absorb the shock of Oriental flavors" that they would come to love. He described the omnipresent pot of bitter tea as "halfway between wormwood and boneset." In spite of everything, they already felt "fairly well settled down."

In contrast to the MCC personnel who had two- or three-year terms of service, the missionaries had five-year terms with the expectation that they would serve multiple terms. For persons with limited exposure to other cultures and languages, James and Arlene were putting down their roots in this new soil fairly comfortably.

Arlene wrote: "Our first impressions of Viet Nam, our home for the next five years, have been very pleasant ones. Our main frustration—the language barrier, and we are confident God will enable us to overcome that in his strength that the gospel may go forward."

They eagerly began Vietnamese language study on June 22 with a twenty-three-year-old Evangelical Christian man, Dao Van Hoa.

After being in country only two weeks, the Stauffers took the first of their many journeys throughout South Vietnam, taking a cross-country taxi to Ban Me Thuot, 650 kilometers north of Saigon in the central highlands. There Harry and Esther Lefever met them and took them to the leprosarium where the MCC unit was located. One day they went with Margaret Janzen, the nurse, and Harry to clinics in surrounding villages. Another evening they celebrated Harry's hunting skills that provided a wild boar for the dinner table.

Back in Saigon, James and Arlene accepted an invitation to a U.S. Independence Day reception at the home of the U.S. Vice-Consul. There they met Alliance missionaries and a few persons from Orient Crusades and Wycliffe Bible Translators.

On June 30, a month after their arrival, Stauffer preached through an interpreter at one of the Chinese churches in Cho Lon, Saigon's Chinatown—the first

The kitchen.

"Mr. Cook."

of many sermons that Stauffer would preach in numerous churches.

The new missionaries studied the Vietnamese tonal language with Mr. Hoa four hours daily six days a week. "We feel like we are making progress, [but] James is having more difficulty than I twisting his 'southern drawl' into a pure Vietnamese accent," Arlene wrote to James' home mid-July. They were practicing their budding Vietnamese vocabulary on the cook, his wife and three-year-old daughter.

These foreigners provided comic relief in many settings. The bicycle James purchased had aluminum handlebars which were not strong enough for the heavier Americans, so he went to the bike shop to exchange the part for steel handlebars. He used the word *bếp* instead of the right word, *thép*. Though the shop owner understood what James wanted, his helpers laughed when he asked for "kitchen" rather than "steel" handlebars! In a letter to his brother, James asked him to pray that they would "soon master the language. It is pretty rough!"

On a Sunday afternoon bicycle ride to the zoological garden, they laughingly observed that while they were looking at the animals, curious people were staring at them "and the animals staring at the whole bunch of us!"

Arlene and James soon met the Evangelical Church President, Pastor Le Van Thai. They also had a visit from Huynh Minh Y, a prominent layman in the Church, now a government official and political advisor to President Diem. Arlene observed that this man was "rather lukewarm toward the existing church." She wrote home: "Although we appreciate his friendship, we can see that he like other malcontents will make our situation here exceedingly delicate—they expect us to atone for any failings the C&MA made in the past."

Stauffer preached one July Sunday at the Hoa Hung Church, one of the six Evangelical Church congregations in the Saigon area. This was the church of their language teacher who interpreted. He and Arlene sang "The Love of God" a cappella. In his introduction, Stauffer introduced the audience to the Mennonite Church and said they had come to Vietnam to evangelize. Evelyn Revelle, the wife of the Alliance Mission Chairman, was in the audience, and James wondered whether she had come to observe this Mennonite missionary!

The Stauffers' teacher told them that a pastor was raising questions about the Mennonite non-resistance beliefs. Knowing that Alliance missionaries were aware of Mennonite opposition to military service, Stauffer hoped this would not keep them from forming good relationships.

James and Arlene traveled 140 kilometers northeast of Saigon one Saturday in late July with Delbert Wiens and the French Protestant pastor in Saigon, Rev. Bertrand DeLuze, to visit the Da Hoa Protestant refugee village that Church World Service had supported. When the CWS representative left the country, Wiens continued liaison with this village. He was frequently called to help work out problems. Thinking Wiens was coming on Sunday, the village leaders were planning a pig roast as a farewell celebration. Wiens promised to return the next day.

On Sunday the Stauffers returned with Wiens, arriving just as the benediction was being pronounced at the church service. In a letter to his parents, James related "interesting discussions" with Ulrich H. van Beyma, a representative of Inter-Church Aid of the World Council of Churches (WCC) from Geneva who accompanied them. Van Beyma gave a rather convincing argument that the Mennonites should work with the Evangelical Church and be part of this Church, even though the Mennonites might retain a separate mission organization. Stauffer reasoned that the Church would not accept their theological understanding of non-resistance to violence. Only if the Evangelical Church leaders would not tolerate the Mennonite convictions would they be justified in starting a different denomination, van Beyma maintained.

To his brother, Stauffer wrote: "Pray that we will never become used to the millions here that do not know Jesus Christ. We are learning that most of the people here do not embrace any system of religion. Sunday is just the same as any other day and with the nationalistic surge running strong, they will not be too interested in the Gospel."

In early August Arlene and James traveled to Da Lat, some 300 kilometers northeast of Saigon, then 200 kilometers further to the coastal town of Nha Trang to visit Alliance missionary friends they had met at the Toronto Institute of Linguistics the previous summer.

Their visit to the Evangelical Church's Orphanage was the highpoint of their Nha Trang stay. Many of the children were orphans of pastors who had been killed during the French Indochina War, 1946-1954. James and Arlene were stirred to hear the children sing. James wrote his parents that their hearts were "gripped" on a visit to a Buddhist temple seeing people "bowing down to wood and stone." They returned to Saigon on a wood- and coal-burning steam train.

James and Arlene were now living outside the Mennonite communities that had nurtured them. Their conservative Mennonite communities mandated a head covering for women (based on the teachings in I Corinthians 11), and men were asked to wear a "plain" suit jacket without lapels. Mission Board expectations were that they continue these patterns in Vietnam. Arlene wore a head covering, and James wore the plain suit in formal settings in Vietnam, though frequently he wore no jacket at all. But there were stirrings of change within the State-side Mennonite communities, and James in a mid-August letter home asked his father to send a copy of the recent report from Virginia Mennonite Conference, the conference to which he belonged, that had passed some new resolution on dress patterns.

James told of spending two days in bed with a terrific headache, and the Adventist doctor diagnosed a viral infection. The following day he still had severe symptoms, and considered going back to the doctor. "But I didn't have enough energy," he wrote home, "and I felt that he had done all he could anyway. So, Arlene read from the Scripture and prayed for my healing. The Lord graciously heard and answered our prayer. I rolled over and went to sleep and when I awoke an hour later the pain and fever were all gone."

D. I. Jeffrey and his wife Ruth invited James and Arlene to visit the youth center they had recently opened near Truong Minh Giang Street. Here was a reading room and a bookstore which was open daily. Each morning there was storytelling for the children. There was an English class in the evenings, using a book of the Bible as the textbook, followed by an evangelistic service. Stauffer noted that many persons had "accepted Christ."

Delbert Wiens left for home August 18. Two days later on Tuesday evening, Arlene, James and Carl Hurst led the service in Jeffreys' chapel. The three sang a trio number, and James preached with Mr. Hoa interpreting.

Writing home, James describes the experience:

> It is a thrill to preach to such eager faces. Most of the group have just accepted Christ in recent months. There are seventy altogether and they are going to start their own congregation. The house was filled to overflowing. There are a few new faces each evening and among them are the ones that are accepting Christ. They want us to conduct the service every Tuesday night, so pray that God will be able to use us in this work. Arlene is going to have a children's meeting on Sunday afternoons at 4:00, too. They are just beginning to have services for the children but Mrs. Jeffrey thinks this is a very fertile field.

James and Arlene received a warm welcome from D. I. and Ruth Jeffrey, veteran C&MA missionaries who had been in Vietnam since the mid-1920s. Now in their late fifties or early sixties, they provided encouragement and support to other congregations in Saigon. Mrs. Jeffrey was the daughter of Jonathan and Rosalind Goforth, well-known Presbyterian missionaries to China a generation earlier. Both D. I. and Ruth Jeffrey were highly respected and greatly loved. Mrs. Jeffrey was an energetic person who originated many programs. The Jeffreys' invitation to them— and their readiness to assist them—laid a good foundation for a mutually respectful relationship between the Alliance and Mennonite missions.

In late September Mr. Hoa, their language teacher, suggested to the Stauffers that some of the people at the center had "accepted Christ . . . just to please the Jeffreys." He said many people were more interested in learning English than learning of Jesus Christ! While undoubtedly so, this ministry developed into the growing, dynamic Truong Minh Giang congregation.

After three months in Vietnam, Stauffer wrote home: "We can truthfully say that we are very happy here. We have found great joy in responding to God's call to this place. We know that some of our greatest testings and trials are still in the future. But praise God for strength for today!"

James and Arlene had just learned with disappointment that the MCC cook and his "wife" were not legally married. The cook, who had a wife and eight children, had met a young widow who moved in with him. Now the younger "wife" was unhappy since he was giving all his money to the other woman! The Stauffers learned that this was a fairly common practice in Vietnam.

James and Arlene had to vacate the MCC house the end of August. Even though Orie Miller had proposed that they live in cooler Da Lat during their years of language study, they decided to stay in Saigon. They liked their language teacher, and delighted in the opportunity to work with the Jeffrey couple. They rented an apartment at 11 Bui Thi Xuan Street, Saigon, near the zoo and botanical garden, and moved on September 12. James was glad they had not brought more "stuff" to Vietnam. Their beautiful house also had problems with termites, silverfish and cockroaches. And both had bouts with "Saigon stomach." Later in the month James was in bed likely with hepatitis. By mid-October James was again feeling well and both enjoyed a live recital by Marian Anderson, the celebrated contralto who had become the first African-American to sing at the Metropolitan Opera two years earlier.

In late September the Stauffers welcomed Glenn and Geneva Stoltzfus to Saigon; Glenn was to become the MCC Director, and Geneva would serve as hostess. With Dr. Krabill in town, the Stauffers invited all the MCC personnel to lunch.

On October 22, 1957, American military personnel in Vietnam suffered their first casualties. Thirteen military advisors were wounded by explosive devices at a hotel and on a bus. Writing home two days later, Stauffer had gone to the American Embassy that morning to get a signature for their official registration and was stopped by a U.S. Marine security guard. He met the vice-consul who told him bombings were thought to be "communist-inspired." The Embassy was trying to keep the incidents quiet. Stauffer wrote his parents that Arlene and he were not alarmed "since this attack was mainly against the military." The Republic of Vietnam was celebrating its second year of independence that weekend; the yellow flag with three red stripes was flying from most houses and shops and even taxis.

Arlene added a note to the letter: "We are getting to the stage in our language learning where I believe we'll see more things happen. With a basic vocabulary now, it is thrilling to be able to understand the gist from a sermon, conversation or scripture passage. Witnessing such spiritual poverty about us increases our incentive to learn this language rapidly. Pray to that end."

Arlene and James sought to maintain a vital relationship with God through prayer and the study of scripture. In every letter home, James shared a Bible passage that had recently meant much to him. In his November 1 letter, he told about meeting eighteen-year-old Nguyen Hung when he and Arlene were riding their bicycles. This young man asked whether he could come to their home and practice speaking English. When Hung came on Sunday morning, James asked him whether he understood anything about Jesus Christ.

"He looked blank and said, 'No,'" James wrote. "There was something about the look on his face that filled my heart with compassion."

Several days later Hung came to their home when Stauffer was studying Vietnamese, and asked about the Christian life and how he could become a Christian. Stauffer invited the young man to read Ephesians 2:1-10, and Teacher Hoa explained the human condition apart from Christ. Hung admitted that this described his life but asked: "Will God receive me?" They assured him from John 1:12 that if he would "receive Christ, God would receive him and make him His Child." As they were explaining this, Hung suddenly exclaimed, "God has saved me. I have received Christ and the burden is gone and a new joy has come to my heart." The three then knelt in a thanksgiving prayer and a dedication of Hung's faith in Christ.

Stauffer learned that Hung's father was a prominent lawyer and that both his parents were members of the Vietnamese legislature. A week later Stauffer said Hung "still had a ringing testimony and was so happy with his new-found faith in Christ."

James and Arlene accompanied Dr. Krabill, Stoltzfus and Hurst to attend an assembly of the Evangelical Church in early November at Vinh Long, 140 kilometers southwest of Saigon along a main branch of the Mekong River. MCC was discussing a proposed joint medical project with the Church.

After attending this assembly, Stauffer wrote to EMBMC Mission Administrators Orie Miller and Paul Kraybill, reflecting on their recent strategizing. "Regarding Mennonite Mission and National Church working relationships," he penned, "we came to Viet Nam under the impression that our work would be largely separate and mostly independent . . . , that there would be only spiritual ties between us and the church here rather than organizational or physical ones. It took us awhile to realize what it is like to be in a country with only one Church. The more we learn to know and observe the Evangelical Church of Viet Nam, the more we feel that our program should be a part of their framework or, at least, in some way be identified with them."

Referring to their July conversation with WCC Representative van Beyma, Stauffer noted van Beyma's opposition to the formation of other Evangelical Protestant churches which would compromise the unity of the Evangelical Church. "He feels that our convictions would be healthy for the Church here and that the Church of Christ needs these different areas and degrees of conviction to complement each other," Stauffer wrote. "Only in the event of refusal or rejection by the ECVN would we be justified in going our own separate way."

Stauffer also mentioned comments of other Christians which could be summed up in the words of Alliance missionary friends: "We know that division will come to the Church in Viet Nam sometime, but we hate to see it come from America."

Stauffer continued:

> If as a result of evangelization we would form congregations as part of the National Church, it would demand a certain amount of give and take on both sides. I doubt if our Board would approve of this plan. We ourselves are not completely resigned to all the implications of such a move. On the other hand, we do not feel at all ready to work toward the goal of an independent Mennonite Church of Viet Nam. This would only add confusion in the minds of the unsaved here. Denominationalism is a great stumbling block to the Oriental mind, and this is the only Asian country that has had a unified Protestant witness.

Stauffer seemed inclined to see the Mennonite Mission place its major emphasis on institutional work—particularly Christian education, while any fruit of their evangelistic work could be incorporated within the Evangelical Church. Yet he recognized institutional work by expatriates would have all kinds of problems.

Shortly after the November 18 arrival of Margaret and Everett Metzler, the new missionary couple, James received Miller's reply. Miller "gratefully noted the progress in language study, for the opportunities that have come to James for preaching and witnessing, for the beginning fruits, for the apparent good relationships being established with MCC workers and program and with the Vietnamese Evangelical Church and the C&MA missionaries." He observed that "the questions raised in James' letter seem to us also the ones that would be normal in a situation in which you are finding yourselves and at this stage. We from this end do not profess to have the answers either, but want to wait and pray with you so that the Spirit may lead us to them together."

Miller said that in his previous conversations with D. I. Jeffrey, Herb Jackson, Gordon Smith and Le Van Thai in Vietnam, "it seemed to be the clear sense of us all that the logic of any Mennonite missionary work would also be a church that would appreciate being related to Christendom at large and to evangelical Christianity through the world Mennonite brotherhood and its Eastern Mennonite Board of Missions constituency. . . . It was also assumed that such church organization would develop and work and grow in healthy spiritual relationship with all the evangelical Christian forces in the country."

On the matter of denominationalism being "a great stumbling block to the Oriental mind," Miller reminded the Vietnamese missionaries that many Asian church leaders "confess that 'evangelical nationalism also presents a serious problem to world brotherhood.'" Because of this, Miller wrote, at the present time it seems that "these nationalism tendencies may need to be counterbalanced with something of continuing denominationalism until in God's own time and under the leading of His Spirit both are resolved into something more in line with God's eternal will."

While having the highest respect for van Beyma "as a Christian person and church administrator," Miller said he does not share his counsel. "Our practical counsel to you now," Miller wrote, "would be to continue to wait and pray and not to feel that you would have to come to firm decisions at once. The MCC work and witness should continue to be helpful, too, in evidencing to C&MA mission and Vietnamese church the felt spiritual ties, and MCC also represents an integral facet of Eastern Board concern. We trust that the witness of these two arms of our church will continue to healthily and integrally supplement each other in Viet Nam."

Miller responded to all the issues Stauffer had raised, leaving no doubts about the direction this sixty-five-year-old mission administrator was guiding the young missionaries.

GETTING A FEEL FOR VIETNAM

Chapter 11

Margaret and Everett Metzler arrived in Saigon on November 18, 1957, nearly six months after Arlene and James Stauffer stepped onto Vietnamese soil. There was now a Vietnam Mennonite Mission (VMM) team.

Like the Stauffers, the Metzlers spent one month en route by ship before disembarking from the SS *Cambodge* at the Saigon docks into the welcoming arms of Arlene and James. The Stauffers took them to their rented home a few blocks from Saigon's Central Market. That evening Margaret and Everett sat down to a meal prepared by "Mr. Cook" and his daughter, Sister Tu. They picked up their chopsticks, their first experience eating with the table utensils favored by much of Asia.

Everett came from Lancaster, Pennsylvania, while Margaret Glick's home was near Minot, North Dakota; they met as students at Eastern Mennonite College. Margaret studied elementary education and taught a few years. After earning his bachelor's degree, Everett stayed on to take graduate courses in Bible and theology and both he and Margaret served as faculty assistants. They were married in June 1956.

The day after arrival, the Metzlers began language study with *Thầy* (teacher) Hoa, along with James and Arlene. Mission administrators had advised the missionaries to spend up to two years studying the language. During the era of French rule, Alliance Vietnam missionaries first studied French, then Vietnamese. Vietnamese was now the official language.

Like the Stauffers, Everett and Margaret had spent several weeks at the Summer Institute of Linguistics (SIL) in Toronto. One of their instructors was linguist William A. Smalley who worked in Thailand with the American Bible Society. The four eager students used a Vietnamese language text prepared by Smalley which introduced basic conversations needed for everyday liv-

SS Cambodge *in Saigon port.*

ing, and progressed into material useful for evangelistic ministries.

On their first Sunday the Metzlers attended the "stimulating Sunday School class and church service" at the American Community Church. Margaret felt this was perpetrating an American mindset, but concluded that it might be alright since they had just arrived.

The following weekend they took a bus to Ban Me Thuot to meet the MCC team. While there they accompanied the mobile clinic to several villages with

Margaret studying language with Teacher Hoa.

Margaret Janzen and Harry Lefever. Back in Saigon, they went with the Stauffers on Sunday to the Evangelical Church's Khanh Hoi congregation near the Saigon docks. Though most of the 900,000 persons who came from the north to the south after the Geneva Accords were Catholic, there were also some evangelical Christians. Many of these who came to Saigon became the core of this new congregation led by Pastor Nguyen Thien Sy. The congregation was making plans to build a church, and Stauffer was invited to preach.

While the Metzlers were gone, James and Arlene had invited to dinner three officers with the U.S. Military Assistance Advisory Group (MAAG) whom they met at the American Community Church. With them Stauffer discussed the Biblical passages that led Mennonites to eschew military service. The men had recently discussed non-resistance at their Thursday evening Bible Study. Writing home, Stauffer said "this war question bothers them more than they realize. They admitted that they had done a lot of thinking on the subject in the past. Pray for them."

Family life became more structured with the two couples living together. In early December Stauffer wrote home: "We resorted to a daily schedule of getting up at 5:30; have devotions, breakfast at 7:00, lunch at 12:00 and supper at 6:00. We are getting more Vietnamese studied." Indeed, the eagerness of the Metzlers to learn the language challenged James and Arlene to keep ahead of them. They now spent eight hours daily in language study. Each studied one-on-one with Thay Hoa one hour both morning and afternoon, with the rest of the time listening to tape recordings, mimicking the six tonal patterns of the language.

Earlier generations of Western missionaries left behind many amenities when they went to Africa or Asia. Nevertheless, they often lived in well-furnished walled villas, eating familiar foods, and traveling in the best transportation available. The Stauffers and Metzlers represented a different mindset. They lived in a simple house like their Vietnamese neighbors, ate Vietnamese food, dressed simply, and got around on bicycles.

The Metzlers were not in Vietnam long before they expressed a desire to live even more simply. In his first letter to Paul Kraybill eight days after arriving, Everett reported that they had cleared their baggage through customs. "[We] are somewhat disgusted at ourselves for bringing so much 'stuff' along," he wrote. "Almost anything needed is obtainable here rather reasonably. We wonder what natives think when they see all our trunks and baggage. We are learning to appreciate the simplicity of their mode of living."

Two more bicycles were purchased the day after the Metzlers arrived. Now, Metzler wrote Kraybill, "All four of us have bicycles . . . to get about. I suppose we make quite a sight weaving in and out of Saigon's multitudinous pedicabs, motorbikes, scooters, street vendors, bicycles and autos."

For several weeks Everett led their evening devotional period from the Sermon on the Mount. When the lights went off one evening, the four sang from memory for an hour and a half until the lights came back. This was a prelude to the four-part quartet a cappella singing they would do in many settings over the next years.

With the Stauffers already involved at the Truong Minh Giang Chapel, Everett and Margaret soon joined them. By mid-December, with around fifty students and others coming to the Saturday evening English program, they were divided into four groups. Few of those attending were Christians, so the new missionaries were eager to help students understand the gospel of Jesus.

On Christmas Eve the four went to the service at the Truong Minh Giang Chapel. Afterwards they went to the Christmas Eve celebration in the large Saigon church on Tran Hung Dao Boulevard. Writing home two days after Christmas, James wrote: "My heart was extra full on that day; this has been the most joyous Christmas of my life. . . .

> [On] Christmas Eve we attended the programs in two different Churches. They had songs, poems, scriptural readings much like our programs in the States. The thing that was so different to us was the elaborate decorations. They had flowers, plants, streamers, archways, illuminated stars, Christmas trees, a star that was pulled across the room on two wires with a blinking red and green light. Then, when it came to rest above the manger scene a photographic flash bulb would go off. They had the three-wise-men scene with the stars illuminated with electric bulbs. In the one church they had Santa Clauses out on the hill side watching the sheep. As the groups would sing, various colored lights would flash off and on. It was really something!

Christmas Eve services at all congregations of the Evangelical Church were elaborate celebrations planned months in advance. Each children's class and youth group had a part in the singing and recitations. The Catholic Christmas Eve services, rich with litanies and liturgies, attracted many people outside the church, and the Evangelical (*Tin Lành* – Good News) churches likewise recognized the opportunities of the Christmas season to announce the Good News of Jesus Christ to the broader community.

In early 1958 James and Arlene traveled with Teacher Hoa to the southern tip of the Mekong Delta. They went 280 kilometers to Bac Lieu on Saturday in response to the invitation given them by Pastor Chi at the November church conference. They slept on cots at the pastor's home. James preached Sunday morning at the local church, and Arlene and Hoa spoke to the youth in the afternoon. They were then invited to go sixty kilometers further south on Monday to the Ca Mau Church where Stauffer spoke both morning and evening. One man confessed his faith in Jesus Christ which confirmed to James the rightness of accepting this invitation. The area around Ca Mau had been controlled by the Viet Minh guerrillas during the French Indochina War. The area pastors said the people were "very receptive to the Gospel" after living under the control of the communist Viet Minh for ten years. The Stauffers met the province chief who had recently promised to give the church a tract of land for a new church building.

James and Arlene found this "to be one of the most interesting weekends that we have had in Vietnam." They had a wild ride back to Saigon on Tuesday, traveling in a new Mercury bus that traveled 110 KPH on a narrow road. Stauffer wrote home: "I was scared and prayed that God would spare our lives. He answered by causing the bus to develop a mild carburetion defect that would not let it go over 90 for the rest of the way. The horn also stopped working which delayed our speed."

Prior to this, Stauffer rarely commented to his family about Vietnamese politics. But now he wrote: "We would like to request prayer on behalf of the political situation here. It seems that the Catholics are gradually taking over and democracy is mostly on paper and not in practice." With President Diem being a devoted Catholic, membership in the Catholic Church was one of the most effective ways to earn positions in the government and the armed forces. Diem believed he could count on these people to oppose communist ideology.

"The economic situation is not too good either," Stauffer ended the letter. "Really, this old world is in an awful mess and maybe the return of the Lord very near."

Sowing rice seed bed.

Transplanting rice.

In a newsletter written to friends four months later, James and Arlene further described this unforgettable journey:

Near the southern tip of Viet Nam lie the two cities of Bac-Lieu and Camau. On Saturday, January 4, our interpreter and we traveled to Bac Lieu by bus through the heart of Viet Nam's "rice bowl." The peaceful countryside had a soul-refreshing effect upon us, especially after living in the heart of Saigon for several months. Here life centers along the canals, which actually divide the land into a group of islands south of the Mekong River. The houses, roads and gardens are concentrated along these canals. Naked children, ducks, water buffalos, and boats navigate the muddy waters. Once we saw a lad standing on the back of a swimming buffalo holding a rope tied to the beast's nose. The added weight of the boy completely submerged the buffalo except for his nose. The resulting effect was not unlike a water-skier in slow-motion. Sights like this made our 175 mile trip to Bac Lieu far from dull.

The two couples had interesting stories to share when the Stauffers returned to Saigon. The previous day a thief entered the front gate at their residence and stole Everett's bicycle. The cook, who was making breakfast, saw him go and took off after him, hollering, "O God, and people of this village, help—he took my bicycle!" The thief then panicked, jumped off the bike and disappeared. The triumphant cook carried the bike back home!

A week later Stauffer spoke at a Friday evening youth rally at the central Saigon church. In his letter home he wrote that two persons "accepted Christ after the service. The one young man has a family and drives a taxi for a living. He had attended a Catholic school and had studied a lot about the Bible and their religion but was not satisfied. He has a relative who explained salvation to him and gradually the Spirit did His work."

The Saturday evening classes at the Truong Minh Giang Chapel were well attended. On the first Sunday in February Everett spoke to the youth at the chapel, and the four sang their first quartet number in Vietnamese. James, for the first time, pronounced the benediction in the Vietnamese language.

That evening a twenty-five-year-old student, Que, invited the Stauffers to her home. James describes this in a letter home: "We told her in as simple terms as possible the Gospel. I have heard of people's mouths dropping open when they hear the Gospel for the first time. Now, I have seen it! She did not have the least idea as to the nature of God's salvation. She came to our home last night and we read some passages with her and gave her a Vietnamese Bible to read. She said she is just curious but we believe she is really hungry. . . . Pray that she will be convicted of sin. She can't quite believe that we are as sinful as the Bible says. She has studied Confucianism but neither she nor her family has followed any religion."

Many Vietnamese families lived by high moral standards. Filial piety and veneration of the ancestors were constant guides to daily living. The prophet Isaiah's words that "all our righteousnesses are as filthy rags" was just as incredible a thought to Que's mind as to many people from the West.

The two couples got a thorough introduction into Vietnamese cultural traditions on the occasion of the lunar New Year. While there are several *Tets* (festivals) throughout the year, *Tết Nguyên Đán* (New Year's Day) is the most important Tet. Arlene and James described these celebrations well in a May letter to friends:

> Tet is a week-long celebration on the occasion of the Chinese New Year. To describe all the aspects of this colorful event would be a gigantic task. We might approach something comparable if we were to combine all the holidays in America into one big occasion. Everyone celebrates his birthday at Tet and is considered one year older then—regardless of his real birth date. New Year's Day according to the lunar calendar came on February 18 this year, but preparation for it began many weeks in advance. Special shops opened around the markets and soon full scale activity equal to our "Christmas Rush" was underway. Some spend a whole year's savings and some go into debt to purchase firecrackers, candy, flowers, clothes, liquor, etc. It is house cleaning time. Bright colored curtains are hung and the house is decorated with spring flowers. Kitchens bustle with activity as special dishes are prepared in advance. New clothes are a must. . . .
>
> On New Year's Eve we went to the temple where thousands gather every year on that night to worship. They bring offerings and wave incense before the altar and, then, prostrate themselves in prayer. After praying they would shake a can containing numbered sticks. The first stick that fell out provided them with a number which was told to one of the many soothsayers that lined

the entrance to the temple. He would open one of his books and tell the person's fortune for the coming year.

After returning we walked down the streets just before midnight. Almost every home had an altar at the front door or sidewalk prepared to receive the spirits of their ancestors. On the altar would be a bowl of rice, roast duck, watermelon and often a bottle of wine. Again we saw the folded hands and bowed knees of these dear people praying to the departed spirits of their loved ones.

James saw within these festivities elements of a wonderful cultural celebration, a harmless but wasteful expenditure of resources—five million dollars spent for firecrackers alone, and "heathenism at its worst" that could be transformed by the power of the Gospel of Jesus.

A month after *Tet* the two couples moved to another house at 48 Ngo Tung Chau Street, Gia Dinh, Saigon's smaller twin city just across the canal to the north and east. Thinking they were paying too much for their small downtown Saigon property, they tried unsuccessfully to bargain for a lower rent. They then learned from their pastor friend of the Gia Dinh Tin Lanh Church that Mr. Tran Van My, the church's treasurer, had just purchased a house with five rooms plus utility space, kitchen and back porch. They agreed to have a well dug and make the needed repairs for a rental fee of only half of what they had been paying. They moved on Friday, March 14, a day so stifling hot they could hardly sleep at night. They purchased additional furniture, and Everett built shelves and cabinets.

Here both couples would live together for more than a year. In their letter to friends, James and Arlene described this house as an answer to their prayers—five kilometers from downtown Saigon, but closer to the MCC house, the Adventist Hospital, and the Gia Dinh Tin Lanh Church. "Here we have lots of trees, mosquitoes, and a yard in front and back which provides a country-like atmosphere," they wrote. "We are still in the midst of a populous area with neighbors on all

Celebrating Tet at Le Van Duyet Temple.

sides. One neighboring house which is easy for us to observe is like a swarming bee-hive since it shelters twenty-five people—mostly children."

The 1958 best-selling novel by William Lederer and Eugene Burdic, *The Ugly American*, was a must-read for Americans traveling to Southeast Asia. These new missionaries did not need this book to show them how not to live as isolated, pretentious, loud and ostentatious foreigners. They clearly modeled a lifestyle that was appreciated by friends they were making among their neighbors and Christians within the Evangelical Church of Vietnam. They regularly attended Sunday worship services at one of these congregations—often the Gia Dinh congregation.

In his first annual report to Eastern Mennonite Missions the end of February, Stauffer wrote: "We thank God for His leading during this initial period of orientation and adjustment. We are happy in the Lord, healthy in mind and body, and contented with the Oriental way of life." He noted the good relationships they had with MCC and with the Evangelical Church. They had been invited to speak in three Chinese and five Vietnamese congregations in Saigon and five in the Mekong Delta, and had attended the annual ECVN Conference. Language study was their primary task.

Stauffer expressed measured concern about government policies. Pastor Kieu Cong Thao of the Gia Dinh Tin Lanh congregation had informed them that a Christian working within the government heard that President Diem recently said that Mennonites would not be authorized to work in Vietnam "because of their opposition to war." James did not take that report too seriously; President Diem was increasingly relying on American aid, and likely would not alienate the United States by denying Americans the privilege of living and working there.

Easter came on April 6. James and Arlene rode their bikes out to the baseball field near the airport where they joined five or six hundred people in an Easter Sunrise service sponsored by the American Community Church. Later James preached at the Truong Minh Giang Chapel. In his

James preaching at the Truong Minh Giang Chapel.

letter home James wrote: "My soul was thrilled as I reviewed this wonderful story and I spoke on the theme: 'The Meaning of the Resurrection.'"

Several days later when riding their bicycles to choir practice, the police stopped Stauffer because his bike lights were not working. He was asked to pay a small fine, but when the policeman learned James was an American, he relented. James wrote home: "I guess one reason they were so considerate is that the US has just granted another large sum to buy new jeeps for the VN police force. Also, the Michigan State University has a crew here to help the efficiency of the Saigon police."

After a year of language study, Arlene and James spent a week in early April 1958 vacationing in the mountainous city of Da Lat, often called the honeymoon capital of Vietnam. The city's elevation of 1,475 meters (4,840 feet) with pleasant temperatures made it an ideal getaway for the French who established the city in the early twentieth century. The Stauffers attended the worship service May 5 at the Da Lat Tin Lanh Church and surprised Pastor Duy Cach Lam who invited them to his home. Holding French citizenship as Paul Richardson, he was the father of Jacqueline Richardson who was studying at Eastern Mennonite College. After James and Arlene returned, Everett and Margaret spent several days vacationing at Long Hai, just north of Vung Tau on the South China Sea, 120 kilometers southeast of Saigon. The Metzlers were looking forward to the birth of their first child.

In a May 21 letter to James' folks, Arlene tacked a note: "In one more week we will have been in Viet Nam already one year. It has not seemed that long—just like one big summer with no unusual change of seasons." In his letter the following week, James said the Immigration Department had just issued them visas for another year. He observed: "It seems like a long time since we left [home] and yet this year has passed rapidly. I certainly hoped that we would be farther along in this language and yet . . . it is soaking in." The rainy season had arrived, and they were enjoying refreshing rains nearly every day.

The Stauffers continued to teach English language Bible classes at the Truong Minh Giang Chapel Saturday evenings throughout 1958, using as their textbook the book of Acts of the Apostles. After the classes a pastor preached a thirty-minute evangelistic message which was a typical Tin Lanh congregational pattern on Saturday evenings. On Monday evenings Arlene taught a beginner English class in their home, and Everett had a conversational class for more advanced students. They also privately tutored some of their new friends they met at the chapel.

The foursome also visited the homes of many of their students. These contacts introduced the missionaries to a more inclusive religious world view. James noted that many "do not follow any religion but are half-way between Buddhism, Catholicism or Protestantism." While expressing a "genuine interest in the Gospel," Stauffer noted that it was common for students to compare the Gospel of Jesus Christ with the teachings of other religions.

The Stauffers and Metzlers enjoyed their shared lives together. The four loved to sing, and were invited to share their voices in a repertoire of four-part a cappella hymns in many churches. They saw the MCC staff as family with whom they met weekly. They found occasion for fellowship and recreation with other missionaries working with Summer Institute of Linguistics, Orient Crusades and the Christian and Missionary Alliance.

PREPARATION FOR MINISTRY

Chapter 12

Wearing two hats—one from MCC and the other from Eastern Mennonite Board of Missions and Charities—Orie Miller flew into Vietnam on June 2, 1958, for a planned stay of nearly two weeks. The following evening he had supper with the two missionary couples at their Ngo Tung Chau Street home. Miller shared with them his life experiences since the recent death of his wife. Writing to James' home, Arlene noted: "His insight into our particular problems here and vision of the future certainly stimulated our thinking."

James Stauffer flew with Miller to Vientiane, Laos, on a brief fact-finding mission to see whether Eastern Mennonite Board might consider placing missionary personnel there. In a "Viet Nam Mission Proposal" prepared by Miller, he noted that the Christian and Missionary Alliance planned to expand missionary activity in Vietnam, Laos, and Cambodia—the former Indochina.

This sixty-five-year-old mission administrator saw significant opportunities for mission in these lands recently freed from French colonial rule. He recommended that Eastern Mennonite Board establish its headquarters and begin missionary work in Saigon. "In addition to the usual community approaches thru preaching, the Sunday school, [and] summer Bible school," Miller wrote, missionaries should utilize "student services, book shops, reading rooms and schools (from kindergarten up)" for mission and church planting. Miller proposed assigning personnel in Vientiane, Laos, and eventually in Phnom Penh, Cambodia, as well as a second location in Vietnam, envisioning a maximum of twenty-five persons.

James Stauffer was designated director and Everett Metzler business manager of the new Vietnam Mennonite Mission (VMM). The monthly allowance for each married adult was set at 5,000 piasters ($69) which Stauffer said was quite adequate. This allowance had to cover food, wages for household help, and personal items. The Mission provided housing, furniture, transportation, and medical care.

Much of Miller's visit was given to MCC agenda. In his MCC report, he noted that the Mennonite Mission welcomed continuing MCC services. Miller, now EMBMC Associate Secretary after twenty-three years as secretary, was here acknowledging that MCC planned to continue working in Vietnam. This represented a somewhat new operational pattern; MCC usually closed short-term relief programs or they were absorbed into long term programs of a Mennonite mission agency.

Miller reasoned that for both Mennonite agencies to work together in Vietnam, there should be some joint administration. The MCC Executive Committee approved Miller's recommendation for a missionary to become part of an MCC Vietnam Administrative Committee, but the new EMBMC Secretary, Paul N. Kraybill, had reservations about a missionary serving in MCC's administrative structure.

After Miller left Vietnam, Dr. Krabill, Glenn Stoltzfus, Stauffer, and Metzler met with Evangelical Church leaders at President Le Van Thai's home in Nha Trang. Thai said the Church had a generally good and sympathetic feeling toward the Mennonites for three reasons. In the first place, the Church appreciated very much the desire of the Mennonites to cooperate and consult with them. Secondly, they sensed that the Mennonites shared similar beliefs with the Church on the cardinal doctrines of the Christian faith. These two reasons were most important. He also appreciated the relief assistance given to the Church.

Krabill and Stauffer reported on MCC and Vietnam Mennonite Mission activities, reviewed Miller's findings and recommendations and asked President Thai for his counsel. Thai suggested that MCC consider food distribution in poor areas of Central Vietnam. On Miller's proposal for a Pax builders' unit, Thai said that the Church had responded with laughter to an earlier proposal for Pax builders. Though they understood the value of interaction with Christians from other countries, they had no interest in such a program, especially since so many poor local Christians were unemployed. Neither was the Church interested in student work camps.

Krabill and Stauffer proposed to Thai that representatives of the Church, MCC, and the Mennonite Mission meet monthly to exchange information and counsel. Pastor Thai responded positively to this idea, and asked them to submit a formal proposal. He invited them to attend the Church's Annual Conference in Tam Ky in early July.

The head of the Church's Relief Committee, Pastor Nguyen Thien Sy, hosted a farewell dinner in his Saigon home for Willard and Grace Krabill on Saturday evening, June 28, with the Stauffer and Metzler couples invited. The Krabills left Vietnam July 3.

The same day Stauffer, Metzler, Glenn Stoltzfus and interpreter Ninh flew in an Air Vietnam DC-6 to Da Nang and took a taxi sixty kilometers south to Tam Ky where the annual Church conference was being held. This took several hours; they had to wait at a ferry crossing since a bridge destroyed during the recent French Indochina war had not yet been rebuilt. They were warmly welcomed by Pastors Thai and Sy who took them out for supper.

Stoltzfus and Stauffer had prepared a letter for President Thai, summarizing the MCC work and projected programs, outlining the plans of the Vietnam Mennonite Mission, and calling for "closer fellowship and cooperation" between the Vietnamese church and the Mennonites, represented by Mennonite Central Committee and the Mennonite Mission. They wrote: "It is our firm desire to correlate our activities with yours wherever possible. . . . We want the Vietnamese Church to be informed as to our activities and our beliefs, and we need the counsel of the Vietnamese Church in making plans and decisions for our programs, inasmuch as our plans affect the Vietnamese Church as well." The Church Executive Committee accepted the proposal to hold periodic meetings.

Stauffer was impressed with the emphasis on prayer within the Tin Lanh Church; nearly all the pastors attended a 6:00 a.m. prayer meeting at the conference, expressing a "real spirit of urgency and fervency in their prayers." Stauffer and Metzler rode back to Da Nang Sunday afternoon at the close of the conference with the Alliance missionary couple George and Harriet Irwin, staying with them that night. The next day they met friends and visited the Church's Bible School before flying back home.

A few weeks later Margaret and Everett became parents when Eric Eugene was born at the Adventist Hospital near their home. The Australian doctor permitted the father in the delivery room during the birth, a contrast to common procedures in the United States at that time. Normal procedure allowed new mothers to rest in the hospital for several more days. Student friends from Truong Minh Giang Chapel brought gifts of fruit, and the church deacon gave them *nước mía* (fresh sugar cane juice.) They were impressed with the generosity of friends, and were reminded that many Christians tithed their income, and would even tithe a gift received.

Now the missionaries no longer relied solely on bicycles or taxis for transportation. A month earlier Stauffer had purchased a motor scooter—an Italian Lambretta. Men generally drove the scooter, while women sat side-saddle on the rear.

The missionaries continued their language study with Mr. Hoa. One Sunday they heard Alliance Field Chairman Jack Revelle say that every missionary must spend the first two years in full-time language study. While they might speak fairly fluently within a few years, it would take many years to master the language. Stauffer found some comfort in these remarks. Arlene shared a brief memorized Vietnamese language expression of faith in church one Sunday in August.

In late August Arlene wore her Vietnamese *aó dài* dress to church for the first time at the Gia Dinh Church. When the tailor had finished the outer tunic a few months earlier, she modeled it at home, and James said she "looked real cute and graceful. . . . With her black hair she will pass for a Vietnamese real well." After wearing it to church, the pastor's wife came over that same afternoon to say how much they all appreciated it, so Arlene was now planning to wear it to most public occasions. James' parents might have puzzled over his comment about this form-fitting tunic worn over pantaloons: "It certainly is one point where I feel we can be 'all things to all men.'"

Stauffer wrote home in August about the discontent of the ethnic minorities against the Diem government for forcing them to move out of the mountains into lower open lands. "The Vietnamese treat these people much like we treated the American Indians," he wrote. This policy encouraged many to support the communist opposition. Reliable reports indicated that some ethnic minorities were going to the Soviet Union to obtain technical training and political education.

The Stauffers continued their visits to other Tin Lanh Churches. In September James preached at the My Tho congregation, seventy kilometers southwest of Saigon. Another Sunday he preached at the Bien Hoa Church—thirty kilometers east—while Everett preached at the Gia Dinh Church near their home.

The reason for the frequent invitations to James and Everett to preach at the Tin Lanh Churches was, no doubt, the anticipation that these Mennonite missionaries might be able to contribute something significant to their churches. Kieu Cong Thao, the Pastor of the Gia Dinh Tin Lanh congregation, served on the Tin Lanh Relief Committee, the Hospital Committee and on the Executive Committee of the Church. He was aware that Orie Miller had recommended that the Mennonite Mission establish Christian schools, and had discussed this with Stauffer.

By this time the missionaries had begun preparing a monthly newsletter—*News and Concerns*—to send to families and friends in the United States. In the September newsletter Everett wrote: "The local pastor, Mr. Thao, continues to ask us to preach in the nearby Evangelical Church when he must make trips away from home. James is to preach this coming Sunday at the monthly communion service." He continued: "We continue to be queried on our future relationship to the National Church. How to maintain the unity of Christ's church and yet not water down some aspects of the Message we feel we must bring will likely always be a problem here."

Paul Kraybill was hesitant to develop the institutions that Orie Miller proposed—like schools and student hostels—that the Alliance Mission had not developed for the Evangelical Church. In an August letter, Kraybill said the Mennonite Mission wanted to maintain close and cordial coordination and fellowship with the Vietnamese church, but did not want to weaken C&MA relationships with the Church by providing services that C&MA chose not to provide.

In late August when Stauffer met with the Tin Lanh leaders, they grilled him about the beliefs and practices of the Mennonite Church. When he told them about non-participation in military service, they seemed to respect that understanding.

The four missionaries often sang a cappella at the Truong Minh Giang Chapel. By this time Nguyen Huu Phien was serving as Pastor of the Truong Minh Giang congregation. Before the 1954 partitioning of the country he was Pastor of the Hai Duong congregation in the North. The Stauffers and Metzlers were invited to the October 11 wedding of Pastor and Mrs. Phien's second daughter, Nguyen Thi Tam, to Tran Xuan Quang, the son of Pastor and Mrs. Tran Xuan Hi. Pastor Hi was Superintendent of the Southern District of the Tin Lanh Church.

A few months later Tam and Quang, the bride and groom, stopped by the Stauffers' and Metzlers' home. Although Quang spoke fluent English, they appreciated that he spoke Vietnamese with them. A decade later Quang would become the first ordained pastor in the Mennonite Church, and Quang and Tam would relate how they were impressed by the simple lifestyle of these young Mennonite missionaries.

October 26, 1958, the third anniversary of the Declaration of the Republic of Vietnam fell on a Sunday. The government asked all churches to have special prayer services for the President and the nation. The four missionaries went to a 7:30 a.m. service at the Gia Dinh Tin Lanh church where several government officials were recognized. The whole populace was asked to fly the yellow flag with the three blood-red horizontal bars. "Our servant thought we should put one out too," James wrote home that day, "but we didn't!"

"Much ado was made about the day, and one feels that nationalism among many is quite strong," Everett and Margaret commented. "Pray that the door will remain open for mission work here. Recently the government decreed that aliens will not be granted identity cards but only 'extension of stay.'"

To visitors, such a universal display of the flags might have suggested a surge of patriotic expression. However, this was patriotism made obligatory by the government of Ngo Dinh Diem. Homes that did not display the flag were visited by officials so Mennonite missionaries soon learned that it might be better to display the flag than to have their household helpers and themselves placed on a list of people to be closely watched.

At year's end Stauffer observed that Everett and Margaret, after only one year of language study, excelled them in conversational ability. But they were all making progress. Language study was hard work. But life in Saigon also had interesting moments, like the men killing a rat in the house and watching the antics of a frog that found its way into their dining room. One day, during a time of meditation and prayer, they spied a frog sticking his head out of a vase on a cupboard five feet off the floor. They chased the frog out the door as it took six or eight feet in each broad jump. At the weekly gathering with the MCC folks a few days later, the frog suddenly jumped from the vase again, hopping under the table and scattering the group!

On Christmas morning Stauffer preached—still with an interpreter—at the Truong Minh Giang Church and they and the Metzlers hosted the MCC folks in Saigon for dinner.

On the first weekend of the New Year 1959, James and Arlene boarded an old bus for Rach Gia, 250 kilometers deep in the Mekong Delta on the Gulf of Thailand where he preached Sunday morning and evening. This was reminiscent of a trip they had taken to Bac Lieu and Ca Mau a year earlier.

The communist opposition against President Diem's rule was intensifying. Stauffer wrote home: "We feel so strongly that this will be a decisive year here in Vietnam. There are many rumors of new threats from the communists toward our little nation here. Only the Lord knows for sure what will happen."

The stakes were indeed rising. What they did not know was that the American Central Intelligence Agency (CIA) in January acquired a copy of Resolution 15 adopted by the Central Committee of the Workers Party in Hanoi, indicating that they were supporting an "armed struggle" to reunify the country.

In late January Arlene and James took the scooter to the Tin Lanh Church in Bien Hoa, twenty kilometers east of Saigon. Only a few persons attended the Sunday worship service; the pastor said that many members were selling in the market—the lunar New Year was only two weeks away. Stauffer expressed a sympathetic understanding: "Their concept of keeping the Lord's Day holy is different than ours. We can hardly blame the Christian woman here for going to market on Sunday morning to buy the day's supply of food. She doesn't have a refrigerator to keep food from one day to the next."

The lunar New Year was Sunday, February 8. Arlene and James spent four days the previous week at the Ban Me Thuot Leprosarium. Here they joined the weekly prayer meeting of MCC staff with the Alliance missionaries and attended the dedication of the new hospital facilities.

Stauffer wrote home describing a three-day Marian Congress in Saigon marking the tricentennial of the formation of the first Vietnamese dioceses in 1659. Bishop Joseph Pham Van Thien ordered from Rome a pink granite statue of the Virgin Mary, the Virgin with a Globe,

which was placed in front of the main Basilica in downtown Saigon on February 16. The Papal Nuncio chaired the ceremony for the *Regina Pacis* (Queen of Peace) statue and closed the Congress.

Given a common Protestant perception of the Roman Catholic Church in this era—five years before Vatican II, views shared by many Mennonites, it is not surprising that the missionaries were jolted by the "pathetic sight" of crowds of 300,000 jamming the streets by the cathedral, many transported to the area by special buses and Vietnamese army trucks. Stauffer noted that the Cardinal stayed in the Vice President's Palace and rode in President Diem's Cadillac with full military escort. There was a daily lecture on the theme of "the Holy Virgin and Vietnam."

John R. Mumaw, president of Eastern Mennonite College, visited them early March, hosted in the mis-

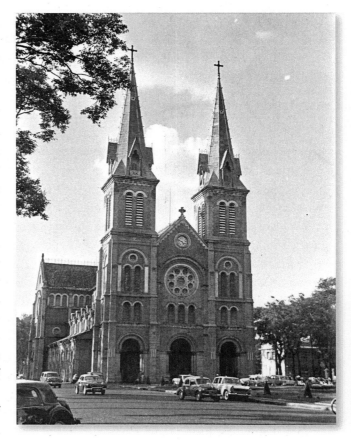

Saigon Notre Dame Cathedral.

sionaries' home. During these few days he interviewed the missionaries, met with the MCC personnel in Saigon, led a Bible study on "Discipleship" with the MCCers and missionaries, and spoke to the Evangelical Christian university students.

Mumaw prepared a report for the EMBMC Executive Committee and the Lancaster Mennonite Conference Bishops' Mission Committee. He said that "the missionaries have a clear sense of call to Viet Nam but they are not clear on what strategy should characterize their missionary advance. [They] apparently have happy relationship with MCC but they are not certain how to relate mission and MCC in the ongoing program."

Mumaw said the missionaries would have to "clarify" the relationship of the Mennonite Mission to the Christian and Missionary Alliance, the Tin Lanh Church and to MCC. He questioned whether "the genius of Mennonite missions can function smoothly within the orbit of C&MA administration." He doubted whether "distinctive Mennonite church elements" could be taught within the Evangelical Church. While not mentioning these "distinctive" Mennonite emphases, he was likely referring to the Mennonite commitment to nonresistance—non-participation in military service—and to nonconformity in lifestyle, including patterns of dress.

Mumaw anticipated a "full scale mission program, including educational and medical work," on the assumption that MCC would phase out all programs within two years, and that a satisfactory understanding could be reached with the Alliance and the Tin Lanh Church to work on "a co-operative but separate basis." The overall aim would be to establish a Mennonite Church in Vietnam "with a balanced program of evangelism, nurture and fulfillment of human need." Concluding, Mumaw wrote, "If this should prove not feasible I would suggest giving the field over to MCC which agency is better adapted to serve a role of assisting other groups."

Paul N. Kraybill, the EMBMC Secretary, was planning a visit in May. In March, James and Everett began surveying Saigon city, noting all schools, cultural-political institutions, business districts, and residential areas in preparation for developing some ministry.

Hoa, their language teacher, left in February to accompany and interpret for Dr. Adrian van den Brandeler, a Dutch attorney representing the World Council of Churches (WCC), who made it his personal goal to visit every Tin Lanh congregation within South Vietnam to understand the needs of the churches. "C&MA is warning the Church about linking up with WCC," Stauffer observed, but the Alliance had "never lifted a finger to help the Church in a social way." In late April the two couples hosted van den Brandeler and another WCC representative, Ulrich H. van Beyma—both stimulating visitors.

In early April the six Tin Lanh congregations in Saigon sponsored two nights of special meetings in a large auditorium. These congregations would have been Tran Hung Dao, Nguyen Tri Phuong, Hoa Hung, Gia Dinh, Khanh Hoi and Truong Minh Giang, all geographic names denoting the area of the city or the streets on which the church was located. The four missionaries sang a quartet number at a Saturday evening meeting.

Arlene told her first Bible story in the Vietnamese language to the girls at the Hoi Duc Anh Orphanage, using flannelgraph to tell the story of Jesus feeding the five thousand.

James was reading a history of Vietnam, most likely Joseph Buttinger's *The Smaller Dragon*, published in 1958, practically the only English language history available. He was struck by the fact that Vietnamese history could be traced back 2,700 years, and that the people had the opportunity to hear the Gospel of Jesus Christ only relatively recently.

MONTH OF DECISION—JUNE 1959

Chapter 13

In a letter to Akron in February 1959, Glenn Stoltzfus noted that William T. Snyder, MCC's new executive secretary, was considering a visit to Vietnam in May. "A visit then would be very useful and timely," he wrote. Paul N. Kraybill, who had become Secretary of Eastern Mennonite Board of Missions and Charities a year earlier, was already planning to come in May for several weeks. Aware that a World Council of Churches representative would also then be in Vietnam, Stoltzfus said that with all these persons converging on Vietnam, May "could well prove to be a month of decision."

A crucial issue for the Mennonite missionaries was their relationship to the Tin Lanh Church. Shall they work independently with the goal of establishing a Mennonite church while seeking to maintain good relationships with the Church, which is what EMBMC administrators were saying, or should all missionary activity be focused on strengthening the witness of the Tin Lanh Church?

Aside from the small Adventist Church, the Evangelical Church in Vietnam was the only Protestant church in Vietnam. It was not only people like Ulrich van Beyma of the World Council of Churches who did not want to see multiple church denominations in Vietnam. MCC Vietnam director Willard Krabill—who had left the year before—also argued quite forcefully that Mennonite missionary work in Vietnam should contribute to building up the Tin Lanh Church rather than introduce another church denomination to Vietnam.

Already in mid-December Kraybill made plans to spend three weeks in Vietnam, Laos and possibly Cambodia, wanting "to get better acquainted with the whole situation and circumstances in these countries." He wanted to further develop the strategy and programs that Orie Miller had recommended; this included where the Mennonite Mission headquarters would be located.

He also wanted "to find ways of relating . . . to and being of assistance to the Vietnamese National Church. We want to do everything that we can to alleviate any fears or suspicion and not put undue emphasis on our particular plans at this point which may be open to misinterpretation," Kraybill wrote. He was prepared to broaden the program "to include any service need or emphasis" that should be part of the mission witness. Lastly, Kraybill said he wanted to "seek to clarify and define" EMBMC's relationship to the Mennonite Central Committee program.

Kraybill concluded: "We are deeply anxious to do whatever is necessary to plan carefully in establishing a witness. We want to gain the confidence of the national church and establish happy working relationships and, of course, we want to pursue an aggressive program of evangelism."

In an internal memo, "Considerations Regarding Viet Nam," Kraybill noted that recent consultations between MCC and several North American Mennonite mission boards seemed to indicate a "new sense of understanding and cordial relationships" between MCC and mission boards as well as "a new sense of the significance of the integration of relief and service to missions."

Kraybill observed that the various Mennonite mission boards favored "a more rapid turnover" of MCC's international relief work to mission agencies, with MCC possibly supplementing their work. MCC, on the other hand, now seemed to be preparing to remain in their countries of service indefinitely and complement the work of the mission boards. This would mean, he wrote, that MCC "would continue to maintain a mobile emergency relief program."

Kraybill preferred to see mission boards take the primary role in international ministries and shape their programs so that they could "quickly and completely give expression to relief and service in a truly integrated fashion." He saw a philosophical or theological problem if MCC carried out long-range programs without a commitment to invite people to faith in Jesus Christ and participation in the life of a church. "What effect will there be on our church and our young people if the 'relief vocation' becomes a long range project with its own type of motivation and expression as against the missionary motivation?" he asked himself. To split "mission" and "service" into separate programs "would be to go against all that experience would teach us," he reasoned.

Kraybill was still pondering Miller's recommendation that one of the missionaries become part of a Vietnam MCC administrative team. Anticipating that EMBMC might assign specialized personnel such as doctors and nurses as the Mission did in other countries, he saw possible administrative problems in the two agencies working side by side.

Kraybill thought there was "some discrepancy in MCC's attitude toward helping missions and working beside them. In India they were reluctant to help a mission, here [in Vietnam] they profess to want to help in their own way of working beside the mission."

In April, Kraybill met with Alliance administrators in New York. He found that "C&MA welcomes heartily our Mission Board to Viet Nam but wishes us to plan for a Mennonite Church as separate from the Vietnamese Church without interfering with the relationships between the Vietnamese Church and the Christian and Missionary Alliance."

The Alliance executives said that Tin Lanh Church leaders tended to want all Protestant activity in Vietnam under the sponsorship of their church. Younger church leaders were especially anxious for assistance they might possibly receive from non-Alliance sources. L. L. King and Robert Chrisman said there was a tendency for some persons to separate from the Tin Lanh Church in order to receive assistance from MCC.

It appeared to Kraybill that C&MA leaders had the impression that MCC was deliberately helping the Tin Lanh Church in an attempt to "prepare the way for the coming of the Mennonite mission who [sic] would then pick up some of the dissident elements that [were] being attracted by this help from MCC." Kraybill assured them that Eastern Mennonite Board had "no intentions whatsoever to draw away or entice folks from the Vietnamese Church by subsidies or any other means."

Kraybill indicated that the administrators seemed "wholly satisfied with my commitments on this. . . . In fact they encourage us to move in the building of a Mennonite Church rather [than] in any way identifying with or even helping the Vietnamese Church."

Kraybill arrived in Vietnam on May 20 and left on June 15. Snyder came on May 31 and left on June 8.

Kraybill accomplished many things on his three-week visit. He spent significant time with the four missionaries, interacted with MCC personnel in Saigon and Ban Me Thuot, met with Alliance leaders, and had two significant conversations with President Le Van Thai and other leaders of the Tin Lanh Church, both in Saigon and in Nha Trang. His severe bout with a twenty-four-hour gastrointestinal attack enabled him to sympathize with missionaries who experienced these illnesses. He was scheduled to leave Vietnam on Sunday morning, June 14. At the airport he discovered that his exit visa was for Phnom Penh, but he was flying to Karachi, so he was not allowed to board the plane. He left on Monday, but had to rebook his entire flight schedule.

Reflecting on Kraybill's visit, Stauffer wrote to his parents: "Paul's visit was a complete success as far as our program here is concerned."

Kraybill's trip report notes that South Vietnam had a population of twelve million, with one-fourth of the people living in the Saigon area. He wrote that the people "are nominally Buddhist" but that ancestral veneration was the strongest religious impulse of the people. Ten percent of the people were Catholic. The Evangelical (Tin Lanh) Church of Vietnam, with 16,000 to 17,000 baptized members, had 120 churches with pastors, and 100 additional churches or worship centers among the minority peoples. The Alliance Mission had 110 missionaries in South Vietnam—half of them serving with the Vietnamese Kinh population, the others among the various minority groups. The missionaries worked separately but in close coordination with the church. Kraybill noted that the Tin Lanh Church was "a spiritual church, fundamental in doctrine and strongly evangelistic . . . , struggling to maintain self-support in line with the rather rigid indigenous policies of the C&MA."

Commenting on the Mennonite Central Committee, Kraybill wrote that the MCC program "has been very effective in meeting its original objectives and it has also served to establish confidence in and appreciation for the Mennonites. Further, it has also made a real contribution to the work of C&MA and the National Church. The MCC program has been the means of strengthening the conscience of the mission and church on its responsibility to minister to physical need and to find wider expression for the life of discipleship."

Kraybill had praise for the Stauffer and Metzler couples, commending them for staying in Saigon for language study, and for their simple lifestyle which enabled them to interact with their community. While they experienced "a period of uncertainty regarding strategy and program," they had a clear sense of call to Vietnam and vision for ministry.

Kraybill then commented on the Mennonite Mission relationship to the Evangelical Church in Vietnam. The raw notes of his May 26 meeting with Pastor Thai and members of the Executive Committee are fascinating to review.

Pastor Thai was highly respected. Born around the turn of the century, he came to faith in Jesus Christ in his youth, and enrolled in Bible school in 1922. After graduation, he effectively served as evangelist, pastor and administrator in various places in Central Vietnam, the south and the north where he was founding pastor of the Hanoi Church. He experienced many hardships which were the lot of all who lived through the revolutionary era of Vietnam. He became President of the Church in 1942. Six days after Ho Chi Minh proclaimed national independence in September 1945, Thai met with the revolutionary leader. In his memoir, Thai describes how Ho Chi Minh asked him to organize a patriotic chapter within the Evangelical Church. Thai explained that Christians were integrated with the people, and supported the revolution through their involvement with youth, labor, workers,' and teachers' organizations. Furthermore, the Evangelical Church did not permit engagement in political activities. Ho Chi Minh allowed the Church to maintain its policy.

James Stauffer and Everett Metzler accompanied Kraybill. Seated at the table with Pastor Thai were [Tran Thu] Quang, Vice President of the Church and chair of the scholarship committee; Church Treasurer Duy Cach Lam (aka Paul Richardson); Huynh Kim Luyen, Superintendent of the Church's central district; Phan Van Tranh, Superintendent of the southern district; Kieu Cong Thao, chair of the hospital planning committee, Pastor of the Gia Dinh Tin Lanh congregation, and friend of the Stauffers and Metzlers; and Nguyen Van Van, a prominent Church layman who served effectively as interpreter.

The edited verbatim conversation went like this:

Thai: "We welcome the Mennonite mission to Vietnam. We long for [your] fellowship with us in the Lord's work. The need is great here; there's a white harvest field. What type of evangelism do you have in mind for Vietnam?"

Kraybill: "Our plans are not yet well developed. We intend to start small and simple. We want to start in Saigon—we believe our headquarters should be in Saigon. The need is greatest in Saigon. We want your advice on where to locate and on other matters. Possible programs may include English classes, Bible study, preaching, home visitation, etc. We will seek to gather groups of believers. Later we will move to outer edges of the city. We wish to avoid mishaps between us and other organizations. Perhaps later on we will move into a rural area. We might possibly use schools."

Thai: "What kind of school? A Bible School?"

(Then there was a discussion about name [of our organization]).

Metzler: On our stamp we have *"Hội Truyền Giáo Tin Lành Mennonite"* (Mennonite Evangelical Mission).

Thai: "What does 'Mennonite' mean?"

[Kraybill then gave a brief history of church.]

Thai: "Your missionaries know the work here. . . . Now more missions are here in Vietnam, e.g., the Worldwide Evangelization Crusade at Da Nang. We wish to fellowship with them. We don't know what their program is. Do Mennonites want to work together with us or wish to work separately—build a separate church?"

Kraybill: "We make it a rule to work in unoccupied territory everywhere else."

Thai: "A Mennonite mission delegation should meet with the Evangelical Church of Vietnam to discuss specific projects."

Kraybill: "Just as we have today, for instance. You would expect us to be ourselves. We must be true to our convictions. We don't want to build on someone else's church. We feel it's a mark of love when two churches coexist side by side in fellowship. Are there other ways we can avoid pitfalls?"

Thai: "In the future we can have representatives of both organizations meet to discuss plans and problems. We can pretty well tell what will cause problems."

Thai: "What is your concept of self-support?"

[Kraybill described the Eastern Board's work in Africa.]

Thai: "Will you work in Vietnam as in Africa?"

Kraybill: "Who knows? We keep flexible according to conditions. Each country is different."

Thai: "We are concerned about new missions' attitudes on the question of self-support. Some give too much, some withdraw too soon."

Kraybill: "We try to walk in the middle."

Thai: "That is a good idea. Self-support is necessary. If church is dependent, when hard times or war comes, then the church has a very rough time. Likewise demanding self-support too soon is like forcing a child to do hard work. We want missions to think in terms of self-support but not too soon."

Kraybill: "We agree with you."

Richardson: "Have your missionaries begun work yet?"

Kraybill: "No, they are still studying language."

Luyen: "Will you use Vietnamese pastors to preach for you?"

Kraybill: "We don't make a practice of hiring other Christians. There are rare exceptions."

Luyen: "How about here?"

Kraybill: "We intend to start small, to gather a group of believers. They, then, will witness to others."

Luyen: "Would you draw away our youth to join you in service?"

Kraybill: "We intend to avoid that. I am glad you raised the question."

Luyen: "We ask because of problems with Gordon Smith. Some poorly qualified students who couldn't get into the Da Nang Bible School were accepted by Gordon Smith."

Thai: "My personal opinion is that it seems late now to begin evangelizing Vietnam. The work so far is superficial; people know of Tin Lanh but don't know what it means. Our Church is not able to evangelize all of Vietnam. If we wait long it will be too late. Ten years ago we invited other missions into Vietnam. We don't know why they didn't come. Perhaps they didn't know the need. Some perhaps wanted to come, but were too cautious, or were hesitant to come.

"There are only two qualifications for persons who come. We request that workers are true to the doctrines of the Bible with no heresy; and that they work in close fellowship with us.

"We report this to the Alliance Mission. My personal opinion is that if such qualified missions come to Vietnam, I think we can loan them workers such as Bible school students. We must make haste to work for the Lord here. Some people think the Executive Committee is bought out by the C&MA. I'm not for sale to anyone—but am consecrated to the Lord."

Kraybill: "We feel honored to have you feel we meet your qualifications. Where do you suggest we work in Saigon?"

[There was no definite reply. Someone suggested Go Vap—a district adjacent to northeast Saigon metropolitan area.]

Kraybill: "We are interested in a more central location for our headquarters. It will not be just an office but also a witness point. How about Ban Co area?"

Quang: "The Nguyen Tri Phuong congregation has a project planned for there, but it's okay for you to begin there."

Kraybill: "Are there large rural areas not yet reached?"

Luyen: "There are many such areas. You must have government permission to go there, however."

Thai: "We think a headquarters idea is good because of the political situation. Beginning in Saigon is best."

Kraybill: "Who should we contact about our plans?"

Thai: "Concerning Saigon, see Quang. Otherwise work through me."

Kraybill's report dealt with the argument that, since there was only one Protestant church in Vietnam, establishing a Mennonite church would contribute to Christian disunity:

It was clear that our witness would not represent the home church as it should if it were identified with the national church. If we took that course, we would have to be dishonest with ourselves in sacrificing at least some elements of our Anabaptist heritage, our interpretation of scripture and our strategy of missions. The alternative would be for us to try to alter that church to suit our liking which would be certainly inadvisable and probably impossible. It was interesting that those who felt we should identify ourselves with this church were usually those who were quite critical of it.

In meetings with Pastor Thai and other Church leaders, Kraybill wrote, "our existence as a separate organization was assumed. . . . They were seeking to assure themselves that they could trust us. After they had done that it was quite apparent that we had their good will and, as far as they were concerned, were completely free to move ahead as we had planned."

It was already known that the U.S.-based Southern Baptist Convention was planning to send missionaries to Vietnam later in 1959, but this was not a factor in the Mennonite decision to pursue a separate program of evangelistic ministry.

Kraybill's report then considered the relationship of the Vietnam Mennonite Mission to MCC. He affirmed MCC's continuing ministries, many which EMBMC was "hardly in a position to serve." He observed that MCC's program had "established confidence and understanding for [Eastern Mennonite Board] among the other mission organizations, church and government," noting that MCC welcomed the counsel of the Mission Board and the missionaries. However, missionaries would not become part of an MCC administrative team.

Kraybill then discussed mission strategy. He saw opportunities for evangelistic ministries in Saigon, a city of three million with only ten Protestant churches, most of them small chapels, and with fewer "than half a dozen missionaries doing full-time evangelistic work in Saigon." He contrasted that with Taipei, Taiwan, a city of 500,000 with one hundred Protestant churches. The Mission would not establish Christian schools since this would largely serve Evangelical Church families and thus complicate relationships with the Church. An earlier proposal to open a bookstore seemed questionable since English language books were now available in downtown bookstores and a small C&MA-operated bookstore carried Vietnamese-language Christian materials.

Orie Miller's earlier vision to quickly expand into Laos and Cambodia was also modified. Kraybill noted the logistical problems of having missionaries in different locations. To work with relatively small programs in several languages would complicate future literature and Bible training programs. Sensing "an unusual opportunity in Saigon," he recommended "establishing promptly a program of direct evangelism . . . consistent with our principles of faith and practice and mission strategy but with sensitive regard and respect for the Evangelical Church of Viet Nam," and in regular conversations with church leaders.

Kraybill recommended that the Mission secure a headquarters site in a residential area near the center of Saigon where the Metzler family would live, with space for ministry activities. The Stauffers would rent another property "farther out toward the growing edge of the city." Both couples were to engage in "direct evangelism, including preaching, personal and home contact, book room and reading room [and] English classes."

Kraybill said that the Mission Board would promptly apply for government authorization for the mission program, and recommended the recruitment of two additional "evangelistic couples." A future program in Laos would be determined by progress in the development of the Vietnam program.

The Mennonite missionaries were highly pleased with Kraybill's visit and their easy exchange of ideas. Orie Miller graciously supported the new secretary's recommendations, saying, "I too rejoice in how the Lord seemed to lead and enable Paul."

Although Snyder's eight days in Vietnam were considerably fewer than Kraybill's more than three weeks, they were no less important. In her diary after Kraybill arrived, Margaret Metzler wrote: "I guess MCC has as many or more problems than we do and they are as eager for Bill Snyder to arrive as we were for Paul."

Snyder described his visit as a "stem to stern" look at the Vietnam programs which was necessary "because both the Mission staff and the MCC staff were not clear on how to move forward in their programs and how to relate to each other." In his report, Snyder "tried to look frankly at the question of whether there is a ministry for the MCC to perform with the coming of a constituent mission board into the country." This involved reviewing and evaluating MCC's programs, and consulting "with a broad spectrum of Christian leaders who might have points of view that would be helpful in reaching [a] conclusion." This included leaders of the Evangelical Church, primarily President Thai; Jack Revelle and Grady Mangham, Chairmen of the C&MA Vietnam and Tribes missions; World Council of Churches Representative Dr. Adrian van den Brandeler; and James Stauffer and Everett Metzler of the Vietnam Mennonite Mission. Snyder and Paul Kraybill consulted numerous times throughout his visit.

Snyder met with the Alliance missionary Dr. Ardel Vietti while visiting Ban Me Thuot, and traveled on to Nha Trang where Pastor Thai showed him the Tin Lanh Orphanage and the new Bible Institute campus; the institute was about to transfer from Da Nang.

Snyder recommended that the Ban Me Thuot medical program be terminated mid-year 1960 with the Alliance assuming full responsibility. The two nurses, Margaret Janzen and Elfrieda Neufeld, might have the option of completing their terms. He recommended that the material aid program be reduced by thirty percent. Snyder also recommended the termination of Harry Lefever's student activities. While it was a significant ministry, he said it would likely "cause awkward working relationships" with the Mennonite Mission since the missionaries were also planning a student ministry.

In a letter sent to C. N. Hostetter, MCC Board Chairman since 1953, and to MCC Akron staff members, Snyder wrote: "I have felt the Lord lead us these days. Paul Kraybill sees daylight completely on the MCC and Eastern Board programs here whereas he did not before coming. Neither did I, but as we went into this together, we came to fully unanimous conviction." Snyder noted that "one round of appointment after appointment," was "exhilarating" because of the high caliber of MCC personnel. He said he and Kraybill came to a "good conclusion on a knotty problem of missions-relief" relationships that would enable two Mennonite organizations with overlapping concerns, vision, and goals to effectively work together in the same country.

In a memo to Stoltzfus, Snyder said he was "confident that we may be writing a new chapter in Mennonite mission-relief relationships," and promised to pray for Stoltzfus and other MCC personnel as they "strive to make these witnesses significant in this needy country."

Snyder's most dramatic recommendation had to do with a medical program to be developed with the Evangelical Church. Already in August 1957 both the Tin Lanh Church and an independent Chinese congregation in Cho Lon, Saigon's Chinatown, had requested MCC assistance with a medical program. Through contact with Ulrich H. van Beyma of the World Council of Churches, both churches learned that WCC's Inter-Church Aid Program might grant matching funds. Thus began a competition between the Evangelical Church Hospital Committee and the Chinese Pastor Hua Hon Long for MCC support in establishing a clinic in Saigon.

In September 1957 Church President Thai had surprised Dr. Krabill by reporting that the church had already raised 300,000 piasters ($4,000) for a proposed clinic and a small inpatient facility, anticipating WCC matching funds. Since both the Evangelical Church and Pastor Long of the Chinese church requested the services of a doctor and a nurse to develop programs in the Saigon area, Krabill saw the possibility of MCC assisting both. Krabill was told that the Chinese church had already begun construction of facilities for a clinic and five inpatient beds.

Pastor Kieu Cong Thao and Mr. Nguyen Van Van, Chairman and Secretary of the Tin Lanh Committee to Appeal for the Establishment of a Hospital, wrote to Robert Miller in November 1957 requesting MCC assistance "especially personnel, equipment and medicine for our future hospital." They wrote: "During these twenty-five years we have been praying God to help us that while we preach The Gospel to our countrymen we might be able to bring them social relief and physical help, because we realize both are necessary."

The Alliance Mission Field Chairman Jack Revelle and C&MA Administrator L. L. King both gave "full approval" to MCC's cooperation with the Vietnamese church in such a project. Though the Alliance did not want to administer medical programs, they did not object to the local churches developing such ministries.

Both the Chinese church and the Evangelical Church in late 1957 sent representatives to visit the hospital in Ban Me Thuot and meet with Dr. Krabill. Robert Miller indicated that MCC was ready to develop medical programs in Saigon with both churches. It was anticipated that one doctor could serve both clinics—at least in the initial stage.

In December 1958 Pastor Thai proposed that MCC assign a volunteer to the Nha Trang Orphanage "with special ability in nursing and teaching." The Evangelical Church's orphanage, administered by Thai and his daughter, housed seventy-four orphans with a primary school for 200 students. It was the only significant social institution of the Church. The Christian Children's Fund provided seventy percent of the support, and MCC already provided food assistance. Robert Miller and Snyder liked this proposal to develop a program with the Evangelical Church outside of Saigon—since the Mennonite Mission was planning to work in Saigon. They suggested that MCC might "even add additional personnel and perhaps a small medical program there if the church would want this."

Snyder was decisive in his June 1959 visit. He announced that MCC would not operate any medical programs in Saigon. In a June 5, 1959, meeting with Evangelical Church leaders, Snyder said that MCC would work at the invitation of the Church in some rural area. He said a new doctor would be coming to Vietnam in August who would work at Ban Me Thuot until mid-1960, and would then be available to work with the Church.

Snyder's decision disappointed Pastor Thao, Pastor of the Gia Dinh congregation near Saigon and chairman of the Tin Lanh Hospital Committee, who wanted the medical program in the Saigon area, even offering his own house to begin the program. It was also a great disappointment to Hua Hon Long, who had been negotiating with MCC for two years. Snyder met with the Chinese pastor, acknowledging that MCC had declared its intention to work with his church, but that no agreement had ever been finalized, and that MCC would now proceed to work with the Evangelical Church.

Snyder's recommendation was based primarily on the clear recognition that more than half of the country's 425 doctors were located in Saigon. Many rural areas lacked even the most basic medical service. A secondary argument was that, with the Mennonite Mission planning to develop programs in Saigon, developing a medical program at another location would help prevent a confusion of agency identification.

The Church would negotiate with Stoltzfus the details of a joint medical program with the operating budget comparable to the current Ban Me Thuot program. An MCC doctor would be medical director and a Tin Lanh Church board would administer the program and be responsible for the spiritual ministry.

A year later the Evangelical Clinic and Hospital opened on land provided by the Tin Lanh Church outside coastal Nha Trang City—adjacent to the orphanage.

BEGINNING THE MISSION WITNESS

Chapter 14

A few days after Paul Kraybill left Vietnam in June 1959 Everett Metzler had a life-threatening experience. In Margaret's diary entry of Saturday, June 20, she noted that Everett had given her a lovely bouquet of roses for their wedding anniversary the following day.

Then she described the harrowing tale of Everett going down their well to retrieve a bucket that had dropped off the rope some time before. She had weakly protested when he told her what he was planning to do. The next thing she knew their household helper was screaming for her to help James Stauffer who had let Everett down the well by a rope tied to his hip. When Everett blacked out due to lack of oxygen, James was hesitant to pull him up for fear he would topple over and fall into the water. When neighbor Sau and other men heard the commotion, they quickly jumped over the fence and helped James wind up the rope. By the time Margaret got to the well with eleven-month-old Eric in her arms, Everett was already pulled up to the top. She writes, "Then I saw that he . . . was hanging on to that bucket. I kept telling him to drop it, but he didn't hear or respond in any way. Just stared, glassy-eyed and rigid into outer space. Finally I pried his fingers loose and they got him out."

Everett soon revived. Margaret wrote that Everett "was none the worse except for a few scratches, and I am left with the horrible memory of it. Oh, we are just so grateful to God for sparing him. . . . Why he stayed still instead of going limp—it is a miracle." Neighbors said that Everett would have suffocated had he been down in the well much longer.

That evening they all went to the MCC house for a farewell dinner for Harry and Esther Lefever and their young daughter Kristen. The next day Everett and Margaret, who was expecting their second child, celebrated their third wedding anniversary with a deep sense of gratitude.

James Stauffer began the process of registering Vietnam Mennonite Mission with the government. He asked counsel of Nguyen Van Ninh, the MCC interpreter, who was becoming increasingly valuable in helping the Mennonites negotiate the Vietnam landscape. Stauffer and Ninh paid a visit to Mr. Huynh Minh Y, a Tin Lanh Church member who was also Vice President of the National Revolutionary Movement, one of the pro-government political parties, and a Deputy Member of the National Assembly. Mr. Y had earlier offered to assist them in contacts with the government. They also met with Mr. Y's son-in-law who had worked with the Vietnamese Ambassador to the U.S., Mr. Tran Van Chuong. Mr. Y advised Stauffer to ask the Eastern Mennonite Board to secure a letter of recommendation from Mr. Chuong, who was the father of Madam Nhu, the wife of President Ngo Dinh Diem's brother who served as First Lady.

The transplanted American missionaries were learning the importance of "who you know" in order to get things done. But even with a good game plan, getting government authorization was not likely to be easy. Even Mr. Y told them the first thing they need to do is pray!

In December at the Vietnamese Embassy in Washington, Kraybill and Orie Miller hand-delivered a letter addressed to His Excellency Ngo Dinh Diem, appealing "for authorization to establish a mission in Viet Nam." Although they did not meet the ambassador who was ill, an official assured them that there "should be no difficulty in securing authorization." Kraybill asked Stauffer to submit the same letter to the President in Saigon with a copy to the Minister of Interior, Mr. Lam Le Trinh. Mr. Trinh had given official authorization in 1958 for the Summer Institute of Linguistics to work in Vietnam.

On January 21, 1960, this letter was presented to the Office of President Diem in Saigon. Six weeks later two men from the Office of the Presidency came to the Metzler's house to make further inquiry about the application, and the missionaries learned that the papers were on the desk of Mr. Ngo Dinh Nhu, the President's brother and political advisor.

In his letter to the President, Kraybill noted the Mennonite concern for human suffering, and wrote: "It is the conviction of this church that as followers of Jesus Christ we should minister in love to human need wherever it is found regardless of race or creed. The various Mennonite groups in North America are joined together in a common concern for such needs and so it was that in 1954 the Mennonite Central Committee . . . began a program of relief consisting primarily of material aid to refugees who were fleeing to South Viet Nam as a result of the partition of Viet Nam into communist-governed and free areas."

"The Mennonite Church," Kraybill wrote, "is a part of the Protestant Church and represents a small group of people who believe deeply in witness and service. While we insist on expressing the love of Christ through social and welfare service to everyone in need regardless of race or creed, we also desire to witness to our faith wherever we find those who have not come to believe in our God."

Attached to the letter was a copy of the EMBMC Charter and a survey of the history and programs of the Mission Board.

Kraybill stated explicitly that Eastern Mennonite Board of Missions and Charities was a member of the Mennonite Central Committee and of the Division of Foreign Missions of the National Council of Churches of Christ in the United States, and attached a letter of recommendation from this agency. He noted the close relationship with and support from both the Evangelical Church in Vietnam and the Christian and Missionary Alliance.

Appealing for official recognition, based on the government Constitution's guarantee of religious freedom, Kraybill wrote: "We will conduct ourselves in the public good and always encourage and promote respect and loyalty to your worthy government.

"We have deeply appreciated the worthy and honorable rule of Your Excellency, President Diem, and it is our hope and prayer that you may be given many years of fruitful service in the cause of enlightening your people and continuing to develop and preserve the democratic ideals which you have so nobly established in your nation."

The Diem government never granted authorization to the Vietnam Mennonite Mission. This recognition was only received several years later under the military government.

While the missionaries continued language study after Kraybill's visit, their primary focus now was on house hunting. Although they had not yet found permanent housing, the two couples—after living together more than a year—decided on separate housing. James and Arlene rented a small apartment at 128 Hai Ba Trung, Saigon, only a block east of the Catholic Basilica, and moved on August 1.

An incident on July 8 at Bien Hoa, thirty kilometers east of Saigon, became a harbinger of things to come. A small guerilla force attacked the living quarters of the U.S. Military Assistance

Advisory Group at night, killing Major Dale R. Buis and Master Sergeant Chester M. Ovnand. These names are the first of nearly 60,000 names inscribed on the black granite walls of the Vietnam Memorial in Washington, DC.

This incident was not prominently reported in the press. The chaplain of the American Community Church, who also served as the MAAG chaplain, related the details of the attack. Communist forces hiding in the jungles completely controlled many areas.

The next weekend James and Arlene left by Lambretta scooter for Vinh Long, 130 kilometers southwest in the Mekong Delta, to attend the last day of the Youth Conference and the first day of the Annual Church Conference of the Tin Lanh Church. D. Ivory Jeffrey, the missionary with whom they worked at the Truong Minh Giang Chapel, was the main speaker. Le Van Thai also spoke. Writing home, Stauffer said they were praying much for the Church that was "facing many problems. . . . Many of the pastors and Christians are poverty-stricken and pastors continue to leave the ministry in order to make a living."

Arlene was at home Monday noon in mid-August when Everett brought a telegram informing them that James' father had died suddenly at age seventy. Arlene was studying language with Mrs. Ngan, a pastor's widow, when Everett brought the small blue envelope to their door. Arlene wrote the Stauffer family: "Mrs. Ngan was very sympathetic as have been many others of our Vietnamese friends as they heard of this loss to our family."

That morning, a friend, Kim Ngan, had come to tell them that her seventy-two-year-old grandfather died on the same day. The Stauffers had visited this family several times, most recently in July. Arlene wrote: "I felt especially led to take several gospels and some tracts with us to give him. His mind was still clear and his eyesight good. We were both able to testify to him in Vietnamese of our great salvation. He read the tracts immediately. Several times he mentioned that he may not have long to live. . . . We do not know whether or not God's word had time to penetrate his heart."

Stauffer was unable to return home for the funeral. Writing to his mother, he expressed thanks that God had granted his father the biblical "three-score and ten years."

National elections were held on Sunday, August 30. Already beleaguered, President Diem refused to allow even non-communist opposition leaders to run. Two candidates who won as independents were refused seats in the National Assembly. In the countryside, many local administrative leaders were being assassinated, and in late September two Vietnamese army companies were ambushed. Vietnamese society was steadily becoming more militarized.

Living downtown, the Stauffers observed some of the activities on Independence Day, Monday, October 26, and "got two good glimpses of the President." In the afternoon they attended a special Independence Day service at the large downtown Tin Lanh Church on Tran Hung Dao Boulevard.

In November the Metzlers and Stauffers heard a young preacher at the Truong Minh Giang Chapel. Le Hoang Phu had just returned from three years' study at the Christian and Missionary Alliance Seminary in Nyack, New York. His dynamic preaching style represented something new in the Tin Lanh Church. Writing to his mother, Stauffer said, "Possibly he will be the instrument that God can use to bring a heaven-sent revival to this dry and thirsty land."

Phu preached at Truong Minh Giang Chapel one week in early January 1960. James and Arlene attended nearly every evening and found this quite inspiring. To his mother James wrote:

"Bro. Phu reminds me of Jeremiah, the weeping prophet. We have never heard anyone in Viet Nam preach with such power and at the same time in a spirit of complete brokenness." Phu joined the faculty of the Tin Lanh Bible Institute where he served until 1975.

In early November Arlene and James were invited to the Jeffrey home along with Garth and Betty Hunt, a young Alliance couple serving in Quang Tri province, just below the seventeenth parallel, the dividing line between the North and the South. The Stauffers were fascinated by the stories of these two couples. They also learned that Herman and Dottie Hayes, the first missionaries of the Southern Baptist Convention, had just arrived in country. Writing home, Stauffer noted that they would be working independently of other missions, and he looked forward to their "fellowship in the gospel."

The Stauffer and Metzler couples celebrated the American Thanksgiving Day with Glenn and Geneva Stoltzfus at the MCC house. The following Sunday Stauffer preached at the Truong Minh Giang Chapel when sixteen youth and adults were baptized. After observing the baptisms by immersion, James wrote home: "Whatever can be argued in favor of or against this mode, I am still happy that our Church practices pouring—if for no other reason than the fact that pouring is more reverent."

Baptism, in the Tin Lanh Church, was the culmination of a process which began when persons "prayed." This prayer affirmed the Creator God, the reality of human sin and separation from God, expressed confession of sin and acceptance of Jesus Christ as Savior and Lord. Persons then made a public declaration in a worship service. New believers went through a period of catechism using the book, *Phúc Âm Yếu Chỉ* (Basic Gospel Guide), before baptism.

A decision to express faith in Jesus Christ was traumatic for some persons due to family opposition. In families that practiced ancestor veneration, the oldest son was responsible to perpetuate the family ritual. Since the Tin Lanh Church forbade the worship of ancestors, families who practiced ancestor veneration usually expressed opposition to the oldest son embracing the evangelical faith. They would have less objection to another child joining the Tin Lanh Church. Arlene told of a student who said to her: "Some of my family are Buddhists, some are Catholic, and several are Protestant. I do not have a faith, but I am somewhere in between a Protestant and a Catholic." The missionaries often heard friends declare: "All religions are the same. They all teach us to do good and avoid evil."

A few months later Stauffer wrote home: "The people here are so anxious to please us that it is easy for them to make a decision [for Jesus Christ] because they know it is our desire for them. Many have already told us that they believe in God and worship Jesus just like we do and yet, at the same time they continue to worship Mary, Buddha, their ancestors, or some other saint or hero—'the more the merrier' idea! Sometimes this mixture of worship is motivated by the desire to take the best from all religions in the search for a perfect religion."

One quiet Sunday afternoon in mid-December James wrote to his mother from their home on Hai Ba Trung Street: "Besides the usual sounds that we have here such as peddlers' calls, children playing, traffic humming, etc., we can hear the bells from the main Catholic cathedral just a block away. This week was a special occasion for them as they observed the anniversary of the 'immaculate conception.'"

Stauffer saw little benefit of this Catholicism over Buddhism or other religions; many Catholic homes had both an altar to Mary and to their ancestors. This attitude toward the Catholic Christian faith was common in the mid-twentieth century within the evangelical Christian community, not only in Vietnam but in the United States as well. Yet writing home two weeks later, Stauffer gave a backhanded accolade to the Catholic Church: "[Christmas] was a most joyous occasion. We enjoyed so much hearing the familiar carols on the local radio station. . . . We have to give the Catholics credit for helping to present the true meaning of Christmas. One newspaper had about two full pages of articles on the birth of Christ. . . . They also had banners across the streets proclaiming Christ as the Saviour of the World, the One Who brings peace, hope, [and] joy."

Margaret's diary entry of December 15, 1959, has an intriguing sentence: "*Chi Bảy* (Older Sister Seven) gave me an earful as to what she thinks of the present government." A half century later no one recalls exactly what their household helper said! While the missionaries were learning about Vietnam from newspapers and magazines, from students and government officials, they were also learning much from the persons who assisted them with housekeeping and babysitting chores. These people who came from the countryside for employment had families back home victimized by the repressive policies of the government.

From the aunt of a household helper, the Metzlers in November learned about a house for sale at 336 Phan Thanh Gian Street, directly across the street from the *Bệnh Viện Bình Dân* (Peoples' Hospital). The same evening they saw the house. Mr. Tran Phuong, a Christian businessman who operated a tailor shop downtown, came to tell them about the same house; he was related to the owner. By the next day both missionary couples agreed that this was a good house at a good location, so Everett wrote to Kraybill, describing the 747 square meter lot with twenty-two meter frontage and thirty-five meter depth. The owner was an old man whose children wanted him to sell and divide the inheritance.

Metzler had already written to Kraybill about whether they could purchase a property in the name of this Mr. Phuong, a member of the Saigon Church, active in the local Gideon organization, "who has been helpful to us and stands in good repute with C&MA and the church." In his later letter, Metzler said "it is more than an interesting coincidence that yesterday as I was going for another look at this property Mr. Phuong met me with the intention of coming to recommend this property to us."

With Kraybill's cabled approval, the agreement of sale was signed January 2, 1960, with permission to take possession of the house two weeks later.

Tran Phuong helped negotiate the price. The actual cost of the property was $17,777 U.S. With repairs and furniture, the total cost would come to $22,468. In arranging a mortgage, Everett wrote Kraybill: "The real issue is our confidence in Mr. Phuong. . . . We have no reason to doubt his reliability as a brother in Christ."

Margaret describes how they inspected the house to decide what repairs to make. "I came away quite discouraged; it seems there is so much to do, and there were people running over the place as if it were public property." It didn't help that the neighbor boys were picking fruit from the papaya trees.

In mid-January 1960 there was an armed insurrection against the Diem government in Mekong Delta's Ben Tre Province, incited by the government's repressive policies. The peasants, angry at being forced to relocate from their villages into large fortified "agrovilles," survived the government's counterattack. The government soon requested the United States to double the number of military advisors to 685 men. Yet the government continued the policy of building "Strategic

Hamlets" hated by the rural population. These programs were later abandoned as ineffective in isolating the people from the opposition forces.

Stauffer wrote in the February 1960 *News and Concerns:* "There is new evidence of increased communist subversive strength here. In fact, the situation is generally described as 'serious' or 'critical.' If what we hear is true it is indeed an urgent matter for prayer!"

Early 1960 found Everett overseeing the renovations to the newly-purchased Mission property, doing much of the work himself. This villa was located on a main east-west street in the middle of District 3 just over a kilometer from center city. The house, surrounded by a yard and patio, was adequate both for living quarters and program activities. At the rear of the property were dependency rooms for helpers to stay and for an office. Margaret and Everett moved with five-month-old Gretchen and soon-to-be-four Eric into the Vietnam Mennonite Mission Headquarters on Leap

Arlene and James at Dakao home.

Day. A few days earlier James and Arlene moved into a rented row home at 42 Nguyen Phi Khanh Street in the Dakao section of District 1.

James preached his first "full-fledged Vietnamese sermon" on Sunday morning, February 14—forty minutes long—at the Truong Minh Giang Church. To his mother he wrote: "This past week I . . . spent a lot of time memorizing my first sermon. . . . I praise God that it went as well as it did but there is still a lot to be desired. Preaching in Vietnamese is not as inspiring to me . . . because of all the mechanics of mastering new words and sounds."

On the last Sunday in February Stauffer wrote his mother: "We just had a visit from a former English student of Arlene's by the name of Phuoc." Eighteen years old, he brought them a bunch of milk fruit—"one of my favorites," James wrote.

Forty-seven years later, in Houston, Texas, Phan Ba Phuoc told this story: "I lived at 111 Ngo Tung Chau Street, Gia Dinh. In 1958 the two missionary families moved down the street a few blocks, and I met them soon after they moved in. One day I saw them at the *Cây Quéo* Market taking photographs and went and talked with them. I had already studied English in school and learned that these missionaries were teaching English in their home, so I went to study. Arlene Stauffer was my first English teacher."

In early February Stauffer and Metzler met with MCC Director Stoltzfus to plan for the upcoming visit of Paul Peachey—sponsored by the Mennonite Central Committee Peace Section.

"We sure have a lot of questions to ask him about carrying on a peace witness in a country that is so seriously threatened by communism," Stauffer wrote home.

Paul Peachey arrived March 14. The next day he flew with Metzler and MCC interpreter Ninh to Da Nang where he spoke to students at the Tin Lanh Bible Institute. Back in Saigon, an anticipated meeting with Alliance and Baptist missionaries fizzled when only one of these missionaries came. Most could not find the Metzlers' new address or received the invitations too late. Peachey was planning to speak on the subject: "The Missionary between East and West."

The evening before he left, Peachey met with MCC and Vietnam Mennonite Mission (VMM) personnel, giving a much appreciated reflection of his understanding of the church dynamics in Vietnam. Peachey observed that they had done "an excellent job in church diplomacy, in establishing wholesome relations under considerable difficulty, and in developing a fruitful cooperation with the Vietnamese Christians." He urged the missionaries to "purge out denominational thinking" and think in terms of one Church of Christ in Vietnam. This would involve their taking on themselves "the burden of the sins and imperfections" of the Tin Lanh Church, and not view these as the problem of the Alliance alone. Peachey urged them to "explore the possibility of associate membership" in the Evangelical Church of Vietnam, converse with church leaders on points of differences, and commit themselves to a ministry of reconciliation.

In March the Eastern Mennonite Board appointed James and Rhoda Sauder to a five-year missionary term to Vietnam. At the Interior Ministry, nine months later, Stauffer was shown "a whole stack of missionary applications" that were waiting for the Minister's signature. The Summer Institute of Linguistics had trouble getting visas for new personnel, and a fourth Baptist couple had been refused visas. The Sauder family never received visas for Vietnam. By the spring of 1961 EMBMC reassigned them to Honduras—their first preference, and where they had an effective ministry for many decades.

On Monday evening, April 4, James and Arlene began evangelistic activities at their home with English Bible classes using a bilingual Gospel of John. They set up thirty-five chairs in their small living room.

"We have not been able to advertise it very much in this immediate community," James wrote his mother the next day, "but when the hour came there were four people here. But people kept coming and by the end of the period we had over thirty. About half of these have never studied English." By using a bilingual Gospel of John "everyone can at least read and understand this life-giving message," Stauffer explained. They planned to teach English two evenings a week.

On Wednesday they had had nearly forty students, and the next Monday more than fifty. So Arlene arranged to teach a beginner class at 7:00 followed by James teaching a Gospel of John class an hour later. James sensed the importance of prayer in their ministry.

The following week Arlene had over fifty students in the beginning English class, and James had more than twenty in the more advanced class. Although some students were studying English in school, they had no opportunity to practice speaking with native English-speaking teachers, so having American teachers was a huge drawing card.

The Stauffers were learning to know their neighbors—some of them middle class. Next door lived a family with several children, one a doctor, one a teacher, another studying medicine. A daughter from another family was studying law at the Saigon University.

Stauffer now discontinued the English Bible class he had taught for nearly three years at the Truong Minh Giang Chapel. As a kind of farewell, he preached there on Sunday morning, May 1, from John 3 on the New Birth. Preaching in Vietnamese, he was told it was a great improvement over his first sermon. To his mother he wrote, "For this we give the Lord all the glory. . . . I really do praise the Lord that I can preach in Vietnamese now. It almost seems like a dream."

On July 3 Everett preached his first Vietnamese message at the Hoa Hung Tin Lanh Church several blocks from their home. Everett and Margaret also taught English two evenings weekly at their new home. The missionaries were finding that English classes using Bible

Everett teaching English class in home.

materials, particularly for the advanced and conversational classes, provided opportunities for students to understand and ask questions about the Christian faith and life. Their classes were crowded.

Margaret also taught a morning class for young women. One was a young neighbor mother, Nguyen Thi Hoang, whose husband, Ho Trung Ty, taught math in a prestigious girls' high school. Margaret found Mrs. Ty "a very sweet little woman."

One day Mrs. Ty stayed after Margaret's English class and "readily accepted" a Gospel of Mark and a booklet entitled *I Chose Christ*. Margaret was reading a Vietnamese novel Mrs. Ty had given by the popular author Nhat Linh, *Đoạn Tuyệt (Rupture)*, a story of modern youth finding their way amidst the cultural traditions. In the July 4, 1960, *News and Concerns,* the Metzlers asked friends to pray for this young neighbor couple. "They are fine moral people, but although he teaches in a Catholic high school, they are not Catholic, and are woefully ignorant of the Bible and Christian faith," Margaret wrote. When she and her husband read the Gospel of Mark, Mrs. Ty said they did "not understand a thing!"

Several weeks later Margaret's diary reads: "Today Mrs. Ty asked me to tell her the whole story of Jesus' birth in Vietnamese. She is surprised to learn that the story we have been studying in English is true. So we started reading the book of Luke together." A few years later Mrs. Ty embraced faith in Christ and became an active leader in the Mennonite Church.

The missionaries had many friends. Phuoc and his mother, whose three sisters lived near James and Arlene, visited the Metzlers expressing a financial need, so Everett gave them a small monetary gift. The missionaries had already learned that small gifts to friends were more appropriate than larger loans; when friends could not repay loans, they avoided you.

Missionaries were given four weeks' vacation each year, and were encouraged to take several short leaves. In May the Metzler family traveled to cooler Da Lat by public bus, with the Lambretta scooter on the roof so they would have transportation in the city. They stayed in very primitive facilities near Villa Alliance, the Christian and Missionary Alliance center.

The Alliance missionaries—175 persons, including children—were then meeting in their Annual Conference. The Metzlers joined them one evening in a "Singspiration." They enjoyed an invitation to the home of an Adventist missionary family with whom they "had a good bit in common." They also traveled outside the city on their scooter, visiting missionary linguist friends with the Summer Institute of Linguistics who lived among the minority people. Everett returned home by scooter—the others by bus.

Stauffer submitted a request in June to the Mayor of Saigon to use both properties as meeting places. Without that permission they would have to limit the attendance to twenty persons. A few weeks later the Stauffers received permission to hold meetings in their home, but it was denied in the headquarters property where the Metzlers lived because it was "not convenient!" Ninh, the MCC interpreter, thought the refusal may have been because the Metzlers' neighbors were relatives of the President and, for security reasons, did not want public meetings next door.

Two months later permission was given to have services in their home any evening and on Sunday. "This came as something of a surprise although we were praying about the matter," Everett wrote the home office. "We had asked Ninh to query the mayor's wife—and secretary—whom he knows, concerning the reasons for the earlier refusal and what could be done to obtain permission. She must have considerable influence at Town Hall as we received in a few days a letter giving permission!"

James Stauffer found the last week of June a time of "special rejoicing for the Lord's working in our midst." During a Monday evening class when he was teaching John 8:1-20 he felt the Spirit's presence as he explained in both English and Vietnamese verse 19, "If you knew me, you would know my Father also." After class several young men stayed behind and asked how they could become Christians. When one man said he wanted to confess his sin and believe in the Lord, Stauffer led them in a prayer of penitence and confession of faith. Two of the three twenty-some-year-old men, Nam, Loc and Nghia, were primary school teachers. They all went to the Truong Minh Giang Church the next Sunday and publically expressed their faith. On Wednesday before English class at the Stauffer residence Nam gave a testimony to his new faith in God.

Arlene gave birth early July to their first child, John Lowell. After six years of marriage, they were delighted. Stauffer would later jokingly attribute the pregnancy to generous helpings of pungent Vietnamese fish sauce which seasoned every meal!

The July 11 issue of *Time Magazine* featured an "eye-opener" article describing the repressive rule of President Diem which James asked his family to read. It described an autocratic, paranoid leader out of touch with the people. Ninh, the MCC interpreter, said "the truth has come out at last!"

Throughout July other young people confessed faith in Jesus at the Stauffer home. The Stauffers planned their first Vietnamese language evangelistic service on Friday evening, July 29. Most of the nearly thirty persons who came were young students. James and Arlene hoped it would become a weekly meeting. The next day Phan Ba Phuoc, the young man they learned to know at their previous residence came to visit them. After a short conversation, the purpose of his visit became clear. "Now I believe in God. I want to be a lamb of Christ," he said. Inquiring further, James learned that Phuoc had made this decision while reading the Gospel of John a month earlier. Thus began James' joyful mentoring relationship with Phuoc to baptism and beyond.

One evening in August, Pastor Dieu, a young evangelist and brother of their former Teacher Hoa, preached on Romans 1:16: "I am not ashamed of the gospel; it is the power of God for salvation to everyone who has faith." Suong, a young English student who considered herself a Buddhist, was disturbed when Dieu said that "only the Gospel provides salvation," and told the pastor how she felt. Yet in early December she declared her faith in Christ at a Friday evening evangelistic service. Another evening Stauffer invited Mr. Do Duc Tri, an articulate Tin Lanh lay preacher; Tri's employment was translating documents for the U.S. Military Assistance Command. Phuoc led the meeting quoting Bible verses which he was memorizing.

In late summer Everett wrote Mission Board Secretary Kraybill, asking whether he might on a trial basis teach English in a private school: "We are seen as professional religious teachers from America who get all their support from abroad," he wrote. "Perhaps we would be more respected if students were not suspicious of our no-fee teaching. They can't understand our motivation for teaching, although we tell them we are missionaries and hope to make acquaintance with them in order to tell them of the Gospel." Everett taught in a private English language school for a time.

In the September *News and Concerns,* the Metzlers reported that their Sunday afternoons were filled as they visited their students and other friends. While each couple worked independently in their homes, the four gathered for a weekly evening fellowship meeting. "These periods of prayer, praise and Bible study are becoming more meaningful as we enter more fully into the work," James wrote home, "We prayed especially that God might soon raise up some spiritual leaders among the friends whom we are witnessing to."

James and Arlene took a week's leave in late September, staying with John and Joan Newman in their villa in Da Lat. James preached at the Alliance missionary children's school Sunday morning. Several weeks later they learned that L. L. King, the C&MA Secretary, had expressed to Orie Miller "sincere appreciation" for the good relationships between the Alliance missions and MCC and Mennonite Mission personnel.

In September Margaret and Everett began a new Sunday evening Vietnamese Bible class in their living room; thirty to forty young people studied the Gospel of Luke. Teaching English was putting the missionaries in touch with many people.

"We are not always certain how effective a means of witness these classes are, but they certainly provide a point of contact," Arlene wrote James' family. James met a young man planning to study in the States: "We had a long talk about 'religion' and he explained many things about ancestral worship and Buddhism. I took an opportunity to witness to him of the reality of Christ living in our hearts. He listened intently but seemed unimpressed."

Margaret and Everett told a disturbing story in the November *News and Concerns* highlighting the growing military activity:

> The other Sunday in our visitation we met a young officer about to graduate from the infantry school. He seized the opportunity to practice the English an American officer has been teaching his class. Asked what he will be doing after graduation, he said, "I am going to Nhatrang to kill the Communists. I *must* kill the Communists." He was in dead earnest about it, too. It struck us anew—the evil that is in men's hearts, and we hang our heads in shame to realize that one of our own countrymen taught him to say that, and to believe it so firmly.

A few days later there was an armed forces attempt to oust President Ngo Dinh Diem. Margaret recorded this in her diary Friday, November 11, 1960. At 3:30 a.m. they were awakened by loud explosions and machine-gun fire. She and Everett laid low after they heard the bullets whiz by. They thought it was a communist attack until they heard a radio announcement that military officers were revolting against the President, demanding that he moderate his autocratic rule to better defeat the growing communist threat. Diem negotiated with them while secretly ordering loyal troops to come to his aid. When they arrived the next morning, fighting erupted around the Presidential Palace where many civilians had gathered to show their support for the rebels. In the ensuing confrontation more than 400 people were killed, many of them civilians. MCCer Don Voth had gone downtown; when shooting erupted he ran from tree to tree to escape the area.

Defeated, the coup leaders fled to Cambodia. Many opposition persons were arrested; some were sentenced to long prison terms. The President continued his dictatorial style, appointing persons to military and governmental positions on the basis of perceived loyalty rather than competency.

Christmas 1960 came on a Sunday. The Stauffers had a full house Friday evening, and another service Sunday morning. In the afternoon Arlene told the Christmas story—using a flannelgraph board—to seventy neighborhood children and gave them candy and greeting cards. In the evening James spoke to the gathering at the Phan Thanh Gian Center where the Metzlers lived.

Stauffer saw the Friday evening evangelistic services as a barometer indicating interest in the Gospel of Jesus Christ. He was happy for a full house and disappointed when only a few persons showed up. He described his feelings like the Southern Spiritual: "Sometimes I'm up, sometimes I'm down!" He was spending more time in prayer prior to the services.

In early February 1961 James, Arlene and six-month-old John had an "almost perfect" time in Nha Trang following James' bout with amebic dysentery which put him in the Saigon Adventist Hospital for two days. They stayed with MCC personnel who a few months earlier had begun the joint medical program with the Tin Lanh Church.

In March Stauffer invited Alliance missionary Paul E. Carlson to preach at a Friday evening evangelistic service. Carlson had served in Vietnam for thirty-five years, and had contributed significantly to Tin Lanh church music. Exceptionally fluent in Vietnamese, he preached on the story of the Pharisee and the publican who went to the temple to pray. Attendance was good that evening.

The only brother of the Stauffers' household helper, *Cô Do*, died in early April, so she went to her country home to be with her family; her father wanted her to stay a month. With their helper gone, James helped Arlene in the kitchen: "There is just about twice as much work involved in preparing a simple meal here," James wrote his mother. James and Arlene were still able to entertain Alliance missionaries Spencer and Barbara Sutherland. Spence had recently spoken at a Friday night service. James found Spence "one of the most friendly" Alliance missionaries, and discussed with him the Mennonite commitment to biblical pacifism—a new insight for Spence.

In the April 9, 1961, national election President Ngo Dinh Diem won reelection with 89% of the vote. When John F. Kennedy was inaugurated U.S. President in January as successor to Dwight Eisenhower, Vietnam was high on the foreign policy agenda. An intelligence report prepared for Kennedy estimated that more than half of the rural area surrounding Saigon was under communist control. Even though Diem continued his authoritarian rule after the attempted coup, the new Kennedy administration in early May authorized sending 100 additional military advisors and 400 Special Forces troops.

Vice President Lyndon Johnson flew to Vietnam to meet President Diem on May 12, hailing him the "Winston Churchill of Asia." American citizens in Vietnam were invited to hear Johnson speak that morning at a riding club; James and Arlene stood near the Vice President and "his charming Lady Bird." At this event Johnson introduced the new U.S. Ambassador, Frederick E. Nolting.

Although Saigon was now attracting political luminaries, the missionaries' greatest interest was the establishment of the church. Stauffer continued regular Bible studies with Phuoc who was studying an English correspondence course, *Life With God*.

Ten months after he had expressed faith in Jesus Christ, Phuoc was baptized on May 28, 1961, at the 42 Nguyen Phi Khanh Street house, four years after Arlene and James arrived in Saigon. James wrote: "This was a milestone for us as we conducted our first baptismal service. Mr. Phuoc has been most faithful since his conversion last July through reading the Gospel of John. I invited him to give a testimony before the message and he almost preached a young sermon but, oh, how I praised God for his testimony. He applied John 14:6 to his own experience and ended with Ephesians 2:8. . . . Phuoc told us that evening that this [was] the happiest day of his life."

MCC WORKS WITH THE EVANGELICAL CHURCH

Chapter 15

MCC's decision in June 1959 to conclude its medical program in Ban Me Thuot by July 1960 set the stage to move rapidly in developing a medical program with the Evangelical Church. Glenn Stoltzfus, the MCC Vietnam Director, outlined the steps the Church should take.

Dr. John B. and Hildegard (Hilda) Dick arrived in Vietnam mid-August. Dr. Dick was not critically needed at Ban Me Thuot at the time, since Dr. James Steiner had come in late June, waiting for a visa for Indonesia, and worked at the leprosarium for seven months. So the Dick family spent some time in Saigon in both Rhade and Vietnamese language study.

In mid-September Dr. Dick and Stoltzfus met with Tin Lanh President Le Van Thai and the Church's Hospital Committee in Nha Trang. They agreed the medical program would be developed four kilometers north of Nha Trang by the Church's orphanage. In late October, Stoltzfus and interpreter Ninh accompanied several members of the Hospital Committee to Ban Me Thuot for a three-day study of the medical program there.

William Snyder, MCC's Executive Secretary, did not want the Church to depend on help from outside sources. "The building and other parts of the hospital should represent sacrifice on the part of the National Church in addition to the contributions that MCC and WCC are making," Snyder wrote Stoltzfus. "A real partnership requires a substantial stake on the part of the National Church. You will know whether this is coming in the form of cash or work or gifts in kind. I think you should encourage it strongly as the only basis for setting up the program adequately."

Stoltzfus did not disagree. However, he pointed out that the Church was "providing land, source of electricity, a house for the Vietnamese director and his family, the director's salary plus half the cost of the hospital building." He expected them to make additional contributions.

MCC and the Evangelical Church in Vietnam signed the agreement for the joint medical program on March 1, 1960—Glenn Stoltzfus and Dr. John Dick signing for MCC, and Le Van Thai signing for the Church.

Partnership was the guiding principle of the agreement. The objective was to provide "good medical care for those in need regardless of their race, religion or economic standing" and to present "a positive witness of the love of Christ." The Church would administer the project. MCC would direct the medical program.

The two parties anticipated having a mobile clinic based in a small hospital and a house for medical personnel. The Church was providing the property. MCC and the Church would each provide half of the funds for the hospital building. MCC would provide the living quarters for its medical staff. MCC would transfer some medical equipment and supplies from Ban Me Thuot and seek to secure other gifts of medical supplies.

The Church agreed to provide a chaplain. MCC agreed to assign one doctor and two nurses, while the Church was to hire other staff personnel. MCC would have one member on the governing board. The agreement was to be reviewed yearly; either party could terminate the agreement with one year's prior notice.

The Church had reportedly raised $4,000, but some of this was contingent on the medical program being established in Saigon. The Church could request $1,960 from World Council of Churches contributions from churches in the Netherlands and Canada.

Tin Lanh Church President Le Van Thai was well-acquainted with Khanh Hoa provincial officials. After receiving a formal request to open a clinic March 10, the Chief of Province, Mr. Le Van Ai, on March 23 responded to President Thai: "In answer to your letter mentioned above, we hereby approve that a clinic be established by your organization on the property of the Evangelical Orphanage (Hon Chong) for the purpose of contributing to the Social Relief and Medical works in our Province and that the same clinic be directed by Dr. John Bernhard Dick.

"Your organization shall be responsible for the establishment of the aforesaid clinic and shall have to conform to the medical and hygiene rules and regulations which are or will be in force."

Alan Hochstetler, the Pax man in charge of upgrading the Ban Me Thuot Leprosarium facilities to accommodate thirty leprous patients, went to Nha Trang in January and presented sketches to the architect to draw up blueprints for the MCC unit house and the hospital building. In March he began construction, collaborating with Duy Cach Lam (Paul Richardson), the Da Lat pastor who supervised the construction of facilities for the Bible Institute that was moving from Da Nang to Nha Trang. By mid-May the MCC unit house was taking shape, and the foundation of the hospital clinic building was being laid. Even though the Church had not yet contributed its promised share of the construction costs, Hochstetler finished the foundation before the onset of the rainy season.

When Geneva and Glenn Stoltzfus left in April, Dr. Dick became Vietnam Director, with Don Voth, the unit leader in Ban Me Thuot, becoming his general assistant. After "a rewarding experience" of ten months at the Ban Me Thuot Leprosarium where they felt a "spiritual warmth" from the eighty inpatient Christian lepers, John and Hilda Dick in June 1960 prepared to move to Nha Trang. Nurse Elnora Weaver was also eager to go to Nha Trang. Elfrieda Neufeld was happy to stay and help train local hospital staff.

The Alliance expressed appreciation for the four years of service MCC gave to their medical program. The chairman of the Tribes Mission, T. Grady Mangham, said they "will long be indebted to each member of the MCC Team who have served so faithfully and have demonstrated a true spirit of cooperation." Quoting from a report, he said they "greatly appreciate the continued cooperation and assistance of the Mennonite Central Committee. Their personnel living at the Leprosarium . . . have made an immeasurable contribution to our work. The medical personnel have given unstintingly of their time and energies and have displayed a sincere concern for the spiritual welfare of the people. The three Pax boys have worked untiringly in the building of the two lovely hospital wings."

Robert Miller reported an exchange between his father and Alliance New York administrators, indicating that "because of their good impression of MCC work in Viet Nam," the Alliance would be happy to work with MCC in the Congo also!

Nurse Elfrieda Neufeld and Pax maintenance man Leland Good remained in Ban Me Thuot when Dr. Dick's family, Elnora Weaver and hostess Ann Ewert moved to Nha Trang in mid-August to begin the medical program. Ann soon terminated. Several days after moving to Nha Trang, Dr. Dick's two-year-old son, Bernard, choked on a peanut, necessitating having the doctor fly his son to Bangkok to have it removed from his lung.

Hospital Board (l to r): Pham Xuan Tin, J. B. Dick, Ong Van Huyen, Le Ngoc Huong and Le Van Thai.

At the Annual Conference of the Tin Lanh Church in mid-August Pastor Pham Xuan Tin, who was fluent in English, was chosen Director of the Medical Program. This conference in Vinh Long was significant in electing Pastor Doan Van Mieng President of the Church following the retirement of Le Van Thai.

The Hospital Board first met in mid-September. Besides Pastor Tin, other members of the Board were Ong Van Nguyen, treasurer, and Le Ngoc Huong, both pastors. John Dick was the MCC representative, and Pastor Thai was designated advisor.

By this time Elnora Weaver and Dr. Dick were seeing fifteen to twenty outpatients daily in an empty house near the hospital site. By mid-October they were examining thirty to sixty patients a day. When the clinic opened, patients were given the opportunity to drop gifts into an offering box. In December the province chief gave permission to charge fees from well-to-do patients, enabling the clinic to realize partial self-support.

They also conducted a few clinic visits to villages ten kilometers from Nha Trang even though the Chief of Khanh Hoa Province had not yet given official authorization. Several times they went to Phuoc Luong, a village of 1,300 minority people who had settled near an old citadel by Dien Khanh, eleven kilometers west of Nha Trang, after fleeing their mountainous village on rafts down the Cai River because they did not want to live under the control of threatening communist bands. (Homer Dowdy tells this story in *The Bamboo Cross*.)

By November the Tin Lanh Church had released only $540 toward the hospital building, far short of their 50 percent commitment. So Robert Miller recommended that construction be halted several months until the church was able to solicit sufficient funds. MCC rejected the hospital board's request that MCC raise its contribution to 70 percent.

This issue was still unresolved when MCC's Board Chairman, C. N. Hostetter, Jr., visited

Man from Phuoc Luong.

Vietnam twelve days in late November and early December. He describes the "dream site" location of the Nha Trang Hospital near the *Hòn Chồng* rocks. "It is one of the most-lovely places I have ever seen," Hostetter wrote. "Patients ought to improve here without a doctor or nurse."

Hostetter agreed that MCC should not provide a greater proportion of funds to construct the hospital which would foster "an unwholesome attitude of dependence." However, he said MCC could "render a better Christian burden-sharing function" by soliciting funds from other sources to meet the Church obligation. After getting Snyder's approval, Hostetter recommended that the World Relief Commission make a cash grant to the church to complete the hospital building. Hostetter, a Brethren-in-Christ evangelist and pastor who had formerly been President of Messiah College, was currently serving as WRC Board Chairman!

Due to the construction delay Hochstetler had transferred to a building project in Korea. Not yet aware of a possible $2,000 WRC contribution, but due to some additional funds they collected, the hospital board authorized construction to resume with the supervision of Pastor Duy Cach Lam. Pastor Tin, the hospital director, also wanted matching funds from the World Council of Churches. Evangelical Church policy did not permit him to directly contact the World Council, so Dr. Adrian van den Brandeler, the WCC representative, suggested that MCC could request the funds for the Church! The hospital construction resumed in March.

With Nha Trang's central location the Dicks had many guests; Dr. Dick said Hilda "had her hands full with guests and our three boisterous youngsters." They met with the C&MA missionaries for fellowship Monday evenings—a "highlight of the week." They also attended the English language worship service at the Orphanage every other Sunday.

In late March 1961 Leland Good reported that security in the Ban Me Thuot area had become "a little shaky." However, he was encouraged to hear that the guerrillas operating in the jungle had told the local villagers that they "did not want to bother the Americans at the leprosarium" because they were working directly with the people rather than with the government.

Several months before, in December 1960, Hanoi had announced the formation of the National Liberation Front for South Vietnam (*Mặt trận Dân tộc Giải phóng miền Nam Việt Nam*) following a gathering in Tay Ninh Province, northwest of Saigon. With ties to the communist Workers Party of Vietnam, the National Liberation Front (NLF) was a coalition of various opponents of President Ngo Dinh Diem. Although many of these opposition leaders were not communist, Diem's government called all of them Vietnamese Communists *(Cộng Sản Việt Nam)* or *Việt Cộng.*

In May 1961 Voth confirmed the deteriorating security. The only road they could travel from Saigon to Da Lat was Route 20, and even that artery had been recently cut when guerrilla forces held Di Linh for six hours. Voth used the term "Viet Cong" which the Saigon regime had recently coined for the opposition forces. Voth noted that two bridges were burned on the road leading from Ban Me Thuot to the leprosarium, but no guerrillas came to the leprosarium.

U.S. Vice President Lyndon Johnson spent two weeks in May on an official visit to Vietnam. After returning home, Johnson said that "the battle against Communism must be joined in Southeast Asia." In a burst of hyperbole, he said, otherwise, "the United States, inevitably, must surrender the Pacific and take up our defenses on our own shores!"

Vietnam's government passed a law requiring all men between the ages of twenty and thirty-three who had completed secondary education to enter officers' training school. The expan-

Alliance Dr. Ardel Vietti with Don Voth and Dr. J. B. Dick.

sion of the armed forces had implications for MCC; MCC's indispensable interpreter was now subject to the draft.

Voth informed John Hostetler, MCC Material Aid Director, that he had been approached by a medical supply officer working with the U.S. Military Assistance Advisory Group (MAAG), indicating "considerable interest" among some military personnel to provide medical supplies to Asian countries. This officer had met Dr. Vietti and Dr. Dick. Such supplies would likely be donated to Protestant voluntary agencies working in Vietnam. Would MCC be able to ship such supplies, Voth asked. Hostetler affirmed "the noble desire of the US military personnel to assist charitable organizations" and said that MCC could arrange shipping provided there was a minimum of strings attached.

When Mennonite Central Committee began its Vietnam program in 1954, it functioned under general authorization granted to all international assistance organizations. Even though authorized to establish a medical program in 1957, it was not until December 1959 that Glenn Stoltzfus signed an agreement with the Government of Vietnam to carry out comprehensive programs.

The contract was to "facilitate and increase voluntary donations and the distribution of food, clothes, medicine and other items, as well as money, by the MCC to needy people in Viet-Nam; realize, as far as possible, the will and intention of those who have made available these gifts of money and goods; [and] facilitate the entrance of the MCC in other fields of service—health, education, social and technical assistance, etc.—that MCC might enter." MCC was to "administer programs of social assistance based solely on the needs of the beneficiary without discrimination. The Vietnamese government would grant duty-free importation of all supplies. The government would provide, insofar as possible, for the unloading, handling, storage and inland transportation of goods to the beneficiaries.

Persons administering material aid programs were to respect the conditions set by the donors—Mennonite Central Committee and the United States government—as well as procedures expected by Vietnam's government.

When Voth transferred from Ban Me Thuot to Saigon in April 1960 to direct the material aid program and assume other administrative tasks, he was determined to follow procedures carefully. It was not long before Voth viewed material aid distribution as a "real burden" and longed to see MCC engage in "more permanent, self-help type of work."

To communicate MCC's philosophy of ministry to Tin Lanh leaders, church members and to government officials, Voth distributed printed materials which he hoped would inspire the Church "in the area of social awareness." Voth emphasized that aid was to be given "without discrimination as to color, race, creed, or political affiliation."

In a report on aid distribution in Central Vietnam devastated by typhoons and floods, Voth cited a case where a congregation sold most of the supplies, using the money for the work of the church. There were other cases where pastors told the people to return the distributed supplies— "give back to God what He has so graciously given them!" Some of these "corrupted pastors" were disciplined by the Church's Executive Committee. To resolve this kind of problem Jack Revelle, the Alliance Mission Chairman, suggested that MCC consider terminating the material aid distributions through the Church.

Aware that the Church's Social Welfare Committee was formed in 1954 to facilitate distribution of MCC material aid, Voth was concerned that many in the Church, including pastors, still viewed the Church as the ultimate recipient of the material aid rather than an "instrument" to distribute aid to all needy people. Voth said that when MCC insists that aid must also go to needy persons outside the Church, pastors will "invariably say that that is the responsibility of the government, of the Buddhists, or of the Catholics."

Voth had "pressed" several pastors to cooperate with village officials and make general distribution to all the needy people—Christian or not. Pastors who did this were pleased. "I hope that we can use our influence to get more of them to try doing it the right way," Voth wrote to Robert Miller. "We may get a reputation for being hard-headed but I am sure that the Church will be a better Church as the result."

A partial solution to the problem of aid going primarily to Church members, Voth perceived, was to make larger distributions in fewer places; relief supplies were spread too thinly over a large area. Voth found it hard to fault the pastors for helping the needy within the church—often the poorest persons in the community.

Members of the Church Welfare Committee would also have to be involved in the distribution. But the committee was unable to supervise distributions because it had no funds to cover travel costs of committee members. Although Stoltzfus had earlier provided funds for committee expenses, Voth did not believe it was MCC's responsibility to provide financial support for this Church committee.

While Voth admitted it was easier to provide assistance without working with the Welfare Committee, he still concluded that it was "extremely advantageous to be able to depend upon the Evangelical Church to serve as our representatives in the outlying areas."

Voth praised Pastor Tran Van De, District Superintendent of the Church's Central District, and missionary D. I. Jeffrey for clarifying to the pastors the purpose of the material aid distributions. In June 1961, shortly before Voth concluded his service, he met with the new Tin Lanh Church President, Pastor Doan Van Mieng, to discuss MCC's relationship with the Church. Much of their conversation focused on the Church's Welfare Committee, which everyone wanted, "but no one wants to support it."

It was not only the Tin Lanh patterns that bothered Voth. In a letter to John Hostetler, the MCC Material Aid Director, Voth gave a classic example of the "burden" of distributing flour received through the American PL480 surplus food program—now called "Food for Peace."

An example of this "burden" was the highly successful MCC bakery program. MCC supplied American surplus flour to the bakery set up at the Hoi Duc Anh Orphanage. Two-thirds of the more than fifty thousand loaves distributed monthly to twenty-seven institutions in the Saigon area were baked at this MCC bakery. Since many of these institutions were eligible to receive surplus flour, they preferred giving a portion of this flour to the bakery as payment for the bread they received. This was not permitted—they were supposed to make a small payment to the bakery for labor and fuel costs. Yet if the institution was unable to do this, there was a temptation to charge recipients a small fee for the bread. This, too, was illegal. "If we simply give the individual recipients flour, we know that they will sell it. If we bake bread we know that flour will be used to pay for the baking," Voth wrote. In spite of the problems with technical irregularities, many children and other poor people were receiving food.

In late April 1961 Robert Miller reported that MCC had recruited Rudolph and Elda Lichti from Reedley, California, to anchor the Saigon base. Lichti, an office manager and field man for a fruit company, would become the Vietnam Director, freeing Dr. Dick of that responsibility. In addition, Pax man Daniel Gerber would be coming to replace Good as maintenance man at the leprosarium.

By the end of June, Dr. Dick and Elnora Weaver began using the new hospital building at Nha Trang. The new facility was dedicated on Sunday, July 9, 1961. Among those in attendance were the Khanh Hoa Province Chief and Rev. Louis L. King, the C&MA representative from New York who had come for the dedication that same day of the new campus of the Church's Bible Institute, just up the hill from the hospital. This was also the celebration of the fiftieth anniversary of the 1911 beginning of Alliance missionary activity in Vietnam.

Pastor Pham Xuan Tin, the Hospital Director who served without salary, in his dedicatory speech said that the Church had the responsibility "to honor, worship and serve the Lord and serve fellowmen." Tin said that believers were not only concerned with "lost souls," but sought to relieve "the suffering of those troubled by disease." Medical help would be given without "distinguishing either religious or economic status." Seven years after first coming to Vietnam, MCCers were hearing leaders of the Evangelical Church express some of the same values and commitment which guided their own call to Vietnam.

Rudolph, Elda and ten-year-old Marlin Lichti arrived in Saigon late August, a few weeks after Don Voth and Leland Good left the country. Dr. Dick spent a couple weeks helping to orient Rudy into the responsibilities of field director. The Mennonite missionaries welcomed the Lichti family who participated in the weekly Mennonite missionary fellowship gathering throughout their term. In September Everett Metzler traveled with Lichti to Laos to investigate relief needs there.

Robert Miller came to Vietnam early October on his first Vietnam administrative visit. On October 5, two days later, Daniel Gerber arrived, and was assigned to Ban Me Thuot.

In late October Lichti was responding to major floods in the Mekong Delta area. The floods somewhat hampered Viet Cong activity in the affected areas. Their forces, however, blew up a train on the track from Saigon north to Nha Trang. With repeated attacks all rail activity ceased, thus crimping internal shipping operations.

As an experienced administrator, Rudy Lichti did not write detailed reports to Akron seeking direction or clarity. The MCC Vietnam presence in the early sixties was quite small. Lichti attended the monthly meetings of the Nha Trang Hospital Board. In December he reported that the hospital board did not prepare a financial report that met his standard. "Their concept of business ethics is an enigma and . . . difficult to comprehend," Lichti wrote. "Accountability isn't a Christian virtue for them." But a month latter he informed Akron that the hospital was self-supporting the previous three months, thanks to small fees and outside contributions. MCC was providing a monthly $250 subsidy.

In the spring of 1962 only a few persons were working with MCC in Vietnam. Rudy and Elda Lichti were in Saigon. Lichti was working with relief to flood victims in the Mekong Delta and negotiating with the Nha Trang Hospital Board to assure smooth working relationships. Nurse Marva Hasselblad had come to replace Elnora Weaver who was leaving. John and Hildagard Dick were medical director and hostess. Gerber was now the sole MCC person at the Ban Me Thuot Leprosarium. Lichti requested that Akron recruit another man to work with him.

Late one night at the end of May, Lichti received the stark announcement that Daniel Gerber was kidnapped! He had been in Vietnam less than eight months.

INCIDENT AT BAN ME THUOT

Chapter 16

R ev. Archie Mitchell, Dr. Ardel Vietti, and Daniel Gerber were kidnapped from the Ban Me Thuot Leprosarium on May 30, 1962.

At dusk that Wednesday evening, armed men came onto the leprosarium grounds, seized and tied up twenty-one-year-old Gerber, then C&MA missionary Mitchell, forty-one years old. Lastly they took Dr. Vietti. She had arrived in Vietnam more than four years earlier at the age of thirty, studied the Vietnamese and the Rhade languages, and assumed responsibilities as medical director at the leprosarium in mid-1960.

A month earlier, nurse Ruth Wilting and Daniel Gerber had announced their engagement to their families and sponsoring agencies. Ruth penned a two-page report of the abduction dated May 30 which she sent home:

> At 7:30 p.m. May 30, 1962 Daniel and I started out for a walk. Prayer meeting was to be at 7:45. It was still light as we started out. On our way back we were surrounded by a group of men dressed in different types of apparel. Their faces were dirty thus giving them a very evil expression. Fear is a terrible thing and we experienced it at that time. But the peace of God flooded our souls as we prayed. They tied Daniel's arms behind him and wanted me to leave him. I stayed for the time. . . .
>
> As Daniel and I stayed together the song "Jesus Lover of my Soul" came to my mind and so I began to sing. Previously I had prayed out loud and the Lord seemed to give the Viet Cong confusion. We had only three men guarding us but all of the men were heavily armed. It seemed to me that there were about ten or eleven men in the group. Soon some of the other men came back with Archie Mitchell. They then tied Daniel and Archie together side by side. They then made me leave and go back to the house. . . .
>
> On the way we met a group taking Ardel in the same direction as the men. This was the last any of the three were seen by us.

The Viet Cong spent two and one-half hours pilfering supplies, taking medicines—particularly penicillin, medical supplies and instruments for amputations and removal of bullets, loading them into the Land Rover. They also took sheets, pillow cases, clothing, towels, and money from the Mitchell and Vietti homes. Before leaving around 10:30 p.m., they lectured the four nurses—Maxine Craig, Dawn Deets, Olive Kingsbury, and Ruth Wilting—and Mrs. Betty Mitchell and their children, Rebecca, Loretta, and Glenn, aged thirteen, ten and eight. Four-year-old child, Geraldine, was sleeping. Wilting said the men told them "how bad we were and that we were only the hands and feet of the head-ones so they were letting us go." The women were instructed not to go the sixteen kilometers to Ban Me Thuot that night, but told to leave the next morning and never return.

Word of the kidnapping reached the Alliance missionaries in Ban Me Thuot by noon the next day. When Vietnam Mission Chairman T. Grady Mangham in Saigon was informed that afternoon, he cabled their New York office. MCC Director Rudy Lichti learned of it that night and cabled MCC Headquarters. Bill Detweiler, Pastor of Kidron Mennonite Church, broke the news to Gerber's family.

Lichti flew to Ban Me Thuot the next day on a military plane. Returning that afternoon, he wrote to J. M. (Jake) Klassen, MCC's Assistant Director of Relief who immediately responded:

> Here at Headquarters we have discussed several times what course of action we should take to facilitate the early release of these prisoners. We are in good communication with Mr. Chrisman [of Christian and Missionary Alliance in New York], with the State Department, and with Daniel Gerber's parents. We are also thinking of the possibility of approaching the problem through United Nations channels. Our biggest hope of course is you, Grady Mangham, and the American Embassy in Saigon. We hope that you will leave no stone unturned in your effort to secure the release of the hostages. At the same time we must be cautious not to build up too strong a relationship between US Government and our workers, for fear that the Viet Cong get the impression that our workers were actually servants of the US Government and hence bitter enemies of the Viet Cong. Perhaps the line we should follow is that the sole purpose of our workers in Vietnam is to help Vietnamese and Rhade tribesmen. We have no ulterior motives other than to help people in need . . .
>
> Do you think that there is anything that we should do at our end here in Washington or the United Nations or perhaps even by approaching North Vietnamese delegations in other state capitals? What information do you have about North Vietnamese Government Embassies in other countries? Would you see any value (or perhaps harm) in such an approach?
>
> . . . May God give you and your coworkers much wisdom to cope with the emergent situation. May he also hold His protecting hand over the captives as well as other members of our missionaries working in Vietnam.

Mangham provided additional details in a letter to Alliance Administrator Robert Chrisman. A week before the abduction on Wednesday, May 23, a special seminar on leprosy opened at the leprosarium with lectures from Richard Buker, a visiting doctor from Thailand. Other C&MA missionary families attended. On Friday night three bridges on the road to town were burned, and two dozen trees felled onto the road three and a half kilometers from the leprosarium. Bamboo spikes were implanted along the sides of the road, and signs posted in both Vietnamese and Rhade warning that no one was to use the road.

On Sunday morning Vietnamese armed forces opened the road and arrived at the leprosarium. The captain requested that all missionary personnel leave. Reluctant to do this, two of the men accompanied the captain to Ban Me Thuot where they talked with authorities, including personnel of the U.S. Military Assistance Advisory Group. It was then decided that visiting missionaries would leave that day, while the personnel assigned to the leprosarium would stay. Since these staff members had been there for some time "with no indication of any ill feeling against the Leprosarium . . . it was thought that there was nothing to fear." Viet Cong forces had attacked an ethnic minority Muong village on Sunday afternoon; missionaries assumed this was the reason the road was blockaded.

Mangham reported that after abducting the three persons, the Viet Cong soldiers accused the others of being government agents, oppressing and betraying the people, and said they were all worthy of death. However, they said the doctor would not be harmed.

"You must turn over the operation and supervision of this work to the national staff here," the guerrillas said, "They are able to carry on without your being here and they will see that these people get proper treatment rather than being oppressed and betrayed as you have done in the past."

The Viet Cong spoke in the Rhade language, although Mrs. Mitchell and the nurses thought there was only one true Rhade man. Some were Vietnamese, and some from another ethnic group who spoke Rhade poorly. Although the missionaries did not recognize any of the men, Ruth Wilting was called by name.

Mangham noted that there was "no violence in the attack and no shot was fired. We are trusting earnestly that the Lord will protect these three and return them to us at an early date."

Five months earlier, in December 1961, when Mangham with his wife Evelyn and their four children were traveling from Saigon to Da Lat, their car and many other vehicles were stopped by Viet Cong guerrillas 113 kilometers from Saigon. Even though they insisted that they were missionaries, they were directed off the road onto a logging trail where they were lectured by the guerrillas claiming to represent the government liberating South Vietnam. After asking Mangham what he did, the guerrilla leader said: "We know you missionaries are here only to help the people of our country. You can turn around now and leave."

The capture of these three personnel stunned the Christian and Missionary Alliance and the whole evangelical Christian community in North America since it was widely believed that missionary personnel would not be harmed by the Viet Cong guerrillas. The incident was reported widely in the American press. Churches prayed for the release of Gerber and the two missionaries.

Reportedly Vietnamese armed forces quickly identified the location of the abductors who by then had joined a larger military unit, but did not launch an attempt to free them, fearing it would lead to much loss of life.

Kingsbury said they "weren't particularly afraid. We were just surprised." She assumed that the captors thought they were seizing three doctors. An *Associated Press* report two months later said the three were "in Communist hands ever since the raid . . . and reportedly are being used to treat the wounded and train the guerrillas in medical aid."

There were many unconfirmed reports about the three being sighted. On September 19 Lichti sent an update to the MCC office, noting that the Akron administrators likely had already received this information from C&MA's New York office.

> The US Embassy requests that no military effort be made to effect the release of those held. This for several reasons: 1. It would endanger their lives. 2. If successful, it would mean that they could not continue assignments in Viet Nam. C&MA is concerned about jeopardizing their continuing program in Viet Nam if they use the military—either US or VN. You are perhaps aware that one attempt was under way to affect their release by military operations. Last Sunday rumors again indicate that a concerted effort is being made to ascertain their whereabouts and get them out either by subterfuge or bribery. The Vietnamese military is becoming concerned about the question of their location as they do not want to plan attacks on areas where they might be. As long as no one knows where they are, military operations will be hindered. The International Red Cross states that it would be a difficult task if not impossible to make contact under conditions here.

Lichti then commented on the personality and commitment of twenty-one-year-old Gerber: "In the months I learned to know Dan," he wrote, "it seemed that he was a 'rugged' individual and should be able to withstand the rigors and privations forced upon him. Above all he has an indomitable faith in God. In discussions with him his final word relative to the questions or problems always was that it was his conviction that God's will for him was being done."

Lichti was hopeful that the three would be released, and he anticipated reassigning Gerber to a leprosarium and orphanage in the Da Nang area established by Gordon and Laura Smith, the founders of the Ban Me Thuot Leprosarium. Unable to go out to the Leprosarium, the Alliance nurses continued their medical services from the Alliance mission base in the town of Ban Me Thuot.

Dr. John Dick continued to develop MCC's Medical Program with the Evangelical Church in Nha Trang, assisted by nurse Marva Hasselblad. Marva's father, Dr. Oliver Hasselblad, President of the American Leprosy Mission, briefly visited Vietnam three months before the kidnappings. In early March he flew to Nha Trang, then accompanied Marva and Dr. Dick in the MCC Land Rover 194 kilometers to Ban Me Thuot to visit the leprosarium which his agency helped support. At the urging of Saigon government officials who had reported Viet Cong activity along that mountain highway, a Vietnamese military escort of young recruits went along to Ban Me Thuot. However, the military escort did not accompany them the sixteen kilometers to the leprosarium.

The Hasselblads and Dr. Dick were greeted by Dr. Vietti who told them that it was good that they had come to the leprosarium alone. "The road in here has a thousand eyes," Dr. Vietti said. "We know that Vietcong lookouts report back on every move we make. We have no idea why we should be under surveillance, but we make a special point of never violating our peaceful purpose in this area. The arrival of one man with a rifle, let alone a truckload of soldiers, could have resulted in a raid. At the very least they would have placed mines along the only road leading in here."

With the number of military personnel in Vietnam increasing, the U.S. Army in April 1962 established the Eighth Field Hospital located by the Nha Trang Airport. It was equipped with x-ray machines and other equipment not even available at the provincial hospital in Nha Trang. The military doctors were happy to come out to the Chan-Y-Vien Tin Lanh (Evangelical Clinic) to help with difficult cases. Though the clinic was considered off-limits to U.S. military personnel from evening through the next morning, doctors loved to come out to this beautiful spot by the South China Sea.

MCC personnel with limited Vietnamese language fluency regularly attended English worship services in Nha Trang at the U.S. Army base. Although Marva usually attended Vietnamese language worship services in the Tin Lanh Church at the Bible school or the Vinh Phuoc congregation near the orphanage, on occasion she was invited to play the organ at the Army base chapel. In a late-May letter home, she describes going to the chapel with the Lichtis who were visiting Nha Trang: "There was a big crowd there this Sunday, including some C&MA missionaries, one of whom gave the message," she wrote. "At the bottom of the order of service, were the words, 'The only service in the world with an Episcopal Chaplain, Southern Baptist Song Leader, Mennonite Missionary Nurse Organist, and Christian and Missionary Alliance Guest Speaker! Congregation, NhaTrang Protestants!' It was all rather nice for a change, especially to hear a sermon in English again."

Hasselblad studied Vietnamese each morning before holding clinic. Like other MCC personnel, she also learned by experience the cultural "dos" and "don'ts." At the end of clinic one day, she asked her valued friend and interpreter, Mimmie, about a discrepancy in the small clinic fee intake that day. Mimmie became upset, went home immediately, and did not come to work the next day. A few days later Pastor Tin, the board chairman, told Dr. Dick, "Marva accused my daughter of stealing. Mimmie will not be working with you anymore." Hasselblad went to Mimmie and explained she was only trying to balance the books, and had not even thought of the possibility that Mimmie had taken anything. After the talk, Mimmie decided to return to work. (Hasselblad wrote about her life in Nha Trang in *Lucky, Lucky* [Evans and Company].)

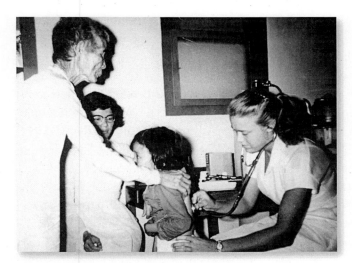
Marva examining patient with interpreter.

The Lichtis stayed in Nha Trang with Hasselblad when the Dick family terminated in late June—until Carl and Phyllis Yoder arrived July 18. During these three weeks volunteer doctors from the Field Hospital came to the Evangelical Clinic. Marva assisted them in performing several operations, and they organized their first dental clinic. Hasselblad describes it:

> By dawn of that day more than a hundred people were already assembled. A few hours later an Army truck arrived, containing a detail of dental corpsmen, two dental chairs, and all the equipment that would be needed. Two Army dentists followed in a jeep. Badly infected gums were treated and, in some cases, surgery was done. While they worked, the dentists explained what they were doing and had me assist at simple things. It was one of the most efficient maneuvers I had ever seen and even included the activities of a cleanup squad at the end.

Dr. Dick had promised to help Phi, an eight-year-old boy crippled by tuberculosis, whenever a surgeon became available. When Major Spencer Walton, an orthopedic surgeon at the field hospital, heard about the case, he flew by helicopter to Phi's village near Tuy Hoa, some 120 kilometers north, and brought him and his mother to the Tin Lanh Clinic. The operation went well, but he needed a long period of recuperation. His Christian mother, whose husband had recently been killed by the Viet Cong, needed to return home to care for other children. After a few days she said to Marva, "I'll just leave him here with you and God."

Dr. Carl Yoder came from Lancaster, Pennsylvania; Phyllis, a nurse, was from Goshen, Indiana. This husband-wife team quickly fit into the clinic. Maj. Walton wanted to help other refugees in Phi's village, so he organized a mobile medical clinic. Carl, Phyllis and Marva flew with three Army nurses and a large supply of medical equipment in two helicopters. In this one day, Hasselblad related, "over 350 patients were examined and treated, over 200 teeth were extracted, more than 12,000 vitamin pills were distributed, and over 200 penicillin injections were administered. . . . For the Yoders this was an intensive introduction to what they were to find in Vietnam in the following months. For all of us it was an enriching experience, our first in full collaboration with the military on a common humanitarian project."

In September Lichti sent a report to Akron entitled "MCC and US Military Cooperation." The report begins novel-like: "The participation of US military medical personnel in the Nha-trang project started quite innocently." Lichti then noted that when a certain doctor came to Nha Trang, Dr. Dick first associated with him socially, but soon they had consultations and the doctor frequently came to the clinic. Lichti said that when members of the clinic board "became concerned about the frequency of the presence of Army vehicles on the premises and stated their concern to us," Dr. Dick assured the board that he would discontinue this association.

Yet when the Field Hospital was set up with six medical doctors, six nurses, anesthetists, lab technicians and many aides, complete with a dental clinic with eight dentists and their assistants, these medical personnel—with much time on their hands—offered their services to the clinic, and they were invited to perform some surgeries. "Their presence became a regular occurrence," Lichti wrote, with their driving out to the Clinic "at will, and left when good and ready. They came in Army jeeps with side-arms and carbines as necessary hardware. We had us a problem."

During the three weeks without a doctor when the Lichti family stayed with Marva, "the Army doctors literally took over the Clinic," Lichti wrote. The hospital board called a meeting one day after Carl and Phyllis Yoder arrived and again stated their concern. They did not oppose the doctors personally, only "the identification with the military which they feel quite strongly draws attention to the Clinic and in this period of turmoil and strife could result in a raid for medical supplies—or the worst, abduction of the doctor and nurses." This was only two months after the Viet Cong had abducted the missionary doctor from Ban Me Thuot.

The relationship with U.S. armed forces medical personnel "brought with it many benefits such as medicines we did not have, free x-ray service, free laboratory service and most of all—specialist know-how. It is apparent that our treatment program was and is being greatly enhanced by these available services," Lichti wrote. But with MCC working under the Tin Lanh board, Lichti was committed to respect their concerns. "It was difficult to request the military doctors not to come except when we call them," Lichti wrote, and there was not yet full compliance. This issue was partly resolved by MCC staff taking patients to the Eighth Field Hospital for surgeries.

A decade later, some MCC personnel at Nha Trang, very much opposed to identification with U.S. or Vietnamese military forces, criticized the hospital board for too much identification with the military policies of the Saigon government. In 1962, however, it was the Tin Lanh board members who were disturbed by U.S. military personnel coming there. Theirs was not an ethical concern, but rather a practical fear that guerrilla forces might abduct the American doctor.

This is a classic example of what became an increasing dilemma for Mennonite personnel in Vietnam—how to live in the broad grey area between the ethical whites and blacks. They wanted to minimize their association with military personnel, especially U.S. forces. On the other hand, it is doubtful that patients who benefitted from medical treatments were concerned about whether the care came from a pacifist medical practitioner or a doctor wearing a military uniform who came to the clinic in a Jeep bristling with guns.

Lichti identified two other areas where MCC was now utilizing support from the U.S. military forces—personal travel and transportation of supplies. After MCC lost ten tons of commodities from a train derailment caused by Viet Cong guerrillas, Lichti asked the Military Assistance Advisory Group to fly medical supplies to Nha Trang, Ban Me Thuot and to World Evangelism Crusade doctors in the Da Nang area. MAAG agreed, so this procedure was being followed for several months already.

Early in 1962 the U.S. Operations Mission (USOM) requested that MCC more frequently observe the distribution of U.S. surplus foods commodities. With deteriorating security Lichti could not travel by road, and frequent flying meant much higher operating costs. Arrangements were made with MAAG to use military aircraft flights. Lichti reported that in the just-over-a-year he was in Vietnam, he had traveled 10,555 air miles; more than half of his travel the previous six months was on military planes. This service was also available to Dr. Yoder.

In his 1962 year-end report, Lichti noted security concerns: "Although we are aware there are calculated risks in living in Vietnam, we feel relatively safe and secure within the cities." Lichti wrote: "There are occasional incidents which tend to make us apprehensive; consequently it is necessary to observe security and safety measures."

In October Lichti reported to MCC's Material Aid Director that the USOM was planning to increase distribution of Food for Peace commodities due to greater VC guerrilla activities. Much of the assistance would go to families of Self Defense Units, Civil Guard Units, and servicemen. Some supplies would go to promoting a hog-raising program, and some would help ethnic minorities struggling with a chronic food shortage. *Did MCC want to continue to handle PL-480 commodities?* Lichti wondered. If not, Lichti questioned the need to maintain personnel in Saigon. However, he said they were "settled in," Elda was teaching some English classes, and their son Marlin was happily studying at the Da Lat Alliance missionary children's school.

The Vietnam Mennonite Mission, along with other mission agencies, was frustrated in 1961 that the government was not issuing visas for new missionary personnel. There was speculation

Rudy Lichti (2nd from r) meeting with interpreter Ninh, Alliance missionary D. I. Jeffrey, and Pastor Nguyen Thien Si.

that this might be due to overt Catholic influence in the Presidential Palace. Although one mission agency utilized the service of the U.S. Embassy to pressure the government to issue visas, Eastern Mennonite Board Secretary Kraybill was reluctant to do this. In a memo to his Executive Committee, he wrote: "We believe in the separation of church and state, and if we resort to the use of the state to coerce another nation into yielding to our desires, we do jeopardize our own convictions and also make it difficult to defend our principles. I would not rule this out altogether depending on the nature of the assistance but this should only be done with extreme care."

Stauffer wrote home after President Ngo Dinh Diem's October 2, 1961, speech to the National Assembly where Diem declared that the country was no longer fighting a guerilla war; government forces were being attacked by large armed units. Besides the growing numbers of casualties, the economy was hurting. Prices were rising and there were food shortages—even rice. James wrote: "Only Divine intervention can save this nation if things continue to get worse. Let us pray earnestly in this time of dire need!"

In that same letter Stauffer informed his mother that Daniel Gerber had just arrived. The Stauffers had casual acquaintance with the Gerber family during the two years James served as pastor in the Kidron, Ohio, community. He invited Daniel to briefly speak to the English language students one evening.

In late October 1961 one of the worst floods of the century inundated the Mekong Delta area. It came at the same time President Diem proclaimed a state of emergency because of the growing communist activity. U.S. General Maxwell Taylor visited Vietnam, and contemplated using the flooding as a cover to introduce several thousand U.S. ground troops who might stay or leave after completing a flood relief mission. Writing home, Stauffer said that a "decision to send American troops in here could have some very serious implications. On the other hand," he wrote, "it is no secret that the Vietnamese Army has more than they can handle and will need some help from somewhere."

The Stauffer and Metzler missionary couples continued their evangelistic ministries, relying primarily on English classes to meet new persons. In a prayer letter published in the March 1962 issue of *Missionary Messenger*, Margaret and Everett referred to Pham Van Luc, a young man preparing for baptism.

"We were thrilled one night after Bible study when our former English student and friend told us that he would like us to pray with him, for he has now decided to follow Christ as his Saviour and Lord," they wrote.

> We knew by his questions and attitude over the past months that Mr. Luc had been seriously considering the claims of Christ. We feel he is sincere and that his is a considered decision, but we know that the road ahead may be rough. Pray for him and for us as we guide him into the riches of the knowledge of Christ.
>
> Mr. Luc is but one of about ten young men and women who have been faithful attenders of our Sunday evening study of Luke during the past year. We pray that this may be but the beginning of a turning to the Lord among this small group.

In this same letter they mentioned Minh, a young woman who confessed faith in Christ at the Stauffer home. She was one of dozens of young men and women who expressed faith in Jesus Christ, but never became members of the Mennonite church. Some of these persons became active members of Tin Lanh churches; others never joined the Christian community. Many of the young men would soon be inducted into the armed forces.

In January the Stauffers welcomed the birth of their second child, Rosemarie. Her birth came just ten weeks after the Metzlers had their third child, Malcolm Dean.

The war continued to expand in 1962. In January the U.S. Air Force began spraying herbicides to defoliate the vegetation to deprive cover to the guerrilla fighters—most of it Agent Orange which contained dioxin, a carcinogenic substance. Eventually it was used over 10 to 20 percent of the entire country. In February the United States established the Military Assistance Command, Vietnam (MACV), headed by General Paul D. Harkins, which now supervised the Military Assistance Advisory Group (MAAG) and directed the conduct of the war. U.S. Secretary of Defense Robert McNamara in May made the first of his many visits to Vietnam.

On February 27 the Presidential Palace, home of President Diem, was bombed by two disgruntled Vietnamese pilots who disapproved of the President's handling of the war. In a letter home, Stauffer described the incident. After hearing several huge explosions, he looked from the balcony and saw the fighter planes diving at the Presidential Palace about a mile away while anti-aircraft guns responded. The radio immediately announced that the President and his family escaped without harm. If fact, Mme. Ngo Dinh Nhu, the first lady, suffered injuries but soon recovered. The palace, however, was severely damaged and had to be rebuilt.

This bombing raid delayed the arrival of EMBMC Secretary Paul N. Kraybill by one day. With Kraybill was Lancaster Mennonite Conference Bishop H. Raymond Charles, the Chairman of the Mission Board.

In a diary entry March 5, 1962, Kraybill wrote about the expanding war with 4,000 US military personnel training and supporting the Vietnamese forces. Kraybill noted that the Stauffer and Metzler families were "well established in their two locations . . . , carrying on English and Bible classes with good interest." He was pleased to meet the "five believers . . . , a very congenial group of young men and women seventeen to twenty years old." That evening Phuoc joined the visitors and missionaries for the first communion service.

Charles and Kraybill visited the MCC-Tin Lanh Hospital in Nha Trang and met with the Lichtis in Saigon. He observed good relationships between the MCC staff and the missionaries. He and Charles also met the Tin Lanh Church President Doan Van Mieng and Vice President Pham Xuan Tin who expressed appreciation for the work of the Mennonites. Kraybill wrote that continued fellowship and mutual respect would enable the Mennonite missionaries "to carry on a witness without any feeling of competition or pressure to merge with their organization."

After learning that the Alliance and Southern Baptist missions were now receiving visas for new missionaries, Kraybill determined to also submit visa applications for new personnel.

Kraybill and Charles left March 9. After five years in Saigon, James and Arlene Stauffer left for a six-month furlough on the same flight.

In his report approved by the EMBMC Board, Kraybill recommended that three additional couples be recruited and sent in 1962-1963 with the maximum of twenty missionary personnel. Kraybill wanted the Vietnam Mennonite Mission office—where the Metzlers lived—renovated for adequate classroom and meeting space and a student hostel in addition to living quarters. Programs were to be developed "with English classes, student work and regular Bible study, evangelistic and worship services."

Eastern Mennonite College (University) was a fertile recruiting ground for missionary personnel, and Kraybill made regular visits to campus. After the May meeting of the Mission Board, he reported to Everett that James and Rachel Metzler and Luke and Mary Martin were appointed for "missionary evangelist service in Viet Nam." A few weeks after visa application forms were submitted to the Vietnamese Embassy in Washington, Everett was "thrilled" to receive a letter from the Interior Ministry authorizing the two families to come for a period of five years.

When the two couples arrived in Saigon September 13, Metzler cabled headquarters, "ARRIVED SAFELY ON SCHEDULE," but "IN" was the only message received in Salunga! Kraybill wrote to Everett: "This acknowledges your cable, the briefest cable we have on record! We are glad to know that the Metzlers and Martins are 'in.' . . . Now that they are 'in,' I suppose the word for you is 'go.'"

The day after arrival we four newcomers registered at the U.S. Embassy and also at the immigration office. The Vietnamese officials there shook their heads in amazement that we had been granted visas for five years! Normally initial visas were issued for three months, with extensions granted for six months or one year. We saw this good fortune as an affirmation of God's call and blessing as we began our ministry in Vietnam.

James Metzler had just graduated from Eastern Mennonite College (EMC) with a bachelor's degree in Bible. Though he had not previously lived overseas, he did have significant cross-cultural experience. As a young teenager, he accompanied his family as they left their insular Lancaster County, Pennsylvania, Mennonite community for rural Alabama to establish new churches. He was very much a foreigner among his school classmates who spoke with a different accent. At recess the kids would crowd around him, demanding "Say 'fahve!'" And when he answered "five," they would all roar with laughter!

Rachel was a registered nurse from Harrisonburg, Virginia, who worked in the Rockingham Memorial Hospital, and whose father was the German language professor at the college.

I had also just graduated from EMC, with majors in Bible and sociology. A farm boy from Lancaster County, eight years earlier I was drafted and, as an alternative to military service, accepted an assignment with Mennonite Central Committee. William T. Snyder invited me to join a thirty-some contingent of Pax men going to Germany to build houses for war refugees. After eighteen months in Germany, I was assigned to Greece for several months. After completing my term, I studied a few months at the European Mennonite Bible School in Switzerland.

Mary Kauffman and I were married a year earlier just after she graduated from EMC with an elementary education degree. She taught one year in the Rockingham County, Virginia, school district. Mary was from Chester County, Pennsylvania. She sometimes described herself as a "hothouse plant" with sixteen years of Mennonite education—from West Fallowfield Mennonite School to Lancaster Mennonite High School to EMC. But her family was very much involved in numerous communities since her farmer father assisted in planting several new churches.

In April both of us couples had interviews at the EMBMC Headquarters at Salunga, and had the obligatory meeting with Bishops of the Lancaster Mennonite Conference discussing theological views to determine whether we could satisfactorily represent the Conference in Vietnam. In July Mary and I took a brief introductory linguistics course where we met linguists William Smalley and G. Linwood Barney, former Alliance missionaries. This course provided us with useful tools for Vietnamese language study. At the Mission Board's request I was ordained a minister.

Our first weeks in Vietnam went by quickly. Two weeks after arrival the Stauffer family returned from their short furlough, welcomed back by their many friends. On Sunday, September 30, Pham Van Luc was baptized. After his baptism Luc gave testimony of his faith in Jesus Christ. Among those present were Phan Ba Phuoc, who a few months earlier had begun working as interpreter for Dr. Yoder in the Nha Trang Tin Lanh Clinic. That afternoon Luc, Phuoc and the missionaries commemorated the Last Supper and a service of foot washing. When Everett and Margaret and their children left for a furlough in the United States, the Stauffer family moved into their vacated residence at what was now being called the Saigon Center.

In a September 27 letter to her sister, Mary reflected on her newly-designated role as a missionary in Vietnam: "We are not first of all American citizens here to help the cause of security in this land but we are first and foremost, Christians. . . . We hope to spend our lives here if God has work for us to do here. We thank Him for the constant peace and assurance that we are in His will. There is no place in the world where we'd rather be right now." And in a *Missionary Messenger* article discussing the influence of different religions in Vietnam, I wrote: "We are here to preach Christ as the only way to God. God has spoken to mankind in history; we are responsible to declare what he has spoken."

Rachel with Teacher Ky.

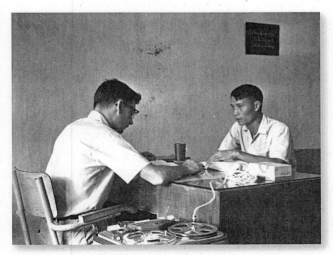

James with Teacher Luc.

The newly-arrived Metzler and Martin couples shared Stauffer's former house at 42 Nguyen Phi Khanh Street located in the Dakao section of District 1. Here we began Vietnamese language study, we men with *Thầy* (Teacher) Chau Hong Luc, and Rachel and Mary with *Cô* (Miss Teacher) Ky. Each would spend two blocks of one hour every morning individually with our tutor while the other listened to tapes and practiced the language drills. Afternoons each spent another hour with the tutor, a few hours listening to tapes, then going out onto the street, sometimes to chat with children, often to the nearby Dakao Market where we would try out the vocabulary we were learning and experience the new culture. Writing home about the challenges of bargaining for every purchase, James quoted his favorite line—from Matthew 25:35: "I was a stranger and they took me in!"

Sample sentences and word and phrase drills were repeated endlessly. Mary wrote home that I was repeating sentence patterns in my sleep. James heard both Mary and me reciting these lines while we slept!

Friday, October 26, was National Day, so we took a break from language study. After watching a two-hour parade downtown of marching units, artillery pieces and tanks, ships on the Saigon River, and planes above, Mary and I viewed an outdoor exhibition of weapons used by government forces. That noon we heard that a hand grenade was tossed into a crowd at an exhibit that we had visited less than an hour before, killing six persons and injuring twenty-six. Welcome to Vietnam!

Our arrival presented a minor challenge to the friends of the missionaries—how should we be called? Phan Ba Phuoc and Phan Van Luc, the two baptized believers, came up with a solution that stuck. In the Vietnamese society, the family name, like *Nguyễn, Phan, Phạm, or Trần,* always comes first, and the given name last. A man's middle name often is *Văn* and a woman's middle name often is *Thị,* sometimes capitalized, sometimes not. People would be referred to by their given names as Mr. Phuoc or Mr. Luc, not Mr. Phan or Mr. Pham. But their friends referred to the missionaries using their family names, as Mr. Metzler, Mrs. Stauffer, or Mr. and Mrs. Martin. But now there were two Metzler families, and how was each to be distinguished from the other? So Everett and Margaret were called Mr. and Mrs. Metzler *lớn,* and James and Rachel as Mr. and Mrs. Metzler *nhỏ. Lớn* and *nhỏ* mean big and little, or tall and short, but in this case meant older and younger.

Addressing the missionaries by their family names was meant as an expressing of respect. However, some short-term Mennonite mission personnel who came later were given Vietnamese names which seemed more satisfactory. Missionaries were also addressed as *Ông* (Mister) and *Bà* (Missus). *Ông* and *Bà* mean "grandfather" and "grandmother," but are also used of persons in a high position. We young adults in our late twenties resisted being addressed in such high terms as *Ông Bà Martin* or *Ông Bà Metzler nhỏ,* but felt we had little choice but to accept the names our new friends called us. We male missionaries were ordained ministers before coming to Vietnam. A pastor or minister was a *mục sư,* and the only way to refer to a minister and his wife was *Ông Bà Mục sư.* Only decades later would some Christian friends refer to us missionaries in terms more in keeping with the Mennonite concept of brother and sister, as *Anh Luke* and *Chị Mary.*

Orie O. Miller, remarried to Elta Sensenig and now associate to secretary Kraybill, visited Vietnam with his wife the first week in December. They visited the Tin Lanh Medical Clinic in Nha Trang. Miller met with T. Grady Mangham, Alliance Mission Superintendent, who reported that there were persistent reports that the three captured persons were active at a Viet Cong base 120 kilometers southwest of Ban Me Thuot. Mangham said that the leprosarium was continuing its program under indigenous staff. Miller also spoke with Southern Baptist missionaries who arrived three years earlier; with Paul Contento, student worker with Intervarsity Christian Fellowship; and with D. I. Jeffrey, C&MA missionary with forty-four years of experience in Vietnam. The Tin Lanh Church now had around 33,000 baptized members. Miller also met with Don Luce, the Vietnam Director of International Voluntary Service; forty-six American IVS personnel worked in educational and agricultural services.

Paul Kraybill had asked that Miller review the direction of the Mennonite Mission programs. In a statement, "Mennonite Mission Role in Viet Nam, 1963-1968," Miller listed three basic principles:

> "We are here to supplement the Christian witness in this country. We want to complement rather than compete.

"We must stress daily discipleship, reveal the true nature of the Church, and demonstrate the Scriptural oneness of all true believers.

"We want to meet the need of the whole man—spiritual, social, emotional and physical."

Regarding methodology, Miller said that "direct evangelism should be our main thrust in Saigon and other population centers," and noted that English Bible teaching provided "excellent contacts and lays some groundwork for future spiritual fruit." He said youth centers could be developed with minimum expense; this would likely be the closest the Mission should come to "institutionalism" in Saigon. An earlier plan for a student hostel needed further study, he indicated.

Miller supported Kraybill's recommendations for renovating the facilities at the Saigon property for student activities and meeting place and wrote that "after establishing a nucleus of believers and conducting Christian workers' training courses," the Mennonite Mission should open other centers in Saigon and its suburbs. "All programming must be flexible and constantly subject to Holy Spirit direction through both national and missionary personnel," he said. Miller's instinct was to maintain flexibility, though there is little doubt that Vietnam's political and military uncertainties weighed in on his concern to be flexible. Miller also anticipated the arrival of another missionary couple in 1963, Donald and Doris Sensenig. Donald was Miller's step son-in-law.

Miller urged Stauffer to immediately begin rebuilding the Saigon property. James drew up simple plans and reviewed them with a Christian contractor, Mr. Bang. Everett and Margaret, now in the States, sent additional suggestions.

A few weeks before Miller's visit, some of the Mennonite missionaries attended a Sunday morning worship service when the Vietnam Baptist Church was officially organized. They adopted a constitution, read the names of around forty charter members, and named Southern Baptist Convention missionary Herman Hayes as the pastor. We noted the more aggressive approach of the SBC missionaries who began preaching services early in English, using interpreters. We Mennonite missionaries, who focused on language learning for a few years, had baptized only two believers.

While we two new couples living at Nguyen Phi Khanh Street did not organize any ongoing activities, we did invite the neighborhood children to a special Christmas program to 150 children packed into the front living room. James Metzler described it in a letter home:

Sunday afternoon found me holding the gate in front of our house so it wouldn't be pushed down. Rachel had made a sign to hang out front to announce our first children's meeting here. They began gathering before 3:00 [p.m.] and by 3:30 they were more than eager. Even though the young believers were to take charge of the meeting, we were glad that Arlene had come to help keep some resemblance of order. When we opened the gate they poured in like water over a spillway. Amazing, they did settle down and learned a Christmas chorus and verse very well in no time flat. They listened real well as Phuoc told the Christmas [story] with flannel-graph. The girls sang some carols in English at the end of the meeting to avoid a rush for the door—so we almost had to coax them to the door one by one. We gave each one a paper with the Bible story in Vietnamese, a picture of the manger scene, and a tangerine. Out of 170 tangerines, we had only about 20 left; so you know the room was full.

At the end of 1962 there were few MCC staff in Vietnam: Elda and Rudy Lichti in Saigon; Carl and Phyllis Yoder and Marva Hasselblad at the Nha Trang Hospital. And Daniel Gerber.

Rudolph Lichti began his 1962 Vietnam Report as follows: "Politically there has been little change in this South East Asia Republic during the past year. Militarily it marks the beginning of the Government's offensive against Communist guerrilla (VC) forces. The US military buildup became evident in December 1961, has continued and US Advisory Units and Special Forces are playing an ever increasing role in the Vietnamese government's determination to win against the VC."

He continued: "The tragic note of 1962 was the abduction of PAX man Daniel Gerber from the Banmethuot Leprosarium on May 30 together with Ardel Vietti, MD, and Archie Mitchell, C&MA missionaries. Concerted efforts have been made to learn their whereabouts, but at this writing we have no information available."

What happened to these three persons? Occasional reports nourished hope that they might be released, but the reports could never be substantiated. Daniel's mother sent several letters to her son through the International Red Cross, but they were never delivered.

An American CIA document dated June 1965, released a few decades later, referred to "a woman doctor and two male assistants captured by the Viet Cong during a raid on a mission hospital in

Daniel Gerber with Ruth Wilting.

Daniel on tractor.

1962; during the next year or so, they were spotted at various times with Viet Cong units in the highlands, presumably being forced to provide medical care. . . . There have been no recent firm reports of the precise whereabouts of any of these civilians; efforts continue to secure their release."

MCC leaders contacted diplomatic missions of the Democratic Republic of Vietnam and of the National Liberation Front in other countries. Alliance leaders pursued similar channels.

The Kidron News of June 4, 1970, reported "reasonable assurance of [Gerber's] safety and continuing ministry behind enemy lines." It referred to a statement that had appeared in the *Alliance Witness* which came from Rhade Christians who "have reported them occasionally in Daclac Province where they are moved north or south, east or west as they are needed." The article stated that they were vulnerable to "friendly ground probes" or Allied bombing attacks. It said that "verbal assurance" had been given that the three were alive and well, but no tangible evidence provided to substantiate this.

When American prisoners-of-war were released following the Paris Peace Agreement in 1973, Vietnamese authorities said they had no information to report on these three persons. Alliance Mission personnel in Ban Me Thuot were to experience more tragedy. Ruth Wilting, Daniel Gerber's fiancé, was one of six missionaries killed in the 1968 Tet Offensive.

After the war, the United States established a program with the Vietnamese government to search for missing American military and civilian personnel. Decades after Daniel's abduction, the Gerber family was given fourteen pages of unclassified material dated November 1992 from the Department of Defense POW-MIA Central Documentation Office which documents an investigation carried out by a Joint Investigation Team from October 22 to November 18, 1992.

The joint Vietnamese American team interviewed a total of twelve witnesses "who provided primarily hearsay concerning the abduction and subsequent killings of three civilian missionaries from a Leprosarium near Buon Ea Ana Village in 1962." The team interviewed persons who acknowledged being part of the party that kidnapped the three. Apparently the guerrillas had received orders from higher authorities to capture and execute three American missionaries who were suspected spies for the U.S. Central Intelligence Agency. The operation involved three separate teams: a security team to protect the area around the leprosarium, a political team to propagandize the residents of the leprosarium, and an execution team to capture and execute the suspected American spies.

No one interviewed admitted to being part of the execution team. However, there was significant hearsay testimony that as the three captives were marched away from the leprosarium, the older man was injured when he fell into punji sticks near the trail and died or was killed and buried there. This area is now tilled farming land. Those interviewed said the other two captives were marched further away and across the Ea Krong River where they were killed and buried. All this presumably took place a short time after their abduction. The joint search team was unable to locate and identify any human remains.

North American Mennonites invariably compare Gerber's disappearance to that of Clayton Kratz, a colleague of Orie O. Miller with the fledgling MCC, who in 1920 was taken prisoner during the civil conflict in Russia and never returned home.

TURBULENCE 1963

Chapter 17

The military conflict intensified in 1963. Many village and hamlet officials were being kidnapped or assassinated, and the government armed forces were suffering many casualties. The 11,000 American military advisors and support personnel providing transportation to Vietnamese units had suffered more than one hundred deaths in 1962. At the end of 1963 the United States had more than 16,500 military personnel in Vietnam with increased casualties.

On January 2, 1963, a government infantry division of 2,500 soldiers attempted to engage a Viet Cong unit at Ap Bac, a hamlet in the Mekong River Delta some sixty kilometers from Saigon. Due to ineptness by the government commanders, Army of Republic of Vietnam (ARVN) troops suffered heavy casualties. Several U.S. helicopters were downed and three Americans died. American officials voiced a growing skepticism that the Saigon government could successfully prosecute a war against the Viet Cong.

A devout Catholic, President Diem increasingly placed his trust in Catholic military officers. Tensions between Buddhist and Catholic religious communities were highest in the city of Hue, Diem's ancestral home, where his brother, Ngo Dinh Thuc, was archbishop. Another brother was a power in regional politics.

When in May 1963 thousands of Buddhists gathered in Hue to celebrate Vesak, the birthday of Gautama Buddha, a local official forbade them to fly the Buddhist flag, even though the Vatican flag was prominently displayed the previous week at a Catholic celebration. This sparked a confrontation resulting in nine deaths, seven of them children, and further exacerbated anti-government feelings, spawning large street demonstrations in Hue and other cities in the South.

These demonstrations confirmed the growing rift between the President and the populace. On June 11 a Buddhist monk, Thich Quang Duc, immolated himself on a major Saigon street intersection. *Associated Press* photographer Malcolm Browne's photograph of this self-immolation caught international attention. When other burnings followed, Vietnam's First Lady Mme. Nhu added fuel to the fire by mocking the *bonzes* who "barbecued" themselves.

Unrest and demonstrations continued. After declaring

The First Lady with Ambassador and Mrs. Nolting.

128

martial law, government troops on August 21 raided Buddhist temples in Saigon, jailing hundreds of Buddhist monks and nuns, students and citizens, causing many casualties. Schools were closed. In response, the Foreign Minister, a Buddhist, resigned. Tran Van Chuong, Vietnam's ambassador to Washington and father of First Lady Mme. Nhu, also denounced Diem's crackdown and resigned.

As this was happening, U.S. President John F. Kennedy tapped Henry Cabot Lodge to replace Frederic Nolting as ambassador. Nolting was known as a firm supporter of President Diem and this change signaled a U.S. willingness to support Diem's ouster if he did not make significant changes, including removing his brother Nhu as chief political advisor. Ambassador Lodge knew that several top generals were already plotting a coup d'état against President Diem.

On November 1, 1963, the generals besieged the Gia Long Palace in Central Saigon. President Diem eventually capitulated and he and his brother Nhu were assassinated. Saigon erupted in celebration as thousands of monks, students and political prisoners were released from detention. The armed forces set up the Revolutionary Military Committee headed by General Dương Van Minh to run the country and named a civilian former vice president, Nguyen Ngoc Tho, as premier. Although U.S. officials publicly disavowed support for the coup, Ambassador Lodge informed President Kennedy that they had prepared the ground for the "coup seed" to grow.

At the beginning of 1963 the Vietnam Mennonite Mission was involved in renovating the headquarters facilities at 336 Phan Thanh Gian Street. The missionaries who had arrived in September continued their full-time language studies.

In a January letter home James Metzler described language study "like a bottomless pit [that] swallows hours in gulps but never gives evidence that they ever existed. . . . It takes hours just to review all the words and sentences that we've studied so far. . . . It is both heart-rending and soul-searching to hear a string of words that sound as familiar as your name, yet your mind and face goes completely blank and you can't think of a thing!"

The following week James, under "the pressures of language study" and with the counsel of the older missionaries, decided to slow the pace a bit. Since James and Rachel were living with Mary and me, it was inevitable that we would compare ourselves with one another. James observed that "language learning is easier for the Martins; they don't view it as a task or work!"

Mary was making good progress and had a good accent. Growing up bilingual—English and Pennsylvania German—Mary now recognized was a great blessing. She had also studied German in high school. I, too, had foreign language experience in Europe. Mary had a keen musical ear—much better than mine, an aid in learning the Vietnamese tonal language. The northern dialect or accent has six tones. The southern dialect has five—combining two of the tones. Although I was learning the phonemes—the sounds of this monosyllabic language—I had great difficulty in distinguishing the difference in tones between *bán, ban, bản, bàn,* and *bạn* (sell, grant, copy, table, and friend)! Even after six months of language study, Mary silently wondered whether her husband would ever be able to speak the language correctly. Language study was hard work for all of us.

We were encouraged to take breaks. A ten-day vacation with Carl and Phyllis Yoder at Nha Trang was very helpful for James and Rachel. James and I observed that Rachel and Mary had some advantages in being able to relate closely with *Cô Nam* (Miss Five), our cook.

When Cô Nam took a maternity leave mid-year, we ate *cơm tháng* (food by the month). Every noon a delivery boy brought prepared food in four aluminum kettles stacked upon each other held together by a frame with a handle. One kettle would have fish or meat, another vegetables, another soup. The largest one was filled with steamed white rice. We ate more rice than we had ever eaten before, often reheating rice for breakfast with fried eggs. We eventually told the delivery boy to cut back on the rice. On Sundays we ate in restaurants.

At the first Sunday morning worship service in 1963 at the Saigon youth center, James Stauffer spoke on the biblical principles of giving and the first offering was taken. The missionaries had not passed the offering plate before—concerned that people might think the foreign missionaries were trying to extract money from the people.

The first two baptized believers, Phuoc and Luc, had been instructed one-on-one before baptism. In mid-February James Stauffer began teaching a catechism class with seven persons present. A week later, two of them, Mr. Hung and Ms. Nguyet, made public their decision to follow Jesus Christ.

James Metzler wrote home about this:

> This past week there have been two more students who have told us that they have decided for Christ. We marvel at the quiet yet certain manner in which the Spirit draws His own to Himself. Students begin in the English classes and learn about Christ. As confidence is built, they begin attending Sunday services. After a while—sometimes a year or two—they give evidence of conviction. The actual step is often in their homes, then they tell us, begin to "move in" with the believers' group and soon give a public testimony. Of course, it is not easy or automatic. Some who seemed to understand the best and we thought were closest to decision, just linger along. And a number who have made a decision have not gone on. But we rejoice for those who have taken their stand.

Around the dinner table we four junior missionaries discussed practices that would reflect a Christian lifestyle in Vietnam. Mindful that Lancaster Mennonite Conference required women to wear a head covering taught by the Apostle Paul (I Corinthians 11), we questioned whether this was appropriate in Vietnam. Although the missionary women wore the traditional Vietnamese *aó dài* dress, they still wore the covering. Committed to the belief that following Jesus meant loving even enemies, our much greater concern was the response of young men drafted for the armed forces.

The war became more personal for us when on March 4 two missionaries with Summer Institute of Linguistics (SIL – Wycliffe Bible Translators) were killed; James and Arlene Stauffer had just visited them a few days earlier. Two families were traveling from Saigon to Da Lat—three kilometers from Dinh Quan—when their vehicle was stopped at a Viet Cong checkpoint. At the sound of a distant shot by a government soldier, the guerrillas opened fire, killing Elwood Jacobsen, Gaspar Makil and one of Makil's four-month-old twin daughters. Makil's three-year-old son was also shot in the leg. The women were not injured. Their deaths now made it clear that missionaries were not exempt from the war. People wondered whether the killings were deliberate or some "mistake." (The story of missionary deaths in Vietnam is told by James C. Hefley in *By Life or By Death* (Grand Rapids: Zondervan, 1969).)

We six Mennonite missionaries—Stauffers, J. Metzlers, and Martins—were invited to sing at the memorial service held in a small U.S. air base chapel at Saigon's Tan Son Nhat Airport, officiated by C&MA Mission Leader T. Grady Mangham. It was attended mostly by missionaries and diplomatic personnel, including U.S. Ambassador Nolting. Jacobsen's body was buried in the Tin Lanh Cemetery near Saigon, while the bodies of Makil and his daughter were flown to his native Philippines.

Mary wrote home: "We are *not* afraid. We only sense again how fragile and uncertain this life is and praise [God] that we can commit ourselves to Him. We have no desire to leave Vietnam. Our hearts are here as much as ever. We *know* God has brought us here and that we are his whether by life or by death. We only seek to bring glory by our lives in our everyday tasks."

In mid-March Vietnamese government officials were angered by a report from the U.S. Senate Majority Leader Mike Mansfield who described conditions in Vietnam as no better than seven years earlier—despite two billion dollars in U.S. aid! Officers with the U.S. Military Assistance Command-Vietnam (MAC-V) were also disturbed since they had spoken of substantial progress in the previous year.

Schooled in the Mennonite understanding of non-resistance in the face of violence, I struggled to find an appropriate perspective on the growing military conflict: "One cannot trust both in the sword and in the power of God," I wrote home. "Perhaps it is only when we live in troubled conditions that we can learn this. I cannot believe that God would abandon Vietnam to communism. Yet even Israel [in Old Testament history] suffered at the hands of nations more evil than herself. I think we should pray that we will be able to continue to preach the message of peace here and even in the North."

In March my language teacher, Chau Hong Luc, returned from a visit to his home area in the Delta's Ben Tre Province and told of a Christian killed by the Viet Cong when suspected of giving information to government personnel. Another Christian was killed in crossfire by govern-

Burial of SIL linguist Elwood Jacobsen.

ment troops. The country people were becoming pawns in the conflict. Both sides demanded allegiance. To refuse could bring death.

The government, under the direction of the President's brother, Ngo Dinh Nhu, was building many "strategic hamlets" all over the country. The purpose of these fortified communities was to isolate the people from the Viet Cong and make it easier for the people to defend themselves from Viet Cong attacks. However, in many cases they made people more vulnerable during VC attacks and provided opportunities for the guerrillas to seize weapons.

Everett and Margaret Metzler returned late March after six months in the States. Mary wrote in her diary: "We've been asking ourselves many questions: questions about our continued involvement in work at the [Student] Center; questions about the value of our contribution there in the past months; questions about the slow progress of the work to this point and the outlook for the future; questions about the outlook of the country politically; questions about the relevance of the Christian faith to many of these people. Yes, even that."

Two more young men were baptized on Easter Sunday, April 14, Lich and Hung. Lich, in his early twenties, supported himself and his aged mother with a good job grinding lenses for an optician. He gave evidence to a growing Christian experience since his conversion in October. Hung, a bit younger, did not tell his family about his decision to follow Jesus Christ until a week before the planned baptism, and his father expressed disapproval. In his testimony, with tears in his eyes, Hung said he believed that he should obey God even over and above his parents. At the end of April Hung and Luc went to Vinh Long Evangelical Church to study in the annual four-week Bible school.

Construction of the headquarters property began mid-April. During that time the Everett Metzler family lived with the Stauffers in a rented property near the airport. English classes were cancelled but the Friday evening prayer meetings and Sunday services met in Dakao area where we younger missionaries lived.

In late April Mary and I vacationed ten days in the Central Vietnam city of Hue, staying with Ethel and Samuel Yoder, a Goshen College professor who was teaching at the University of Hue. They were the parents of Phyllis Yoder, a nurse in Nha Trang. In Hue we visited Robert and Mildred Davis, C&MA missionaries who were training a core of students in evangelistic ministry.

While we were in Hue, Rudy Lichti came to review MCC Material Aid Distribution Programs and invited us to go with him to Quang Tri where we met C&MA missionaries Leroy and Nancy Josephson. This was near the seventeenth parallel demarcation line between the North and South. We then traveled west on Highway #9 to Khe Sanh where we met Wycliffe linguists John and Carolyn Miller and on to the Lao border at Lao Bao where we stayed overnight in a pastor's home. Along the way we made a brief stop at the Cam Phu home of Worldwide Evangelization Crusade missionaries Roy and Daphne Spraggett; the following January the Spraggetts were injured when their house was blown up by explosives.

The government confrontation with the Buddhists on May 8 occurred the week after we flew home from Hue. Many Buddhist leaders did not support the militant anti-communist stance of the Diem regime, wanting to resolve the growing armed conflict politically. Interpreting the government repression in religious terms, they demonstrated in Hue, Saigon and other cities. On June 11 around 400 Buddhist monks marched in Saigon to the intersection of Le Van Duyet and Phan Dinh Phung Streets, a few blocks from the Mennonite Center, where Thich Quang Duc immolated himself. James Stauffer had gone downtown for business on his scooter and came upon this macabre scene before the police arrived.

The Buddhist struggle for greater recognition continued. In Saigon many demonstrations were staged at the Xa Loi Pagoda also located near the Mennonite Center. Riding bicycles or scooters from our home in the Dakao area, we often saw demonstrations and tried to avoid them.

High school students often stopped by our home after school to practice English, although now we wanted to practice speaking Vietnamese. Some students stopped visiting us when we insisted on speaking Vietnamese. Once a student friend persisted in speaking English, I doggedly continued speaking Vietnamese; neither of us would give an inch! Some students asked us to explain the Bible to them in English, arguing that they could understand it better in English than in Vietnamese. There was some truth to that assertion; many people were not familiar with some terms in the Vietnamese Bible.

Xa Loi Pagoda.

Buddha statue at Xa Loi Pagoda.

A friend from Mary's home community developed a friendship with a Buddhist student studying at New York City's Columbia University. When Nguyen Thi Hong returned to Vietnam with her master's degree in education, we invited her to our home for dinner in early April. Hong was busy in Saigon, teaching, translating educational materials and helping to prepare national high school exams.

A few months later Hong told Mary that she was planning to join the Catholic Church and then marry her fiancé, Tran Nhu Chuong. Both Hong and Chuong came from Hue. Their planned marriage surprised us, especially in the midst of the ongoing inter-religious Buddhist-Catholic conflict in Hue. James, Rachel, Mary, and I attended their wedding reception in Saigon in late July and their church wedding the following day. Mary and I continued a warm friendship with their family throughout our years in Vietnam.

The rebuilding of the Saigon Center property was completed by mid-August at a cost of around

$9,000 U.S. The public facilities were upstairs—a large meeting room capable of seating 150 people, a reading room, and a classroom. The large meeting room could be partitioned into classrooms. The outside stairway went up to the third floor patio, partially under roof, where students could go for study or recreation.

Everett and Margaret and their three children moved into the first floor of this house on August 21, the day President Diem declared martial law and his special military forces violently raided Xa Loi and other Buddhist temples and jailed more than a thousand Buddhist monks. The planned September 1 dedication service for the student center was postponed because students were reluctant to gather at such a large venue for fear of being arrested. A 9:00 p.m. to 6:00 a.m. curfew also kept people off the streets. Schools were closed.

Informing the home office that Saigon was under "strict military rule," Everett wrote: "The Buddhist struggle has become political and the government has allowed some very brutal things to happen in the raiding of pagodas and suppression of demonstrations. Our best source of information is the Voice of America and eyewitnesses to some of the events. Last Sunday morning a very upset young man was in our services. Afterwards he asked that we pray for him. Three of his friends were killed at Hue in riots."

Although Everett admitted the political climate was "quite unstable," he still urged the Donald and Doris Sensenig family to travel to Vietnam as planned. "We continue confident of the Lord's intentions for us to be here as his witnesses," Everett wrote. "We count on the Church's prayers."

The Mennonite missionaries not only related closely with MCC personnel, but also kept in touch with the Mennonite volunteers in International Voluntary Service. Carl and Phyllis Yoder, and IVSers Gene Stoltzfus, Willie Myers, and John Witmer were at a Saturday evening gathering mid-August at the Stauffer home; James, Rachel, Mary and I invited the IVS men to our home for lunch on Sunday.

Stoltzfus and Myers had just arrived in country in July. Phuoc, the first baptized believer, had left his interpretation job with Dr. Yoder and was now working with IVS near Da Lat. He was shaken up a few months later when the Jeep they used was shot up, injuring the driver. The attackers asked where the American and his interpreter were—they said they wanted to kill them.

Don and Doris Sensenig arrived with two-year-old Anne and four-and-a-half-month-old Lynne on September 6, 1963, after being diverted to Thailand due to a coup attempt in Saigon. Both Doris Mellinger and Donald Sensenig were from Lancaster County, Pennsylvania. Both graduated from Lancaster Mennonite High School and Eastern Mennonite College. They had just completed a two-year voluntary service assignment in New York City where Don took courses at New York Theological Seminary, graduating from New York University. Their arrival raised the Mennonite Mission personnel to ten, only one-half the missionary personnel that Orie Miller had envisioned in 1956 but now considered by the Mission Board as a full contingent.

The Sensenig family moved into a house in the Phu Nhuan area where Everett and Margaret and family had lived when the Center property was being rebuilt. Characteristic of the humor that Don brought to the missionary team, Don told of giving money to their cook helper, *Cô Do*, to "buy some dysentery" at the vegetable market! Assuming that food bought there might be contaminated with bacteria, we all had to exercise care.

The new facilities at the Saigon Center were dedicated on Sunday, September 22. Pastor Doan Van Mieng, the Tin Lanh Church President, preached the dedicatory sermon. Among the

Mennonite Mission Headquarters and Saigon Student Center.

160 persons who attended were many Tin Lanh pastors. On Saturday afternoon 125 persons came out to an informal tea. The English language classes had already begun with more than 200 students—most of them high school and university students. The Gospel of Mark was used as the text in some of the advanced classes.

The struggle between the Saigon government and the Buddhist community intensified. With the United States assuming a growing political and military involvement, we missionaries became aware that we were viewed as Americans.

"As we returned home one evening," Mary and I wrote to friends late September, "a woman stopped at our gate asking if we would help her. We invited her into the living room. Sobbing, she told how the monks at her pagoda were forced to leave and were replaced by unknown monks"— likely government agents. The woman asked us to do something about this wrong! A few days later when we were downtown, at the rear of a shop a distressed mother and her son described the arrests that morning of hundreds of high school students.

"You probably sense the situations we face because we happen to be Americans," we wrote. "We want to sympathize with those who are troubled. We must also try to understand the intentions of this government, which have sometimes been misrepresented. Yet, in this time of crisis, we want to be faithful in proclaiming the message of the kingdom of God."

A rather bizarre incident involving the Alliance Mission and the Evangelical Church occurred late September. A Vietnam Press release in the English daily, *The Times of Vietnam,* reported that a delegation of three missionary leaders and two pastors, including the Evangelical Church President, had paid a visit to the Gia Long Palace and presented a written statement to President Ngo Dinh Diem praising his "wisdom and strong faith," expressing "absolute loyalty" to him and promising to continue to pray for him, his government, and the armed forces.

A small group had indeed visited the President, but Revelle, the Mission Chairman, maintained that they had not written the statement and that he refused to read it to the President when asked to do so. When the press refused to print a retraction of that article, the Church in its periodical assured pastors and others in a strongly worded statement that the delegation did not present the statement to the President as the local press reported.

"We are trying to avoid becoming worked up by such incidents," Everett wrote our Mission Secretary, "but find it difficult not to be interested in the political affairs that affect the lives of our friends and fellow Christians."

By the beginning of October the atmosphere in Saigon seemed more normal and martial law was lifted. Ambassador Lodge, however, was aware that some military commanders were still plotting to remove President Diem from power.

James and Rachel and Mary and I were now in Vietnam a full year. Don was studying Vietnamese with Luc, our former teacher. With young children to care for, Doris was only studying part-time. I continued my study with Dang Thai Hung, a Christian young man from Central Vietnam. We were learning much about Vietnamese life from those with whom we regularly interacted—our household helpers, our teachers, and the students who came to visit us.

In mid-October Mary and I took a vacation in Nha Trang, staying at the MCC unit house with the Yoders. Phyllis was busy helping Carl in the clinic; Marva Hasselblad was on a three-week vacation with her sister in India. I had taken along Tolstoy's *War and Peace*, but most of the time Mary and I just relaxed in the house by the sea—framed on one side by a sweeping mountain range and on the other with the huge jumble of rocks that is *Hòn Chồng*.

Mary wrote in her diary: "How could one describe this lovely spot! It seems that the wonder of it nearly cast a spell on me for several days. I couldn't settle down to do any of the things I wanted to cross off the list. I could only sit and drink in all the grandeur." It was just like others had said—it seemed that a sick person could here be restored to health without any medical intervention. When seeking relief from stress throughout the following decades of life, Mary's thoughts transport her back to this magnificent beachside setting.

Pham Xuan Tin, the Chairman of the Tin Lanh Clinic Board of Directors and professor at the newly-relocated Bible Institute, showed us around the seminary located on the hill above the clinic. Though the dormitories had room for 200, there were currently only seventy students; national conscription was cutting into the eligible student pool. Students spent two years in residence at the school. After an in-service practicum of a year or two with an organized congregation they returned for their third year of classes. After graduation they would be commissioned as *truyền đạo* (evangelist) and assigned to lead a new congregation or assist a pastor in a large congregation. Only after a few years' experience at the age of thirty with the affirmation of the congregation and church district could they be ordained as *mục sư* (pastor). The role in each position was essentially the same, except that the *truyền đạo* had more limited responsibilities in conducting religious ceremonies.

In late October, Robert Miller reported to Rudy Lichti that USAID officials in Washington had asked MCC to consider expanding American food distribution in Vietnam. Akron was willing to do this only on the basis of Lichti's own investigation of need and ability to respond. If expanding, Lichti was to arrange for volunteers to supervise distributions to minimize costs. However, Miller said the program would have to be "kept completely separate from the USOM program and should not be in any sense an instrument of the US government."

In October the Vietnam Mennonite Mission began having occasional "conferences" to discuss mission strategy. We were now ten persons—all living in the Saigon area. Three of the five couples were still engaged in Vietnamese language study. Writing to the home office late October, Everett reported that our team felt a need for "a more direct evangelistic thrust" in work with students, and were planning a series of evangelistic preaching services four evenings with two missionaries and two local pastors as speakers.

In spite of the anti-government agitation and persistent rumors, Everett said we had "been able to carry on normal activities at the Center." He continued:

> We are puzzled with conflicting reports concerning the political situation. I fear that I tend to lean toward the pessimistic viewpoint in evaluating [them]. We know too many individuals whose stories flatly contradict the "rosy viewpoint that all is going well" and yet one cannot easily determine what is fact and what is fabricated. We do know . . . that two students living near here were taken during the night, that one of the believers was picked up on the street on the morning of a student demonstration and detained four days along with thousands of others, that many are living in fear. The other week a former acquaintance stopped in. His emaciated body confirmed his story of a four-month imprisonment in one of the many "re-education" camps about the country. The story he told sounded almost identical to the stories of Nazi concentration camps during the war. I am inclined to believe it.

Since some of his previous letters failed to arrive in the States, Everett sent this letter by APO, the U.S. military post office.

A few days after Everett sent this letter, on November 1, a military coup d'état deposed President Ngo Dinh Diem. That Friday morning we missionaries met at our house for prayer fellowship and a business meeting. Don and Doris stayed with Mary and me for lunch.

We first heard shooting after siesta around 2:30 p.m. We went out on the balcony and saw neighbors looking up the street where a national police building was located. Small groups gathered, asking what was going on. Later we heard the roar of A-1 Skyraiders bombing and strafing targets and the answering anti-aircraft fire. By evening it seemed quieter and a friend came to visit and joyfully reported that President Diem had been ousted.

The armed forces took over the radio station, announcing that most of the armed forces were against Diem and naming the generals supporting the coup. Since gunfire continued we knew there was still opposition. It was All Souls' Day, a Catholic holiday, and our neighbors suspected that generals who supported Diem might have been away from their posts that day.

Mary wrote in her diary: "Now it's nearly 11:00 and has been quiet for at least three minutes, I believe. Gentle rain is dripping on the roof. Perhaps after a Psalm, we'll go to bed."

After reading Psalm 91 and prayers, we retired but didn't sleep until midnight. We were awakened at 3:00 a.m. Saturday morning by "huge heavy explosions" which continued for a few hours.

Co Nam, our cook, came before 9:00 a.m. saying that everyone is *vui lắm* (very happy). Since Mary and I had planned to go to the library Saturday morning, we hopped onto the scooter and went out. The library was closed, so we drove around. Many specific targets had been damaged or destroyed—an armed forces camp shot up, a radio station bombed. Pro-government newspaper offices were being sacked, and homes of hated government officials burned. At the end of Hai Bà

Trung (Two Sisters) Street, a recently-erected Hai Bà Trung statute had been shot up, one figure without a head, the other figure only dangling by its steel reinforced feet.

Vietnamese legend has it that Trung Trac, around the time of Jesus Christ, was so infuriated when the Chinese lords assassinated her husband, a landlord, that she and her sister led a revolt that briefly freed the Vietnamese from Chinese domination. The trouble with this stately statue was that it was made in the likeness of Mme. Nhu and her oldest daughter. Mme. Nhu was responsible for implementing a family law that was denounced by many, and was criticized for her unswerving support to the autocratic rule of her brother-in-law president. Fortunately Mme. Nhu was out of the country—visiting the United States.

At the grandiose post office, soldiers lounged around several tanks. Mary waited outside by the Notre Dame Cathedral while I was in the post office. She scurried behind the church when shots rang out—trigger-happy soldiers were demonstrating their weapons to young admirers.

Back home for lunch, Co Nam returned from market with a report that the President was dead! We didn't believe it since we had heard that he surrendered. That evening a short bulletin in a Vietnamese newspaper reported that the President and his brother Nhu had committed suicide. On Sunday it was reported that they died from injuries sustained in the fighting. Only later did we learn that the brothers were assassinated after surrendering.

Co Nam, more aware of political realities than many domestic helpers, was *buồn lắm* (very sad) at the demise of the President. She was almost in tears as she described how many people loved the President while they hated Nhu and his wife.

The missionary group had planned to meet at the home of Margaret and Everett on Friday evening. With the coup underway and a curfew imposed, we knew the meeting would be cancelled so stayed at home. Don and Doris Sensenig, in country only eight weeks, did not hear the curfew announcement and rode the scooter with Anne and Lynne through the vacated Saigon streets to the Saigon Center!

People accustomed to war and fighting for twenty years took the coup d'état in stride. Even though heavy tanks moved in to blast the camp of forces loyal to the President, traffic was running nearly like normal a few blocks away. Thirty-three persons were killed and 233 injured—two-thirds of them civilians. After President Diem was deposed, the national flag, flown during the Republic Day celebrations a week earlier, was now unfurled in support of the Revolutionary Military Council. Saigon appeared to be in a holiday mood.

The Ngo family was now blamed for all of Vietnam's troubles. The Military Council expressed an anti-communist line and released information purported to show that the former government had secret contact with the government of North Vietnam; presumably the North would have been willing to cease hostilities if Americans forces were withdrawn.

The Military Council permitted greater personal freedom after the coup. Yellow-robed Buddhist monks were again seen on the streets; the universities reopened. The arrests of high officials and the dismissals of others caused some administrative confusion. Most of the people, though happy about the ouster of the old government, were still non-committal about the new government, waiting to see what it accomplished.

Four nights of evangelistic preaching at the Mennonite Student Center, postponed from early September due to martial law declaration, were rescheduled to begin October 31. There was good attendance that evening but the other meetings could not be held due to the 7:00 p.m. to 5:00 a.m. curfew following the coup d'état.

Three weeks after President Diem was assassinated, on Friday, November 22, President John F. Kennedy was assassinated in Dallas, Texas. Due to the time zone difference, we learned of it Saturday morning. Like millions of other Americans, we remember what we were doing when we heard the shocking news; we missionary men were meeting at the Saigon Center for Bible study and prayer. When President Lyndon B. Johnson proclaimed November 25 a national day of mourning for all Americans, we decided that it would be proper to dismiss English classes Monday as a sign of respect. Vietnam's leaders also ordered their flag to fly at half-mast for three days. Some friends came to our home to express sorrow over Kennedy's death. Others, particularly Catholics who mourned the death of President Diem and aware of the U.S. complicity in the coup, wondered aloud whether this was the hand of divine justice.

We missionaries spent the American Thanksgiving Day evening in the Stauffer home. Margaret Metzler had just given birth to Andre Jon, their fourth child. On Friday evening we had a Thanksgiving program for students at the Center. Mary told the story of the Puritans. I introduced the program in Vietnamese—with many linguistic mistakes!

James and Rachel spent several weeks house-sitting the Da Lat home of John and Jo Newman, an Oriental Crusade couple on a short leave. After returning to Saigon, they moved into a small row house while Mary and I stayed in our Nguyen Phi Khanh Street house.

In a December 1963 *Newsletter* to friends, James and Arlene Stauffer described a growing concern: "It has been *too* long since we have seen any friends accepting Christ," they wrote, "and we are deeply concerned. We can no longer blame it on inadequate facilities or a tense political situation. Then what can be hindering the Spirit? Interest in our English classes remains good. Each Friday night on the average of 100 students come to see a film, converse in English, sing or hear a lecture and a variety of special features. However, attendance at our Sunday services is at a low ebb."

James Stauffer leading Bible study at the Saigon Student Center.

Margaret and Everett were also praying for those "who seemed to be sincerely seeking Truth, but turned away at one point or another."

Pastor Le Hoang Phu, professor at the Tin Lanh Bible Institute in Nha Trang, spoke at a series of evangelistic services at the Saigon Student Center after Christmas. We were encouraged that fifty to seventy persons attended these meetings. Several students asked questions about the Christian faith but only one person expressed a desire to follow the way of Jesus. Combining teaching and preaching with friendship evangelism, we missionaries recognized that not all would embrace the Gospel of Jesus Christ, yet believed—as in Jesus' parable of the soils—that some who heard the Word would accept it and become followers of Jesus.

Ms. Nguyen Thuy Nguyet was baptized on Sunday, December 29. She took this step against the wishes of her Catholic family. She gave witness to her growth in the Christian life. Nguyet told how she had worked in a government orphanage before the coup d'état and was accused of being a communist. Arrested, she was severely tortured in prison because she refused to sign "confessions" which would implicate her friends. With her hands tied behind her back, she was hung up by her thumbs. Other tortures impaired her hearing. Now her accusers feared she would squeal on them because of their false accusations; instead she spoke of God's forgiving love. (Many years later, after the victory of the communist forces, it was reported that Nguyet had at some point become a secret, active participant with the National Liberation Front.)

The Lichti family joined the five Mennonite missionary families Christmas Day. Rudy Lichti's year-end 1963 Viet Nam Report noted that the provisional government established by the military officers was in full control and there was now "open optimism." He wrote that the war continued "to take its toll in lives as well as [make] economic development, particularly in rural areas, next to impossible, and United States military and economic aid [continued] to prop up the economy."

Lichti reported that the medical program at Nha Trang operated at capacity under Dr. Yoder's direction. The clinic was averaging 3,000 patients monthly and the twenty-five hospital beds were usually full. The medical supplies and medications MCC purchased or imported were supplemented by donations from U.S. Operations Mission and from the U.S. Eighth Army Field Hospital in Nha Trang. Many patients from the Evangelical Clinic were taken for surgeries performed at the Field Hospital or by USOM-supplied doctors operating at the provincial hospital, with post-operative care given at the Tin Lanh Clinic.

U.S. Defense Secretary Robert McNamara came to Saigon again in late December to review the military state of affairs, his first visit after the military coup. While publicly optimistic, McNamara reported to President Johnson that the Viet Cong had seized control of more areas. If this trend were not reversed within a few months, he said it would likely lead to a "Communist-controlled state."

BOOK TWO

PARTNERSHIP
1964-1970

U.S. EXPANDS MILITARY ACTIONS 1964

Chapter 18

We five men of Mennonite Mission—Everett Metzler, James Stauffer, James Metzler, Donald Sensenig and I—continued our Saturday morning prayer and Bible study sessions. We finished reading Harold Bender's *The People of God* and were now discussing Elton Trueblood's *The Company of the Committed*. On Thursday evenings we five couples regularly met, alternating at different homes; we were currently studying the Apostle Paul's first letter to the Corinthians to see what practical principles we might learn in guiding the young Mennonite church.

In a January 1964 letter home, I expressed concern for the believers, especially one young man who had told Stauffer that he did not want to associate with us for a year. I wrote: "For all our joy at the reality of the Christian fellowship where all are committed to following after Christ, it seems so few want to join us. . . . We realize that we are not primarily called to amass huge numbers of people into a church. But we believe that if we are faithful others will want to join us in our witness to Christ."

The letter closed with an observation that every news release about the war "seems more pessimistic than the previous one. . . . We still do not know how best we can carry out the job of peacemakers."

On January 30 General Nguyen Khanh ousted the three-month-old government of Gen. Duong Van Minh and Premier Nguyen Ngoc Tho, catching U.S. policymakers by surprise. There was official American concern that Khanh might advocate neutralism. President Lyndon Johnson quickly pledged support when Khanh promised to pursue a tough strategy against the Viet Cong.

James Metzler, in the February *News and Concerns* newsletter, noted that there was now "an increasing pessimistic atmosphere. . . . Frankly, we do not know what request we should ask you to offer to God for this situation."

In her diary February 7 Mary mockingly jotted an incongruous quote by an American Congressman about the Vietnamese government's leaders: "Why don't they take our advice? If we don't know what's good for Vietnam, who does?" She wrote on: "And President Johnson said all that's needed for victory in South Vietnam is to get rid of the guerillas plaguing the people. Indeed, yes! But that's an impossibility. At least as long as the US seeks to drive them away by force. They can't be driven away because they live here. They're citizens of this land."

After a student demonstration in Saigon demanded that Gen. Duong Van Minh be returned to power, on February 8 Khanh announced a government with himself as premier and Gen. Minh as a figurehead chief of state. New Year, *Têt Nguyên Đán*, followed five days later.

One day in early February I went by the Tan Dinh Catholic Church a few blocks from home and listened to a priest's homily to several hundred people. As I walked home by the scooter repair shop I met the mechanic who repaired our vehicle. He asked me to sit down, so we talked for nearly a half hour. With eleven children, he told how he had a hard time making ends meet; he was worried that his children could not get the education they needed. Though all children could get a basic sixth-grade education, a child had to be really brainy or have money to get into middle and high school, he explained.

When I told my mechanic friend that I wanted to more fully understand Vietnamese life, he said I was not willing to do this—live on the food they eat, have our children run around with torn clothing, unable to go to school! When I told him I would be willing to suffer some things, he replied, "When difficulty comes you'll get on a ship and leave!" It was difficult to argue with him.

Paul Kraybill and Donald Lauver visited Vietnam in mid-February. Kraybill's last visit had been two years earlier. Lauver was Lancaster Mennonite Conference Bishop's Representative to churches in Asia established by Eastern Mennonite Board of Missions. We missionaries had heard stories of how bishops once attempted to insure that new believers in east Africa followed the lifestyles expected of members in America, so we did not know what to anticipate from Lauver. We were pleased to find him very understanding and supportive.

Sunday, February 16, the day after the two men arrived, became a day long remembered. I was using Everett's new 50 cc motorcycle and had come to the Saigon Center for the morning worship service, parked and locked the bike. When I came downstairs to leave it was gone; I had failed to attach the heavy chain and padlock!

After this worship service, Kraybill and Lauver went with most of the missionary families to the late morning worship service at the International Protestant Church which was then meeting in the Kinh Do Theater, several blocks from the Center. Afterward our visitors took Rudi and Elda Lichti and the five missionary families out to lunch. In the afternoon we had a communion and footwashing service at the Center which included Phuoc, Luc and Lich.

Lauver spoke at the evening service at the Center. At 7:45 p.m. we heard a series of explosions which targeted Kinh Đô Theater where we had been that morning. Three Americans and one Vietnamese person were killed and fifty persons were injured. This incident occurred a week after another explosion at a ballpark near the airport killed two Americans.

Writing home about these attacks, I said: "We are not worried. Our trust is in God. We do not want to handle our lives recklessly, but neither will we run at all danger. . . . I would rather sacrifice a little for the cause of Christ and the Church. After all, men are giving their lives for less noble causes."

Kraybill wrote in his Deputation Diary:

> One sees abundant evidence of the grisly and grim war that is tearing at the heart of this country and which is spreading fear, terror, destruction, and despair and uncertainty, and the future is bleak and somewhat hopeless. We face here a more uncertain and unpredictable situation than on any of our other fields. The change in government, the deteriorating security, the incessant progress of the Communist guerrillas, and the vicious counter attacks by the government forces supported by the United States army are leaving their scars on the people and one feels helpless and heartbroken that this country of fine, intelligent, gracious, and friendly people must be so caught up in such a deplorable and tragic situation. . . .
>
> The task here is difficult. After one and one-half years of constant language study, a missionary is only beginning to speak publically in Vietnamese. Urban work is difficult. One needs to find ways of relating to people in this complex, urban situation. . . . The more receptive group here seems to be the young people, but many of them are extremely busy because of schoolwork and often distracted and confused by the political situation. It is gratifying, however, to realize how many friends have been made and how many very warm relationships have been established and not a few . . . have expressed themselves as believers and are receiving further instruction.

We discussed a possible focused evangelistic witness in the Dakao area of Saigon where we lived. In her diary, Mary asked, "Are we being aggressive in our witness? In what ways can we be aggressive but not offensive?" Hung, my language teacher, had little appreciation for our approach to sharing the Gospel of Jesus: He said we should go from house to house, seeking to evangelize, rather than expecting that anyone would come to us. We were not convinced that this was the most appropriate approach.

Kraybill and Lauver left for Hong Kong on February 19. In his diary that day, Kraybill wrote: "One leaves Saigon unable to be very confident about the future. For the people this grinding war with its brutality seems more and more futile and frustrating. . . . It seems clear that the United States policy will probably change, but whether US will step up the war with American troops or accept neutralization is still impossible to predict." Kraybill hoped that leaders would embrace a policy of neutralism that might "keep the door open for missions for a few more years." He could not have imagined that this war would continue for another decade.

Three days later Kraybill returned to Saigon for several more days to interact with MCC administrators, Executive Secretary William Snyder and Associate Director of Relief Wilbert Shenk, during their one-week visit.

Five years earlier Kraybill had asked whether two Mennonite agencies could effectively work together in Vietnam. It was now clear that there was a happy relationship. Snyder viewed Kraybill as "one of the most creative mission leaders in the Mennonite church," and enjoyed working with him. "Out here where Christians are outnumbered so drastically, we must learn to work together even more than we do back home," Snyder wrote.

Snyder observed that the war was "not going well" for the Saigon government; he predicted that the war would intensify and that the United States would become more prominently involved.

Snyder met with many officials of the Vietnamese government, U.S. Agency for International Development, and voluntary organizations, and spent significant time with personnel of International Voluntary Services (IVS), the agency he served as board chairman. IVS first came to Vietnam in 1957, and was primarily involved in community development and educational services. Snyder was surprised to learn from Don Luce, IVS Vietnam Chief of Party, that fifteen former IVS personnel continued to work in Vietnam with USAID after they completed their two-year IVS assignments.

Three Mennonite men were working with IVS in Vietnam in 1964, all graduates of Goshen College: John Witmer, Eugene Stoltzfus and Willie Myers. Snyder met with them "to determine how they [were] getting on and particularly whether the war situation [was] creating any problems in their Christian pacifist position." He learned that the men had been asked to carry sidearms which they refused to do. This then became the IVS position, Snyder explained, due to "the simple logic that carrying arms would do very little good and might even make it more difficult if on their many trips into the country they were picked up by the Viet Cong." The young men discussed problems relating to the military forces. "IVS is a terrific test for the Christian pacifist in a military situation," Snyder said, "but these men are carrying on well." Snyder encouraged the men to maintain relationships with MCC and the Mennonite Mission personnel.

In a letter to Orie Miller, Snyder wrote: "These IVS men have come through far better than I anticipated, and their association with the military has made them even more convinced in their

Christian pacifism. I think we have a rather good group in IVS, but such an assignment is only for the very strong."

Snyder and Shenk visited MCC's "topnotch" medical program in Nha Trang, the bakery in Saigon, and reviewed all aspects of MCC work with Rudy Lichti. "Our program is known all over the country and is fully accepted by the Vietnamese church, other missions, and the Mennonite mission," Snyder reported. "It is good to realize that MCC is looked upon as a strong ally, and I believe that we should continue in the country but keeping it under constant review because the next year will be one of significant change either toward neutralization or toward increased tempo of the war. In any event, the Vietnamese people will stand in need of the kind of assistance that we are giving and the churches will also appreciate our being there with them."

In a letter to the Akron office, Snyder expressed praise for terminating director Rudi Lichti's good administration. But with MCC's proposal to move into more social services, Snyder said it would be helpful to have a director "of the Paul Longacre type."

Snyder and Shenk recommended that the Mennonite Mission develop an MCC Family Child Assistance sponsorship program—to be approved by the Minister of Social Action. This would eventually be implemented at a community center in Gia Dinh, Saigon's smaller twin city to the northeast.

Don Sensenig, in the March *News and Concerns*, summed up the visit of Kraybill and Lauver: "We sought their counsel on such problems as giving a peace witness in a country at war, the relation of the mission to the developing church, how to complement and work with the existing national church. We appreciated very much their thoughtful suggestions. . . . Together we made some plans for expansion."

Since we already had a student center, Kraybill proposed a new community-centered ministry which would include English language classes but with a stronger focus on ministering to needy families—likely through a child day-care program. Bible study classes and worship services would, of course, be central. Kraybill also proposed that the Mission assign personnel to specific areas of ministry such as student services and literature.

Kraybill encouraged us with a meditation and prayer the evening before he left. Mary wrote in her diary a few days later:

> He pointed out two things for us to keep in mind. The Gospel is communicated in an atmosphere of love. We need not go about acting like we have what everyone else wants and therewith preaching it to them. But our contacts . . . must show love.
>
> We should not be dismayed by the lack of response we'd like to see. This reaction in effect says the program is ours and we must bear some shame for its lack of effectiveness or success. If it is truly God's work we will continue sowing in faith with our eyes on Him and not on how the results are turning out.

Kraybill emphasized demonstrating "love in action." In an uncertain future in Vietnam, Kraybill indicated "the time may come when we are forbidden to preach. Then our presence alone will speak of God's love."

A Vietnam presence. Yes. We would continue to foster relationships in an effort to share the Good News of the kingdom of God. We would continue to invite Vietnamese pastors and other Christians from the Tin Lanh Church to preach evangelistic sermons. We would continue to teach the scriptures and preach, inviting people to accept the claims of the gospel. But in this war-torn land that would soon see hundreds of thousands of American GIs overrun the country, we would eventually view our mission a bit differently. It is not that we were ever forbidden to preach. But the times challenged us to share the Gospel of peace in appropriate ways.

Although the Anabaptist movement of sixteenth-century Europe—the forerunner of the Mennonite churches—was uncompromisingly evangelistic, severe persecution influenced the survivors to pursue a quieter witness which continued into the nineteenth century in North America. Then American Mennonites followed other churches in proclaiming the Gospel of Jesus Christ in other lands.

Our passion in Vietnam was not to "save souls," but to enable people to hear and accept the gospel which would transform their lives and guide them in becoming faithful followers of Jesus Christ and witnesses to his love.

More than seven centuries earlier, St. Francis of Assisi reputedly said: "Preach the Gospel and if you must, use words." While not discounting the value of large public preaching campaigns, we Mennonite missionaries—in this time and place—were more comfortable with friendship evangelism. "Friendship Evangelism" was championed within the Mennonite churches by Arthur G. McPhee in his book by that title (Grand Rapids: Zondervan, 1978). Mission as "presence" is articulated by Calvin E. Shenk in *A Relevant Theology of Presence* (Elkhart, IN: Mission Focus, 1982).

The acting director of the Eastern Mennonite Board of Missions missionary team in Somalia had been stabbed to death in July 1962 by a *mullah*, a trained religious leader. It was clear that the only way the mission there could continue was through an evangelism of "presence." Kraybill likely had this in mind when he articulated the validity of "presence evangelism."

Vietnam was not Somalia. In Vietnam we were free to proclaim the Gospel of Jesus Christ through various methods—public preaching, community visitation, literature distribution and other ways—and we did. But with the growing and ever more dominating U.S. military forces in Vietnam, our missionary team—all of us Americans—felt the need to distance ourselves from that strong political and military presence. Many of our friends from other mission agencies welcomed the American GIs. Vietnamese opinion was divided. Some of our Vietnamese friends welcomed the growing American involvement in Vietnam—others strongly opposed American policy. There was still the legacy of Western colonization melded to the spread of the Christianity. Many Vietnamese associated the Evangelical Christian faith with the United States of America in the same way they connected the Catholic Christian faith to colonial France. We did not want to perpetuate that relationship. While we could not avoid being seen as Americans, we wanted to develop ministries demonstrating caring concern for people and in that context proclaim the essence of the gospel. A phrase used by Marshall McLuhan in 1964, "The medium is the message," resonated with us at that time. A message reinforced by a military presence is not the Gospel of Jesus Christ.

President Johnson was in office only three months when, at the end of February as U.S. Secretary of Defense Robert McNamara returned from Vietnam, he and his staff reviewed various possible responses to the Vietnam issue inherited from the Kennedy administration. There was a clear assessment that the Viet Cong forces had made significant gains in the months following the overthrow of President Diem. While publically predicting that most of the military advisors could be withdrawn from Vietnam the following year, the Department of Defense was drawing up plans to attack North Vietnam and had already authorized clandestine operations by South Vietnamese forces. Johnson did not want to allow a communist state to expand on his watch.

James Metzler, in a February 19 letter to *Missionary Messenger*, wrote: "Regarding the current political situation, even if we could accurately describe it, it's likely to be quite different by the time you read this. . . . Many of our Vietnamese friends express their opinions with one word, *lộn xộn,* which means just that—confusion."

In early March the U.S. Defense Chief made another fact-finding trip to Vietnam with General Maxwell Taylor, the Chairman of the Joint Chiefs of Staff of the armed forces. Besides conferring with Vietnamese and American officials, on March 9 McNamara went to the countryside to demonstrate support for Gen. Khanh. The March 20, 1964, issue of *Time Magazine* describes this well:

> McNamara and Khanh took off on a barnstorming tour, crisscrossing the guerrilla-infested Mekong Delta and hitting three provincial centers in one day. Their plane was trailed by another carrying two squads of Vietnamese paratroopers, who were to be dropped to protect the V.I.P.s had they been forced down, and was escorted by a half-dozen AD6 fighters. On the ground the pair plunged into a round of grassroots politicking that left locals gasping. At Can Tho, 80 miles southwest of Saigon, McNamara and Khanh ignored a blazing oil-storage tank—set afire by Viet Cong mortars only the night before—and drove to the town square. There McNamara and General Maxwell Taylor, chairman of the US Joint Chiefs of Staff, each grabbed one of Khanh's stubby arms high in a victory salute. McNamara then wowed the crowd by shouting lustily three times in Vietnamese: "Viet Nam muon nam"! (Viet Nam forever). The act proved such a crowd-pleaser that the barnstormers repeated it everywhere.

McNamara's declaration was actually comical amusement for the crowds who were summoned by authorities to gather in the town centers to meet the celebrities. We who studied the Vietnamese language had learned the dangers of pronouncing phonemes with an incorrect accent. Instead of what he wished to say, *Việt Nam Muôn Năm!* (Long Live Vietnam!), McNamara was declaring, *Vịt nam muốn nằm!* (The southern duck wants to lie down!). Vietnamese newspapers reported his mispronunciation which, ironically, expressed the sentiments of many people who wanted an end to the war.

I preached my first Vietnamese sermon on Sunday evening, March 1, at the Saigon Student Center. I had prepared this fifteen-minute sermon weeks in advance with the help of my language teacher, had recorded and listened to it, and had preached it at least thirty times! I was feeling more at home in the Vietnamese language, though the tones were still giving me a bit of trouble. That evening Mary added a page to my letter home: "Now [Luke's] sermon is history. In my biased opinion it was very good—he gave it naturally and with ease. And he should have after saying it so often! . . . Some others complemented him on it, too."

Mary gave her first public speech at the Student Center a few months later on Sunday evening, May 10. In a letter home, she expressed delight that we could now speak and be understood!

Don and Doris were also progressing well in language study, even though they had a special challenge with two small children. And Anne was now speaking Vietnamese she learned from the babysitter and neighbor playmates. James, Rachel, Mary and I continued

Children's activities at Dakao house.

our study, spending more time preparing speeches and conversing with our tutors about various aspects of Vietnamese culture. Mary also agreed to coordinate a program of children's activities that Phuoc and Luc were planning in our home. While we were delighted at our ability to converse with friends, there were times when we were still unable to express a simple idea correctly.

Formal Sunday morning worship services began at the Saigon Student Center in March. Everett preached on Psalm 73 on March 15, and James Metzler preached his first Vietnamese language sermon that evening on the blind man who received his sight. James described the sermon to his parents as "more-or-less successful."

In a letter home, James told of showing Bible films borrowed from the Baptist Mission. Aware of the difficulties in communicating effectively, he wrote: "To most of [the students] it just sounds like the myths and legends that they have heard about Buddha or their national heroes. But to those who will believe, it becomes the precious truth that saves."

After General Khanh announced plans to draft all able-bodied men, in late March I wrote home about Luc's fear of being drafted into the armed forces. He had considered the possibility of refusing service and going to prison; this would likely entail being beaten and tortured. "We certainly cannot advise him against going into the army and yet Luc's decision may have far-reaching consequences for our future witness here," I wrote. "You certainly will realize how tactfully we must express these concerns of ours in a young independent nation with strong national feelings that is threatened with subversion within and without, and which relies on a draft to get men to fight. . . . We don't want to be kicked out of the country for interfering in political affairs."

In April Everett wrote a perceptive article, "Context for Trust," that was published in the *Missionary Messenger:*

Vietnamese society is not inclined to allow the individual to readily make decisions on his own as does American society. The opinions and prejudices of uncles and aunts as well as parents and older brothers and sisters need to be considered in any decision-making. Although many parents will say that their child may choose his own religion, when it come to the point of accepting baptism, neglecting ceremonies celebrating the death of ancestors, and active witness of Christ, traditional beliefs and social mores create strong pressures to conform.

The civil war casts a threatening shadow over the lives of young believers. The young men all face the draft as [there is] yet no provision for conscientious objectors. No other evangelical group has taken a position opposing participation in armed conflict, so these young men are standing alone. Pray for them as they try to be true to the Lord using neither illegal means to dodge the draft or rationalizing to compromise the Gospel standard of love.

With five missionary families and an MCC couple in Saigon, we had significant opportunity for fellowship among ourselves, so we associated less with personnel of other missions than the Stauffers and Metzlers had done earlier. It was thus a great treat to be invited to an all-missionary banquet early April by Bob Pierce, Director of World Vision, the agency he founded in 1950. Pierce spoke to sixty missionaries, nearly half of whom were Wycliffe Bible Translators personnel attending a conference in Saigon.

Rudi and Elda Lichti regularly joined the five missionary couples in our weekly evening fellowship meeting. We five couples occasionally met for a longer conference to discuss significant issues and do long-range planning.

We five men also met as a Mission Council to take care of business matters. After noting that some members of the Tin Lanh Church were attending the Sunday morning services at the Student Center, we encouraged them to attend services in their own church to avoid the perception that we were enticing Christians to identify with the Mennonite church. And in our reluctance to associate with U.S. military personnel, we discussed whether to accept gifts from the Saigon Protestant military chapel. Naval Chaplain Harry R. Miller had donated a tape recorder, and Everett formally expressed thanks. We agreed that we could accept such gifts "when they don't weaken our witness." Several months later Chaplain Miller donated $300 to the Mission to purchase furniture and books for use at both the Student and Community Centers.

Referring to the Mission Council, Everett commented to Kraybill: "I feel we have a group that works together well despite our personality differences. We thank God for this."

Don Sensenig told of their years of voluntary service and study in New York City when personnel would meet regularly to discuss strategies of witness and service. While most of the group were of similar minds, one person would frequently disagree. Discussing this with his stepfather, Orie Miller, Miller reminded him that whenever ten persons work together, there always will be one such person!

We did not have such a person on our missionary team in Vietnam for which we were indeed thankful. We appreciated this congeniality as we struggled with issues associated with increased American political and military involvement. Although we shared different opinions, holding some views more intensely than others, we were quite a compatible team.

At Mission Council meetings late May and early June we discussed the matter of governmental recognition for Vietnam Mennonite Mission. After learning that the Baptist Mission had petitioned the government under Gen. Minh, and now under Gen. Khanh, for formal recognition, Everett spoke with an official of the Ministry of Interior who suggested our Mission submit a letter to the Ministry, updating them on our work and asking for action on the request for registration that the Mission had submitted in January 1960. This Everett did. On October 11 the Mission received a letter in the Vietnamese language from the office of Premier Khanh, the translation as follows:

> Temporary Permission
> While awaiting formulation of regulations for all religious groups practicing religion in Viet Nam, the Viet Nam Mennonite Mission is granted temporary permission to operate in Viet Nam. The above organization may be active only in purely religious activities.
>
> 18 September 1964
> Prime Minister of Government
> General Nguyen Khanh

We did not fully recognize the importance of this "temporary" authorization for the Vietnam Mennonite Mission. In his letter to Paul Kraybill, Everett wrote that "we feel this is a step forward but do not feel overly optimistic that it means very much in the present situation."

We eventually learned that it meant very much. Under the French colonial empire the Roman Catholic Church had official status. But the government had not yet promulgated comprehensive regulations covering all religious groups. This document enabled us to purchase property. We would never receive anything beyond this. And when the Mennonite Church sought to register under the Socialist Republic of Vietnam decades later, it appealed to this document as evidence that the Vietnam Mennonite Church was a recognized church prior to the 1975 revolution and unification of the country.

U.S. Secretary of Defense McNamara returned to Saigon May 12. Three days before his arrival, a young Viet Cong operative was arrested while trying to place a large explosive charge under the bridge that Ambassador Lodge and Secretary McNamara would take from the airport into the city. Aged seventeen, the electrical worker was sentenced to death and publicly executed by a firing squad on October 15, thus becoming a poster boy for the Viet Cong. After the 1975 revolution, this main artery into the city, then called Công Lý (Justice) Street, was renamed Nguyen Van Troi Boulevard. Many cities and towns throughout Vietnam today have streets bearing his name.

The day before Troi was arrested, the military government executed Ngo Dinh Can by firing squad at Saigon's Chi Hoa Prison. The fifty-three year-old younger brother of President Ngo Dinh Diem was arrested following the coup which deposed his brother, and convicted by a military court of murder, corruption, extortion and misuse of power. He had been a virtual warlord ruling central Vietnam with an iron hand from Phan Thiet north to the seventeenth parallel. Another brother of the President, Ngo Dinh Thuc, the Archbishop of Hue, was in exile. A sister, Elizabeth Ngo Dinh Thi Hiep, a person of deep Christian faith, continued to hold the Ngo family together.

Mary and I spent several days in late May in Da Lat, staying with Joan and John Newman. We accompanied Newman in his Land Rover out to ethnic Koho villages. On one trip he showed a movie on the life of Jesus with a generator-powered projector, and we stayed overnight in the pastor's house. On Sunday morning we went to the Da Lat Tin Lanh Church, located three blocks from the beautiful newly-built market.

In May Gen. Khanh signed a decree abolishing Diem's restrictions on Buddhists, granting them the same rights as Catholics. Buddha's 2,508[th] birthday was celebrated on May 26. At the end of a busy street in Saigon a huge memorial with the image of the young Buddha was erected. The Buddha's birthday had not been celebrated in such a big way in the previous 100 years since France entered Vietnam.

The multicolored Buddhist flags waved from many homes and shops all over the city. Living near a small pagoda, James and Rachel could hear Buddhist sermons and litanies broadcast by loudspeaker from five in the morning until ten at night. In a June letter Rachel observed that people now found it "easier to be a good Buddhist."

Buddhist bonzes.

Indeed, the Buddhists were becoming a force to be reckoned with. Their demonstrations in 1963 against the Diem government, orchestrated by Thích Trí Quang, had led to the military coup in November. Gen. Minh and his military government gave them permission to organize the Vietnamese Buddhist Reunification Congress which met in Saigon December 21 to January 3, 1964. This Congress established the Unified Buddhist Church (or *Sangha*) of Vietnam (UBCV) which unified many different Buddhist sects in the country. This resurgent Buddhism now challenged the war policies of the Khanh government.

The assassination of Catholic President Diem and the recent execution of his brother disturbed Catholics who held a fierce anti-communist position; they feared a Buddhist attempt to end the fratricidal war might lead to a governmental embrace of neutralism which they viewed as a step toward communist rule. Some 35,000 Catholics clogged Saigon streets on Sunday, June 7, in an anti-communist anti-neutralist demonstration. Mary and I were caught in a traffic jam on our way to church at the Saigon Youth Center that morning.

It was not clear whether the Unified Buddhist Church supported neutralism or supported continuing the fight against the Viet Cong, and this ambivalence disturbed most Catholics and other anti-communists. Having now gained some political power, the Buddhists were not prepared to relinquish it. This set the stage for a series of Saigon street demonstrations that continued throughout the year, at times quite violent.

Mary and I again had difficulty traveling to church on Sunday, July 19, when Catholics organized another anti-communist demonstration on the occasion of the tenth anniversary of the signing of the Geneva Accords July 20, 1954. The earlier Diem government had designated that day as *Quốc Hận*, the National Day of Shame.

In late June, Lieutenant General William Westmoreland succeeded Gen. Paul Harkins as head of all the U.S. forces in Vietnam. President Johnson also named Gen. Maxwell Taylor to replace Henry Cabot Lodge as ambassador; Taylor arrived July 7.

The Vietnam Mennonite Mission activities continued as usual. With the support of young people from the Evangelical Church, Margaret organized a two-week Summer Bible School at the Saigon Center for sixty neighborhood children. Everett and Margaret commented: "You ought to hear them sing, memorize, and watch them drink in the story. They know none of the Bible stories. We are hoping that this warm response from our immediate neighborhood will lead to a larger ministry among adult neighbors."

Mary and I began teaching English language classes at the Saigon Student Center three evenings weekly and we delighted stopping on our way home for refreshing *sinh tố* drinks made at a street cart from tropical fruit, sugar and shaved ice. I also taught an English class once a week at a private high school near our home.

In late June James Metzler smarted from a second episode of pick-pocketing in four months. Besides the loss of money was the hassle of replacing the ID cards lost. My time came later. I collected first-day covers when new stamps were released by the central post office downtown. Standing in line one day to have the stamps cancelled, I checked my hip pocket and my wallet was gone! Accusing those around me of taking it was futile. Humbled, I left the post office that day, vowing never to carry my wallet in my hip pocket again!

On July 27 the United States announced that more soldiers were being sent to Vietnam, bringing the number to more than 20,000. Mary wrote home:

> Politically, we don't feel that things are getting any better. We doubt that 6,000 additional US men will improve things. You've likely read about the increasing number of VC incidents. *Stars and Stripes* reported over 9,000 in the past week, the highest ever except for the week following the coup. The Vietnamese Christian Church is also in need of our prayers. . . .

Margaret with neighbor children in Vacation Bible School.

We often wonder what is the best way to give a peace witness in this land in such a time as this. Here and there people ask and we have shared our beliefs about war. Many indicate this is what they are looking for in a Christian. But we do not go about loudly proclaiming our position. We don't want to be kicked out of the country as subversives. We are not anti-government. But it seems more and more evident that military might is not the answer to this country's problems.

In late July several South Vietnamese patrol boats attacked two islands in the Tonkin Gulf, and North Vietnam accused the United States and South Vietnam of those raids. U.S. naval ships were patrolling the Gulf collecting intelligence, and on August 2 the *USS Maddox* and three patrol boats from North Vietnam exchanged fire. Planes from a U.S. carrier strafed the small boats, sinking one and disabling the others. Two days later at night the *Maddox* and another ship erroneously claimed they were attacked; U.S. authorities reacted by sending planes from the carriers *Ticonderoga* and *Constellation* to hit torpedo boat bases and fuel facilities along North Vietnam's coastline.

President Johnson addressed the nation, denouncing the "unprovoked" attack on U.S. ships in international waters. Over the protests of Oregon Senator Wayne Morse and Alaskan Ernest Gruening, the joint session of the U.S. Congress on August 7 passed the Southeast Asia Resolution (Gulf of Tonkin Resolution), granting the President authority to conduct military operations in Southeast Asia without a declaration of war.

While the heavy bombing raids were described as a response to North Vietnam's attack on American ships, the United States had actually been preparing this for many months. Gen. Khanh used the crisis to impose press censorship and declare a state of emergency, decreeing a curfew from 11:00 p.m. to 4:00 a.m.

Having suffered military defeat ten years earlier, the French called on South Vietnam to embrace a policy of neutralism to avoid an expanding war. Catholic students, however, rejected this appeal and demanded that the armed forces attack the North. At the same time they were doing everything possible to stay out of the armed forces. One sensed a growing divide between the population of the cities and the people in the countryside who did not want to fight a war.

One Sunday morning in mid-August Everett Metzler preached from Psalm 91. This was relevant, I wrote home, because people in Saigon were digging trenches as protection "against the arrows that fly," fearing retaliation for the American bombing of North Vietnam.

"The US stand against N. Vietnam has served as propaganda for the North and for the Viet Cong in the South," I wrote. "The communists can now say that America, and not S. Viet Nam is the enemy. America is gaining the same reputation that France had had. And remember 1954. One Saigon newspaper editorially likened the US attacks on N. Vietnam bases as an encounter of David and Goliath—as the encounter of a strong and a weak nation. Likely the United States represented Goliath in their minds. Whether they knew the end of that battle or not was not mentioned."

NEW PROGRAMS

Chapter 19

By mid-year 1964 the decision was made for the two Metzler families to work together at the Saigon Student Center and Mary and I were assigned to work with James and Arlene Stauffer in developing a community service center. In July we found an old two-story French villa for rent a few blocks from the Gia Dinh City Center and the large Ba Chieu Market. The owner agreed to rent it for 8,000 piasters ($110 U.S.) monthly, paid two years in advance. Everett Metzler described the area to Paul Kraybill as a mixed community with civil servants, army officers and laborers with no Protestant church nearby. This became the Mennonite Community Center.

The Martins would live upstairs at the Community Center location while Arlene and James would live nearby. Renovations for the Martins' apartment were nearing completion when U.S. bombers began pounding North Vietnam, and the owner "half-seriously" suggested that a bomb shelter should be built. Although Everett thought it might be a good idea, it was not pursued. No one anticipated the fighting that would come in this area four years later.

MCC's Director to succeed Rudi Lichti had not yet arrived, so Everett spent a few hours daily at the MCC office, authorizing aid allocation to areas where people were displaced by military activity. Rachel and James Metzler were both "out of commission" for several days early August with what appeared to be dengue fever. A few weeks earlier Don had been sick with what was diagnosed—after his recovery—as cholera, this despite having been inoculated against the disease.

Mary and I met frequently with Arlene and James in early August to plan for the activities of the new center. We planned to offer six free English classes using as text Frank Laubach's *Stories of Jesus*. We would have a reading room open at designated times. And we would open a morning daycare center for thirty children from needy homes. The Mission Council agreed that a daycare program would be good, but expressed concern that the Community Center "avoid creating for itself the image of a welfare center."

There would be regular evangelistic services. In keeping with our policy of informing the Tin Lanh Church of our activities, the Council asked James Stauffer to report our plans to the pastor at the Gia Dinh Tin Lanh Church located two kilometers from us and to the area district superintendent.

Mary and I moved into the community center at 62/262/1 Phan Văn Tri Street on August 20. Two days later I came down with dengue fever. It was now my turn to

Gia Dinh Mennonite Community Center.

154

experience the fatigue and intense total body aches of this mosquito-transmitted disease. A week later, while my fever had subsided, Mary noted in her diary that "his eyes have the same blank, sick stare all the time and he walks around so weakly as if in a dream."

Ten days later I was feeling well. But I had missed the informal evening downstairs on Saturday evening, August 29, when a group of twenty-six persons—local Christians, missionaries, and staff—welcomed the new MCC representatives Paul and Doris Longacre who arrived two days earlier. Our cook, Co Nam, served chicken corn soup.

The Longacres arrived at an inauspicious time. There were demonstrations in the streets calling on Gen. Khanh to resign. When he did step aside, there were murderous counter-demonstrations. Mobs roamed the streets carrying pipes, cleavers, and knives. Gen. Khanh then arranged to form a ruling triumvirate including himself, Gen. Minh and Lieutenant General Tran Thien Khiem. Although we lived only four kilometers from this near-anarchy in downtown Saigon, Mary noted that we could "go to sleep to the sound of crickets [and] awake to the sound of a rooster crowing." However, since our house was located on one of the approaches to Tan Son Nhat Airport we frequently heard the roar of fighter bomber planes overhead.

While the Stauffers, Mary and I were prepping for the new outreach in Gia Dinh, James and Rachel moved into a densely-populated area of small houses near the Saigon Student Center—so they could work more easily with Everett and Margaret. They and we were now in Vietnam nearly two years.

James Metzler was writing an article in mid-September when Air Vice-Marshal Nguyen Cao Ky sent planes over Saigon, threatening to bomb the headquarters of generals trying to oust Gen. Khanh. James asked, "How does a child of God who proclaims peace fit into this picture?"

James could no longer ignore reports that so many Viet Cong guerillas were being killed. He could no longer condemn one side as guilty and pronounce the other side just. No more could he say: "My country—right or wrong." While having no affection for communist atheistic materialism, he suggested that "our godly materialism" was no more pleasing to God.

Paul and Doris Longacre were taking their new life in Saigon in stride. In a letter to Wilbert Shenk, MCC Assistant Director, Overseas Services, Paul wrote: "You would probably be interested in knowing how we weathered our first coup. In spite of its seriousness it was somewhat amusing. Each weekend has provided some special entertainment free of charge. The first Sunday were the riots; the second, a Catholic funeral; the third, the massive Buddhist funeral parade; and now the coup."

In his September 1964 monthly report, Paul wrote, "A month's stay has already convinced me of the need for MCC here in Vietnam. Some days when I see the multitudes of Americans milling about the downtown area my certainty falters, but a testimony from a local pastor or a letter from an up-country missionary reporting on the need for material [aid] provides the reassurance needed. . . . We are experiencing God's continued protection and are able to go about our work with calm assurance that we should be here and want to remain."

Mary and I were learning to know our new Gia Dinh community. While not as densely populated as much of Saigon, there were houses everywhere, some masonry dwellings, with many ramshackle houses built in the "hedges and byways."

We needed local personnel to help implement our mission activities at both the Saigon Student Center and the new Community Center. The Mission Council recognized that employing

Tin Lanh seminarians might strain relationships with the Tin Lanh Church. We were hopeful that Phan Ba Phuoc, the first baptized believer, now working with IVS, might come back to Saigon to work with us. Two of our Tin Lanh language teachers, Dang Thai Hung and Chau Hong Luc, wanted to continue working with us.

Phuoc consented to be the bookroom monitor at the Community Center. In his reply to Stauffer's invitation he wrote, in excellent English: "As you know, I have been working for International Voluntary Services as interpreter for over one year. I enjoy helping the Montagnard (tribes) people very much. But I felt that I have missed something in the field of spiritual relationship and fellowship with our Church. I have been praying the Lord very much for about three years. Thanks to my faith and prayers God answers me now and I think that I should serve Him as a humble servant with all my heart, strength and soul."

Phuoc was taking a significant cut in salary to come work with us. But security was better in Saigon than in Bao Loc; a few months earlier someone shot at him and his IVS colleague when they were traveling a main highway.

We distributed a thousand invitations to the Community Center Open House, Saturday, September 19, and planned a series of sermons on the Gospel of John beginning that Sunday afternoon. Shopping for the first time at the Ba Chieu Market, preparing for the Open House, Mary had her wallet snitched. It contained only the piaster equivalent of seven dollars, but she lost a favorite photograph.

Aware that people valued education highly, we planned to introduce a Bible correspondence course on the Gospel of John. To my parents I wrote: "Pray that in these early days and weeks we will be able to make contacts with neighbors and friends that will lead to their becoming disciples of Christ."

Many neighbors came to the Open House. We were also pleased that five adults from the community came to the Sunday afternoon Bible meeting. We introduced the Bible course on John for them to study at home and James Stauffer then preached. Mary had her hands full with thirty in a children's class. Everett observed it was "apparent that the community is not hostile to the presence of the Center and witness."

Phuoc as bookroom monitor.

Students in the reading room.

September 19 coincided with *Tết Trung Thu*, the Children's Autumn Festival. Co Nam's daughter, Huong, was enjoying her lighted lantern that evening out by the alley with other children, including five children from one neighbor. We were reminded of their poverty when the oldest child said to the younger ones: "When we have money we can have lanterns, too."

Interest in English language classes was high. Many of the 188 who registered were students, but older women and some men—civil servants—signed up. We were planning to use *Stories of Jesus* as textbooks, even though we noted that students seemed to be more interested in the "English" than the "Bible" aspect of the class. I had used the same materials when I taught a three-month class at the Saigon Center; there I had emphasized proper pronunciation but now I was hoping to emphasize the meaning of the Bible stories.

By the next week more than two hundred persons had signed up for the English classes, more than we had hoped for. Thirteen families brought children to enroll in the soon-to-open daycare. Five community adults attended the Bible hour the second Sunday afternoon, although not the same persons who had come the previous Sunday!

Edgar Metzler, Executive Director of MCC Peace Section, spent a few days in Saigon late September. One evening he spoke to more than one hundred persons at the Saigon Student Center on the topic, "The Christian and the State." A few Tin Lanh pastors accepted our invitation. Several expressed thanks for the lecture.

Metzler also met with Paul Longacre and the Vietnam Missions Council to discuss options for Christian youth in light of compulsory military service. We reported that a couple men in our Mennonite fellowship had already been deferred, and one man dodged the draft by providing false information. While the Ministry of Defense's new draft order allowed for deferring religious leaders, none of the Christians in our group had expressed interest in requesting this. In light of our presumption that none would refuse military service if drafted, Metzler proposed that the medical corps might be an opportunity for a Christian witness so we resolved to inquire of the small Adventist Church to learn what choices their young men made. We questioned whether we foreign missionaries should take the initiative in pleading for exemption for Mennonite believers, but noted that official Mennonite Mission recognition would be an asset if any believer sought exemption on religious grounds.

Sensenig learned that the Adventist Mission was able to secure deferment in four categories: ordained pastors, intern pastors, student pastors, and essential workers—those who worked in the hospital and printing press. In addition, the Adventists had their own program of training medical corps cadets beginning with men at age seventeen. Any draftee could request service in the armed forces medical corps; men with some prior medical training were more readily assured acceptance into the corps. After basic training, recruits did not need to carry weapons.

My brother Raymond arrived in Saigon by ship in late September for a two-month stay on his way to the States. Three years earlier he had gone to Somalia on an agricultural development assignment with Eastern Mennonite Board of Missions, and later served in Tanzania. Ray wanted to learn to know Vietnam and its people through teaching English. He taught one class at our new Community Center, and soon arranged to teach English in several private high schools.

Raymond's visit prompted some intense conversations about our mission strategy and practice. After a Sunday morning when I preached—in Vietnamese—at the Saigon Student Center, Raymond engaged us at the dinner table, saying that if he could only see three persons attend a meeting after working here for seven years, he "would make some drastic changes." Of the two hundred English language students at the Student Center, only one student attended this worship service, and only two or three came to the evening program. Though a young woman recently said she wanted to be a Christian, I admitted that "there is little response in terms of building a church."

In the October 1964 *News and Concerns* Everett and Margaret also expressed concern about the apparent lack of interest in the gospel message. "We are disappointed," they wrote, "in the response of our student groups. It is hard for youth to be anything but pessimistic now, and many of them turn to [an] 'eat, drink and be merry for tomorrow we die' philosophy of life." Although some large crowds had gathered for cultural activities, it did not appear that many were interested in hearing the Gospel of Jesus stories.

But there was already some optimism at the new Community Center that the gospel seed falling on "good ground" might reap a harvest. When Pastor Thai Van Nghia from the nearby Gia Dinh Tin Lanh Church preached on Sunday afternoon, October 18, a young man, Nguyen Huu Lam, said he wanted to be a Christian. The following week Lam said he wished to attend a Bible school and wanted to be baptized. A fifteen-year-old student in one of my classes, Co Huong, also told me she wished to follow Christ and I had prayed with her. She said she made her decision after reading two tracts she received in the reading room. She immediately told her Buddhist parents who said she could follow any religion she desired.

We were hopeful that the child daycare program would not only provide a needed service to the community but also create opportunities to share the gospel message. This program opened on October 19, directed by Ms. Huynh Thi Dung and assisted by Ngo Thi Bich. The first days a few of the children cried all morning, but soon the thirty-two youngsters had a great time playing, singing and listening to Bible stories, learning hygiene and social responsibilities. Dung was also teaching them to write.

Ms. Dung had given up a higher-paying job at the American Embassy to direct the morning daycare center six days a week. Mrs. Nguyen Thi Bay served as the cook to prepare snacks for the children and Mr. Phan Tư Dung, an older man, served as the caretaker.

Ms. Dung guiding children.

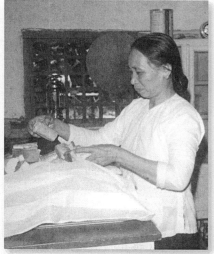

Mrs. Bay preparing sandwiches for children.

In late October Prime Minister Gen. Khanh was forced to resign and was replaced by Saigon's former mayor, Tran Van Huong. Khanh retained his position as commander of the armed forces, however. But intergovernmental infighting continued for the next several months.

On November 3 Lyndon Johnson defeated Barry Goldwater for the U.S. presidency. Our students held to a variety of opinions. Some students had said they hoped Goldwater would win and expand the war to North Vietnam. Just two days earlier, Viet Cong guerrillas infiltrated the U.S. air base at Bien Hoa, thirty kilometers east of Saigon, killing five Americans, wounding more than seventy and destroying or damaging twenty-six planes. Mary was awakened by the continuous, rhythmic explosions of mortar rounds. In their Saigon home Everett and Margaret at night heard the rumble of government artillery attacking suspected Viet Cong positions. People were more cautious about leaving home in the evening.

In November newspapers announced that there would be no exemptions from compulsory military service. But Everett learned that pastors and evangelists in the Tin Lanh Church were "exempted across the board." Hung, one of the believers baptized a year earlier who had gone to Nha Trang to work, was now drafted into the local militia.

With around 23,000 U.S. "military advisors" in country and four months before 3,500 combat-ready Marines waded ashore in Da Nang, the U.S. Defense Chief McNamara declared on November 10 that the United States had no plans to send combat units to Vietnam.

The 1964 Pacific typhoon season was one of the most active in recorded history. With Vietnam's long coastline vulnerable to these yearly storms, Central Vietnam was struck by a series of tropical storms and typhoons from September through December. After a typhoon in mid-September, MCC released some material aid supplies to the government. Materials could only be shipped by rail as far north as Quy Nhon. Supplies further north had to be shipped by freighter to Da Nang.

American military advisor with Vietnamese unit.

Longacre and interpreter Ninh visited Nha Trang, Da Nang and Hue October 8 to 15. Due to poor security, they were unable to travel outside the cities. Paul emphasized to Pastor Vuong, the District Superintendent of the Tin Lanh Church in Da Nang, that the first shipment of supplies could be distributed to the Christian ministries. The second shipment, however, was to be distributed without discrimination to all typhoon victims. A local C&MA missionary hinted that supplies distributed to Christians might be sold and the funds used to repair the church buildings damaged by the storm, but Longacre insisted that not one sack or carton was to be sold!

On November 12 Longacre accepted an invitation from Deputy Prime Minister Nguyen Xuan Oanh, Minister of Social Welfare, to accompany a group of fifty persons including four Cabinet ministers to survey Central Vietnam after being battered by two typhoons within ten days. First flying in a military aircraft to Da Nang, they boarded army helicopters to survey the flooded areas with stops in Quang Ngai, Tam Ky and Hoi An. A storm surge as high as eight feet had swept away villages near Tam Ky with much loss of life. National Road #1 and sections of the coastal railroad were washed away, with vast areas remaining inundated with flood waters. Most of the fall rice crop was destroyed.

The government, U.S. Operations Mission, and voluntary agencies all had to coordinate aid distribution with the military which had the only means to transport goods. The Evangelical Church Social Action Committee was distributing MCC-donated bread that normally was allocated to the Saigon area. Longacre also released thirty tons of food—bulgur, wheat flour, cottonseed oil, and MCC canned beef—and clothing to this Committee. Sixty tons of supplies sent to Da Nang in October had just arrived, allowing this aid to also be distributed to the newest flood victims.

Longacre was impressed that the Vietnamese people—accustomed to storms—took this disruption in stride. Though still raining, he observed many families salvaging their personal effects, shoveling mud from their houses, and washing their beds and sleeping mats. In a letter to Akron he wrote: "If you have next to nothing, it takes little time to get back to next to nothing." Still he acknowledged that it would be a struggle for those who lost their water buffalo, pigs and their rice crop.

Humorous stories emerged from the tragedy—a U.S. army major in Quang Ngai told Paul that, after many hours of rescuing marooned victims by helicopter, they noticed some familiar faces; apparently some of the peasants enjoyed their rides so much that they managed to become marooned a second time!

Wilbert Shenk informed Longacre that MCC was sending another large shipment of aid and that Church World Service and Lutheran World Relief were prepared to send food, blankets and clothing from their Hong Kong warehouses—and funds. Inter-Church Aid of World Council of Churches in Geneva was also prepared to respond. A generous gift was received from Germany's *Brot Für die Welt*.

Paul flew to Qui Nhon November 19—on a military flight because Air Vietnam flights were fully booked a week in advance. He hoped to be able to release seventy tons of food there but learned that it had not arrived because the Viet Cong had blown up the train forty kilometers south of the city! The next day he caught another military plane to Da Nang where he learned that only twenty tons of the total shipment had been distributed—most of this by C&MA missionary Orrel Steinkamp making repeated runs in his Volkswagen microbus!

Longacre described to Shenk the ethical dilemmas in food distribution:

> This relief business is intricately tied up with the war effort. The American Army is not just in it because of their Western humanitarian concern. . . . This relief is presently military strategy. Today Mr. Evans of USOM relief said that yesterday there was a meeting of important military strategists . . . who decided that no relief was to go to areas that are under Viet Cong control. Mr. Evans, the humanitarian that he is, said this was unfortunate and that there was considerable opposition to the decision. I think this is utterly in error and I intend to make protest to the American military and Vietnamese military insofar as the latter is involved in the decision. Simply because VCs control an area, relief is forbidden and the people destined to starve. . . . MCC *must* speak out against such action on the part of the US government.

In his letter to Nguyen Xuan Oanh, head of the Inter-ministerial Flood Relief Committee, Longacre said that MCC was "opposed to the intentional use of relief goods as a military weapon

[and] counter to the spirit and intention in which they were given." Refusal to assist storm victims in these areas would also result in "greater antagonism to the Government." Concluding, Paul wrote: "In the face of such great disaster, a person's need should be the only criterion in judging his eligibility for relief supplies."

Longacre was invited to share his views with other members of the Inter-ministerial Flood Relief Committee. He was assured that people were not starving, and that the Committee had sent food to all areas they intended to help. The Committee was projecting that they would have to feed 750,000 people for four months.

Although 80 percent of the flooded area was controlled by the Viet Cong, the majority of the population now lived in government-controlled areas. Paul learned that Committee members, in collaboration with the military authorities, had indeed decided not to give aid to areas under the VC control. "It is no secret that relief or the refusal to provide relief has been a tool of the military," he informed Shenk. "In several instances the Government forces have announced to a certain area—controlled by the VC—that aid was to be parachuted in. When the aircraft came they dropped bags of sand, and as the VC came to grab the loot the aircraft shelled the spot. This is the type of thing I had hoped would not happen in the relief efforts and against which my letter was addressed."

In mid-December a typhoon struck Nha Trang, further down the coastline, dropping eleven inches of rain within twenty-four hours, eroding the railroad bed. Vietnamese freighters were booked long in advance, so Paul checked with the U.S. Navy to see whether they could send supplies there.

In a later letter to U.S. Navy Chaplain Harry Miller, thanking him for a cash gift to MCC, Longacre said that MCC was "deeply indebted to the military" for getting aid to the flood victims when there was no other transportation available.

Longacre was pleased that the Tin Lanh Church solicited assistance from church members after the earlier floods, and by late November had raised over $1,000, half of which they were giving to the government Relief Committee. At the end of the year when Longacre met with Pastor Doan Van Mieng, the Tin Lanh Church President placed a high priority on repairing the damaged church buildings. In light of the massive relief needs in Central Vietnam, Longacre discontinued an earlier pattern of distributing Christmas Bundles to the children of pastors.

Although Saigon did not get heavy rain from the Central Vietnam typhoons, temperatures were cooler. One night in mid-November the temperature dropped to 19° C (66° F), prompting students to ask us whether it ever got colder than this in America!

Many of our friends had family members living in Central Vietnam. Arlene and James organized a sewing day at the Gia Dinh Community Center in mid-November to sew clothing for flood victims. Using cloth donated by MCC around sixty women—students, friends, and neighbors—spent several days sewing at both the Gia Dinh Community Center and the Saigon Student Center.

Since Mary and I lived upstairs at the Community Center, people frequently came by to visit. Writing home, I said that we were "often interrupted by guests. I don't really mean interrupted, but since we do not know when guests will stop in we can't really plan for them. There have been times when it seemed a bother, but when we realize we are here for this reason, it even becomes enjoyable. I suppose Nicodemus dropped in unexpectedly, too."

All missionaries had students and others who dropped by at any hour for conversations. Few people had phones—even we did not have a phone at the Community Center. Although the people could not contact us in advance, we could usually arrange our time to accommodate them. A high school student, Nguyen Thanh Hoa, often visited us. Coming from a North Vietnamese Catholic family who had migrated south in 1954, he was strongly opposed to the Communist North. "If I learned that a brother supported the communists," he told me one day, "I would kill him!"

Mary, in a diary entry, once commented on "the broken heartstrings" of those who came from the North in 1954 and 1955. When visiting us these guests might say, "In the North . . . ," and would then describe the four seasons, the glorious past, the beauties of Hanoi, the coolness of the winter, and the correctness of the Northerners' speech. Mary wondered whether anyone really cared when we say, "In America . . . ."

Two days after Raymond left Vietnam, on November 22, Mary and I flew to Nha Trang for a ten-day vacation. We stayed in the MCC unit house with Carl and Phyllis Yoder and Susan, their adopted Vietnamese-American daughter. Mary and I were looking forward to the birth of our first child in February. The Nha Trang Evangelical Hospital was becoming well-known for restoring sight to persons handicapped by cataracts and other eye problems. Carl invited us to observe a surgery.

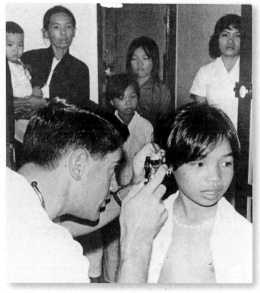

Dr. Yoder examining patient.

While we were gone, thousands of people in Saigon, led by Buddhist leaders, demonstrated their opposition to Prime Minister Tran Van Huong. The two Metzler families got whiffs of tear gas several times as police tried to break up demonstrations. All schools closed, even kindergartens. Buddhist leaders announced a policy of non-violent non-cooperation with the government.

Back from vacation, Mary and I continued working with the Stauffers in the day-to-day activities of the Community Center. It was not unusual to experience misunderstandings among staff members, often due largely to different cultural expectations. Mary described one such incident in a December diary entry.

Arlene wondered why Phuoc and Dung told her they were discontinuing the Tuesday evening children's Bible class. Inquiring, she learned that because Mary had suggested to Phuoc that *she* would drop the Sunday afternoon Bible class because the same children were coming to their Tuesday evening class, they understood this to mean that *they* should drop the Tuesday evening class since she wanted only one class—and wanted to teach it herself!

Phyllis with Susan.

Arlene described an earlier incident that also involved Mary. Mary and Ms. Dung had been in the storeroom looking for towels to use in the nursery. Returning after leaving for a moment, Mary looked for a striped towel she remembered seeing—so three matching striped towels could be used for the nursery. When she could not relocate that one striped towel, she had said, "*Không sao,*" meaning "It doesn't matter." Mentioning the "lost" towel seemed to imply that Dung likely took it!

In late November Paul Kraybill wrote to us missionaries suggesting that, given the deteriorating political and military situation in Vietnam, it might be strategic for some of the Vietnam missionary personnel to transfer to other places. Since Eastern Mennonite Board of Missions wanted to begin a program in Hong Kong, Kraybill proposed that one of the five Vietnam couples transfer there. Everett in his December 11, 1964, response said that the missionary team was shocked by the letter since we did not view the situation "quite so near collapse" as the American press viewed it. Even if the North and South would accept a negotiated political settlement, we believed we could continue to work freely for some time. We could not support the reassignment of any personnel unless we received replacements in Vietnam. The Stauffers did agree to a short assignment of several months until their August furlough date, provided they could then return to Vietnam after a year's furlough.

Sunday, December 13, was a special day for Phuoc, the first baptized believer. He and Sang, a seventeen-year-old bride, were married by the Tin Lanh pastor of the Bao Loc Church at the Saigon Student Center. We missionaries sang "O Perfect Love" and a Vietnamese wedding song set to the tune of "Old Black Joe." Phuoc had met Sang while working with IVS in Bao Loc.

That Sunday afternoon we presented certificates to ten people at the Gia Dinh Community Center who had completed the home Bible study course on the Gospel of John. Some of them continued another course and several indicated their faith in Christ. Nguyen Thanh Phong, the young pastor of the new Go Vap Tin Lanh congregation, preached that Sunday afternoon. In my letter home, I wrote:

> Six persons came forward at the invitation after the sermon to publically show their willingness to accept Christ as Saviour. Several of these had told us previously of their faith in Christ, but this was the first that they publically declared their faith in him. We believe the Spirit of God is working in the hearts of those who allow his word to speak to them. I am sure that none of us could have given as forceful a call as the one that Mr. Phong gave. While we must preach and teach what God has shown us, it is still the Vietnamese who can best speak to the Vietnamese. James is planning to begin an instruction class for them after Christmas.

In that same letter I sent a translation of a letter from Hung, the believer who was inducted into the local militia in Nha Trang:

> One person destroys what another has built, a job that I desperately hate. Why does one wear a uniform, carry a gun? To kill! Kill whom? Kill people who are not really enemies, whom one does not know. It is really a repulsive business. Knowing that this is a dirty road, why do I walk it? How can I escape this road when people are on the lookout for me, threatening to punish me if I seek to evade them?
>
> As a child, I cannot resist. I cannot walk the road I wish. But because I am a child of the Lord Jesus, I will live in the face of these difficulties. The Lord will not leave me. I call on the name of the Lord to deliver all the people of the world, and especially the people of Vietnam, from war. I also ask you all to pray for this.

On Tuesday that week we five missionary families had an all-day spiritual retreat in a fruit orchard belonging to lawyer Trinh Dinh Thao, located near Lai Thieu beyond the Saigon's Tan Son Nhat International Airport, now being used by many military planes.

The Community Center planned a program before Christmas with readings, singing, film and pantomime to tell the story of Jesus' birth; more than one hundred persons attended. Another evening the Gia Dinh Tin Lanh Church presented a program in the back patio.

On Christmas Day, with James and Rachel Metzler and the Longacre family at Nha Trang, our missionary team had dinner at the Community Center where Mary and I lived. My twenty-five-year-old cousin, John M. Martin, in the U.S. Air Force in Thailand, had come to Saigon on temporary duty and visited us a few days earlier, so we invited him to our Christmas dinner which we spread in the enclosed patio attached to the rear of the house. John told us about the terrific explosion at the Brinks U.S. officers' billet on Hai Ba Truong Street Christmas Eve that killed two Americans and injured many people. He had been in a shop only a block away and expected the building to cave in! On his occasional visits with us he always wore civilian clothes, a good idea since the area was considered off-limits for American military personnel.

On Tuesday evening, December 28, around ten persons who had recently expressed faith in Jesus Christ came to the center for the first catechism class. James Stauffer introduced the course on the *Christian Life*. In contrast to the traditional Vietnamese setting where the teacher lectured and the students memorized material, he wanted this class to be more informal with discussion. James wrote home: "Do pray that these babes in Christ will go on to maturity and be willing for water baptism and church membership."

In this same letter James also expressed praise to God that Nguyen Thi Hoang (Mrs. Ho Trung Ty), a long-time friend of Margaret Metzler, had just expressed her faith in Christ that week and was experiencing a new joy. She was earlier hospitalized by an illness. Her husband was currently receiving no salary because the schools had been closed.

In a December letter to friends in the States, the Stauffers wrote:

> We were told missionaries must learn to live with fear—that is, cope with and conquer it. We are learning. Despite constant crisis and uncertainties in the political situation here, we live fairly normal lives. To Saigonese the United States bombings in North Vietnam last August evoked a dread similar to the fear that gripped Americans during the [1962] Cuban crisis. Air raid shelters were constructed; rice was hoarded. These tensions resolved only to be replaced by others. Schools are still closed after some bloody student demonstrations protesting the new civilian government. Martial law and a five hour curfew each night also continues. In the country, sometimes only a few miles outside Saigon, death and terror reign. War is a sinister and ruthless reality. To many peasants, neutrality or communism itself could not be worse than this ugly war. Living near the airport as we did until recently, we constantly heard the drone of heavy planes, shrill whine of jets, and chop-chop of dozens of helicopters going on their ominous missions. Frogs grew silent last night as big guns in the distance shattered the stillness and rattled light fixtures and window panes.

Arlene and James assured their friends that the missionary team was still upbeat, singing together in our weekly gatherings. One of our favorite choruses: "I will sing of the mercies of the Lord forever."

CHURCH GROWTH

Chapter 20

On Sunday afternoon, January 10, 1965, forty or fifty students and neighbors attended a farewell gathering for the Stauffer family. They anticipated returning to Saigon the summer of 1966—after several months in Hong Kong and a year's furlough in the United States. With John, Rose, and Carl in tow, they left for Hong Kong by ship on January 15.

It was now my responsibility to oversee the various ministries of the Community Center and also assume pastoral responsibility for the church taking root there.

Don Sensenig, by now quite fluent in Vietnamese, was prepared to teach English language classes. He and Doris with their two daughters—Anne and Lynne—moved into the house vacated by the Stauffer family, located one kilometer from the Community Center in a long alley off busy Le Quang Dinh Street. A neighbor earned his livelihood by turning five-gallon metal kerosene containers into pails to carry water, either by hand or on both ends of a shoulder carrying pole. The bang-bang din only ceased at night. We referred to this place as the "Tin Can Alley." Anne and Lynne were soon quite at home with the neighborhood children.

Two more young men made decisions to follow Jesus Christ the Sunday afternoon a local Bible colporteur spoke. From a Buddhist home, these brothers were first introduced to the gospel by an older brother who had studied a Bible correspondence course some years before. "So again we see evidence of God's Spirit at work," Mary wrote home, "giving the increase where others have sowed the seed."

In late January we missionaries sat down with three of the believers, Phuoc, Luc, and Lich, to hear their suggestions for church development. Differences in language, customs and living standards had given rise to some misunderstandings we tried to address. They suggested that we should distribute more printed materials, plan more gatherings between the believers of the downtown Saigon Student Center and the Gia Dinh Community Center, and have more singing in services with stronger preaching. We noted the importance of leadership training and involving the believers in the life of the church. Jim Metzler, who coordinated our literature program, reported that he kept fifteen titles of assorted Vietnamese gospel tracts for distribution at the Saigon Student Center, and that one hundred and fifty tracts were taken from the racks every two days. He had prepared and printed a small booklet of Scripture verses. He and Margaret Metzler also prepared a tract that was published in April, *A Life that is Fitting for You.*

We then formed a joint committee of missionaries and local believers to plan the Sunday services. In mid-February Everett and Luc met with Phuoc and me to plan the joint meetings for Christians from the two centers. We scheduled a once-a-month joint gathering alternating between the two locations.

Mary and I were enjoying our life in the Gia Dinh community. Since our house did not have glass windows, we could hear the sounds of our neighbors. A large extended family lived in the house to our left. The matron of the home had several daughters and sons. Each son married in turn and brought his wife to the family home. The youngest wife had the lowest pecking order, and was often harassed and forced to do many of the household chores. To our surprise the family invited Mary and me to a *Tất Niên* dinner, an end of the year celebration before *Tết,* the lunar New Year, February 2. We and one of the sons, an Air Vietnam pilot, conversed in both English and Vietnamese. This invitation was another affirmation that we were indeed welcome in the community.

That evening Mary and I walked through the community before midnight, observing the many families who set up altars outside their homes to welcome ancestors home for the great holiday. We went down to the well-known temple in the center of Gia Dinh that honors Field Marshal Le Van Duyet who helped develop the country at the turn of the nineteenth century. Here hundreds of people offered prayers wafted on the smoke of joss sticks seeking good luck for the coming year.

During the Tet holidays we visited the family of Mrs. Le Thi Hai who lived on our right. Mrs. Hai, her son, and her niece had attended some of our Bible study classes. Her husband, fluent in English, had once studied in a Catholic School in Hong Kong and also expressed interest in the gospel. In a letter home, I said that "we are attempting to see/make the message of Jesus Christ meaningful to a culture influenced by Confucius, Buddha, and other men and ideologies. We are trying to communicate to an urban culture," something I noted American Mennonites found difficult. I said there was "interest and even response to Christ's message, but that it [was] more difficult to guide these interests into meaningful and devoted commitment to a new way of life."

We organized a four-evening series of evangelistic lectures after Tet which were well-attended, bringing a number of neighbors to the center for the first time. The first evening we showed a film, "Something to Die For." Speakers were Don Sensenig, Navigators missionary Vernon Betsch, and pastor friend Nguyen Huu Phien.

On February 7 the Viet Cong attacked an American helicopter base and barracks near the Central Highlands town of Pleiku, killing nine American military advisors and injuring more than one hundred. The next day U.S. President Johnson implemented a prearranged plan to evacuate dependents of official American civilian and military personnel. The American Community School in Saigon closed, and Eric Metzler was without a school. After one week, however, the parents of thirty children with U.S. citizenship organized the Phoenix Study Group with Margaret Metzler serving as teacher of grades five and six. Phoenix Study Group became the elementary school for the Mennonite missionary families' children and operated until April 1975. The 150-student elementary and high school the Christian and Missionary Alliance established in Da Lat in 1929—where Lichtis' son Marlin had studied for three years—chose to evacuate to Bangkok; at the end of the year it permanently relocated in Malaysia.

The United States retaliated for the Pleiku attack by bombing North Vietnam. After the VC on February 10 blew up a military barracks at the central coastal town of Qui Nhon, killing twenty-three Americans, there were more retaliatory bombing raids on targets north of the seventeenth parallel. On February 13 President Johnson ordered sustained bombing of the North—called Operation Rolling Thunder—which continued until October 31, 1968, nearly four years.

The evacuation of American dependents had a positive side for us missionaries which Everett and Margaret described in the March 1965 *News and Concerns*:

> The evacuation of Americans' wives and children makes it more clear to people here that our family is not supported by the [US] government and that our work is really very different from

that of most Americans here. Our [English language] students have expressed appreciation when they find out that we hope to continue on and will as long as we have opportunity to teach them God's Word and are allowed to do so. However, it has made us think more seriously about our work. Often we feel urged to work hard while we can. . . . We have felt a little anti-Americanism (such as taxis refusing to pick us up) but on the whole we are keeping on as before.

Following the bombing of the North there were reports that thousands of Chinese troops had moved into North Vietnam. In a letter home, I wrote that "truly we don't know what a day may bring forth." Voicing the sentiments generally held by our missionary team, I wrote: "I still believe America's goals in Vietnam will not be realized. There may be room for a compromise, and this is probably what Washington is hoping for. Perhaps the struggle in South Vietnam will go on for years, or even generations. It is about time that Washington admits the actual reality about China, and the fact that a country like China is going to have a lot of influence among its neighbors in Asia, as well as in the entire world."

A few days later I wrote a letter home in the middle of an attempted coup d'état which began Friday, February 19, 1965. Vietnamese radio stations began broadcasting martial music, and the American Armed Forces Radio Service announced that "things are still fluid." A group of officers were trying to oust Gen. Nguyen Khanh who had ousted "Big Minh" a year before. The announcer on the Vietnamese radio was condemning Khanh for all sorts of things—establishing a military dictatorship, being indecisive, vacationing when he should have been working to save the country, dividing the armed forces and the country, and leading the country into the hands of the communists.

Afraid of having the electricity cut off, I scootered downtown to get batteries for the radio, driving by the Vietnamese naval headquarters which was in rebel hands. AE1 Skyraiders were flying over the city with their loaded bombs. We learned later that Air Marshal Nguyen Cao Ky was trying to force the coup leaders to withdraw their forces. But Ky was persuaded to support the officers trying to oust Khanh, and after several days Khanh was out—without any bloodshed. On February 25 he was sent out of the country as a roving ambassador!

Paul Kraybill, the EMBMC Secretary, visited Vietnam while this power struggle was going on. He arrived on February 23 and left on the same Pam Am flight as Gen. Khanh. Kraybill described this in his trip diary:

> The airport was a bustle with guards and soldiers and all kinds of dignitaries. United States Ambassador Maxwell Taylor, General Westmoreland, Prime Minister [Pham Huy] Quat of Vietnam, and many other important people arrived for the ceremonies. We boarded the plane and after the ceremonies in the airport, General Khanh came out walking past the honor guard and accompanied by a crowd of friends, newsmen, and photographers and the party that was going with him. . . . It was an interesting and rather dramatic episode in international politics. These people in Vietnam are getting quite adept and sophisticated in their coups. One could hardly think of a more dignified and auspicious way to send a man into exile!

Though Kraybill's visit was short, he was able to review the Mission programs. In a diary entry, he commented on "a remarkable spiritual response" at the Gia Dinh Community Center. About the fellowship lunch Wednesday noon he wrote: "I was quite gratified to see a group of twenty Vietnamese gathered together, including baptized members, believers, and a few Christians who are employed as bookroom monitors, nursery teachers, etc. . . . It was a happy and thrilling experience to share with this group and sense the growing way in which the group is finding itself and relating to our workers and to the witness here in Saigon. This group will certainly have to be the nucleus of the congregation and church here in Vietnam."

Kraybill met with Doris and Paul Longacre and was gratified "to see the fine relationship that exists between the MCC couple and the missionaries and to realize that they are actively participating in the work of the mission."

In Kraybill's meeting with the Mission Council—Everett and James Metzler, Donald Sensenig and me—we reported that the U.S. policy was not succeeding. We said that the Viet Cong intended to wear down the United States and South Vietnam. We sensed growing anti-Americanism in Central Vietnam and even in the south. We told Kraybill that we "should recognize that the political situation could deteriorate [further] and we be forced to leave." We believed, however, that we had great opportunities for continued ministry in Vietnam and would consider leaving only if our presence could no longer contribute to building the church. Should we be forced to leave, we would likely go to Hong Kong where James and Arlene Stauffer could offer support.

Asked how the political crises affected occasions for Christian witness, we said that the mandatory military draft meant losing contact with many young men. While some young people expressed a reckless disregard for life, the war and political crises led others "to seriously consider the meaning and end of life." We admitted having become bogged down with programs, but felt that good responses at the Community Center had made us aware of new opportunities for witness.

Impressed by those he met at lunch, Kraybill said this group of baptized, non-baptized, and Tin Lanh Christians needed to develop a congregational consciousness. We should "let them be Christian," not require certain criteria before they enter our fellowship. We must be flexible, not putting too much emphasis on baptism, but incorporate into the group all those who express faith in Christ—even invite them to share in the Lord's Supper. They should choose their own congregational elders and other leaders, though a missionary might chair the group for a time. Kraybill said we were to "raise pertinent issues" on themes like forgiveness, peace and reconciliation, and help the young believers find appropriate responses.

We asked Kraybill how we can affirm the growing Christian faith of new believers while at the same time objecting to their participation in the armed forces. He said the first generation church may not fully express biblical love and peace; nevertheless we had to emphasize these themes in our Bible teaching and preaching.

Kraybill supported our proposal to expand our child care facilities at the Gia Dinh Community Center. He also agreed to our proposal to recruit additional short term personnel who would become self-supporting through teaching English. He recommended small increases in missionary allowances and authorized an out-of-country air fare to Hong Kong, Singapore or Bangkok during each worker's term. With James Stauffer gone, I was asked to serve as the Mission chairman.

Mary was not involved in the conversations with Kraybill, having given birth to our first child Sunday evening, February 21. I took Mary to the Adventist Hospital Saturday evening at 11:30 p.m. due to the 12:00 to 5:00 a.m. curfew. After visiting the hospital Sunday morning at 6:45, I returned to teach the Bible class at 9:00, but did not preach the sermon I had prepared. Steven was born just before 6:00 p.m. I was pleased to be permitted in the delivery room. Following normal procedures, Mary stayed a few days in the hospital.

When we studied the language and culture, we learned to never say "No" when asked if we had children. The correct response was "Not yet!" To say "No" would imply that we did not want to have children! We were now happy to say we had a child.

Following the afternoon worship service the next Sunday our friends wanted to see mother and son. We had an unscheduled "open house" as they found their way into the bedroom. Our neighbor Mrs. Hai, who had worked as a midwife, bathed Steven each morning, and often stayed to enjoy him, becoming like a grandmother to him.

We had a household helper to assist with household chores. Co Nam, a great cook, had left several months before. Co Hai was now helping.

The idea that we would have household "servants" was problematic for new missionaries. It conjured up images of colonialists who demeaned persons who worked under them. Yet given the way of life in Saigon requiring someone from each household to daily go to the market, cook on charcoal stoves and do all the laundry by hand, it would have been difficult without the aid of household helpers for us to concentrate on formal language study, prepare and teach Bible and English language classes, and carry on a program of community visitation, let alone care for young children. Servants were grateful for the employment. Not all our helpers lived in; some went home each evening. Many of our household helpers also had servants at their homes who naturally received a lower wage than what we paid. Interacting with servants enabled language learning especially for the women and provided insights into the Vietnamese culture. Experiencing the war vicariously through them helped us to understand the life of the people and enabled our children to quickly become fluent in the language.

In a special report written as he left, Kraybill noted the "rather successful communist penetration of South Vietnam" which the United States perceived threatening to end the "free world influence" in Southeast Asia. Commenting on the challenges the missionaries faced daily, Kraybill wrote:

> It is clear that the Lord has called us to Vietnam, and it is also clear that there is a need in Vietnam for a witness of the Gospel of Jesus Christ that adds some dimensions to the understanding of the Gospel which the evangelical church of Vietnam does not express. In light of this and in light of the recent encouraging response, we all came to a very clear conclusion that we want to plan to stay. . . . Unless we plan confidently and carry on our program positively with definite goals in mind, we will simply be marking time waiting to see what happens, and in the end nothing will be accomplished.

On March 2 Everett sent greetings to the Annual Mission Board Meeting that was soon planning to meet: "Though we have seen rapid changes in this country during the past year we are convinced that the situation presents to us great opportunities to live and proclaim the message of Peace. We request . . . prayer that in the midst of uncertainty, tension, and fear we may be faithful Stewards of the Gospel."

I wrote home on March 6, 1965—the day the United States "crossed the Rubicon."

> Today the first of two divisions of US Marines arrived in Da Nang. This is another step in the gradual escalation of the American involvement in the war in Vietnam. Johnson apparently feels that this is the only way to salvage anything here. But greater American participation and direction provides good propaganda for the VCs. Some Vietnamese are now telling me that the US will now confront China, while others say American's determination to help VN will keep VN in the 'Free world' bloc! Time and blood and negotiations will tell. We want to be ministers of peace.

Two weeks later I wrote home about a conversation with an English student—a civil servant and father of several children. Even though a refugee from the North who did not like the communist regime, he said that the Viet Cong would eventually win the struggle. He, like many others, was sick and tired of war and said that he would not oppose communism. He considered both the governments in the Soviet Union and the United States good.

Another friend who worked in the Information Ministry conceded that the majority of the people in the South support the VC or at least tolerate them. But he said it was because the people are uneducated. He claimed that through a program of psychological warfare, people could be convinced that the United States was helping the people of Vietnam; when they understood this, they would support U.S. and South Vietnam policies.

His arguments were ludicrous. I recalled a recent incident when a pilot in a spotter plane saw a VC flag flying over a town only ten kilometers from Da Nang city. Planes were called in to strafe and bomb the town, killing many people including twenty school children. Were the VC blamed? Of course not. The Saigon government and the Americans who supplied the planes and the bombs were blamed.

I also described the arrest of Dang Thai Hung, my former language teacher and bookroom monitor at the student center. Everett, Phuoc, and I went to see him at the local police station where he and twenty other young draft dodgers stood behind a barbed wire barricade. Many were ashen-faced, but Hung managed to smile. We were able to talk together for a while. At his request, we asked for his release so he could enlist in a branch of the armed services where he might not have to carry a gun. The assistant police chief was polite but, obviously, would not release him. The men were then trucked off to the Quang Trung Army Center, becoming some of the 100,000 new recruits who were being inducted into the army. I considered the possibility that perhaps after training he might at some point confront his brother who was earlier captured and forced into service by the Viet Cong.

Mary, in a March 29 letter home, wrote: "This morning's *Saigon Post*, English daily, contained excerpts from an editorial in the *N. Y. Times* saying that the US is committed in [South Vietnam] to the point of no return. A likely possibility for carrying out this commitment is the sending of 250,000 US ground troops to V. N. We hope we don't see that day. Even now, with the almost daily raids on the north we're almost ashamed to be Americans. And some people around us think we're agents of the US 'imperialists.'"

The following day the VC managed to drive a car laden with explosives to the American Embassy on Saigon's Ham Nghi Boulevard, killing twenty-two including two Americans. We heard the explosion—several kilometers away. A new American Embassy would later be opened on Thong Nhat Boulevard—this one would be breached in the Tet attack three years later. Everett wrote Kraybill that we missionaries did not sense that we were in any great danger. Any possible hostility expressed toward us would be because we are Americans, not because we were missionaries. Regardless of how people felt about the growing American role in the conflict, Everett said "most Vietnamese deeply resent the fact that Americans are shooting and bombing Vietnamese."

Beyond the sadness of the expanding war was the joy in participating in a service of baptism at the Gia Dinh Community Center on Easter Sunday, April 19, when nine persons were baptized, bringing the total number of baptized Christians to fourteen. Phuoc was the worship leader, Don Sensenig preached the sermon—his first in Vietnamese, and Everett performed the baptisms. The auditorium was full with fifty persons. We publically announced the service only after some people expressed interest in coming. Following baptism each of those baptized was invited to speak briefly. In a letter to friends that evening, I described the service and those who were baptized.

Vu Thi Qui bounded to her feet when opportunity was given for testimonies. Nineteen years old and the oldest in her family, her parents came to the service. They were nominal Buddhists and venerated ancestors in their home. They had visited Mary and me a few weeks earlier and expressed pleasure that their daughter had decided to follow *Chúa* (God, the Lord). Qui's father was in the armed forces and seldom at home, and they were glad that we were giving their daughter spiritual teaching. They said their daughter's life was different since she decided to follow Christ. Qui said that at first she feared coming to the Center, but learned that the missionaries welcomed everyone. She had made a public decision to follow Christ Sunday afternoon, December 13, when Nguyen Thanh Phong, a visiting pastor, spoke. Qui said that she had just read the passage where Jesus tells the disciples that nothing would be impossible if they place their faith in him. Qui admitted that her faith is too small to move mountains, but declared: "I believe in Christ, and I will obey all that I promised here this morning."

Nguyen Thi Hoang (Mrs. Ho Trung Ty) was overcome with emotion when she stood up to speak. Forty years old and a mother of four sons and a daughter, she and her husband were troubled with matters of faith for several years. Though they had Catholic friends, their family was nominally Buddhist, and they sought to practice *làm lành lánh dữ* (do good—avoid evil). This was not adequate for her. They were interested in the *Tin Lành* (Good News, Gospel) faith, but many of their friends thought little of this, perhaps because many poor, uneducated people were attracted to it. When Mrs. Ty was hospitalized, Margaret Metzler gave her a Bible and other literature to read. Here she embraced the Good News of deliverance and found a sense of peace. At Christmastime she told her husband, a high school teacher, that she believed in Christ and then told Margaret who continued Bible study with her.

Nguyen Huu Lam was twenty-one years old and—like other youth—faced conscription but hoped to enter Bible school. Lam quoted John's Gospel that Jesus has shown us God, and Acts 4:12 where Peter declares that "there is no other name" by which we can be saved.

Nguyen Van Tu, thirty-one years old, worked as a telegraph operator in Saigon. He and his thirteen-year-old daughter lived with his mother. He appreciated the fellowship of other Christians at the Center. "I am very happy that I could share in the baptismal service," Tu said. "April 19, 1965, is the date that will remind me of my salvation."

Hai, an English language student eighteen years old, was a typical young man. He liked to have a good time and had just gotten a guitar, an answer to prayer. He said that an existential philosophy of life as expressed by Jean Paul Sarte, accepted by many youth, was not satisfactory for him; he desired the forgiveness of God. He made a decision to accept the Lord at a preaching service one Sunday afternoon. He said he was now happy. Hai's father was in charge of the local Buddhist pagoda, Quan Am Tu, and his mother operated a business in Saigon.

Hieu was fourteen years old. He was an avid reader and had studied the Bible with us for several months. He expressed faith in Christ after studying the Gospel of John course. Hieu had a cheerful personality and witnessed of this faith to his friends. Though he had long told us that he wanted to be baptized, he was hesitant to tell his parents. But a week earlier he had discussed this with his parents, and they told him he could follow any *Đạo* (way, religion) he chose. "I am happy to give witness to Jesus Christ," he said.

Minh, fifteen years old, was a friend of Hieu. Although he had studied the Bible in some of our classes, I did not know him well. His family resembled that of Hieu's family. In his testimony, Minh expressed faith in Christ and desired to see others believe.

Tran Van My was the son of Mrs. Hai, our neighbor and "grandmother" to our son Steven. Though he said that he was happy to be baptized, we knew that his mother had encouraged him to take this step in faith. She also believed in Jesus Christ, but told us that she could not yet be baptized because her husband's parents would object.

Truong Thi Kinh, a niece of Mrs. Hai, was fourteen years old, like My. She said she believed in Christ and had experienced forgiveness.

This day was a highlight in the young Mennonite church and encouraged us to develop a distinct congregational life. In 1964 Eastern Mennonite Board of Missions had approved new policies for overseas missionary work that emphasized that missionaries were "considered members of the overseas church wherever established congregations exist." This was seen as crucial for the missionaries' identification with the church to which they were sent. While maintaining membership in a "home church," it meant that we missionaries were also "fully subject to the discipline and life" of the local church. This was different from the C&MA policy; their missionaries were not considered part of the Evangelical Church of Vietnam. They were very much involved in evangelism, Bible teaching and church planting, but the local church was distinct from the mission. Kraybill, deeply committed to the understanding that all Christians were brothers and sisters of one another, could not understand this dichotomy.

It would take some time for the church organizational pattern to develop. However, as with the persons who had earlier been baptized, there was now a new sense that these new believers were one with us and we were one with them, and we tried to communicate that understanding to them.

Yet in many ways we who had come from a much different culture were not "one with them." In a letter home a week later, Mary wrote about a conversation I had with an English student. I was teaching the story of Jesus' encounter with the "rich young ruler" where Jesus told him to sell all he owns and give the proceeds to the poor. After class a student asked me whether I expected to get into the Kingdom of heaven! Sensing his possible line of reasoning, I asked the student if he thought we were rich. His answer: "Yes!"

On April 25 Nguyen Nam Hai and his wife participated in the Sunday afternoon service at the Gia Dinh center. A young pastor of the small Chanh Hung congregation on the southern outskirts of Saigon, Pastor Hai taught language to James Metzler, and his wife had taught both Rachel and Mary. He gave a well-illustrated message about the Holy Spirit in the Christian's life which the new believers appreciated. With Pastor and Mrs. Hai we discussed the possibility of calling a Vietnamese pastor. We felt a need "for one of their own people to shepherd the flock in a way we foreigners cannot do," Mary wrote home. "We had hoped for one to come from our own group, but at this time all in our group are too young or too young in their faith for such responsibility."

This concerned the Mission Council, and in May took action to invite Tran Xuan Quang to serve as "advisor-pastor" for the developing group at the Gia Dinh community center. Both he and his wife, Nguyen Thi Tam, had graduated from the Tin Lanh Bible School several years before. They both came from families of pastors. Quang worked with the Navigators in their large Bible correspondence course program, and had preached at a few of our Sunday afternoon meetings.

After checking with the Navigators director, we invited Quang to give designated time to supporting the developing church. Though busy with correspondence work and occasionally preaching Sunday evenings at the Truong Minh Giang congregation where his father-in-law was pastor, Quang agreed to teach the five o'clock Sunday afternoon Bible class at the community center.

Two weeks after the Easter baptisms we had a Communion service. We also had a service of foot washing—patterned after Jesus' teaching in the Gospel of John. Mary noted in her letter home that we "were thrilled to see the new Christians participate in this," along with our janitor, Mr. Dung, a member of the Tin Lanh Church that did not practice this. "For us who have done this all our lives, it is easy to do it without true humility," she wrote. "After studying it together with the new Christians . . . it meant more to me than ever before."

We missionaries did not ask the new Christian women to wear the prayer veiling because it did not seem relevant. But we thought footwashing did have significance and we washed one another's feet with light conversations and joyous hearts—quite in contrast to the solemn way we had practiced this in our congregations in the States.

In late April we missionaries were all invited to the Longacre residence to welcome Dr. Linford Gehman who was succeeding Carl Yoder at the Nha Trang hospital and clinic. A few days later Gene Stoltzfus and Willy Myers stopped by to see us; they were completing their two years' service with International Voluntary Service. Gene planned to return to Vietnam after a short home leave, and Willy planned to recruit for the IVS Washington office. Everett and Margaret hosted a fellowship meal at the Saigon Center on Thursday evening, May 20 for Linford, for Carl and Phyllis, and for several IVS men.

We missionaries traveled around the city on Italian-designed Lambretta motor scooters. The Sensenigs had a mishap that fortunately was not more serious. Heading downtown on Le Van Duyet Street from their home in "Tin Can Alley" with their family of four on board, Anne's seat—which was attached over the spare tire—came loose and fell to the street with Anne in it! Doris felt her going but could not catch her. A small Renault taxi following them stopped quickly and Don and Doris ran back to pick her up. Crying and with a lump on her forehead where she hit the street, Anne was taken to the Adventist Hospital. Thankfully there was no fracture although her one eye swelled shut for a time. She was soon her normal playful self, but told Doris later that she had thought she was going blind! The previous year both Don and Anne were thrown from a scooter when a car turned in front of them. We needed little convincing that guardian angels were watching over us in Vietnam.

May weather is often very oppressive; the daily rains have

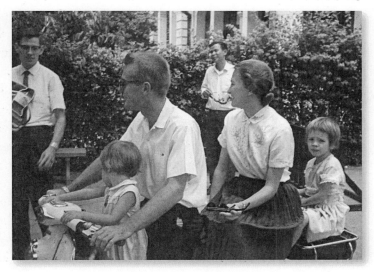

Sensenig family on scooter.

not yet arrived to relieve the muggy heat and humidity. Near the end of May 1965 Mary and I flew to the mountains of Da Lat where we stayed in a C&MA-owned chalet. Going to the Tin Lanh church Sunday morning we met newly-baptized Mrs. Ty and her husband who were vacationing with their whole family. In Da Lat we met other missionaries who invited us to dinners and teas. Most of them worked among the various ethnic groups around the city. Among them were an older couple, Herbert and Lydia Jackson—she a graduate of Messiah College.

Mary and Hong with Steven and Bobi.

We discovered that Nguyen Thi Hong and Tran Nhu Chuong whose wedding we had attended lived only ten minutes' walk from our chalet, so we visited together and compared babies! Their daughter Thuy Phuong (Bobi) was eight months old, Steven only three months. Hong was headmaster of the prestigious public Bui Thi Xuan girls' high school, and Chuong was a professor of group dynamics at the military academy.

Back in Saigon, electricity was rationed because the VC had bombed several of the transmission towers of the Da Nhim electric generating station near Da Lat. This hydroelectric system was built by the Japanese as World War II war reparations and had just begun sending the power to Saigon. Since the power station in Saigon-Cho Lon could not provide enough electricity, we were often without lights or the use of our French-style ceiling fans. We resorted to using kerosene pressure lamps in our English classes.

In early May, Major General Nguyen Van Thieu, head of the Armed Forces Council, entrusted the government to civilian Premier Phan Huy Quat. Over the next weeks Catholics expressed opposition to Quat, fearing that he might advocate a policy of neutralism. By mid-June he resigned and Thieu again assumed the role of chief of state with Air Marshal Nguyen Cao Ky as de facto premier. In a letter home Mary wrote: "The change back to military rule seemed the only possible solution to the deadlock over the proposed resignation of several ministers of government. Now one side is happy. How long will the other be still? Many predict a continued series of coups. Judging from the past two years, this is most likely. "

On June 19 Ky (of Brigadier General rank) was officially named premier. Many of us missionaries had seen this dashing officer at the airport several months earlier, and suggested that it wouldn't be long until he would become the country's leader. In spite of low expectations, the Generals Thieu and Ky continued to hold various top government posts for the next ten years.

The war kept expanding. Around 7:30 a. m. on Friday, June 18, we heard a rumbling noise as our house vibrated with the window curtains swinging back and forth. We thought it might be an earthquake or shock waves from government troops blasting some underground VC tunnels. Later in the day we learned that B-52 Stratofortress bombers from the U.S. Strategic Air Command had dumped hundreds of tons of bombs on a two square mile area of Bình Dương province

B-52 bombers carpet bombing.

Bomb crater.

forty kilometers north of Saigon called the Iron Triangle. Each of the twenty-seven B-52s dropped fifty-one 750 pound high-explosive bombs. The horrific explosions felt like a small earthquake forty kilometers away. This was the first use of the B-52 bombers in the war.

The cousin of Margaret Metzler's cook was one of the hundreds of Army of the Republic of Vietnam (ARVN) soldiers killed in the week-long battle of Dong Xoai, a district capital 150 kilometers north of Saigon. This ARVN defeat prompted the introduction of more American combat troops.

At the Sunday afternoon Bible class at the Gia Dinh center June 20, Don taught on the subject, "The Christian and his relation to the state," mentioning the dilemma of the Christian and the army draft, something facing every young man. I wrote home: "We are not going to advise our friends to disobey the government. We are trying to teach them to obey the teaching of Christ. . . . A few people yesterday shared their concern that, if drafted, they should not take the gun to kill their fellowmen." Teacher friend Hung, forcefully inducted into the army a few months earlier, was grateful not be assigned a combative role.

On Friday evening, June 25, a huge explosion at the Floating Restaurant anchored at the Saigon Riverfront at the end of Tu Do Street killed dozens of people including nine Americans. We missionaries had eaten there a few times, and exactly a week earlier Mary and I celebrated our fourth wedding anniversary at another floating restaurant just a few yards away. Hearing about this incident, Paul Kraybill wrote Everett: "Our minds and hearts are with you continually and, of course, the explosion on the Floating Restaurant brought back many memories of pleasant meals there and also some of the suspicions that I had even then about the security of that place. I am confident that this has been a reminder . . . of extreme caution in frequenting places that are known for their attraction to Americans."

Two days after this incident, Mary and I went to the International Protestant Church. We seldom attended because of the many Sunday activities at the community center. If we could get away, we usually preferred attending services at a Tin Lanh congregation. Yet sometimes we liked going to the IPC for a change. Preparing a letter home the next day I wrote:

> On Sunday the [American] pastor prayed for the protection of American and Vietnamese soldiers dying for freedom, and that freedom would be preserved in the South and the North liberated from the godless Communism. I confess I cannot pray that way. At least he didn't pray that all the communists would be killed. It seems to me that the minister of the Gospel of Jesus Christ must be above power struggles. He must identify with truth and justice. But must he identify with one party in a conflict because he believes their badness is not [as] bad as the badness of the other party? Is it possible, as I like to think, to praise both parties when their aspirations are noble and to speak out against evil which is perpetuated by both sides?

That Sunday afternoon a large group participated in a special musical program at the community center. This was also the farewell for Phuoc, the assistant at the center, who was leaving to work with US Operations Mission. We were sorry to see him leave, but our Mission was unable to compete with US government salaries. He had been receiving the equivalent of $50 U.S. per month, and we offered to rearrange his schedule to pay $70, more than an experienced government secretary could earn. However, with his good English language skills, Phuoc would be receiving twice that wage—needed income for the young couple. He was assigned to Vinh Binh, Tra Vinh province, a very insecure area in the Mekong Delta, and he and his wife attended the small Tin Lanh Church there.

Nguyen Quang Trung, a twenty-two year-old English student and Christian from the southern Mekong delta area who was active in the Gia Dinh Tin Lanh congregation, accepted our invitation to replace Phuoc in July at the Gia Dinh center bookroom. This was the beginning of Trung's life-long relationship with the Vietnam Mennonite Church.

We recognized the value of good staff persons who were able to do much more than we could do. We were sorry when Ms. Dung also asked to resign her position directing the day care nursery in order to study in a Bible college in the Philippines.

I still vividly recall a conversation I had one afternoon with Ms. Dung and other staff members some months earlier. In the country three years, I observed that—culturally—Americans and Vietnamese have a somewhat different understanding of truth-telling. Though liars are found in both cultures, some Americans bluntly say they will tell the truth even if it might hurt someone. In contrast, I observed, most Vietnamese tend to give a more nuanced response to questions—designed not to antagonize the inquirer. Even Christians in Vietnam shared

Don Sensenig teaching English.

this trait, I said. With fire in her eyes, Ms. Dung demanded to know if I was saying that Vietnamese Christians lie! Chastened, I backtracked and attempted to give a more nuanced Vietnamese explanation!

Don and Ms. Dung organized a vacation Bible school for children aged five to fifteen the last week in June. More than 150 children came to the two classes that were taught primarily by teachers from the Gia Dinh Tin Lanh congregation on Chi Lang Street, two kilometers away.

We registered many students for the summer English classes at the community center where Don, Mary, and I taught. We invited them to a series of evangelistic meetings three evenings in early July. Among the speakers were Ms. Ada Lum, with Inter-varsity Christian Fellowship, and Le Vinh Thach, a Tin Lanh theological student who had just returned from London.

On Sunday morning, July 4, James Metzler preached at the community center on the theme, "Children of God." That afternoon Stephen Cary, the assistant executive secretary of American Friends Service Committee (AFSC), spoke on "The Basics of Christian Service."

Cary came to Vietnam to consider service opportunities for AFSC and stayed several months with Everett and Margaret at the Saigon Center while meeting throughout the country with American and Vietnamese authorities. Woodruff Emlyn joined Cary for a short time. Everett said that the two Quakers helped us "to see more clearly our responsibility to protest and publicize."

Around July 4 a delegation of Protestant, Catholic and Jewish leaders under the aegis of the Fellowship of Reconciliation came to Saigon to meet with officials to encourage an end to the fighting. After several of the visitors paraded on the street with placards calling for an end to the war, the group was escorted by Vietnamese police to the airport. While ambivalent about their tactics at that time, I would later praise those who very publically challenged the American military policies.

I expressed anger when I wrote home mid-July, a day the sky was filled with fighter bombers and with helicopters ferrying troops out and bodies back:

> The United States has set out to do some impossible things. She cannot expect to get what she wants here. The war here is not really a civil war. . . . Many people side with the VC because they are sympathetic with their cause or because of expediency. A minority are anti-communist. Many consider communism and war equal enemies. . . . The United States is not fighting for democracy here. It is fighting for its own nationalistic self-pride. Much as I hate to see people die in this war, I have no more pity to see an American die than a Vietnamese. Because the war is really a struggle between the Americans and the forces of communism rather than a struggle between the northern and southern Vietnamese, the Americans should be willing to sacrifice thousands of men on the altar to the god of Mars rather than allow the innocent Vietnamese to suffer. . . . The US must pay the just price for her involvement here.

My anger likely was stirred in part by our pain for Co Khuyen, our new household helper who learned that her only brother was killed in the fighting near Pleiku in the central highlands on May 30, and she had not heard about it for six weeks! I wrote: "Only when you have lived here can you know the meaning of a son in the family to perpetuate the family interests. Until recently an only son has been exempt from military service."

I bought an Air Vietnam ticket for Khuyen to fly to Kontum to learn more details of her brother's death. She planned to return in five days. Even though she had a return flight ticket, she was told she would have to wait a month before she could return on an Air Vietnam flight; people were afraid to leave Kontum by bus because the VC controlled the countryside. She managed to return on a military flight with some Wycliffe Bible translators.

Lam, the new believer, told me a friend was killed in combat—a friend he had introduced to me only a few months earlier. And Hung, who in March was forcibly inducted into the armed forces, came home on a short leave reporting that many of the young men who were forced into the armed forces with him had already been in battles and some had been killed. Others had deserted the ranks and drifted back into Saigon.

I wrote home: "I never want to forget the war around us, and we cannot; yet at the same time I rejoice in what is going on around us here, the development of the Church of Jesus Christ. We are concerned at times for the spiritual growth of the believers, and at other times we rejoice. Yesterday was a time of rejoicing. "

After the Sunday evening Bible class Qui said: "This is the best Bible class ever. " She then described how her interests had changed. Fine clothes and expensive jewelry had been her delight, but now she realized that the inward life was more important than the physical. Some things she once enjoyed now sickened her. Tu also told how he had grown spiritually. He previously spent time with friends in the wrong kind of entertainment which wasted both his money and his health. He said he had better health since he decided to follow Christ.

"To me, these are evidences of spiritual growth and understanding," I wrote. "But we are not teaching that it is wrong to drink or wrong to go to the movies. We do not have a list of 'don'ts' for the Christian life. . . . We believe the Spirit of God can lead these believers. We want this to be Christ's church—not ours. "

We were now having a joint worship service the first Sunday morning each month for believers from both centers. Each Sunday afternoon we planned an evangelistic preaching gathering at the community center. Most Tin Lanh churches traditionally had evangelistic services on Saturday evenings, with only a few Christians attending. I observed that Vietnamese liked to meet with a large group. "So I think we are right culturally and theologically when we try to have the Christians attend the evangelistic meetings," I wrote. "The whole church becomes involved in evangelism. The people are attracted to the warm Christian fellowship, too. "

After Mr. Phong preached, a young man who had heard Qui and Tu speak the previous week told us he wanted to follow the way of Christ. He was Trung Tin, meaning "faithful," and we hoped he would live up to his name. A few days before Duong Thanh Chau, a friendly nineteen-year-old man, had told us of his desire to follow Jesus Christ. Chau was baptized on the fourth Sunday of Advent along with four others. He was an apprentice in the newspaper trade who often could not come to the Sunday services. He was strongly committed to the life of the congregation, even later when he was attached to a local naval unit. (Decades later I again met him and learned that he was still active in the life of a church.)

Four others were baptized on December 19. Tranh, thirty-eight years old, whose wife and children lived in Nha Trang, was a chauffeur for an army colonel; though in the army for fifteen years, he still could not get discharged. He had wanted to be baptized earlier. There was another Mr. Chau, a married man in his upper twenties who was inducted into the army. Ms. Hue was a quiet twenty-two year-old who had learned of Jesus Christ in our Bible classes and Sunday services; Hue's family opposed her decision to become a Christian, but apparently relented. Le Van

Thao was an eighteen-year-old English student who came to faith in Christ through the message of the English Bible classes and Sunday services. He was later inducted into the armed forces and Don Sensenig, Nguyen Quang Trung and I visited him a few years later at his post in the Mekong delta city of Vinh Long. (I also visited this gentle man in the nineties.)

While we missionaries sensed our calling to guide the believers in the way of Jesus, we were also learning from them. In a letter home, I told how Tranh had been summoned home to Nha Trang because his eleven-year-old daughter was at the point of death. Some relative had given her medicine which caused severe hemorrhaging. She fortunately recovered. When we asked Tranh what medicine the relative had given, he said he did not ask because he did not want to make the woman feel badly. Such forgiveness! The deed was done and could not be undone, so why probe and further hurt the relative who was already feeling badly about it.

One Saturday in late July James Metzler and I drove out to the military cemetery several kilometers from our home. "This is the place of the dead," I wrote home. "They had funeral services for fourteen men on Saturday morning. The broken bodies are washed, wrapped in grave clothes, placed in coffins which are nailed shut. After a ceremony they are hauled out for burial."

While we generally felt secure in the city, we kept hearing stories of life in the countryside. In a letter home early August I described the experience of the family of Sensenigs' household helper. After their neighbor was killed by government troops, her father realized that he, too, was in danger of being shot while out in his rice fields. The Americans and South Vietnamese forces had designated the area a "free strike zone," so anyone there was considered fair game. Yet he chose to stay because he didn't know where else to go or what else to do. Then one day an artillery shell crashed into the kitchen right after her mother had gone to the well for water. That settled it; they decided they had to leave. But where could they go?

The great loss of life among the people of the countryside disturbed us missionaries. U.S. officials acknowledged that they might kill two or three civilians to every guerrilla fighter killed. I wrote:

> I am disturbed that Christians in America are not speaking out against this . . . policy. More and more the Americans are viewing this as a struggle between the United States and China. And more and more people are saying that since this is the case, it is better to fight in Asia than on the shores of America. This is nothing but selfishness of the highest order. Earlier, American leaders have said that the troops are fighting here only at the request of the Vietnamese people to defend their country against Communism. Now many American authorities here say that American troops will stay here even if the Saigon government would ask them to leave.

That week there were twenty-one "peace mongers" on trial *in absentia* in Saigon, charged with "undermining the morale of the armed forces and engaging in subversive activities." Under an order promulgated by the Prime Minister, advocating talks with the National Liberation Front to bring about cessation of fighting or proposing a policy of neutralism was considered subversion punishable by death. One of these persons was Trinh Dinh Thao, a sixty-three year-old lawyer and one-time law partner of Nguyen Huu Tho who was now president of the National Liberation Front. Thao had done some legal work for our Mission a few years before. "Perhaps these are the kind of people that Jesus pronounced blessed," I wrote.

In late July U.S. President Johnson ordered an increase of American military forces in Vietnam from 75,000 to 125,000, and promised to send more if he determined it necessary.

Monthly draft calls were raised from 17,000 to 35,000. Most members of Congress supported the President.

Chau Hong Luc, our language tutor now working as a bookroom monitor at the student center, enlisted in the quartermaster corps. With draft age raised to age thirty-five, he hoped to avoid being arrested, given brief training and sent out to kill and be killed.

In mid-August, I talked with the pastor of a nearby Tin Lanh Church who predicted difficult days ahead for the church and for missionaries as well. Noting that American missionaries had a major influence in the development of the Tin Lanh Church, he said we should consider publically disassociating ourselves from the American policy—although we "must stay clear of politics!" He mentioned occasions when American missionaries prayed publically that God would bless the efforts of the U.S. and ARVN troops in their effort to defeat their enemy. This mindset, he said, contributed to the killing of a young pastor by the VC only a few weeks before.

Margaret Metzler wrote to friends:

> Pray God to show us how to witness meaningfully in the context of war. . . . We feel the effects of the war more and more. . . . A neighbor's son came home wounded the other week. . . . Acquaintances tell us they dare not return to their homes in the country to harvest crops. Salt is very scarce, price of rice and charcoal have gone up higher. This brings suffering to the poor class—most of the people. If you could just walk with us through the government hospital on the outskirts of Saigon and see room after room full of maimed men–arms, legs, faces blown off forever–you would know in a new way how ungodly war is.

Margaret then expressed the sentiment that was growing on all of us: "We plead with you to speak out against this war in every way possible."

"In spite of the devastating war we live in, our work continues," Margaret said. Students continued to crowd the English classes at the Student Center. Everett was resuming a Sunday afternoon Vietnamese Bible study, and James and Rachel planned the Friday evening bilingual activities with lectures, Bible stories, music and films.

The growing congregation at the Gia Dinh Community Center on Sunday afternoon, August 1, formed the first organizational structure of the Vietnam Mennonite Church chosen by the group—a *Ban Đại Diện* or Representative Committee. Already in mid-February, two missionaries and two believers—Phuoc, Luc, Everett and me—had met to plan for joint services between the two centers. Luc and I prepared in advance a slate of five persons. Staff members of the community center who were members of the Tin Lanh Church were not eligible to serve, but could cast votes. Nguyen Quang Trung moderated the election. Vu Thi Qui and

Everett leading a Bible study—Phuoc and Luc.

Nguyen Van Tu were chosen to serve with Everett and me. By voice vote Luc was elected to serve as treasurer. By early September, this church committee had met twice. Qui and Tu were quite free to share their opinions and to participate in the life of the church. The church developed additional organizational structures in following years, but the *Ban Đại Diện* remained as the core church council of the Gia Dinh congregation.

Tran Xuan Quang began teaching the Sunday afternoon Bible class at the Community Center on August 29. We used materials the Baptists had published on the life of Jesus Christ. We were pleased with Quang's support of the growing church and anticipated more involvement as he learned to know the members of the congregation.

After learning that the Baptists received deferments for three pastors, in late August I requested draft deferments from the Ministry of Defense for Nguyen Quang Trung and Nguyen Huu Lam. We arranged for Lam to study at the Tin Lanh Bible Institute in Nha Trang. Lam's family paid his tuition; our Mission contributed a subsidy to the school. Although the Ministry spokesman said Lam could begin school, our center staff urged him to wait until he had the papers in hand. On October 13, Trung and Lam received six-month deferments "for religious reasons." Lam then flew to Nha Trang. Lam's late entry into his classes and a weak background in Bible studies handicapped him greatly. Both men were able to extend these deferments.

Additional nursery facilities were constructed at the Community Center during the summer of 1965. Writing to the Mission Office, Everett said that "sometimes we feel a bit like Jeremiah must have, buying land during siege time. However, if we are going to move forward in witness there, some sort of more adequate facility is a necessity." With the owner's support, we arranged for Mr. Bang, the contractor, to construct a 12 x 6 meter frame building at the rear of the property. The day care nursery with space for forty-eight children moved into this new building early October. Ngo Thi Bich, Co Dung's former assistant, now directed the program, assisted by church member Nguyen Thuy Nguyet.

The frustration and agony of the American war finally prompted the Vietnam Mission Council on August 11 to take action to prepare a public statement concerning the war. Everett Metzler, James Metzler, Donald Sensenig and I were entering new terrain. Was it appropriate for us to do this? To whom would we address the statement? What would we say? We asked James Metzler "to prepare a preliminary paper for us to work on together."

Tết Trung Thu, the mid-autumn children's festival, the fifteenth day (full moon) of the eighth lunar month, fell on Friday, September 10. The day care nursery organized a party that evening, and quite a few parents came. Do Duc Tri, the bespectacled lay preacher of the Tin Lanh Church who worked as a translator for the US Military Assistance Command Vietnam, preached an engaging sermon. After the meeting we served cookies and drink. It became rather wild when 150 children crashed the gate, but the kids thought it was great, so we considered it a success!

Since it was a holiday, that morning Don and I had ridden out of the city in our old fire-engine-red Lambretta scooter to participate in a student work camp. Mr. Thuat, the director of the camp, lived near us and was an English student at the community center. He was a friend of Harry Lefever and other MCCers who had left Vietnam six years earlier. The camp was in Thanh Loc, a town north of Go Vap twenty some kilometers from us. The people here were mostly Catholic refugees from Central Vietnam, displaced by severe flooding from areas controlled by the Viet Cong. This camp was a testimony that Lefever's vision for work camps and other youth activities was continuing. Thuat was anticipating 120 campers who would work a few weeks to build sixty twin houses to house 120 families.

I had just had a conversation with two of my English students—high school teachers—who bitterly complained that the Vietnamese had become victims of a power struggle between two world power blocs. One expressed fear that the Vietnamese people would be exterminated. Another said bluntly that if the U.S. wants to fight, it should fight with their soldiers, not Vietnamese soldiers. He said that in joint American-Vietnamese military operations, Vietnamese soldiers were put into positions where they would take most of the casualties.

In late October 1965, the Stauffer family returned from their interim Hong Kong assignment for a short visit before home leave in the States. James spoke at the dedication service for the new day care facilities on Sunday, October 24, attended by nearly one hundred persons. The most exciting part was a dedication pledge, prepared by Don and Doris Sensenig. We invited the baptized Christians, staff members from both centers, the missionaries and other new Christians and those who wanted to identify with the church to read this together—more than twenty-five persons. This public commitment dramatically announced a new Christian community within our Gia Dinh neighborhood.

In the nine months James and Arlene were gone from Saigon, they observed that the city had taken on a more haggard, war-weary look. Shops and houses needed a face lifting. Sanitation had deteriorated. Vehicles were shabbier, streets dirtier and people sadder. Smoke and smog hung heavy over this once beautiful city. Its main arteries heaved and swelled with increased military traffic. And above the din of the city were "the everlasting arms" as someone described the chopping helicopters and loaded bombers.

Even though the day care nursery had just moved into the new building, we considered a major shift. When the center opened a year earlier, community parents said that a primary school was more urgent than a day care program. Without experience operating a school or a staff member qualified to head up a school, we put this on hold. But the Mission Council in early October considered a proposal by Mrs. Phan Tuyet Nga to open an elementary school in our facilities. She had been principal of an 800-student school in Da Nang related to the Tin Lanh Church. Her husband, a low-ranking air force officer, was transferred to Saigon so she wanted to open a school here. Paul and Doris Longacre highly recommended her for having improved the Da Nang school. Paul Kraybill and the EMBMC Executive Committee approved our proposal for an elementary school program.

When the Mission Council and Margaret Metzler met with Mrs. Nga in late November, we proposed that the Mission would operate the school and she would be named principal. Don Sensenig was appointed chairman of a School Advisory Committee which included Margaret and me. The Ministry of Education approved the application Mrs. Nga submitted and preparations were made to open the school the end of January 1966.

In September, the government changed the exchange rate to 118 piasters to the dollar for personal funds, the most significant change since mid-1956. (Program funds still had to be exchanged at the 73.5 rate for a time.) This 62 percent boost when exchanging dollars enabled the Mission to raise staff salaries, as well as increase our missionary allowances—based on a cost of living index.

John Mumaw, president of Eastern Mennonite College (University), visited Saigon for a few days in mid-September, accompanied by his wife. He had recently married Evelyn King whom we knew as the Dean of Women. To welcome them at the airport in style, we decorated the MCC blue Ford Falcon with flowers as was the typical Saigon practice for a bride and groom! Mumaw preached at the Sunday morning and afternoon services at the community center and they enjoyed a noon fellowship meal with church members, staff and friends. He also led an evangelism workshop for us missionaries.

Mumaw prepared a positive report for Eastern Mennonite Board of Missions. He wrote: "Fellowship with this [missionary] group was very warm. We were deeply impressed with their composure and vision. There in the midst of military action they expressed concern about our going to India. Isn't it strange how bad things look away from home!"

Mumaw was pleased to meet the Longacres. He wrote: "Paul and Doris Longacre are a happy choice of MCC for their job in Viet Nam. They are warmly related to the Mission personnel and take a genuine interest in the witness of the Church. . . . Perhaps we are at a point in history where relief and mission will be more closely coordinated in our total ministry of reconciliation. "

As chairman of the Mission responsible for implementing policies, I discussed with Mumaw the pattern of women wearing a head covering, something we had not asked of the women in the church. We now reasoned that if the new members of the church did not wear head coverings, why should the missionary women?

Eventually the missionary women discontinued the practice. The Eastern Mennonite Board of Missions and Charities operated under a Foreign Missions Polity of Lancaster Mennonite Conference, adopted in 1949. Although missionaries were asked to adhere to the uniform church practices of Lancaster Conference, the polity stated that "where the native church lives in conditions that are very different from the home church . . . , church polity for the foreign mission churches should be worked out and administered according to local needs and circumstances. " In deference to the practice within the churches in the States, the women wore a head covering when on home leave.

In early October, I was invited to a gathering called by Tin Lanh President Doan Van Mieng to consider the formation of a Vietnamese Evangelical Fellowship as a member of the World Evangelical Fellowship (WEF). Others attending represented the Tin Lanh Church, the Christian and Missionary Alliance, the United Christian Church (with headquarters in Da Nang) and independent Chinese churches. The Baptists were invited but sent no representatives. The Church of Christ was not invited because they claimed to be the only true church! We could subscribe to the WEF constitution and felt positive about working together with other church groups. Kraybill affirmed our joining the association. It seemed a primary motivation for forming such a fellowship was a desire to keep the Tin Lanh Church from participating in the East Asia Christian Council which had fraternal relationships with the "liberal" World Council of Churches. Although the various evangelical churches in Vietnam had good relationships, a Vietnamese Evangelical Fellowship was never formally established.

In the November *News and Concerns* newsletter, Everett and Margaret described the expanding war. More helicopters and fixed-wing aircraft were flying from Saigon's Tan Son Nhut airport making it now "one of the busiest in the world." Streets were clogged with increased military traffic. Huge tractor trailers carrying munitions and supplies competed with all kinds of vehicles—cyclos, blue and cream-colored Renault taxis and sleek Mercedes, causing monumental traffic jams. New hotels and billets were being built to house the foreign troops. Living costs were also rising, putting a pinch on salaried workers. American troops now replaced the defeated French soldiers who left the country a decade earlier.

The Metzlers noted continued interest in studying English at both our centers; many students had to be turned away. While providing a much appreciated service for students, and using English classes to communicate the Gospel story, we recognized that the Americans' need for English-speaking drivers, laborers, secretaries, typists, and even bargirls, helped fuel the interest in English language classes. Yet we realized that among our friends who had come to faith in Jesus Christ we had generally made our initial contact with them through English language classes.

Friends of International Voluntary Service were shocked to hear of the ambush shooting of twenty-four year-old Pete Hunting on November 12 near Can Tho, the largest city in the Mekong River delta. He was the first IVS volunteer killed in Vietnam. On his second term of service, he was IVS supervisor for the Mekong Delta region. He shared an apartment in Can Tho with IVSer Harold Kooker, a graduate of Eastern Mennonite College. Many of us attended the memorial service at the International Protestant Church. (See Jill Hunting's *Finding Pete: Rediscovering the Brother I Lost in Vietnam* [Wesleyan University Press, 2009]).

Bui Thi, a seventeen year-old high school student, came to live with Mary and me in November. David Luellen, an American teaching English in central Vietnam, took a liking to Thi and wanted to take him to the United States where he could continue his education. David got his parents from western Pennsylvania to adopt him. Thi's adopted name was Brian Timothy Luellen. When Luellen concluded his term, Thi stayed with Alliance missionaries waiting for the adoption papers. When this family left for furlough, Thi came to our home. He knew enough English that we could converse in either language. Friendly and talkative, he became "Uncle Tim" to nine-month-old Steven.

This was the beginning of our relationship with Thi's family. When MCC began work later among refugees in Quang Ngai, the MCC volunteers learned to know Thi's father, mother and siblings. Thi's father was a respected hamlet chief in Quang Ngai province and left the countryside for the refugee camp with his family to avoid assassination by the Viet Cong. Thi's mother died of illness during their years in the camp. In the early seventies the family moved to an area northeast of Saigon to develop new agricultural land and our family visited them in their primitive grass house. During the 1974-1975 school year, Thi's youngest brother, Quang, lived with us while attending high school in Saigon and became like an older brother to our three children.

In early December, the hamlet chief and another official in the area of our community center were assassinated—likely by the Viet Cong. Gia Dinh city was divided into districts, wards and hamlets. Both good and corrupt officials were targets; the assassina-

Bui Thi

tion of good officials was a blow to effective government control of an area, and killing corrupt officials was viewed as a benefit to the people.

Even though we lived in an area that was off-limits to American military personnel, we had no great security concerns. There was some indication that many among whom we lived understood that we were not part of the official American presence. Everett once heard the caretaker at the Community Center reprimand the neighbor children for calling me *Người Mỹ* (American). "You should call him *Giáo sĩ* (missionary)," Mr. Dung had said, "because he is not involved in the killing and bombing that other Americans do here."

We learned that Phuoc's uncle was among hundreds of Army of the Republic of Vietnam soldiers killed late November when two battalions were mauled in an attack on their regimental headquarters in the Michelin rubber plantation at Dau Tieng in Binh Duong province—some seventy kilometers northwest of Saigon. Many died when U.S. planes mistakenly bombed an ARVN relief unit.

In the December *News and Concerns*, James and Rachel wrote: "With the recent battles resulting in casualties by the thousands instead of hundreds and with the ominous visit of Mr. McNamara, everyone is quite preoccupied with the war. As we read and hear many tragic stories, we must struggle to avoid the extremes of becoming calloused or overwhelmed. Only the peace of God can keep our hearts and minds stable in Christ."

James and Rachel were inviting students to their home near the Saigon center on Sunday evenings for an English Bible class, using as guide Phillip's Gospel of John entitled *One Way for Modern Man*. The bilingual Friday evening program at the student center attracted nearly one hundred persons, mostly English language students. Students were picking up various Gospel tracts, several hundred each week and several persons confessed faith in Jesus Christ.

In early December, Nguyen Thanh Phong, pastor of Go Vap Tin Lanh church, invited me to preach Wednesday evening in the military prison near his home. This was a reciprocal invitation, for we had invited him to preach several times at the community center. The huge Quang Trung military complex was situated on the northeast edge of metropolitan Saigon. Lining the streets were dozens of barracks and other support facilities. I had already visited the hospital there. Here in the prison were hundreds of men awaiting trial. Charges against the men—some only teenagers—ranged from draft dodging to insubordination and graft. I assumed that some were objectors to war—among them some Christians. Pastor Phong told me that some men cut off their trigger finger in an effort to avoid military service. While the Tin Lanh Church publically disavowed support for any political group or faction, most of their members in the cities and towns volunteered or were drafted into the Army of the Republic of Vietnam. Those of officer rank were accorded respect in the church. The Tin Lanh Church also appointed chaplains to the armed forces.

I had misgivings about accepting the invitation. How could I avoid being perceived as an American whose government followed a policy requiring *them* to join the ARVN forces? Yet out of respect to Pastor Phong I agreed. It was a strange experience to speak of God's love to a large crowd of 700 men standing in the open prison courtyard. I would have loved to privately talk with many of these men, assuming some might have shared concerns similar to mine. I wondered what gospel the men really heard that evening; I suspected that many viewed this American missionary as part of the increasingly massive American presence in Vietnam.

The Christmas 1965 programs at the two centers were well attended, with 150 and 200 persons. There was lots of music, including a Vietnamese song by the missionaries' children and local children. On Christmas Day, Mary and I invited our missionary families, the Long-acres, and Dr. Christopher and Lois Leuz—then working in Pleiku—to a dinner in the rear open patio of our house. The children loved using the day care nursery playground equipment.

Four days after Christmas Mary and I left for Malaysia on a three-week vacation.

Christmas program at Community Center.

Don leading singing at community Christmas program.

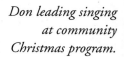

Community church choir singing.

MCC RESPONDS TO WIDENING WAR

Chapter 21

An Associated Press release early in 1965 described "three young American medical missionaries working in beautiful but dangerous surroundings" near the coastal town of Nha Trang in an area "frequently raided by the Viet Cong." It referred to Dr. Carl J. Yoder, his wife Phyllis, and Marva Hasselblad—both nurses—Mennonite Central Committee personnel at the Evangelical Clinic.

Following the November typhoons and floods that ravaged the area, Viet Cong guerrilla forces operating in the mountains came to the lowlands, raising security concerns for the personnel at the clinic. The hospital board, mindful of the kidnapping of the doctor from the Ban Me Thuot Leprosarium three years earlier, recommended that the American staff members go in to Nha Trang city overnight; they did overnight for a few days with the family of an American doctor friend who worked in the provincial hospital.

The Evangelical Church in Vietnam celebrated the dedication of the new wing of the Chan Y Vien Tin Lanh on Sunday, January 17. The new wing doubled the clinic's inpatient facilities to thirty-five beds. In his speech Dr. Yoder, the medical director, said that the Good News Clinic "offers more than just medicine for physical ailments and pain. We are . . . a Christian hospital where a patient can also find relief from sadness, fear, hate, envy, anger, strife and even death. This is the importance of the 'Good News' in our name. When one believes and has faith in Jesus Christ, joy replaces sadness, confidence replaces fear, love overcomes hate, peace removes strife, and even our most powerful threat—death itself—is overcome." Funds to build the addition came through MCC from the World Council of Churches (WCC).

Top: Carl Yoder at the dedication with interpreter Pastor Le Hoang Phu. Left: Evangelical Clinic-Hospital at Nha Trang.

Hospital admissions for 1964 averaged around sixty per month. From 150 to 200 patients were treated in the clinic each morning four days weekly. The chaplain reported that fifteen thousand people heard the Gospel preached during the clinic hours and that 352 persons had confessed faith in Jesus Christ.

MCC Vietnam director Paul Longacre was still involved in the allocation of aid to victims of Central Vietnam typhoons and floods. He and Ninh, his associate and interpreter, had in mid-January visited Da Nang and met with Pastor Nguyen Xuan Vong, the Tin Lanh District Superintendent. Many of the supplies were flown from Saigon on U.S. Operations Mission flights—the only way to get the aid out. Longacre was pleased that at least fifty percent of the supplies were distributed by the Church to persons outside the Church. Pleased with their organization, the government's flood relief committee asked the Church to distribute some of their supplies. MCC also distributed $13,000 in cash grants to those with severe losses. While most of this went to Christian families, each of the twenty-nine congregations in the devastated areas was given a small amount of funds to be distributed beyond the church community.

The expanding war, which by April had "generated" more than 300,000 internally displaced persons or refugees with many more expected within the next year, led to many concerned Americans asking the question, "Why are we not doing more to help the victims of the conflict?"

Wilbert Shenk, MCC's Assistant Director of Overseas Services, reported on MCC's Vietnam work at a March 1965 meeting of the Asia Department of the National Council of Churches' Division of Overseas Ministries in New York. Boyd Lowry, Associate Director of Church World Service, the service agency of the NCC, submitted a proposal that would have MCC administering a joint MCC-CWS program.

Robert Miller came to Vietnam one week in early April. He observed the Nha Trang medical program and saw the two bakeries in Saigon that provided 162,000 loaves of bread each month for orphanages and other institutions. He met with officials of the Ministry of Social Welfare and had conversations with the Mennonite missionaries, with C&MA mission director T. Grady Mangham and with Pastor Doan Van Mieng, President of the Tin Lanh Church, who expressed appreciation for all the flood relief to the churches.

Mangham told Miller that the WCC in 1964 had asked him to propose assistance projects; this inquiry he referred to the Tin Lanh Church which decided not to receive funds from WCC directly. It was clear that both C&MA and the Tin Lanh Church preferred to have WCC and CWS work through an MCC-administered program than have these agencies develop their own programs.

Prior to Miller's visit, Longacre prepared several "occasional papers." One dealt with strategies for relief assistance. Paul argued that distributing material aid through the Evangelical Church in order to "create a sense of social consciousness in the church by showing through deeds what should be done" was a failed policy. Church leaders, he said, seldom responded to local crises, usually declaring: "Our people are so poor, we cannot do anything!" In the ten years since the Church's Social Welfare Committee was formed, Longacre said the Church had shown little initiative in pursuing assistance projects on its own.

Although MCC had decided the previous year to reduce aid distribution, the expanding war meant that need for assistance was now increasing. "As long as there is acute need for us and our supplies, our presence is necessary," Paul wrote. He proposed urging the Welfare Committee to motivate Church leaders to solicit resources from the Tin Lanh Church to help the needy rather than function only as an instrument for distributing MCC supplies.

In another paper, Longacre discussed long-range planning for the clinic-hospital in Nha Trang. Paul was unhappy that the Church seemed unwilling to support the clinic financially, even reluctant to pay the chaplain's salary. MCC, he wrote, should continue to insist on the Church's obligation to this ministry. He proposed, however, that MCC allocate resources to train nurses.

Another paper called for clarification of MCC's relationship to the U.S. government. It was appropriate for MCC to work with the Vietnamese government to help people realize a better life, Paul reasoned. However, MCC now had to rely on the U.S. forces to transport goods. More troubling was the U.S. effort to enlist voluntary agencies to carry out objectives of the American administration. "MCC's purpose is not to win the war and save these people from Communist domination," Paul wrote. "Our purpose is rather to help these people simply because they are in need of a 'cup of cold water'!" As a Christian agency advocating a peaceful resolution to conflict, Paul insisted that MCC had "a unique responsibility and opportunity to validly protest against the U.S. military operation" and creatively show a "more excellent way" of loving service.

Longacre illustrated the problem. Missionaries "vocally and violently opposed to the Communist movement" often assisted the Evangelical Church in material aid distributions; thus the MCC material aid was distributed with "a strong pro-Government, pro-American flavor," he wrote. On a few occasions Longacre had released supplies to USOM provincial representatives. In one case MCC blankets and clothes were given as a reward to hamlet chiefs for moving their hamlets as part of a military maneuver; a USOM representative claimed that "MCC goods are far superior to anything else and thus make worthy gifts!"

To deal with this "ulcer-creating" problem, Paul suggested that MCC avoid military transportation as much as possible and avoid allocating aid supplies to USOM which usually gave them to the provincial chiefs for distribution. MCC also needed to prepare print materials explaining the source and purpose of the aid, and protest to Vietnamese and American officials any practices causing civilian suffering. MCC personnel should also be more forthright in expressing these concerns to C&MA missionaries and Tin Lanh pastors, Paul said.

Shenk responded to Longacre, noting that MCC entered Vietnam in 1954 "with the tacit approval of C&MA, and [had] ever since planned programs in relationship with the Evangelical Church." Given the theological stance of the Alliance mission, Shenk said that it was "hardly surprising" that the Church had not engaged in organized response to physical need. But the fact that the Church now works with MCC in responding to physical need shows that the Church is embracing this ministry. Shenk urged Paul to "dialogue with church leaders and pastors concerning the theological meaning of Christian service. "Rather than engaging in protest action against American military policies at this juncture," Shenk wrote, "we prefer to invest our time and energies in constructive service," always seeking to involve Christians deeply concerned about helping others.

There was indeed evidence that MCC was appreciated by the Church and the Alliance Mission. The C&MA missionaries' June 1965 conference sent greetings to the Akron MCC office: "We wish to express our gratitude for the generous assistance that you have given to us, which has so helped us in the furtherance of the Lord's work here in Vietnam."

MCC Executive Secretary Snyder also wrote to Longacre: "You are in a wartime situation and at best things are messy. We must calmly assess the situation in Vietnam . . . and decide where our limited efforts must be directed in the difficult political and military situation that has developed." Indicating that he clearly heard and understood Paul's anguish, he continued: "We can sympathize with your feeling that you cannot identify with the U.S. government under certain circumstances and that you must have greater control of the services and commodities that come to you for distribution."

Acknowledging Paul's frustration with the local church, Snyder said MCC administrators had seen slow progress in the relationship with the Alliance and the Church. "I pray that you will look beyond the frustrations of the United States government, the Vietnamese government and the local church to see the needs of the unfortunate victims of war and to concentrate our attention on meeting those needs," Snyder wrote. "If we must modify our program to keep our witness clear, we must be prepared to do so. However, there will be times when events will transpire that will be far from our liking but we must always weigh this to determine if, on balance, we are doing an adequate piece of work in the name of Christ."

Asked to comment on the CWS proposal to provide assistance through MCC, Longacre said one option would be to "say 'no' to the CWS offer to help, and curtail further MCC's material aid program." This could be "a real protest against the U.S. actions here and our own involvement in helping to win the war. We are involved a great deal regardless of how we try to avoid it, especially in the material aid program." However, recognizing the increasing needs, it did not seem easy to curtail assistance.

Paul suggested that since there were acute medical needs, MCC might develop a new medical program that would not need to rely on American logistical support as did material aid distributions. After two visits to Pleiku, in mid-June Paul made a formal proposal that MCC build a small clinic in Pleiku to primarily serve the ethnic minorities. Acknowledging that security in Pleiku was tenuous because guerilla forces encircled the town of 20,000, he predicted that within two months the situation would change—either the Viet Cong forces would have taken the town, or they would be pushed further away.

In April, Paul reported increasing numbers of internal refugees due primarily to the U.S. and Vietnamese bombing raids against suspected VC installations that forced people to evacuate to safer areas. "Since the care and feeding of these people is a real psychological part of the war effort, the Government with USAID's help is doing everything in its power to provide for these people," Paul wrote. While the church should respond to the needs of the people, he said, it was challenging "because almost everything we do appears to be or is turned into part of the whole Western effort to defeat the Communists."

By May, Church World Service announced a preference for working within the MCC structure rather than reestablishing a separate program. Frank Hutchison, CWS Director for South and Southeast Asia, was coming to Vietnam to plan for this. Robert Miller reported that the Alliance Mission also supported having Church World Service work with MCC.

Other international relief agencies were considering aid programs to Vietnam. Both East Asia Christian Conference and World Vision anticipated developing programs. Stephen Cary was surveying relief needs for the American Friends Service Committee. Snyder wrote Longacre: "We have no illusions that the AFSC may have the answers to the very difficult situation, but we have seen them operate in other countries and on the whole they do an effective job on the political level which we Mennonites do not begin to touch."

Longacre also affirmed developing an MCC Family Child Assistance sponsorship program at the Mennonite Mission Community Center, confident that they "would not exploit the program in an undue manner for evangelization purposes."

Nurse Marcella (Marcy) Weber from Ontario arrived in Saigon late June to replace Marva Hasselblad at the Nha Trang Tin Lanh Clinic. Church World Service recruited four short-term nurses who arrived about the same time. Jean Dickason and Barbara Stallwood were assigned to work at the Saigon Adventist Hospital, and Barbara Carlson and Helen Devitt went to the Nha Trang Clinic. Marcia first engaged in language study; Barbara provided additional training to local clinic staff. MCC also recruited Christopher and Lois Leuz from Doylestown, Pennsylvania, who arrived in October and Emma Lenzmann, an experienced nurse from British Columbia who arrived a month earlier. These three spent a few weeks for orientation at the Nha Trang clinic before moving to Pleiku to develop the new medical program for ethnic minorities.

U Thuang Tin came to Vietnam representing East Asia Christian Conference. EACC imported fifty tons of rice and other foods to help feed ethnic minorities. Alan Brash, the EACC Secretary for Mission and Service, affirmed their intention to serve those in need "irrespective of their political allegiance—to the south, the north or the Vietcong." Backing up this pledge, Brash reported that their first assignment of medical supplies had already been sent to Hanoi, and that further aid was planned.

The World Relief Commission (WRC), the relief agency of the National Association of Evangelicals, entered Vietnam with C&MA blessing. An Alliance missionary in Hue, Robert L. Davis, was named the WRC Vietnam Director. The Commission worked initially in Quang Tri and Thua Thien (Hue) provinces just south of the seventeenth parallel, establishing vocational training centers and developing a school lunch feeding program.

In late June, newly-named Premier Nguyen Cao Ky and his foreign minister, Tran Van Do, spoke at an "international aid day" event to recognize the contributions from the international community. Since Paul and Doris Longacre were out of town, Nguyen Van Ninh, MCC interpreter and Administrative Assistant, asked me to represent MCC at this event. While interested in seeing and hearing these high level officials, I was ambivalent about attending—not wanting to be identified with the political struggle in Vietnam. U.S. Ambassador Maxwell Taylor and General William Westmoreland, head of U.S. Military Assistance Command-Vietnam, were there. Medals were presented to several aid missions and private agencies giving aid to the country. While MCC was recognized, Longacre learned later that Catholic Relief Services, CARE, and MCC were to receive medals, but this was postponed to a later private ceremony for fear Buddhists would object since they were not represented by a similar service agency.

In late July, Longacre learned that USAID's Advisory Committee on Voluntary Foreign Aid in Washington proposed assigning persons to Saigon to set up a coordinating committee for voluntary agencies. Paul said this was "utterly ridiculous" since there was already a well-functioning coordinating committee. A more acute need was help in transporting relief supplies, Longacre said, like providing an amphibious landing ship to deliver supplies for the agencies!

While busy with the expanding programs, there were also humorous moments at the MCC office. In August, Paul forwarded to the Akron office a letter he received from an American GI along with the familiar label from a can of MCC beef. Airman First Class Robert Woller bought the meat at a public market in Da Nang because, he said, "the food in our chow hall has been un-eatable!" Apparently the recipient sold the meat to buy rice enough for several days. Lots of goods originating from the U.S. military commissary were also sold on the black market. Since such commodities were sold quite openly, Saigon missionaries referred to them as "gray" markets, and we sometimes bought favorite food there.

Carl Kaufman transferred from Hong Kong in mid-August to assist Longacre. When Gary Dewarle came the following month, Gary helped Paul in Saigon with material aid distribution while Carl went to Nha Trang to provide support for the clinic staff.

To implement the expanding service program in late summer, MCC elicited assistance from two Mennonite missionaries—Everett and me. Everett worked with

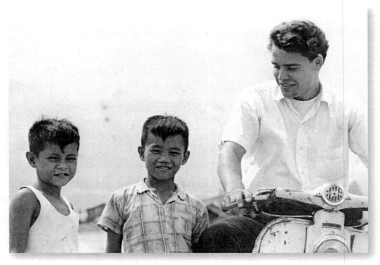

Carl Kaufman with village boys.

Paul to inaugurate the new medical program in Pleiku while I assisted in renting facilities in the Saigon area and, later, in developing MCC's Family Child Assistance program at the Community Center. We were both pleased to support MCC in these programs.

In September, Bernard Confer of Lutheran World Relief (LWR) also expressed interest in working with Mennonite Central Committee. At their September 17 and 18 meeting, the MCC Executive Committee affirmed MCC's readiness to work cooperatively with other agencies:

> Moved and passed to approve general planning for the Vietnam area within the context of the following policy considerations:
> We want to maintain sensitive and close relationship to Vietnam church.
> In the emergency period ahead, we work cooperatively with other interested agencies and offer services as needed and deemed advisable by the [new] administration.
> That we respect the goals and autonomy of each agency.

The Executive Committee supported developing a new major medical project (Pleiku), plus two additional short term medical projects. They also approved recruiting ten to fifteen professional personnel to be sent to Vietnam as soon as possible, including doctors, nurses, material aid workers, social workers, and persons experienced in refugee resettlement. Ten to fifteen additional Pax men, conscientious objectors to war who would give service in lieu of military deployment, were to be recruited to assist in medical work, material aid distribution and other service; MCC would issue an invitation to the Church of the Brethren to help recruit such personnel.

After the EACC sent medical aid to North Vietnam, the Executive Committee also approved "an initial $500 be allocated for medicine for North Vietnam to be channeled through East Asia Christian Conference." This was MCC's first contribution to "the other side."

Dr. Howard A. Rusk, pioneer in rehabilitation for the physically disabled, led an American government fact-finding group to Vietnam in August. Following this President Johnson asked the American Council of Voluntary Agencies for Foreign Service to send a delegation to further determine refugee needs. Asked to appoint a member to this group, MCC invited Willard Krabill. It was already seven years since Krabill had left Ban Me Thuot. Other members of the delegation included Hugh Farley, Church World Service; Bernard Confer, Lutheran World Relief; Fr. John McCarthy, Catholic Relief Services; Judge Robert Hansen, national vice-president of CARE; and a representative of International Rescue Committee.

This delegation made a whirlwind tour of South Vietnam October 18-23, visiting areas of large refugee concentrations, observing how governmental and non-governmental agencies were alleviating some of the refugee needs. The delegation concluded: "The motivations of the voluntary agencies are humanitarian, often religious, and seldom political. Governments are normally and properly concerned with political and security objectives. It is a tribute to both parties, however, to find them working in collaboration in Vietnam in such an effective way to meet human need, with respect on each side for the other's integrity."

Dr. Krabill gave a personal report in Elkhart, Indiana, on Thanksgiving Day, November 25. He described Vietnam as "a beautiful country with a sick soul—weary from the long ravages of war." Krabill said that voluntary agencies would have to expand their programs. However, the greatest need, he said, was to "quit making refugees. . . . No effort should be spared in ending the war."

In mid-September, Longacre reported that there were now over 600,000 refugees, of which one-third had been resettled. Most of these left their country homes to avoid American and South Vietnamese air and artillery strikes. Though recognizing that MCC could not ignore the obvious refugee needs, Longacre again asked the question that was troubling him for months: "What constitutes a proper theology and practice of relief and service in a guerilla war situation?"

Paul had just come from meetings with U.S. officials who emphasized refugee assistance as part of psychological warfare—popularly called "winning the hearts and minds of the people." They stressed the importance of rank and file Americans giving support to voluntary agencies so that they will feel a part of what the United States is doing in Vietnam. Not wanting to join the official drumbeat, Paul said that MCC must work in projects with limited logistical needs so as to minimize association with military forces, must genuinely focus on alleviating obvious needs without considering their psychological warfare value, and develop projects that "show people the Kingdom of Christ."

Robert Miller noted Longacre's concerns. Miller said that Stephen Cary, the AFSC Administrator who just returned from his stay in Vietnam, emphasized the importance of placing civilian personnel in Vietnam to show that there are Americans other than the military forces.

Again in early October, Paul expressed his misgivings about a large joint CWS-MCC ministry which would rally American Protestants to support U.S. goals in Vietnam and do little to stop the cause of the human suffering. "By patching up and building structures for the refugees," Paul wrote to the Akron office, "we will be making it more palatable for the U.S. and South Vietnam to create more of the same."

Since an enlarged program would require more MCC administrative personnel, Paul proposed that he serve as assistant to a more experienced director. At least one new staff person, he said, should be given the task of reporting Vietnam developments to U.S. churches and urging American officials to show military restraint. By virtue of the service this larger agency would be giving to refugees, this person would have a strong forum from which to speak and a clear right to speak. Paul, using a forceful figure of speech, said that rather than succumbing to President

Johnson's arm-twisting, MCC should through interpretive reporting "knife the psychological war-mania in the back."

Longacre also insisted that new personnel coming to Vietnam be given three months of full-time language study. "There are too many Westerners here now who can make no contribution at all in person-to-person relationships with Vietnamese people and who give the impression that study of the language of the people they are supposed to be serving is not worth the time or effort," Paul wrote. "We should be different." This advice was followed.

Church World Service, at a meeting in Nashville of the Division of Overseas Ministries of the National Council of Churches on October 5, announced that they were recruiting "some thirty trained Christian doctors, nurses, social workers, child care experts, agronomists and other specialists to mount a 'dynamic, humanitarian American presence' among the Vietnamese people," working under MCC, and that they were raising an emergency fund of $250,000 "to strengthen and greatly expand existing aid programs now being operated in South Vietnam by Christian agencies."

CWS Executive Director James MacCracken said the American churches were "deeply concerned about the refugee victims of this tragic conflict," not only in South Vietnam but also in the North. He said that they would appeal to the World Council of Churches and financially support efforts "to help these refugees in the north who are beyond our reach."

In late September, Paul asked Akron to cancel the shipment of second quarter 1966 surplus food commodities. There was already a good supply of materials in the warehouse for normal distribution, and Longacre wanted to cut back on food distributions which required military logistical support. The U.S. psychological warfare teams, he said, had plenty of resources to give help after battles. To give emergency material aid assistance to refugees immediately after military operations would make MCC part of the operations and would be harmful to MCC's image, Paul said.

Security did improve in the Pleiku area, enabling progress in developing the medical program there. Everett and Paul met with Tin Lanh and C&MA leaders who gave enthusiastic endorsement to the project. The Church president took action to appoint a board and C&MA Pleiku missionary Charles Long and Pastor Truong Van Sang requested land and sought approval from local government officials. Dr. Chris and Lois Leuz and nurse Emma Lenzmann went to Pleiku early November. They began by examining patients at the C&MA leprosy clinic.

While Everett worked with Longacre to develop the clinic program at Pleiku, I scouted Saigon for rental properties. The MCC office moved to 83 Cong Ly Street in downtown Saigon. A few years later Vietnam Christian Service would move their office to a rented prop-

Em Dem gate.

erty adjacent to the Mennonite Mission office and student center on Phan Thanh Gian Street. In late November, MCC rented a property on Le Quang Dinh Street, Gia Dinh, which would become the first home for the many volunteers, the place they studied the language, and their guest home when they came to Saigon from assignments in the provinces. Several motel-type rooms were built behind this spacious one-floor villa. The name attached to the front gate—Êm-Đêm (Tranquilty)—stayed.

Writing to the Mission board home office early November, Everett reflected on his role with MCC:

> I do still feel that our mission here is primarily church building but would be open to whatever seems to be the Spirit's directing as sensed by all parties concerned. The urge to 'do something' in the present situation is felt more strongly by all of us here these days as the tempo of war increases. . . . There still seems to be something basically wrong about our coming as Christians to heal and help where our fellow countrymen have killed and destroyed if at the same time we do not register a strong protest and appeal to all the fighting parties concerned to stop the destruction.

Under Premier Ky's orders for full mobilization, Ninh in October was called into Officers' Training School at Thu Duc—just east of Saigon. Since the Mennonite Mission had successfully petitioned for deferment for two persons engaged in religious activities, we helped Longacre petition the Ministry of Defense for a temporary deferment on the grounds that Ninh was indispensable for MCC's ministries. Ninh was released in November.

Robert Miller and CWS representative Frank Hutchison spent nearly three weeks in Vietnam in November, visiting all the areas with large refugee populations, speaking with Vietnamese and American officials, and with representatives of numerous voluntary agencies and missionaries. Ove E. Nielsen, Assistant Director of Lutheran World Relief, also spent several days in Vietnam consulting with Hutchison and Miller.

Miller was amazed at the changes he observed since his previous visit only seven months before. In a letter to William Snyder November 17, Miller wrote: "The United States buildup here is truly massive. Military personnel, trucks, jeeps, planes dominate the scene in the towns we visited. USOM is also expanding and rapidly building up its staff in Saigon and at the regional and provincial level."

We missionaries supported the expansion of MCC programs. Yet with some ambivalence we also asked whether MCC should continue in Vietnam. Could MCC maintain an identity distinct from the America which was raining death over the countryside? Aware that many American military personnel gave assistance to children in orphanages, we wondered whether they saw this as partial penance for their destruction of life.

In December, we learned that my brother, Earl, was considering an MCC Vietnam assignment. In a letter home Mary wrote: "Earl, we would surely love to have you in Vietnam. Of course, we realize the dangers for a young American who can easily be mistaken for a military person. But the VC aren't always too choosey about that, anyway. . . . We trust your decision, along with MCC's, will lead you to the place God is planning to use you."

Atlee Beechy was invited to direct the new joint agency. Beechy, a Goshen College psychology professor who had served as Dean of Students, had experience in relief work in Europe following World War II, and served on the MCC Executive Committee.

Within weeks of Miller's return to Akron, three agencies on January 6, 1966 signed a Memorandum of Understanding as follows:

> The name of the program shall be "Vietnam Christian Service." It shall serve refugees and other people in the emergency situation in Vietnam.
>
> The program shall be supported by the Mennonite Central Committee, Church World Service and Lutheran World Relief.
>
> The program shall be administered by the Mennonite Central Committee.

The memorandum stated that each agency would name a representative to a consultative committee which would "give guidance on policy and program matters" to MCC, and MCC was to report regularly to this committee. Within six months, program and agency relationships were to be reviewed. During this initial period the committee members would consult at least monthly.

MCC was beginning a uniquely new experience.

PUBLIC STATEMENTS AGAINST THE WAR

Chapter 22

William T. Snyder, MCC's Executive Secretary, at the request of the Executive Committee meeting in Chicago June 2, 1965, sent to U.S. President Lyndon Johnson a letter expressing "deep concern over the enlarging war in Vietnam with its consequent toll of human suffering."

Snyder referred to MCC's relief and service programs in Vietnam the previous decade, and plans to increase their services in response to the growing need. He called for economic development rather than military activity. He said aid must be given to needy persons regardless of political persuasion. And he urged a negotiated settlement to the hostilities, concluding with a plea to "move in the direction of peace by an escalation of compassion rather than an escalation of conflict."

The delegates to the General Conference Mennonite Church, at their sessions in Estes Park, Colorado, on July 15, expressed deep grief "over the course of action being pursued in Vietnam." Noting MCC's letter to the President the previous month, a June resolution by the Church of the Brethren, and a paid ad in the April 4 *New York Times* placed by the Fellowship of Reconciliation (FOR), these delegates called for a "reappraisal of the United States government policy in Vietnam."

While abhorring "subversion and aggression of the communists in Vietnam," the statement called on the United States to "halt and disavow the bombing of noncombatants, the torture of prisoners, and other such acts of war." It called for a negotiated settlement that would unite Vietnam without prior insistence on a specific political or economic order. The delegates pledged to pray for government leaders and to provide support to Vietnamese refugees through Mennonite Central Committee.

On July 28, President Johnson announced that the number of U.S. troops in Vietnam would be raised from 75,000 to 125,000. Three days later Everett Metzler wrote to EMBMC Mission Secretary, Paul N. Kraybill, "Increasingly we must face the question of the validity of our being here unless we can somehow find some way to disassociate ourselves from the American image and effort here. We need to protest more actively."

Everett noted with approval the FOR statement. He said "we missionaries need to prick the conscience of the church in America. We should make it clear that we fundamentally disagree with American policy in Vietnam. . . . The struggle here is basically a U.S. versus China issue and the Vietnamese are the ones who are made to suffer the brunt."

Thus, after months of escalating American military activities, the Vietnam Mission Council on August 11, 1965, unanimously agreed to issue a public statement concerning the war.

Likely the most opportune time for making a statement had already passed—after the President had made a commitment to use the military might of the United States to defeat the Viet Cong. After Secretary of Defense McNamara returned from a Vietnam visit, President Johnson, on July 21, initiated a series of high level conversations about the ongoing Vietnam policy, involving National Security Advisor McGeorge Bundy; Secretary of State Dean Rusk; William Bundy, Assistant Secretary of State for East Asia and Pacific Affairs; Under Secretary of State George Ball; Ambassador to Vietnam Henry Cabot Lodge; Cyrus Vance, Deputy Secretary of Defense;

CIA head Richard Helms; Army Chief of Staff, Harold Johnson; and others. At the conclusion of those meetings, President Johnson announced the troop buildup, promising that additional troops would be sent as needed. (For a synopsis of those conversations, see George McTurnan Kahin, *Intervention*, [New York: Alfred A Knopf, Inc., 1979, 1986]).

Our decision to prepare a statement came after months of agonizing discussions and prayer. We missionaries were schooled in a two-kingdom theology—the kingdom of Jesus Christ and the kingdom of the world. Since the general social order was "outside the perfection of Christ," Christians were to have no part in civil governments. While civil government was also instituted by God to maintain order in an imperfect world, it was not the duty of Christians to tell government how to rule. Rather, they were to pay taxes and obey laws unless these laws were in conflict with God's higher law.

Each of us missionaries had a personal sense of call to proclaim the gospel of Jesus Christ and were commissioned by the church in the United States. We were now alien guests within the Republic of Vietnam. Our visas stipulated that we were authorized to carry out religious activities. And the authorization granted to the Vietnam Mennonite Mission by the government of Gen. Nguyen Khanh in September 1964 stated that the organization "may be active only in purely religious activities."

Even though we knew that the Alliance missionaries generally supported the U.S. military involvement, Everett and I met with T. Grady Mangham, C&MA Vietnam Chairman, on August 24 to get his view of the political and military situation. The future seemed quite unpredictable. China had threatened to send troops to support their southern neighbor, leading to a larger conflict. A few observers held to a slim hope that North Vietnam might offer some concession to reduce hostilities.

We asked Mangham whether American support of the war hindered the work of the Tin Lanh pastors or of the missionaries. Grady thought not. He said that in certain areas of South Vietnam where churches were recently established, the VC had tried to demonstrate—sometimes effectively—that the coming of the missionaries coincided with the increasing U.S. aid to the government. One area supervisor of the Tin Lanh Church in Central Vietnam reported that 85 percent of the churches in his area were in zones controlled by the VC. The people from these villages often fled to towns to escape American and Vietnamese bombing and strafing raids or VC harassment. However, pastors who stayed in the VC-controlled areas were generally allowed to travel around. When these pastors were accused of supporting the Americans, they would reply: "The American missionaries have told us not to follow them or America, but to follow God." Mangham said that some pastors in the larger towns had contact with Americans they knew to be Christians and it did not seem to affect their witness. He told of a pastor who heard a radio report from Hanoi which admitted that the Front for the Liberation of South Vietnam was having difficulty in its program to "liberate" the South, attributed partly to Christian ethnic minority people and Vietnamese pastors who refused indoctrination.

Everett and I told Mangham that we Mennonite missionaries were considering preparing some statement expressing our opposition to the U.S. military involvement in Vietnam. Mangham said that their Mission and the Tin Lanh Church only released public statements when there were erroneous news reports or when the public misinterpreted some Mission or Church policy.

This is what the American military intervention had become for us American Mennonite missionaries; we believed that—unless we speak—people would assume that we supported the American military actions! We Mennonite missionaries agreed that we must release a statement. To whom would we address it? What would we say?

In early September, the Mission Council decided that the statement should be directed to our constituency, the church in the United States. James Metzler read a statement to which we offered critique. It would still be a few months before we would release a final statement.

Responding to Everett on September 20, Kraybill wrote:

> I wish we could talk face to face about some of the questions we all have regarding the current situation. It is certainly a frustrating and discouraging situation to say the least, and one feels terribly helpless to know how to raise a protest against the course of events. I have noted with much interest the various statements that are being issued by church groups. The controversy over the various approaches to the Vietnam situation continues here in this country although it is not as strong and marked as it was earlier. . . . It is difficult for us here to really know what is right and how to say the right thing when the situation there is so complex. I am concerned that the church here is increasingly aware of its true role as a church and does not compromise its principles by simply becoming another political protest group.

Kraybill asked us to keep him informed of our thinking. He had recently met John A. Lapp who reported his conversation with the missionary team during his two-day stop in Saigon a month earlier. On his way home from an assignment in India late August, Lapp spent two days in Saigon, meeting with the Longacres and the missionary families. He also spoke to students at the Saigon Student Center one evening.

Kraybill continued his letter:

> I agree with John Lapp and with Mr. Mangham that for you folks to make a statement is a rather precarious proposal, unless as Mr. Mangham says you are in a position of being publically misunderstood.
>
> The course of events, of course, is not predictable and one would hope that regardless of whatever changes may occur, one always can maintain a neutral stand that will enable you to continue your work and service regardless of the tide of events. One has the feeling that when you begin to make statements you are almost forced to continue that pattern or your silence will be construed to mean something that you had not intended. If one is not in the habit of making statements, then it may be easier to maintain a position that is known and understood than if one is expected to comment frequently and fails to do so and then is misinterpreted because of that. Here at home, I think it is in order for the church to speak to itself about its attitude although I have mixed feelings about statements being made to Washington.

Everett continued the conversation with Kraybill in early October. "We appreciate your counsel in this," he wrote. "I think the Mission group is still minded to make a statement to the Church at home, at least."

Everett referred to the view expressed by Stephen Cary, AFSC representative who had made the Saigon Mennonite Center his base for three months as he traveled all over South Vietnam. Cary related many stories to Everett and James Metzler—stories he heard from American GIs. Helicopter gunners told how they killed women and babies among suspected Viet Cong farmers, and how they leveled an entire village with rocket fire because some VC guerrillas fled into the village. Cary, Everett said, pointed out to us that "our Saigon postmark and position does obligate us to speak out." He continued: "One gets the impression that Washington is putting on the pressure to stifle and ridicule any protests against what our government is doing here. [Although] we do have difficulty in determining what should be said, to whom, and with what purpose, we do feel we need to have something to point to as representing our position in the conflict here."

When the 264 delegates to the general conference of the Mennonite Church met at Kidron, Ohio, in August 24-27, they adopted a statement declaring that the church "must question the moral basis of the American involvement in Vietnam." Questioning the validity of the arguments for U.S. intervention, the delegates said that they "recognize that it is not within our province to propose specific solutions." However, the statement called on the nation to recognize its "hazardous course" and "retrace misguided steps." Recognizing the Church's own failures to always "love mercy and do justice," the delegates pledged dedication anew "to the ministry of love among the peoples of Southeast Asia."

Gospel Herald, the official organ of the Mennonite Church, on September 28 published "A Message from Mennonite General Conference to the Constituent Congregations Concerning the War in Vietnam." This statement lamented the "weak, confused and divided" Christian community in the United States, a country which in "a spirit of arrogance" had again gone to war. While the statement deplored the atrocities committed by the Viet Cong, its primary concern was not "the sins of other nations [but] rather the brutal warfare waged by the forces of our own country. . . . That our nation should embark on a course so hazardous, while enjoying the passive or even active support of professing Christians, is symptomatic of the profound confusion, even apostasy, among the churches in America. This is most distressing to all who hold to the biblical principle of love and nonresistance."

Carefully worded, the statement then urged the congregations of the Mennonite Church, and "all others who will hear," to seriously consider the context of the Vietnam crisis. It observed that "history has moved beyond the time when Western powers can presume to play the role of international broker among the nations of Asia (or Africa or Latin America)" and to recognize the powerful forces of nationalism, cultural dignity, and security from hunger. It observed that "atrocities characterizing American and American-supported military action are glossed over" by much of the mass media. Arguments in defense of American policy like "containing" China, defending a weak state from external aggression, or "to honor our commitments . . . lack a genuine moral basis." Most surely, the statement continued, "negotiation is preferable to military escalation."

The statement urged every congregation of the Mennonite Church to serious reflection, conversation and prayer regarding the war in order to give an appropriate witness, and to "renew our common commitment to the way of peace" while giving sacrificial service to the victims of the war.

There had been many demonstrations by American college students against the war in 1964, and the following spring "teach-ins" were organized in many universities discussing the background of the conflict. Now in October 1965, a hundred religious leaders met in New York City and formed the Clergy Concerned about Vietnam. This later broadened to Clergy and Laymen Concerned about Vietnam.

Paul E. Peachey, Executive Secretary of the Committee on Peace and Social Concerns of the Mennonite Church, was in conversation with his counterpart in the General Conference Mennonite Church, Stanley Bohn and with Edgar Metzler of the MCC Peace Section. On November 5, 1965, these three committees met as a task force at Goshen, Indiana, and acted to request that the *Gospel Herald* and *The Mennonite*, the official papers of the two large denominations—Mennonite Church and General Conference Mennonite Church—devote a special joint issue as a congregational action manual on the war in Vietnam.

Since the Lancaster Mennonite Conference representative was unable to attend this session, Paul Kraybill, Eastern Board Secretary, did not hear these plans until late November. After receiving a request to provide material for this special issue, Kraybill immediately called Snyder. Both had reservations about contributing to a project without more background information. Kraybill asked Everett to send the statement the Vietnam Mission Council had prepared—it was basically written in September but had not yet been sent out. He asked that we not release it until first cleared through his office. "I am sure that your statement could be a very meaningful contribution," Kraybill wrote, if it can be included within a carefully arranged outline of other publicity materials. He acknowledged being "deeply torn and confused by the tragic, heartbreaking" escalation of war in Vietnam, but insisted that the information and concerns be presented in a way that would not further confuse or alienate people.

Orie O. Miller, who had long served as EMBMC Secretary and had championed the Mennonite non-resistant peace stance throughout his life, informed Kraybill that persons from this joint session had concluded that it was both "urgent and timely for our constituency to speak forthrightly, clearly and boldly regarding the Vietnam agony." Their request for EMBMC and MCC participation "needs considered response and readiness for involvement as the Spirit would lead," he said.

In early December, Peachey informed the editors of the two papers, John Drescher *(Gospel Herald)* and Maynard Shelly *(The Mennonite),* that both MCC and the Mission Board would prepare materials describing their program involvements and objectives in Vietnam. Kraybill and Robert Miller were invited to join the task force. Snyder praised Peachey for the vision of the task force "in keeping before the program planners and administrators the need for clarity of thought on our Christian witness in the Vietnam situation."

Writing to Everett, Kraybill said that the Mission Board was ready to speak

> but [we] want to be cautious that we do not confuse our people more than we help. There are so many voices trying to speak today, many of them polarized either on the extreme left or extreme right and very few who have a creative spiritual accent. . . . To identify ourselves either with the pro-military or the anti-military pressures here in the United States may compromise our neutral position which we feel is essential to the unique kind of ministry that we want to be able to give regardless of the political climate or circumstance. We are also concerned about reconciliation of the opposing elements rather than polarizing more rigidly the controversy that is raging about us here in the States.

Everett acknowledged Kraybill's letters, saying that we missionaries generally concurred with Paul's concerns, though we "would lean a bit farther left."

Snyder sent another memo to the task force on December 22, affirming the importance of this publicity. Observing the complex relationship Mennonites had with Vietnamese Christians, Alliance missionaries, the Vietnamese government and the American military, he wrote: "Our voice on Vietnam will be heard in all these quarters, especially within the Christian church, and I think it must be a highly responsible voice."

Writing just two weeks before MCC signed the Memorandum of Understanding with Church World Service and Lutheran World Relief to create Vietnam Christian Service, Snyder expressed reservations about MCC leading Vietnam Christian Service. "Frankly," he wrote,

I am somewhat apprehensive whether we can, as an historic peace church, lead the Protestant forces as we have been asked to do in Vietnam. If we pull out all the stops in our criticism of US government foreign policy by asking withdrawal of United States from Vietnam, I think we will likely pull apart from the larger body of Protestants who presently want to work through us. On the other hand, if we are somewhat moderate in tone, I believe that we may have an opportunity to influence these denominations on a scale that we have not hitherto had opportunity to do. It is clear to me that our words and our deeds in Vietnam must go together and that the acid test of what we say in the *Gospel Herald* and *The Mennonite* must be what we do in Vietnam and in our own communities.

Snyder called on Mennonite church communities to urge persons with technical and professional skills to volunteer for service in Vietnam and to back them up with an outpouring of program funds to demonstrate our concern for the people of Vietnam. Taking on "some of the sufferings of the people of Vietnam" would demonstrate the seriousness of our concern.

The joint issue published in *Gospel Herald* on January 25, 1966 was a significant achievement. *The Mennonite* issue of the same date was nearly identical. The lead article "Vietnam: Soul-Sick and War-Weary" by Willard S. Krabill, described the Vietnam he had seen and heard in late October as a member of the government-sponsored visit. He called for increased assistance to the growing number of refugees, but said that "the greatest need in the Vietnamese refugee problem is to quit making refugees. . . . No effort should be spared in ending the war."

Paul Peachey in "Vietnam, 'Hour of Truth'" described the historical context of the U.S. self-interest in Vietnam as a "chapter" of America's confrontation with China. Theologian John Howard Yoder gave answers to the question, "Why Speak to Government?" He emphasized that God is on the side of the poor, and that violence is no basis for social peace. It is not appropriate, Yoder wrote, for the United States to attempt to police the world—policy-makers cannot be trusted to be also the judges of their own actions.

Larry Kehler, Information Secretary at MCC, submitted an article entitled "What is MCC Doing?" and Paul N. Kraybill prepared a piece, "What Is Eastern Board Doing?" Kraybill closed his article with a "Statement of Purposes for the Eastern Board Program in Vietnam" endorsed by the Mission Board Executive Committee. This statement reaffirmed the church's refusal to support the war and urged the church to see opportunities for witness and service. It asked the church to pray for all involved government leaders, Christians, and "all the suffering people" in Vietnam. It committed the Mission to "continue a positive program of witness . . . as long as humanly possible" and called on the church to "sacrificial self-discipline . . . to make possible an enlarged program of witness and service."

On December 8, Everett Metzler sent the "Statement of Concern" prepared by the Vietnam Mennonite Mission Council. Addressed to Christians, especially those within the Mennonite churches, the statement asked persons to learn the historical background to the conflict. It described the human tragedy of the people who have no voice in choosing their fate and questioned the validity of the American military involvement. Inasmuch as Vietnamese viewed America as a Christian nation, it noted how the war made the Gospel communication more difficult.

This statement signed by the four members of the Mission Council—James Stauffer was on furlough—was rather mild. Mindful that we missionaries were guests of a foreign country whose leaders relied on U.S. support, the statement makes no mention of the Vietnamese government or its policies. Nor does it explicitly criticize the American government. When we first went to Vietnam we would have claimed to be non-political. By this time we had learned that we could not be viewed as apolitical; we were among the tens of thousands of Americans pouring into Vietnam. Just by being in Vietnam we had made a nonverbal statement. Our written statement made it clear that we did not support American military policies—even if the majority of other missionaries did.

Kraybill reported to us—before the Statement of Concern was published, that it "was well accepted" by local church and mission leaders who read it.

Richard Benner, the missions' editor for the Mennonite Board of Missions, had written to us missionaries in late November inviting us to write a short opinion on the question: "What should the Christian worker do in Vietnam in light of the military struggle?" Benner wrote: "Since the politicians can't tell us what the U.S. is doing in Vietnam, maybe some of our workers can tell us what non-resistant Christians should be doing there."

Several of us wrote personal responses to this question, more directly critiquing American policy than in our joint "Statement of Concern."

James Metzler suggested that the most realistic witness might be to leave the country, given that many people "considered us to be part of the total war effort." Yet he could hardly think of leaving because the opportunities to witness and serve were so obvious. Perhaps our response called for us to accept misunderstanding, and above all, seek to end the carnage.

Everett Metzler, eight years in Vietnam, wrote that appeals must be made "to all parties in the conflict to turn from war as an instrument of policy," even though dissent from the war policy of the Saigon government was considered treason. Specifically, Everett said, we must "disassociate ourselves and our mission from the US military establishment here . . . , place ourselves in the shoes of Viet-namese people as war ravages their countryside," and give ourselves to ministries of healing.

This special joint issue enabled American Mennonites to express anguish as their nation rapidly accelerated its military intervention in this small country in Southeast Asia. Although Kraybill had early reservations about participating in this project, he later thanked the editors for the opportunity to contribute to informing the church community.

Mahlon Hess of the Eastern Board information office thanked Louis L. King, C&MA Foreign Secretary, for providing information on the Evangelical Church in Vietnam, and sent a copy of the special issue of the *Gospel Herald*, reporting that it "seems to be having a good ministry among our congregations." The C&MA office requested six additional copies.

In the annual report prepared for the March 1966 Mission Board Meeting, Everett alluded to the special January edition of the *Gospel Herald*, and wrote: "The massive American commitment to take a stand in Vietnam has lessened for the time being the possibility of a collapse which would necessitate the evacuation of missionary personnel. This in turn has made it increasingly difficult to avoid undesirable identification with the American effort here as the American presence is more the character of an occupation rather than 'assistance.' This problem is complicated by the lack of hesitancy of other missionaries to identify with the American effort."

It would not be the only time we missionaries spoke out; Kraybill may have been correct when he in September told Everett: "When you begin to make statements you are almost forced to continue that pattern or your silence will be construed to mean something that you had not intended." However, given the massive American military intervention coupled with Gen. West-moreland's strategy of attrition—killing as many people as possible—there was no way that we could have remained silent!

"We do want to continue our opposition to war, and this does not exclude a protest about the war in Vietnam," Kraybill wrote.

> But this opposition is based on the fact that we are opposed to every war on the basis of Christian principles and do not want to be identified with the draft dodgers, draft card burners, and others who are getting a lot of publicity now and whose opposition to war is more a matter of political conviction or humanitarian and particularly directed to this specific war rather than an ongoing conviction against every war. Our opposition to the Vietnam War must be of a different quality and nature than this, and this does become a problem to maintain the kind of Biblical posture that is valid now and will continue to be valid regardless of the political circumstances.

Kraybill was articulating moderate core convictions of the Mennonite churches, as he continued, "We are strongest when we continue the conviction that we had before this conflict and hope to maintain after this conflict, namely, that war is wrong and that we are opposed to it and want to protest its evils in every form."

Kraybill was concerned that speaking to governmental leaders, marching in demonstrations, and making foreign policy pronouncements might negate our "pilgrim stature" in the world. "We have a unique Christian mission in all of this and I hope that we can maintain it. I know that you understand and accept this but I simply say it in trying to think through the whole problem with you."

Instead of backing away from Vietnam, Kraybill advocated greater commitment: "We want to increase our involvement in Vietnam and underscore our willingness to take seriously the tremendous physical and spiritual need there. We had nothing to do with this war, hence I do not feel we need to be guilty at all for participating in the ministry to human need. There are people there who are the innocent victims of suffering and destruction and our program should continue to strengthen its compassionate ministry to these people."

Everett thanked Kraybill for his thoughtful letter, but wrote: "As Christians we feel we must be doing something to end the conflict. . . . We are grateful that over the years our church has not been standing on the outside talking but has been making significant efforts to be true to her responsibility as a New Testament Church in social service and other activities consistent with our peace testimony."

Yet Everett took issue with Kraybill's assertion that "we had nothing to do with the war." Everett insisted that to some degree "we are guilty by association in the fact that we are Americans and cannot change this. He wrote: "It remains for us to demonstrate by love in action that we are of a different motivation than most Americans here."

Metzler and Kraybill expressed different stances—perhaps a difference between living within the war zone and living half a world away, perhaps a distinction between younger and older persons in the church, our readiness to move away from a quiet nonresistance to a more engaged Christian pacifism. Kraybill acted and wrote out of deep spiritual conviction concerning the way of Jesus. Tidy theological formulations did not suffice for those of us in Vietnam who lived daily with the conflict. To us there was a more desperate demand to attempt to pull the contestants apart, the need to stop the powerful Uncle Sam who had traveled ten thousand miles from home to fight Uncle Ho in his own land.

VNCS ERA BEGINS 1966

Chapter 23

On January 6, 1966, Church World Service, Lutheran World Relief, and Mennonite Central Committee signed a Memorandum of Understanding to partner in Vietnam Christian Service (VNCS), with MCC administering the program; this was approved by the MCC Executive Committee on January 14. By this time many new personnel were already in Vietnam. By year's end VNCS would have sixty-four international volunteers compared with only five persons serving with MCC two years earlier. A significantly larger budget would enable VNCS to begin many more programs.

MCC was committed to continuing a close relationship with the Evangelical Church of Vietnam (ECVN). In the Vietnamese language "Vietnam Christian Service" became *Tổ Chức Xã Hội Tin Lành* (or Protestant Social Organization). For some people *Tin Lành* represented a specific *evangelical* understanding of Christianity. However, since the Evangelical Church was the dominant expression of Protestant Christianity in the country, most Vietnamese thought of *Tin Lành* as *Protestant* in contrast to Catholic Christianity.

Some Alliance missionaries and Tin Lanh Church leaders were not pleased that VNCS used the *Tin Lành* name. In South Vietnam's struggle with a communist-led guerrilla force, some Church leaders were also uncomfortable with Mennonite expressions of peace. With other agencies coming in response to the growing war, Tin Lanh leaders could seek support from World Vision or from World Relief Commission, the service agency of the National Association of Evangelicals—in which the Alliance Church held membership. The Tin Lanh Church President, Pastor Doan Van Mieng said it was alright for the new agency to use *Tin Lành* in its name.

Atlee Beechy, the first Executive Director of VNCS, arrived in Saigon on February 11. Beechy negotiated an eight-month leave from Goshen College in Goshen, Indiana where he taught psychology. He had a wealth of experience working with Mennonite service programs. During World War II, as a conscientious objector to war, he was leader in a Civilian Public Service Camp. After the war he served as MCC's European Area Director for two and one-half years. Wanting a person with broad experience, William Snyder in early December invited Beechy, aged fifty-one, to direct the new program.

Beechy arrived at Saigon's Tan Son Nhat International Airport just a few hours after American Vice President Hubert Humphrey arrived for a five-day visit. In his first letter to Robert Miller, Beechy thanked Miller "for arranging . . . such a fine reception. The flags and banners were flying and there was a good delegation to meet me at the airport." Beechy's wife, Winifred, came a few months later.

Beechy and Paul Longacre attended a reception the next day at the American Embassy in honor of the Vice President. Here they met U.S. Ambassador Henry Cabot Lodge and Ambassador at Large W. Averell Harriman. Meeting the Vice President, Atlee and Paul told Humphrey about "the growing concern of American churches for the agony of Vietnam" and the work and goals of Vietnam Christian Service.

Paul Longacre now served as VNCS Associate Director. Longacre wrote home: "It is going to be a pleasure to work with Dr. Beechy. His thoughtful, considerate way of dealing with people and problems will provide real learning opportunities for me. His competence, maturity, and manner will be essential ingredients in the future with our involved structure—MCC plus LWR plus CWS equals VCS—with different people of different backgrounds we need his capacities here."

At first Vietnam Christian Service used the acronym "VCS." But "VNCS" had a nicer rhythm. More importantly, those opposing the Saigon government were called "VCs"!

Doris had given birth to the Longacres' first child, Cara Sue, just five weeks earlier. Though he would be on the road—or more aptly, in the air—a great deal of time in following months, Paul was a most devoted parent. He wrote home: "[Babies] are one of the most time-consuming creatures every created—but a most enjoyable way to consume time." Aware of the tragedy of the expanding war, he wrote: "Doris and I enjoy our little darling immensely but we do it with a vague sense of uneasiness, knowing that there are so many parents close to us who cannot thus enjoy their children. . . . While Doris was in the hospital an old Vietnamese nurse who cares for the babies in the nursery began to talk and weep one day as she told Doris of her own son who had been killed in the war just three months before."

After their daughter was born, Longacre wrote to the President, concerned that Johnson would escalate the war following the failure of a Christmas peace initiative by the United States.

Doris also wrote home about a fortunate-within-an-unfortunate experience:

> The . . . day I came home from the hospital Paul had an unfortunate experience. He was riding home on the motorbike with his small briefcase strapped on the back, and someone snatched the briefcase—probably someone on another bike. He and Everett Metzler immediately went to the nearest police station and reported it. About fifteen minutes after Paul got home a policeman came here to the house and took Paul along to the station where they gave him the briefcase with everything in it except the money—7,000 piasters or about $50.00. Since it contained his passport, Vietnam identification, MCC financial records, and other important papers, we were most fortunate to get it back.

Paul and Doris Longacre moved into the roomy villa on Le Quang Dinh Street, Gia Dinh, on February 1. A small sign on the gate identified its name—*Êm Đêm (Tranquility)*. The large back yard was a virtual fruit orchard with sapodillas, cainito, mango, lemon, papaya, and coconut palm trees. The banana trees had to be cut down to build the new motel-type rooms where volunteers lived during their two-month intensive Vietnamese language studies. Nhung, the savvy businesswoman wife of interpreter Nguyen Van Ninh, purchased most of the furniture and appliances.

Church World Service recruited Bill Luken to serve as accountant and Ross Orr came as material aid coordinator. Gary DeWarle served as Material Aid Assistant. Eight MCC volunteers arrived in mid-February—nurses Mary Pauls and Ruth Yoder, Dr. Christopher and Lois Leuz, David and Sue Neufeld with their one-year-old son Mike, and Pax men Paul Kennel and Earl Martin. Pauls and the Neufelds were from Ontario, Canada—the others from the United States. A month later three persons recruited by the Brethren Service Commission arrived—Mary Sue Halstern, Rufus Petre and Bill Herod.

In December 1965, Naval Captain Archie Kuntze, head of the Military Exchange operated by the US Navy, sent letters to US non-government agencies, offering limited commissary privileges, ostensibly to ease the demands by American civilians on Vietnamese markets. The offer was made to organizations "solely supporting the US and South Vietnamese efforts" in Vietnam. Although Paul knew the intent was meant to exclude business people, he asked for further clarification; after all, MCC was generally opposed to U.S. policy in Vietnam! Kuntze said they would modify the statement MCC would have to sign.

Longacre reasoned: "Accepting the privilege and eating American food would place us one step farther away from the Vietnamese people and one closer to the military. It would tend to mute our protests against the U.S. military activity."

Still Paul noted how the use of the commissary might be helpful for up-country units having difficulty getting good food. Like many things in Vietnam, many issues were not so black and white. Beechy later reported to the Akron office that they requested commissary privileges for Doris Longacre, the *Êm Đêm* hostess, and for Ross Orr, the VNCS material aid director. They were "strongly urging limited use" by the MCC volunteers so they would rely on the same markets as the Vietnamese people. However, Beechy did not impose this on CWS personnel.

Although Mennonite missionaries were also offered commissary privileges, they were cool to the idea, and none ever requested a card.

Atlee Beechy and Paul Longacre with language teachers at Em Dem.

Everett Metzler developed the language and orientation program for the new VNCS personnel, implemented as soon as they arrived. The students spent eight hours daily in Vietnamese language study. Planned lectures included discussions about government structures, political history, Vietnamese religions, the Evangelical Church, students, the minority peoples, USAID, voluntary agencies, and International Voluntary Service.

On Saturday afternoon, March 12, Beechy and Longacre discussed security matters with old and new staff members. Though the meeting was scheduled several days earlier, the timing was perfect. The previous evening several VNCSers came on the scene of a grenade attack at a nearby police station just after the incident occurred. And very early Saturday morning three American barges on the Saigon River—two kilometers away—exploded with 350 tons of ammunition. Beechy observed: "Most of the places housing military or certain other types of Americans have barbed wire fences,

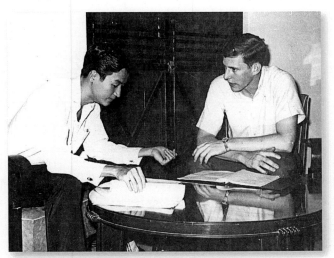

Paul Kennel at language study.

sometimes high netting and guards. Our position to date has been not to accent our American identification with the above. Theologically and realistically this seems best. We plan to place a sign identifying ourselves on the front gate. This will include our symbol and will be in Vietnamese." *Êm Đêm* was never attacked.

Using a prepared outline, "Guidelines Related to Security Matters," Beechy and Longacre encouraged personnel to avoid two extremes—"a daring obliviousness to existent dangers or a frenzied fear of the almost nonexistent dangers." They said staff members should share security concerns with others, be conservative about traveling, know the way to their destinations, limit travel to only business in areas with limited security, travel only during the day and avoid travel in military or USAID vehicles, avoid announcing travel plans, and avoid regular travel routines. When traveling by air, personnel were to use Air America (used by USAID personnel) if possible because there was no charge. The second priority was Air Vietnam, the national airline. Military planes were only to be used as a last resort.

Longacre accompanied Beechy on his first visit to central Vietnam in late February. Beechy was impressed with the good reputation of the Tin Lanh Clinic and hospital in Nha Trang. They discussed possible expansion with the staff and the board. Flying on to Quang Ngai, they stayed with Alliance missionaries Woody and Charlotte Stemple. As the only missionaries in the province, the Stemples expressed great interest in having VNCS develop ministries among the one hundred thousand refugees there. They also met with the pastor of the local Tin Lanh congregation and with eight licensed pastors from the surrounding area, many of whom had earlier assisted MCC in distributing material aid supplies to flood victims.

The two men also met with USAID officials and with an American army major, one of three hundred American military advisors in Quang Ngai. They visited the provincial civilian hospital guided by a U.S. captain, a member of a U.S. Military Provincial Health Assistance Program team. Beechy felt "sick and angry" when the captain described young boys severely burned by napalm as "unfortunate victims of the war." In an engagement near Quang Ngai earlier in the week, more than a hundred ARVN soldiers were killed or wounded. One soldier, shot through the neck and spine and paralyzed, was evacuated to Saigon on the same plane they traveled, accompanied by a medical corpsman and the soldier's wife.

"The trip was most helpful to me," Beechy wrote. "It gave me a sense of things which no amount of study could give me. The scars of war are deep. The ministry, if it is to help in the healing process, must be deeply compassionate."

Beechy took time to write a letter to John Brademas, the Representative to the U.S. Congress from Indiana's Third Congressional District. Saying he was "deeply troubled," Beechy noted that U.S. Administration officials were pursuing a hard line approach to North Vietnam while at the same time saying they were prepared to negotiate. He wrote:

> One problem with those who briefly visit Vietnam is that they do not have the time to listen to what the Vietnamese people are saying. Recently I talked to a high ranking university official. He said, 'we are the war-weary people.' Visitors usually do not talk to the villagers whose homes have been bombed and burned and whose families have been broken. Most have not visited the hospitals where the disfigured and the bruised are found. The two eight year old boys I saw at the Quang Ngai Civilian Hospital several weeks ago come back to haunt me time and again. They

were very friendly but had been terribly burned by napalm bombs. They are indeed the innocent and unfortunate victims of the war. The civilian to military casualty ratio is varyingly estimated as being from 6-10 to one. I am also troubled as I see and talk to the young American soldiers. They do not lack in courage but one senses a kind of bewilderment and uneasiness about the whole thing. Most are desperately looking forward to the day when they can go home.

Beechy noted that many informed people viewed American policies "with considerable cynicism," believing the United States was in Vietnam for its own self-interests. While not minimizing "the evils of communism," he expressed concern that the U.S. response "must have some consistency with the goals we seek or we destroy ourselves in the process and the ends we want slip away in the chaos." This was the first of many interpretative letters Beechy sent from Vietnam to American officials.

In early March, Frank Epp, editor of the weekly *Canadian Mennonite*, came to Vietnam for two weeks at the request of MCC to visit projects and prepare publicity materials. He met one evening with VNCS and Mennonite mission personnel at Everett and Margaret Metzler's home. Initially having "serious reservations" about MCC being in Vietnam, he left "convinced that we belong."

Beechy soon became acquainted with Saigon government officials with whom MCC had worked, with USAID officials, and with administrative persons of the various international non-governmental voluntary agencies. In mid-March, he met with representatives of the Council of Voluntary Agencies, identifying the critical need for training local personnel in nursing, social work, agriculture, mechanics, and home economics. Paul Longacre had just been named chairman of the Council.

As host and hostess of the Saigon VNCS center, Paul and Doris welcomed many visitors. In February they hosted Holdeman Mennonites and a leader of the Korean Episcopal Church who came to contact units of the Korean armed forces in a chaplaincy role.

The Longacres also entertained others who lived and worked in Vietnam: Rev. and Mrs. Gordon Cathey, the pastoral couple of the International Church; Ms. Elizabeth

Duc Anh Orphanage administration showing the bake oven to Bill Luken and Atlee Beechy.

Brown, Vietnam Director of Foster Parents Plan; and Rev. Theodore H. Evans, Pastor of the Anglican Church in Saigon. The Anglican Church had just contributed $2,500 US to build better facilities for tubercular patients receiving treatment at the Nha Trang Hospital.

The MCC home office in Akron, Pennsylvania also entertained Pastor Doan Van Mieng, President of the Tin Lanh Church, when he visited the United States in April. Parents of Vietnam missionaries and MCC personnel who lived nearby were invited to meet him. Mieng expressed thanks for the help the Mennonite Central Committee gave to the Evangelical Church. Mieng said the Church had been able to maintain a relatively neutral stance in the conflict. Although the Church was growing despite the war, Mieng declared: "The people of Vietnam are tired of war and want peace, but nobody knows what the future holds. All we can do is trust God. He is the loving God, and promised to be with us to the end."

Forging MCC Vietnam into Vietnam Christian Service was a significant challenge for all parties, from the top administrators in the States to those on location in Vietnam. William Snyder said the second meeting in March with the VNCS Consultative Committee, involving Frank Hutchison (CWS) and Ove Nielsen (LWR), "moved the ball further."

Robert Miller prepared a preliminary statement on "Vietnam Christian Service Objectives and Philosophy" and another on "Guidelines to Vietnam Christian Service Relationships to United States Agencies in Vietnam" which were shared with new personnel.

The statement on relationships with U.S. agencies began with a clear inference that the United States is the perpetrator of the war: "The United States government is engaged in military and economic wars in Vietnam. The U.S. government is using large quantities of material and personnel resources to fight these wars directly and through assistance to the South Vietnam government."

While appreciating support from the U.S. and Vietnamese governments in implementing VNCS service programs, the statement is explicit about minimizing the use of American civilian and military facilities, with a deliberate "desire not to be used for political purposes by USAID, the U.S. military, and other governmental agencies."

Representing the concern of American churches for the agony and suffering of the Vietnamese people, VNCS was committed to carrying out "a personalized, efficient ministry to human need, a ministry of Christian presence in the midst of disorder and suffering, and a witness to the reconciling power of love."

The draft statement on VNCS Objectives and Philosophy stressed the importance of "genuine and close identification with the Vietnamese people, emphasizing the principle of self-help." While seeking to carry out an "impartial ministry to persons in need," VNCS wanted to continue MCC's concern of relating

Pastor Doan Van Mieng meeting Elizabeth and Daniel Martin.

"helpfully to the Evangelical Church and other Christian groups." Seeking to be "flexible in approach, structure, and pattern," VNCS hoped to implement "a team concept in which each member participates in the planning, the carrying out, and the evaluation of the work."

VNCS developed rapidly. When, in late March, Beechy sent a memo to Charles Mann, head of USAID Vietnam, he attached a list of the twenty-five members of the VNCS team. Eight were working at Nha Trang, three in Pleiku, three in Quang Ngai, two in Hue with World Relief Commission, and six support people in Saigon. Half of the personnel were working in medical programs.

While asking Mann how VNCS might facilitate long range resettlement of refugees, Beechy indicated "a responsibility to work toward peace, to plan for the day when it will come, and to orient our planning so that we may be most effective when it comes. . . . We consider this to be a tremendous task and we plan to stay around to assist in it after the fighting stops."

Work toward peace. MCC was committed to work with its partners to minister to the victims of war, but was equally dedicated to finding ways to end the carnage. Mann affirmed VNCS's objectives.

Longacre and Beechy made frequent visits to central Vietnam. There were the medical programs in Nha Trang and Pleiku, the World Relief Commission (WRC) projects in Hue, and ministries to refugees in Quang Ngai. While waiting for a flight at the Da Nang airport late March, Longacre counted twenty-three fully-loaded jets taking off for bombing raids.

Robert Miller and C. N. Hostetter, Jr., the chairman of both the WRC and MCC boards of directors, met in early March with Louis King, the C&MA Foreign Secretary. King expressed great appreciation and respect for Paul Longacre. King proposed that VNCS assign to World Relief Commission only persons recruited by MCC. Beechy and Longacre opposed such a policy but promised to be "sensitive" in assigning personnel. Likewise when Methodists asked about having a distinctly Methodist project, Beechy dismissed this idea. Personnel would be placed in teams according to personal skills and specific needs.

Large numbers of U.S. ground troops continued to arrive throughout 1966, so that by the end of the year the number of American GIs had more than doubled to 380,000. Casualties also increased; more than 5,000 GIs were killed and 30,000 injured. The Army of the Republic of Vietnam (ARVN) and the Viet Cong forces also suffered heavily due to a greater number of skirmishes.

The relentless American bombing of transportation networks in the North continued. Though the United States claimed that their bombers were not attacking civilian targets, there was conclusive evidence that residential areas were being bombed. A January 1967 CIA report estimated that eighty percent of the 24,000 casualties of bombing raids over North Vietnam were civilians.

In early February 1966, U.S. President Lyndon Johnson conferred with Prime Minister Nguy-

US fighter bomber returns from bombing mission.

en Cao Ky in Honolulu, promising that the United States would help South Vietnam "prevent aggression," develop the economy and establish "the principles of self-determination of peoples and government by the consent of the governed." He said he would monitor their efforts to build democracy, improve education and health care, resettle refugees and reconstruct the economy.

The *New York Times* reporter R. W. Apple, Jr. told of Gen. Ky speaking with reporters late one night at the February 6-9 conference, telling them what was wrong with the country, saying that Vietnam needed a revolution. Just before the Prime Minister left the gathering at 2:15 a.m., one of the correspondents asked him who might be able to lead the revolution. Ky replied half-jokingly, "There is only one person who could lead it—Ho Chi Minh!"

It was soon clear that the United States was quite unable or unwilling to fulfill its promise to help build a true democracy in Vietnam. South Vietnam was embroiled in political turmoil. With the support of the ruling National Leadership Committee, on March 10 Prime Minister Ky dismissed the popular General Nguyen Chanh Thi as commander of I Corps, which encompassed the five provinces south of the Demilitarized Zone. Thi was known to support negotiations with the Viet Cong to find a political settlement for the conflict. The Venerable Thich Tri Quang and other Buddhist leaders who had contributed to the overthrow of President Ngo Dinh Diem in 1963 strongly protested the dismissal of Gen. Thi, a Buddhist. Though they called for a non-violent struggle against the policies of Ky and Chief of State General Nguyen Van Thieu, violent anti-government demonstrations broke out in Da Nang, Hue and many central Vietnam towns.

While not advocating support for the Viet Cong, Tri Quang and others within the Buddhist-oriented political community were more inclined to advocate neutrality than in vigorously pursuing the war. With the Catholic community strongly denouncing any accommodations with communist forces, the stage was set for violent conflicts which raged for some time.

Over several months, the Johnson Administration conducted a series of reviews of the Vietnam situation. Some of President Johnson's advisors recommended disengagement from the war through political accommodation with the other side. In the end, however, Johnson chose to defeat the Viet Cong militarily. Demonstrations in Central Vietnam against Prime Minister Ky were decidedly anti-American. VNCS persons working with WRC in Hue evacuated to Saigon after demonstrators burned the United States Information Services library on May 26 and the U.S. consular office five days later. Many ARVN units in central Vietnam rebelled against the Saigon government. The stand-off eventually ended in June after Ky pledged elections for a constituent assembly that would lead to a civilian government.

Missionaries and other Mennonite personnel in Vietnam during these months continued to speak and write about the immense human suffering and devastation the war was causing. However, since it was not politically expedient for the enigmatic Thich Tri Quang to clearly elucidate the goals of the dominant Buddhist community, it was only later that we recognized the significance of their struggle to end the war. U.S. officials—by their actions—made it clear that they were taking charge of the war and were unwilling to end the conflict except on their terms.

Beechy visited Hue briefly in the midst of the anti-government demonstrations in early April. He enthusiastically described the WRC programs: "The work with pigs, poultry, crop, and feeding patterns are all underway." A vocational training school building was being built with pressed mud bricks. More than one hundred refugees worked on the project—receiving relief food as payment.

Atlee wrote: "The Hue project holds real promise provided the political situation permits the further implementation of the vision. The vision of lay leadership is sound. The many facets of the projected program reflect strong creativity. The technical leadership and the personal spiritual dedication of the staff appear strong."

Saigon was not immune to the demonstrations that wracked central Vietnam. Longacre described an anti-American gathering at Saigon's Central Market on March 31 with banners reading "We want American Friends, not Bosses," and "Americans, let us be independent."

"The U.S. Government cannot expect to put 250,000 men into a country as small as this," Longacre observed, "and expect that the local people would not resent it."

In the midst of street demonstrations there were also some lighter moments. On Good Friday, April 8, a monkey loose in the neighborhood came swinging down a hole in the attic of the Neufeld home, scaring Sue while Dave was downstairs playing with Michael. After her screams the monkey soon disappeared back up into the attic.

On Easter Sunday, April 10, eighteen VNCS staff members with visiting CWS leader Frank Hutchison gathered in the open Em Dem courtyard for an Easter sunrise service. Christopher Kimmel, just evacuated from Hue because of the anti-American demonstrations there, led the service. Beechy writes about it: "Meditating on the cross and the resurrection seemed particularly appropriate at this time. Through the singing of hymns, the sharing of the Easter story, and the sharing of testimonies and prayer we were linked to the suffering of the Vietnamese people and the Christians throughout the world. The distant but distinctive sound of bombs dropped by B-52s and the noise of low flying helicopters and other aircraft brought a strange and paradoxical dimension to the gathering. The resurrected Christ stands for hope amidst the confusion, disorder, and despair of our day."

A few days later, A. J. Muste, a well-known Christian pacifist activist, and five others from the Committee for Non-Violent Action came to Saigon, hoping to steer the U.S. policy toward a peaceful resolution of the conflict through negotiations with the National Liberation Front. Several came to the VNCS unit house to meet Beechy and other volunteers. Soon after they arrived, three loud explosions and nearby gunfire nearby sent people scurrying to the center of the house under a table. Muste quietly said, "I'm too old to worry about my safety. I'm staying in my chair." Beechy stayed sitting in his chair, too. Nothing more happened. Later they learned that the VC had tried to blow up a police station about a block away. Beechy described the evening as "paradoxical—somewhat humorous and tragic."

At a later press conference downtown, Muste asserted that they had "a moral obligation to say here where the fighting is going on what we have said in the United States. . . . We are friends of both anti-communists and communists in Vietnam. We wish you could solve your problem without violence." The press conference was broken up and the party escorted to the airport.

In April and May new persons arrived, and the six persons completing two months of language study went on assignment. Some of them were already speaking Vietnamese quite well.

In April, Edgar Metzler, Executive Director of MCC Peace Section, corresponded with Beechy about how to best carry out the church's ministry in Vietnam. One issue was the matter of security. Metzler implied that MCC-VNCS should be less security conscious. So Beechy asks, "What do we mean by security? Which kind are we talking about? How is it measured? Who should do the evaluating?" Beechy noted that during mass demonstrations, some with an anti-American tone, Americans were asked to stay off the streets. Why did authorities ask Americans to stay off the streets—because of danger or for political reasons? What would be the consequences of ignoring the government's request?

In the few months since he arrived, Beechy noted that there had been three incidents only one hundred meters from the VNCS center where people had been seriously injured or killed. One was an attack on a police station; the other two involved Americans.

"As field director," Beechy wrote,

> I also face some responsibility for the welfare of our workers. What is the nature of this responsibility? Even though I may be ready to risk my own life, to what extent do I have the right to ask others to do so?"
>
> Our immediate and ultimate security obviously rests in God. Our workers, in the main, seem to have a kind of relaxed but realistic attitude toward this area. There have been times when I have wondered about the possible impact of a group of persons deliberately working in very insecure areas with the full awareness that there would likely be some persons captured or killed. In other moments I ask myself just how much different that would be than what we are now doing. It is a matter of degrees.

Beechy indicated that consideration had been given to assigning medical and community development personnel in Long Thanh, a district town forty kilometers northeast of Saigon. With a U.S. Special Forces Camp and a heavy Vietnamese military presence there, Beechy doubted that VNCS personnel could divorce themselves sufficiently from the military presence to clearly project a Church sponsorship. Traveling to Long Thanh also required movement through insecure areas.

A second issue was how to best give a witness for peace. "At this juncture I do not believe it advisable to designate one person to carry such an assignment," Beechy wrote; "the climate at this time would likely not permit an open aggressive program of pacifistic teaching." However, Beechy said there may be "growing sympathy for this approach . . . due in part to an increasing weariness of the war." Rather than designate one person to this task, Beechy said he wants to see several of the Saigon administrative staff speak out. Beechy said he found unusual opportunities to give a witness through the course of his work. "The explanation of who we are and what we are doing here is called for almost daily," Beechy wrote.

The third area for discussion was the degree of freedom VNCS needed to work in Vietnam. VNCS had to have, Beechy wrote, "some freedom as to where and how we work, the right to clear identification of our goods and services, and opportunity to interpret our goals. The deliberate or subtle attempts to use our work for political or military goals by any governments or private agencies" would be determining factors. These were the reasons, Beechy said, which caused MCC to withdraw from Poland and Hungary in 1948. "These issues are involved and complex," Beechy wrote, "The black and white we see shows up too often as gray."

Another concern, Beechy wrote, is "the moral problem of what our Government is doing to the people of this country, to ourselves, and to the world. . . . Surely we must find ways to protest and witness against current policy. This must be done at all levels and in as comprehensive a way as our spiritual and creative resources permit."

A few days later Beechy wrote a postscript to his earlier letter to Edgar Metzler:

> The question of Guidelines for our work in South Vietnam raises the question as to whether we should be thinking about some Guidelines for possible work in North Vietnam.

I would be inclined to be flexible or liberal in order to work there. I think, however, we might give some attention to the matter even though it may seem hypothetical at this time. What kind of supervision or direction would we accept?. . . I have also been wondering, to what extent do we speak to non-United States governments? The question is applicable to the governments of both South and North Vietnam? I gather that we are less inclined to do this than to evaluate the morality of our own government. There are times when the unrepresentativeness of the government here and some of its actions seem very serious in the total fabric of things. There also are times when I think the evil or immoralness of the government of North Vietnam is somewhat overlooked in our deep concern about the evil in our own government's actions. The Church, if it discharges its function of bringing judgment upon all men and all systems, has indeed a large and comprehensive task.

This "hypothetical" question Beechy raised in 1966 had to be addressed in 1975 when MCC proposed a large post-war assistance program to Vietnam.

The Buddhist struggle against the government which began March 10 with the dismissal of the popular Gen. Thi in central Vietnam continued throughout the summer—sometimes simmering, sometimes boiling over. The *Viện Hóa Đạo*, the Institute for the Propagation of the Faith of the Unified Buddhist Church (*Phật Giáo Việt Nam Thống Nhất*), was located only a few blocks from the Mennonite Mission headquarters. This Institute was established only after the overthrow of President Ngo Dinh Diem in late 1963. During the summer there were frequent demonstrations which formed at the Institute with the groups marching by the Mennonite center on Phan Thanh Gian Street.

In response to the virtual rebellion against the government forces, Prime Minister Ky on Sunday, May 15, sent 1,500 crack troops to Da Nang to restore control. The following day Beechy suggested to Robert Miller that the present government would likely "not be able to survive much longer." There was even speculation that central Vietnam might secede and seek accommodation with the Liberation Front and North Vietnam, or that the government would be replaced by a pro-neutralist government where Buddhist political figures would have a strong-

Street demonstrations.

er role. Beechy also brainstormed about possible options should some expatriate personnel be asked to leave the country.

Beechy's wife, Winifred, arrived mid-May. The international VNCS team now totaled 29 people. Newcomers James Bowman, Kenneth Keefer and Sanford Stauffer were in language study. Bill Luken, the short-term business manager, left in May. There were a growing number of Vietnamese staff members including a son of Doan Van Mieng, the President of the Evangelical Church. Tran Xuan Quang joined the team June 1, working with Ross Orr in the material aid department. Quang had begun teaching a Sunday afternoon Bible class at the Mennonite Community Center the previous year.

Ruth Yoder, one of the Nha Trang nurses, had an unforgettable experience in late May when flying to Saigon. She and a young Vietnamese woman managed to get seats on a small single-engine Pilatus Porter plane operated by Air America. The take-off was fine. After gaining some altitude, Ruth settled back in her seat to read the letter she had just received from her mother; the work schedule at the Tin Lanh Clinic was so hectic she had not read the letter when it arrived. Aware of the political turmoil and the street demonstrations, her mother's greeting expressed concern for her safety. Before she finished reading the letter, the engine sputtered and stopped. Ruth looked out the front windshield and said to herself, "Something's not the way it should be!" The propeller wasn't spinning—it just stood straight up and down! Chomping on his cigar, the pilot tried to restart the engine. It didn't start. Peering out the side of the plane, he said: "I'm gonna hafta find a place to put this baby down!"

The pilot spotted a dry rice paddy field way below, too short but the best available. They circled the area as the gliding plane lost altitude, then drifted to a bumpy landing on the rough rice paddy field. At the end of the field an embankment ripped off the landing gear and the plane skidded to a stop. Silence. Everyone was alive. Neither the pilot nor the two passengers were injured. Moments later a Jeep with American soldiers came bumping to the scene. They checked everyone out, then agreed to take the three back to the Nha Trang Airport. Ruth recognized the crash site—near the old Citadel at Dien Khanh, several kilometers west of Nha Trang. The MCC doctors and nurses from the Tin Lanh Clinic had come here to treat minority people who had fled guerrilla forces in the mountains.

Back at the airport, Ruth found another plane to Saigon's Tan Son Nhat Airport, then caught a taxi to Em Dem, the VNCS unit center. It was time for the evening dinner and everyone was invited to the table. After the prayer of thanks, everyone began eating their meal blended with conversations about the happenings of the day at the office and the challenges of language study. Part way through dinner, Ruth caught her breath, and said, "Oh, by the way—," then told her story.

Doris Longacre's task of supervising the Em Dem unit home was no less challenging than Paul's work of supporting the field personnel. In a letter home, April 8, she wrote: "Life at our hotel is busy and never dull, except that sometimes having such a crowd of people around can be a bit tiresome. Most of the time I like it pretty well—there are days when I wish for my own little home for three to have privacy and the privilege of doing my own housework the way I want it." She said the four female household helpers and the gardener-yardsman-watchman were "a good group of people to work with."

On June 4, she wrote: "I have spent a lot of time this week trying to settle fights among the servants. They are very suspicious of each other taking things. I don't need to worry much about our things being stolen because they do all the worrying that is necessary and more. . . . If I fired servants for taking little stuff I would look a long time before I would find better ones to replace them. I am more interested in trying to help them with the Christian virtues of loving each other and getting along with each other."

Flexibility was necessary to manage a Saigon Guest House in 1966. In another June letter Doris told about the difficulty Sue Neufeld and son Mike had to get a flight back to Quang Ngai. Once they had already been on a plane with seat belts fastened and were told to get off. Doris wrote: "Here we don't unmake the beds until about twenty-four hours after the person has left, and usually don't make beds until someone actually arrives."

Doris was appreciative of skills among the volunteers in language study: "We finally got a couple of Pax fellows here who know how to fix things. Are they great to have around! They've gotten an old Speed Queen washer back into the service after it was out for about a year, plus a number of other services. Here one doesn't dare throw away such things as old washers. . . . The phenomenon of the junk yard is unknown here. . . . Old cars never die—they don't even fade away. They keep running."

USAID encouraged Longacre to place VNCS agriculturalists in Phan Rang. One official said: "I don't suggest that you go there for the agricultural skill and medical help you can give but for the restoration of hope and reconstruction of the social fabric you can bring. This is what will be needed and this your people can give."

Paul mused on why Mennonites, historically an agricultural people, had so few trained agriculturalists. Young people were leaving the farm for medical and social work even though food production was a more basic need.

Beechy encouraged VNCS personnel to become acquainted with the Evangelical Church which had about 50,000 members, both learning from them and witnessing to the international character of the Christian church.

In a June letter to ECVN President Doan Van Mieng, Beechy noted that VNCS was "being built in the tradition and spirit of the earlier Mennonite Central Committee program. The objectives of giving needed materials and services to people in need irrespective of religion, politics, social level, of bringing the Christian presence into the very fabric of the program, and of giving a witness to the cross of Christ and to the power of reconciling love are essentially the same as in the earlier program," he wrote. "Those of us working in Vietnam Christian Service deeply appreciate the Evangelical Church in Vietnam. Your hopes, achievements, problems, joys, and disappointments are ours, too. We have learned much from you about faith in the midst of difficulty and much about the evangelical task of the church. . . . We want to reaffirm our desire to continue this relationship."

Beechy then explained that VNCS was reducing its material aid program significantly, and would no longer need to rely on the Church's pastors to assist in aid distribution. This would also relieve the pastors of needing to decide who receives and who does not receive assistance.

In a letter home mid-June, Longacre expressed anger regarding the position of a prominent American Christian leader who supported the U.S. military policy in Vietnam so that missionaries could continue to evangelize! We knew missionaries in Vietnam who held similar views. Singapore church history Professor B. Violet James in her doctoral thesis asserts that Alliance missionaries generally supported the war they believed enabled them to continue to proclaim the gospel of Jesus.

Within American Protestantism were churches interested primarily in calling people to personal salvation and those committed to ministering to all people in need in the spirit of Jesus. The MCC workers to Vietnam twelve years earlier knew missionaries who represented the first view—all social ministries were a waste of limited financial resources. In 1966, however, most of the Alliance missionaries welcomed the work that VNCS was now involved in. An Alliance missionary from Hue was now directing the Vietnam programs of World Relief Commission. The Evangelical Church of Vietnam, once only a channel to funnel assistance to needy people, was now working with MCC in directing medical programs in Nha Trang and Pleiku.

Nguyen Van Van, a prominent lay leader, was invited to speak about the Tin Lanh Church at an orientation session for new personnel. Asked whether Tin Lanh leaders and others knew about the Mennonite position regarding war and violence, Van said they did. Asked whether some in the Church were sympathetic to that position, he said that refusal to serve in the armed forces is "somewhat illegal" in Vietnam, but he had heard Tin Lanh Church members say that the "Mennonites are right." Van said the Mennonite position is respected and that it was very good for Mennonites to be in Vietnam at that particular time. VNCS persons sometimes wondered whether they were inadvertently contributing to the war effort.

Beechy traveled to Pleiku three days in early June to visit personnel. Pleiku was being developed as a large military base. Dr. Leuz introduced Beechy to a U.S. army chaplain who wanted to help support the new clinic. Beechy saw relationships with U.S. military personnel both "a resource and a potential threat." He said the clinic would welcome voluntary contributions from military personnel but would try to avoid close identification with them.

Prostitution accompanied the deployment of foreign military forces into Vietnam. Traveling northeast of Saigon towards Bien Hoa, Beechy observed that the highway leading into Saigon was lined with bars and bar girls "looking for business." In a letter to the MCC Peace Section describing this "sad and disturbing situation," Beechy referred to an agency that "encourages social contacts and then advertises an adoption service for the mixed children which result." The agency promised to complete all the adoption papers and furnish an Amerasian child for a fee of 32,000 piasters ($270 US).

Spending a full day in June with the Nha Trang Hospital Board, Beechy and Longacre were "reassured" of the Evangelical Church's commitment to the medical program. In a letter home Longacre wrote: "In many ways it would be easier to operate a project by oneself than attempt to cross cultures in doing a work." Yet the benefits of working with an indigenous organization "far outweigh the liabilities," he said. With Ruth Yoder's experience teaching nursing courses, the board supported a proposal to develop a one-year assistant nurses training program.

In late June, Beechy met Rev. Calvin Thiel-

Chris Leuz observing progress in building Pleiku clinic.

man, Pastor of Montreat, North Carolina, Presbyterian Church and a close friend to Billy Graham and to Lyndon Johnson—whom he served as campaign manager when Johnson ran for the U.S. Senate! In 1965 and now again in 1966, Thielman came to Vietnam as the President's personal envoy. He was accompanied on this visit by Fr. Daniel Lyons, SJ, who was associated with the American Security Council, an anticommunist pro-military organization. The two men had just completed ten days in Vietnam, hosted by Gen. Westmoreland. Beechy heard Thielman preach Sunday, June 26, at the International Church. On Monday evening, Paul and Doris and Winifred and Atlee were invited to a reception for the two men given by Wells Klein, USAID liaison officer. On Wednesday evening, Beechy was at a dinner in their honor given by Charles Mann, head of USAID. Writing to the Akron, Pennsylvania, office Beechy said that in "brief encounters with Thielman and Lyons, I sensed a warm evangelical spirit in the former and a militant hawk in the latter." In their discussion of Christian pacifism as expressed by Mennonites and others, Thielman said "there are moments when I have the uneasy feeling that they may be right."

Meeting again Thursday morning, Thielman kept his accompanying military brass waiting while he and Beechy continued an intimate exchange. Beechy said Thielman recognized more clearly than in 1965 "the dichotomy and conflict of our country devastating the country and at the same time trying to help the people. He has a disturbing uneasiness about the suffering we are causing, particularly the civilians, as we fight communism." Thielman promised to express this "moral problem" directly to U.S. Ambassador Lodge.

Paul and Doris were planning to attend a worship service in a Vietnamese congregation Sunday morning, July 3, but Doris was asked to play the organ at the International Church since the regular organist was gone. Paul was apprehensive that the service would "probably be more patriotism than worship"—patriotism expressed as support for U.S. military activity in Vietnam.

Paul's hunch turned out to be true—too much for Doris. Beechy tells the story in his diary:

> Doris Janzen Longacre made a strong witness for peace in this morning's worship service at the International Church. There was a fairly heavy dose of American nationalism and militarism present in the service. Doris was the organist. At a certain point Doris said she simply could not take the idolatry of nation worship. After two verses of a hymn that emphasized this theme she stopped playing, got up and walked out. She said she can't fully explain what happened except that she was over-powered with the travesty of it all. Later she had a good exchange with the pastor.

On June 29, U.S. bombers attacked fuel storage areas near Hanoi and Hai Phong, the port city, prompting Hanoi authorities to order the evacuation of the city's population except for essential workers.

On July 11, the MCC Board Chairman Hostetter and Executive Secretary Snyder sent a four-page letter to President Johnson, expressing "a contradiction and paradox in our efforts, trying to help the people, on the one hand, while at the same time our government [is] engaged in an escalating war devastating the countryside and creating enormous and tragic suffering for the civilian population. The time has come," they wrote, "when we can no longer maintain faith with the homeless, the hungry, the orphaned and the wounded to whom we minister unless we speak out as clearly as we can against the savage war in which our country is engaged."

The letter deplored the tragedy of over 3,000 American deaths but insisted we must also be aware of the deaths of over 400,000 Vietnamese. It noted the "war weariness" of the people.

Snyder and Hostetter wrote:

> We are concerned about the future in Vietnam because as Christians we feel called to identify with the misery and suffering of the Vietnamese people. We recognize that our presence as Americans in Vietnam may be interpreted as part and parcel of the total war effort there. We are willing, as God gives us strength, to suffer with our Vietnamese brethren and serve with them in meeting their needs. But we do not want our efforts to be a palliative on the conscience of a nation seeking to do good on one hand while spreading destruction on the other. Therefore we must in good faith and in integrity to those we seek to aid in Vietnam, make as clear to you as we can our opposition to escalation of military efforts which increase the dimensions of human suffering.

Their letter called on the President to place the welfare of the Vietnamese people over "national pride," and urged the United States to some "bold initiative" to end the bloodshed.

Following up on this letter Hostetter and Snyder together with Paul Peachey, Robert Miller, and Edgar Metzler made plans to meet July 13 at the White House with Ambassador William K. Leonhart, special assistant to the President who worked directly on Vietnam matters.

Several new MCC recruits arrived early July: Jesse Gingrich from Oregon, Carolyn Nyce from Doylestown, Pennsylvania, and Patricia and Douglas Hostetter, a sister-and-brother pair from Harrisonburg, Virginia. Later in the month, Dr. Harold and Esther Kraybill came, as well as Paul and Loretta Leatherman and their three children, sixteen, twelve, and ten years old. Paul would replace Beechy as executive director.

In early July, Neil and Marta Brenden and Gerald and Judy Aaker arrived, both couples recruited through Lutheran World Relief. Church World Service recruited two others who arrived in July—Virginia Callahan, who was assigned to do secretarial work in the Saigon office, and Alfred Stoffel, a medical doctor from Switzerland. Given the growing American military presence, VNCS wanted to further internationalize their expatriate personnel.

Beechy was pleased with the personnel the agencies were recruiting for Vietnam Christian Service. He described four essential qualifications for VNCS personnel. They had to have competence in some skill and needed to have "general cultural adaptability." This meant that "the volunteer must have profound respect for Vietnamese and their patterns. The person must be sensitive to the great conflict going on within this culture and to the devastating impact which the war situation is making on the culture."

Further, Beechy wrote,

> The volunteer must have an above-average emotional or psychological maturity to work here. He must be courageous without having a martyr complex or without being foolhardy. He must live with insecurity and not be overwhelmed or imprisoned by it. He must see the needs of the people in perspective. He must be able to relate effectively to others—both Vietnamese and Americans. He should have a healthy appraisal and acceptance of his own strengths and weaknesses. He must be self-reliant to a considerable degree, be able to assess a fluid situation, and go to work without all the usual family and community structures.

Lastly, "The volunteer must have a genuine Christian experience," Beechy wrote. "If we are to represent the Church, I think we obviously must have dedicated Christians in it. I do not prescribe a traditional pious definition to 'Christian' but think the qualification is crucial. The volunteer must be sympathetic to the Church. The quality of his faith and expression does not need to be unusual or dramatic in any way, but it must be genuine. He should be able to give positive expression to his faith in his own individual style. He should respect the national church on matters even if he does not agree with that position."

Beechy said this "means more than a legalistic compliance about not doing certain things in front of members of the church." Mentioning smoking, he said some persons thought VNCS stricture against smoking was due to Mennonite sensitivities. Rather it had to do with sensitivity toward Tin Lanh Church members; many of the staff persons at the office and at the service centers were members of the Tin Lanh Church who abstained from this habit.

The sixties was also the era of the mini-skirt, daring in North America but considered more scandalous in Vietnam. Many VNCS women chose to fit in with the culture and to wear what typical Vietnamese wore—loose trousers with blouse.

With the arrival of new VNCS team members who were in language and cultural orientation, a "sort of a spiritual life conference" was planned a weekend late July at Em Dem unit house with Ted Evans, Pastor of the Saigon Anglican Church, leading discussions around the theme, "Our Task in Vietnam." Invited by Rev. Evans to preach the Sunday sermon at the English language Episcopal Church in Saigon July 24, Beechy followed the scriptural passage of I John 4:15-21 (Love for God, love for others). The sermon was entitled "God's People: The Compassionate Community."

In his sermon, Beechy said:

> To proclaim the good news, to speak the prophetic word of judgment, and to be the compassionate community are interrelated parts of the vocation of God's people. The compassionate community is obviously made up of persons who are parts of a fabric of relationships . . . , those who take seriously their commitment to God in a deep, genuine sense of care for the ultimate, total welfare of persons. This means first being a caring person, coming from an experience of God's Grace, his and others' care for you. What *doing* there is emerges from this inner core of *being*. Recently I asked one of our volunteers why she came to Vietnam. Her answer was, "a belief that God cares for what is happening here, and I'm here to be a channel of that care."

Beechy cited examples of people who were moved to give: a friend whose family was making monthly contributions to VNCS, recent gifts from the Hiroshima Union Church of Japan, from a Vietnamese businessman, and from an American author.

Mr. Trong, the baker who baked bread for MCC's feeding projects, gave around $2,500, likely motivated in gratitude for the successful heart surgery his wife had in Paris; this was used to purchase an X-ray machine for the Nha Trang Hospital. A gift of $100 came from Hiroshima Union Church in Japan. A check for $2,500 came from Norman Cousins, editor of the *Saturday Review*, with whom Beechy corresponded. This was used to provide program services in Quang Ngai refugee camps.

Concluding his sermon, Beechy said:

> Perhaps the day will come in our civilized and advanced age when prejudice, hate, fear, violence and war will not only seem illogical and wasteful, but also unnecessary—a day when chariots of iron become the plowshares of the paddy fields. In the meantime God's people must seek to eliminate those things which cause prejudice, hate, fear and violence. They must, in reality,

be the compassionate community—translating into their relationship something of the creative, restorative, healing, eternal caring Spirit of God. . . . May you feel the Spirit inviting you to more active membership in the compassionate community.

Though Beechy did not know it until after the service, in attendance that Sunday morning were Ambassador and Mrs. Henry Cabot Lodge. In his memoirs, Beechy wrote: "Mrs. Lodge had appreciative words for my message, but the Ambassador was silent. I was not surprised!"

Before leaving Vietnam, Beechy wrote to Ambassador Lodge expressing thanks for the assistance given by the Embassy and USAID personnel, mentioning several persons by name. Having worked closest with the USAID liaison person Wells Klein, he expressed appreciation for the way Klein respected the voluntary agency status of VNCS. In this letter to Lodge, Beechy wrote, "We regret the need for services such as our agency is rendering but we are grateful for the opportunity of working in this place at this time." Leaving Vietnam, Beechy said he "will carry . . . deepened concern for the agony present in so many phases of the situation here. Although I disagree with certain aspects of our policy here, I do not minimize the difficulty and complexity of the problem. You have my best wishes and prayers as you work at this demanding task."

In his memoirs, Beechy describes a time he was visiting up-country relief projects and was hosted by "a veteran Western missionary" who expressed thanks to God for good weather which "helps our boys blast those Viet Cong. The Lord surely is on our side." Grateful for the hospitality the missionary gave, but surprised and troubled by the host's comments, Beechy asked if the church is dependent on the military to bring the Good News to the Vietnamese. "And how will the Viet Cong who are killed in the raids hear the Good News?"

After the exchange, Beechy said, "We remained friends!"

The day before he preached at the Episcopal Church, Beechy spent a few hours with Mr. Ton That Thien, the forty-two year-old highly respected managing editor of the *Viet Nam Guardian*. A well-educated man who worked with Ho Chi Minh and later Ngo Dinh Diem, he was strongly nationalistic but rejected the communist approach of Ho Chi Minh. Thien told Beechy that the Vietnamese were not fooled by high altruistic-sounding phrases about the United States being in Vietnam to protect the rights of the Vietnamese. The greatest need for Vietnam, he said, was for peace.

With Beechy unable to extend his term, MCC recruited Paul Leatherman to serve as executive director of VNCS. At the end of July, Atlee and Winnie flew with Leatherman to Pleiku by Air America, making stops at Da Lat, Nha Trang, Qui Nhon and Da Nang, taking seven and one-half hours to reach Pleiku! On the flight from Da Nang to Pleiku they conversed with Dr. Nguyen Phuc Que, the government Commissioner for Refugees. They returned to Saigon in only fifty minutes on a military flight—no other planes were available.

Beechy and Leatherman traveled to Quang Ngai in early August. Here VNCS was working with more than seven hundred families (4,000 people) in two refugee camps—one lining national highway No. 1 north of the provincial capital, the other west of the city near the airport. The scope of the intended programs included agriculture, small industries, recreation, family and child welfare, and public health. Sanford Stauffer, who had come in April with James Bowman and Kenneth Keefer, was beginning a feeding program at the Rung Lang camp to provide milk and bread for six or seven hundred school children just before their classes. Earl Martin was working with one of the school teachers to develop a recreational program for the children.

On August 1, Beechy gave his "final word" to his VNCS co-workers, emphasizing that "*being* precedes the *doing*."

"What is our task?" he wrote:

> In one real sense we are the Church at work in this place, this situation with all its suffering, its dislocation, and its chaotic confusion. In the midst of this we are called to be the "fellowship of the caring."
>
> Acts of service must emerge out of a real sense of caring, out of a deep response to God's care.
>
> This caring must be genuine.
> This caring must be personal.
> This caring must be sensitive to human aspirations.
> This caring must be free from condescension.
> This caring must not be used to make others feel obligated, but rather to help others discover again a sense of self-respect.
> This caring is not deterred by hostility, by rejection, or by lack of appreciation.
> This caring opens the way for hope to emerge and for the one cared for to start caring again.
> To live means to care, and
> To care means to live.
> This is our vocation.

Beechy introducing Leatherman to Pastor Doan Van Mieng.

Beechy closed with the Apostle Paul's final greeting to his Philippian friends: "I thank my God upon every remembrance of you."

In his memoirs Beechy wrote, "To build an image that Vietnam Christian Service represents the church, not the American government or USAID, was a formidable challenge. I believe this goal was achieved to a considerable degree, though not completely. Of course, the battle was not fought only in Asia. The same questions were being discussed by Americans in churches and relief agencies all over North America."

Winifred and Atlee Beechy left Vietnam on August 15. Again in his memoirs Beechy wrote: "As the plane left the runway and headed out toward Hong Kong, Winifred and I felt a measure of relief. But an overwhelming sadness also swept over us, for the faces of the children and the old in the refugee camps, the hospitals and the underside of Saigon have been indelibly written into our hearts. . . . In the days ahead they will return to haunt us, to drive us to do everything within our power to halt this great human tragedy and to urge sensitive people everywhere to reach across the world and help in the rebuilding of hope and life among these people."

WITNESS IN TIME OF POLITICAL UNCERTAINTY

Chapter 24

The 1966 lunar New Year, *Tết Nguyên Đán*, fell on Friday, January 21. On what is the most celebrative day of the year, Phuong, a day care child at the Mennonite Community Center, died. Relatives told us the sad news. They said she was conscious until her death and talked about dying. She told her parents that she had "confessed her sins" at the nursery. What she had heard and understood about God's love from our Tin Lanh teachers in day care we do not know. Although the parents were not Christians, they initially asked us to help arrange for burial in the Tin Lanh Church Cemetery—then decided to bury the body near their home. Though many of the center staff persons were away for the holiday, several of us were able to go to their home. Mary described it in a letter home:

> We went and had prayer and scripture reading at the home and also at the grave. Phuong was the oldest of three children in a poor family. Her mother sells bread along our street. At the time of burial the parents wore the same clothes they had worn the day before when they came to our house. The parents, a few relatives, Mr. Yung, Mrs. Bay, Miss Qui and Luke and I made up the 'funeral.' If we hadn't gone, there wouldn't have been any ceremony. When everything is ready, they pick up the casket, carry it out, drive to the cemetery and bury it. The little sister was there and likely knew everything that had taken place from the time the child breathed its last until it was placed in the ground. No hurrying off of the body to a funeral parlor. Everything is done at home. On our way out to the street, everyone continued firing fire-crackers [for the Tet holiday] and playing cards as before. No one bothered to take notice that anyone had died.

Government and Viet Cong leaders had agreed to a Tet cease-fire truce for a few days. In Mary's letter home, written after the truce ended, she wrote: "Last night and the night before—it was distressing to hear the usual mortar and plane activity after a kind of 'peace' for several days. We had forgotten how terrible it sounds."

Luc, one of the believers, related how he had gone to the Mekong delta town of Sa Dec to celebrate Tet with his brother. His bus passed the scene of a bus that had struck a mine fifteen minutes earlier, killing twenty-nine passengers and injuring the rest. In Sa Dec he observed the fighter bombers in action. On the way home he saw bodies of soldiers lying by the road.

Bui Thi, the young man from Quang Ngai who lived with us, was also quite sad at Tet when he learned that his mother was being detained by Viet Cong forces. Though fire-crackers were popping all around, Thi was not in the mood to celebrate.

President Johnson had ordered a halt to the bombing of North Vietnam December 24, 1965, and initiated a concerted international effort to explore the possibilities for a negotiated settlement of the conflict. With the United States unwilling to recognize the National Liberation Front, the North claimed the U.S. was not acting in good faith. At the end of January, Johnson ordered the bombing to resume.

In the annual report of the Vietnam Mennonite Mission early February, Everett wrote that the massive American military commitment, while lessening the likelihood of an early collapse of the Saigon government, had "made it increasingly difficult to avoid undesirable identification with the American effort here as the American presence takes on the character of an occupation rather than 'assistance.' This problem is complicated by the lack of hesitancy of other missionaries to identify with the American effort." Noting that we needed to continue to stress evangelism and lay leadership training, Everett wrote that we missionaries tried to "remain in the background, assisting in areas where our foreign-ness will not detract from the message of the Spirit."

"Our Mission sees its role here as supplementary to that of the existing Evangelical Church and other mission groups," Everett wrote. He described the ministries of the Saigon Student Center and the Gia Dinh community center, noting the growing congregation. Fourteen persons were baptized the previous year, bringing the total number in the Mennonite fellowship to twenty-seven; this included the eight missionaries.

The young church center was maturing. Following the practice of the Tin Lanh Church, we observed Communion the first Sunday of the month. We also practiced the ritual of foot washing after Communion on Sunday morning, February 6. Twenty-one believers—missionaries, baptized believers, and Tin Lanh staff members—shared in this service.

That evening, Mary and I attended the wedding of Co Ky, the first language teacher of Rachel and Mary. Mary observed that "she did a good job of looking sad as all good Vietnamese brides are supposed to do."

The following week we had evangelistic meetings at the community center. Le Vinh Thach, a young man who had just earned a master of divinity degree from London University, preached two evenings and Don Sensenig and I each preached once with Tran Xuan Quang interpreting. We were now calling Quang the "associate pastor." One young man confessed faith in Jesus Christ.

While the day care nursery continued at the Community Center, on February 2 the *Rạng Đông* (Dawn) School welcomed its first students. Mrs. Phan Tuyet Nga, a teacher and

Happy school children.

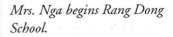

Mrs. Nga begins Rang Dong School.

school principal with many years' experience in Da Nang, began with sixty students in first grade. Since some of the community children were unable to go to school, many were more than six years old. Mrs. Nga planned to offer classes in three more grades after she received official authorization from the Department of Education.

Vietnam's statutes on compulsory elementary education were not enforced since there were not enough public schools. Private schools abounded, but poor families were unable to afford even minimal tuition charges. With fathers absent, often in the armed forces, and mothers selling in the local markets, older children from poor families were often required to care for younger siblings. Rang Dong charged reasonable fees of fifty piasters a month ($0.42 US), but no poor child was turned away.

A new term of English classes resumed after Tet. Two hundred and seventy students studied at the Student Center and more than three hundred students were enrolled at the Community Center, most using materials on the life of Jesus. Don, Doris, Mary, and I taught classes at the Community center. Ms. Vu Thi Qui, baptized a year earlier, also taught two elementary classes. In a letter to friends, Mary wrote that the English Bible classes "provide a setting for those who want to learn of Christ without obliging them to enter a church. The primary incentive of most students is the desire to learn English, but several say they have been attracted to Christ through the classes here."

Everett and Margaret, who taught English classes at the Student Center, told friends of their growing conviction "that the Lord still has much work for us to do. Of course there are many questions and problems in our minds; however, there is an over-all feeling of sureness of our calling to keep on as long as doors are open."

Mary and I entertained many of the new MCC-VNCS personnel in our home. Dr. Fred Brenneman came to work two months at the Nha Trang hospital. After Atlee Beechy arrived, we discussed with him and Paul Longacre procedures for initiating the MCC Family Child Assistance program, a family-to-child sponsorship program, at the community center.

In March, Everett reported that Saigon was "getting hotter, dustier, noisier." Heavier traffic led to the introduction of one-way streets, including Phan Thanh Gian, the street by the student center. "The American presence is felt more and more," Everett wrote. "A Vietnamese friend riding in a taxi that was waved on by an American MP (military police) heard the driver complain bitterly: 'My own country and I can't drive and park where I wish!' He added that the Americans have already taken over the best houses and buildings and are more likely to take everything over. He echoes the feelings of many. Pray that we might be 'wise as serpents and harmless as doves' in this situation."

I accepted an invitation to attend a conference for all evangelical pastors and missionaries

Ms. Qui with family at Tet.

in Vietnam held on March 1-4 at the former Alliance missionary children's school in Da Lat. Many pastors and evangelists from the various ethnic minorities were among the 390 pastors and missionaries who met. We prayed together, ate together, and roomed together. The main speaker, Rev. Dr. William C. Newbern, former missionary to China and now President of the Alliance Seminary in Hong Kong, spoke from his wealth of experience. He drew many parallels between China, Hong Kong and Vietnam. Rev. J. Oswald Sanders from Singapore, the General Director of Overseas Missionary Fellowship, gave expositional messages on themes of the Holy Spirit and commitment for the future. It was for me a moving experience to be in the company of so many committed Christian workers. Many of the pastors had come from areas under the control of the VC or in areas heavily contested. I met some of the Christian leaders of Phuoc Luong, near Nha Trang, who had fled harassment from communist forces operating in the mountains.

Returning to Saigon, I met the newest member of the missionary family. On March 2, James and Rachel received Brian James Metzler from an orphanage into their home; they were able to complete adoption procedures before furlough in late summer.

Mary wrote home about the "good Sunday" March 6, when Don preached at the morning worship service. Mrs. Phan Tuyet Nga, Principal of the Rang Dong School, spoke about her life of faith, telling how her parents strongly opposed their decision to become Christians. Her husband's family now had nothing to do with them. Although she had offers from other Saigon schools, she preferred to work in a Christian school. Having a strong personality, Mrs. Nga was also very congenial and sensible.

Both the morning service and the special evening music program were well attended. A young friend of one of the recently-baptized believers expressed his belief in Christ. Mary observed that several young women attending the services seemed "very open and ready to believe but they don't feel free to become Christians." She wrote home: "Girls are supposed to follow their husbands and—before marriage—follow the family's religion. . . . We always encourage them by saying that they can believe in their hearts anyway. . . . Ba Hai, too, has not yet been baptized and everyone considers her a part of the fellowship." In a letter to friends we expressed our joy "for the privilege of sharing in the building of the Church of Christ."

We planned an evangelistic service every Sunday afternoon, with a morning worship service once a month which included the believers from the Saigon youth center as well. Later this became a weekly service. We were grateful to have Quang leading the Sunday afternoon Bible study class, encouraging the new believers. Quang was now participating in more of the activities of the center.

In early March, we missionaries attended a series of meetings at the International Protestant Church led by a former army chaplain. Writing home, Mary noted the IPC ministry to American military personnel in Saigon, expressing a view our missionary team would have affirmed: "We have not felt called to especially minister to this need, but we must caution against a feeling of distaste, disgust, and maybe even hatred for the American military [personnel] here."

The March 28 *Newsweek Magazine* featured several women who lived in Saigon—among them Margaret Metzler. Margaret noted that people hearing us speak Vietnamese "wonder if [we] belong to the CIA." Yet when they recognize us as missionaries we are given "a certain immunity" from Vietnam's political struggles.

The last weekend in March, we eight missionaries—Margaret and Everett, Rachel and James, Doris and Don, and Mary and I—sang several Passion and Easter hymns as an octet at a large

Catholic university student-sponsored choral program at one of the large Catholic churches. We hoped that this would lead to more friendships with Catholic Christians.

A city-wide evangelistic campaign sponsored by the Asian Evangelists Commission began Saturday evening, April 2, and continued through the following Saturday, with the meetings in a rented soccer stadium in the Cho Lon section of Saigon. I invited some of our English students to go the first evening, attended by five thousand people. Evangelist Dr. G. D. James from Singapore was the speaker the first night.

Even though our missionary team was not inclined to sponsor large events like this, we saw this organized campaign having significant value. In an April 4 letter home I wrote: "It will help make the public aware of Tin Lanh, the Good News. It will make the Christians more aware of each other. It is an opportunity to invite many into the fellowship of the church by personal acceptance of Jesus Christ." It also provided training and experience for a few young people from our church who were invited to serve as counselors.

Since in the public's mind Evangelical or Protestant Christianity tended to be associated with America, we were particularly pleased that all the participating evangelists were Asians. One morning we four missionary men met with Rev. Kazuomi Tsuchiya from Osaka, Japan, one of the visiting evangelists. Tsuchiya was acquainted with leaders of the Mennonite Church in Hokkaido and served as speaker on the Mennonite Brethren radio program, *Asanohikari* (Morning Light), in Osaka. He told us that the cause of Christ was "being hindered in Japan" because of the U.S. Vietnam involvement. In every discussion of Christianity the Vietnam issue is brought up, he told us. Tsuchiya said that many American missionaries in Japan were disturbed by the strong Japanese nationalistic spirit, yet when asked about Vietnam they would without fail defend the U.S. Vietnam policies, not even raising any questions about the "rightness" of those policies in view of the Scripture and the teachings of Jesus Christ.

Our missionary team sang as an octet one night. We invited students and parents of the nursery and kindergarten children at the Community Center to go along, borrowing the old MCC Willys Jeep, and renting buses. Throughout the eight evenings several hundred people responded to the invitations to place their faith in Jesus Christ. In spite of attempts by planners to follow up these persons, a much smaller number of people eventually were baptized and received into a church. A few of the students who went with us one evening made a public commitment of faith, and several joined a new catechism class I began on May 8.

Easter Sunday, April 10, followed the end of the special meetings. That morning the Mennonite congregation met in the open patio at the Gia Dinh Community Center for a sunrise service at 6:00 a.m. followed by a fellowship breakfast.

These were the days of frequent street demonstrations. Fearing that Prime Minister Nguyen Cao Ky's administration might be replaced by a neutralist government, the Johnson administration in April conducted a full-scale reassessment of its Vietnam policy. Under-Secretary of State George Ball—ever the devil's advocate—called for U.S. disengagement. Other advisors informed the President that public sentiment overwhelmingly supported negotiations with the National Liberation Front and a peaceful settlement. In the end, however, Johnson chose to continue his war policy and fully support Ky's government.

Our term of English classes at the Community Center ended in late April. Over 200 people came to the closing program, well-planned by Don and Doris Sensenig and Ms. Qui. Nearly every class had a part, telling or acting out a Bible story. We offered a five-week summer class which began late May.

On Sunday, May 1, Jacqueline Thimm spoke to fifty persons packed into the auditorium at the Community Center. A native of Da Lat, Jacqueline had come in February to help administer the estate of her late pastor father. She and her husband Arno were busy with church ministries in Germany. We urged then to consider an assignment with Vietnam Mennonite Mission. Having an international team could have made a significant contribution to our ministries. Jackie filed papers to adopt an orphan before she returned to Europe with her mother.

James Metzler, in May, wrote an article for the Mission Board journal, *Missionary Messenger,* describing a visit to a morgue for ARVN soldiers: "Fifty bodies lying side by side on stretchers . . . , stiff, swollen, mangled, and scorched black . . . , still wearing boots, fatigues, and even a few helmets." He told how family members slipped silently up and down the rows, with handkerchiefs over their noses, checking identification cards or pictures, even prodding with sticks for a better look to identify bodies "for the wailing women waiting outside."

Observing that war feeds on illusions from each side in

James Metzler preaching at Easter service with Pham Quang Tam interpreting.

Students telling story in English.

Jacqueline Thimm speaking at Community Center.

the conflict that they alone are fighting for the cause of freedom and justice, James wrote: "What a bitter irony! A nation is being demoralized, an ancient culture is being wiped out, and a weary people being crushed—all in the name of their own best interests." These illusions were nurtured by half-truths from each side. People accused the other side of using propaganda—unaware or unwilling to admit that their side also used propaganda. James referred to a recent conversation with "a veteran missionary in Vietnam" who insisted that "America never uses propaganda!"

Writing for the mission magazine, James spoke to those who embraced the Mennonite commitment to non-resistance. "It is easy for us as a church to claim noninvolvement in this conflict," he wrote. "We wash our hands in the basin of conscientious objection to war. Thus it is possible to fully support the actions of our country by our attitudes but still be absolved of any personal guilt before God." This position is untenable, James insisted. Unless we resisted the atrocity that the United States was perpetrating on the Vietnamese people, we were affirming it. "Silence can only mean consent—where there is opportunity to speak," he declared. "To us the question isn't whether we should be involved or not. It is rather—how can we represent the concerns of Christ in our involvement?"

In the May 1966 *News and Concerns,* Don and Doris Sensenig commented on the political unrest and the military activity—factors that affected the work of the church, The Mennonite Mission and Vietnam Christian Service. They invited readers to pray with us for Vietnam and our ministry. "Or perhaps God is calling you to DO SOMETHING MORE," they wrote.

What was that "something more" that Don and Doris suggested? We missionaries were struggling about how we should respond to the expanding American military involvement. We had written a letter of concern in late 1965. We had moved beyond the safe quietism of a let-the-government-do-what-it-chooses-to-do stance to the place where we had to speak out against the terrible bloodletting and destruction the United States was visiting upon the Vietnamese people. Sensenigs were now implying that our families and friends, our churches and community leaders also needed to speak out—to protest the military policies of the U.S. government.

Our mission secretary Paul Kraybill visited Vietnam May 8 to 14—Sunday to Saturday. He described Saigon much differently than on his previous short visit in February 1965: "Saigon is busier than ever, crowded with people—the noisiest place I have ever been," Paul wrote. The sounds of fighter bombers, helicopters, and artillery combined with the street activity—army trucks, scooters and motorcycles all added up "to an unearthly din that beats at your senses and intrudes on every conversation from early morning until midnight."

Kraybill's Sunday afternoon arrival at Saigon's Tan Son Nhat International Airport allowed him to speak at the 4:00 p.m. evangelistic service at the community center. The average attendance at the evangelistic services was twenty to thirty persons with fifteen in the Bible class and a concurrent children's Sunday school with twenty to forty children.

Kraybill came back to the Community Center on Monday to meet with the Mission Council and to observe the nursery and primary school with over 170 children enrolled in kindergarten through fifth grades. First grade was running for three months and kindergarten for one month. There were 300 persons enrolled in the English language classes, almost as many as at the Saigon Student Center.

Kraybill met with the chairman of the Alliance Mission, T. Grady Mangham, who reported that their missionaries were able to continue their work in spite of the war; four Tin Lanh church buildings had been destroyed. Although Christians were not suffering religious persecution, many were suffering due to the war—just like everyone else. Kraybill also met with Atlee Beechy and Paul Longacre at the VNCS office and shared an evening meal at Em Dem. He was well-impressed with the caliber of the VNCS staff members he met.

Kraybill described getting "caught in one of those paradoxes of the situation in Vietnam." Wanting to visit one of the VNCS up-country units and unable to get Air Vietnam tickets, he flew with Everett and me in a large C-130 troop transport plane to Pleiku in company with troops and war correspondents. After meeting with Lois and Christopher Leuz and other personnel there, we flew back to Tan Son Nhat Airbase on a C-47, the military version of the DC-3.

In his trip diary Kraybill wrote:

> It was an uncomfortable experience [to get] a feel of the massive military power that the United States is pouring into this nation. Ironically, I heard repeatedly from the lips of the Vietnamese that probably eighty percent of the population representing the common people, villagers, and country people are desperately eager for the war to cease. They have little concern who wins but are anxious for peace. Regardless of what political developments follow peace, they cannot be worse off than they are now in the constant fear and danger that faces them. They have little to lose, even if communism would take over, so they are only concerned that the war comes to an end.

Kraybill and the Mission Council met with the Representative Committee *(Ban Đại Diện)* of the Gia Dinh congregation. Kraybill wanted to see the new believers take more responsibility for owning and directing the total ministry of the mission and church. He wrote in his trip diary: "It was indeed gratifying to sense the understanding and spiritual grasp of these folks and to have this tangible opportunity to participate with Vietnamese in a discussion of church organization and development."

That evening Kraybill had a "most enjoyable and refreshing" fellowship tea with the entire believer group. Forty persons came—twice as many as on his previous visit. He read a letter he had just received from the believers' fellowship in Somalia, expressing their hope that the Christians in Vietnam would become "peacemakers" in the midst of the war. The group expressed appreciation for this greeting—especially touched by this was Ho Trung Ty, a high school math teacher whose wife was active in the congregation.

In his diary just before he left, Kraybill wrote:

> While my first impressions on reaching Vietnam were the impressions of war and military power, it was most refreshing to be here long enough to begin to get closer to the lives of these people and to participate more realistically in the everyday work of our missionaries. As one began to get beyond the more obvious signs of war, one learned that our missionaries are calm and relaxed and assuredly continuing their ministry in a rather normal fashion. Then to get involved with the church and to sense the work of the Spirit in this place with the developing group of believers and the new opportunities that continue to face us, one sensed that the work of the Lord is going on here and that the things we read in the newspapers in America do not really tell the whole story.

Kraybill recommended that one missionary couple be assigned to each center and that a third center be opened—also with a community-oriented witness program, together with a small youth hostel and a systematic program for training lay workers.

Kraybill also affirmed missionary assistance to Vietnam Christian Service. He also asked me to "give special attention to developing avenues of peace witness, particularly among Evangelical Christians, and recommended that the Mission Council plan for translation and [printing] of appropriate peace statements and literature for careful distribution as a part of a witness to our peace position."

Luke and Dorothy Beidler were planning to join the missionary team in late summer and Kraybill recommended that they, after several months' language study, devote three-fourth of their time to self-supporting work like teaching English in the university.

After returning to his office near Lancaster, Pennsylvania, Kraybill sent a letter to the parents of the missionaries along with his travel diary. "I want to assure you," he wrote, "that I was remarkably impressed with the calmness and assurance with which our folks in Saigon are facing their tasks in spite of a disturbing and unsettling war situation."

Things were relatively quiet in Saigon during Kraybill's visit—the earlier street demonstrations between Catholics and Buddhists had tapered off. However, on Sunday, May 15, the day after Kraybill left, Premier Ky sent 1,500 government troops to Da Nang in an effort to end the rebellion which followed the dismissal of General Nguyen Chanh Thi. This touched off street protests which continued for weeks. But the government prevailed, and effectively ended the Buddhist aspiration for a negotiated solution to the conflict. The war would continue for many more years.

The Vietnam Mission Council, made up of the ordained missionaries, reviewed Kraybill's recommendations. I agreed to write a letter of greeting to the annual C&MA missionary conference and write a separate letter to their chairman expressing our desire for further fellowship with their missionaries "on various subjects of mutual concern, including peace and war."

James and Arlene Stauffer were planning to soon return from home leave and our Mission anticipated they would again assume leadership at the Gia Dinh community center. I wrote to them about our thoughts of organizing a Bible training program for the believers. Rather than focusing on training pastors, it seemed that a lay leadership training for all interested believers was more appropriate for this stage of church development. I was currently teaching a Sunday morning Bible class for those considering baptism.

After a communion service and foot washing service June 5, the congregation elected a new *Ban Đại Diện*. Committee members were Nguyen Thi Hoang (Mrs. Ho Trung Ty), Vu Thi Qui, Duong Thanh Chau, with Bible teacher Tran Xuan Quang and me as ex officio members.

The congregation expressed lots of enthusiasm. Although the nursery had a week's vacation, the teacher, Ngo Thi Bich, did not want a vacation so she with her husband, Nguyen Quang Trung, and Nguyen Huu Lam planned a Bible School for sixty to seventy community children! Lam was home after his first year at Nha Trang Bible Institute.

Don Sensenig and I flew to Quang Ngai on Monday, May 16 for four days, working with Dave Neufeld about plans to renovate the house that VNCS had purchased. In addition to spending time with the VNCSers we also spent time with David and Mary Stickney of the American Friends Service Committee who had opened a day care center.

My brother Earl quickly made friends in Quang Ngai. When walking around a house VNCS was considering renting, Earl stepped onto an ant hill and children who were following us hollered *"Kiến cắn, kiến cắn!"* (The ants are biting!) as they attacked his sandaled feet. The next day as he walked down town, young kids pointed to him yelling, *"Kiến kìa!"* (There's Kien!) The name stuck; Earl was Kien.

105 mm canon.

Security perimeter at airfield.

While Quang Ngai seemed like a peaceful town, we saw a huge U.S. Marine convoy and tanks rumble down the main street. At night 155 mm artillery guns sent 100 pound projectiles eighteen kilometers into the countryside. Earl told how he had watched fighter bombers conduct air strikes just outside the town. Don and I flew both ways in two-engine C-123 military planes since all Air Vietnam flights were booked weeks in advance. Without insulation the engine noise was so loud that we could not talk to one another. I noted the irony of disapproving US military policies while relying on their logistical services.

Mary gave birth to Becky Joanne on Saturday, June 11. Mary and I were delighted—so was Steven. Our friends were pleased. "The oldest should be a boy," they said, "and then it's nice to have a girl!"

Just two weeks after Becky's birth Jean Louise Sensenig was born, joining her sisters Anne and Lynne. There was a dedication service for both infants at the worship service in the Gia Dinh congregation early December.

Our fifty-two year-old neighbor was not free to assist in bathing the new-born as when Steven was born. An experienced midwife, Mrs. Hai went back to work in a maternity hospital because her husband's salary in a government office was no longer sufficient to support the family. She was active in the church even though she did not yet dare to alienate her husband's family by being baptized. Mary told friends that when Mrs. Hai in late 1965 was ill, her husband encouraged her not to pray to the ancestors or she would lose her faith in Christ. Still she heard her neighbors' comments that she was ill because she was following this new American religion! Even after she recovered, she still experienced fatigue and lack of appetite. One day she said to Mary, "I don't know why we're sick all the time. Aren't you praying for me?"

My mother had written to Mrs. Hai, thanking her for the support she gave us during Steven's infancy. Soon after Becky was born, my parents received a letter written by her husband. Having studied in Hong Kong, he wrote in English. His comments about us applied to the entire missionary team: "The noble mission that the Martins have undertaken in this country has substantially contributed to the lasting friendship among our people. Besides we all consider them an acquisition to our neighborhood. So we are eager to be in any way as useful to them as they, with the help of the Almighty, can be of service to our people."

Rachel Metzler's mother died the same day Jean was born. This encouraged discussion about whether James and Rachel might consider taking their furlough a year early to lend support to her father. James and Rachel were enjoying parenting Brian whose adoption papers were signed in court on June 17. They left Vietnam on August 30, just after Brian's final adoption documents were issued.

The Everett and Margaret Metzler family also planned to leave on furlough around mid-August. However, when Kay Turner—a Quaker who stayed with them for a short time while working on a project in Saigon—offered to help Margaret take care of the children during the flight, she and the children arranged to leave in July. Everett left August 12.

On a brief visit to Saigon, Goshen College Bible Professor C. Norman Kraus spoke one evening to students at the Youth Center. Everett reported in the July *News and Concerns* that students were crowding the Saigon Youth Center cramming for exams. The bookroom monitor at Saigon Center was among the 80 percent of his high school group who failed baccalaureate exams so crucial for getting into university.

In the newsletter, Everett wrote about recent military engagements close to Saigon. One could see planes bombing and strafing from the roof patio of the student center. He described the deepening Vietnam tragedy: "Increased American military involvement only heightens the resolve of the other side to fight on to victory over the 'foreign invader.' Thus the cure for the sickness is more and more becoming the cause for the malady, with no face-saving option left for either side but a drawn-out war to the end."

Everett continued: "I am more and more convinced that the Church of Christ must get involved by becoming aware of what is going on here and in appealing to both sides to bring an end to the senseless slaughter. Surely Vietnam is our 'brother in need' in terms of I John 3:17 and we cannot say it is none of our business what happens here. We *are* involved–even if we do nothing– for silence is understood as consent and approval. Pray for the Church here that she might be more faithful to her Lord in this hour of trial."

In late July, Mary wrote home about the experiences of our household helper's family. A month earlier Tuyet's mother in the countryside had sent us some juicy mangoes. Now their orchard was destroyed by bombing and chemical burning. It was no longer safe to plant rice.

The word was slowly getting around to the rice farmers in the Mekong River delta that their best chance for survival—if suddenly surprised by a helicopter—was to keep working in the fields while the big bird hovered

The ubiquitous Huey chopper.

overhead. To run to a tree line or seek some shelter would certainly invite withering machine-gun fire. A part-time guerrilla fighter and a simple peasant farmer looked the same—black pajama garb, conical hat, long-handled hoe. Yet American helicopter pilots claimed they could tell the difference. If they ran, they were Viet Cong, and therefore, fair game! One of the Mennonite staff members had this experience in his garden. Praying fervently, he hoed frantically until the helicopter flew away.

Several years earlier, James Stauffer had arranged for fifteen-minute English *Way to Life* tapes produced by *The Mennonite Hour* to be aired early Sunday morning on one of the Saigon radio stations. This program offered a Bible correspondence course, "God's Great Salvation"; inquiries were few. James Metzler picked up this responsibility after Stauffers left. This correspondence course was also offered to our English students. While not many people enrolled in these courses, it was still significant. In a commentary published in the December 1966 issue of *Missionary Messenger*, Metzler shares the comments received from a middle-aged Buddhist man who worked as a secretary in a top government office in Saigon. This father had studied the life of Jesus in one of our English classes before enrolling in this course. After completing the twelfth lesson he wrote—in English:

> God loved the world so much. But alas!—after many churches destroyed, thousands of innocent men dead during the war, everywhere tears . . . , will God do nothing to relieve this unhappy world?
>
> After studying these twelve lessons, I have the idea that the believers—the Christians—must love everyone, whether he is white, black, or yellow; and serve everyone whether he is a Buddhist, a Christian, or a Moslem. I think a good believer agrees with this philosophy of Buddhism: "One should forget himself for the happiness of others."
>
> But alas! Since I was a young boy until now, I have seen the followers of Jesus Christ (certainly I don't say all of them) often do very bad things in our country—especially during the war to shake off the yoke of French domination. They have caused much blood to flow. And recently in Saigon you have seen thousands of Christians with knives in their hands sowing terror in the streets as they went; and afterward they gathered in a church. What do you think of that? Will they be punished? And will a still more severe punishment fall on their leaders?
>
> I sometimes read the Bible when I was a schoolboy, but I never paid any attention to the words of God. But a new idea came to me when I read your answers on my Lesson 4: "I could never kill another man, even in self-defense." I must wait until I am 45 to ponder this sentence written by a Christian. And if someday I still want to be converted, it will depend a great deal on your statement. I think a religion is strong, not by its strength over others, but by its submission and love.

The missionary comings and goings in August were a game of musical chairs that affected all but Mary and me. The Sensenig family moved to the Saigon youth center when Margaret and Everett went on furlough. The returning Stauffer family moved back to the house they had first rented in "Tin Can Alley" that the Sensenigs just vacated. Dorothy and Luke Beidler, Mission Associates, arrived August 26 and moved into the Ban Co area house where James and Rachel had lived, near the Saigon student center.

Luke told how community people reacted when they heard he and Dorothy were going to Vietnam. Why would anybody choose to go there? We missionaries heard a wide range of comments about our decisions to leave a fairly comfortable and predictable life for an unknown experience in Vietnam. When Sensenigs were making plans to leave three years earlier, Don candidly mentioned that a desire to see the world and experience adventure was a small part of his motivation. While a brother in the church questioned the legitimacy of that motivation, that in no way diminished the sense that God's Spirit was prompting him—and all of us—to represent the church in Vietnam, living and working among the people, sharing the gospel of Jesus Christ.

Even after we were in Vietnam for years, many community people also wondered why we had come. Given that political intrigue was intertwined with a devastating military conflict, some people wondered—usually not out loud to us—whether we were really working for the American CIA. Other people, aware of our religious commitments, assumed that we were there doing good deeds to assure that we would be amply rewarded in the next life!

The Stauffers arrived on August 29, just one day before James and Rachel left. James Stauffer assumed pastoral responsibilities in the congregation and he and Arlene gave direction to the community center. VNCS also had their comings and goings at this time. Paul Leatherman came to replace Atlee Beechy as VNCS Director.

We felt that the Lord had blessed our ministry at the Gia Dinh Community Center. As a foreigner directing the Center, I did not micro-manage the nursery, school and the bookroom staff. Rather than arbitrarily making decisions when there were differences of opinion, we discussed various options until we could reach a consensus. The staff appreciated clear-cut decisions. Even though life in Vietnamese communities was generally fairly harmonious, people freely expressed differing opinions. "Ten people, eleven opinions" was a frequently quoted Vietnamese proverb.

A few months earlier some personnel misunderstandings and conflict at the Community Center came to a climax when several staff persons threatened to leave unless one person left. We called a staff meeting that began quite stormy. I thanked God that we came to a good resolution. There were currently ten staff members at the Community Center, most of them Christians from the Evangelical Church.

Ms. Qui was again teaching beginner English classes at the Community Center, using the *English for Today* textbook. Don was using a book about the life of Jesus, *The King Nobody Wanted*, and in the advanced class I used J. B. Philips' *New Testament in Modern English*.

Attendance at the Sunday morning and afternoon services at the Community Center was good. By now many staff members from the Evangelical Church were asking to become members. Considering them associate members was no longer adequate. The Mission Council asked me to discuss this with Phan Van Tranh, the Superintendent of the Tin Lanh Church Southern District. Pastor Tranh said that within their church pastors usually wrote letters of introduction to other congregations and suggested that this would be acceptable. It was clear that the Tin Lanh Church considered us a sister church and had no fears of our "stealing sheep."

The young Baptist pastor from nearby Go Vap, Do Vinh Thanh, preached at the Sunday afternoon meeting August 21. Five persons responded to an invitation to faith in Christ, two young men and three young women, ranging in age from eighteen to thirty-five. All these had been attending frequently during the previous months. Mentioning this in a letter to Kraybill, I commented: "While we don't always see the response we might hope for, I think we're mistaken to assume that Vietnamese just don't respond to the message of the gospel."

Inflation was causing a sharp rise in the cost of living. A few years earlier we missionaries began receiving allowances based on the cost of living index, indexed to a 1959 COL base of 100. In July 1965, it was 136. Now a year later it was 244, nearly 80 percent higher! We missionaries chose to receive a lower allowance than authorized; it did not seem right for us to receive a much larger amount when the earnings of people around us were much less.

Don Sensenig commented on the inflation in the September *News and Concerns*, then described a conversation about the war, an example of widely varying viewpoints:

> Some Vietnamese Christians, including leaders, continue to think of war as the proper way to deal with Vietnam's problems. A pastor said [yesterday] he believes America will soon send more troops to Vietnam, so the Vietnamese troops can invade North Vietnam, which will draw China into the war, and America will then bomb China, and that will be the beginning of World War III. He welcomed these steps as the solution to the problems of Vietnam!!! Pray that we will be able to share a different viewpoint effectively, that we will be peacemakers, that the church in Vietnam will be a peacemaker and will find Christ's work and Christ's way in this confused and terrible mess.

Thoughts of the war were ever with us. In September, Mary wrote to friends: "Tonight's news was as usual: so many [bombing] missions over North Vietnam, so many planes shot down and pilots missing, so many sorties flown in the country (South Vietnam), so many VC killed, so many VC "structures" damaged or destroyed, so many sampans destroyed. Day after day, destruction of property, land, resources, life, and hope continues." As Americans, she wrote: "we share in the responsibility for this. We cannot wash our hands of it. As we see and hear the awful effects of what "we" are doing, our hearts are heavy. Pray that, by the Spirit's leading, we may know how we can best be peacemakers in this land of war and hatred."

A national election on September 11 chose a 117-member Constituent Assembly to draft a new constitution. A week or so later Don met one of my former English students, a high school teacher who had moved to Da Lat, who was elected to this assembly. He expected to be working on this draft constitution for six months.

James Stauffer, in one of his first letters home after returning to Vietnam, wrote: "Every now and then we meet someone who seems hostile to us but it is surprising how generally everyone here in Saigon seems to be resigned to the American commitment. . . . No one can predict a near end to the conflict." In September all missionaries in the Saigon area were invited to a fellowship meal to hear Dr. Eric F. Fife of Inter-Varsity Christian Fellowship speak. While enjoying association with the other missionaries, James and Arlene expressed dismay at "their unquestioning acceptance" of American war policies.

James and Arlene were happy to be back in Vietnam, challenged by the believer group and new persons who had recently come to faith in Jesus Christ. He and Arlene gradually picked up the responsibilities at the community center from Mary and me. James taught the Sunday morning Bible class in their home.

I flew to Da Nang in late September on a VNCS assignment to investigate refugee relief needs, staying with C&MA missionaries Leroy and Nancy Josephson. In early October I accompanied VNCS director Paul Leatherman to survey medical needs on Con Son Island, a harsh prison island built by the French.

The Mid-Autumn Children's Festival, the fifteenth day of the eighth lunar month, fell on the last week in September. The Rang Dong School principal Mrs. Nga had planned a big celebration, and more than 100 parents and 240 children came to the event. The gifts of cake and candy had to be given the next day because so many other children crashed the party.

The first weekend in October the Stauffers' cook went to her home in the Mekong River delta sixty-five kilometers southwest of Saigon, just after a "friendly" mortar shell landed on her uncle's house while they were sleeping, killing four and seriously injuring two others. She asked to stay for the funerals. James wrote in the newsletter: "This strikes close home to us and yet this is just one of many such incidents that never even reach the papers. All the horrors of this war are not being told and many people even here in Saigon seem to justify it in light of the final aim—to stop communism. May God bring peace, is our hope and prayer."

Saigon now seemed peaceful most of the time—only a few grenades tossed now and then! But the army was conducting raids across the city to round up the armed forces deserters and draft dodgers, even using helicopters to spot those who climbed roofs to hide out.

In October, Tran Xuan Quang, James Stauffer, and I represented the Mennonite Mission at a meeting with the Office of Mobilization under the Ministry of Defense. The Director, Colonel Bui Dinh Dam, called Protestant groups together to discuss changes in the law granting deferment to religious leaders. Besides the Tin Lanh Church, there were also representatives of the Christian Church (related to World Evangelization Crusade in Central Vietnam), Baptist, Church of Christ, and Chinese churches. The chair of the meeting, Lieutenant Colonel Nguyen Phu Sanh, said that under the current laws religious leaders could be deferred for only six months—with possible extensions—and, for Protestants, only in two categories, *mục sư* (pastor) and *truyền đạo* (evangelist/licensed pastor).

Doan Van Mieng, President of Evangelical Church, reported that most of their pastors and evangelists had been deferred but some of the evangelists were drafted. He requested the Office of Mobilization to defer twenty theological students each year. Most of the other groups represented had also been able to receive deferment for a few persons.

I reported that two Mennonite evangelists were deferred—Trung and Lam. Although I did not consider this the setting to make a case for conscientious objection to war, I did state our desire to serve in a non-military capacity.

During the discussion time, Lt. Col. Sanh asked why there were so many Protestant churches. Pastor Mieng explained that there was "a spiritual unity" between the different groups and cited the Mennonites as a body that believes the Gospel should be proclaimed both by verbal witness and by deed in helping those in need.

When we asked whether the Mennonite church could receive deferment for staff engaged in church social ministries, Sanh said we should submit more information for them to study the matter—the rationale, the number of persons, and the period of deferment sought.

In closing, the Lieutenant Colonel said that the Office of Mobilization would propose to the Ministry of Defense that pastors and evangelists (licensed pastors) be given long-term deferments. He also said that it was reasonable to request deferment for theological students.

I submitted a request to defer up to five persons each year in categories of pastor, evangelist or theological students. "Evangelists" would be of two kinds—those primarily involved in evangelism, and those primarily involved in social projects.

In a letter home in late October, I wrote: "If Christians (peacemakers) worked as hard to bring about peace as the governments work to fight militarily, perhaps there would be some fruit." I told about a tragedy that struck a neighbor family the night before. Their twenty-two year-old son Dinh was killed while on patrol in Cho Lon, Saigon's Chinatown. Dinh was one of the first students to register for English classes two years before and his brother Hieu was one of the first community youth baptized. When Dinh and another brother reached draft age, they volunteered with the National Police, likely thinking that they could avoid induction into the army. He and other policemen were approached in a heavy

Funeral for Dinh.

rainstorm by Viet Cong wearing police uniforms and gunned down.

I went to their home to express condolences. The family consulted the oracles to learn the most auspicious day for the funeral for assurance that his soul would be at rest. They had a very elaborate funeral.

Luke and Dorothy Beidler arranged to teach English classes at the Saigon University in addition to their classes at the student center. Luke and Don also taught a few classes weekly in a U.S. Embassy-related school near the student center. Luke became a partner to James Stauffer and Don Sensenig in regular weekly early morning tennis games.

On National Day, November 1, the third anniversary of the overthrow of President Ngo Dinh Diem, the government had its usual parade and celebration. The Viet Cong fired 75mm recoilless rifle rounds for over an hour into downtown Saigon, killing and wounding many people. Mary and I saw both Phuoc and Luc at church that weekend, and both men expected that they would soon be drafted into the armed forces. They told stories of the suffering of the people in the Mekong River delta. Phuoc was now working as interpreter for an American USOM doctor at a province hospital where 400 civilians came monthly for treatment of war injuries. This doctor knew one village in Vinh Binh province where 500 people were maimed or disabled by loss of an arm, leg or eye! "Communism would be better than this," Luc declared.

Stauffer preached at the church the first Sunday morning in November on "The Christian Warfare." Two persons, a school teacher and a young man, confessed faith in Christ. Thirty some adults and ten children stayed for a fellowship meal. Robert Miller, on a long visit with Church World Service and Lutheran World Relief representatives, spoke at the afternoon service. He expressed the concerns of the American Christians about the Vietnam conflict.

Luke Beidler, now doing the monthly financial reports, helped me prepare the 1967 Mission budget. With the wild inflation it was difficult to project the costs. The Mission Council approved a 75 percent increase over the current year. I wrote to our home office: "With American troops still pouring in, defoliation spray killing crops, bombing and strafing preventing farmers from working, and floods in the western provinces, prices cannot become lower." The daily newspaper reported that the American armed forces bought 30 percent of the vegetables produced in the Da Lat area.

Some of us missionaries attended the American Thanksgiving Day service at the International Protestant Church. The preacher was Colonel Burton Hatch, a chaplain ordained by the Grace Brethren Church. That afternoon I was downtown—on my tenth trip—working to license two used Lambretta scooters that Stauffer had purchased in the States which were sent out with the Biedlers' personal unaccompanied baggage. Even though Kraybill recommended we get a car for Mission use, scooters were more convenient for getting around the city.

In August, Ernie Frey from Fulton County, Ohio, came to Vietnam, drilling wells with Layne Company. He and Mabel joined our weekly missionary prayer group. On Thanksgiving evening, they invited our missionary families out to the restaurant on the top floor of the Majestic Hotel—overlooking the Saigon River and the docks. Afterward we sang songs around the table. Two days before Thanksgiving we missionaries hosted all the local VNCS personnel for a tea with lots of singing. Many new personnel were completing their language study and ready to go to their assignments.

Everett—on furlough—asked for an update on what was happening in Vietnam. I hardly knew what to say—the "war machine" had become so powerful. I reported that some VNCS personnel were interested in working in zones controlled by the Viet Cong and suggested that it should not be too difficult to make contact with the VC. I said that we do not need "to be 95 percent sure of success before we try some peacemaking."

Since both Mennonite Mission and MCC-VNCS personnel were in Vietnam with the approval of the Saigon government, I asked myself whether the government would tolerate our working in VC-controlled areas. The *Saigon Post* had just reported that the American Friends Service Committee recently donated $4,000 to the International Committee of the Red Cross to assist victims of the American bombing in the North.

On December 4, the Viet Cong penetrated the defense perimeter and mortared the Tan Son Nhat Airport, causing American casualties. We slept through the attack. Three days later, Tran van Van, a prominent member of the Constituent Assembly, was assassinated by the Viet Cong during morning rush hour—just a few blocks from the Saigon student center and the VNCS office. Three weeks later, Dr. Phan Quang Dan, another prominent member of the Constituent Assembly, survived an assassination attempt.

In early December, the Eastern Mennonite Board of Missions office received a telegram from the chairman of the American Council of Voluntary Agencies for Foreign Service, inviting them to send a representative to the White House Executive Office on Monday, December 12, to meet with Vice President Hubert Humphrey. The telegram said that the Vice President wanted to personally express the thanks of the President for "the relief of suffering in war-torn Vietnam." H. Howard Witmer, one of the bishops on the Mission Committee, was asked to go.

The Vice President told agency representatives that they had "stepped into the front lines of the fight against human suffering." He assured them that the administration would give continued support and cooperation in their "efforts to shelter the homeless, to feed the hungry, to heal the sick." Addressing those who assembled, Humphrey said:

> I am privileged to meet today on behalf of President Johnson with leaders of America's voluntary organizations who are serving so well the innocent victims of the war in Vietnam.
> It is, I believe, so very appropriate that in this Christmas season, this time of selfless giving, you [who] are giving so much to so many be recognized and thanked by your grateful Government.

In doing so, you reaffirm—in action—our President's pledge of the Manila Conference [in late October]. You continue thereby a tradition which is as old as this Republic—citizen action to assist those in need at home and abroad. . . .

Through the voluntary agencies, American donations of money, food, clothing, and technical services are reaching the innocent victims of aggression in Vietnam. . . . Our common goal is freedom for the people of Vietnam—freedom from oppression . . . , freedom to harvest their crops . . . , freedom to raise their children in a land that we hope and pray will be at peace in the days ahead.

Neither MCC nor EMBMC considered their ministries part of the policies of the American administration. However, it was glaringly clear that the American administration considered them and other voluntary agencies part and parcel of its Vietnam policy.

In October, Mary experienced a health concern. With tuberculosis endemic in Vietnam, we had routine chest x-rays every few years at the Adventist Hospital. After the U.S. Third Army Field Hospital opened in Saigon in the vacated facilities of the American Community School, the Adventist Hospital often sent x-rays to the army hospital. Their radiologist spotted a tumor attached to a spinal nerve while reading Mary's x-rays. Although it was believed benign, all doctors recommended its surgical removal as soon as possible.

At the dedication service at church for both Jean Sensenig and our daughter Becky on December 4, there was prayer for Mary's healing. Mary wrote home that she truly had a "peace of mind." We missionaries also had a special service of prayer and anointing for healing on Thursday evening, December 15, when we spent most of the evening singing.

Mary preferred not to leave Vietnam for the thoracic surgery. Doctors at Third Field Hospital offered to perform the procedure at a time they had few casualties. Although we would have preferred not to use the services of the U.S. military, this seemed like the best option. The surgery was delayed due to anticipated casualties from an American military offensive in the "Iron Triangle" northwest of Saigon. The successful surgery was performed in early February.

At the Gia Dinh Congregation on Sunday morning, December 18, two young men, Hung and Tien, were baptized. Both men expressed how they came to faith in Christ. Tien said it was his loneliness that brought him to Jesus.

Christmas season 1966 was busy. We missionaries sang at the annual Christmas singing sponsored by the Vietnamese American Association one evening. The primary school and nursery gave an excellent Christmas program at the Community Center.

We missionaries got together for a Christmas soup and sandwich feast on Monday, the day after Christmas. Mary and I hosted this dinner in the downstairs patio at the Community Center. Most days this area was filled with children. Besides the Stauffer, Sensenig, Beidler families and us four, Ernie and Mabel Frey were there. A special guest was Elta Miller, Don's mother and the wife of Orie O. Miller; she had flown out to meet her youngest grandchild and spend Christmas with the family. We also shared in Dorothy Beidler's grief at the death of her brother Kenneth and her father's injury in a motor vehicle accident.

On New Year's Eve, the warring parties declared a truce—to extend until January 2. Yet each side charged the other with violations of the agreement.

There were now 280,000 U.S. troops in Vietnam, with nearly 100,000 more supporting the war on ships or in Thailand. More than 5,000 American soldiers were killed and 30,000 wounded in 1966. There were tens of thousands of Vietnamese military and civilians deaths on both sides of the conflict.

VNCS CARING AMID CHALLENGES
AND CONTROVERSY

Chapter 25

MCC would have liked Atlee Beechy to stay longer as the Executive Director of Vietnam Christian Service. Beechy likewise enjoyed the challenge of working with the VNCS ecumenical team and might have wished to stay longer, but Goshen College wanted him to resume his duties there. Paul Leatherman assumed the duties as executive director shortly before Atlee and Winifred left on August 15, 1966.

Leatherman was familiar with the work of Mennonite Central Committee because he was employed for more than a decade as the traveling representative of Orie O. Miller's Miller Hess Shoe Company in Akron, Pennsylvania. He was an outspoken critic of U.S. Vietnam policies, saying the United States should never have become involved. It was not easy for Loretta to take their three children into a war zone, however. Sixteen-year-old Jeanette was enrolled as a high school junior at the International School in Bangkok, Thailand. Twelve-year-old Don and ten-year-old Karen studied in Saigon's Phoenix Study group. The Leatherman family moved into a rented house I found on Le Quang Dinh Street—the same street as Em Dem, the unit house, about a kilometer away.

Leatherman wrote to the home office: "The responsibility of this position is now bearing down on me and it appears quite demanding, challenging and, I am sure, quite rewarding. We feel your wholehearted support, as well as the support and prayers of many people around the world."

Longacre helped orient Leatherman. The two Pauls traveled to Nha Trang early August to attend the hospital board meeting. In late August, fifteen VNCS personnel were involved in language study, some having just arrived while others were preparing for their assignments. Leatherman asked Robert Miller to slow down assigning people to Vietnam until Saigon administrators were able to adequately place those who were already there! Miller agreed that some time was needed to consolidate and to build programs.

A program proposal under discussion was a large feeding program for school children in refugee camps. While Beechy was still in Vietnam, consideration was given to a proposed three-party agreement between the government's Commissioner of Refugees, USAID Office of Refugee Coordination and VNCS. Under the proposal, VNCS would provide the expatriate administrative staff and USAID would provide most of the food from PL-480 commodities, though VNCS might supplement this with some MCC canned meats. VNCS would support its personnel but USAID would cover most of the program costs including local staff wages. Feeding programs at the Rung Lang and Phu Nhon refugee camps in Quang Ngai were seen as pilot projects possibly leading to additional feeding programs in four central Vietnam provinces. Wells Klein, the USAID liaison officer, was "pushing this idea very hard." Miller, who had discussed this with Beechy in the States, liked the proposal—provided it could be done without VNCS losing its identity as a church-related organization or becoming too closely identified with USAID. Miller preferred having VNCS form a contractual relationship with the Vietnamese government's Commissioner of Refugees rather than with USAID—even though the funding might come from AID.

In his hesitation Miller reflected the unease expressed by the MCC Executive Committee in July. While permitting the proposal to be considered, they expressed concern that "there may be problems of too great identification with the United States government in Vietnam if an AID contract is signed."

In late August 1966, Paul Longacre visited Di Linh district town outside Da Lat. Jerry and Judy Aaker, assigned as project leaders there, were looking forward to working among Koho ethnic minority refugees in agricultural and medical work. They and other personnel spent additional time studying the Koho language.

When flying out of Da Lat's Lien Khuong airport, Longacre noticed large quantities of fresh vegetables being airlifted out by the U.S. military. He asked the GI in charge where they were going and in what amounts and learned that they were shipping out between twenty and thirty tons a day to the various U.S. military units around the country. This practice had only begun a few weeks earlier and already the prices of vegetables in the Saigon market had more than doubled. Incensed that these vegetables are going to the U.S. military forces when they should be going to parts of the country that lacked fresh vegetables, Longacre wrote a letter of complaint to Gen. Westmoreland, commander of all U.S. troops, with a copy to the US Ambassador, identifying this as another instance where the U.S. military is much more interested in the morale of its troops than in the welfare of the Vietnamese people.

By August, programs were functioning in several Quang Ngai refugee camps and another one was starting at Tam Ky. Several VNCS personnel were working in the greater Hue area with World Relief Commission. In addition to the expanded program at the Nha Trang Clinic-Hospital, a team was developing the Pleiku Clinic—the second cooperative program with the Tin Lanh Church. The twenty-bed hospital facility was to be completed in early 1967. VNCS also signed an agreement with the Department of Health to provide a doctor and nurse for a district clinic in Nha Be, just south of Saigon. In Khanh Hoi, Saigon's District 4, social workers Neil and Marta Brenden were guiding a program which included a day-care center for twenty children and a public health nurse, Carolyn Nyce, was conducting hygiene classes for mothers.

Vietnam saw an increase in the number of medical providers with the introduction of the Military Provincial Health Assistance Program (MILPHAP), a joint program of USAID and the U.S. Military Assistance Command-Vietnam (MAC-V) that placed military medical teams in provincial hospitals. Begun in late 1965 after the U.S. troop buildup with heavier military action projected, by early 1966 there were six teams in place with fifteen more projected. By May 1968 there were twenty-two teams from the American army, navy or air force. Each team had three physicians, a medical administrative officer, and twelve enlisted technicians.

These teams provided services to the Vietnamese people. The Agency for International Development was spending huge budgets providing services to the government and people, helping to manage the economy, building schools and dispensaries, assisting in agriculture and public health, constructing roads and bridges. Thousands of dedicated USAID employees worked to improve services to communities and to "winning the hearts and minds" of the people. But by 1966 the military activities dwarfed the work of USAID civilian personnel.

Leatherman and Longacre attended the dedication of the Pleiku clinic facilities on Sunday afternoon, September 18. This event coincided with a conference of the ethnic Jerai Church. Pastor Doan Van Mieng, the Tin Lanh Church president who addressed the 400 people at the dedication service, accompanied Longacre to Pleiku three days earlier by Air America. Pastor Truong Van Sang chaired the hospital board which included two other Vietnamese pastors and Pastor Brao of the Jerai ethnic minority.

The Quang Ngai team was getting to full strength. Besides David and Sue Neufeld were Sanford Stauffer and Earl Martin. Pat Hostetter joined them in September and Tharon McConnell, a nurse, would join them later. Paul and Doris visited Quang Ngai in late August.

In late November Earl reported:

> I'm getting up to my ears in things to do these days. Once again I am beginning to live on a schedule. Often in the mornings I go to Rung Lang camp to check out the garden and meet some of the families. At 12:30 p.m. Pat and I just started teaching English at Rung Lang in order to get to know some of the youth of the camp. I have an enthusiastic bunch of about twenty-five fellows. By the time we pedal back from camp it's about time for my 2:30 Vietnamese class with a Tin Lanh man teaching me for an hour. At 3:30 for three days a week Pat and I are going to the Trung Tam Duong Lao (Senior Center) to work with the old people trying to get some small industry going in the center. The old codgers seem to be taking to the idea real quickly; some of them have had some talents which they hadn't used for a while and are finding it fun to get busy again. We have been working with bamboo, making rugs, embroidery, making fish nets, some metal work and some wire work. Then the other two afternoons we're planning to have an hour of recreation with the school kids at Rung Lang. So some days I'll be going out to the camp at least three times.

Earl wanted to live at the camp but realized that this might put others in danger of harassment. He wrote: "The last couple days we've been seeing a bunch of Marines in the camp—apparently they want to win friends and influence people also. It's hard to imagine the resentment I felt toward them for being in 'our' camp. First of all they have created the refugees and now they come and want to make friends. I'm sure it's great psychology."

Before Tam Ky was chosen, VNCS checked out the Da Nang area, the second most populated area in South Vietnam after Saigon. Since Everett Metzler had gone on home leave and James Stauffer had returned to Saigon, I was now giving half time to VNCS, supervising the language program for new personnel and was available for other assignments. I spent four days in Da Nang late September 1966 investigating refugee needs. VNCS decided not to open a service unit here; though Da Nang had many refugees, the government could more easily assist them and large U.S. military bases provided employment for thousands of people.

Doug Hostetter moved to Tam Ky late September to work with refugees in Quang Tin province. Two months later he wrote to his parents:

> The war and its struggle are very real here. Pray that my presence will not add to the conflict but help to heal it. I am the only American in the town outside of the guarded compound. I hope I am not endangering the family I am staying with. . . .
>
> I have done some serious thinking and talking about peace and war in the last two months and have made some decisions just this last week. I have decided that since I worship a God who is bigger than national or ideological boundaries, I will stay here working even if we are overrun by V.C. I am telling the military that they shouldn't feel responsible and I won't run if security deteriorates. This is not a hurriedly made, rash decision but has been made over two months of

talking, thinking and studying—as far as I'm concerned, it is the only Christian possibility. Of course I will continue to try to be sensitive to the leading of the spirit in all situations. I have much peace and freedom because of my decision. I think I am finding the meaning of Luke 9: 23 and 24 ["If anyone would come after me, let him deny himself. . . . Whoever loses his life will save it."], at least for this situation. My life and future are now in God's hands and I will consider whatever happens as His will. This frees me to live a sane and happy life where most military men are pulling out their hair.

This stance put Doug Hostetter on a collision course with local official Americans. Just that month, November 1966, the United States combined the U.S. Agency for International Development, Central Intelligence Agency (CIA), and the Joint United States Public Affairs Office (JUSPAO) into the Office of Civil Operations (OCO). The head of the Tam Ky OCO unit was a military officer.

One of the least likely developments was the proposal from the Ministry of Health for VNCS to place a medical doctor in Con Son, South Vietnam's well-known prison island located in the South China Sea 180 kilometers from the coastal town of Vung Tau. I made plans to accompany Longacre to the island, partly to see whether there might be opportunities for a spiritual ministry there. When Longacre came down with dengue fever, Leatherman and I went.

On Saturday, October 8, we flew to Con Son on a C-47 of Continental Airlines that was carrying supplies to the island for the Raymond, Morrison & Knudsen (RMK) group, the giant construction consortium that was building a permanent communication station on the island for the U.S. Coast Guard. The RMK medic took us into town, about fifteen kilometers by a winding road.

There we met Major Nguyen Van Ve, the undisputed chief of the island. He was irritated when we first met; he had not been informed that we were coming. After reading the letter of introduction from Dr. Thieu of the Ministry of Health, he was courteous and cooperative. He showed us through the three prison camps which we were told held 3,600 prisoners. We were told that some were political prisoners—suspected VC who had not been tried or sentenced and were there for re-education. Others were common criminals and political prisoners serving their sentences. We learned that the day before our arrival, two C&MA missionaries had been on the island distributing New Testaments and other gifts to the prisoners. These two men had been introduced to ministries with the military forces of the Republic of Vietnam by Mrs. Ruth Jeffrey, who with her husband D. I. Jeffrey had served in Vietnam since the 1920s. Much of their support came from World Vision. World Vision also imported large numbers of wheelchairs which were donated to injured Vietnamese war veterans.

Besides the prisoners on Con Son were civil servants (700 with families) and three companies of Regional Forces (about 1500 men and families) who guarded the island. Despite the nearly 6,000 inhabitants of the island, there was no resident doctor! We met the Chief of the Con Son Hospital—a young man who had only three years of nursing training—who welcomed having a doctor. Major Ve invited us to dinner, and arranged overnight lodging and breakfast. We were fortunate to meet a former English student of mine, Bui Cong Dong, an assistant to Major Ve, who shared much information with us.

Leatherman recommended assigning a doctor to the island as soon as possible. He noted that it could have some "far-reaching political implications" because of the many political prisoners on the island; VNCS would be unable to publish details of its work there. Leatherman also noted that VNCS might also be able to place an agriculturalist on the island to experiment with various food crops and animal husbandry. With VNCS commitment to serve anyone in need regardless of racial, religious or political affiliation, it seemed a good place to assign personnel.

We stayed overnight in the home of the captain in charge of the regional forces, hoping to return on Sunday. But there were no flights to the island Sunday or Monday, so we did not return until Tuesday! In those two days Paul and I soaked up sun walking on the beaches, swimming, and eating American food in the RMK camp. We really appreciated the unexpected vacation! Leatherman and I foresaw the era—forty years later—when luxury hotels would be built on this beautiful island. Eventually Dr. Alfred Stoffel was assigned to work here.

As Vietnam Christian Service neared the end of its first year, Robert Miller spent two weeks early November in Vietnam along with top CWS and LWR administrators visiting all of the projects. They attended a meeting of the Council of Foreign Voluntary Agencies in Vietnam which Paul Longacre chaired, had a luncheon meeting with several top USAID administrators, an afternoon meeting with US Deputy Ambassador William Porter, and a dinner with the Minister of Health and Social Welfare and several of his deputies. They met Dr. Nguyen Phuc Que, the Commissioner of Refugees, and Major General James William Humphreys Jr., USAID's assistant director of public health in Vietnam. It is no wonder that Longacre wrote home after the visitors had left: "Visitor fatigue!" But he continued: "In spite of the mental strain,

Top: Refugee Commissioner Dr. Nguyen Phuc Que.
Left: Robert Miller and Paul Longacre making field inspection.

physical as well, the visit of our bosses was very helpful. It gave a lot of time for program evaluation and planning for the year ahead."

Vietnam Christian Service (*Tổ Chức Xã Hội Tin Lành*) was developing well. This coordinated ministry of American Protestant churches helped to project the image that the Tin Lanh did indeed respond to social needs to assist the victims of war and other disadvantaged people and was not solely concerned about bringing people to Christian faith.

Vietnam Christian Service, like Mennonite Central Committee earlier, wanted a close relationship with the Evangelical Church. While many MCCers—as well as staff recruited by Church World Service and Lutheran World Relief—were happy to identify with the Tin Lanh Church, for others it was a struggle. Those who enjoyed puffing tobacco or sipping wine were invited to forgo this pleasure if they were assigned to work in settings where they would have close association with Tin Lanh Christians.

The issues were more than life style, however. It involved different cultural perceptions and theological views. Earl Martin, after working six months in Quang Ngai, dared to express this in letters to VNCS administrators in Saigon.

Beginning calmly enough, he wrote: "I found it hard enough to tolerate some of the religious irrelevancies in the States where I could understand them and influence them with my ideas, but here in Vietnam . . . I find it harder to take." Then he let it all out:

> This morning was all it took. I've been building up resentments and frustrations about being associated with the Tin Lanh Church for a long time and this morning I could take it no longer. The church 'service' lasted over two hours. 'I was mad from the first song. Pat was playing the organ, and . . . all of a sudden wondered why in the heck we Americans were taking the jobs away from the Vietnamese just because we could do them better. I asked the Vietnamese organist why he didn't play and he answered "because Pat can play better. . . ." I enjoyed singing in the choir, but I can't help but think that this big tall white-faced bearded American standing in the middle must have drawn some attention.

He continued: After the music "a bunch of old men gave some sort of 'testimonies'." Then they had the announcements, and "some more songs, responsive reading, and more Scripture. Then [the pastor] preaches. Either his watch was broken or he forgot to bring it with him." Following this the treasurer or secretary asked people to publically pledge how much money each would give to buy gifts for the children at Christmas. When they "yell out their name and how much they're promising to give toward the project, then, in my haughty opinion, they're going too far."

When we missionaries first arrived in Vietnam, we had similar reactions about some patterns in the Evangelical Church but had generally come to accept the church as it was. Publically announcing the amount we were contributing to the church was not what we were taught—"do not let the right hand know what the left hand is doing"—but it fostered generosity and accountability, important in their church.

Earl reacted against the Church evangelism as "a fire escape from the leaping, lashing fires of eternal hell." He described a stereotypical Tin Lanh personality as one who does not "smoke, drink, play cards, play billiards, play chess, dance, and go to movies." And "though maintaining a relative non-involvement in politics," Earl wrote, "Tin Lanh in general is supportive of the war effort and C&MA is flagrantly supportive of a misled U.S. national policy in Vietnam. Having ideological pacifistic affinities, I believe this fact seriously jeopardizes the effectiveness of a positive witness for peace in this land."

In a positive note, Earl observed that "associating with the Tin Lanh group does give [one] a group of young people who already have some social cohesion; their group already has some workable structure. . . . I believe these youth can be challenged by social needs around them and stimulated to action with a bit of direction." Further, he noted that "Tin Lanh youth seem to possess a stability and common purpose amid the uncertainties of this war situation. While many youth around them have a fatalistic outlook, evidenced by lack of skills and large numbers of school dropouts, the Tin Lanh kids are bound to each other and bound to their God. This resource could potentially be used well in service to our community."

A week later Earl sent a copy of that letter to Mary and me with additional comments:

> I think you understand the things I'm talking about. . . . I sometimes feel like a phony spending so much time with a group I am not really sold on, but I still firmly believe . . . that there is some good potential in working with this bunch of kids. And while I would like to get more involved in Buddhist and perhaps Catholic youth, I suspect that I'll continue a rather close working relationship with the Tin Lanh bunch. I just started teaching English two nights a week at the church and last night, the usual preaching night, I pinch-hit for Woody [Stemple] who's in Danang with his wife who nearly died because of an [illness] but who is now doing fine, and I had an opportunity to share my convictions on love and pacifism by parabolically speaking of ants and anthills instead of people and countries. I have a close relationship with the pastor and most of the youth of the church and some of the other people.

Sam Hope, VNCS's Director of Personnel Services, and a minister in the Presbyterian Church in the United States, prepared a Personnel Recruitment and Job Description dated November 1966: It reads: "Working in Vietnam is no picnic. It is always frustrating and sometimes disillusioning. At times it is exciting and thrilling, but more often it is slow and discouraging. The needs and problems are urgent, but the solutions take infinite patience and perseverance. . . . It takes an exceptional person to work in the war-torn 'hell' of Vietnam. It is essential that personnel arrive in Vietnam with as realistic expectations as possible."

Hope cited three basic requirements—personality, skills and Christian faith. Regarding personality, the statement reads: "Emotional security is essential. Is the person flexible, friendly, broad-minded, creative? There is no room for personalities who are rigid, authoritarian, perfectionistic or judgmental. Job assignments and locations can change overnight. Unit living is often in simple quarters with little privacy. The person must be able to 'roll with the punches' and make the best of constantly changing situations and problems."

Under the heading "Christian faith," the statement reads: "Christian convictions and motivation are obviously required for all VNCS personnel. This includes a concern for and a sensitivity to the suffering of the Vietnamese people. It is essential that our Christian faith be strong enough to understand and respect a wide range of convictions regarding personal piety and social customs. In Vietnam, love is needed even more than courage."

Harold Kraybill described the unity of VNCS personnel from many denominational backgrounds "very thrilling." Dr. Kraybill with his wife Esther had spent a few months in Nha Trang before coming back to Saigon for their Vietnamese language training. With reminders of the war all around, he was happy that VNCS was giving a Christian response to human suffering.

A VNCS Program Review and Projected Planning prepared by Paul Leatherman, dated December 1, 1966, reported sixty-four VNCS personnel representing twelve major Protestant groups. Eight persons were from Canada and one from Switzerland; the rest were from the United States. Regarding skills, six were doctors, fourteen nurses, three medical assistants, four social workers, five home economists, two child welfare workers, eight community development workers, five agriculturalists, three agricultural assistants, one mechanic, one architect, nine administrative persons and three hostesses. A similar number of Vietnamese staff included social workers, nurses, interpreters, administrators and secretaries.

Billy Graham arriving for meeting with Tin Lanh pastors.

While many of Mennonite missionaries and VNCS personnel struggled with the theological and political mindset of some evangelical Christians in Vietnam, we also disagreed with the stance of American evangelical leaders like evangelist Billy Graham. When we missionaries and VNCS leaders learned that Graham was planning a Christmas visit to the American soldiers, we asked to meet him to share our concerns about what the war was doing to the Vietnamese people, what American policy was doing to the American conscience, and how the American Christians' support of the American policy in Vietnam was hindering Christian evangelism in other countries. Leatherman phoned "Pentagon East," the Military Assistance Command, Vietnam at the Tan Son Nhat Airbase to make the appointment.

Graham and his party arrived on Monday, December 19. The next day he spoke at a prayer breakfast sponsored by International Christian Leadership. I didn't attend this breakfast but James Stauffer appreciated the meeting. At noon, missionaries of all agencies were invited to a dinner with Graham and his staff at the Rex officers' restaurant on Nguyen Hue Boulevard. Cliff Barrows led in singing, Bev Shea sang a solo, and Graham spoke briefly. Both Mary and I met him. On Wednesday morning Graham addressed a gathering of enthusiastic Vietnamese church workers: pastors, evangelists, and church leaders, calling them to evangelize the country as they are empowered by the Spirit of God.

I had followed Graham's ministry with interest, having first heard him preach in 1955 at Neckarstadion in Stuttgart, Germany. In 1957 I heard him again during his long campaign in New York's Madison Square Garden, New York City.

I wrote home:

> You of course know that Billy Graham is in Vietnam. A year ago there had been reports that
> he was coming to Vietnam. I had written asking him not to come since I felt his prominence as
> a church leader would tend to indicate that the American Christians support American policy in
> Vietnam. He didn't come last year, but I don't think it was because of my letter. When I heard
> he was coming this year I didn't write since I think it is clear to the world what America is doing
> here. His coming after American policy has been set is not as serious as if it had come at the time
> President Johnson was making some of his basic decisions regarding Vietnam. Still his coming as
> a guest of [Gen.] Westmoreland and for the sole purpose of speaking to American troops suggests
> that he is showing a good deal of support for the American military policy in this land.

Late Wednesday morning, December 21, after his meeting with Vietnamese church leaders,
Paul Leatherman, Paul Longacre, Neil Brenden, Lance Woodruff and I met Rev. Graham. With
Graham and his staff were several chaplains, including Lieutenant Colonel Fairchild, the top Protestant chaplain in Vietnam. Leatherman asked Neil Brenden, a Lutheran, to be the spokesperson.
After briefly describing the work of VNCS, Brenden said that the VNCS volunteers believed
that Graham's association with the American military policy was hindering the acceptance of the
Christian gospel in Asia. Graham said he had heard this line from Mennonites before. He said he
came to Vietnam as a call from God to minister to the soldiers in the same way as he conducted
his evangelistic campaigns.

Writing home, Paul Longacre described the encounter:

> We all were quite disappointed with the meeting. I came away feeling that we are in a dark hour
> in the history of "American Evangelical Christianity!" We attempted to raise some questions from a
> Christian perspective about the American involvement in Vietnam in the course of presenting our
> program. We got a cold response: "I heard all those things before and they're not valid." He gave a
> five minute rebuttal saying, "we gotta watch China—no open Christians there, and she will have
> nuclear missile capabilities in x number of years, [President] Johnson has superior knowledge and
> information so we should not question his policy," and other useless arguments. The thing that was
> so depressing to us was the fact that just a month ago we had an appointment with US Deputy
> Ambassador [William] Porter on business matters and he literally poured out his heart about the
> difficulties of the US involvement here. Billy Graham, a Churchman in contrast, spoke as the Gov-
> ernment policy apologetic.

Longacre concluded: "If American Evangelical Christianity thinks that American military
and economic power is the only way to solve the world's problems, it is a dark hour for the world,
for America, and above all for the Church."

Leatherman later said that this was the "most discouraging meeting" he had in his two years
in Vietnam.

When we addressed Graham with our concerns, Chaplain Fairchild tried to defend
American policy. Graham said the world does not confuse American Christianity with American
policy since America is not a Christian nation. Regarding Vietnam policy, he told us after the
interview was over that he had never publically made a statement regarding American policy in
Vietnam. Yet to us, his actions spoke more loudly than his words.

In his 1999 autobiography, *Just As I Am,* Graham said he went to Vietnam during the Christmas seasons of 1966 and 1968 at the invitation of Gen. Westmoreland, the commander of US forces in Vietnam. He noted the times of fellowship with missionaries, military chaplains and Vietnamese pastors, and said that Pastor Doan Van Mieng, the president of the Evangelical Church, invited him to return to Vietnam to conduct an evangelical crusade.

"When I arrived in Vietnam during one of those trips," he wrote, "reporters asked if I supported the President's policies. My answer was always the same. 'My only desire is to minister to our troops by my prayers and spiritual help wherever I can.'"

In my letter home, I reflected, "Has anything come out of this meeting? I'm not sure. We do at least have the satisfaction that we have presented one point of view which he likely will not hear from any other source."

At the same time that Graham was in Vietnam, Francis Cardinal Spellman, Archbishop of New York and military vicar to U.S. Catholic military personnel, was also visiting Vietnam December 23 to 28. He declared that the Vietnam War was "a war thrust upon us—we cannot yield to tyranny," and told the U.S. soldiers that they were there for the "defense, protection and salvation not only of our country, but . . . of civilization itself." Anything "less than victory is inconceivable," he said. The Vatican was unhappy with his statements, and a Vatican spokesperson declared that the Cardinal "did not speak for the Pope or the Church." Billy Graham did not have to answer to a pope.

U.S. administration officials insisted that they were doing what they could to end the conflict. In early December, Ambassador Lodge asked the Polish member of the International Control Commission to inform North Vietnam that the U.S. was willing to meet with their officials. Hanoi accepted the proposal for talks at the ambassadorial level without repeating their earlier demand that the U.S. first cease their bombing raids in the North. But Hanoi refused to meet with American diplomats after U.S. planes bombed the Hanoi area on December 13 and 14.

As an agency committed to helping victims in need without political considerations, the Mennonite Central Committee was increasingly troubled in providing aid only to those within the political control of the Saigon government. The MCC Peace Section had taken action on July 31 and November 20, 1965, asking that ways be found to provide relief assistance to North Vietnam. There were attempts by Peter Dyck in Algeria and Vernon Reimer in India to arrange for an MCC visit to North Vietnam to discuss providing relief assistance, but these efforts were unsuccessful. Dyck reported that he and Tony Enns had spoken to a "nameless gentleman" in the Algiers office of the Democratic Republic of Vietnam on October 25, offering material aid. They were told that material aid, medicine and personnel were not needed. What was needed, they were told, was to "condemn the imperialist American aggression."

VNCS 1967—A PIVOTAL YEAR

Chapter 26

Thursday—February 9, 1967—was *Tết Nguyên Đán,* the Lunar New Year. Vietnam Christian Service arranged for the entire international staff to gather that weekend in Da Lat for fellowship, recreation and inspiration. A few VNCSers complained about missing the New Year celebrations with their Vietnamese friends in the areas they were serving, but most made it to Da Lat.

Relating to the massive American occupation was becoming more complex. Paul Longacre, in a January letter to friends, described how the U.S. in November 1966 combined the field operations of USAID, the Embassy, CIA and JUSPAO (Information Services) under the Office of Civil Operations (OCO) with the objective of making significant progress in "pacification" within six months. Paul wrote that one of America's "blind spots" was thinking that another "instant program" would help them accomplish their elusive goals. "Furthermore," he said, "in an effort to get American consensus behind the war effort, so much one-sided propaganda has been issued by the Government that a U.S. messianic complex seems to have been formed concerning the war. This makes the destruction of a nation and its people a righteous goal."

"The U.S. is taking more and more control and autonomy away from the Vietnamese," Paul wrote.

"Again, I sense a growing anti-American feeling . . . , not the street-riot variety but a much more sophisticated, subtle 'I do not like what you are doing to me' feeling. A leading Vietnamese businessman told some of our people that the Americans' taking over more and more Vietnamese areas of responsibility is creating an intolerable situation. . . . To another one of our people a Vietnamese doctor said, 'It's just a matter of time until I join the Communists. I hate communism; I don't like what they do, but I cannot take the present situation.'"

Longacre said "one of our own people put it well to a visiting dignitary the other week when he said, 'The question is not whether we are going to have to negotiate out of here on less than victorious terms, but it is whether we should do it now or in five or ten years. . . . ' A lot of . . . international prestige, lives, money and property could be saved if the US people could decide that the time for this is now." How prophetically true this was!

VNCS continued staffing the two medical programs with the Tin Lanh Church in Nha Trang and Pleiku. Another doctor worked at a government district dispensary in Nha Be, ten kilometers south of Saigon city. One doctor worked in the psychiatry unit at the large Cho Quan Hospital in the city. In an unusual placement, a doctor worked with prisoners on the prison island of Con Son. Assistance was given to refugees in Quang Ngai and Tam Ky in central Vietnam as well as through the World Relief Commission programs in Hue and Quang Tri province near the Demilitarized Zone. VNCS also developed services to refugees among the minority ethnic people in Di Linh and Pleiku. In Saigon there were community services in Khanh Hoi (District 8) and at the Mennonite Community Center. Here are brief descriptions of the activities at each place, as well as crucial issues addressed.

Côn Sơn: After the unusual request from the government's Ministry of Health for VNCS to place a medical doctor on Con Son, South Vietnam's well-known prison island located 180 kilometers off the coast of southeast Vietnam, Dr. Alfred Stoffel began his assignment there in March 1967, the only medical doctor on the island with a population of six or seven thousand, of which more than two thousand persons were military or civilian personnel and their families. In his first report prepared ten days later, the Swiss doctor said he was spending most of his time in the hospital wards of the prison camps with up to 200 inpatients. He found typhoid, beriberi, leprosy, tuberculosis, mental disorders, and other diseases—many patients seriously ill. There was an acute shortage of all kinds of drugs and nutritious food.

In his next report, Stoffel indicated that the situation in the prison camps was "quite serious"; he had no Streptomycin to treat one hundred patients suffering from tuberculosis. Stoffel wrote that the prisons were "very well managed and kept," and that the camp commander, Maj. Ve, and his assistant affirmed his work. However, he indicated that "there are still many things I see and hear which are extremely grim," things he was not able to disclose. Although pleased he could offer solace and limited medical treatment to the prisoners, he wrote: "I am often depressed when I leave these places of concentrated suffering."

In his May report, Dr. Stoffel said he received the things he had asked VNCS to send on the supply ship. Stoffel wrote:

> The medical situation in the prisons is not good. . . . In one prison there are not even beds; the patients lie on the floor and I have to crawl around to examine them. Before they never had been properly examined and had been left in the care of some prisoner-nurses. Every day now I work myself through the hospital ward of one prison. There are always serious cases among them, of TB alone about one hundred. Work is difficult there because of lack of drugs, equipment, nursing facilities, and also because sometimes the prison wardens are reluctant to let me do my duty. It is inevitable, of course, that I see things which would better be hidden. The prisoners by now know me well and I believe they trust me and some are obviously glad to see me every week. I don't doubt that I can do something to help them a little; it may not be spectacular, but it satisfies my ambition.

In his September report, Dr. Stoffel acknowledged receiving medical supplies. He said that sick patients were now getting meals with canned meat twice a week—meat VNCS had sent. Not only was this treatment against beriberi, Stoffel said this was "something, I believe,

> they will never forget. From time to time the prisoners get some presents from Government officials or Missionaries who come here for half a day. But then there are always speeches, pamphlets, etc. For the average prisoner this is like a bribe with either a political or a religious purpose. I wish some of the well-meaning gentlemen, who after their optimistic speeches go swimming and to a banquet with the commandant, knew what prisoners think of them. For that reason I try to give whatever you send me in a quite different way. There must not be any ties to a present. People here know it comes from American Christians, that they get it regularly and that nothing in return is asked of them. Also I don't bring it to the prisoners myself like a Santa Claus, but hand it out to the prison nurse in charge. Maybe this kind of present, which is new to them and quite unexpected, impresses them more and makes them think. If not, words would be useless, too. Anyhow, I feel a strong improvement in the morale, especially in prison Nr. 1 (with detained

people for political reasons) and prison Nr. 4 (with all the crippled men), and this has been acknowledged lately by Capt. Tran.

Occasionally the prisoners thank me, usually in the form of a (more or less secret) speech held by one they delegate for that purpose. They know that my life here is not too easy and that I fight a rather hopeless war against negligence and corruption in our department. They tell me that they feel that I like them and don't despise them and that they are very grateful for it. This of course helps my morale, which often suffers badly under the lack of cooperation by the prison authorities and under the humiliating circumstances I have to work occasionally. I am not free to do what I should. Also we have very little drugs, practically no equipment and no technical aid. What I can achieve is therefore not spectacular. But I try to give something more, a message without words, unknown here, and which I hope will be heard by some and not forgotten.

The report is signed, "Yours sincerely, Alfred Stoffel."

The files contain no more reports from Dr. Stoffel. Paul Leatherman, in his memoirs, tells how Dr. Stoffel returned to Saigon "under great stress." He had learned that there was a detention center on the island where prisoners suffering all sorts of illnesses were not being treated. While he brought with him some documentation, the doctor insisted that it not be made public. He left Vietnam within a few days, afraid for his own life. It was more than three years later that American congressional representatives visiting Vietnam reported to the world the existence of the "tiger cages" where some 400 political prisoners suffered under gruesome conditions.

Leatherman later said his greatest regret as VNCS director was a failure to accompany the doctor to the United States to report these abuses to the sponsoring agencies and to the U.S. Congress. The doctor, however, was not up to this.

———————

Nhà Bè and **Long Kiển:** Arranged by the Vietnamese health ministry, VNCS provided a doctor and nurse—Jesse Landhuis and Helen Snavely—who worked with Vietnamese personnel in a district dispensary just ten kilometers south of Saigon. Most of the materials were provided by the government. The doctor and staff saw 1,800 patients each month, spending mornings at Nha Be and afternoons at Long Kien.

Saìgòn: The VNCS administrative office was in Saigon. The **Xóm Chiểu** Community Center was developed near the Saigon River docks in District 4 (Khánh Hội). Social workers Neil and Marta Brenden, public health nurse Carolyn Nyce, and ten Vietnamese staff worked here. The services included a child care center, sewing

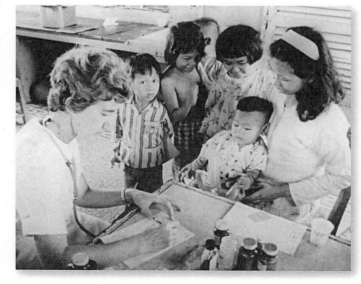

Anne Falk at Binh Loi Orphanage.

classes for young women, nutrition classes and an MCC-funded Family Child Assistance (FCA) sponsorship program. Marta also worked with the staff of the Mennonite Community Center in the northern outskirts of Saigon to develop the FCA and educational assistance programs. By the end of 1966 VNCS had also begun a small program in District 2 in a slum area closer to the VNCS office, cooperating with a government clinic and beginning a sewing class and other assistance programs. Carolyn, in a 1967 year-end report, said her work at Xom Chieu was satisfying but at times frustrating when patients did not follow proper procedures.

Dr. Marilyn Strayer, in March 1967, began working in the psychiatric ward of Saigon's Cho Quan Hospital, caring for 170 non-paying psychiatric patients. She expressed frustration due to lack of medications, but by June was more optimistic because she was able to discharge some patients with hope of eventual recovery. In September, she and a Vietnamese doctor were assigned an additional ward, bringing their patient load to three hundred. Nancy Hope was doing crafts and a recreational program several mornings weekly. Anne Falk, who left Tam Ky due to security concerns, gave lectures to students on psychiatric nursing. Dave Neufeld, earlier in Quang Ngai, was visiting families and finding placements for patients ready to be discharged. Marilyn also was pleased to conduct a twice-weekly health clinic at the Mennonite Community Center.

Martin Strayer provided architectural and engineering services and spent time with local architects to become familiar with their practices. In April, Strayer reported helping Summer Institute of Linguistics in Kontum. In addition to designing various buildings for VNCS he assisted in developing plans for remodeling and rebuilding Saigon's Cho Quan Hospital. When Prime Minister Nguyen Cao Ky and the Minister of Health visited the hospital, they were pleased with Strayer's work and Ky promised additional funds for hospital construction.

Other VNCS staff persons were involved in English teaching, either as an assignment or in spare time. One staff member taught English at the Regina Pacis School for home economists.

Di Linh: Di Linh is 225 kilometers northeast of Saigon on Highway #20, eighty kilometers from Da Lat. Here VNCS placed a community development team composed of a public health nurse, an agriculturalist, a home economist and a community development worker, working primarily with Koho ethnic minority people who had fled the mountains to escape warfare. Jerry and Judy Aaker were unit leaders; Jerry developed good relationships with community leaders. A nurse, Judy was spending much time in the government's district dispensary. Lee Brumbeck was developing an agricultural program; Richard Milk, an agriculturalist assigned to Hue, made recommendations. Betty Tiessen worked with public health in the Go Jung refugee camp; June Sauder gave a short stint teaching village women how to prepare USAID food commodities.

In a major battle only five kilometers from Di Linh on February 24, 1967, the town was nearly overrun by VC troops massed in the area. The district chief, two American advisors and thirty ARVN troops were ambushed and massacred, and several civilians killed. Judy treated a young captured VC who Jerry said "looked no different from any other Vietnamese kid we see on the street every day."

When Aaker became VNCS program director in mid-1967, Dean and Marta Hancock replaced the Aakers, with Dean serving as unit leader.

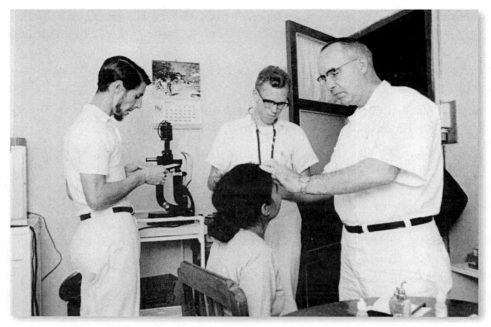

Dana Troyer (r) providing additional training for Drs. Gehman and Kraybill.

Nha Trang: Here VNCS continued the Tin Lanh medical program. Throughout 1967 two doctors, Linford Gehman and Harold Kraybill, were on the staff. Dr. Dana Troyer spent three months—February to May—performing surgical eye procedures and giving additional training to the staff doctors Gehman, Kraybill, and Pleiku doctor Chris Leuz. Together they performed a total of 170 surgeries. Trachoma was common. The unique eye care program of the Evangelical Clinic and Hospital was well-known throughout central Vietnam.

The normal inpatient census was forty-five. Close to 3,000 outpatients were treated monthly. The clinic additionally treated 250 TB patients. Nurses Emma Lenzmann, Ruth Yoder, Mary Sue Helstern and the doctors provided training for the hospital and clinic staff. Yoder made plans to begin a one-year Nursing Education Program.

The staff was affirmed in providing excellent medical care. They now had a functioning x-ray machine, thanks to the Chinese man who operated the MCC bakery in Saigon. They still lacked a laboratory. Esther Kraybill managed the unit household; Eugene, the Kraybill's first child born in early 1967, was a joy to them and the whole community.

Pleiku (and Đắc Tô): Pleiku is in the central highlands 550 kilometers north of Saigon. The medical program with the Tin Lanh Church, opened in 1966, continued to develop; the twenty-bed hospital was completed by year's end. Dr. Christopher Leuz and nurses Mary Pauls and Barbara Stallwood were providing service to nearly two thousand outpatients monthly. Lois Leuz also began nursing duties in the clinic in March.

Home economist Jessie Gingerich and Rufus Petre worked on the experimental farm and training center one kilometer north of town that International Voluntary Service developed for the minority Jarai and Rhade (Ede). They taught nutrition and food preparation, health, and other family sciences; the nursing staff assisted. Twenty students—thirteen men and seven women—graduated in May 1967.

There were many military skirmishes around town. Lois reported in August that she and an Alliance nurse traveled to a village by army helicopter to give BCG inoculations to prevent tuberculosis, and local officials insisted they be escorted into the village from the landing site by armored personnel carriers! The Tin Lanh Clinic made plans to inoculate all the children in Pleiku's public and private schools.

Pauls enjoyed her clinic work. In April she and Carolyn Nyce, visiting from Saigon, flew to Kontum to visit legendary Dr. Pat Smith who operated the Catholic Minh Quy Hospital.

When Petre left in mid-year, IVS assigned Del Epp to the agricultural farm. Jonathan Newkirk went to Dac To, ninety-five kilometers north

Jessie Gingerich teaching sewing.

of Pleiku, where he developed a feeding program and self-help handicraft project for refugees. Newkirk also traveled to Nha Trang, Quang Ngai, and Dong Ha to repair vehicles.

Quảng Ngãi: In Quang Ngai, a coastal town nearly half-way between Hanoi and Saigon, 860 kilometers from Saigon, a VNCS community development team worked among the thousands of refugees who fled the countryside. In January1967, Canadian David Neufeld, Quang Ngai unit leader, reported that in the previous nine months they had worked primarily in the Rung Lang refugee camp with 458 families (2,500 people). He chafed under the pressures of the Vietnamese government and the US Office of Civilian Operations (OCO) which viewed the VNCS refugee services as part and parcel of their total program. Dave said that he would not raise "the question of identification" if the refugees were physically starving but since they were relatively well cared for he believed that he was a "traitor" to himself, to VNCS, and to Christ if he became "part and parcel of the government-military war effort." He was later reassigned to Saigon.

In contrast, Fred Gregory in February was feeling quite positive about his involvement in providing milk and bread to 1,320 refugee children each morning in Bau Giang and Rung Lang refugee camps. He then enrolled 600 more children—both from a Tin Lanh refugee camp and children from the community. At the end of May he had added one more camp, including one considered in an "insecure" zone, for a total of 3,000 children. Observing that people receiving handouts were not always gracious recipients, he "witnessed jealousy, greed, corruption and anger along with happiness, love and gracious acceptance of what was given."

Some of the team members worked closely with local Tin Lanh Church leaders and with C&MA missionary Woody Stemple. VNCS visitors to Quang Ngai would sometimes stay in Woody and Charlotte's home.

Tharon McConnell and Sue Neufeld assisted the government nurse at the Rung Lang refugee camp; Tharon held a clinic three times weekly at the Tin Lanh camp, seeing at least thirty patients at each clinic. Pat Hostetter and Earl Martin organized children's recreational activities and adult educational programs in refugee camps and in an old peoples' home.

Unit members were brainstorming every Thursday evening for several months with Quang Ngai provincial officials, sharing ideas and possibilities for community development. Earl found this "window into how the local government worked intellectually stimulating," but he and others expressed concern about how OCO considered the VNCS ministries

Tharon McConnell treating child.

an integral part of their program. This issue was further acerbated by the May 15, 1967, Executive Order of President Johnson creating the Military Assistance Command, Civil Operations and Revolutionary Development Support (MAC-CORDS), the brainchild of Robert Komer, Johnson's special assistant for pacification in Vietnam. This brought the whole OCO "pacification" program under the US military command of Gen. Westmoreland.

"Identities continue to trouble us," Earl wrote.

> Who are we as a Christian presence here? Who are we in relation to other governmental agencies working in Vietnam?. . . The present USAID man in charge of refugees, Ernie Hobson, seems even more intent than his predecessors to coordinate and homogenize the efforts and goals of all agencies working in the area of refugees. For these reasons of political entanglement, I should hope VNCS

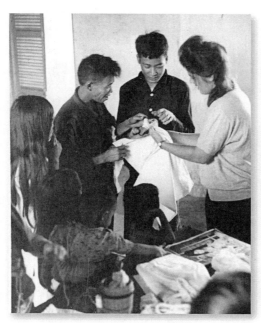

Pat Hostetter relating to older persons.

Earl Martin with school boys.

would attempt to concentrate even more efforts in the less politically fraught areas of medicine and agriculture and education rather than in refugee community development which is so dependent on commodities which is USAID's strength. And I'm not sure that we are distributing USAID's commodities any more effectively than they or the [government] refugee office cadres could do.

In early May 1967, the First Brigade of the American 101st Airborne Division initiated Operation Malheur I in Quang Ngai province, a series of "search and destroy" operations as part of Task Force Oregon. Operation Malheur II followed in June and July with air assaults against an area west of the Ve River valley in Nghia Hanh district. Part of this operation involved forcibly uprooting 10,000 civilians and bringing them into Nghia Hanh district town. People were transported from their villages by helicopter, 170 in one Chinook helicopter.

Since this evacuation was hurriedly made, no food or shelter was prepared for the people. With afternoon temperatures around 100° Fahrenheit (38°C), living conditions were horrible. Gregory said "the urge to help could not be restrained." So he, along with Neufeld, recruited Tin Lanh Pastor Tuoi and other members of his congregation to help. Using a corn-soya-milk (CSM) mixture with several pots and small kerosene stoves, they began feeding people the first day. Since they could not travel to Nghia Hanh district town until 9:30 in the morning for fear of road mines, they cooked some CSM before they left Quang Ngai, worked all day, finishing the feeding operation by 5:30 p.m. when they returned to Quang Ngai. This hectic schedule continued for two weeks until they were able to find a permanent location at Nghia Hanh to store the supplies and cook the food. By then Gregory had arranged for a crew of ten local persons working full-time to feed 8,000 people daily. He was still saddened that the people had nothing to do all day long. He wrote: "These early days were the most taxing, both physically and emotionally, that I can ever recall going through, but yet the feeling of satisfaction at helping people who had been crushed was in itself almost overwhelming. For the first time I have met and given to people in desperation."

Mother with children at Nghia Hanh camp.

The evacuation of these refugees was especially traumatic. In late June, Sanford Stauffer flew into Quang Ngai where Neufeld met him and together they went to Nghia Hanh where they picked up a coffin for a boy, one of many who had died from gas poisoning; before bombing an area American soldiers used tear gas to force people from a cave. Several other people were taken to the Quang Ngai Hospital in serious condition.

On October 20, Neufeld sent a letter to the editor of *The Saigon Post* in response to an article they had published, "*US Tear Gas Use Saves Lives of Viet Innocents*." Neufeld described the death of the boy from tear gas overdose.

Although Jim Mays, the Quang Ngai USAID chief, told Sanford Stauffer that they would soon have things well managed, Stauffer wrote: "The situation in the Nghia Hanh area is worse than I have seen anywhere as far as planning and management of the movement of refugees is concerned." The quick response of the VNCS team alleviated this critical situation.

USAID liked the VNCS refugee feeding program and continued to press a proposal for VNCS to develop a country-wide program. Most unit members signed a July 12, 1967, letter to Paul Leatherman, VNCS director, regarding a "VNCS – CORDS Feeding Contract." It read: "It has come to our attention that there has been continued consideration of the possible contract between Vietnam Christian Service and the Civil Operations Revolutionary Development Support with respect to refugee feeding. We . . . entertain some misgivings about entering such a commitment and would like to express several reasons for these uncertainties."

Such a large program, the letter said, "would be another step in sacrificing our freedom of a unique ministry . . . and would inevitably stifle the independence we now enjoy as a team of service-minded volunteers." The central concern, the writers feared, was that such "a contract with CORDS would identify [VNCS] more closely with the total military effort" and was not consistent with Church programs. They believed that to become involved in a large "commodity distribution" program would negatively impact VNCS's "service-centered program." The writers also expressed a concern that a program allied with official American policies might have negative effects on future programs.

This was not an ultimatum. "We would beg your careful consideration of this matter," they wrote. "We pledge our continued support to the guiding principles of Vietnam Christian Service." It was signed by Sanford Stauffer, Earl Martin, Tharon McConnell, Pat Hostetter, David Neufeld and Sue Neufeld.

Robert L. (Bob) Miller and Fred Gregory did not sign this "petition." In a July 28 report sent to Jerry Aaker, who was now serving as associate director for up-country projects, Fred disagreed with the sentiments expressed in the letter.

Taking issue with fellow unit members, Gregory wrote, "To me it is a sad day when our primary concern

Fred Gregory in refugee camp.

is our 'identity' rather than meeting the needs of the people. I have felt this feeling so strong since coming to Quang Ngai. . . . As long as people are in need and there is someone to help, I don't care who gets the credit for the job. My primary concern is not to further the political position of VNCS or to spend a great deal of time establishing our 'image' if it detracts from the job of meeting and helping those in need."

Two positions—each expressing a powerful argument. Those who signed the letter did not object to giving food to refugees who were dumped into Nghia Hanh district town. On the other hand, if VNCS signed a contract with USAID, it seemed that VNCS would be participating in the CORDS strategy of "pacifying" the countryside, would need to prepare to care for refugees "generated" by U.S. military operations, and would thus become an important cog in the entire military operation.

Gerald Aaker visited Quang Ngai early August, talking with each team member, especially with Bob Miller who was named unit leader when the Neufeld family moved to Saigon. The unit discussed a longer term response to the Nghia Hanh refugees. The feeding program headed up by Gregory was now running smoothly with the Tin Lanh pastor directing the program under VNCS supervision. Martin was planning activities for the refugees. Aaker concluded that there was "still a great deal of struggle for several of the staff about VNCS role and function in Vietnam," which VNCS administrators would have to define more clearly. "The intense idealism of some of our people must be channeled and used without restricting it," he said.

In December, Earl wrote to Paul and Doris Longacre, telling them that some "men from the mountains" had come into the Nghia Hanh refugee camp before Christmas demanding the kitchen key of Ong Van and sampled the Sunkist raisins. Ong Van successfully begged them not to take the raisins and CSM powder but they took several cooking pots with them. MCC-VNCS thus inadvertently provided a little assistance to "the other side!"

Tam Kỳ: Quang Tin province, like bordering Quang Ngai province to the south, was a hotly contested area during the war. Tam Ky town, the province capital, was eighty kilometers south of Da Nang, South Vietnam's second largest city but just fifty kilometers north of Quang Ngai town.

VNCS assigned two community development persons, William Herod and Douglas Hostetter, to Tam Ky to teach English in the high schools, support youth activities and to develop handicraft production among the refugees. Nurse Anne Falk worked with the government nurses in the refugee camps. June Sauder, a home economist who arrived in January 1967, anticipated starting a sewing class for young girls in Vuon Lai refugee camp, home to 1,375 people.

Doug wondered how much they should work through the provincial government. In discussing a possible program with the chief of a refugee camp, he learned that the camp chief had to send proposals to the provincial refugee chief who would submit them to Saigon for approval. "With this kind of efficiency," Doug wrote, "we may as well be working for USAID."

Paul Longacre, program director, visited Tam Ky early February 1967. Herod was living at the high school in town. June and Anne were living temporarily in a USAID house until a new house became available. Hostetter, the unit leader, lived nearby. He and Herod had quickly established good community relations through teaching English at several high schools and involved the students in their visits to the refugee camps.

Sunday evening, February 5, Longacre said, was a night "no one cares to repeat again, if possible." The four unit members talked with Longacre until 10:00 p.m., then watched jets bombing and strafing an area five kilometers west of the town. Doug stayed with Bill that night and Paul retired to Doug's bed in the small house behind the house where Anne and June lived. They heard intermittent small arms fire and artillery until 1:00 a.m. "Then everything broke loose," Paul said.

> Our end of Tam Ky was under attack and the house we were in was on the front line—MACV two blocks to the east, USAID one-half block to the south, the ammunition dump 100 yards to the north and the VC everywhere to the west. We three camped under the bed in the east section of the house. The first series of blasts lasted for three-quarters of an hour. The initial blast largely coming from the VC and the latter from the inside going out. Around 2:00 a.m. the firing broke off to sporadic out-bursts except for a few intensive bombardments. At 4:30 three of the USAID fellows came over to the house to check on us and requested us to come to the USAID compound.

The USAID and MACV compounds, the provincial headquarters and some ARVN camps were the targets of the VC attacks. At least one ARVN soldier and a civilian man were killed. Longacre suggested that Anne and June leave immediately for the VNCS conference in Da Lat, and wait a few weeks before returning. The "few weeks" would stretch on and on; Anne and June never returned to Tam Ky.

This attack was the largest VC attack on the town in many years. Since there were warnings of a possible attack the USAID compound had installed a new machine gun on their roof and placed more concertina wire around their walled compound. By contrast, Doug and Bill had no wall and no guard. Doug wrote home: "We believe that if we claim to love both sides, no protection may be our best witness and perhaps our best protection."

"I, like most Vietnamese people, have learned to live in the 'eternal now,'" Doug wrote, "I sop the present of all the joys and sorrows that it has to offer but I neither look back on the past nor am anxious for the future. Matthew 6:25-34 has really come to life and makes some sense" ("Do not be anxious about your life. . . . Do not be anxious about tomorrow. . . . Let the day's own troubles be sufficient for the day.")

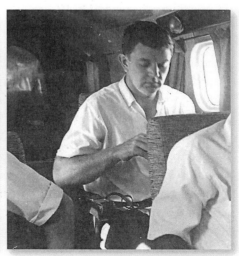

Doug Hostetter with Buu of the literacy program.   *Dave Neufeld in the air.*

Doug and Bill were receiving concrete evidence that the community was accepting them. A stolen bicycle was returned and young thieves were now even picking up clothing that blew from their clothesline and returning the items. The men did not want a car in the unit, deciding that a three-wheeled Lambretta motorcycle with cargo box would be sufficient to haul items around town.

An observation of Doug was a portent of things to come: "Relationships with USAID seemed to be a bit strained after the VC attacked the town. I am not sure if it was just jealousy that we were living unguarded and unharmed or if the reasons were deeper. They indicated that they thought our pacifism was offensive to them and said that if they found that we were trying to influence the Vietnamese people along those lines 'we would not be around long.'"

Following the attack, Doug said he and Bill were a "redemptive presence," assisting two families whose homes were destroyed and helping rebuild the Ky Phu Tin Lanh church.

When I visited Quang Ngai in mid-April, Dave Neufeld and I flew to Tam Ky one day. At the Tin Lanh church I met the pastor I had met at a conference. Doug was away vacationing for a few days and Bill came to meet us. He said security seemed better than a few weeks earlier, but wryly commented that he likes to "keep his prayer life up-to-date." While we were there the 155 mm artillery pounded suspected VC positions in the countryside.

Bill was enthusiastic about his work, teaching and upgrading English educational courses. He spoke about conflict between them and the strong-willed Tam Ky pastor who was requesting more assistance for Tin Lanh refugees and wanted to accompany Doug to the refugee camps to preach and distribute religious literature! VNCS could not, of course, accede to the pastor's wishes.

In late April, through early June, the U.S. First Marine Division initiated Operation Union and Union II against units of the Peoples' Army of Vietnam operating in the Que Son Valley. In his May report, Doug noted "the continuing poor security" in Tam Ky. He and Bill were both staying in single rooms at the Duc Tri High School. They had given emergency aid to families who suffered from American military action and to other victims of VC military activity. They placed two sewing machines in the Ly Tra refugee camp after the government refugee office donated 1,000 meters of cloth to the families. Doug arranged for his high school English students to teach a children's summer literacy course in the camp. In May, Doug accompanied a priest and forty students and five teachers for three days to a small island off the coast. And the last weekend in May he accompanied Tin Lanh friends to the Tin Lanh youth convention in Da Nang that was held as part of the larger Evangelical Church conference. There he met missionary James Stauffer—both were from Harrisonburg, Virginia.

A storm was brewing between Doug and the USAID personnel now working under CORDS. Doug's visits to nearby villages in areas deemed insecure by the official Americans would eventually raise other issues. In an April letter home, he told how he had traveled into VC territory and accidentally discovered some camouflaged fox holes and a mortar pit that were recently dug—directly across from the ammunition dump and less than 300 yards away from where he and Bill lived. "Aside from the fact that a woman saw me there and likely told the VC I was spying, I was faced with an impossible moral question: report it and get the VC killed, or don't report it and let the city and ammunition dump suffer," Doug wrote. "I didn't report it, feeling it would violate my neutrality."

For Colonel Bryerton, who headed the USAID/CORDS unit in Tam Ky, that was the problem. How could an American in Tam Ky claim neutrality? In a letter home early July, Doug wrote:

Things with USAID have gotten worse. Colonel Bryerton, USAID province representative, now feels that I'm likely a VC spy. After all, I don't support the US position on the war. (Some people can see only black and white). He is trying to get me kicked out of the country. He has no authority over me, but being a colonel, he may have pull in many places. Pray that God will take control of the situation. I would really hate to leave the country now but would rather do that than support the US war here. Don't worry. I'm sure things are in God's hands.

Leatherman wrote a "highly confidential" letter on August 2, 1967 to Paul Longacre—now in the Akron office serving as Director of Overseas Services—regarding Doug's situation at Tam Ky. Leatherman was tipped off by Doug's sister Pat a few days earlier that Doug might be facing difficulties in Tam Ky because of his expressed views that VNCS should be working in both "secure and insecure areas." Lance Woodruff, the VNCS media person, was going to Tam Ky to do a story so Leatherman asked Lance to observe what was going on. Lance returned August 1 and reported that the AIDS-CORDS representative indeed was not getting along well with Doug. Col. Bryerton was convinced that Doug was not helping the needy people but was spending much time and energy involved in political discussions with the area Vietnamese! Lance reported that Col. Bryerton had already initiated action to have U.S. Deputy Ambassador, Henry Koren, expel him from I Corps, the tactical zone comprised of five provinces below the Demilitarized Zone.

That evening, August 1, Woodruff and Aaker met with Leatherman to discuss this situation and Ninh also dropped by. Leatherman was advised to ask Doug to come to Saigon before authorities took this drastic action. Leatherman wrote: "I did not concur with this suggested procedure as I feel this action is too hasty. I have not received any official word in this office about this problem from any government agency." Since Aaker was planning to go to Quang Ngai and possibly Tam Ky on August 2, Paul asked him to contact Doug "and suggest that he come to Saigon for consultation."

Leatherman continued:

If Doug is speaking with various youth groups and taking a strong anti-US war policy with these groups, this I feel, would definitely be involved in political discussions and he could be subject to censure. If, on the other hand, Doug is speaking with his Vietnamese friends on the level of Christ's teaching regarding man's relationship with his fellow human beings and how a Christian should act when men come into conflict, then I would feel this would not necessarily be in the realm of political discussion and activity. It may be that Doug has not been discreet in voicing his convictions. We will need to try to establish the facts of what has transpired.

I recognize the seriousness and implications to the VNCS program and work in Vietnam . . . if it should become necessary for Ambassador Koren to ask Doug to leave. I also recognize the tremendous implications to our own Mennonite stand if I would find it necessary to ask Doug to leave Tam Ky because he is no longer remaining neutral in the conflict, but might actually be lending active support to the enemies of the present government in power.

Leatherman asked Longacre for his immediate reactions.

Gerald Aaker did meet with Doug and Bill in Tam Ky. He also met with Col. Bryerton. In Jerry's words,

Col. Bryerton stated to me that it was nothing personal, but that Doug's influence in this small community is very great and is working at odds with the purpose of the CORDS program. They do not want any kind of confrontation, and certainly little publicity if possible. "Can't you just transfer him; he can't be that important to your program?" I question if the actual incidents can be stacked up as significant in and of themselves, though if it came to a confrontation, enough could be found against VNCS as far as the US structure is concerned. I think it can be summed up as the fact that "We just don't trust him!" That is, Doug goes about the community avoiding the Americans and becoming dissociated with them whenever possible, and at the same time making significant contact with Vietnamese people. When put together with his adamantly professed anti-war stand, there is bound to be a clash.

In his report, Aaker continued:

I think Bill Herod's feelings in this matter should be firmly considered (keeping in mind the fact that Bill is also a very strong pacifist). Bill says CORDS is not trying to control or strong-arm VNCS, that Bryerton is possible to work with, that they will allow us to run our program as long as we don't interfere with their program, and this is in fact what we are asking of them. Bill has more contact with USAID people, but is also thoroughly exposed to the Vietnamese people, and I am very pleased with his method of approach and results. I am not under-rating what Doug is doing, and I am not critical of him on those grounds. But, if in fact Doug is working as more of a political activist than as a community development worker where he should be concentrating on "projects," perhaps VNCS would have a difference with him, and his activities would be detrimental to [VNCS] purpose and goals. . . .

As for the program and involvement with the Vietnamese, I feel the two fellows there are making a valid contribution, and if we push this matter and make an issue out of it unduly, there would be a strong possibility we could not work there later.

Aaker apparently had discussed with Bill the possibility of Doug leaving, for Aaker writes that Bill indicated that he could carry on in Tam Ky alone if Doug left.

In a letter home August 5, Doug tells his folks that Aaker was there "to investigate the rumor that USAID was trying to get me kicked out. So I had to go through the whole business of trying to justify myself." He continued:

I really appreciated Jerry's attitude. He is not a pacifist or a Mennonite so I'm sure that he would have good reason to condemn me. He did bring home one rather startling fact. My views on a peace witness and an impartial Christian witness to all parties involved in this conflict are now a minority in VNCS. Could it be that a Mennonite who really believes in a peace witness will have to join the Quakers to do so? The Quakers have taken a strong stand on peace in Vietnam while the Mennonites are drifting into a nice comfortable USAID-type of witness. And now they want to make sure that we come into no conflict with USAID. It looks like VNCS can go through the red tape of getting me kicked out--which means I likely have less than two months in Tam Ky. This may be best, but where does a Christian organization draw the line on allowing others to dictate what kind of 'good news' they can bring? At some point I am afraid that we just become an instrument of the state.

Leatherman asked Doug to come to Saigon to fully clarify and discuss the issues—with the possibility of being assigned back to Tam Ky. Doug interpreted this as VNCS's reluctance to stand up to U.S. officials only interested in pursuing the war. Leatherman maintained that he fully supported Doug but that it was essential that Doug come to Saigon so the issues could be clarified.

After some time in Saigon, on September 4, Doug was told to return to Tam Ky for one week, then come to Saigon for further conversations—most likely to be given a new assignment. Leatherman asked Doug not to travel into NLF areas, concerned that this presented risks for VNCS as an organization; Leatherman wanted to have a policy decision from the supporting agencies before authorizing this.

Back in Saigon, Doug was in limbo. This changed when Doug's colleague in Tam Ky, Bill Herod, became very sick with hepatitis and was medically evacuated to Nha Trang. The Saigon VNCS office then asked Doug to return to Tam Ky. Telling his parents that he was planning to return on September 27, he wrote: "I will need your continual prayer support as I go back and try to pick up our projects."

Heavy rains flooded the Tam Ky area, requiring massive cleanup work. But in a letter home October 10, Doug wrote: "Tonight Tam Ky is beautiful and peaceful. It is really kind of great to go out at night because at night I own the whole town. The GIs and CIA may use it during the day, but at night, it is their enemy. But for me it is my friend both day and night."

In his October report, Doug commented on the conflict with the official Americans in Tam Ky:

> Relationships with USAID have been very good this month. However, Col. Bryerton has been on home leave the entire month, so we have not met since I have returned. I have heard that the CIA were unhappy when they heard that I was back, but I have had no direct contact with them either. I do not expect any more problems in this respect, but the political tensions are crackling and anything could happen. I have been very "hard put" to know how to answer honest questions by sincere students concerning the rising anti-war sentiment in the US as well as VN. Living in a Catholic HS with kids who are struggling with the religious, moral and national problems of war presents opportunity, a challenge, and danger. Pray with me that I will be able to speak not only truthfully, but wisely as well, and still not betray my responsibility.

Paul Longacre in the Akron office responded to Doug's report: "Be assured of our prayers for you and the other VNCSers, particularly those in difficult places such as Tam Ky. We pray for your well-being but, more important, for your continued faithfulness.

"Obviously, we all are glad the past several difficult months are past. Your attitude and perspective in threading your way through this with us was deeply appreciated. It was, and is, genuine; God bless you."

Over a period of several weeks there were several meetings between voluntary agency officials and Ambassador Ellsworth Bunker in Saigon, as well as conversations between top agency officials in the United States and State Department officials in Washington. By mid-November, a memorandum from the Military Assistance Command CORDS headquarters made clear that CORDS did not have the authority to restrict voluntary agency personnel.

Huế: World Relief Commission established the Vocational Training School and demonstration farm five kilometers from Hue city with classes in agriculture, carpentry, blacksmithing, sewing, hat making, basket weaving and nutrition. VNCS personnel—Chris Kimmel, Paul Kennel, Kenneth Keefer, Harley Kooker and Jerry Sandoz—were the core of the WRC team.

Chris Kimmel at Hue agricultural training school.

VNCSers Richard and Juliet Milk spent several months in Hue. An experienced agriculturalist, Dick gave good leadership at the farm. In an April 1967 report, Juliet indicated that things were tense in Hue. Dick was then teaching an agricultural course at the training school and demonstration farm to several dozen students. VC guerrillas were visiting the area each night; one night the previous week a force of 300 VC came to the training school and the neighboring village making speeches. They examined the equipment and supplies at the center, but did no damage. On April 24, just ten minutes after the Milks returned to Hue from the farm, three Vietnamese officials were ambushed and killed by VC dressed in ARVN uniforms; Paul Kennel happened on the scene a few minutes after the ambush. One of the men killed was the assistant chief of Nam Hoa district and another was the local head of Chieu Hoi, the Open Arms Program that encouraged VC defections. Juliet wrote: "For some reason this seems to have all Hue 'jittery. . . .' We have not felt unduly alarmed, nor felt we should leave yet—but I wanted to 'clue' you in. Last week leaflets were scattered about Hue saying they would take Hue and there was fighting near Seven-tier [Thien Mu] Pagoda. Fifty-one VC were killed in one assault. In spite of this, last week was a 'relaxing' week."

Juliet wrote that Doug Hostetter had spent a week's vacation in Hue; Gary DeWarle, working with material aid in Saigon, had also spent a vacation helping the staff at Hue. As the ancient imperial city, Hue had much to offer vacationers.

Early in the year, Jerry Sandoz reported that Kimmel, Kooker and he were enjoying singing in the choir of the MACV chapel. With limited Vietnamese language skills, VNCS personnel in some locations regularly attended chapel services with U.S. military personnel.

Mark and Sue Weidner reported from Hue in late April that they were "finally settled" in their house. Mark was involved teaching grades eight to ten in Hue's public vocational school.

VNCS director of personnel Sam Hope, a Presbyterian Minister, visited Hue mid-May. The evening before he arrived the VC had fired thirty mortar rounds onto the MACV compound, around five hundred meters from the VNCS house where the men lived, and a Vietnamese Catholic priest known to team members was assassinated.

Following the vocational school closing ceremonies for its second term in mid-June, Sandoz spent some time in Da Nang, 110 kilometers south, expediting shipping supplies for the Hue programs. The VNCSers often stayed with Alliance missionaries Leroy and Nancy Josephson when they were in Da Nang. While Sandoz was gone the VC tried to burn several villages near the school, telling the people they would be safe if they went to the school which they considered Tin Lanh property. Reporting this Sandoz wrote: "This shows that the VC feel that we are not their enemies—at least for the present."

After leaving Tam Ky in February and spending a brief time in Di Linh and Saigon, June Sauder was assigned to Hue. Flying from Saigon to Hue, June met three new agriculturalists, among them USAID Tom Ragsdale who would become a close friend. As the only trained home economist in what was called I Corps, June worked with a Ms. Tuyen of the government agricultural services and the USAID staff. June enjoyed her work at the WRC vocational school relating to the teachers and was excited about teaching English two nights weekly at a youth center in Hue.

But the ever-present war was disquieting. June wrote in July: "The war situation does get to be rather discouraging at times. As I say this, I am thinking of what both the VC and Americans are doing to these people." A few days before preparing her report, sixteen men, women and children were killed in a village only two kilometers from the training school. And one of their teachers came from a village that was bombed by American planes; he feared most of his family had been killed. "Hearing all this makes me wonder if we are really meeting the needs of these people in the midst of such confusion," June wrote.

In August, June reported a program to evaluate the nutritional value of CSM, the corn-soya-milk combination that USAID was now providing for their refugee feeding program. When Pauline and Harlan Hochstetler arrived in October, Pauline worked with June on some projects.

Kimmel was appalled at all the food, clothing, soap and other commodities flooding the country and corrupting the society. In some ways, he said, this is "doing more to destroy this country than the VC." To him it appeared that these goods distributed by the U.S. government, the Protestants, and the Catholics were received "as a bribe to support the Government of Vietnam and the United States policy in Vietnam."

In late August, Keefer, Kennel, Weidner and Sandoz spent several days helping missionary linguists John and Carolyn Miller in Khe Sanh, 130 kilometers northwest of Hue.

Gayle Preheim with K'Roh.

Đông Hà – Quảng Trị: Quang Tri was the northernmost province of South Vietnam, just below the seventeenth parallel and the Demilitarized Zone (DMZ). By 1967, large numbers of soldiers from North Vietnam crossed the DMZ, and the towns of Dong Ha and Quang Tri, seventy kilometers north of Hue, were frequently attacked. Here Gayle Preheim and Robert L. Miller (later in Quang Ngai) distributed food, blankets and other relief supplies to refugees, many of them ethnic minorities who fled from the mountains.

Here refugees displaced by American military action were generally receiving good care. American military forces assigned engineers to civic action teams to construct the camp facilities and medics who visited the camps regularly. With USAID warehouses filled with cement and metal roofing, the leader of a relocated village told Preheim and Miller that he could get as many supplies as he wanted! While there was generally plenty of food, it was not the most nutritious. Using the corn-soya-milk (CSM) food combination donated by USAID, VNCS set up fourteen mixing and feeding centers in six villages serving more than thirty hamlets—feeding more than three thousand children. The health benefit of CSM feeding was quite evident; after only two months, the incidence of skin diseases had decreased and the children had clear white eyes.

Personnel from the Vietnamese government, USAID, U.S. forces and voluntary agencies coordinated programs. VNCS furnished classrooms to a new school in a refugee camp and donated school kits to several hundred children. WRC also organized a village vocational training program.

By April 1967, the security in the area deteriorated. Miller and Preheim sandbagged the floor of their Land Rover vehicle for protection against possible road mines and installed a bunker in their back yard. Friends of theirs died in land mine explosions. When personnel director Sam Hope visited them in mid-May he found them relaxed with a "mature and realistic attitude toward their circumstances." After visiting Dong Ha, Jonathan Newkirk praised them: "These fellows up here are the unsung heroes of VNCS to me. Nowhere else in VNCS are there conditions like these. I see a job well done in the worst of conditions." When near year's end Hope again traveled to Dong Ha, the plane was hit by ground fire as it neared the runway; a passenger across the aisle took a bullet in his foot.

William Snyder, MCC's Executive Secretary, and William Keeney—from the MCC Peace Section—spent two weeks in early May 1967 in Vietnam. They met with all the VNCS personnel except with Dr. Stoffel. They met Evangelical Church pastors and C&MA missionaries. They met U.S. and Vietnamese officials and persons serving with other voluntary agencies. They met several times with the Mennonite missionaries.

Asked about giving a witness for peace, Keeney noted that Doan Van Mieng, the President of the Evangelical Church, "cautioned against advocating a polity which may be construed as involving the local Christians in disloyalty to the government." The Evangelical Church sought to uphold an apolitical stance, Mieng said, although most of the leaders would prefer not to live under the Viet Cong. Because VNCS uses the "Tin Lanh" name, Mieng expressed concern that some people might view VNCS work as that of the Evangelical Church. Thus, while MCC relationships with the church were cordial, Keeney noted that an aggressive politically-oriented peace witness might lead to alienation from the Evangelical Church. Keeney also observed that Alliance missionaries tended to support the military policies of the U.S. administration, seeing America as "raising a shield against godless Communism" and anticipated that the Vietnam conflict would eventually be resolved in a way that "would allow the Christian church to flower" among the Vietnamese—similar to the standoffs between the two ideologies in Korea and China/Taiwan. Keeney said C&MA missionaries seemed to fear "the Mennonite peace position" even more than a wariness regarding the close working relationship MCC had with less theologically conservative Lutheran and Church World Service personnel in VNCS.

The Saigon director of the Office of Civil Operations told Keeney and Snyder that he "is aware of [the Mennonite] stance on war, is unhappy with it, but feels we are doing a service the government cannot do and so tolerates the dissent." Keeney said that two of the MCC personnel in VNCS "were told rather bluntly by OCO representatives that if they speak too actively against American policy, they would be unable to remain and continue the work." Keeney observed that "with the present dependence on American government support for transport and permission to operate, too direct an attack of American policy would jeopardize the [VNCS] program of service."

The OCO was put under military direction in CORDS at the time of Keeney's and Snyder's visit. Wade Lathrum, the OCO Director, tried to assure them that the new structure would not affect voluntary agencies. If the change would force voluntary agencies to become "only a part of the military effort," Keeney said, MCC "would need to refuse and would be forced out." Acknowledging that some people have suggested that MCC should withdraw from Vietnam as a protest against the US military policies, Keeney said such action "would probably be worthwhile" if it could bring an end to the war. But such action would have little impact, he said, and "would only leave us with no testimony in Vietnam."

Keeney's report highlighted both the strengths and weaknesses of the Vietnam Christian Service structure. "Not all the VNCS partners share the Mennonite position," he wrote. Some persons were pleased to have the US government active in Vietnam, though they recognized that the massive political and military intervention created huge problems. "If the MCC is to cooperate with other Christians in a service program," Keeney wrote, "their convictions must be respected even though we need to retain the freedom to discuss our differences. To force them to identify completely with our nonresistance convictions would jeopardize the whole effort of cooperation."

Keeney called for a clearer articulation of the theological basis for the Mennonite opposition to the war so it would be clearly distinguished from the radical pacifistic anti-war protestors. With the Mennonite missionaries' understanding of the war's violent disruption of Vietnamese society, Keeney said we need to express our concerns to decision-makers in Washington and inform our church constituencies and other Christians "to counteract the influences of an idolatrous nationalism" and express the Christian perspective of compassion and love.

He recommended the formation of a small local advisory committee for peace concerns made up of Mennonite missionaries, MCC-VNCS persons, Quakers, and Mennonites in IVS to identify needs, assess local resources, plan program strategy and maintain contact with the MCC Peace Section. Missionary personnel would carry primary responsibility for engaging other missionaries and the Tin Lanh church leaders in a biblical understanding of peace. Keeney anticipated that the Peace Section would also recruit a person who would be able to visit Vietnam quarterly to give support to this committee and prepare interpretive materials for use in the United States and Canada.

Keeney sensed that some VNCS personnel did not view the Peace Section as an integral part of MCC and saw his visit as MCC's "CIA to check on their righteousness!" Thus he emphasized the importance of integrating peace concerns into the orientation of all MCC personnel and providing resources to enable them to carry out a relevant peace witness.

Keeney said that "the situation in revolutionary societies may require some new approaches which might deviate from present MCC policy." Noting that "revolutionary societies do not afford a great degree of security or easy communication," he wondered whether this called for some type of person-to-person international multi-racial "peace commando teams" to work in these areas, offering technical skills and developing community programs.

Keeney's "peace commando teams" would take shape two decades later with the formation of Christian Peacemaker Teams in 1986, following Ron Sider's call at the 1984 Mennonite World Conference for the church to develop a "nonviolent peacekeeping force."

Snyder and Keeney, along with Paul Leatherman and James Stauffer, met with T. Grady Mangham, the chairman of the Alliance Mission, concerned that MCC maintained good relations with the Tin Lanh Church and with C&MA now that MCC was leading a broad Christian coalition in Vietnam Christian Service. Mangham invited Leatherman to attend the annual June conference of their missionaries in Da Lat.

Paul Leatherman attended a session of this conference. Mangham introduced Leatherman to the missionaries giving a full background of MCC's earlier work, and Paul sketched the details of the VNCS program, emphasizing that VNCS was keenly interested in the well-being and spiritual maturity of the Tin Lanh Church. Many of the missionaries expressed appreciation for his presentation. Snyder sent Leatherman's report of this meeting to the MCC Executive Committee. Noting the good relationship MCC has with C&MA, Snyder wrote: "We sometimes feel that the Christian and Missionary Alliance approach causes trouble for us, but I think we should see that we cause them about as much anxiety."

There is an amusing footnote to Leatherman's report. He returned to Saigon from Da Lat on a USAID C-46 plane that had just delivered a load of Kellogg Pop-Tarts that World Vision sent to a missionary for distribution. They would be eaten without first being toasted!

Several days after returning from Da Lat, Leatherman attended a special International Aid Day celebration in Saigon where he—as VNCS representative—was presented the Order of Merit of the Republic of Vietnam in recognition of his "good will and efforts in contributing to the achievement of various social welfare services." The award was presented by Deputy Prime Minister, Nguyen Luu Vien. Awards were given to representatives of other foreign voluntary agencies and military units.

We missionaries supported working with the MCC Peace Section in articulating a strong theological base for a peace witness. We anticipated opportunities to share our understanding of the gospel of peace with the larger Christian community—among other missionaries and within the Tin Lanh Church. We also hoped to prepare and publish appropriate peace literature for distribution.

Although Snyder and Keeney supported the continued development of Vietnam Christian Service, events over the next few months would threaten a pattern of cooperation the Mennonite Central Committee had with official United States government structures.

The initial MCC assistance to Russian Mennonites in 1922 was aided by the American Relief Administration which handled MCC's food remittances without charge. U.S. government support to American private voluntary agencies was formalized in 1946 with the creation of the Council of Relief Agencies Licensed for Operation in Germany (CRALOG), formed by the joint efforts of Washington officials and the relief agencies.

This decades-long relationship between voluntary agencies and the U.S. government was perceived to be beneficial to the agencies and contributed to a positive image for the U.S. government in recipient countries. This pattern continued into the era of the Vietnam conflict. The March 1967 report on "Assistance Programs of U.S. Non-Profit Organizations" in South Vietnam of the American Council of Voluntary Agencies for Foreign Service (ACVAFS) makes this statement: "Agencies registered with the Advisory Committee are eligible for certain benefits, including government grants of agricultural commodities under PL 480 legislation; reimbursement by the Government for the overseas shipment of these foods and their own donated supplies."

As a member of this Council, MCC in 1954 registered its Vietnam programs. In the early years when MCC personnel on field complained about too close a relationship with American governmental organizations, Akron administrators would remind them that this is an occasional complaint in many countries where MCC worked, nevertheless a problem one had to accept when working in an area of acute needs when normal administration infrastructures were nonexistent or had broken down.

But these arguments were no longer adequate in 1967 for many MCC Vietnam personnel, and increasingly so for agency administrative personnel in Akron as well. MCC-VNCS persons serving in Quang Ngai, Tam Ky and elsewhere were raising many questions. It was no longer just a rejection of the American political and military policies vis-à-vis Vietnam. It now involved a fundamentally different process in which the United States carried out those policies.

In mid-1966, the MCC Executive Committee had authorized VNCS to consider a contractual arrangement with USAID for a large-scale refugee child feeding program in multiple locations, though they voiced concern that it might involve an unacceptable connection to the US government. Again in December, the MCC Executive Committee authorized the VNCS Director to negotiate a contract with USAID and the Vietnamese Commission for Refugees office. However, several weeks before the projected signing of a contract the executive committee scuttled these plans when on May 27, 1967, the Saigon VNCS Director was told to hold off in order to "maintain a VNCS identity and integrity to the greatest degree possible in the face of stronger military control of South Vietnam by the United States forces." This action came right after William Snyder's visit to Vietnam and the executive order by President Johnson creating the Civil Operations and Revolutionary Development Support (CORDS), placing all U.S. operations in Vietnam under military management.

Even though VNCS had not contracted with USAID to carry out any projects, VNCS received material aid supplies from USAID and relied on Air America logistical support. And the CORDS man in Quang Ngai told Earl Martin that he was part of their "pacification" team!

In late August, Sam Hope, VNCS's personnel director, wrote to Paul Longacre, now the Overseas Director at the MCC Akron office, on the subject of "The Role of Volunteer Agencies." Hope had earlier written a well-documented article entitled "Why We Cannot Win in Vietnam" which he had shown and discussed with the USAID liaison officer at the American Embassy,

Gardner W. Monro, who told Hope it was "dynamite" that could seriously jeopardize Vietnam Christian Service and other voluntary agencies in Vietnam.

Hope now informed Longacre that he, Paul Leatherman and Program Director, Jerry Aaker, had spent many hours in the previous weeks discussing the role of voluntary agencies in Vietnam. Hope said his article and the specific situation of Doug Hostetter in Tam Ky, where the U.S. Deputy Ambassador in Da Nang had declared Doug Hostetter *persona non grata*, served to illustrate the urgency for voluntary agencies to clarify their status.

Hope continued: "Due to recent MAC/CORDS military authority over USAID and pacification programs, there is increasing pressure to 'get on the US team' and be more whole-hearted in our support of US activities. They want a unified esprit de corps, and when VNCS personnel seek to maintain a separate and independent identity, the 'military mind' becomes both disgusted and suspicious."

Among VNCS personnel there were two schools of thought, both legitimate and Christian, Hope said, and "we are not in a position to make a strong recommendation one way or the other," and thus need the guidance and counsel of the VNCS Consultative Committee. Many VNCSers, Hope wrote, hold the following position: "I believe that war and/or the U.S. presence in Vietnam are wrong and immoral. I came to Vietnam under the impression, as stated in VNCS Objectives, that the independent, distinctive, Christian, church-related sponsorship of our agency would be emphasized. I refuse to be 'on the U.S. team.' And do not want my services to be interpreted by the Vietnamese people as being part of the U.S. efforts. I cannot remain silent and it is my Christian duty to express the difference in my motivations to serve in Vietnam."

"Others feel just as strongly," Hope wrote, "'I am here to serve the Vietnamese people any way I can, regardless of the limitations. I want to serve the suffering and needy, and do not want VNCS personnel engaging in secondary activities that would jeopardize the working relationship of VNCS in this land. I do not care who gets the credit for my help, including the American government.'"

The Saigon VNCS administrators, Hope wrote, came to the following "tentative conclusions":

> "We should not seek to influence Vietnamese against their government. . . . We have no right to engage in Vietnamese politics in any way. . . . We have no right to actively oppose or obstruct US personnel in Vietnam [and] military policies made in Washington. We do have the right to oppose US policies in Vietnam by writing and/or talking with US citizens who make or influence policy, including US reporters. . . . We have the right to refuse to cooperate with US intelligence efforts among Vietnamese with whom we work."

Hope then asked these questions:

> Is it not true that VNCS is to be distinctly Christian and church related, as contrasted with humanitarianism and secular relief agencies? If true, then does it not make a difference "who gets the credit" for our work? Is not our image and identity important? If our work does not witness to Christ, then why should the church sponsor it? If I merely want to help suffering people in need, then why not do the same work with CARE, IVS, or USAID? . . . Was not the US involvement in Vietnam a part of the basic motivation to create VNCS in the first place? Was it not thought of

by some of our personnel and/or sponsoring agencies as an "atonement" on the part of American Christians for the suffering our nation was here to inflict on the Vietnamese people? Did we not come to witness to a better and more effective way of helping the Vietnamese people? In the long run, would VNCS not contribute to the alleviation of suffering in Vietnam if it could influence the US policy-makers to de-escalate or withdraw from the country?

James MacCracken, the head of Church World Service, responded to Hope's letter. He saw no problem with Hope's arguments except for the last question: "Would VNCS not contribute to the alleviation of suffering in Vietnam if it could influence the U.S. policy-makers to de-escalate or withdraw from the country?"

MacCracken disagreed with Hope's implied answer to this question. While both the National Council of Churches and the World Council of Churches had gone on record condemning the American military intervention in Vietnam and the escalating warfare, MacCracken said it was not appropriate for Church World Service to become political or associate with either a hawk or dove stance. CWS was endeavoring to minister to acute human need without regard to "the accident of geography, race or religion," he wrote. At the time VNCS was forming in 1965, it was recognized that VNCS would have to rely heavily on the American government for logistical support.

Ellsworth Bunker had replaced Lodge as U.S. Ambassador in March and Leatherman made plans to meet with Ambassador Bunker to discuss a whole range of issues. One recent order from the Embassy downgraded access to Air America flights on which voluntary agencies relied for logistical support. On September 14, Leatherman met Ambassador Bunker at the Embassy, together with Elizabeth Brown, Foster Parents Plan; Peter Ewald, representative of American Friends Service Committee; and Don Luce, International Voluntary Service Chief of Party and current chair of the Council of Foreign Voluntary Agencies in Vietnam. These representatives protested to the Ambassador the pressures they felt to become part of the "American team" and insisted they needed freedom to determine their own programs with Vietnamese authorities and to assign their personnel. The Ambassador told them that the refugee problem was a political matter, and said that voluntary agency representatives should not speak publically about political matters. He said they did not have the right to oppose U.S. or Vietnamese government policies and that no aid could be given to the Viet Cong.

In Leatherman's memoirs written thirty years later he recalls the meeting with the Ambassador:

We presented to him a very strong case indicating that there would be an extremely strong backlash in the US if it were learned that this change of priority status effectively shut down the work of the voluntary agencies. In the midst of this discussion Ambassador Bunker said he was informed that VNCS operated several hospitals. "Is this true,'" he asked. I described our medical program. . . . Then he asked, "Are you treating any Viet Cong (VC) in your hospitals?" I replied that we did not ask patients for their ID cards. If they were sick and needed hospital care they were admitted. If a wounded person appeared at the hospital the doctors repaired their wounds. Next he asked about our feeding programs in refugee camps. I told him about our large feeding program for children in these camps. Again he asked, "Are you feeding children of the VC?" I answered again as I had previously that we do not check ID cards of the persons in our feeding program. If they are hungry and starving we feed them. Ambassador Bunker then standing almost nose-to-nose with me said, "You know the VC are the enemy. If you are feeding the VC and treating them in your hospitals, this is treason and you know the penalty for treason." The Spirit gave me words to speak, so without hesitation I said, "Mr. Ambassador, VNCS is here doing the work of the church. We follow a book that you may or may not be familiar with. It commands us to feed the hungry, to heal the sick, and to clothe the naked. I know what the penalty is if we do not do that."

Within a half-hour after the meeting, Leatherman received a call from the Ambassador's assistant telling him he should quickly return to straighten out his "problem" with the Ambassador. Leatherman said he had no problem with the Ambassador; if Bunker had a problem he should call him! Leatherman met the Ambassador on several later occasions but this encounter was never mentioned.

Don Luce and many other IVS staff also viewed the growing numbers of refugees as an ethical issue, not merely social or political. Following a large staff meeting the weekend of July 4, many concluded that they needed to speak out and drafted a letter addressed to President Johnson.

Calling the war "an overwhelming atrocity," they wrote: "We are finding it increasingly difficult to pursue quietly our main objective: helping the people in Vietnam. In assisting one family or individual to make a better living or get a better education, it has become evident that our small successes only blind us to how little or negative the effect is in the face of present realities in Vietnam. Thus to stay in Vietnam and remain silent is to fail to respond to the first need of the Vietnamese people—peace."

This letter was signed by forty-nine IVS volunteers, nearly one-third of their 170 personnel. This letter was presented to the U.S. Embassy September 19, 1967, then released later that evening to *New York Times*. Four IVS personnel resigned, including Luce and two Mennonite volunteers, Gene Stoltzfus and Willy Myers. The next day Ambassador Bunker agreed to meet with them, calling their handling of the resignations and the letter "unethical and discourteous" but showed scant interest in discussing the motivation for their actions.

In reporting these developments to William Snyder, Leatherman thought there might be more IVS resignations, adding: "This might also encourage some VNCSers to take the same action."

This dramatic action by IVS was both condemned and applauded. IVS had a contractual agreement with the U.S. government and was fully funded by USAID. George Goss, CORDS Chief of the Refugee Division, called a meeting on September 20 in Saigon which involved representatives of fifteen voluntary agencies. Goss said he called the meeting because a *New York Times* article described a "deteriorating relationship between CORDS and the voluntary agencies." Goss said he was not aware of a problem. He said it was contrary to U.S. government policy to control the programs or statements of voluntary agencies. If a problem existed, Mr. Goss said, he wanted to remedy the situation.

Don Luce said that IVS had two primary areas of concern: the general concern about the war and the question of whether their personnel could work within the present structure of CORDS. Luce then read from a resignation letter from Willy Myers, IVS Team Leader in the Mekong River delta area. Since the USAID Mission had placed all field operations under U.S. military command, Myers said this structure had made it more difficult to serve Vietnam's needs effectively. He gave two examples: IVS staff were often under pressure to assist in American-dominated priority programs and found it difficult to respond to needs expressed by Vietnamese people. Secondly, the negative attitude Vietnamese had toward the massive American military and civilian presence made it difficult to have a genuine relationship with the Vietnamese people. Myers now viewed IVS work as "part of a sugar coating on the undesirable aspects of the American Effort in Vietnam," and no longer wished to be part of that.

Luce then cited examples of CORDS interfering in IVS personnel placements, and CORDS reaction to staff members who criticized U.S. Vietnam policy. Goss admitted to being aware of the IVS problems but said he was not aware that other agencies had similar issues. Gardner Munroe, the USAID/CORDS liaison officer, expressed concern with Luce's descriptions and said that government officials have no right to tell voluntary agencies what to do. Munroe asked whether other agencies received similar pressures.

C&MA missionary, John Fitzstevens, serving as Vietnam director of Christian Children's Fund, said they had no trouble. Bob Pierce, the founder-director of World Vision, said they had the highest praise for the cooperation they received from the U.S. government and military.

Elizabeth Brown, Vietnam head of Foster Parents' Plan, said that constructive civilian programs cannot function adequately under military control since the function of any army at wartime involves killing, destroying and promotion of fear. Several persons strongly disagreed with her characterization of the military forces and expressed strong support for the American military engagement.

Paul Leatherman said VNCS had not experienced any opposition to any of their programs but said there was a "subtle determination" from the U.S. military to make things difficult for those who were not officially part of USAID/CORDS. He noted that when personnel from some agencies expressed opposition to the "extensive creation of refugees," they are told not to express their dissent.

VNCS administrators in the United States also pressed their insistence that voluntary agencies needed to have autonomy from the massive American military and political giant. USAID called a meeting October 5 in Washington with voluntary agency representatives. William Snyder presented a memorandum to James M. Grant, the Assistant Administrator of USAID for Southeast Asia, indicating how the transfer of the USAID program to CORDS put pressure on VNCS to relate its programs to "immediate military objectives."

"This takes the form of subtle and indirect pressure for voluntary agencies to gear their programs toward military goals," Snyder said. "Personnel in certain areas have been advised not to give supplies to certain villages because of their political sympathies. Our team in Quang Ngai was strongly urged to establish a feeding program for the refugees . . . being gathered after forcible removal from their villages as a military tactical program. Likewise, voluntary agency priorities on USAID aircraft have fallen since CORDS was formed."

Snyder said that VNCS staff must have full freedom to develop their own programs, with a clear understanding that personnel have no obligation to report information of a political or military nature to governmental authorities.

Ambassador Bunker had cabled the Department of State two days prior to this meeting, saying that USAID should reassure voluntary agencies that "their integrity and independence of operation in Vietnam have not been nor will be jeopardized in any way by the U.S. mission," and indicated that the Embassy would respect the independence of voluntary agencies to initiate and carry out their programs subject to the approval of the Vietnamese government.

This assurance came from the U.S. Embassy in a very explicit November 11, 1967 letter on the subject of "Voluntary Agency Support" from the Office of the Assistant Chief of Staff, CORDS, Headquarters of the United States Military Assistance Command Vietnam, to the CORDS deputies in the four military regions in South Vietnam. In this letter, L. Wade Lathram, the Deputy Director of the Saigon USAID office, noted that there were currently twenty-six U.S. international and third country voluntary agencies accredited to the Vietnamese government and the U.S. Mission carrying out programs in the fields of health, social welfare and refugee assistance. These programs, he said, represented a major contribution to the Vietnamese people and that it was U.S. policy "to encourage and assist the agencies to continue and expand their programs and to enlist the participation of additional agencies." Seven of these twenty-six agencies had contractual agreements with USAID. "The Mission has agreed to provide air transportation for agency staff, air transportation and warehousing for voluntary agency commodities, logistical support for field personnel for their welfare programs, as well as to keep the agencies informed of U.S. programs and operations relating to agency activities," he wrote.

"Please always bear in mind that it is mission policy to respect the sovereignty and independence of operation of all voluntary agencies consistent with GVN agreements and USAID obligations," Lathram wrote.

> It is particularly important that CORDS representatives not interfere with agency prerogatives to confer with GVN official at all levels of the Government.
>
> Although CORDS personnel are responsible for assisting the GVN to coordinate Volag contributions and participation in provincial refugee and welfare program in order to achieve maximum program coverage while avoiding duplication or overlapping effort, such *coordination should be carried out in such a way as to preclude charges of interference in and control of Volag activities*. Voluntary agency personnel . . . are subject to necessary security regulations and measures, but matters of agency internal administration and discipline are sovereign to the agencies concerned [Italics original].

USAID also raised the priority status on Air America aircraft to #2 priority for international staff of the voluntary agencies. Since Vietnamese staff persons only had #5 priority, meaning that they could get reservations only late afternoons before their desired flights, VNCS planned to arrange for them to fly on Air Vietnam when possible.

Lathram's memo was a clear message that the Johnson administration could not afford to alienate the Americans who provided support to the voluntary agencies—and on whom they counted for support of their policies. And for VNCS, it meant—among other things—that Doug Hostetter could continue his service in Tam Ky without harassment from the local USAID-CORDS office. In the Statement of Guidelines of June 1966, VNCS had written that it would "clearly and creatively interpret our goals . . . and our desire not to be used for political purposes by USAID, the U.S. military and other governmental agencies." The clear statement of VNCS clarifying its relationship to U.S. governmental agencies was confirmed.

This could not, however, resolve the different points of view among VNCS personnel. Jonathan Newkirk, a member of the Oregon Yearly Meeting of Friends and a graduate of George Fox

College, Newberg, Oregon, now involved in feeding refugees, sent a personal statement on September 8 to the MCC Peace Section. In it he wrote:

> I did not come to Vietnam to protest this war. I came as a positive expression of the love of Jesus Christ through social channels that were acceptable to my country as an alternative to military service. I base my convictions concerning 'Positive Pacifism' on the ministry and teachings of Christ. To me Christ's life is an example of a positive witness. Jesus did not campaign against the Roman Government or the political plans of the Jews. He repeatedly refused to become involved in the political aspects of the day. He taught that we were to go and preach the gospel and that the results of his gospel was that man loved one another and therefore took an active interest in the whole being of that man. There is no place that I can think of that Christ told us to be against something. He preached the merits of his way, not the shortcomings of the other way. . . .
>
> I understood . . . when I came to Vietnam that VNCS was a non-political organization, set up to meet through Christian love the needs of all people resulting from the war. To continue to meet these needs I feel that we must remain non-political, and by non-political I don't mean neutral. To me a neutral position is a political stand. I feel that VNCS can work in Vietnam and not enter into the political controversy of whether United States involvement is right or wrong. We are here to meet the needs of the people and not to criticize someone else. Through criticism we jeopardize our ability to remain in the country.

Newkirk expressed concern for VNCS's Vietnamese staff should the agency be forced to leave. He also said that—as guests of Vietnam—it was improper to criticize their government.

Ivan J. Kauffman, the Executive Secretary of the Peace Section, replied to Newkirk, thanking him for his "clear and thoughtful way" he had expressed his concerns. Kauffman agreed that VNCS was in Vietnam as "a positive expression of the love of Jesus Christ" and that Jesus "preached the merits of His way, not the shortcomings of the other way."

"However," Kauffman wrote, "I think that many of us would not be able to agree with you that protest is incompatible with a positive ministry in the spirit of Christ. We would in fact feel that at times protest is a necessary part of a positive witness. . . . Many of us would also have to disagree with you that it is possible to be uninvolved in the political aspects of life." While agreeing that the VNCS emphasis was on positive service rather than negative protest, "we see the situation as a matter of both-and rather than either-or." Kauffman specifically questioned whether VNCS could work in Vietnam and "not enter into the political controversy of whether United States involvement is right or wrong."

Kauffman included in his letter a statement the Peace Section was preparing: "We cannot serve the victims of the war in Vietnam without speaking against those activities of the United States which cause the suffering we seek to alleviate. Our consciences will not allow us to clothe and feed and heal refugees while remaining silent about a policy which needlessly generates new refugees each day."

Paul Longacre, acting Asia MCC Director in the Akron, Pennsylvania office, in an article published in a Mennonite Church paper acknowledged that VNCS personnel did "not have a consensus of opinion on how they see their role of meeting human needs in Vietnam." Some persons, like Linford Gehman at the Nha Trang clinic and hospital, were treating persons who would have been sick even if there had not been a war. Others who worked with refugees felt their services encouraged military commanders to create thousands more refugees. The burden of protest had to come from the American people.

"Christian responsibility demands that the church speak," Longacre said.

But from what stance can the church best speak? Can we speak from Vietnam, where a vocal protest easily becomes a widely political stance? MCC was invited by the church and by the Vietnamese government to serve in Vietnam in a relief role. . . . A publicized protest by relief workers may be a denial of this invitation and result in our inability to continue serving.

Thus, MCC workers in Vietnam are not really free to protest. Yet they cannot watch the disintegration of a people and a society without speaking out. The church and individuals here must give expression for them. If we fail to speak, we make it impossible for them to work in Vietnam. Our failure intensifies their dilemma.

Our cries to US policy makers concerning the war in Vietnam have more substance because, as a church, we are there. We must continue to serve the Vietnamese people in their time of greatest suffering by both relief efforts and vigorous pleas to our government to change its destructive course in Vietnam.

WORK AND WITNESS
WHILE THE WAR GRINDS ON

Chapter 27

Paul N. Kraybill, secretary of Eastern Mennonite Board of Missions, was visiting Vietnam as the calendar ushered in the New Year 1967. Accompanying him were two Lancaster Mennonite Conference bishops, David Thomas and Donald Lauver. Thomas was the Conference moderator; Lauver was a member of the Bishops' Mission Committee and the Conference representative to overseas churches established by Eastern Mennonite Board of Missions. In the early twentieth century bishops were the guardians of church order. Now newly developing churches in various countries were finding their own way in matters of faith and practice and we were confident that the bishops would see beyond specific cultural practices to celebrate the lives of those who had recently embraced faith in Jesus Christ and were active in the growing church. In a December 30 letter home, Mary wrote that we were looking forward to their visit.

In her next letter home, Mary wrote:

> Sometimes we think of bishops as men who wield a big stick. We certainly haven't found them to be that. They are encouraged by signs of new life in the church at home and are ready to accept and work with the church here even though it isn't built on the same pattern as what they expect at home. The foundation is the same—Christ, and by study of the Word and the leading of the Spirit, the church here must decide together what applications of these principles are meaningful. We cannot dictate to them what the pattern must be.

After the three arrived, the Mission Council briefed them on current developments and the entire missionary group joined in a fellowship meal on the rooftop patio of the Saigon student center. The next morning, Sunday, January 1, Lauver preached at the worship service at the Gia Dinh Community Center. A communion service and foot washing service followed; many of the twenty-one baptized members were there and participated. Kraybill spoke at the afternoon meeting with thirty-five persons attending. On Wednesday evening, Thomas preached an evangelistic sermon to an overflow crowd of one hundred persons. Thomas found the missionaries "dedicated to a Biblical witness;" Lauver observed that the missionaries were "happy and relaxed" with a clear "sense of direction."

With a congregation taking shape at the Gia Dinh Community Center, this was an important time for missionaries, local Christians, and mission and church leaders from the sponsoring church to together consider appropriate expressions of the Christian faith and life. We discussed the question: "How much should the Mennonite fellowship be separated from the practice and life of the Evangelical Church?" We missionaries maintained that asking women to wear a head covering as was done in the United States did not seem appropriate within Vietnamese culture. And the "holy kiss" encouraged in the Apostle Paul's epistles and practiced in the American church could be expressed by a Vietnamese "double handshake." A much more important issue was the question

Paul Kraybill (r) visiting Lam at Bible Institute with Donald Lauver and David Thomas.

of members entering military service. We missionaries reported that, in general, believers had no strong objection to military service, although there was a lessening of a pro-war attitude typical of some of Saigon's youth. Two church members were deferred from the draft for religious reasons and we were anxious to seek deferment for others working with the church. We were aware of the political implications of urging members to refuse military service. There was also the question about the appropriateness of dictating what church practice should be. Bishop Thomas asserted that the issue would not be solved by "pressing our point," and said we should look at questions such as these "by going to the Word and letting the Spirit show us the way."

In a letter home, I wrote: "Donald Lauver and David Thomas observed much and commented little. Just as on Bro. Lauver's last visit [February 1965], we sensed that they are aware that Vietnam is not Lancaster County. The church's expression of its obedience to Christ cannot possibly be the same here as at home. Our duty is to preach and teach the Word; the Holy Spirit can be trusted to do his work."

One day I flew with the three men to Nha Trang. Kraybill was eager to visit the Evangelical Hospital where Kraybill's cousin, Dr. Harold Kraybill, served as medical director. We also toured the Evangelical Church's Bible Institute where we met Nguyen Huu Lam in his second year of study.

Back in Saigon, the men met with T. Grady Mangham, the C&MA Mission chairman, and with the President of the Tin Lanh Church, Doan Van Mieng. Mangham reported that they were planning to enlarge the Alliance missionary team to a total of 150 versus the current ninety, with 120 missionaries serving at any given time, promoting and stimulating evangelism. Missionaries did not serve as pastors to congregations. Pastor Mieng spoke about the war which he viewed as a struggle against international communism. He reported that nine church buildings were destroyed by American bombing. He said the "church is suffering along with the people of Vietnam, but this is giving opportunity for witness and evangelism" in areas such as central Vietnam where the church was growing. The Mennonite Mission hosted a tea at the Saigon Youth Center for local Tin Lanh pastors one afternoon; these pastors expressed appreciation for the various Mennonite ministries.

Kraybill affirmed the continuation of the programs of the Saigon Student Center and the Gia Dinh Community Center and proposed renting another property in the Gia Dinh area with facilities for a student hostel and a worker training program. The couple residing there would focus on Bible instruction and lay worker training. The Mission would also open another center in Saigon, the city now approaching a population of four million. This would likely be in Phu

Tho on the growing northwestern edge of the city. The mission secretary also expressed continued support for the programs of MCC-VNCS.

The three men left January 6. In his diary that day, Kraybill quoted what for us missionaries had become common wisdom: "If you don't leave Vietnam more confused than you were when you arrived, you haven't stayed long enough!" He continued:

> It is striking to note how often one is confused by the contradictions and enigmas and imponderables of this perplexing situation. Yet in the midst of all this, our workers are increasingly finding a sense of direction and purpose in their witness and they do go about their work with a minimum of distraction and interference by the political situation. And so we leave Vietnam, troubled and perplexed by the political situation and the uncertain future of the country, yet confident and assured that our team there has a real mission and is reasonably relaxed and completely committed to the job that is waiting to be done.

A few days after the New Year's truce ended, U.S. military forces, on January 8, launched Operation Cedar Falls—the biggest operation of the war—in the "Iron Triangle" thirty to forty kilometers northwest of Saigon, an area B-52s had been bombing for a long time. This brought many casualties to the U.S. Army Third Field Hospital in Saigon. U.S. planes resumed air strikes in the Hanoi area January 15; U.S. intelligence confirmed that many civilian houses were destroyed.

Luke and Dorothy Beidler, who joined the missionary team only six months earlier, were now teaching English in the Saigon University in addition to helping at the Mennonite student center. In the February *News and Concerns*, they asked friends to pray for Don Sensenig who was leading a Sunday morning Bible class for ten students at the student center.

They wrote:

> Men may cry Peace, Peace, but there is no peace. Here in our living room a Vietnamese university student spoke for an hour last night about America's war to contain Communism. I think he symbolizes a new rise of sentiment against big America and our nagging involvement into all areas of Vietnam. He specially despises the fact that the US supports a corrupt government and is producing a new upper class of corrupt richness. As a student at the Saigon University of Medicine he had joined the other students in protesting against a group of deans who in his own words "are not good men, but because they are pro-American and have been educated in America, they get this place of honor and responsibility." But what can we do, he says? "If we demonstrate they will raid our houses at night and cart us off to the frontlines like they did some of my friends already. So we just will not go to classes."
>
> We missionaries are American, what should we say? While many of us do not choose to join 2-3,000 clergymen who march on Washington, let us in our own way shoulder our responsibility in prayer, in charity, and in creative witness to Jesus' own words.

The Beidlers were referring to a demonstration at the White House the day before, organized by Clergy and Laymen Concerned about Vietnam (CALC), calling for a halt in the bombing of North Vietnam. James Metzler, studying at Eastern Mennonite Seminary while on furlough, went to Washington early that morning for this gathering with a local pastor Eugene Souder, and with two professors, Samuel Horst and Jacob Jacobszoon. Metzler spoke with two Virginia congress-men and walked by the White House for an hour.

James's diary documents significant energy devoted to the Vietnam War issue over the next days and weeks. Harrisonburg, Virginia, area persons who attended the rally purchased a full page advertisement to publish the ten-page CALC statement in the Saturday, February 4, issue of *The Daily News Record*, signed by thirty-some Mennonite and Church of the Brethren persons. The next evening, James preached at the Pike Mennonite Church; afterward a group of church leaders surrounded him "and started firing away because of the ad in the paper—like Christ and the Pharisees!" A month later, James and others who signed the statement had a conversation about the Vietnam issues with Virginia Mennonite Conference leaders. Rachel, too, spoke to a Women's World Day of Prayer event and at other settings. James joined twenty others on Eastern Mennonite campus in a fast for peace in Vietnam.

The last week in February was Service Emphasis week on Eastern Mennonite campus. Among the speakers were William Snyder, Atlee Beechy and Everett Metzler—also on furlough. Gene Stoltzfus (IVS) and James were featured on a local television station on Vietnam. The last weekend in February James traveled to the Souderton, Pennsylvania area where he spoke on Vietnam at a Special Day of Prayer. This inspired a telegram by Bishop John E. Lapp to President Johnson.

In early March, he and Rachel were back in Pennsylvania where James spoke on Vietnam March 8 at the Mission Board annual meeting. His message was entitled, "The Nonresistant Christian in Vietnam." Paul Kraybill affirmed the message James gave.

One of the strengths of the Eastern Mennonite Board of Missions was the close relation-ship between the missionaries and the congregations of Lancaster Mennonite Conference that supported the Mission Board with prayers and gifts. Many of the missionaries came from these congregations. Since the missionaries were known personally, their message was more readily ac-cepted; their concerns could not be easily dismissed.

The lunar New Year came on Thursday, February 9. Saigon celebrated by exploding millions of firecrackers, more than we had ever heard before. Soldiers fired their weapons—one large cali-ber bullet crashed through the roof of the VNCS house where Ernie and Mabel Frey were staying. When the short Tet truce ended, the war resumed with great intensity.

Mary and I prepared the March *News and Concerns* telling about Bui Thi, the student who had lived with us for a year and was still waiting for his visa for the United States. During the lunar New Year holidays he visited his family in Quang Ngai. A year before the infamous My Lai massacre in Quang Ngai province, Thi was already describing soldiers' atrocities against civilians. We wrote:

> Refugees told Thi of the cruelty of the Korean soldiers' operations in that area. They engage in all evils so prevalent in wartime—extortion, murder, pillage, and rape. This contrasts sharply with American propaganda which pictures the Allied forces as well-disciplined who always treat the people with respect. Thi was told that the soldiers often kill everyone in a village—men, women and children—if anyone in the village shoots at them. American soldiers on operations may try to spare civilians, but they still call in air strikes which also indiscriminately kill civilians in a more impersonal way. Thi is anti-VC, but is becoming more aware that the medicine for the cure is perhaps more deadly than the disease.

Soon after Tet the VC lobbed several mortar shells toward the US military headquarters in Saigon from a house near the Beidler house. Don Sensenig and Luke Beidler were standing outside the student center when a loud boom startled them as a nearby house exploded, sending debris flying through the air.

Writing home in late February, James Stauffer described watching planes dive-bombing an area a short distance away. There was a growing anti-American sentiment, Stauffer observed: "some of the big construction companies are going to lay off thousands of workers. . . . So, we must work while it is day. More and more our group is convinced that we must be more diligent about our business and not get too worked up over the situation here."

Not get "too worked up" over the Vietnam situation? That was hard. The next day, February 25, Dr. Martin Luther King, Jr. delivered his "Casualties of the War in Vietnam" speech in Los Angeles. Referring to the tens of thousands of women and children killed in the war, King said that these casualties are enough to cause all people "to rise up with righteous indignation and oppose the very nature of this war. . . . By entering a war that is little more than a domestic civil war, America has ended up supporting a new form of colonialism covered up by certain niceties of complexity," he declared. "Our participation in the war in Vietnam is an ominous expression of our lack of sympathy for the oppressed, our paranoid anti-Communism, our failure to feel the ache and anguish of the Have Nots. It reveals our willingness to continue participating in neo-colonialist adventures. . . .

"It is time for all people of conscience to call upon America to return to her true home of brotherhood and peaceful pursuits," King thundered, "we cannot remain silent as our nation engages in one of history's most cruel and senseless wars."

King's call resonated with us missionaries. James Metzler would soon be returning to Saigon with renewed dedication to protest the evils of the American War and Mary and I were preparing to return to the States where we would find the Mennonite practice of a quiet disengaged non-resistance an inadequate response to the American war that was killing hundreds of thousands in Southeast Asia. James Stauffer preached a sermon at the Gia Dinh Tin Lanh Church early March, using the text, "Blessed are the peacemakers."

On March 25, Dr. King led 5,000 anti-war demonstrators in Chicago, declaring that the Vietnam War was "a blasphemy against all that America stands for." Three days later the Quaker-supported yacht *Phoenix*—in defiance of U.S. prohibition of trade with North Vietnam—arrived in the port of Hai Phong with medical supplies valued at $10,000.

In March, President Johnson appointed Ellsworth Bunker to replace Ambassador Henry Cabot Lodge. Bunker strongly supported the war policies of the U.S. and Saigon governments, and retained his post until 1973. The U.S. defense department announced an increased use of the toxic herbicides and defoliants known as Agent Orange—packaged in orange-colored drums.

On March 20, President Johnson, Secretary of State Dean Rusk, and Secretary of Defense Robert McNamara met with Chief of State Nguyen Van Thieu and Premier Nguyen Cao Ky in Guam to discuss political and military strategy. The next day, the North Vietnamese press agency reported a February exchange of correspondence between President Johnson and Ho Chi Minh on ending the war. President Ho Chi Minh rejected the offer, saying the U.S. had to cease all military action against North Vietnam before they would consider talks.

On Easter Sunday, March 26, around thirty-five persons gathered for an Easter Sunrise service in the front patio of the Community Center, then shared a breakfast in the back yard.

After being in Vietnam since September 1962, Mary and I were planning a year's furlough. Mary wrote to friends:

> We are at home here and enjoy living here. It's possible we won't even feel at home in the States! But we are certainly looking forward to our furlough, mostly because of a desire to see and fellowship with you and others dear to us. We pray for and anticipate many times of joyful fellowship together. We hope the doors of communication between us and many of our American friends will be open as we can mutually profit by this experience. We believe we need the help of American Christians in finding ways to be truly Christian in our situation. And maybe, with our now different perspectives, we can see more clearly how American Christians can be more Christian in their situation. But we're not coming with the answers.

We would be engaging our friends, especially within the churches we would be visiting, with our interpretation of what the American military involvement was doing to our adopted country and its people. There were some powerful voices calling for a radical new approach, among them Dr. King who delivered his "Beyond Vietnam" speech April 4 at the Riverside Church in New York City. King declared:

> "This is the first time in our nation's history that a significant number of its religious leaders have chosen to move beyond the prophesying of smooth patriotism to the high grounds of a firm dissent based upon the mandates of conscience and the reading of history. . . . No one who has any concern for the integrity and life of America today can ignore the present war."

To those who argued that the civil rights leader was getting off target in addressing the issues of the war, King asserted,

> I have to live with the meaning of my commitment to the ministry of Jesus Christ. To me, the relationship of this ministry to the making of peace is so obvious that I sometimes marvel at those who ask me why I am speaking against the war. Could it be that they do not know that the Good News was meant for all men—for communist and capitalist, for their children and ours, for black and for white, for revolutionary and conservative? Have they forgotten that my ministry is in obedience to the one who loved his enemies so fully that he died for them? . . . We are called to speak for the weak, for the voiceless, for the victims of our nation, for those it calls "enemy," for no document from human hands can make these humans any less our brothers. . . . I speak now . . . of the people who have been living under the curse of war for almost three continuous decades now. I think of them, too, because it is clear to me that there will be no meaningful solution there until some attempt is made to know them and hear their broken cries.

We learned later that this speech was drafted by Vincent Harding, an influential leader within the Mennonite churches from 1958 to 1966.

In late March, I flew to Hue with Mark Weidner where we rented a house for Mark, Sue, and their daughter. We visited the other WRC locations where the VNCSers were working. I met Paul Kennel, and was impressed with the good work that he and others were doing. When Mary and I had flown into the Phu Bai airport four years earlier, it was a sleepy airfield. Now it was bustling with American fighter bombers and transport planes ferrying troops into battle. We saw a U.S.

Marine Jeep drive from the airport with blindfolded war prisoners. Mark and I had planned to return to Saigon on an Air America cargo plane. When the flight was scrapped, we waited several hours and returned in an Air Force C-130 Hercules.

Soon after returning to Saigon, in early April, our family took a short vacation to Da Lat where we stayed with John and Joanne Newman who were working with the Koho ethnic people under Overseas Crusades. Joanne was a gracious hostess who saw hospitality as her special calling. I went with John one day to visit an agricultural and technical high school being built with World Vision funds for the Koho. A week earlier the Sensenig family was vacationing there and Don had gone with John to visit the school. In the short time between their drive down and back, a mine detonated on the road under a Vietnamese military truck, killing four soldiers.

Working among ethnic minorities in an area where guerilla forces operated, some of us wondered whether the missionaries offered intelligence reports to American authorities. After the war, when asked whether he provided intelligence information to American CIA agents, Newman said he did not, but said that some of the ethnic minorities with whom he worked did report to the intelligence agency.

Mr. and Mrs. Peter Wiwcharuck were house guests of the Newmans while we were there. Now working with the World Relief Commission in the Hue area, Peter was a former naval officer who served a year as Canadian representative on the International Control Commission, the agency set up to monitor the implementation of the 1954 Geneva Accords. Wiwcharuck described his six months in North Vietnam and what he learned about the Evangelical Church in the North after many of the Protestants, including pastors, came South. Wiwcharuck said there was significant religious freedom for a few years but then many of the church buildings were closed. Some of the church buildings were used for shelters after serious floods and never returned to the congregations. After searching, he found the Tin Lanh church in Hanoi and visited with the pastors. Every able-bodied person had to have a productive job of some kind; none of the

Ethnic minority village in Dalat area.

pastors could give full time to pastoral responsibilities. The old pastor told him they had a thriving congregation and that several young men were in training as church leaders. Peter could not find any church buildings in Hai Phong. The church building in the city of Vinh was reportedly used as a granary. (This was one of the few buildings in Vinh to survive the American bombing raids. In spite of the repeated request by the Church to return the building, it was destroyed by the authorities in 2002.)

Before leaving for furlough, Mary and I also wanted to visit my brother Earl in Quang Ngai. Since there were no Air Vietnam flights from Da Lat to Quang Ngai, we flew from Da Lat to Da Nang on Air Vietnam. Leaving two and one-half hours late, we arrived in Da Nang around 1:00 p.m. We assumed that we would stay in Da Nang for the night and attempt to get an Air America flight to Quang Ngai the next day. Having carried out assignments for VNCS, I had authorization to fly Air America. After picking up our baggage, I checked at the Air America desk about a flight the next morning and learned that their last plane to Quang Ngai that day was leaving in ten minutes. Fred Donner, the Air America dispatcher in Da Nang, delayed the flight and insisted that since I had standing travel orders he was going to send us all to Quang Ngai! To my great embarrassment he pulled several passengers off the already fully-loaded plane and put Mary and me, Steven, Becky, our helper and our luggage on the plane and we were off to Quang Ngai, arriving at 2:30 p.m. The irony of a Mennonite missionary "pulling rank" on an airline later recognized as operated by the American CIA! This was Vietnam.

Relating this story to Donner more than forty years later, he said his family was living at the Alliance missionary residence at that time. If he did not get us to Quang Ngai that day, we might have showed up on their doorstep for the night!

We had enjoyed cool pleasant weather in Da Lat; in her journal, Mary asked, "Why doesn't the Lord call us to Da Lat?" In Quang Ngai it was shockingly hot, dry and dusty. But we enjoyed watching the area farmers harvest their rice. One evening out in the fields beyond the town we viewed a spectacular sunset. The western clouds allowed shafts of the sunlight to radiate to the zenith of the sky above us and then, in a mirror image, to converge again on the eastern horizon. Such a sunset we had never seen!

We stayed with Earl in the unit house. On Thursday, we went with Earl and Pat to one of the refugee camps VNCS served and visited the American Friends Service Committee rehabilitation center where technicians made and fitted prostheses for war amputees. We were invited to dinner that evening with Alliance missionaries, Woody and Charlotte Stemple. (Charlotte describes their Quang Ngai experiences in *My Vietnam*, [Xulon Press, 2010]).

Dave Neufeld was then unit leader. Tharon McConnel and Sue Neufeld, both nurses, were involved in public health. Fred Gregory was in charge of a bread distribution program. Earl and Pat Hostetter, in a budding romantic relationship, both taught English classes in the refugee camp. Their good language skills contributed to good community relationships.

In one of the refugee camps we met Bui Thi's family, who had fled an area controlled by the Viet Cong only a few months before. We attended the Tin Lanh church in town Sunday morning; I was asked to preach that afternoon at the Tin Lanh refugee camp. On Sunday evening, we joined the unit for their weekly worship time with lots of singing. I visited a reformatory where hundreds of people were detained—many because they were suspected VC. With Earl I went to the provincial hospital where hundreds of civilian war victims lay.

Two of the staff members of the Gia Dinh Community Center married when we were away—Nguyen Quang Trung and Ngo Thi Bich. The pastor of the Gia Dinh Tin Lanh congregation officiated. Trung worked in the reading room and helped in the church; Bich had worked with day care nursery. Trung and Bich, both members of the Tin Lanh church, would soon become members of the Mennonite congregation. They flew to Da Lat for their honeymoon, the first either of them had flown. Around the same time Pham Van Luc and Vu Thi Qui, both from the Mennonite congregation, announced their engagement.

In April, the free day-care nursery was combined with the Rang Dong elementary school under one principal, Mrs. Nga, for more effective administration. More than 250 children enrolled in what the community people often called *Trường Mỹ*, the American School. Children of poor families received scholarships. James Stauffer and Mrs. Nga took twenty of the school children to the hospital for chest x-rays; they all had active cases of tuberculosis.

The congregation at the Community Center was now meeting for worship every Sunday morning. Sunday afternoon meetings had more variety, usually with singing or talks in English. We did not encourage everyone to attend both meetings. The semi-weekly chapel-type services at the Saigon student center were discontinued due to poor attendance. Instead, Sensenigs and Beidlers planned informal Saturday afternoon recreational activities to interact with students. Don Sensenig wrote in the April *News and Concerns*: "We continue to look for ways of witness that are vital to their lives and aspirations."

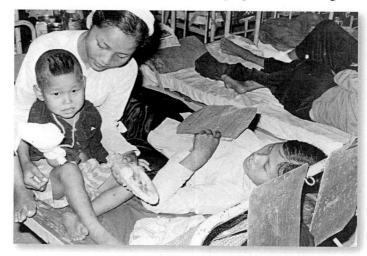

Mother consoles son who lost his hand in a bombing raid.

In early April, Sensenig served as interpreter for three doctors from the Committee of Responsibility (COR) representing the American Medical Association, who visited thirty-five provincial hospitals throughout South Vietnam in search of civilian victims of napalm bombings. The Committee was a newly-organized group of medical professionals and other private citizens horrified by the casualty toll among Vietnamese citizens. They found fewer child

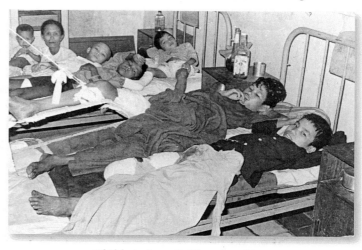

Child victims of village bombings.

napalm victims than expected but found many injured by bullets and artillery, mortar and bombing strikes. More than half the surgical cases were war-related. In the Quang Ngai provincial hospital eighty percent of the total patients were surgical cases and eighty percent of these were war-related. Doctors spoke of lack of supplies. Vietnamese doctors quickly amputated arms and legs because they did not have the time or skill to save injured limbs. It seemed that few children survived napalm attacks on their villages. There also were not as many victims as in the previous year since many of the country people were already forced off their land and were now living in refugee camps.

After visiting the Long Xuyen provincial hospital in the Mekong River delta, the driver of the Jeep carrying Sensenig and the COR doctors was hurrying back to Can Tho city before dusk when Viet Cong forces controlled the road. Hitting a deep pothole, the back seat passengers were tossed off their seats and one of the doctors was knocked out when his head struck the roof. Stopping, they laid the unconscious man on the ground. A military doctor accompanying the group had his pistol at the ready while the hapless doctor was revived.

The U.S. armed forces placed medical teams in many provincial hospitals. These Military Provincial Health Assistance Program (MILPHAP) teams, first assigned in November 1965, worked under the supervision of the provincial medical chief. Working both in provincial and district medical facilities, some with limited water and electricity, they provided good care and sometimes evacuated patients to U.S. military field hospitals. Over the next few years, the COR mission and ongoing program brought one hundred severely injured children to the United States for treatment.

Paul Longacre and I visited the Mekong River Delta three days in late April. We went first to Can Tho, the third largest city in South Vietnam—after Saigon and Da Nang—then west to Long Xuyen, a prosperous town on the lower branch of the river. Returning to Can Tho we met Willie Myers, who was serving as team leader to some thirty IVS volunteers. The next day Myers took us to Sa Dec where we visited a Catholic priest who told us that many members of his parish supported the National Liberation Front. Fr. Joseph Marie Ho Hue Ba, the Catholic representative on the Central Committee of the National Liberation Front, was born in Sa Dec. He reportedly had earlier taught in a seminary and was active in peace movements.

During the sixties, there were frequent discussions about the makeup of the National Liberation Front formed in 1960. Those who supported the U.S. Vietnam policies said the NLF was merely a front for carrying out the instructions of the Vietnam Communist Party. Many who opposed U.S. war policies downplayed the communist orientation, insisting that the Front was a legitimate political movement with a broad representation of persons struggling for independence from foreign domination. There was truth to both arguments. Even though there was broad non-communist support, much NLF activity was coordinated through Hanoi.

With the congregation at the Community Center growing, we began a weekly Bible study and prayer gathering in the homes of the new believers. One week in May, church members met in the home of Nguyen Van Tu who lived with his aged mother at the edge of the city next to rice fields, surrounded by bamboo and coconut palms—a quiet and peaceful setting. The group met around a table with kerosene lamps, sharing their joys and problems with Tu's mother and many children listening quietly in the background. Tu was the only Christian in his family and recently had been attending the services more regularly. We were happy that Mr. Ho Trung Ty was now accompanying his wife to the worship services.

When the English classes resumed, Stauffer enjoyed teaching his English class using as a text-book *The King Nobody Wanted*, the life of Jesus. Mary taught one English class; I taught two classes on Monday, Wednesday and Friday evenings from 6:15 to 8:15 p.m. and often stayed for another hour of conversation. Since we lived upstairs at the Community Center, this was convenient. With home Bible studies on Thursday evenings and our missionary fellowship meeting on Tuesday evenings, Mary observed that Saturday evening was our only evening free for entertaining.

Conversations with advanced English students were stimulating. A student, Nguyen Van Hai, presented me his reflections on peace in Vietnam—both in Vietnamese and English. This came shortly after thirty-three-year-old Buddhist teacher Thich Nu Nhat Chi Mai immolated herself publically in Saigon, calling for peace. "Folding hands I kneel" was a piece of poetry she left behind. In it she asked:

> Why do Americans immolate themselves?* / Why does the world demonstrate?
> Why is Vietnam silent? / Not permitted to speak Peace? . . .
> I still my hands, O people! / More than twenty years already,
> Much blood spilled--bones scattered, / Don't exterminate my people!
> Don't exterminate my people! / Folding my hands I kneel.
> (* *Reference to American Quaker Norman Morrison who immolated himself in 1965*).

Identifying himself as Buddhist, Hai said he was not as holy, magnanimous or unpretentious as Nhat Chi Mai who died imploring for peace for Vietnam. Nevertheless, "facing the spectacle of the ever more irrational, indiscriminate and cruel war," even if he could do nothing to bring peace to the country, he still had to envision peace and national unity for the people. In English, he wrote:

> As a Vietnamese, I can no longer bear the sight of the Vietnamese blood pouring out; to us it is not the blood of the soldiers from our side or from the other side, it's only the blood of hundreds, thousands of innocent people...
> As a Vietnamese, I cannot tolerate anymore, the sight of foreigners destroying our beautiful country, poisoning our youth's minds, killing our people with any modern weapon they could think of. As a Vietnamese, I never want North and South Vietnam fighting against each other, killing each other, only because of contradictory opinions on politics between countries.

In May, the Community Center finally began enrolling families into MCC's Family Child Assistance (FCA) sponsorship program which was planned more than a year earlier. Mrs. Bich served as caseworker and worked under the supervision of Marta Brenden, the VNCS social worker who had introduced an FCA program in the Khanh Hoi section of Saigon. Teenagers from families with limited income were enrolled in courses learning trades so that they would provide additional income to their families in a relatively short time. The center organized its own sewing school taught by Co Van (Bay). Boys were enrolled in private electrical or mechanics schools. North American sponsors were sent files of the children they sponsored and occasionally letters were exchanged. Mrs. Bich knew the community well. Arlene Stauffer and Marta often went with her to visit the families. Ten students were enrolled the first month. Paul Kraybill was pleased with this MCC-EMBMC cooperation, noting that the FCA program was "an excellent example of the tie-in with relief assistance and mission witness."

Mrs. Bich in FCA office.

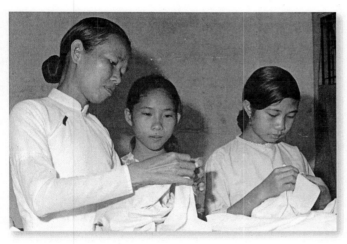

Ms. Van organized a sewing school.

With 379 students enrolled in Rang Dong primary school that summer, the Mennonite Mission requested support from another MCC sponsorship program—the Educational Assistance Program (EAP). We eventually enrolled 150 children into EAP, one quarter of the later 600 school enrollment. Like FCA, EAP sponsors received files of the children they sponsored and the children received uniforms and tuition.

James Stauffer, director of the community center, also arranged for a twice-a-week afternoon clinic with MCC volunteer Dr. Marilyn Strayer. On these afternoons, the patio at the center was full of women with babies waiting to see the doctor who worked out of the school office. Mrs. Nga, the school principal who had pharmacy training, also assisted. This clinic became a much appreciated service of the community center.

In a letter home, Mary remarked: "All this amounts to a lot of activity. . . . Living among crying physical needs, we feel we must do something to help in a physical way. . . . How much time should we be spending in social concerns and how much in evangelization? We feel the two must go hand in hand."

In the June *News and Concerns,* Don Sensenig wrote that the Sunday morning Bible class at the Saigon student center was "quite encouraging at present" with about ten persons regularly attending, most of whom were "sincerely seeking for God's presence and power in daily life." Students were daily crowding the center facilities to study for year-end exams.

Premier Ky announced that he would run for president and campaign posters were appearing all over Saigon proclaiming "The government of Nguyen Cao Ky is the government of the poor." Chief of State Nguyen Van Thieu indicated that he might also run for president. By late June the Armed Forces Council resolved this matter by announcing that General Thieu would run for president and Gen. Ky had to accept the vice-presidential slot!

The Mennonite Mission was invited to a Tin Lanh pastors' retreat in Da Nang in late May and the Mission Council asked James Stauffer to go. Stauffer stayed with Alliance missionaries while attending the conference. One day he went with C&MA missionary Leroy Josephson to see the head chaplain of the U.S. Third Marine Corps. Josephson presented the chaplain a list of thirteen churches in that area that were either totally destroyed or heavily damaged by U.S. Marine operations. The Third Marine Division had established a Protestant Chapel Fund which gave assistance to local congregations, sometimes helping churches build schools. James wrote: "The irony of it is—as fast as they built them up in some areas they are destroying them in others. This is a strange war. And there seems to be no end in sight."

Stauffer told about the death of a Tin Lanh farmer who was shot in the head as he worked in his field during an American military operation thirty kilometers from Da Nang. His pastor brought him to a hospital in Da Nang where he died. The pastor described to Josephson and Stauffer how senseless and tragic those military tactics were. "When a village hears that the soldiers are coming, all the men with the VC flee and the soldiers pass through and find mostly women and children. They arrest a few suspects and sometimes destroy the homes, but as soon as they leave the VC come right back. Nothing has been accomplished except to make the life of the people more difficult."

In a June 20 newsletter to friends, James and Arlene reflected on the ten months since they returned to Vietnam for their third term of service. "These months have been by far the busiest and most gratifying of our ten years in Vietnam." they wrote. "Behind us lie years of difficult language study and a groping about for proper techniques and strategy in a new field. Church building moved very slowly in an uncertain war-weary context. Our sojourn in Hong Kong allowed us to witness the Holy Spirit at work building his church there. Then we were overjoyed to hear of the developing congregation and an educational program at our Gia Dinh Center. The prospects of assisting this young church emerge and becoming involved in its 'growing pains' excited us."

The Stauffers described the Rang Dong School with nearly 400 children under the leadership of Mrs. Phan Tuyet Nga, the principal. Some of the teachers were Christian; they met together for morning devotions before classes each day. "We are not restricted in teaching the Bible and Christian ethics, and have unusual opportunities to influence children from non-Christian homes," they wrote. Parents were invited periodically for lectures, films and special programs where the Gospel of Jesus was presented. The nursery school children received a hot lunch each day and all the children got sandwiches made from bread baked in the MCC oven at the Hoi Duc Anh Orphanage.

The Mennonite congregation, on the last Sunday in June, organized a picnic retreat with the Go Vap Baptist congregation in the rear yard of Em Dem, the VNCS house. There were around thirty-five persons from the two Mennonite centers and twenty-five from the Baptist Church. The Baptist pastor, Do Vinh Thanh, brought a message based on II Chronicles 7:14: "If my people, who are called by my name,

Paul and Doris Longacre with Cara Sue.

shall humble themselves…" I had a long association with Pastor Thanh who invited Mary and me out to a restaurant a week later. Widowed two years before, his four-year-old son was living with relatives.

Paul and Doris Longacre completed their three year MCC assignment and left Vietnam with Cara Sue on June 16. Ernest and Mabel Frey were leaving July 28.

With our plans to return to the States for furlough after nearly five years in Vietnam, Mary and I were invited to dinners at the homes of friends—both missionary and MCC colleagues and some of our Vietnamese coworkers, like the caretaker at the Community Center. It was also special to be invited to the home of the President of the Tin Lanh Church, Pastor and Mrs. Doan Van Mieng.

We timed our travel schedule to attend the Eighth Assembly of Mennonite World Conference in Amsterdam. Having read on the subject of the church in communist countries, I wanted to briefly visit Moscow en route to Amsterdam.

We left July 15, 1967. Our flights took us to Bangkok, then on to Calcutta (Kolkata) where we stayed at the MCC center. Here we met Devadoss Maddimadugu who would travel to Vietnam the following February to work as lab technician at the Nha Trang Evangelical Clinic. We secured visas to the Soviet Union in New Delhi.

We stayed at the historic Hotel Metropol in central Moscow three nights. Stepping outside the hotel we suffered a jolt of cultural shock. In contrast to the graceful promenading on the Saigon streets, we witnessed the stout Moscow population scurrying to their jobs.

Before leaving Saigon, I had written to Michael Zhidkov, the English-speaking pastor of the Baptist church in Moscow and a leader of the All-Union Council of Evangelical Christians-Baptists. We wanted to meet some church leaders unofficially to register our sadness for the American fighting in Vietnam and our desire for peace. We also wanted to meet Viktor Kriger, a Mennonite pastor associated with the All Union Council of the Evangelical Christian Baptists. Mary and I went to the Baptist office, gave our greetings, and were invited to stay for lunch with the church staff. Again a cultural jolt—as soon as the "Amen" sounded the thanks for the meal everyone grabbed spoons and wolfed down their borsch in five minutes. This was no comparison to the polite invitation of a Vietnamese host who picks up chopsticks and invites the guests three times before they pick up their chopsticks and join him in the meal.

We flew to Amsterdam on July 22, the day before the Conference convened. We met friends—Paul Kraybill, William Snyder and others. The assembly met under the theme: "The Witness of the Holy Spirit." The stirring Sunday morning sermon response by Vincent Harding titled "The Peace Witness and Revolutionary Movements" confirmed that we were indeed living in changing times.

Harding began with the words from Isaiah 61 that Jesus quoted when he was given the opportunity to speak in the synagogue in Nazareth. Stating a conviction that most Mennonites "know and care very little about the explosive worlds of color and revolution," Harding recited the "voices of revolution" which included an unnamed member of the Vietnam's National Liberation Front:

> No brutal force in the world, not even that of American imperialism, can bring to their knees a people who have pledged themselves to die rather than to live in slavery. We have endured the sufferings of twenty years of unrelenting warfare; that is why, more than any other nation in the world, we want peace, a life free of bombing, where all families would be reunited and could

freely rebuild their lives in happiness and prosperity. But we want a real peace, a peace that gives freedom, and not one obtained under the crushing heel of the aggressor.

Revolutionaries "often consider the good Christians of the West as some of their major enemies," Harding declared. "They see America as the leader of counter-revolution for the world." Noting that Mennonites seldom hesitate to seek justice for themselves, he asked: "What do we have to say to others who seek justice? How shall our 'peace witness' be valid if it refers only to *their* quest for justice and not ours . . . ? What is our peace witness when we live as citizens of the nations that make peaceful revolution impossible?"

The final offering at the assembly was designated for Vietnam—to be divided equally for relief needs in the North and in the South.

We had tentative plans to travel to Germany, but our Pennsylvania homes seemed best for the health of our two young children suffering from diarrhea. The flight to New York City experienced technical problems, forcing our plane to first land in Boston. Waiting four hours at Kennedy airport, our families welcomed us back at midnight.

Living in metropolitan Saigon with responsibilities at the office across town, I would daily ride the Lambretta motor scooter the ten or fifteen minutes amidst the sea of vehicles on Le Van Duyet Street across Cau Bong Bridge onto Hien Vuong Street straight to Dan Chu traffic circle, then take Tran Quoc Toan Boulevard, left on Cao Thang Street, then another left onto Phan Thanh Gian Street to the Vietnam Mennonite Mission office. There were frequent traffic incidents, mostly minor due to the relatively slow speed of the traffic, but occasionally fatal. It often occurred to me that, were I to be killed, either by some crash or by a grenade tossed into a crowd, life would continue to go on for others. Most people would not even know that I once existed!

Reflecting on how the Vietnamese people could live with two decades of war, it was clear that life went on in the midst of difficulties. Babies were born, children went to school, young people married and adults got jobs to support their families. Now our small family was back in the United States but life and work for others continued in Vietnam.

As soon as we left Vietnam, our upstairs apartment at the Community Center was turned into an English language classroom and Stauffer's office.

And more people were embracing faith in Jesus Christ. James wrote home: "Several more people have found the Lord during the last few weeks. Tho, a young man who interpreted for the clinic, is one. A man who came to the clinic was another. Two young girls who help and teach in the school are happy in their new faith. One is the sister-in-law of the school principal, Mrs. Nga."

Stauffer asked his mother to pray for the five persons being instructed in the way of Jesus on Sunday mornings at 8:30 a.m. He wrote: "It is quite a mixed group—some of the mothers can't read and some of them are school teachers. Some young and others old." He noted that attendance at the Sunday morning worship service was fourteen to twenty and thirty to forty persons attended the English-Vietnamese afternoon program.

On August 1, the Mission rented a two-story house at 8/12 Nguyen Thien Thuat Street, Gia Dinh, located in an alley only ten minutes' walk from the Community Center. After repairs and renovations the Sensenig family moved into the top floor and began enrolling up to ten young men to begin the hostel program which had long been envisioned as a training center. This was the fourth house the Sensenig family had lived in since coming to Vietnam four years earlier. By the end of September, four young Christian men were living in the downstairs hostel, with several more expected soon. Some were students; others had jobs. Don's goal was "to provide a Christian community and atmosphere, with opportunities for lay training and Bible study." The Sensenigs would also assist the Stauffers in activities at the community center.

Everett and Margaret Metzler and family returned from furlough to again occupy the living space at the office and student center. Everett wrote to the home office: "Saigon is something of a shock again. After Tokyo and Hong Kong efficiency, Saigon gives one an initial impression of chaos and artificiality. But we are rapidly feeling at home and are grateful to be back. The children are getting in on their third Summer Bible School for the summer—at the International Protestant Church. Friends have made us feel very welcome. Adjustments include doubling the price of almost everything, getting used to the noise, relating to servants, and remembering the keys to this [Vietnamese] typewriter."

The national elections on September 3, turned out as predicted: General Nguyen Van Thieu and Air Marshal Nguyen Cao Ky were elected president and vice-president with thirty-five percent of the total votes cast. The other votes were scattered among ten different civilian candidates—one billed as a peace candidate. A former government minister of economics, Au Truong Thanh, was forbidden to run because he advocated negotiations with the National Liberation Front; he was arrested three weeks later. A few weeks after the elections there were demonstrations in several cities—supported by many Buddhists leaders—denouncing the election results, but the election was eventually validated by the Constituent Assembly.

Arlene Stauffer had a harrowing experience one evening in early September. The area around "Tin Can Alley" suffered a power outage that afternoon. When James left home, just before 9:00 p.m., to visit the Sensenigs who lived a kilometer away, he did not bother to close the front gate. Arlene also left the front door open. She was sitting at the dining room table reading by candle light when she heard a noise near the bedroom. Taking a candle to investigate, a robber confronted her with a pistol and asked for their money. Arlene told him they were missionaries and did not have much money at home.

The robber spoke English at first, but soon they were speaking Vietnamese. To Arlene he seemed like one of her English language students. She told him of God's love and asked whether she could pray for him. He did not object but kept nervously looking around as if fearful that someone was around or that James might come home.

Arlene had washed her hair which was still hanging loosely and the candle ignited her hair. Dropping the candle she tried to beat out the flames. The robber helped her extinguish the flames, then searched around a bit more. As he prepared to leave with a few items, Arlene kept reminding him that he would have to give account someday for his evil deeds! He listened a bit, warned her not to yell, snuffed out the candle and ran out the door.

James described this incident to his mother, praising the Lord for protection, concluding, "Well, we're going to keep our gate locked more now, especially when the lights are out!"

James and Rachel Metzler returned to Vietnam early September. In the October *News and Concerns* they described their life since returning. They lived with the other Metzler family for a month and had just rented a three-room house in the western part of the city, across the street from the Phu Tho race track where small horses ran each week.

They also reported the resignations of International Voluntary Service personnel Gene Stoltzfus and Willy Meyers and the letter IVS sent to President Johnson two weeks earlier. Their action, he wrote, was "a well-publicized protest against the increasing U.S. military effort being carried out against the Vietnamese people [and] symbolized the pressure which is growing on all of us."

In this 1967-68 school term, Dorothy Beidler was teaching twenty-four fourth graders at Phoenix Study Group, the small private American school where Eric, Gretchen and Malcolm Metzler, John and Rose Stauffer and Anne Sensenig studied.

Dorothy Beidler teaching elementary school students.

On Saturday, September 9, the church celebrated the wedding of Pham Van Luc and Vu Thi Qui, members of the Mennonite church. This was followed by a seven-course meal for 200 guests in a local restaurant.

In mid-October James Stauffer wrote his mother:

> We are following with keen interest the anti-war demonstrations in the States. . . . The truth is coming out. Oh, that our leaders might see the folly and tragedy of the war they're waging. Yesterday's *Saigon Post* carried headlines about the refugee situation. Allied forces have deliberately created 300,000 refugees this year. The director of refugees is complaining because sometimes he is only given one day notice to prepare for thousands of new refugees. He reported that 10,000 refugees in the northern section are facing starvation because the only way they can be supplied is by helicopter. So far, the military has none to use for this purpose.

Stauffer noted that around two million persons were registered as "refugees" and another two million were displaced because of the war—nearly one-fourth of the seventeen million population in South Viet Nam. "The gulf between the suffering countryside and the booming cities is widening," he wrote. "[Those of us in Saigon live] in a completely different world. Oh, we feel some effects of the war—the streets are full of pot holes, and the electricity has been off a lot here of late. Prices are still going up every month. But TV sets and motorbikes are selling like hot cakes."

In October, Winston O. Weaver, CEO of a construction company in Harrisonburg, Virginia, active in the Mennonite community and board member of World Vision International, met with the missionary men. Stauffer enjoyed the visit with Weaver who challenged them to "a greater prayer effort," but noted that they confronted Weaver with "some misgivings" about World Vision because "they work so close with the military and are rather strong anticommunistic."

The same week Everett and Margaret commented in a letter to *Missionary Messenger:*

We are more convinced than ever that to make Christ known here it is imperative that we disassociate ourselves as much as possible from the "American image" present here. America and the evangelical faith become more and more identified as one and the same. Unfortunately, many missionaries openly support the US and fraternize with and support the US military program. A long-time Vietnamese Christian friend who works in a high office told me that more and more people are asking him about the relation of evangelicals and the US military. Their past would condition the Vietnamese to assume that the religious activities of the Western missionaries are part and parcel of the larger military effort. (This was often true during the days of French colonialism.) We have therefore prepared a statement to share with our Vietnamese friends to try to clarify our identity.

Luke and Dorothy Beidler wrote in the November *News and Concerns:* "In our work here in Saigon we know that often we are misunderstood. Teaching English, providing a clinic, running an elementary school, and most seriously, even preaching the Gospel, often we are seen simply as another arm of the larger American effort. . . . This past month we spent a lot of time in the 'garden' praying and agonizing over this problem." They then quoted the October 25 statement in full:

Statement of Mennonite Missionaries to Vietnamese Community

Since we are Christians and also American citizens we feel it is imperative in the present situation to make the following statement to our Vietnamese friends.

We have come to Viet Nam to share our faith in Christ and to demonstrate God's love and concern for all men. We are sent and supported by Christian friends of the Mennonite Church in America to whom we are responsible. We are not here as representatives of any government or government agency.

We affirm that the church of Jesus Christ is universal and should not be identified with any particular people or political system. We confess that Christianity has often been identified with Western nations and their interests. We believe that many people are rejecting Christianity because of this association.

However, we affirm that the dynamic of Christ's way is love that is willing to suffer rather than coerce. We confess that often Christianity has been identified with the use of military and other coercive force. We believe that this is true in Viet Nam today.

We are deeply moved by the tremendous suffering and grief being endured by many Vietnamese people. We believe that the military force causing most of this hardship is not in their interest and cannot solve their problems.

We plead and pray for a change of heart and methods.

The statement was translated and posted in English and Vietnamese. However, several Vietnamese staff members expressed strong opposition to the statement. James Metzler wrote in a letter to his father that the "Vietnamese believers are so opposed to saying anything about the situation that it is doubtful if we can use it." In the Saigon world of doublespeak, a statement that missionaries were not part of the U.S. government could suggest that they were! However, a main concern of staff members was that, given the strong military stance of the government, they themselves might be interrogated by the police. The statement was afterwards only given to people who inquired.

The first Sunday in November, five persons were baptized at the Gia Dinh church, bringing the total baptized membership to twenty-six. Mrs. Anh, a mother of five young children, was a teacher at the Rang Dong School. Two other teachers were also baptized, Ms. Ngo Anh and Ms. Bich Lien. Bich Lien, who assisted in one of the kindergarten classes, had followed the Cao Dai religion and was vegetarian. Mr. Tho was an interpreter for Dr. Marilyn Strayer at the twice-a-week afternoon clinic at the Community Center; one of his brothers had run for the presidency of the country in September.

The fifth person baptized was Mrs. Xinh, a poor illiterate woman whose husband, Mr. Thanh, was dying of tuberculosis. She was one of forty mothers and grandmothers aged thirty to sixty years of age taking literacy classes at the center—organized by the school principal, Mrs. Nga. The class met four nights weekly; on Saturday evening they had a lesson on health and sanitation.

Most of these struggling people who lived in *Đồng Ông Cộ* (Mr. Co's Field), a cemetery near the Gia Dinh Community Center, were unofficial refugees from the war who had moved here for safety. They lived in shacks—many of them on top of graves. It was not unusual to visit a family and find a grave marker under the table on the dirt floor. Eventually the stone or concrete marker would be removed or covered up.

James and Rachel Metzler and young son Brian were back in Vietnam only two months when James wrote to Paul Kraybill the end of October: "I feel constrained to share with you my misgivings concerning our presence in Viet Nam at this time."

The Metzlers had just moved into the small house by the Phu Tho race tracks to share a Christian witness in this community. Although James found the Vietnamese language difficult, it was not the challenge of teaching or preaching in a different tongue that disturbed his peace.

"You already know, of course," James wrote,

> . . . from my writing and speaking that I am moved very deeply by the situation here. Throughout the summer months, I've been doing a good deal of reading . . . and the more I learn the more disturbed I become. . . . I feel that the situation is deteriorating rapidly. The escalation of brute force which the American military appear driven to . . . brings me to a crisis point.
>
> Thus I believe the time is fast approaching, if not already here, when we must disassociate ourselves from this evil campaign—for our personal consciences' sake as well as a witness to true Christianity. As I have shared with the [Mission] Council, I already feel as though I do not belong here; the entire spirit and atmosphere which envelops us all is totally foreign to our own spirit. . . . We simply have not been able to stand apart from it. . . . Everyone and everything is being forced to line up—there is no political neutrality. There is but one issue in Viet Nam and everything is related to it.

While James admitted that it "is still possible to bury oneself in daily programs and forget the larger issues of identification and suffering," he could not shake off the idea that "our very presence in the midst of this military-political-social struggle implicates us directly with what our nation is doing."

Alluding to the letter IVS personnel sent to President Johnson and the resignation of key IVS leaders six weeks earlier, James acknowledged that our work as missionaries was not as closely related to government as that of International Voluntary Service.

> Yet, because of the impact America's action is having on the image of Christianity, I feel our association with it is doubly serious.
>
> Thus I believe that a strong, clear witness against this immorality (and the Christians' involvement in it) is *the witness* which we should give and the one which will make the greatest impact for Christi-

anity in this country and throughout the world. The past election and the response to [the] IVS stand convince me that a good majority of the Vietnamese are longing for someone to speak out for them. But regardless of the impact, we still face the question of being party to what is going on.

In his letter to Kraybill, copied to members of the Mission Council and me in the States, James admitted that while the other members of the Mennonite missionary team were "deeply troubled" by what was happening in Vietnam, they had not come to think that they no longer belonged in Vietnam. The missionaries were preparing statements to release, James noted, but "we apparently are not ready to jeopardize our mission program or our visas by expressing our true feelings too publicly." And James was uncertain about "how much to stir them up by [his] own constant agonizing." He asked for Kraybill's response amid a suggestion that he might need to ask for a reassignment to some other country.

James enclosed a copy of "An Open Letter" he had written to Lyndon B. Johnson several day earlier. In the opening paragraph, he gave historical analogies for what he was experiencing in Vietnam. Having lived in Vietnam for several years, he wrote: "I feel like one of the Germans who could hardly believe what he saw Hitler doing to the Jews. I fear that history will view America's treatment of the Vietnamese peasants in the same category. Therefore I am compelled to openly identify myself with their cause."

The letter observed that the United States had allied itself with an aristocratic ruling class against the rural peasants, and suggested that the destruction raining down on the people in the countryside would enhance the appeal of communism.

I responded to James' letter, paraphrasing the words of Jesus, "Agonize with those who agonize!" Rachel, James, Mary, and I had arrived in Saigon on the same plane in September 1962; we had lived together for a time on a small one-way street in Saigon. We were still close together, even though now I was twelve time zones removed, studying in seminary.

I assured James that I respected his convictions. I, too, was struggling with how to express our views of U.S. military policies when speaking to church audiences. In a Mennonite congregation the previous Sunday, I said that we must oppose this war because all wars are wrong and must seek to bring about peace. Afterwards, I was troubled, feeling that the audience had understood me to say that we should support the Johnson administration's efforts to bring about peace! We needed to find new ways to protest U.S. military policies, I wrote, and "inaction is worse than making a few mistakes."

I believed that we American missionaries should stay in Vietnam—even be willing to suffer for doing right. Only then would it be redemptive. Americans in Vietnam could hopefully "be prophetic voices against the evil being done by our government."

Kraybill responded to James, also expressing respect for his "conscience and convictions." He noted that mutual respect is essential "if we are to maintain Christian integrity in our struggle for the right answer." It was clear, however, that Kraybill did not agree with James' reasoning. Protest, he wrote,

> . . . may mean running the risk of being misunderstood by both sides in the struggle. . . . It may be possible that an exaggerated protest may only say indirectly that we are guilty. . . . Should we not concentrate on emphasizing that "our" nation is not "our" nation, but that we are symbols of a faith and a conviction that . . . stands apart from the acts and deeds of a nation with which it is falsely identified. I am not sure that withdrawal will do very much to change America's im-

age, but I do have a feeling that involvement might help to change the Christians' image and it is toward that that I feel we must work.

Kraybill said he has no intention to argue Metzler from his position, respects his right to make his own decision, and would stand by him in sympathy and understanding. Kraybill hoped, however, that James would not jeopardize the witness and conviction of others who do not agree with him. If James asked to transfer to some other country, Kraybill said he would attempt to implement it. James expressed thanks for Kraybill's "sympathetic understanding and acceptance" and said that he and Rachel are quite willing to continue their witness in Vietnam "for the present."

Kraybill sent some of the Kraybill-Metzler dialogue to William Snyder for his comments. In his reply to Kraybill, Snyder wrote:

> James is too strong in saying that we "are party to" or are "implicated directly with" US policy. Not if we declare publicly that we are not! IVS'ers [who resigned from the agency] may go back to Vietnam under other auspices—they are not saying that being there is wrong. From my standpoint, we must have freedom as a mission and MCC to work within the things to which called BUT our leaving the field would be a dis-service to the Vietnamese because our voices are stronger—much stronger—if we speak from involvement rather than uninvolvement. I hope he stays. I would like to meet the mission brethren when Atlee and I are there [in January].

James also shared his concerns more widely. In a commentary published in the December 1967 issue of *Missionary Messenger*—written weeks earlier—Metzler alludes to conversations with Mennonites in the States who asked what would happen to our missionary work if the US troops left the country! "Imagine Anabaptists preaching the Word under the shadow of the cannon," he asked! In light of the continuing military escalation by the United States bringing death and destruction on the people of Vietnam, Metzler wrote:

> It is crucial for the church at home to think clearly with us regarding our position here. How much longer should we stay in Vietnam? . . . We too are Americans; it is simply impossible to disassociate ourselves to any clear extent—in the eyes of the Vietnamese, fellow Americans, or the onlooking world. . . . Since our work is viewed as part of the pacification program (and we are winning friends for the US), are we serving a military cause any less than noncombatants? Our relief and service projects are all part of "the other war," the refugees having been deliberately created by the US forces. And statements of support must be signed before even entering the country. So our presence itself has political implications; one doesn't become involved in politics only if he witnesses against this evil.

James concludes, "True, our primary task here is evangelism. But what is the greatest witness the church should be heralding to these people and the world? Perhaps our apparent support of our government's program here is the only witness people are really hearing. . . . Pure religion worth sharing is still, first of all, identification with the oppressed and suffering ones."

Mission Secretary, Everett Metzler, wrote to Kraybill, saying: "We all are deeply disturbed by what is happening about us and at times question our usefulness to the Kingdom in this mess. But most of us feel that our reasons for continuing include the necessity of witnessing to the supra-nationalism of Christianity and its very relevance to Vietnam-type situations. This is going to demand that we stand up and be counted and may also get us into hot water but I think that we are all ready to take that chance."

Everett noted that, in addition to preparing a statement to post locally, members of the Mission Council were considering a statement addressed to Christians in the United States. "We felt it especially imperative to make a simple statement to the Vietnamese as to our relation to the U.S. presence, our purpose, and our support," Everett wrote. "We are hearing more and more questions about the relation of Protestants and missionaries to the U.S. effort here. On numerous occasions we have been asked if we are CIA agents."

In the same December issue of *Missionary Messenger,* James Stauffer asked:

> Could it be that our proclamation of the "good news" is drowned out in the roar of planes and guns? Can we blame "our" message for falling on deaf ears when "our" bombs and bullets are making orphans and widows—filling hospitals and graveyards? The emblem of the cross which we preach is also boldly displayed on military bases, uniforms, and even chaplains' jeeps.
>
> As a mission family we are being forced to clarify our position in relation to this growing military venture. The military establishment is taking over . . . every civilian effort that is useful to their policy. . . . We may soon need to make clear by public declaration our convictions and attitudes. . . . Some may construe this to mean that we are moving into politics. Actually, the opposite is true! We want to move away from being identified politically. Most Vietnamese consider us to be an arm of American design in Southeast Asia. Many are surprised to learn that we are not supported by the US government.

Stauffer then referred to an incident that happened the week before. When Lam, the evangelist from our church, was speaking to someone about the gospel of Christ, a neighbor angrily retorted: "Christianity is part of the USA's plan to take over our country."

"We need to make clear that this is *not* the case," Stauffer insisted, "that we are *not* supporting or even sympathetic to our country's policy, that we are *not* sent out by them or have any organizational ties with them."

Further, he said, "Along with this negative protest should go an affirmative statement of call and purpose: that we are, first of all, members and citizens of God's kingdom, that we are called by God and the church to minister to the whole man, that we believe in the use of love rather than force, that we are peacemakers, that we are here to share with the Vietnamese the message of reconciliation which gives them peace with God and man through Jesus Christ. Then, our message of Life may become more credible in this dying land!"

In late October, the missionary men—James Stauffer, Everett Metzler, James Metzler and Donald Sensenig—began crafting a statement to release publicly. Initially the intention was to release one to the general public and another directed specifically to the Christian churches. James Metzler was asked to prepare the first drafts, but the others also drafted statements. There was vigorous discussion within the missionary team about what to say. By early November the two statements were ready to be sent to Paul Kraybill for his review and to me for my comments.

The Advisory Committee on Peace Concerns, proposed at the time of the May visit of Snyder and Keeney, met in Saigon November 18 and 19. Everett chaired the meeting. Others participating were Donald Sensenig, Paul Leatherman, David Neufeld and Douglas Hostetter. Gayle Preheim was unable to attend. The group reviewed materials and discussed action plans.

One question discussed was whether to focus primarily on the particulars of the Vietnam conflict, or to deal with the broader question of Christian participation in any military actions. The committee assigned Everett and Don to sponsor a meeting with local missionaries of other agencies—preferably before Christmas—to express concerns for peace.

On November 13, Everett sent Kraybill a draft of the "Letter to American Christians" aimed at American Evangelicals—a *Christianity Today* audience." He also sent a second draft aimed at a general American audience; this one was never released. These were written in the context of "considerable heart searching, prayer and discussion," Everett wrote. "We realize that this type of thing may have unforeseen and possibly undesirable consequences," Everett concluded, "but we all feel that we need to take that risk rather than remain silent for the sake of the present and future Christian witness here."

Kraybill gave a surprising affirmative response: "My initial reaction to the statements . . . is very positive. I share with you a complete agreement that we should be speaking to Christians to help them understand what is happening and to give a witness to our understanding of Christian love and the meaning of our peace witness. I think your . . . 'Letter to American Christians' speak[s] very eloquently to the kind of witness we should be communicating." Kraybill made a few suggestions for ways of strengthening the statement. A week later he reported that the Mission Board executive committee had discussed the "Letter" and expressed a "genuine sympathetic concern and understanding of the issues" the missionaries faced. However, the executive committee members took no official action regarding the missionaries' plans to release this statement.

Everett mailed me the draft statements and I likewise made a few editorial suggestions. Although Mary and I discussed possible visa implications if I signed the statement, I asked that my name be added to the other members of the Mission Council. In my November 24 reply I wrote:

> I have always appreciated the consensus that we usually reached when we struggled with difficult problems. I believe it can be the same now. I do not think we should underestimate the possible consequences of making these statements. On the other hand, we cannot ignore the consequences of keeping silent. I have shared the problem of our identification with the US military and political policies in Vietnam with some folks in congregations who are generally cautious of our speaking to the government, and they feel that we as Christians have no choice but to make clear our position if, in fact, we are being identified with the US policy. I believe Lancaster [Mennonite] Conference will support this action if they understand the problem.

In Kraybill's response to Everett, he questioned the frequent use of the word "our" in the statement being prepared. The repeated use of "our," Paul said, seems to suggest that our church or we missionaries are part of the total American destructive policies in Vietnam. Everett replied: "We feel that no matter what position we take as a church in regard to war and the state, we are still Americans, and although we disavow any guilt because we are non-participants in war, yet we do not come away quite pure. We are guilty by association and likely there is no way to totally disassociate ourselves from what our country is doing here until we no longer call the U.S. 'our' county. Which of course is the point behind our making statements."

Kraybill said the missionaries were free to circulate the statement as they desired. However, in a later letter he returned to this "our" argument: "I still feel rather deeply about the 'our' matter," he wrote. "I have some problem in principle with the idea that because I am a citizen of a certain country, therefore I am guilty by association of all of that country's evil and sin. I . . . feel that a preoccupation with this may only defeat our desire to disassociate ourselves."

The December 1967 *Letter from Vietnam to American Christians,* was published in the January 16, 1968 issue of *Gospel Herald,* the official publication of the Mennonite Church and the March issue of *Missionary Messenger.* It also appeared in the March issue of *World Vision Magazine.* The Committee of Concern on Vietnam in Harrisonburg, Virginia, headed by Eugene Souder—printed several thousand of the statement which were distributed to the congressional offices of all the senators and representatives in Washington.

The Letter identified the writers as Mennonite missionaries who were not speaking "as political commentators or final authorities." Rather, being witness to the increased suffering of the people, we were compelled to declare our "concern for the moral issues" of American actions in Vietnam.

The Letter referred to the long struggle of the Vietnamese for independence with the Americans replacing the colonial French, noting that many who once supported American assistance were "now fearful of domination and destruction." But this basic issue was now "overshadowed by the war itself and the way it [was] being conducted."

"We do not condone the atrocities and terror of the other side," the statement said, while asserting that the United States was primarily responsible for the "massive destruction of their life, property, and social order." We believed "that such primary reliance on military force [was] insuring defeat of the goals being sought."

The letter then noted how the American involvement negatively influenced peoples' perceptions of the Christian faith:

> The world gets the impression that the Christians' God is behind our country's action in Vietnam. They see pictures of church leaders and chaplains with the US troops and hear that our president prays God to bless "our pilots" on their missions of destruction. Since we are generally regarded as a Christian nation, Christianity itself is entangled in America's military ventures and political policies.
>
> This is a call to all Christians to become aware of the image being given to our faith. We sense a continuing rejection of this religion of the wealthy, white, warring West, for which we all bear responsibility. We fear that nations may close their doors and multitudes will be deaf to God's call because of the American Christian's participation in and support of this war.

The Letter did not criticize the South Vietnamese government, nor did it propose specific corrective action. But it did call for a change of policies:

> In light of these serious offenses against social justice, human life, and the Christian faith, we therefore plead for a true consideration for the interests and needs of the Vietnamese majority; a change of heart which will not only admit but also accept the consequences of past failures and mistakes against these people; a change of policy and tactics which will show them that our primary concern is for their own well-being, self-respect and independence; a tolerant spirit which would not force others to line up with us, but rather seek to understand their feelings and views; [and] a fresh demonstration of our confession that in Christ there is no East or West.

The Letter was signed by James Stauffer, Everett and James Metzler, Donald Sensenig, Luke Beidler, and me.

In late November James Stauffer wrote his mother: "Oh, the sorrows of being draft age in this troubled land." He then described conversations with young Christian men. One expected to be drafted into the army within a few months. "He doesn't want to go but like the rest feels there is no other choice," James wrote. "Don and I are having some good conversations with these young believers. They know what some Christians do about war but they feel it wouldn't work here. We believe the Spirit is at work and we want to keep on being peacemakers."

Stauffer then described visiting in the home of a very militant Catholic student. "They think that America is doing the right thing," he wrote. "They would even advocate atomic bombing of China. It was pathetic to see the hate and extremism in their words and attitudes."

Stauffer continued: "There is a lot of fighting going on all around us here again. We are about two miles from the Saigon River and every night there is shooting going on there throughout the night. This war is awful. The fighting at Dak To has taken the heaviest toll of lives on both sides yet. Don Sensenigs received a letter from a medic from his home community that is serving here. He said there are so many women and children getting killed. This war (or any war) is so senseless!"

In the December *News and Concerns*, Everett and Margaret Metzler wrote: "Total mobilization clouds the future of all young men and their families. . . . More and more we are hearing, 'What is the point of fighting?' The optimism that U.S. officials perennially articulate is not shared by us or many Vietnamese." They noted that around 200 students had registered for English classes at the Saigon youth center, many of them young men "hoping that a knowledge of English will be helpful if they cannot escape the mobilization that is to affect all men from eighteen to thirty-three years of age with the new year."

After Phan Ba Phuoc expressed interest in being a missionary to the ethnic minority people, the Mennonite Mission requested a deferment so he might be able to take seminary training the following year. But Phuoc was not deferred.

In early December, James and Rachel sent a letter, printed later in *Missionary Messenger*, thanking people for praying for their work in Saigon. "It is not easy to accept identification with the horrible, immoral things which our fellow Americans are engaged in here. In the midst of such destruction, disruption, and demoralization, it is difficult not to become hardened, bitter, or discouraged."

After nearly five years in Vietnam, Mary and I were happy to be back in the United States and to introduce our children to two sets of grandparents and to our wider family. We lived in a mobile home near Mary's parents. Kraybill suggested that I enroll in a two-year seminary program, and I found this academic year exciting.

Weekends were busy. I accepted many Sunday morning invitations to preach. There were frequent Sunday evening engagements as well. Mary and I were invited to talk about Vietnam —about its people and culture. We told about the war and the terror it was bringing to the people. Often asked specifically what the Vietnamese people thought about the war and the American involvement, I would explain that the Vietnamese themselves did not share a common agreement about the war. Some people, I would explain, were very much opposed to the communist ideology and were very grateful for the American military forces there. Then there were those strongly opposed to the American political and military involvement in their country. Most of the people were somewhere on a continuum between those two views.

I soon concluded that this was not adequately representing the concerns of the people I had learned to identify with. Struggling to find a satisfactory way of speaking to Mennonite audiences,

ARVN soldiers.

I explained that, while the Vietnamese people did not agree about a political solution, there was strong agreement that the war itself was the overriding concern. The strategy of attrition and the massive American military firepower was bringing death to hundreds of thousands of combatants and civilians, and people wanted peace.

I was schooled in the Mennonite view that we Christians committed to the way of the Kingdom inaugurated by Jesus Christ were called to live a life of nonresistant love in all our relationships. Leaders of nations lived by the rule of power politics in the kingdom ruled by the powers of the world. While we could condemn the Vietnam War—indeed all wars—as evil and outside the will of God, we still had to respect our national leaders who, in spite of wars, still attempted to bring some order into human society. Now, however, I could not support the policies of the United States government which had chosen to fight in a poor Southeast Asian country and was raining death on its people.

On October 17, just a month after he resigned, I heard former Vietnam IVS leader, Don Luce, speak to 300 persons at a meeting sponsored by the Princeton University Faculty Council on Vietnam. I wanted to join some seminarians going to Washington to participate in the demonstrations sponsored by the National Mobilization Committee to End the War in Vietnam, but I had commitments at home and in churches.

Even though the issues of the war were complex, I knew that I needed to take some specific steps to help bring peace to Vietnam. "Inaction is worse than making a few mistakes," I had written.

I later took part in a large anti-Vietnam-War demonstration in Washington. I was initially disturbed to see a contingent of anarchists marching, and asked myself why I was keeping company with people who held those views. But I quickly resolved this concern. I did not need to agree with all the positions of others. I was willing to join with others committed to stopping the American reign of terror bringing death to so many. In 1961, the Mennonite Church had affirmed a statement on *The Christian Witness to the State* that supported a much more active peace witness than had previously been affirmed. I was convinced that we needed to confront the authorities who were perpetuating the war on an innocent people.

How my thinking had changed in five years was highlighted in my interactions with the pastor of my New Holland, Pennsylvania, church. Drafted during World War II, Frank Shirk served in several Civilian Public Service camps including a mental hospital in New York State. Released after the war ended, he volunteered to serve two years with an MCC building unit in

France. I as a fifteen year-old lad had great admiration for him. Later he became pastor of our congregation.

Our friendship was tested during our year in the States. I respected Frank's time-tested views of non-resistance and non-involvement in governmental policies as practiced by the church. Yet I was compelled by my Vietnam experience to a more active confrontation of the U.S. government's military policies in Vietnam. The gospel stories of Jesus required an interpretation adequate to the situation in which we lived. The story Jesus told his questioner who asked, "Who is my neighbor?" not only pointed to binding up the wounds of the injured man. It asked, "What must be done to prevent the robbers from beating up and killing others who come down the road?"

People from most congregations were supportive. But the seismic changes of the sixties decade were taking a toll within Lancaster Mennonite Conference. After the Mennonite Church adopted a new *Mennonite Confession of Faith* (1963), a significant minority of Lancaster Conference leaders requested a release from the Conference in 1968 and formed the Eastern Pennsylvania Mennonite Church.

I was not the only person asking the leaders of the New Holland congregation to rethink the church's position vis-à-vis the United States government. Soon after our family returned to the States, a men's group—which included the pastor—received a letter from my brother Earl. Responding to a letter from their group, Earl rather dramatically described some recent incidents which brought death to the child of a refugee woman with whom he worked in Quang Ngai.

"You gentlemen asked honest questions about how you could legitimately become involved in these 'miscarriages of justice' and then you went on to assure me and yourselves that you are praying for peace in Vietnam," Earl wrote,

> . . . and for this I am grateful. I don't mean to be cynical but what if I should tell this woman that I have a group of friends in America who are praying for her. And I know your prayers are sincere but if she asks a fish, can we give her the stone of sterile words?
>
> I believe that sincere prayer will stir people to action. . . . I think I'm just a bit troubled that if the church is really concerned about the injustices going on in the world, why is she so hesitant to become involved in speaking out against these wrongs and seeking a stronger course of action to rectify these maladies? If the church is really concerned, why does it continue to make the nation-state its god? Why do we continue to think in terms that probably God is on our side? . . .
>
> In this crucible of international dealings and power politics I am beginning to understand that in a democracy, as we are privileged to have, silence most often means assent. I hope the church will not fail.

By the end of 1967, the number of U.S. troops in Vietnam was nearing the half million mark. More than nine thousand U.S. soldiers died during the year, and more than one hundred thousand Vietnamese.

TET MAU THAN 1968

Chapter 28

MCC Executive Secretary, William Snyder, was planning another visit to Vietnam in early January 1968 with Atlee Beechy, the first VNCS director. MCC Asia Director, Paul Longacre, said it was time "for a real hard look at VNCS." Vietnam Christian Service had been functioning for two years and most of the international personnel were in Vietnam for more than a year, some nearly two years. It was time to review VNCS's organization pattern and how it was viewed by the Evangelical Church, the Mennonite Mission, and the Vietnamese government.

Longacre told them to listen to the personnel on field assignments—persons like Sanford Stauffer who traveled frequently throughout South Vietnam. From them Snyder could get perspectives beyond that of the Saigon administrative team: Director Paul Leatherman, Personnel Director Sam Hope, and Program Directors Gerry Aaker and Neil Brenden. "One of Atlee's primary tasks," Longacre wrote, "should be to study what is happening to people working in such a difficult situation and under such tremendous pressures." During 1967, ten persons terminated early, six for medical and four for personal reasons.

Referring to the cooperative effort of MCC, Lutheran World Relief and Church World Service, Longacre said that CWS administrator James MacCracken does not want VNCS "to do anything that will compromise the traditional Mennonite Central Committee pattern of service." However, Longacre reflected,

> In several areas I think we may be compromising our position in accommodation to the other groups and the personnel they send. Our living is a bit too affluent. We are probably closer to the USAID and C&MA missionary pattern of living than to the Vietnamese; commissary privileges are too attractive. The traditional MCC pattern of living in units is very modified in Vietnam. Privacy is worshipped. . . . The pressure of . . . producing statistics is probably too great. It's subtle, probably does not all come from CWS, but it may be telling on the integrity of the whole effort and compromising MCC's tradition. CWS is always yelling about needing the most professional, most skilled, most competent highly-trained specialists in Vietnam. Some of these persons are needed, but I think the emphasis may be deterring us from our most unique ministry.
>
> More attention needs to be given to our identification in the country. We are dependent upon the US government for logistical support . . . , but [this] can easily lead on to other compromises. Identification often relates closely to productivity. To really get something done one often needs to use US government or military resources. Is our productivity expectation too high, which forces us to compromise our position, or the needs of [those] we are trying to serve so great that compromise is an ethical necessity?

Doug Hostetter was asking why assistance was given to only one side in the conflict while living under the protection of the U.S. and South Vietnamese government. Longacre said this question must be addressed: "Are we taking every opportunity to minister to the other side? Are we preoccupied with security? Is MCC really recruiting and placing clear-thinking dedicated personnel in locations such as Tam Ky where effective ministry to both sides can take place?"

Although the war continued unabated, there was hope that it would eventually end, so Longacre said that VNCS also had to initiate post-hostility planning.

Paul Leatherman, VNCS director, said the main goal of the Snyder-Beechy visit would be evaluation and program planning. "Hopefully a five-year program projection with various alternatives which would include both the contingency of a continuing war and also sudden peace at some future date," Leatherman wrote.

The 1968 lunar New Year, *Tết Mậu Thân*, was coming January 30. Plans were made for all VNCS personnel to meet in a retreat at Da Lat University over the lunar New Year holiday, February 2 through 7.

Snyder and Beechy arrived in Saigon on Sunday, January 28. Snyder, a member of the International Voluntary Service executive board, spent the next day with IVS administrative group. It was a stressful day because IVS was dealing with the mysterious assassination two days earlier of David Gitelson, a very effective agriculturalist in the Mekong delta who was known to have a Viet Cong safe travel pass.

In a letter to his home pastor, Rev. Floyd Bartel, Snyder wrote:

I have never had an afternoon and evening of greater soul searching as an American and as a Christian than the time I spent with these IVSers. Most of these people are not conscientious objectors—in fact some of them have military service behind them—but all are troubled with the US government policies on Vietnam. There is a growing anti-Americanism everywhere, not only on the part of the Viet Congs but also the general populace of Vietnam. The reason is that the US has practically taken over the operation of this country and in addition, is creating thousands of refugees in both rural and urban areas as the bombing and shelling continue. I don't want to oversimplify, but those of us who are concerned people must urge our government to reconsider its present policies that are taking us to disaster.

Several members of the Mennonite Economic Development Associates (MEDA), Ivan Martin, Henry J. Pankratz, and A. A. DeFehr, arrived in Vietnam the same day. On Monday, Beechy went with them to visit the VNCS medical project in Nha Be, just south of Saigon.

On Tuesday morning, these visitors spent most of the morning with the Mennonite missionaries to bring them up-to-date on VNCS planning and "to get their viewpoints on the Vietnam situation." Snyder was pleased with the MCC-VNCS support of the sponsorship programs at the Gia Dinh community center.

"The great thing about the missionaries," Snyder wrote, "is that they see so clearly the immorality and the problem created by the American presence as it is now being felt through the war effort. There is no clearer position being taken by Mennonites at home or abroad than by this small group of Eastern Board people. They have reinforced my conviction that we must continue to speak to the authorities at home on the issues of the war and what it is doing to these people."

The next day was for the history books. Tuesday night and early Wednesday morning, January 31, the Viet Cong attacked several spots in the Saigon area, among them the ARVN headquarters at the Tan Son Nhut Air base. The most spectacular attack came against the U.S. Embassy in downtown Saigon. Sappers planted explosives at the thick concrete fence, blowing a hole through the eight-foot high wall, and quickly entered the Embassy grounds. Although the grounds were secured by American reinforcements within six hours, this daring attack belied Gen. Westmoreland's declarations that the VC were being defeated and that there was "light at the end of the tunnel."

Within a short time VNCS confirmed that all their Saigon personnel were accounted for. But the Viet Cong had simultaneously attacked more than one hundred cities and towns throughout the country on January 30 and 31. On February 1, VNCS cabled Akron that they had "no information yet from units but assume everything is OK," an optimistic assessment based only on hope. The VNCS medical personnel who worked at Nha Be were in Saigon when the attacks began.

James Stauffer wrote to his mother:

> Well, at last the war has come to Saigon. Things have been just too quiet and gay to be true. Not exactly quiet because all day Monday (29th) the firecrackers were building up to one great gigantic climax at midnight. Most of the people seemed to be having a happy Tet. At 2:50 a.m. on Wednesday (31st) things changed. We were awoken by a loud explosion followed by small arms fire. Mortar rounds were pouring into the downtown area about two miles from us. I went up on the roof and could pinpoint the sound by the Post Office tower. Fighting would break out at other points around the city. The circling flare-ship went into action over the downtown area. It was soon joined by two more plus Huey choppers and Skyraiders. For the rest of the day we were to hear the constant drone of aircraft.

While Stauffer described the military activity bringing death to the city, yet from his relative safety he viewed with fascination the high tech Allied military machines:

> During a lull in the morning I went over to the [community] center. While there I saw for the first time the Hueys with machine guns in operation. They were circling about a mile away at the edge of the city. Even from that distance the sound of their guns was deafening. In the afternoon we saw the Cobras, a revised version of the Huey, operate about a mile away in another area. This was even more awesome. They fired rockets and mini-guns. The mini-gun is a small bore machine gun with seven barrels that rotate so each barrel has a chance to cool. They can fire 6,000 rounds a minute. The sound is hard to describe—perhaps the nearest thing to it is a fog horn on a ship. It is just one big "Burr-r-r-r"!
>
> We saw and heard the Skyraiders diving down firing 20mm cannon, rocket and dropping bombs. Last night they provided "fireworks"—that is, we could see the tracer bullets and the flash of their rockets igniting, etc. The Hueys were also operating downtown and the streams of red tracers were pretty if it wasn't so tragic.
>
> Several very sharp firefights broke out around us. About 9 p.m. I was up on the roof watching one about a mile away. I could hear the bullets zinging above me. Then another one broke out at a police station about one-half mile away. It only lasted about two or three minutes but was sure hot, thick and fast.

The Stauffer and Sensenig families living in Gia Dinh city northeast of metropolitan Saigon soon established contact with Everett and Margaret Metzler at the Saigon office. But nothing was heard from James and Rachel Metzler, who had moved to the Phu Tho area of northwest Saigon a few months earlier to begin an evangelistic witness there. From the rooftop of the Saigon Student Center, it was quite evident that the Phu Tho area—just two kilometers away—was caught up in the fighting. And Luke and Dorothy Beidler were in Da Lat for a short vacation break.

On February 2, the story of the attacks in Ban Me Thuot bringing injury and death to Alliance missionaries sent shockwaves throughout the missionary community. The view that missionaries were not targeted by the VC was no longer a safe assumption. Five Alliance missionaries were killed: N. Robert Ziemer, Carl Edward and Ruth Stebbins Thompson, Ruth Wilting and Leon Griswold. Carolyn Griswold died later. Missionary Betty Olsen and Henry (Hank) Blood, a linguist with the Summer Institute of Linguistics, were captured along with Mike Benge, a former IVSer who was now working with USAID. (Olsen and Blood died in captivity. James C & Marti Henley tell this story in *By Life or by Death* and *No Time for Tombstones* [Harrisburg, PA: Christian Publications, 1974].)

Ruth Wilting had been engaged to Daniel Gerber, the MCC Pax man abducted from the Ban Me Thuot Leprosarium in May 1962 along with Archie Mitchell and Ardel Vietti. After the abduction, the expatriate leprosarium personnel moved into the C&MA facilities in Ban Me Thuot. Later, Ruth went to Pleiku where she held clinics for leprosy patients and engaged in evangelistic work. Now Ruth became a casualty of the war that had claimed her fiancé nearly six years earlier.

At 5:30 a.m., on January 31, Rachel and James Metzler were awakened by the sound of "fireworks." Soon louder explosions convinced them that they were hearing rifle and exploding mortar fire. They and Brian huddled against an inside wall for protection. When the disturbance died down they relaxed. As they prepared breakfast their next-door neighbor, the owner of their house burst through the side door and in a loud whisper shouted, "There are Viet Cong out in the street!" He warned them to close all doors and shutters and stay out of sight. He told them that at 5:30 a.m. many guerrilla soldiers moving portable guns and carrying VC flags had passed by and that six dead bodies lay on the street, including two American military police. Then the owner's wife ran into their kitchen, reporting that an American in civilian clothes had stopped his jeep in their driveway. Concerned that one of the other missionaries might have come in the Jeep station wagon looking for them, James hurried to the front door, seeing a man he did not recognize. James watched, dazed, as the man darted from tree to tree, wildly firing his pistol in the direction of the Viet Cong AK-47 automatic rifles.

Telephone service was hard to secure in Saigon, and expensive, so the phone at the Saigon headquarters was the only phone the Mennonite Mission had. Not wanting to risk life trying to contact the others, the Metzler family stayed put. The radio was still playing its normal soothing music and had not yet announced that the VC had attacked other areas of the city. Assuming that the Americans and South Vietnamese troops—the ARVN—would be counter-attacking the VC, the Metzlers quickly built a bunker inside their small house, for the tin roof, fiberboard ceiling and four-inch honeycombed brick walls were not much protection against a modern arsenal of weapons. Arranging three steel drums in the back bedroom with a mattress on the floor and boards and other mattresses on top, they prepared for a long siege. They packed suitcases with valuables and necessities should they decide to flee.

By noon helicopters were swarming overhead firing rockets and machine guns into the street intersection near their home. James describes it in *From Saigon to Shalom* (Scottdale, PA: Herald Press, 1983):

> As we huddled together in our bunker, I faced stark, uncontrollable fear. With emotions already strained from the hours of suspense, I kept repeating Psalm 23 and the Lord's Prayer, but it did nothing to ease the trembling.

The terrifying din of war swirling around us defies description. The mini-cannons on the US helicopters right overhead sounded like the worst gear-grinding noise one can imagine. This was punctuated by the hiss and explosion of the rockets they fired. Beneath that was the steady chatter of tanks and rifle fire. All around us bullets were popping, while fragments pinged on the tin roof and concrete courtyard. Afterward I counted twelve holes in the side of the dormer above our room, several of them as large as a fist.

As the battle noise died down, the Metzlers heard a man shouting "House on fire!" A rocket had struck a new house just two doors away, located across an alleyway from a lumber shed. Neighbors quickly formed a bucket brigade and managed to extinguish the flames. Not everyone was so fortunate; James saw billows of smoke from fires consuming homes nearby. Everyone was edgy as the VC forces roamed the area. Sweaty American GIs walked through their house in a house-to-house search for guerrillas. The armed forces set up a camp and munitions dump in the race track across the street to resupply the helicopters, thus making the area a prime target for VC mortar attacks. Electricity was cut off and by the second day there was no water.

In those days of waiting, James reflected on life and death. If a rocket had obliterated their house they would have become mere statistics of the war. If the VC had come into their house with guns blazing, they would have been killed as hated Americans. Few neighbors would have had any understanding of why they were there at that particular time in history.

"I concluded that night that I simply was not ready to die for a cause I couldn't believe in, much less support," James wrote later. "Though I would continue to work and witness as best I could in that broken, bleeding land for two more years, I would never feel the same about being in Vietnam."

By Sunday, February 4, five days after the first attack, things had quieted down so that James and Rachel considered risking a dash with Brian by scooter to the Mission office. Then Don Sensenig appeared at the door and through tears said, "Praise the Lord, you're safe. We surely were worried about you."

Don told them that Margaret and Everett were inviting them to come to the headquarters building, so they quickly gathered a few items and left. Since the office was located across the street from the People's Hospital, they considered this a fairly safe place. The ARVN, however, did build a sandbagged pillbox on the front sidewalk of the Mission office. A few days later, James heard a radio message reporting that a VC battalion was operating in the area of the Phu Tho race track from where James and Rachel had fled.

Doris Sensenig wrote to her parents in her matter of fact style: "The city folks got a taste of [war] the last few days and there was nothing nice about it."

Doris said she awoke the morning of January 31, poked Don, and said, "I don't think that's firecrackers." Don eventually got up and prepared to leave for an early morning tennis game with James Stauffer, but Doris still thought she heard machine gun fire!

Don spent most of Wednesday and Thursday on their house roof with the binoculars, and was concerned that government soldiers would want to use their house for observation which might draw fire from the VC. The Sensenig and Stauffer families and VNCS personnel who lived nearby were able to stay in their homes. The Sensenigs had forty "refugees" staying in the first floor of their house—many of them families of Mennonite community center staff.

Luke and Dorothy Beidler, vacationing in Da Lat, were in real danger. Da Lat had been a kind of peaceful island in the midst of the Vietnam conflict and there were reports that leaders from both sides of the conflict came there to recover and rest. But early January 31, the VC seized all the roads leading into the mountain city and sent in a large number of troops. Beidlers were staying in the area of the former Alliance missionary school compound where several missionaries lived; this area was now surrounded by guerrilla soldiers. Their most apparent danger was from ARVN artillery, but they did not know the intentions of the Viet Cong soldiers. Some of the missionaries wanted to wait it out, believing that local VC would not harm them because they had tried to project a neutral stance. But news of the killings of their missionary colleagues in Ban Me Thuot shook them. One of the C&MA missionaries had a pistol ready in case they were attacked, saying, "If they come to try and get us, I'm going to take some of them with me." He did not say where he was taking them.

On February 3, they requested evacuation. A U.S. Army signal company sent a heavily armed convoy into the missionary compound and evacuated thirty-four persons—Beidlers among them—who were flown by helicopter to the U.S. air base at Cam Ranh Bay on the coast. The VC did not interfere with their leaving. This experience convinced the Beidlers that, should it ever be deemed necessary to flee the country, they would leave early rather than rely on later evacuation by military forces.

On the first day of the attacks, more than two hundred injured persons were admitted to the Binh Dan Hospital across the street from the student center and office. A week later traffic was again flowing normally and many markets had reopened. Yet fires were still burning only a few blocks away. Everett wrote to Mission headquarters: "We pray that this madness will soon end. We want to assure you that we are taking reasonable precautions and that we do not feel in any great danger."

Nha Trang was also attacked, but the area around the Evangelical clinic and hospital on the edge of Nha Trang was not invaded by VC forces. Yet U.S. military personnel urged the VNCSers to leave the hospital area at night. On Thursday, February 8, pastors and other friends around the hospital urged them to go into the center of town due to reports that North Vietnamese troops of the Peoples' Liberation Army were in the area. Most of the staff went into Nha Trang, but Dr. Gehman and Ruth Yoder stayed. The next evening, a helicopter landed in the front courtyard to take all the VNCSers into the city during the night. They traveled back to the clinic in the morning.

A few days later, Atlee Beechy visited Nha Trang, and he and James Bowman spoke with a Colonel Weigman, expressing thanks for his concern, but emphasizing that they prefer to get their security information from the Evangelical Hospital staff.

The VNCS staff at the Pleiku Clinic spent a whole day huddled in an inside bathroom, There was a skirmish near the house where the single people lived; all the staff were able to flee the gruesome scene to a nearby airbase. The Viet Cong then used the headquarters house as a fortification from which to shoot at American and ARVN forces.

In the central highlands north of Pleiku and Kon Tum, the town of Dat To was attacked on January 30, and the market and surrounding houses were bombed and destroyed by the next morning. There were relatively few civilian casualties, however, and VNCSer Bill Rose was able to distribute clothing and blankets through the Catholic and Evangelical clergy.

The VNCS team in Di Linh was lifted from the area by American army helicopters. In Quang Ngai, though the area was attacked, the unit personnel stayed. The district town of Nghia Hanh was completely taken over; Earl Martin, who worked there, was in Quang Ngai at the time.

Most of the refugees at Nghia Hanh fled the camps and returned to their native mountains and valleys to the west. VNCS provided CSM, other food and clothing to some 7,000 people in the Rung Lang and Bau Giang camps on the edge of Quang Ngai.

The VC captured the provincial headquarters in Tam Ky and held it for two days, occupying other parts of the town for six days. Although the VC soldiers were around the unguarded high school compound where Doug Hostetter and Bill Herod lived, they did not come into their rooms. When food was not available in town, the local pastor invited the two men to his home. On February 3 when Doug went to the home of a friend, an ARVN soldier, who lived just outside town, the road was still littered with bodies "from the ages of four to seventy!" The people had organized an anti-government, anti-war demonstration that morning, and government troops were ordered to fire on them. The marchers carried only bamboo walking sticks!

Doug described to his parents "the worst night [he had] ever spent." At 1:00 a.m., January 31, he was awakened by the sound of AK-47 automatic rifles outside his window; he instantaneously fell to the floor while shooting continued. An hour later, several VC soldiers went house to house, knocking on doors and questioning the occupants. When they came to a house just seven meters from his room, Doug was "never . . . so scared" in his life. He wrote: "I had always imagined how I would answer the VC if they ever came into my room, how I would calmly explain in perfect Vietnamese what I was doing and why I was here. Well, when I heard them next door, my knees and arms were shaking uncontrollably and my stomach was doing flips. I don't think I could have even spoken a word of Vietnamese if I had been spoken to. . . . I could plainly hear every word that the VC said even after they had entered the [neighbor's] house." Not knowing whether the guerrillas holed up or left the area, Doug waited, then crawled back to bed at 4:00 and slept fitfully until daybreak.

(Years later, Doug learned that an older brother of Le Dinh Sung, a local artist and his closest friend in Tam Ky, had been a high-level NLF official in the province. After the war this brother was appointed province chief in the new government. Doug says: "I came to realize that Le Dinh Sung and his family were true friends to a young American who had made a sincere attempt to live at peace in the midst of a bitter and deadly war. I also realized that on the many occasions when the NLF took over Tam Ky while I was there, God's protection had received some assistance from Le Dinh Sung's brothers on the other side.")

Gayle Preheim was at Dong Ha, the town in Quang Tri province seventy-seven kilometers north of Hue and just twenty-two kilometers from the Ben Hai River, the demarcation line between North and South Vietnam. Here VNCS persons worked at providing vocational training, digging community wells and feeding refugee children. The U.S. Marine Corps had set up a major command and logistics base in Dong Ha. At the end of January there were reportedly 66,000 troops from the northern People's Army of Vietnam (PAVN) in the province. In his diary for January 31, Preheim wrote:

> Tonight there is an almost constant rumble of war. . . . Rifle and machine gun fire could be heard across the river on both sides of town. . . . Here in Dong Ha, they drove around with big speakers saying Hue and Quang Tri [twelve kilometers south] had been hit, to be on the alert. I considered going to the base for the night, but decided against it. These are the people I live and work with. I can leave; they cannot. I could not face them if I left. I'm tired but really rather afraid—not so much of tonight, but the future of things up here.

On February 2, he wrote: "Just 15 minutes ago the word reached us that the NVA had entered town. The first we knew . . . was when people started running. The news spread like wildfire. Everybody locked up and put the lights out. The town is now dark and dead except for soldiers in the streets."

Preheim was concerned that the presence of VNCS personnel might endanger the friends and coworkers. Even though friends encouraged them to spend several nights at the U.S. military compound for safety, Prehiem wrote: "Not only is this definitely not in keeping with the philosophy of our organization, but it is an inconvenience to the military who are busy enough fighting a war."

One week after the Tet offensive began, the VNCS Saigon office had still not received any message from their six persons working with World Relief Commission in Hue: Harlan and Pauline Hochstetler, Kenneth Keefer, Paul Kennel, Jerry Sandoz and June Sauder. All that was known is that the VC had seized large parts of Hue city. It was not until late February 8, that Akron received a cable from William Snyder: "All Hue personnel safe." This was perceived as a miracle—an answer to the prayers of many people.

The People's Army of Vietnam—from the North—seized virtually the entire city of Hue, holding parts of the old citadel in the northern part of the city for a month. There was massive loss of life among all parties. The VC flag flew over the Old Citadel on the north side of the Huong River until February 29. All VNCS personnel lived on the south side of the river.

At 4:00 a.m., on January 31, June Sauder was awakened by artillery fire, and soon Pauline and Harlan Hochstetler joined her huddling in the inner hallway of their house at 38 Nguyen Hue Street. When dawn arrived, they peeked behind window shades, startled to see soldiers in unfamiliar uniforms and quickly realized that they were not ARVN troops. At another house more than a block away, four MCC guys were also shaken by the battle sounds—Paul Kennel, Jerry Sandoz, and Kenneth Keefer, all working with WRC, plus Harley Kooker, visiting them from Dong Ha. During a lull in the fighting around 9:00 a.m., they jumped into a pickup truck and drove to the house where June and the Hochstetler couple were staying, still not aware that North Vietnamese troops were swarming around the city. Soon they also saw the men in khaki uniforms camouflaged with tree branches carrying mortar tubes and machine guns through the streets. (Omar Eby tells this story in *A House in Hue* [Scottdale, PA: Herald Press, 1968]).

January 31, was a long day. Lunch was not appetizing. While sitting in the living room during the afternoon, a bullet zipped through the window screen between the heads of two of the guys. That night, before a fitful night of sleep, the seven recited together the Twenty-Third Psalm.

The next day—Day 2—they saw two of their friends from USAID being marched down the street with their arms tied behind their backs; one was Tom Ragsdale, an agriculturalist friend of June. That night, as artillery shells exploded nearby, the seven hurried down into the ten-by-five foot bunker built under the floor of the hallway which they had cleaned out that day. Shortly after breakfast the third day they heard an American truck coming down the street and watched in horror as People's Army of Vietnam troops opened up with machine guns, killing both U.S. Marines.

On Saturday, Day 4, Paul, Ken and Harley hurried over to their house, quickly grabbing food, water and other supplies and scurrying back. Outside their house they met two Americans who warned them that PAVN troops still occupied the area. On Sunday, they saw these troops outside, and throughout the day and into the night there was heavy fighting all around them. Heavy artillery shells rained down in the area; while none struck their house, some fell within one foot of the walls. Much of the day and night were spent in the bunker.

On Monday, Day 6, they again saw PAVN troops on the street. June's cook, Chi Hai, who had come over a few days earlier, warned them not to step outside the house because the soldiers were around the house. They were now rationing their food and water. That evening heavy artillery again pounded their area and many of them spent the whole night in the bunker. The next morning they surveyed the damage; all the drapes were knocked down and the windows blown out; the living room facing the street had several gaping holes. On Wednesday morning, Day 8, allied tanks were firing on the street. When by mid-morning they no longer saw PAVN troops on the street, they voiced hope that their ordeal might soon be coming to an end.

On Day 9, Thursday, February 8, they heard and saw children playing amid the rubble. When American Marines came down the street they hurried out to meet the surprised soldiers who took them to the MACV compound where they were questioned by international journalists who relayed the news to the world, then boarded a military landing craft on the Perfume River for a seven-hour ride south to Da Nang. The seven were indeed grateful for surviving this terror—thankful also that no military force had been used to protect them or to rescue them.

Their house was the only house in Hue occupied by Americans that the VC did not enter. And several of their marked vehicles were parked outside the house. Were the soldiers told to avoid their house? This is not known. (A few years later, however, when Kooker was in the States he received from an official U.S. agency translated notes of VC documents showing the exact times the WRC persons went to work at the training school. The document said "they are no threat to our cause.")

For a few days after the initial Tet attacks in Saigon, a twenty-four hour curfew prevented VNCS personnel from working out of their office and Snyder's room at the Majestic Hotel became the center of operational response. Dr. Linford Gehman, who had earlier come down from Nha Trang, soon joined Dr. Marilyn Strayer and several nurses in caring for the many displaced persons.

ARVN forces in Saigon used artillery to destroy buildings that provided cover for the VC forces. Hundreds of civilians died in Saigon and thousands were made homeless. Early on the third day of the offensive, VC forces occupied a large two-story building at an intersection just a block from the Stauffer home. The VC told the civilians to leave and began firing at police and military personnel with machine guns. ARVN forces counter attacked, but feared the B-40 shoulder-launched rockets the VC were firing. Eventually, Huey helicopter gunships armed with rockets and machine guns attacked their positions. When rockets started several fires that spread to nearby homes, Arlene and James packed a suitcase in case they needed to flee their home. After fifty-two hours the VC faded away from this area.

"There is no end in sight," Stauffer wrote. "Last night we were awake most of the time from 3:30 on listening and watching a new battle develop about 1 ½ miles away. Thousands of people have been streaming down our street all morning."

Several Viet Cong local force battalions attacked Vietnamese military headquarters in the Go Vap area, located only a few kilometers from the Mennonite community center and the VNCS unit house, Em Dem. Vietnamese and American units countered with a massive military response that destroyed hundreds of houses. Many of the homeless sought shelter in schools and other large buildings or erected temporary shelters. The government refugee ministry asked Americans to keep away from the scene of relief operations for fear of snipers.

David Neufeld, a Canadian, pondered what it meant to be a Christian pacifist in Vietnam. Just after promising families who were digging through the rubble of their homes that he and others would return the following day with water and other assistance, he learned that Social Welfare Minister Nguyen Phuc Que had asked all voluntary agency international personnel to stay out of the stricken areas for a few days. After being mistaken for an American by neighbors who refused to allow him to use their phone, obviously not wanting to interact with Americans, Neufeld was "just about ready to leave Vietnam." He wrote. "The only Christ I know is the one who is also the Prince of Peace. When people fail to disassociate us from the American political and military effort, we really bring more hell and heartache to Vietnam than we do relief and comfort."

Pastor Tran Xuan Hi surveying damage to Thu Duc Tin Lanh church near Saigon.

T. Grady Mangham, now working in the C&MA New York office, flew to Saigon to take part in the memorial service on February 12 at the International Protestant Church for the missionaries killed in Ban Me Thuot.

Snyder prepared to leave Vietnam while Beechy stayed on to interview VNCS personnel. The two men prepared a memorandum regarding planning for 1968. It was "providential," they said, to face the crisis of the Tet offensive with the VNCS team. "It also gives us a clearer picture of the problems you will confront in the weeks ahead." In something of an understatement, they wrote: "Under present circumstances we do not feel that the longer term post-hostilities program can be given the adequate consideration necessary."

In a report to Mennonite churches in North America, Snyder and Beechy praised the dedicated and courageous relief workers and missionaries serving and witnessing under very tense and difficult conditions and called the church to "intensified prayer," to continued Bible study and effective practice of the church's peace witness and to support the relief ministries and reconciling work of the church including a witness to government leaders.

With programs disrupted and questions about ongoing security, many agencies asked dependents of service personnel to temporarily leave Vietnam. All VNCS wives and children were encouraged to evacuate to a nearby country for up to one month. Single women could also choose to evacuate but men were expected to remain at their assignments unless there were unusual circumstances. It was not clear whether personnel could return to Di Linh and Hue. There were also questions about returning to Pleiku since the clinic was located near an air base.

In the midst of these uncertainties, Doris Sensenig suffered an appendicitis attack; she got to the Adventist hospital before the evening curfew and underwent surgery the next morning. Luke and Dorothy Beidler helped the Sensenig family with cooking and child care. They told hair-raising stories about their Da Lat experience, the helicopter evacuation to Cam Ranh Bay and return to Saigon three days later.

The Mennonite Mission also authorized wives and dependents to leave temporarily. Rachel Metzler and son Brian left for Malaysia on February 17, along with several VNCS personnel, where they stayed at the Christian Convention Center on Penang Island. With the Phoenix Study Group planning to resume classes for the children on February 26, it was not clear when or whether Doris, Margaret and Arlene would leave with their children.

Though Saigon was still an armed camp, by mid-February curfew hours were shortened and markets had reopened. Missionaries became involved in local relief operations in the Gia Dinh areas near their homes. James Stauffer bought large quantities of rice wholesale and sold it at cost to families around the community center. Don Sensenig, James Metzler, Luke Beidler, Dave Neufeld, and Gayle Preheim worked with Go Vap Baptist Pastor Do Vinh Thanh and others in delivering water, bread and other food to the thousands of homeless persons in the area; most of them were crowded into school buildings and churches. No one else was providing this assistance.

This involved some risk from VC snipers still in the area. Although the Saigon government requested that Americans not become involved in the relief work for fear of snipers, it seemed that the real reason for attempting to "ground" the Americans was that the government wanted to be seen as the benefactor to the victims of this tragedy. Nevertheless, the missionaries found something to do. They were able to gain access to American controlled docks on the Saigon River and delivered eighty loads of wooden pallets and other packing materials which the displaced persons used to build temporary shelters and for firewood.

Don wrote to his folks in mid-February: "Luke [Beidler] and I are gone practically all day every day in various tasks connected with assistance and relief—hauling lumber, firewood, water, rice, liaison with others assisting refugees, trying to plan for immediate future and longer term rebuilding, etc. The situation is now much improved." The curfew hours were now 5:00 p.m. to 8:00 a.m., instead of an earlier 2:00 p.m. curfew. Interestingly, curfew began for international "white-faces types" at 7:00 p.m. instead of two hours earlier! "We feel our Gia Dinh center is strategically located to be of much help in ongoing relief," Don wrote.

Don told of being down at the docks getting a load of rice where he had a conversation with a man who lost several members of his family "mostly to American and Saigon government actions: helicopter machine gunning, bombs, strafing from planes, which are gunning for VC in heavily populated areas, and which mow down the people with the VC." Sometimes people were warned to flee an area before bombardment—other times, they were not warned; "the people [were] sacrificed to the military objective."

American radio reports spoke of allied forces killing ten Viet Cong while losing only one of their own soldiers. Don wrote: "It's a terrible thing, and it's an aspect of the war our self-righteous Embassy, military, Pentagon, White House, never, never mention. Their platitudes and 10-to-1 kill ratios they keep preaching just infuriate me. Some of those wool-headed hawks in our government are either just plain stupid and ignorant or else they are closing their eyes to some terrible realities. I have half a notion one of these days I'm going to go into the Embassy just to register my own personal feelings with someone, based on what I've seen and heard."

Closing with comments which hardly reassured his family, Don wrote: "We hope you all don't worry too much about us. We are living quite normally these days. Things are definitely much better and improving daily."

In the following week Doris wrote home to her family:

> The last two nights haven't been quiet . . . on the outskirts of Gia Dinh. Refugees were pouring back into the different centers again yesterday. There is no end, it seems. It is impossible to believe US casualty reports because we know many reported V.C. deaths are really civilians caught between the two sides. Much of the suffering is from the US government side, using big fire power in crowded areas to get a few VCs. . . . Don, Luke, Jim M. are still helping haul rice, firewood, lumber, etc. I'm glad for the 7 o'clock curfew because we can have the evenings together. They have been working real hard. We play Rook in the evening since I'm home from the hospital. It's quiet until we go to bed and then the shooting usually starts. The girls play as usual.

Mary and I were with our children in the States, living in a mobile home set up near her parents' home. During the first days of February, we tuned our small black and white TV set to the Vietnam news. Friends thought it fortunate that we were in the States during this urban fighting. We had mixed feelings, however. We did not like being absent from our Vietnamese friends and missionary colleagues during this difficult time.

Many U.S. and ARVN soldiers were killed in the Tet Offensive, thousands of civilians killed and injured and many persons left without their homes—nearly 400,000 in the Saigon area alone. Nevertheless, American and South Vietnamese leaders soon declared a huge Allied victory! Relying on their overwhelming firepower, they had inflicted staggering losses on the other side.

(So many southern guerrilla soldiers died that the role of the People's Army troops from the North became more prominent. This would have long-term implications for the revolution; when the war ended in 1975, the highly rigid Marxist northerners more easily pushed aside the less ideological southern revolutionaries.)

Before the Tet Offensive, VC troops had been told that these attacks on large population areas would result in a popular "uprising" of support for them. This did not happen. However, given the optimistic reports by Gen. Westmoreland and others in late 1967, the Tet Offensive dealt a serious psychological blow to the United States. Americans greeted the reports of Tet victories with skepticism.

Newsweek correspondent, Francis Sully, and Senior Editor, Arnaud de Borchgrave, interviewed some of the missionaries in mid-February. A few days earlier James Metzler sent an open letter to President Lyndon Johnson, citing the immorality of using massive firepower in Saigon—destroying many lives and much property. He noted that allied forces shot residents fleeing fires that incinerated their houses. While expressing distress for the suffering inflicted by the VC, he noted that the VC forces were more disciplined. "This is no attempt to tell the military how to wage war," he wrote, "but how can such a mighty nation brag of victory when fighting guerillas in city streets with planes and tanks? What justification is there for attacking snipers in densely populated areas with rockets and artillery?"

On February 27, Bishop H. Raymond Charles, the President of Eastern Mennonite Board of Missions, and Mahlon Hess sent a letter to the pastors of the Lancaster Mennonite Conference calling for a Day of Prayer for Vietnam on March 3. They called the *Letter from Vietnam to American Christians* "a thought-provoking statement of the basic issues in the conflict which was having a wide ministry."

Hess, of EMBMC information services, said: "People are eager to hear from persons on the spot whose judgment they trust, since so many things about the war are giving them doubts. Some other church groups [say] this is the clearest statement of the issues they have yet seen."

Clergy and Laymen Concerned about Vietnam organized a second mobilization in Washington, DC on Monday and Tuesday, February 5 and 6. With other seminary students I attended this event. Coming immediately after the beginning of the Tet offensive, it enabled the two thousand participants to get the attention of senators and representatives in a unique way. Speakers included John C. Bennett, Harvey G. Cox, William Sloan Coffin and civil rights leader Martin Luther King, Jr. Coffin called for civil disobedience. King asserted that the United States was not winning the "unjust" and "unwinnable" war. Tying the struggle for peace in Vietnam and the struggle for civil rights in America together, King said those working for civil rights and justice in the United States should also be striving for peace in Vietnam. He declared that "a genuine leader is not a searcher of consensus, but a molder of consensus. . . . There comes a time when one must take a position that is neither safe, nor politic, nor popular, but he must take it because conscience tells him it is right." King was assassinated two months later.

The Committee of Concern on Vietnam in Harrisonburg, Virginia, headed by Eugene Souder, printed 20,000 copies of *A Letter from Vietnam to American Christians*. Five thousand of these were distributed at the Washington meeting, and Souder got permission from the Sergeant at Arms to distribute these to all congressional offices—senators and representatives alike. Requests for the statement came from many states. A United Presbyterian pastor in Ohio requested a thousand copies. Souder declared: "We believe God led in the writing of this statement by our Mennonite missionaries. It can be a useful tool to help bring light and understanding to a most involved and difficult problem."

During this Washington event, I joined a small group to speak with Edwin Eshleman, the Republican Congressman from Pennsylvania's 16th Congressional District (Lancaster County). Though "hawkish" about the war, he advocated abolishing the draft.

The Tet Offensive continued in parts of Saigon for a few weeks. On Sunday, February 18, the Mennonite congregation had their first formal worship service in three weeks at the Community Center. James Stauffer wrote home: "We praise the Lord for protecting us to this moment." He then reported that three thousand civilians were killed by the fighting in Saigon and eight thousand injured, 80 percent caused by American planes and tanks. Everyone, he wrote, was more afraid of the Allied fire-power than of the VC forces. The Mennonite Community Center was distributing 500 loaves of bread daily and the clinic was giving cholera and plague shots. VNCS bought materials for mosquito nets, and the girls' sewing class and neighborhood women sewed these nets for distribution to the thousands of families whose homes were destroyed.

Doris Sensenig wrote home about a wild night at their home on February 20 when a student in their hostel went berserk. Hung had studied in Australia three years and spoke English well. Before coming to the hostel he had experienced mental illness. On this day, he got upset when his mother informed him that their house in Da Lat had been damaged in the fighting. Agitated by some nearby shooting that night, Hung declared he was an American citizen—Don Tennessee by name! He punched Don in the nose and demanded the keys to the VNCS Volkswagen pickup truck Don used to haul wood for refugees. Don tried to reason with him because the police were enforcing a strict curfew—if he drove out he would get shot. Hung replied, "How can their bullets hurt me? I'm the emperor!" Since Hung was trained in judo and had manhandled police, Don finally gave him the keys, then asked a neighbor who had military phone connections to try to get a message to the nearby roadblock that this man was mentally ill—not an attacking VC. Hung had trouble starting the pickup, but eventually took off. He had only gone a block when soldiers fired into the truck. Hung jumped out and ran, catching a bullet through his chest; fortunately, he survived. So did the VW pickup truck; though riddled with forty-one bullet holes, the truck still ran!

Doris ended her letter home: "After that night, I decided I wasn't strong enough to cope with that sort of thing and planned to go to Penang for a rest. It just left me weak and exhausted. But that might happen to anyone, I guess. The girls slept through it all, thank goodness. They sleep soundly every night, no matter how loud the artillery. Jean is the only one who seems to mind it and she doesn't understand it. Lynne asked if there is shooting in Penang and I said no, and she said 'hurray!' This is a hurray, isn't it?"

The missionaries spent significant time discussing whether to leave or stay. "It won't take too much more to get us out," Stauffer wrote home February 21. With a sentiment expressed by others he wrote, "I don't see much point in dying simply because we are Americans. If we would be killed because of our faith in Christ it would be a different matter." The next day, however, Paul Kraybill cabled a strong recommendation that the women and children, at least, transfer temporarily to another country. In a follow-up letter, Kraybill said that—should there be more attacks—the men might find it more difficult to stay if the wives and their children were there.

Dorothy Beidler—who was seven months pregnant—and the Sensenig family made plans to go to Malaysia. But the Everett Metzler and Stauffer families were staying because the Phoenix Study Group had just reopened in dispersed locations for their school-age children, even though the enrollment had dropped from 160 to only sixty-five students. The rocket attacks on Saigon's Tan Son Nhat air base continued almost daily.

Meanwhile, Don Sensenig, Luke Beidler, James Metzler and VNCSer Dave Neufeld continued with direct relief assistance. It was a confusing time—Americans and Canadian Dave trying to bring relief to the victims of American bombing raids with VC snipers still in the area. A clear rationale for their service was elusive—they only knew people had needs and they were in a position to help. Don coined the phrase which they all embraced: "Don't think! Just work!" In a mid-February memo to Orie Miller, the seventy-five-year-old MCC executive secretary emeritus, Bill Snyder said that the missionaries were helping the victims and also providing a good perspective to the MCC-VNCS administrators. "This is a rather exciting place for everybody," he wrote. "Although there are risks, there are also possibilities."

VNCS personnel in other places were finding things to do. In a March 3 letter from Tam Ky to "fellow Christians," Doug Hostetter told how that on the second day of the fighting, a Christian from one of the refugee camps came to report that much of the camp had burned. After determining that there was no fighting in that area, Doug and a student friend went out in their old Ford pickup truck to see what could be done. By two o'clock, some thirty Christian high school students were there cleaning up the still-burning rubble. Even though Tam Ky was still under a twenty-four hour curfew, Doug got permission from the police chief to run the road blocks. Each day he would pick up the students and return them home in the evening. The students made large banners identifying themselves as Christian high school students so they would not be shot at. Over the next two weeks, the group grew to over sixty students. They cleaned up homes burned by the VC and homes destroyed by American artillery, homes in government-controlled areas as well as homes in insecure areas—around 200 houses. Doug provided the transportation, shovels, cola and French bread. They went through twenty-two cases of drinks and hundreds of loaves of bread! "To be able to get in and actually involve myself in trying to heal some of the scars of war was personally one of the most thrilling experiences of my life," Doug wrote.

It was easy to be misunderstood, Doug wrote. Just before Tet, American military forces going through the village of Quang Co had killed nine villagers who were protesting the war in a demonstration at the village market. Doug's friends told him not to return to the village for some time to allow hostilities against the Americans to subside. By the end of February, Doug was the only VNCSer in Tam Ky since Bill Herod had completed his term of service. His friends and the community leaders told him he was wanted, understood, and should stay.

Doug thanked his "fellow Christians" for their prayers and other support. Describing his experiences of the previous month, he asked: "[How] can I possibly explain to you a bombed village, a terrorized refugee camp, a public execution, a group rape by 'civilized' men of one of my high school students, a rotting corpse or a dead child?" Most of the damage in Tam Ky was caused by allied rockets, helicopter gunships and tanks, Doug reported, but in Thang Binh village north of Tam Ky the VC destroyed nearly one hundred homes and killed many civilians.

New personnel coming to Vietnam were delayed for a short time. But Devadoss Maddimadugu arrived on schedule from Bangkok on February 28. A member of the Mennonite Brethren Church in Andhra Pradesh, India, he was trained as a laboratory technician at the M. B. Medical Center in Jadcherla and the M. B. Hospital at Wanaparthy and worked briefly at the MCC center in Kolkata (Calcutta). Doss was assigned to the Nha Trang clinic and hospital.

Atlee Beechy left Vietnam February 17. In a report to MCC, Akron, he said that the Tet offensive created nearly 400,000 new refugees, half of whom had their houses destroyed, according to Dr. Nguyen Phuc Que, the Social Welfare Minister and Special Commissioner for Refugees. This was in addition to more than two million others uprooted previously. Beechy noted increased pressure on voluntary agencies to make their resources available to the government, thus making a clear church identity more difficult.

Beechy commented on the close relationship between the Mennonite missionaries and VNCS. He also observed that relationships with the Evangelical Church in Vietnam remained cordial, but noted that the Church was relating more closely to

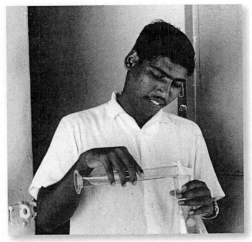

Devadoss Maddimadugu in Nha Trang Clinic lab.

World Vision and the World Relief Commission. "There seems to be some movement in the Church and among certain C&MA personnel toward a greater acceptance of social welfare as a legitimate part of the Christian expression," he wrote. "I believe we have been helpful in encouraging this development. On the other hand, the growing identification of C&MA personnel with the US political and military aims remains another factor which needs to be recognized in our relationship patterns."

In a telephone conference call on February 19 with Paul Longacre, James MacCracken (CWS) and Ove Nielsen (LWR), Beechy noted the strength of the VNCS leadership team in Saigon. During his Vietnam stay, he had interviewed fifty-eight of the total sixty-seven international VNCS staff members. A few persons were requesting termination or reassignment, but most of the people wanted to stay in Vietnam unless circumstances changed drastically. Ruth Yoder expressed a common sentiment, saying that she "definitely wants to stay in Vietnam if at all possible, but not at the price of being dependent on the U.S. military defending her."

Beechy reported in this phone call that the warehouse where VNCS material aid supplies were stored was intact and the supplies were in good order. But later the warehouse was raided on three successive nights while ARVN soldiers were standing guard! Raisins, MCC beef, and other commodities valued at $22,000 were stolen and bundles of clothing ripped open and strewn all over the place. Everett photographed the stands of a nearby black market that was doing a brisk business selling the raisins and MCC beef. The VNCS treasurer, Abner Batalden, then chairman of the Council of Voluntary Agencies, sought reimbursement for the losses and was told to present a request to the minister of national defense.

On February 20, Longacre wrote to Executive Secretary Snyder—who was still traveling in India—urging him to return to Akron since there were some critical questions to process. Ivan J. Kauffman, the Executive Secretary of the Peace Section, was recommending that VNCS terminate its Vietnam programs.

Arguing the case for MCC to withdraw from Vietnam, Kauffman wrote: "In terms of the 'battle for men's minds,' the United States has been decisively defeated in the Vietnam War." This meant, he wrote, that the political structure of the Saigon government with which MCC had worked since 1954 now existed "only as a puppet of the U.S. military forces there." Kauffman noted that U.S. military and political leaders were discussing the possible use of tactical nuclear weapons. He also referred to the destruction of the Mekong River delta town of Ben Tre on February 7. Associated Press correspondent Peter Arnett, writing about the decision to bomb and shell the town regardless of the number of civilian casualties, had quoted a U.S. major saying, "'It became necessary to destroy the town in order to save it." Kauffman questioned whether a viable non-communist government in South Vietnam existed and suggested that an American occupation of the South might be the only alternative to withdrawal. He argued that this called for a total—at least substantial—MCC withdrawal from Vietnam. If any MCC presence remained, Kauffman argued, it would have to be "clearly and publicly" separate from "the aims of the U.S. occupation forces." It would also have to rely on "carefully selected and specially trained and motivated individuals" rather than built around specific institutional projects.

Longacre, in a "partial response" to Kauffman, wrote: "Both you and I have been saying that South Vietnam will ultimately be controlled by some form of Communist-dominated government. This is the wave of the future and we must recognize it." The alternative would be political and military domination by the United States. Noting that VNCS had to change, Paul agreed with Kauffman that one of the greatest services the church could provide in Vietnam was sending volunteers with the "ability to listen and absorb some of the hostilities and frustrations of the Vietnamese people caught in these tragic circumstances."

Yet Paul said MCC had to listen closely to the voices of Vietnamese Christian leaders. He quoted Tran Xuan Quang, a VNCS staff member who would soon become the first ordained minister in the Mennonite Church in Vietnam. "This is no time for the church to pull back in Vietnam," Quang said. "This is the time for her to move out with the good news. My fellow Vietnamese have spent their lives gathering things and now see them go up in smoke. They have sought security only to find death coming to them everywhere. What else but the Christian faith can bring to man a sense of reality?"

Longacre said it seemed apparent that MCC needed to make "a more vigorous effort" to establish an identity with the National Liberation Front. But Longacre cautioned that MCC could not unilaterally change VNCS. Church World Service and Lutheran World Relief would also have to be involved in a change in VNCS programming. Snyder said he and Beechy agreed that VNCS needed to make "some drastic program revisions" but that neither VNCS nor the Mennonite Mission contemplated complete withdrawal.

In early March, Sam Hope expressed his views of VNCS's ongoing ministry in a memo to Leatherman. Although expecting more VC attacks, Hope said that VNCS needs to remain in Vietnam and maintain its identity and visibility. He argued that even a reduced staff would be "a great psychological and symbolic value" to the Evangelical Church and to the many friends VNCS had made over the years. In addition to providing services, Hope said that VNCS would function as a "listening post" to provide interpretation of the war to the Christian church in the United States. Without the ethical concerns injected by missionaries and VNCS personnel, among others, the moral tone of the US community in Vietnam would suffer, he wrote.

Another paper circulating in the VNCS office noted how VNCS as an independent group could report the terror and destruction the people experienced. To leave would silence this voice. This is especially important, the writer commented, because "the local churches feel they must be loyal to, and uncritical of, the present government."

These writers made an important point. The Saigon government considered public opposition to its policies treasonous and citizens who spoke out were subject to arrest, interrogation, torture and long prison terms. Persons working with international organizations could more easily express their views. Those who spoke, however, had to be fair. A likely alternative to the Saigon government was a communist-dominated government—also not very attractive to many people.

Official America wanted voluntary agencies to stay. In an April 2, 1968, message from the Embassy, Ambassador Ellsworth Bunker said that improved security indicated no reason for nongovernmental organizations (NGOs) to curtail activities. They should maintain current level of services or expand, he said. All agency personnel would continue to be offered APO mail privileges and travel on Air America.

In early March, Dr. Que, the refugee commissioner, proposed that VNCS could make a significant contribution by helping to construct houses for those whose houses were destroyed.

Marty Strayer, an architect who sometimes had difficulty in finding a niche in his field, was asked to be in charge of a housing project in Gia Dinh, assisted by Dave Neufeld and Mark Weidner from VNCS and missionaries Don Sensenig, James Metzler and Luke Beidler. Gayle Preheim worked with another housing project.

Dorothy Beidler and the Sensenig family left for Malaysia on March 4, with Don planning to return soon. The missionaries had asked members of the Mennonite congregation whether it was appropriate for the missionaries to leave. While understanding it was alright for the women and children to leave, some said all could stay; their lives were not endangered by the missionaries' presence. None of the members of the local church had been injured or suffered loss. That would change within a few months.

VNCS decided to terminate its programs in Quang Tri—near the DMZ—and in Di Linh where they worked with ethnic minority people. Lee Brumback, however, wanted to return to Di Linh in spite of personal risks, and he was allowed to return on the condition that he send weekly reports. Lee acknowledged that visits to distant villages were out of the question, but he argued that he could continue his agricultural work in thirteen villages near Di Linh as well as in two refugee villages.

The men assigned to WRC in Hue returned to the city to carry out emergency relief aid there, but by early April Paul Kennel, Jerry Sandoz, Harley Kooker and Ken Keefer were working out of Da Nang city. Some of them were assisting at a trade school run by the Christian Youth for Social Service (CYSS), a fledgling organization of Evangelical Church university graduates and professional people who were inspired by MCC and other international Christian agencies to carry out service ministries.

By early April, many of the activities at Quang Ngai were back to pre-Tet levels except for the programs at Nghia Hanh district. Earl Martin and Pat Hostetter celebrated their wedding with friends on March 23—just one week after the infamous March 16 My Lai massacre of hundreds of civilians by the Charlie Company of the American 23rd Infantry Division only fifteen kilometers from Quang Ngai town. However, it would be more than a year and a half later before the world learned of this cover-up, further fueling the American anti-war movement. Whispered reports of many civilian massacres by American and Korean troops circulated in the Quang Ngai area but these were routinely officially denied.

General Earle Wheeler, Chairman of the U.S. Joint Chiefs of Staff, went to Vietnam after the Tet Offensive to evaluate the military situation with Gen. Westmoreland. Westmoreland considered the Tet Offensive a victory for allied forces which had exacted a heavy death toll on VC forces. The VC had also failed to spark a "peoples' uprising" of support. On the other hand, the Viet Cong attacks did undermine the allied "pacification" program so that now the VC were operating with relative freedom in the countryside. When he reported to President Johnson at the end of February, he presented his and Westmoreland's recommendation for more than 200,000 additional U.S. troops with a proposed ceiling of more than 730,000 U.S. military personnel. To accommodate this request would require calling up military reserves. To deny the request would concede U.S. inability to impose a military solution. President Johnson ordered Clark Clifford, who had become Secretary of Defense in mid-January after McNamara's resignation, to conduct a thorough review of the war. With around 525,000 troops already in Vietnam, Clifford persuaded the President to deny Westmoreland the additional 206,000 troops he sought, though he authorized sending 22,000 more soldiers.

On Sunday evening, March 31, President Johnson spoke to the nation in a televised speech, announcing that he had unilaterally ordered a halt to bombing North Vietnam—except in the area around the DMZ. He said that the administration was "prepared to move immediately toward peace through negotiations." At the end of his speech Johnson stunned Americans by announcing that he would not run for reelection.

On April 2, after consulting with other MCC staff and with William Keeney, Peace Section chairman, William Snyder sent a night letter telegram to President Johnson, saying: "Your decision to move toward the conference table by ordering the cessation of bombing in most of North Vietnam is a step that we strongly endorse." Acknowledging that "the road to peace" would not be easy, Snyder wrote: "We believe that your message to the people of the United States and the world last Sunday evening strikes the right note." Snyder said MCC was asking its constituent churches to renew their prayers for peace and pledged that MCC would look for opportunities to increase its developmental programs in Southeast Asia.

I wrote to my missionary colleagues in Saigon on April 2. That evening I had heard a speech by R. W. Apple, Jr., New York Times reporter who had left Vietnam several weeks earlier. Apple viewed Johnson's "bombing pause" as a "non-pause," and did not expect Hanoi to accept the President's terms. Apple told his audience: "The North Vietnamese think they're winning, principally because they are!" He said that the United States would be unable to impose a military solution because Hanoi could send several more divisions south. Commenting on the failure of the "pacification" program, Apple referred to a village north of Saigon that had been "pacified" eleven times during the two and a half years he lived in Vietnam!

Apple said there was growing opposition to U.S. policy; many common people were troubled because so many civilians were being killed by allied military activity. While morally serious, Apple said it hardly represented a threat to the Saigon government. Another growing form of anti-Americanism, however, was coming from those who supported the Saigon government, particularly the Catholics and was a reaction to the pressure Ambassador Bunker was putting on President Thieu to pursue American policy goals.

I had already typed a letter of thanks to President Johnson for his offer of "unconditional" peace talks but then decided not to send it, questioning whether his offer was sufficiently generous for Hanoi to accept. However, to my surprise the next day, April 3, Hanoi radio announced the government's readiness to meet with U.S. representatives.

In an April 4 letter to Paul Kraybill, Everett reported that Saigon governmental officials were "much disturbed" by these developments. Metzler said that the VC controlled nearly the entire Mekong River delta except for the towns. Government troops were still seen all over Saigon. There were reports that another wave of attacks on the towns and cities could be expected in May.

On April 28, Hanoi reported the formation of an urban front called the Alliance of National, Democratic and Peace Forces which called for an independent, non-aligned South Vietnam. The Alliance was headed by Mr. Trinh Dinh Thao, a highly-regarded Saigon lawyer who had once done legal work for the Mennonite Mission on property matters. Thao had reportedly declined the presidency of the National Liberation Front when it was formed late 1960. Thao favored political neutrality to end the conflict and the government security police had interrogated him on several occasions. Knowing they would be arrested by the Thieu government, the Alliance leaders now went into hiding. Charges were indeed brought against them and they were all sentenced to death in absentia. In June 1969, the Alliance merged with the NLF to form a Provisional Revolutionary Government (PRG) which was quickly recognized by the world's socialist countries.

While the men of the Vietnam Mennonite Mission continued their involvement in local relief services, James Metzler had already made clear to the missionary team and to Paul Kraybill that he could not continue to serve in Vietnam. Stauffer, in mid-March, wrote that the Metzler family would "most likely be leaving us." He noted that James "feels more strongly than ever that the political implications of our being here are such that he cannot stay on and be true to his conscience. The rest of us may reach this stage soon, too." Kraybill assured Metzler that they would discuss this matter in person during his upcoming April visit.

Many American missionaries in Vietnam identified with the "free world" commitment to save South Vietnam from coming under the control of a communist government and related comfortably with American military personnel—from the lowest-ranking combat troops to the highest officer personnel. Since we Mennonite missionaries were all recognized as Americans, there was no way that we could fully convince anyone that we were not—in some way—part of the dominating American political and military presence in Vietnam. The succinct statement coined by Canadian Catholic philosopher and writer Marshall McLuhan, *The medium is the message* said it well. We could try to live simply within the Vietnamese community and proclaim the Good News of the gospel of Jesus Christ through words and deeds. Yet most of the population would still view us as part of the American political and military presence in Vietnam.

The Mennonite missionaries had some evidence to substantiate their perceptions of the views of other missionaries. In an early April letter to Paul Kraybill, Everett wrote: "You may be interested in some of the things we discussed in Council yesterday. . . . Four missionaries of other societies have to date reacted to copies of our [Letter to American Christians]. Responses varied from mild disagreement to rather violent disagreement. Some expressed appreciation even if they do not agree completely. Some feel that such statements only encourage the enemy and shorten the days that it will be possible for Western missionaries to preach the Gospel in Viet Nam."

This *Letter from Vietnam to American Christians* eventually got the attention of the wider evangelical community in the United States. Several prominent Christian leaders asked C&MA leaders for their position on American Vietnam policy. Franklin Irwin, the Vietnam field director, responded to Rev. Stephen Olford in May 1969 expressing support for American policies. "The Vietnamese asked us to come and help them drive back an invader, who was trying by murder, force and war to subjugate all the peoples of South Vietnam," he wrote. For America to desert this "gallant, little nation, fighting for its life and freedom" would be both immoral and unchristian.

T. Grady Mangham responded to an inquiry from Donald McGavran, Professor of Mission at Fuller Theological Seminary. Writing in December 1969, Mangham supported continuing the war policies. Although aware of the atrocities and horrors of the war, he was convinced that the alternative, a communist rule, was "frightening, almost unthinkable." Already in January 1967, Mangham, in a letter to Louis L. King, said that the U.S. "must support the South Vietnamese people in their resistance against a Communist takeover."

On April 8, when the missionary men were busily involved in local relief efforts, the Mennonite Mission received a telegram informing Luke Beidler that Dorothy had given birth to their first child, a daughter, in Penang, Malaysia. Don Sensenig had already returned from Malaysia and Luke had been planning to be at Dot's side for the occasion. Luke left two days later. A staff member of the Community Center, Nguyen Tuyet Nga, also received word that her husband was injured when an army truck hit a mine killing nine soldiers.

The Mennonite church at the Community Center celebrated Easter, April 14, with a sunrise service. This was followed by a breakfast for over one hundred people. Devadoss Maddimadugu, now in language study, attended the worship service. The previous day had been designated by President of the Evangelical Church, Pastor Doan Van Mieng as a special day of prayer for Vietnam.

Paul Longacre and Ove Nielsen, of Lutheran World Relief, spent the last two weeks of April in Vietnam. In a memo on May 2 to Paul Leatherman, they authorized $150,000 to build housing units in the Saigon area. Except for Dong Ha in Quang Tri province, all the programs would continue. However, administrators were to give special attention to security issues at Pleiku, Dat To and Di Linh before personnel returned. They met with the entire VNCS international personnel. Some persons were completing their terms of service, a few requesting reassignment out of Vietnam but most were prepared to complete their terms. Forty-five international personnel remained and new personnel were scheduled to arrive in the summer. Dean Hancock was named Director of Program replacing Gerald Aaker. VNCS staff learned that Robert W. Miller, MCC Overseas Director, would be succeeding Paul Leatherman who was completing his two-year term as director.

EMBMC Secretary, Paul Kraybill, and Assistant Secretary, Harold Stauffer, visited Vietnam April 25 to May 3. Harold, on his first visit to Vietnam, noted the "barbed wire barricades, sandbag bunkers, and the presence of military vehicles and personnel everywhere." He observed that conversations frequently referred to pre-Tet and post-Tet, symbolic of the significance of the Tet Offensive. He noted the high morale of the missionary team. Commenting on the church development he said the congregation was eager to have a Vietnamese pastor. "This would facilitate close cooperation of the missionaries in a supportive role but would also allow for less actual dependence upon the missionaries and would allow for continuing congregational leadership in the event missionaries would need to leave at some point in the future," he wrote.

Kraybill noted the congregation's "emphasis on peace and service" even though their belief and doctrine was similar to that of the Evangelical Church. He was impressed with the creative initiatives the missionaries had demonstrated in caring for victims of the fighting. Referring to the massive destruction caused by Allied planes that bombed residential areas in the effort to dislodge VC fighters, Kraybill wrote: "One wonders why we want to be identified with a nation that calls itself Christian [when it tries] to protect itself by such unbelievable violence in somebody else's homeland." Still he affirmed that "it seems right that we are here and that in some small way we seek to minister to those around us who know us not as Americans but as Christians with a concern to share Christ's love by word and deed."

Kraybill and Stauffer met with C&MA's Irwin and with Evangelical Church President Doan Van Mieng. Pastor Mieng reported that seventy Tin Lanh Christians lost their lives during the Tet Offensive; four church buildings were destroyed and several more damaged. The two mission administrators also met with Paul Leatherman and Paul Longacre. The way MCC-VNCS worked with Vietnam Mennonite Mission at the Gia Dinh Community Center "symbolized something of our conviction that witness and service must go together rather than be separated," Kraybill wrote.

Among the "priorities and guiding principles" for the future, Kraybill and Stauffer recommended the following: "Development of a systematic program of Christian education and lay worker training in the Gia Dinh congregation," greater Vietnamese involvement in all levels of programs, and clear steps taken to provide a Vietnamese pastor for the congregation. It was anticipated that Mary and I would return in July and that James and Rachel Metzler would be reassigned if a suitable position became available. These recommendations were approved by the EMBMC executive committee.

Just two hours after Paul Kraybill and Harold Stauffer left Vietnam on May 3, a taxi packed with explosives detonated in Saigon. Arlene Stauffer was downtown shopping only two blocks away. And early Sunday morning, May 5, Arlene and James were awakened by incoming mortar and rocket explosions. The VC 1968 May Offensive was under way. The police soon had roadblocks set up all over the city. In Everett's May 9 letter to Kraybill he writes of watching the "latest marvels from the U.S. air arsenal," the Bell AH-1 Cobra attack helicopters lazily circling then diving down to discharge rockets. There were reports that Viet Cong soldiers had infiltrated into the Gia Dinh area. After a government security man was assassinated, neighbors told Mrs. Nga and Mrs. Bich—the primary school principal and the director of the Family Child Assistance program at the community center—to leave the area for their safety. The Mennonite Community Center was closed.

In a letter written home on May 7, James Metzler told of hauling fifty bags of rice from a warehouse in Cho Lon, Saigon's Chinatown, to a soccer field beyond Gia Dinh where more than four thousand people were living in long open sheds—two of which VNCS helped build. The government did not have enough trucks. He also worked with the young Baptist pastor, Do Vinh Thanh, dispensing cash for the first six permanent houses VNCS was building.

"It's a different type of life than I ever expected to live," James wrote, "I guess I've stopped asking moral questions about our being here."

James described how a group of poor mothers from the church and community had made 600 mosquito nets which were distributed with additional clothing and soap. "We're very happy the way our little congregation is catching on and entering into the same type of work," he wrote. With these opportunities for ministry, James said he was "almost ashamed to write of leaving." He told of discussions with Paul Kraybill about possibly transferring to the Philippines to relate to an Anabaptist group in a teaching ministry for which he felt better suited.

James wrote to his three brothers: "A seven o'clock curfew is pretty nice in some ways. So much is happening that I guess we're getting to think the abnormal is normal."

James reflected on the possibility that he and the other missionaries and their families could easily become war casualties: "Several months ago I was resisting such ideas, feeling as though we were so identified with the whole program that our life would only be slung on the heap of other meaningless sacrifice. But the breakthrough of our witness in the States and my close involvement with the refugees the past two months have now given me the peace I needed for the thought of sealing my witness in this way should the Lord desire it."

James' reference to "our witness in the States," referred to the wide distribution and acceptance of the *Letter from Vietnam to American Christians*.

"I just wish I could take you to visit the place where I'm now spending almost full time," James continued,

Victims of fighting at Community Center for mosquito nets.

Bread for distribution.

It's a community of about 200 families on the edge of the Saigon air base. Nearly all of them came from Quang Nam in Central Vietnam three or four years ago. They were largely self-supporting as a group, with many looms for making cloth. It all went up in smoke when the Americans discovered [around] 30-40 VC in the area. The US used helicopters and rockets. One factory owner said he's not planning to repair the machines because they would be destroyed again. He expressed some anti-American sentiments, thinking I was a Frenchman because of my beard. He was quite troubled when he learned I was American, but I assured him that I felt as sad and disagreed as strongly as he did. The GIs are always saying how they want Charlie* to come out and fight—yet they'll destroy a whole village, jeopardizing hundreds of lives, to wipe out a VC squad without suffering any casualties. (*VC or Vee Cee in NATO phonetics was Victor Charlie. This was often shortened to Charlie.)

On May 20, James wrote home: "Well, I guess I have really taken Don's place in refugee work all right. Thanks to God's grace and opening of doors, I've been able to move ahead. . . . It's tiring work because of the long hours, depressing situations, and discouragements; yet I'm finding a great measure of satisfaction in being able to relate to people and their need meaningfully."

On Thursday, May 23, as Stauffers left a dinner at the Gia Dinh Community Center honoring departing VNCSer Marta Brenden who had supervised the sponsorship programs, they came to a roadblock and the guards yelled "VC!" Large numbers of Viet Cong wearing ARVN uniforms had infiltrated into an area north and east of the large Ba Chieu Market in Gia Dinh. James and Rachel fled to the Saigon center when shooting broke out. On Friday morning, ARVN soldiers were shooting from the roof of their house! On Saturday, some VC soldiers came within two blocks of the Stauffer home. On Sunday, morning a sound truck went through the area asking everyone to leave because of impending military action. The Stauffers also left for Saigon headquarters. VNCS personnel vacated the Em Dem unit house and other houses in Gia Dinh. The church did not meet for worship. On Monday morning, May 27, all the staff from the Community Center fled, reporting that the Viet Cong occupied the area; Trung and Bich and their infant daughter left their home with only the clothes on their backs.

Abner Batalden, the VNCS treasurer, sent a cablegram to Akron on Wednesday, May 29, reporting a twenty-four hour curfew in a quadrant northeast of the Ba Chieu Market, which included the Gia Dinh Community Center. It was believed that there were 500 Viet Cong troops deeply dug down in *Đồng Ông Cộ* (Mister Co's Field) adjacent to the community center.

American helicopter gunships attacked the dug-in Viet Cong soldiers with rockets. Trung reported that the Community Center was broken into, so Everett drove out on his scooter. While a few people were still in their homes, no one was in the alley—rather scary. Trung met Everett at the center. ARVN soldiers had shot the locks off the doors and ransacked the place but were unable to open the safe. As Everett stuffed important files and valuables into a suitcase, he located the key to the safe and emptied the contents as a firefight in the neighborhood grew louder. After emptying the safe they beat a retreat, sweating as they had trouble getting the scooter started. When Everett counted the money at the Saigon office he found that it was the piaster equivalent of almost $3,000 U.S.! The funds were intended for staff salaries and community rebuilding programs.

On Sunday, June 2, James Metzler tried to get more clothes from their house. Stopping a block away, he watched a Skyraider drop a bomb in the vicinity of their house. James's one outfit of clothes had to be washed out each evening.

After helping refugees near the airport for three weeks with the Baptist Preacher, Do Vinh Thanh, James and others decided it was better to help the refugees close to the Mennonite Community Center. They managed to take a van loaded with French bread to an area where helicopters were firing into a row of homes where the people cheered when the food arrived. James was not keen in dealing with ARVN troops; these soldiers demanded a quarter of the load before permitting them to enter that area.

Pastor Thanh, James and a Catholic priest worked together with the assistant province chief one day to find a place for refugees who were asked to leave a camp. Skyraiders bombed the area thirty minutes after the people left. "To be among those people made one wish he could cry his heart out and then forget it all," James wrote. "It is so hopeless in so many ways." They soon opened a new aid distribution point at the Neufeld house near the Mennonite Community Center. Rachel helped Anne Falk and Dr. Strayer conduct a clinic. Although frequently exhausted, James wrote home that they were "finding a real satisfaction in helping" where they could.

On June 4, much of Gia Dinh was still under a twenty-four hour curfew and helicopter gunships continued attacking targets near the Mennonite Community Center. In a letter to parents of MCC personnel Paul Longacre reported that the recent fighting was more destructive—in numbers of homes destroyed and civilian casualties—than the main Tet offensive four months earlier. He wrote that "the Viet Cong tactic seems to be to infiltrate a specified area and let the ensuing battle devastate it." For the civilians it meant "suffering heaped upon suffering."

In a letter to Everett June 7 Paul Kraybill wrote: "We are remembering you in prayer." He referred to the assassination of Sen. Robert Kennedy a day earlier which he said "has shaken this nation to its roots." This followed the assassination of Martin Luther King, Jr. by two months. Kraybill said that President Johnson appointed a commission to study the cause of the violence in the United States, but did not even hint that there was "any relationship between this and the ongoing violence and slaughter in Vietnam."

The Viet Cong launched several rockets into Saigon the night of June 6 from eleven kilometers northeast of the city. One of these rockets landed near the main entrance to the Binh

The Buddha statue survives the destruction in the Dong Ong Co area.

Months later vegetation returns.

Dan Hospital across the street from the Mennonite Student Center where Everett Metzler's family lived and other missionaries were staying. The ARVN had placed a sandbag guard-post by the gate to the student center where an alleyway led into a congested resident area. A soldier sleeping on a cot by the guard-post died when struck in the throat by shrapnel; three others were wounded. Apparently two other persons at the hospital were killed and several wounded. The intended target of this rocket might have been the police station at the end of the street or it may have been randomly launched.

By the morning of June 7, the military action by the Mennonite Community Center in the Dong Ong Co area was over and residents returned to salvage what they could find. Four families from the Mennonite congregation had lost everything and eight more families found their houses damaged or ransacked. Mr. Tu's house was completely flattened—nothing could be saved from the rubble. The house of Trung and Bich had holes in the roof from shrapnel and falling cartridge cases from helicopters; the locks were broken—likely by ARVN soldiers—and clothing and valuables stolen. The government brought a bulldozer into the area to cover up bodies found in foxholes and tunnels.

Everett and James Metzler salvaged materials still at the Community Center where ARVN troops had billeted for a few days. By the middle of June VNCS personnel had not yet returned to Em Dem and the Stauffers' home was still considered a bit insecure. VNCS had just rented the large house adjacent to the Mennonite Student Center near downtown Saigon which would become their main office, a storage area, and a third floor apartment.

Uncertain when things would return to "normal," the Mission Council suggested that we, the Martins, delay our return temporarily given the still dicey security situation. For some time Mission secretary Kraybill was hoping to place experienced overseas personnel in Hong Kong, and he spoke to us about an assignment there. We wanted to return to Vietnam but said we would consider an assignment to Hong Kong if it was not suitable to return to Vietnam.

By late June, Loretta Leatherman and the children were all back in Saigon after a few weeks in Bangkok. In spite of an occasional rocket landing in the city which could be a bit unnerving, things were running well. Paul Leatherman quoted Aase Dybing, VNCS information person, who in a recent newsletter had closed by saying, "But despite everything, it is not as bad to be here as outsiders think." Don Voth, a trained agriculturalist who had worked in Vietnam with MCC from 1958 to 1961, was spending several weeks as a consultant to the VNCS agricultural projects and he was quite relaxed and thankful that he had come.

By the end of June, the Stauffer family returned from their brief out-of-country leave and moved back into their Gia Dinh house and VNCS personnel were back at Em Dem. The Community Center damage was being repaired and Mrs. Nga, the Rang Dong School principal, made plans to reopen the school on July 1. Though there were only one hundred students at first, by September, 350 children were enrolled in half-day classes. By November, the number of students had increased to 500.

"For the first time in weeks we met for worship and fellowship at the Gia Dinh Center this morning," Everett wrote to Kraybill June 30. "It was a quiet and reverent group that met." Several women whose children were involved in the MCC sponsorship programs attended. "One lady gave a testimony of how the Lord kept her family from harm even though her home was destroyed and considerable livelihood gone," Everett wrote. "It tears one around to see some of these folks who have so little to begin with lose everything that they have. Yet they seem to be able to 'take it' in stride much better than we could."

Luke and Dorothy Beidler, who had come two years earlier, in a July letter thanked the mission supporters for their prayers. "We can't know the mind of God in the way He will choose to write the history of small Vietnam or of proud America," they wrote, "but whether viewing the situation from here in Saigon or there in the States, it's life-saving to believe that God is in control." They expressed delight at the "little extra happiness" God granted them in the person of their daughter Marta who was born in Penang three months earlier.

The Beidlers lived in a simple row house one block from the Saigon student center. They wrote:

> Students come often to visit us. They pause a bit confused and look again to see if they have the right house number. One student stated the problem when he offered to find us a more magnificent house!
>
> On an average Sunday morning we have about six visitors. Some come only to talk English. . . . But there are others whom we have learned to know as real friends. We value their opinions and find their advice honest and helpful. On the other side, they are young searching Christians, and we can share our faith experience with each other.
>
> Sometimes we have doubts about being in Vietnam during the present trouble. We wonder if our witness can be heard because we are often seen first and finally as Americans. Perhaps it was a US bomb that leveled one's store and house or took the life of a friend or relative. We asked a Vietnamese friend about this one day. His answer came to us as a word from the Lord. He said it so simply, something like this—"Oh, you help so much. You have helped me think about my life. At first I came to the Mennonite Center with a friend. Then I decided to study in the English classes. After that I went deeper and attended the Bible class Sunday mornings. Now, where can I go to talk about my ideas? I think of you."

In a commentary published in the October *Missionary Messenger*, James Metzler told about a conversation with a visiting church official. After describing his work he was asked: "But are you a missionary or a relief worker?" He observed:

> Our view of the whole gospel for the whole man has made it seem natural for us to get involved in the physical and social situation in Vietnam. . . . We're aware that it's not acceptable in this culture for anyone of honored position, such as a teacher of religion, to be seen with dirty hands. But in this desperate situation, loving service which is given freely will surely [overcome] that obstacle. In fact, we're more fearful of creating too great an impact.
>
> For when a Vietnamese receives help or gifts, he incurs a keen sense of obligation and indebtedness. Some have used this cultural trait to buy a following. This poses an acute problem for us. Yet Christ didn't refuse to give needed bread just because He would have some "bread followers." Rather, the danger serves as a pricking reminder that social service can't replace preaching. The Word and the deed must be presented in a unified witness.

Observing the missionaries' response to the obvious needs, a young Mennonite from the States commented, "This is the kind of mission work I can believe in."

Seven Tin Lanh staff members of the Community Center transferred their membership to the Mennonite church on July 7. This included secretary and evangelist, Nguyen Quang Trung and his wife, Ngo Thi Bich; and Nguyen Van Ngai and his wife, Phan Thi Tuyet Nga, the school principal. Tran Xuan Quang was formally designated Associate Pastor and was assisting in material aid distribution at the Community Center. Quang was beginning a catechism class for twenty people who made a confession of faith. Quang's wife, Nguyen Thi Tam, was also involved with relief projects of the local congregation. James Metzler was still bringing 1,400 loaves of French

Ruth Yoder with student nurses.

bread daily to the center for distribution to 700 families and supervising the work of producing 500 mosquito nets weekly for distribution.

VNCS was also getting on with their programs. Don Voth was working with Lee Brumbeck in Di Linh. Dean Hancock introduced Swiss nurse, Elizabeth Roggli—recruited by MCC—to her assignment at the Nha Trang Clinic and Hospital. Esther Kraybill was very upbeat about life at Nha Trang where she served as hostess. They had begun a weekly prayer meeting where more than thirty of the hospital staff got together. The Kraybills' two children, Eugene and Charlene, were getting along fine.

Ruth Yoder, co-director with Nguyen Dam Cuc of the new nursing training program at the Nha Trang Hospital, reported in July that eight students were involved in the one year program. Emma Lenzmann and Tharon McConnell assisted in teaching. The students were doing clinical work in the Khanh Hoa Provincial Hospital. At the August 11, dedication of the School of Nursing, both government officials and Tin Lanh leaders spoke highly of the program which complemented the services of the well-known Clinic and Hospital, one of the two outstanding places in South Vietnam performing eye surgeries. The staff bade farewell to Marcie Weber, Emma Lenzmann, and Linford Gehman who had completed their assignments.

In Tam Ky, Doug Hostetter expressed excitement about a literacy program he initiated. Working with thirty high school students from three youth groups—Catholic youth at the reception center, Buddhist youth from the Tu Hiep refugee camp, and Cao Dai youth working in the Vuong Lai refugee camp—literacy courses were organized for 600 children ages six to twelve years old who had never been in school. The bamboo handicrafts program was selling products in shops in Da Nang and Chu Lai. Doug was disbursing limited aid materials as part of the sewing program and literacy classes and kept a supply of clothing and blankets on hand for emergencies, but was not distributing any U.S. government food commodities.

In the Saigon office, with Leatherman leaving, Abner Batalden served as acting director until Robert W. Miller arrived in September. Jim Bowman was office manager. Paul and Loretta and their family left Vietnam on July 5.

"Serving in Vietnam radicalized us," Paul said. Living in the midst of war "we saw our tax dollars dismember and disembowel those whom we knew as friends in Christ." This led to a decision to withhold tax monies used for military expenditures—not paying what Caesar wanted.

POST-TET DEVELOPMENTS

Chapter 29

Already in the spring of 1967—a year before the Tet Offensive—some of the MCC field personnel with VNCS were carrying on a conversation with Professor John Howard Yoder who taught theology and ethics at the Goshen Biblical Seminary in Goshen, Indiana.

Having attended Goshen College, Pat Hostetter knew Yoder and she and Earl Martin wrote to him in mid-May 1967. Aware of his concerns and his involvement with the MCC Peace Section, they asked: "Why do we not have a program of assistance to North Vietnam?" Further, "How can we, as the Church which senses equal responsibility to all men, irrespective of political affiliation, afford to work closely with the South Vietnamese government program . . . when it is their express purpose to be selective in their assistance?"

Yoder welcomed their inquiry. Already in mid-October 1965 when Church World Service asked MCC to lead a united relief program in South Vietnam, Yoder expressed the importance of assistance to war victims on both sides of the conflict. Writing to the executive secretary of MCC's Peace Section, he asked: How can we genuinely say that we have attempted to serve in "the territory under Viet Cong control when there have been no feelers extended to the [National Liberation Front] either through the offices they have maintained in Prague or in Algiers, or through the International Red Cross?" At that time there was speculation that Daniel Gerber and the other two persons kidnapped in 1962 might be working in a VC hospital—perhaps on the Cambodian side of the border. Yoder suggested that MCC propose fielding a multinational team of medical personnel—including Canadians and Europeans—to take the place of the three persons held.

In March 1966 the MCC Peace Section European Committee discussed correspondence between Yoder and Dr. Herbert Landmann from the German Democratic Republic about sending medical supplies to North Vietnam and recommended that MCC send someone to North Vietnam to determine relief needs among Christians there. A few weeks later, the Peace Section Executive Committee took action to, among other things, "reiterate our request to the MCC Overseas Office and to other Mennonite relief agencies (Canada, Netherlands, Germany) to continue efforts toward relief operations in North Vietnam and in National Liberation Front territories."

In June 1967 Yoder wrote a longer letter to Pat stressing the importance of emphasizing to co-workers that war is wrong. Further, they should share with Vietnamese friends "the universality of God's concern and the absolute identification of Christ with man in his suffering" to help them understand God's identification with them. Their third audience is North American churches. He wrote: "It is extremely easy to be satisfied [that] we are doing good work, and . . . that it is not the business of the church to tell government how to do its work."

"We must not be judgmental or irresponsible as we continue the search for alternatives. We must not give the impression that we think there is one easy recipe for moral purity or heroism. The conversation must be continued with your field colleagues, with those who share this concern and those who do not, and with your family and friends at home in the course of your normal correspondence," Yoder concluded. He signed the letter, "Respectfully yours, John H. Yoder, Associate Consultant."

In September 1967, Pat and Earl wrote a two-and-a-half page letter to Yoder, saying that they were happy with the kinds of things they were able to do in Quang Ngai—feed malnourished children, provide meaningful occupation for those whose lives were disrupted, help children, alleviate medical problems, and establish person-to-person relationships to help restore a sense of individual worth. Yet they were restless.

> We understand . . . that we are working in a country which is at war. We understand that we are operating in a context of power politics and national interests. And we accept the challenge of working in a complex . . . situation where not all is ideal. . . . We cannot support the policy which is creating the refugees with whom we work, but inasmuch as they are the victims of an unfortunate situation, we are eager to cast our lot with them and assist them in every way possible. We would prefer that our service be seen as a purely humanitarian and Christian effort to alleviate human suffering and not as some political gimmick to win the hearts of the people to some prescribed persuasion.

They were happy to work with Vietnam Christian Service which they considered "one of the most impartial . . . , non-political, humanitarian services" in Vietnam. "But if truly we are non-political," they asked, "why are we then working on only one side of the seventeenth parallel? Why have we chosen to work on only one side of the many real and imaginary fences erected here in South Vietnam?"

Was it only "political expediency," they asked, that VNCS was working only in areas controlled by the South Vietnamese government? Would working in North Vietnam or in areas of the South controlled by the National Liberation Front preclude working with the South Vietnamese government? Had this question been raised with Vietnamese government officials? In light of the many agencies now working in the South, was it necessary to choose between one side or the other? Perhaps it would even be more legitimate to work on the "other" side, the two suggested.

Would the NLF and the Democratic Republic of Vietnam welcome assistance from VNCS? Had anyone inquired? Who would assume the responsibility of asking? And if these questions are not being raised by the agency officials, does it "by default . . . become our responsibility to seek these relationships on the grassroots level by making contact with NLF leaders on the province or district level?" they asked.

Earl and Pat sent a copy of this September letter to Paul Leatherman, the VNCS Vietnam director, and to Paul Longacre, who had been serving for a year as Acting Director for Asia at the MCC Akron office.

Longacre quickly acknowledged that the "very pertinent" questions they raised needed to be studied, "particularly as the war becomes more intense." He noted that Frank Hutchinson, the CWS administrative member of the VNCS team, expressed a concern that VNCS might "be too closely linked up with the U.S." in engaging in refugee programs such as the assistance at Nghia Hanh, and should possibly restrict their programs to established refugee camps. (Nghia Hanh was where the Allied forces dumped thousands of refugees without giving assistance.) Longacre expressed interest in seeing all their correspondence with Yoder.

William Keeney, who was with William Snyder in Vietnam in early May, was aware that Paul Leatherman, the VNCS director, had asked Doug Hostetter to leave Tam Ky and come to Saigon for consultation about reports that he was traveling to areas partially controlled by the Viet Cong.

Keeney wrote to Yoder late September: "The treatment of Doug disturbs me. I think he may be sacrificed for program and for interests of church relationships. I am also disturbed that Peace Section has not been informed and brought in more directly when we have expressed concern so often at the point where this case is most directly involved."

In late September, Yoder wrote to Pat, Earl, and Doug, hesitant to intervene in the administrative process and noting that significant progress was made that summer by MCC Canada giving aid to North Vietnam. He suggested that it should be possible to find a way to provide humanitarian aid to the other side in the South—by finding a way to move out from the government-controlled areas of South Vietnam or by coming in from a neighboring country.

Ruth Yoder, who arrived in Vietnam early 1966, also had occasional correspondence with Yoder. Before she left for Vietnam he had said to her: "Be careful you don't become grist for the American military mill." In April 1967, Ruth answered a letter that Professor Yoder had written to her in December. Prefacing her remarks, she wrote: "The only certain thing about the 'true' situation in Vietnam and what to do about it, is that anyone who knows for sure doesn't understand what's going on here. Those who really know the situation best are the most cautious in saying what *really* is happening—what all the delegations come to find out in three-and-one-half days."

Ruth wrote that some VNCS personnel were concerned about finding a way to help in "those other areas," and suggested that Doug Hostetter was "learning first-hand the practical problems in what sounds like the only real Christian way of giving help" to both sides. Noting the difficulty for field personnel to give assistance in areas controlled by the Viet Cong, Ruth wrote: "It isn't a matter of being afraid of getting shot. It's a matter of having set up some contact with someone in there so that getting shot will at least mean something to those you are getting shot for." She rhetorically asked why any of "three major fighting groups"—Viet Cong, South Vietnamese forces and American military—should trust "non-military young Americans coming into the situation right now?"

Ruth said that she and her coworkers at the Nha Trang Evangelical Clinic can treat people on both sides of the conflict—since they do not ask for ID cards—without getting into trouble with the community. "I'm glad VNCS is concentrating on services rather than distribution," Ruth wrote.

On February 1, 1968, right after the beginning of the VC Tet military offensive, Yoder sent a sharply-worded letter to Longacre. Carefully explaining that his letter was not directed personally to him, Yoder said that for over two years—since November 1965—the Peace Section had been asking that MCC relief work be "carried on in such a way and in such places that it would demonstrate our moral condemnation of war and our desire to help on the other side."

MCC had begun contacting Democratic Republic of Vietnam embassies in Europe to inquire about giving help to North Vietnam. But Yoder believed that MCC could find ways within South Vietnam to work on both sides. During the Algerian struggle for independence from France, 1954 to 1962, Yoder said that MCC had maintained contact with the Algerian National Liberation Front. MCC worked through the French voluntary agency Cimade which criticized France's policies both in France and in Algeria. Mennonite personnel in Algiers lived in the Arab section of the city and in no way identified with the French military personnel. Thus in Vietnam, where the need to disavow identification with the US military activity was so much more crucial, Yoder argued that MCC could most certainly find a way to contact NLF-Viet Cong personnel if there was the will to do so. Some possible ways, Yoder suggested, might involve working through Laos or Cambodia or moving into some "insecure" town in South Vietnam. Yoder also insisted that—since journalists were able to establish NLF contacts in Vietnam—it should not be difficult for MCC to meet with NLF personnel in Saigon or Da Nang. Unless MCC found a way to reach out to the other side, Yoder argued, MCC's commitment to serve all those in need was being compromised. Unless MCC made a serious attempt to do this, Yoder said he could no longer counsel people like Pat and Doug Hostetter and Earl Martin to patiently work through official agency channels!

Preoccupied with the crisis of the Tet Offensive, Longacre sent Yoder a preliminary response. Each VNCSer, Longacre wrote, "is making some effort to establish his identity as something other than that of the U.S. government." Longacre agreed with Yoder that "the Vietnam program has not been daring in its faithfulness, in its boldness to demonstrate that Christian service is to both sides." Still he maintained that the Vietnam program did "reflect the desires of the church." This response did not satisfy Yoder who quickly replied: "You did not explain that there is, or that there is not, an MCC policy, explicit or implicit, against relief efforts on the other side. You do not say that it has or that it has not been discussed. . . . Only an active concern to help on both sides would be the testimony that you are really trying to rise above political partisanship."

Longacre immediately informed Executive Secretary Snyder that Yoder was convinced that the Overseas Office apparently had "a definite policy—written or unwritten—that says we are only going to minister to one side in the Vietnam conflict. . . . Only some direct attempt to establish communication with leaders of the NLF will satisfy him."

Yoder again wrote to Longacre a month after the Tet offensive, beginning with a quotation from one of Doug Hostetter's letters. Doug had written: "Previously, in Tam Ky, we were able in a small extent to witness to this great love [of God]. We were able to aid and give assistance to people on both sides of the political and geographic boundaries. Twice, in fact, I was invited to come into areas not occupied by American forces to see personally if there was some way in which we could help these people. In both instances, I was prohibited from doing so by our Saigon office."

MCC administrators now faced the issue of integrity. Though he doubted that it was so, Yoder had been told that it was not possible for VNCS personnel to contact people in the NLF areas of control. It now appeared that the MCC Overseas Office was distorting the facts! Unless the MCC Overseas Office could resolve this issue, Yoder would have to contact the executive committees of MCC and the Peace Section as well as the executive offices of Church World Service and Lutheran World Relief.

William Snyder immediately wrote to Yoder, referring to Doug's allegation that VNCS administrators refused to let him accept invitations to go to areas partially controlled by the National Liberation Front. "I have read Doug's entire letter and feel that it is an honest attempt to state the dilemma that all of us have in the Vietnam situation at the moment," Snyder wrote. "Leatherman spoke to me about Doug's interest in accepting a Tet invitation from friends in 'VC territory.' I found that Paul Leatherman was very concerned about Doug's personal safety. . . . Paul had a hard time in making this decision because he wanted to do the right thing with full sensitivity to Doug's feelings. I told Paul that I would back him in asking Doug not to accept the invitation."

Snyder mentioned the mounting anti-Americanism and the mysterious killing of IVSer David Gitelson—many believed he was killed by South Vietnamese or American intelligence personnel. Snyder said many people believe there is no place "secure" in Vietnam. Yet the fact that

VNCS personnel in Hue were not harmed in the Tet offensive might suggest that VNCS had been "coming through to 'the other side,'" Snyder wrote.

"We need your help in planning for the future, John," Snyder wrote, "but we need it on a broader basis than selection of isolated incidents such as Doug's report. Part of our problem in Vietnam or elsewhere is the tension between Freedom and Order organizationally with the knowledge that those who are assigned administrative responsibility cannot always come down on the side of unlimited freedom for the individual within situations that are subject to varying interpretations."

MCC was making plans for Atlee Beechy to contact diplomatic offices of the Democratic Republic of Vietnam and the National Liberation Front in the summer of 1968—a continuation of contacts previously made. In May Jacob Classen had met in Phnom Penh with an NLF representative who said that—instead of sending medical supplies—it would be better to agitate for an end to the American military involvement.

Longacre wrote to Nha Trang's Dr. Gehman in early June, asking whether he would consider working in DRV or NLF areas if it could then be arranged, or later in North or South Vietnam after some settlement, even possibly "replacing Gerber and his associates if [MCC] would have reasonable assurance that these persons would be able to treat civilians and not military casualties." MCC would consider "a team of two or three, probably another doctor and a nurse," Longacre said. He wrote: "We feel that you have the necessary skill, depth of commitment and stamina, and general 'cool' needed for such an assignment."

Paul Leatherman terminated his assignment early in July, leaving Abner Batalden, VNCS business manager recruited by Lutheran World Relief, as the interim VNCS director. Before Leatherman left, he and Batalden discussed a draft of VNCS Guidelines which Paul Longacre prepared; this was to be a supplement to the VNCS Service Objectives and Philosophy prepared two years earlier.

In a letter to Bernard Confer, the LWR executive director, Batalden commented on the bizarre relationship VNCS had with official American entities in Vietnam. He gave examples: VNCS expresses a desire to cooperate with USAID in Vietnam, now operating under Civil Operations & Revolutionary Development Support (CORDS), "but even in our guidelines we indicate a suspicion of them and a desire to set up programs that are clearly separate." Another example: "We indicate the urgent need of security from the military, but in the indoctrination of our staff we encourage them to have nothing to do with the military." Even Leatherman, Batalden said, had observed that "we are in danger of 'talking out of both sides of our mouth.'"

Many VNCS personnel criticized these proposed guidelines saying that they were contradictory, idealistic and paternalistic. Some saw the statement as a list of "dos" and "don'ts," an attempt by MCC administrators to impose their concerns on persons recruited by the other two agencies.

The new VNCS Guidelines approved by the VNCS Consultative Committee in August as a supplement to the June 1966 VNCS Objectives and Philosophies acknowledged that "whereas VNCS strives to maintain a nonpolitical identity, it is accepted that all VNCS personnel and programs can be construed as political." VNCS would coordinate its activities with existing government structures but remain autonomous in program planning, but "may enlist the support of CORDS/MACV or GVN to meet needs it cannot accomplish independently." Reliance on allied military or U.S. government facilities and services were to be "held at a minimum."

The Guidelines stated that "VNCS assistance is to be given to individuals in need without discrimination to race, religion or political conviction." The only motivation in carrying out programs should be "the Christian response to ease the suffering of the people of Vietnam."

VNCSers were encouraged to live in Vietnamese neighborhoods, eat local foods and communicate in the Vietnamese language as much as possible. Personnel were to refuse to give intelligence for either side. Newsletters or articles for publication or interviews with reporters were to be cleared with the director in advance. VNCS personnel were urged to learn the local language, immerse themselves in Vietnamese culture, and participate in the activities of the Evangelical Church.

In mid-July, MCC Executive Secretary Snyder informed Philip Habib, Deputy Assistant Secretary of the U. S. Department of State, with a copy to James Grant, Assistant Administrator of USAID for Southeast Asia, that Atlee Beechy planned a summer visit to National Liberation Front and Democratic Republic of Vietnam missions in Europe, Africa and Asia. He noted that MCC has always attempted to serve needy people "irrespective of political affiliations, race, or creed." Snyder was very explicit: "Consequently, we are desirous of meeting civilian human need in areas now controlled by DRVN or NLF," though "under no illusions about the difficulty in making such arrangements."

On his assignment, Beechy took with him a statement introducing the Mennonites and the Mennonite Central Committee. Noting that our first loyalty is to God, it said that Mennonites as followers of Jesus Christ reject violence and war and work for reconciliation and peace among all people. It described MCC's work in Vietnam since 1954 and its current work within Vietnam Christian Service. It said that "Mennonites believe their Christian responsibility has not been fully discharged by working only in certain areas of South Vietnam" and desire to "assist the civilian population in . . . North Vietnam and in areas under the administration of the National Liberation Front." Among other materials, Beechy presented the Mennonite missionaries' 1967 "Letter from Saigon to American Christians."

Beechy met with DRVN or NLF representatives in Paris, Berlin, Prague, Algiers, New Delhi and Phnom Penh. While some meetings were quite perfunctory, Beechy frequently had extended conversations with representatives. In Berlin, Dr. Beechy met Dr. Landmann who reported on the MCC gift of medical supplies to North Vietnam and how he had spoken with the Minister of Health "about the Mennonites and their deep concern."

At the end of his assignment in August 1968, Beechy wrote a lengthy letter to President Lyndon Johnson reporting on his summer contacts with NLF and DRVN representatives.

In Saigon, the missionaries continued their work with enthusiasm.

"I will praise the Lord at all times," James Stauffer began his letter to his mother in late July 1968. "This past month has been one of the busiest of my life. . . . Fortunately, we don't have to do all this ourselves. We have some good helpers, some otherwise! But we could use the Martins and hope that they will be able to come direct to Saigon rather than spend time in Hong Kong."

The previous Sunday, July 21, there was an "overflow crowd" at the worship service. "The Lord seems to be using the recent events to bring many to Himself," James wrote. "There are over thirty in the believer class and over a dozen accepted the Lord after the class. We pray that each one will truly meet the Lord and be a genuine follower."

This was the beginning of a significant influx of new persons into the church. In their interactions within the community begun more than three years earlier, missionaries shared the gospel of Jesus Christ and invited persons to accept this Way. We stressed to the staff that the educational, social and medical services offered were not dependent on whether people accepted the gospel message. Many of those who believed during those first years responded to invitations given by pastors and lay preachers from the Evangelical Church who had been invited to preach. Especially when the American military and political involvement in the country became more marked, it seemed more authentic to see people respond to invitations from their fellow countrymen than from us American missionaries. Now with the deprivation and desperation that followed the Tet offensive when many lost everything, there undoubtedly were those who considered a close identification with the church might enable them to receive additional material benefits. Yet there was a genuine gratefulness that *Ông Trời,* the God of Heaven, whom Evangelicals called *Đức Chúa Trời* (God), had indeed protected them, and they were prepared to commit themselves to God and to Jesus Christ as Savior and Lord.

With the Sensenig family now on furlough, the missionaries in Saigon were James and Arlene Stauffer, Everett and Margaret Metzler, James and Rachel Metzler, and Luke and Dorothy Beidler. When they were together Thursday evening, July 25, they agreed to cable Eastern Mennonite Board of Missions requesting that the Martins proceed directly to Saigon. They envisioned me helping both James Metzler with relief assistance and James Stauffer supervising some of the social programs at the community center. In addition, I was to establish a lay leadership training program for the growing congregation.

On July 27, Mary and I received a phone call reporting that the Vietnam Mission Council was asking that we come directly to Vietnam rather than go to Hong Kong. We were now delighted to return to Saigon even though the armed conflict continued.

Paul Kraybill, the Mission secretary, had mixed feelings about our returning to Vietnam. The earlier request of the Mission Council to delay our return to Vietnam was an incentive for him to reassign us to Hong Kong. We had agreed to go temporarily to Hong Kong until it seemed appropriate for us to return to Vietnam. My assignment in Hong Kong was "to study and explore . . . opportunities for Christian peace witness; gain understanding of present-day China and implications of this for future developments in Asia; study and explore all available information regarding the church in China; [and] project possible guidelines for future development of a Christian witness to the people of China."

Kraybill said it was clear that we "should go to Vietnam." Yet he was disappointed that we were not pursuing the Hong Kong assignment. We left Pennsylvania August 16. Since I had already made plans for contacting various persons in the crown colony, we went first to Hong Kong. In our two weeks there, I interviewed various people and prepared a report for the Mission Board.

Kraybill said our brief visit underscored the need to place someone in Hong Kong. And in a letter to Everett, the Mission secretary in Saigon, Kraybill said that he wants one of the Vietnam couples—now with some overseas experience—to transfer to Hong Kong. Although Mary and I preferred to stay in Vietnam, we informed the missionary team that we would consider Hong Kong if this was the consensus of the group. Although none of the other families expressed much interest in transferring to Hong Kong, Everett and Margaret Metzler eventually agreed to move there.

We arrived in Saigon September 4 and moved into the Gia Dinh house that Sensenigs had rented a year earlier. The former youth hostel downstairs was replaced by a sewing class taught by Co Van, also called Co Bay (Ms. Seven); forty-two young women were enrolled in sewing and embroidery classes. The office for the Family Child Assistance (FCA) program was also downstairs, coordinated by Mrs. Bich, assisted by Mrs. Nguyen Thi De and Mrs. Nguyen Tuyet Nga (Three staff members had the name Nga, a poetic rendering of "moon." To distinguish from the school principal, dark-complexioned Nga was "black Nga" and the stout Nga was "fat Nga." Neither term was derogatory). James and Rachel Metzler rented a house on Bach Dang Street—a block from the main Ba Chieu market and three blocks from us—where they organized English classes for one hundred students.

On Sunday we met with the congregation at the community center; they had just begun meeting upstairs in what had once been our family's living room! Tran Xuan Quang was serving as the associate pastor and VNCS interpreter Nguyen Van Ninh was teaching the adult Sunday school class. Around sixty persons attended the Sunday morning worship services. "We surely feel like this is where we belong and we're glad we're here," Mary wrote home.

The community center at Gia Dinh was very busy during these months. A new VNCS doctor, Joanne Smith T, was now serving in the clinic at the community center.

VNCS authorized expending two million piasters ($17,000 U.S.) to build homes for families near the center. James Metzler and Luke Beidler worked with this project. VNCS secured inch-thick steel rods that were welded into 4 x 8 meter frames which, when covered with canvas, became the

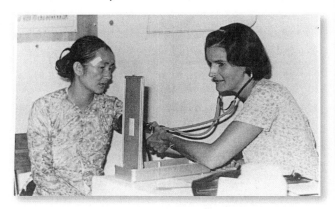

Joanne Smith T at Community Center.

walls of the house, set on mortared brick footers. On top came rafters and aluminum roofing. The total cost was around 25,000 piasters ($215 U.S.) per unit.

James Metzler described this in the December issue of *Missionary Messenger,* the Mission Board journal. "We don't expect—and sometimes don't get—much gratitude for our work," Jim wrote. "The bitter resentment against our country for such awful destruction is usually unexpressed but clearly sensed. We must be content to remain unwanted, even when our resources are freely shared.

"Thus we are doubly happy for every indication that God's loving concern is shining through our efforts. The community's interest in our witness and services has greatly increased since the fighting. A number from the village testify that Jesus is a true comforter to them in their difficulties. They are sharing some definite answers to their prayers of childlike, fervent faith."

I soon became involved in this project; by early October, we were averaging one house per day. As the families secured resources, they bricked in the sides and finished the floor, thus getting quite adequate living space. VNCS gave an additional one million piasters ($8,556 US) to continue rebuilding homes. The program concluded in November with 130 houses rebuilt.

There were staff turnovers in many VNCS projects. Dean Hancock traveled with Gayle Preheim to Di Linh September 7. After working with housing in the Saigon area for several months, Gayle was eager to pick up the agricultural project there. Security was dicey; the Viet Cong had attacked the community twice in the previous two weeks and had taken up positions near the VNCS house, causing the VNCS men to hide out in the basement stairway. But the U.S. Military

Building houses in Dong Ong Co area.

James Metzler with a family at their new house.

Assistance Command-Vietnam was bringing in an engineering company of 300 men to build the highway from Di Linh to Da Lat, and later Di Linh to Saigon, so less VC harassment was expected. After meeting with the CORDS personnel in Bao Loc, Hancock agreed for Preheim to be assigned to Di Linh.

Assigned to World Relief Commission, Paul Kennel was assisting in building a new high school for the Tin Lanh Church in Da Nang and preparing to build another high school at nearby Hoa Khanh which would be staffed by young Evangelical teachers. Kennel was the go-between in getting cement and rebar from USAID, lumber from the U.S. armed forces, cash donations from U.S. military chaplains, and had applied for an Oxfam grant. Ken Keefer and Harley Kooker worked with Kennel in repairing a school in Hue. Carpentry and sewing classes were running at Phu Bai (site of the Hue airport) and they were hoping to get classes restarted in Quang Tri.

These three young men were key members of the World Relief Commission in the Hue area. WRC asked MCC to release these men to WRC but Longacre said it was important for the men to return to the States at the end of their three year terms, after which they could volunteer to return to Vietnam with WRC.

Robert and Jean Miller arrived with their family around September 12, he to assume the role of VNCS director. They moved to a rented house near the Dan Chu (Democracy) traffic circle in Saigon, a few blocks from the newly-rented VNCS office at 330 Phan Thanh Gian Street. Thirteen other new international personnel arrived in September; Everett again coordinated their language studies.

The summer exploratory MCC contacts with "the other side" had repercussions in Saigon for Miller. In late October, James Stauffer wrote home:

This evening the Mission Council met with Bob Miller, the new VNCS director. He wanted to share with us some of the problems he's facing. This week some USAID officials talked to him and feel that he needs to pledge more active support to the U.S. and Saigon governments. They have picked up things here and there that make VNCS appear to be aiding the enemy. The same day the girls that work in the VNCS office were typing up Atlee Beechy's report of his visit with NLF representatives to mimeograph for VNCS personnel, and were greatly upset by it. Bob called the [VNCS] executive committee together and they wouldn't say a word so he felt somewhat alone. Since he had no support from the committee he had all the papers burned but now feels that he perhaps didn't do the right thing. It isn't easy to be a peacemaker here.

Robert and Jean Miller family arrive.

Some of the Vietnamese staff members generally supported the American military objectives. All, however, feared possible arrest, torture and imprisonment since advocacy for political accommodation with the other side was considered a criminal offense.

Mennonite church member Pham Van Luc graduated from the junior officers' training school in Thu Duc and was assigned to command a small company of Popular Defense forces in the Mekong River Delta. Luc and his wife, Qui, spent an evening with Everett and Margaret. Everett said Luc was "torn between the wrongness of it all and his responsibility to his family and country. He has no enthusiasm for the business, but can find no way out. His is the plight of many."

After the Tet offensive, the Saigon government announced the total mobilization of all men from the age of eighteen to thirty-eight. Two of the Mennonite church leaders, Tran Xuan Quang and Nguyen Van Ninh, were just below the maximum age.

James Stauffer wrote home about a local boy who had gone AWOL:

This afternoon I was called upon to intercede for a youth who is helping to build houses for those in our programs. His mother will be baptized this Sunday. The boy, Thanh, also believed about a year ago but never went on. He has been attending regularly for a month, however. He was arrested by the security forces guarding in our village. He didn't have proper papers and was actually AWOL. When we started the rebuilding program he was home from the Army for one week. He wanted to help during that time. When [the week] was up, he kept on and worked for over a month now. They were accusing him of being a VC. So his mother wanted me to testify that he wasn't. I hesitate to do this because I have no way of proving that he isn't. On the other hand, I did know the family and I told them of their relationship to us. The officer seemed satisfied and he was moved by the mother's pleas and agreed to let him go, providing he reports back to his unit on Monday. One hardly knows what to do in situations like this.

On September 29, fourteen new believers were baptized. Each of them was asked to give a testimony. One of them was Ms. Van, the teacher of the sewing class. In her testimony she read II

Newly baptized group.

Corinthians 5, "If our earthly house is dissolved, we have another house not built by human hands." This passage spoke uniquely to her because she had lost her house just a few months before.

Mentioning the baptisms in the October *News and Concerns*, Margaret and Everett wrote: "Though perhaps not all the motivation is the highest among these thirteen women and one man, it is possible to see a real work of the Spirit in some of them. The Thursday evening prayer meeting has been started again among believers in the Gia Dinh area and is proving to be a meaningful activity."

James Stauffer noted that some of these new believers "have been bringing others to the Lord." Much credit for this, he said, was the witness of Mrs. Trac, who served many years as a "Bible woman" and personal worker in the Evangelical Church. She now attended the Mennonite church at the community center. Arlene said Trac's method is simply to "brag on the Lord."

In a three-page November newsletter to friends, Arlene and James wrote about developments the previous year:

> For the first time many prayed and found God real. They found deliverance and forgiveness—joy in pain and suffering—eternal life. Now they come to church praising God, spontaneously testifying to their simple faith in prayer meetings—and witnessing to their neighbors about what God is doing for them. The blind, the lame, the widow, the beggar, young and old—often illiterate, happy in answers to prayer. It is a new, exciting, contagious thing God is doing among us. Isn't it wonderful that we can watch it happen—that God let us be here in "Dong Ong Co" (our village) at such a time as this? Last month fourteen were baptized, uniting with the church. Each week new ones pray. A class of twenty is under instruction. We are grateful for the prayers of God's people the world over—grateful for the sincere, devoted staff of workers God sent us—the evangelists, Bible lady, the assistant pastor and his wife, the sacrificial labors of the medical team, the social workers, janitors, school teachers and principal who work hard, long and prayerfully.

After we returned to Vietnam, Mary had begun teaching Bible stories Friday afternoons to the girls in the sewing class that met downstairs in our house. These girls were learning these skills through the Family Child Assistance program, a program I was directing. There were ninety-three families enrolled—with authorization to go to 150 cases. Mrs. Ngo Thi Bich was the primary caseworker. There were currently 120 children receiving tuition and other support in the Rang Dong School through the Educational Assistance Program and we were hoping to increase this to 150 cases. Thirteen parents had also taken out small loans, mostly for merchandise for selling in markets; the average loan was the equivalent of around $34 U.S.

In their rented house near Ba Chieu Market, James and Rachel arranged the downstairs for a classroom and study room, with a library and reading room in the garage. This small youth center quickly attracted 130 students in five English classes. Pham Quang Tam, son of an Evangelical Church pastor, taught two of the classes. Tam was trained as a pilot in the United States. He was drafted but due to an eye problem was not flying, instead instructing in helicopter maintenance. Nguyen Quang Trung monitored the reading room. While well located, it was also dusty and noisy, with large army trucks and even convoys of tanks passing by. Students enjoyed Sunday evening discussions and James organized a Sunday morning Bible class for interested students. Rachel was assisting in the Gia Dinh community center clinic.

New English classes started at the Saigon student center in September, but classes were smaller than before Tet. An Evangelical Christian student group was also using the facilities one evening a week and a Bible Story Hour for neighbor children had been recently started. The Beidlers lived nearby. Dorothy was teaching the five older Metzler and Stauffer children, using Calvert materials, and Luke was teaching English in the Saigon University. Luke had also recently begun teaching conversational English to some seventy Buddhist monks at an institute on the outskirts of Saigon.

Throughout the summer and fall, there were ongoing procedural discussions between the United States and North Vietnam leading to the eventual Paris peace talks. In late October, Everett Metzler reported to the Mission Board office that the newspapers in Saigon were "full of rumors, speculation and reactions to the politics of de-escalation. Some feel the U.S. is about to sell Vietnam out to the communists. Most just want peace and are willing to accommodate to some degree."

In a national address October 31, President Johnson announced the cessation of bombing raids over North Vietnam. We found it amusing that, while the President agreed to admit the National Liberation Front into the peace talks, he insisted that the U.S. was not giving them "recognition in any form." In the presidential election in the United States November 5, Richard M. Nixon defeated Hubert H. Humphrey. When he was confirmed as candidate at the August Republican National Convention in August, Nixon pledged through negotiations to "bring an honorable end to the war in Vietnam."

After the election, James Stauffer commented: "We can but pray that Nixon will be able to bring peace to this troubled land. There is no easy way as long as both sides are determined to have their way. Many Americans are predicting that the war will be over in '69 or '70, but I haven't found any Vietnamese that optimistic." Stauffer had just met some visiting church leaders from the United States and was appalled at their support for the war. "They don't seem to question any of the basic issues or the way it is being conducted," he said.

We all believed that peace was "still a long way off." In a December letter home, I questioned whether the Saigon government wanted a political settlement, somehow hoping that they would be able to defeat the other side militarily—even willing to risk an expanded war and perhaps a nuclear confrontation. One promising sign was that the local press was discussing post-war issues.

Both Stauffer and I referred to the American war tactics. Gen. Westmoreland, the commanding American general from 1964 to 1968, pursued a "search and destroy" strategy, anticipating that this would weaken the ability of the other side to pursue the war. Large numbers of southern Viet Cong and People's Army of Vietnam (PAVN) soldiers from the North died from aerial bombing and napalming and from heavy shelling from artillery on land and from naval ships offshore. This strategy also resulted in hundreds of thousands of civilians killed. (Nick Turse documents the war on civilians in *Kill Anything That Moves* [New York: Henry Holt, 2013]).

Given the desire of the Vietnamese people to rid their country of foreign military forces, it is questionable whether any strategy would have enabled the United States to "win" the war. But the policy of attrition—to kill as many soldiers as possible while minimizing one's own losses, made the war so savage. It also encouraged the killing of civilians to inflate the "body-count" ratios. As the counters said, a dead Vietnamese is a dead VC. Westmoreland's successor in June 1968, General Creighton Abrams Jr., relied more on a "clear and hold" strategy.

Nineteen sixty-eight was the deadliest year in the long war. More than 16,000 U.S. soldiers died, bringing the total U.S. deaths to 31,000 along with 200,000 wounded. The U.S. troop strength at the end of the year was more than one half million—537,000 soldiers in Vietnam, with hundreds of thousands more in Thailand and on the South China Sea. Nearly 30,000 ARVN soldiers and around 200,000 on the other side were killed. Tens of thousands of civilians died.

Vietnam Christian Service personnel gathered in Saigon early November. Soon after the conference, Fred Gregory concluded his two-year term. In contrast to some VNCSers who were not too keen to relate closely to the Evangelical Church, Fred emphasized the importance of working closely with the Church. In his termination report, he wrote: "Perhaps our most meaningful contribution to Vietnam will be to give the vision of concern and Christian compassion to the Church so it can be the Christian presence of reconciling love to all men so that this 'presence' can be indigenous as it should be, rather than a foreign presence." (Fred went on to a career in international development, including nearly twenty years with World Concern, first as director of international development and later as president.)

While no one was under the illusion that the war was over, there was planning for "post-war Vietnam." In November, William Snyder wrote that MCC plans "to continue in Vietnam for an indefinite period of time." Noting the cooperation that MCC had for many years with the Evangelical Church, Christian and Missionary Alliance and the Mennonite Mission, Snyder said that MCC wanted to continue these relationships. Experiencing a satisfying relationship with its VNCS partners, Snyder said MCC was "willing to continue administration of the Vietnam Christian Service program as long as the present emergency continues." He said that MCC's greatest potential after the conflict ends would be its personnel resources, its experience in Vietnam, and the positive church relationships it has had.

Referring to conversations with representatives of the NLF and DRV, Snyder said MCC "hopes to serve the Vietnamese people irrespective of the political solution to the conflict." The World Council of Churches was also discussing post-hostilities planning. Paul Longacre went to Geneva early November to take part in these discussions.

Reading Snyder's comments, Paul Kraybill foresaw a "greater degree of cooperation" between MCC and Eastern Mennonite Board of Missions. "Perhaps we will be able to be some kind of a bridge or buffer between the World Council groups and the Evangelical Church," he said.

Kraybill's comment about Mennonites being "a bridge or a buffer" between churches who identified themselves as Evangelical and the conciliar churches in the World Council of Churches ecumenical movement was increasingly recognized during this era. Mennonites held to many basic biblical and theological positions of the theologically conservative churches, while being at the same time committed to service programs that put them into association with churches united in Church World Service of the (American) National Council of Churches and the World Council of Churches. The largest American Mennonite denominations were neither members of the National Council of Churches nor the National Association of Evangelicals. Another factor was that Mennonite church bodies were relatively small, thus not as overpowering or dominant as larger churches tended to be viewed.

In a December letter home, James Stauffer spoke of the growing Mennonite Church:

> Praise the Lord with us for those that are coming to the Lord. Almost every Sunday there are several who accept Him. Last Sunday, December 1, I was especially thrilled to see a middle aged man believe. His wife was baptized in September. He has been attending regularly and has perhaps believed for some time. But he wanted to make a definite, public decision. He has been watching the workers and missionaries here for the last three years, he said. We feel this kind of commitment will be genuine. Several of those new believers are being sorely tempted. . . . Pray for them!

Another fourteen persons—three men and eleven women—were baptized December 22. One of the men was blind; one of the women suffered from leprosy. Ly Tuyet Nga worked in the clinic of the community center; she was hoping to go to the Nha Trang Evangelical Clinic the following year for a year of nursing training.

When writing home on Christmas Eve, I commented on the church welcoming "the blind and the lepers." I also noted that in contrast to our observation that Vietnamese men often made significant faith decisions first and then wives would follow their husbands, here at the community center, church women often made the decision first. In our community, women were frequently the heads of homes since the men were drafted into the armed forces; some were killed while others deserted their families.

These baptisms brought the total Mennonite Church membership to 66 persons plus the ten missionaries. Baptisms seemed to be the way we Mennonite missionaries measured the growth of the church. We never recorded the number of people who expressed faith. In contrast, the Tin Lanh Church would report how many people *tin Chúa* (believed in the Lord) in a certain period of time. Those who believed in the Lord were said to have experienced the "salvation of their souls" (*cứu linh hồn*). While the Tin Lanh Church would also record baptisms, they emphasized the number of those who made an initial profession of faith.

One of the practices we missionaries introduced into church life was our tradition of footwashing. When the congregation grew, we again discussed whether to continue this practice. Nguyen Van Ninh, the long-time MCC interpreter and VNCS personnel director, was in on the discussion. His family was seen as quite well-off and thus on a higher social level. In earlier years, he was not active in the church, but was now a committed member of the congregation. Someone in the group asked a practical question, "Would anyone in the church be willing to wash the feet of Mrs. Hai who has lost toes to leprosy?"

With little pause, Ninh responded: "If no one else wants to, I will!" We washed feet.

More than four hundred persons came to the Mennonite Church's Christmas program Saturday evening in the rear patio. A feature of the Sunday morning service was recitation of Philippians 2:1-11. Several illiterate women memorized the passage. Someone donated a roasted pig for a Sunday dinner, so we had roast pork sandwiches after the worship service and baptism.

We missionaries sang Christmas morning at the Truong Minh Giang Church where Arlene and James Stauffer had ministered a decade earlier. Mary and I hosted our missionary colleagues and their children for dinner. We all were thankful for the opportunities we had to give expression to the gospel in Vietnam.

POST HOSTILITIES PLANNING

Chapter 30

On January 1, 1969, Earl and Pat, nearing the end of their terms, went with our family to My Tho. After engaging a skipper on the Tien Giang branch of the mighty Mekong River, we went to Phoenix Island where the Coconut Monk (*Ông Đạo Dừa* – Nguyen Thanh Nam) lived with his followers. An engineer who had given up his work in the pursuit of peace, he embraced an esoteric blend of beliefs which included symbols of the Christian cross and the Buddhist swastika. At the entrance to his community were images of the Virgin Mary and the Buddhist Goddess of Mercy, *Quan Thế Âm*. We did not meet the famous monk who urged peace among the warring parties––he had gone to Saigon in an unsuccessful attempt to meet President Nguyen Van Thieu.

After long arguments about the arrangement of the table, the Paris Peace Talks opened on January 18 with four parties, the Democratic Republic of Vietnam, the National Liberation Front, the United States, and the Republic of Vietnam.

Two days later, Richard Milhous Nixon was inaugurated as the new president of the United States. Elected on a promise to end the war, he said in his address: "We are caught in war, wanting peace. . . . After a period of confrontation, we are entering an era of negotiation. . . . The peace we seek to win is not victory over any other people, but the peace that comes with the opportunity for all the peoples of this earth to choose their own destiny."

It soon became evident that Nixon was not prepared to quickly end the fighting. Neither was Hanoi ready to give up the fight. Although North Vietnam charged that the new American president was pursuing the same failed policies of President Johnson, most members of the U.S. Congress were ready to give Nixon some time to resolve the conflict.

In his inaugural address, Nixon had also said: "I know that peace does not come through wishing for it—that there is no substitute for days and even years of patient and prolonged diplomacy."

Years of prolonged diplomacy! Nixon was not going to be the first American president to lose a war—the war would continue. He would pursue a policy of "Vietnamization," replacing U.S. forces with a greatly enlarged Army of the Republic of Vietnam (ARVN).

In mid-February, Everett Metzler surveyed the scene: "The B-52s and regular artillery barrages testify to the fact that Saigon defenses are under pressure, and that life in the countryside has not improved," he wrote to Paul Kraybill. "Our prognosis is more of the same. We see no sudden end to the fighting. The NLF isn't going to just fade away. Unless there is a radical change in U.S. policy or in 'the powers that be' here, there is no prospect for peace in the near future. Too many who have power now are afraid of peace."

Thus, four years later, at the end of President Nixon's first term in office, there was still no peace agreement. Along with hundreds of thousands of conscripted soldiers from both North and South Vietnam and large numbers of civilians killed, 27,000 additional U.S. military personnel lost their lives before the peace agreement went into effect on January 27, 1973.

The large number of MCC personnel who arrived in the country in 1966, the year VNCS began the cooperative program, were now completing their three-year assignments. Mary Pauls, who was leaving in February, admitted in her January termination report that one of her "short-comings" was her neglect to submit monthly reports—common to many MCC volunteers. She believed that "the work will speak for itself." She and Dr. Christopher Leuz had worked at the Alliance leprosy clinic before the Pleiku clinic and hospital opened in September 1966. Later she worked in public health in thirty-five villages around Pleiku, concentrating in twenty-five of these. Better hygiene already resulted in fewer skin infections and prevention of hookworm. She was pleased to work with the provincial medical chief in a "rewarding program" of BCG vaccine inoculation in the Pleiku schools to protect against tuberculosis which even provided some immunity against leprosy.

"I am very grateful for the opportunity I've had to work with this organization in Vietnam," Pauls wrote. "It is with regrets I leave my beloved villagers in Pleiku."

In March, Doug Hostetter also wrote a termination report. Although he had raised many questions during his time in Tam Kỳ, he wrote:

> I have thoroughly enjoyed my tour and feel that I have learned much about Vietnam, her culture, her people and her war, to mention nothing of my greatly increased understanding of my own country, government, culture and myself. Although there have been many hard, difficult and unpleasant experiences, I feel that these, too, have been a part of the educational and hopefully maturing process. I leave Vietnam with a sense of accomplishment and fulfillment. No, I have not stopped the war, built a large institution or saved many lives through medical skill, but I have seen people change. I have seen hate . . . exchanged for tolerance or even love, cynicism move into idealism, suspicion change into trust.

While he appreciated many things about VNCS, Doug expressed concern about the "ideological split within VNCS" which made it difficult for many volunteers to follow their convictions—especially in regards to active peacemaking. This "split" did not follow denominational lines. "There are many Mennonites who are not seriously interested in reconciliation while there are many persons from others agencies who are deeply concerned along these lines," Doug wrote. To resolve this issue, he said the recruiting agencies needed a commonly agreed ideology and purpose.

The year 1969 also saw the beginning of a community development program in Ban Me Thuot. Sanford Stauffer was there a short time before his term ended. In August, Kurt and Frieda Sawatzky began working there.

One day in late January at the Gia Dinh community center, I chanced to open the small wooden mailbox attached to the inside of the large entrance gate to the center. We never checked this mailbox because we received all our mail at Box 991 at Saigon's central Post Office. Inside were two folded and slightly rain-stained letters. Both carried the seal of the People's Liberation Front, Saigon-Cholon-Gia Dinh Sector. Not wanting anyone to see me with these letters, I quickly folded them and placed them in my pocket, returned home on my scooter and set about to translate them.

We surmised that they might have been in the box for several months. While neither was dated, it was clear that one was written earlier and addressed specifically to "Miss Bích" who gave leadership to the Family Child Assistance program. The letter said: "We have heard from some compatriots directly, and also from the general public, expressions of indignation about injustices in the relief assistance of the Evangelical Organization (*Hội Tin Lành*) in which you play an important role."

The letter continued:

> As we see it, everyone must bear a load in war-time, but it is the poor class which must bear the heaviest load because they have heretofore lacked and now lack even more. This is why any charitable work must concentrate on helping this class. There is no reason—under any kind of sentiments—to make a mistake about this matter. Furthermore, no charitable organization can go along with injustice or an indifferent party spirit which affects the significance of the charitable work and causes the organization to lose its respect among the people.
>
> We ask you to reexamine your work. If it is as the compatriots . . . have said, you must immediately change it. We also strongly warn anyone who purposely goes against the common advancing movement . . . , we shall deal with them strongly with an appropriate punishment.

The other letter was directed to the "Board of Directors, Evangelical Organization in South Vietnam," and was less ominous, even quite warm with praise. "We are extremely touched and grateful for the charitable work of your organization in helping with relief . . . and . . . also helping to supply lumber to rebuild houses. Again we express our gratefulness to your organization."

However, the writers also expressed a few of their "opinions." The charitable work of our mission is very good, the letter said, "but because it is not closely inspecting the activities of some of its personnel, the significance of your work is lessened." The letter claimed that in giving relief assistance, some of our staff members had "selfishly taken advantage even to the withholding of relief supplies, demonstrating authoritarian attitudes." They said that this had been reported to our organization and wondered whether it had yet come to our attention. The problem was continuing, the letter said, and urged us to "remedy the situation." The letter closed with sincere greetings and wished us good health.

Much of the letter was written in standard communist political rhetoric that we were familiar with. We had no doubts that the letters came from a local NLF unit, but were hesitant to share the letters with the staff of the social service center, fearing negative reaction if government personnel should learn that we had received messages from the National Liberation Front. However, since one letter was directed to Miss Bích, and the other letter criticized the actions of our staff personnel and even warned of drastic action unless these problems were corrected, it seemed appropriate to show the letters to key staff members. Miss Bích was not greatly concerned by the letter addressed to her; she said she had received other occasional comments from the community.

We were not aware of irregularities which supposedly were reported to the Mission. We had literally given assistance to several hundred families and attempted to do this fairly. In a letter to the Salunga Mission Board office, Everett wrote that the letter indicated that "at least we are known to the other side in a way that we wish to be known." We changed no policies and received no further letters from "the other side."

The social ministries of the Gia Dinh community center also came to the attention of the government's Social Welfare and Relief Ministry. One of the VNCS expatriate social workers supervised our staff who worked with the MCC sponsorship programs. Since VNCS worked with the Ministry of Social Welfare in training social workers, our community center was chosen as one of the institutions to provide a month-long practical experience for a class of cadres, working with the clinic and with the Family Child Assistance program.

One day Mrs. Bich learned that the husband and father of one of the FCA families was killed in the war. A child in the family had been accepted into the program to learn a trade. The mother, Mrs. Thoi Lap, supported the family by selling at the market. We accompanied Bich to express our sympathy for their loss and saw that she received some financial help. The war deprived many families in the Dong Ong Co area of husband and father.

The Thoi Lap family mourns the loss of husband and father.

Orie O. Miller came to Saigon for three weeks in late January to visit his son Robert's family. Representing the Mennonite Economic Development Associates (MEDA), Orie proposed a small income-generating project for members of the church and other community families with limited incomes.

The principal of the Rang Dong School, Mrs. Phan Tuyet Nga, and her husband, Nguyen Van Ngay, agreed to develop this program raising and marketing broilers. Beginning with $500 U.S. in capital, they would purchase and care for one hundred chicks for a few weeks when they would be distributed to families, each raising twenty chickens until marketed. Mr. and Mrs. Quang, James, Arlene, Mary and I would make up the board of MEDA-Vietnam.

The program got off to a fairly good start. In a May 31 report to A. A. DeFehr, secretary of MEDA Southeast Asia, the first ten families involved were satisfied with their profits. However, the problems inherent in a volatile wartime economy were already articulated in an attached letter. The best chick breeds had to be imported from Japan and the government restricted these imports to encourage local hatcheries. Poultry feed also had to be imported—some of it from Singapore. We received a second $500 infusion into the program in August.

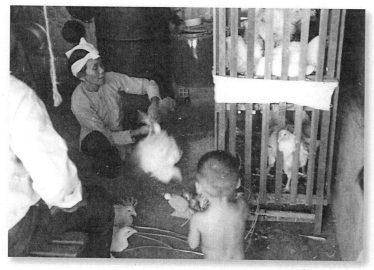

Family raising chickens.

The program suffered serious setbacks in mid-1970 when two consecutive lots of chickens ended up with losses due to diseases and low broiler prices. Most families asked out of the program because they were unwilling to do the work with no profit. An attempt to work with fewer larger producers was unsuccessful. Even though the local MEDAV committee was able to borrow additional funds at a lower rate than what MEDA charged, the poultry project was discontinued. Two major currency devaluations in 1971 and 1972 reduced the assets to the dollar equivalent of $246.05 when the account was liquidated in December 1972.

On Sunday morning, February 9, 1969, Everett, Margaret and James Metzler took Orie Miller with them to attend the worship services of the Evangelical Church in the Mekong River city of My Tho. They were stopped mid-way because the Viet Cong had mined the highway; traffic was stalled for several miles. After waiting an hour, they returned to Saigon. James Metzler later said he wished he had taken a picture of Miller standing looking at the long line of traffic "just to show that Orie Miller can be stopped!" Miller was again stopped a few days later when leaving Vietnam. Americans were routinely granted fourteen-day courtesy visas, but he had inadvertently overstayed this complementary visa and had to go through the red tape of securing an exit visa to leave.

Miller recommended to Paul Kraybill that the Mennonite Mission expand to another area in Vietnam, suggesting we should consider Da Nang, some city or town in the Mekong River delta, or even a ministry among the minority people "as the political situation allows." Pastor Doan Van Mieng, the president of the Evangelical Church, told Miller that Mennonites were welcome to go "anywhere in Vietnam."

In January, the Gia Dinh congregation formally invited Tran Xuan Quang to become pastor; he promised to prayerfully consider it. At the worship service on Tet, the lunar New Year, February 17, he announced that he and his wife had decided to accept this invitation. Everyone was delighted. On the second day of Tet the church council visited the homes of members. Quang said they visited around forty homes and drank thirty cups of tea.

At the suggestion of Pastor Quang, the congregation collected $57.00 which was sent to Mennonite Central Committee to aid victims of the conflict in Biafra (Nigeria).

On the fourth day of Tet, Everett and James Metzler and I walked through the area around the community center, visiting many families whose houses had been rebuilt after the May 1968 fighting. Among the homes we visited was that of Mr. and Mrs. Vo Van Hoa, both of whom had been baptized in December. They also dedicated their children to the Lord. Their oldest child, Be Hai, had accepted Christ by faith and was in the instruction class for baptism. Mr. Hoa told us that this was their first Tet since they were living for the Lord—a wonderful time. Other years they borrowed money for various purchases and ended the season with large debts. They now had greater freedom. They still had only canvas sides on the house which VNCS helped them build. Above the table written in chalk were the words Mr. Quang used as his text in the Tet sermon and suggested as the verse for the year: "As for me and my house, we will serve the Lord."

During Tet holidays, Mary and I visited Bui Thi's mother who was in the Binh Dan Hospital, just across the street from the Saigon student center. She was suffering from cervical cancer and received radium treatment. Margaret had visited her several times. (Thi was now studying at Edinboro University near Erie, Pennsylvania, while most of the family members were living in a Quang Ngai refugee camp.) After treament Thi's mother returned to the refugee camp where she died six months later.

The seven-day Viet Cong Tet ceasefire ended on Saturday, February 22, and the next day they launched rocket and mortar fire into Saigon and many other cities, towns and military bases. One rocket landed near the International Protestant Church in downtown Saigon on Sunday afternoon after the conclusion of a baptismal service. Since there were rumors of a VC attack, ARVN soldiers went door-to-door in some parts of the city, looking for weapons or propaganda leaflets. On Thursday morning they came into our Gia Dinh home. When they realized who we were, they left before searching the whole house.

Describing all this to my family, I wrote: "Some people try to point out that, were it not for the Vietnamese and American armies here, we would not be able to be here either. There is a certain amount of truth to this. But if [the Americans] weren't here, there would likely not be a war, and perhaps it would be possible for us to be here anyway. I generally feel safer if the troops are not around. To me the sight of a soldier with a steel helmet, a gun with bayonet, having ammunition and grenades around his belt, is not a very pleasing sight."

One morning the following week, nine VC rockets had fallen into Saigon. "I guess we are getting a bit fatalistic about such things," Everett wrote to Salunga. "I don't think that Saigonese are rushing to build bunkers as was the case last summer during the rocket season."

"We fear that our new President Nixon will be under great pressure to retaliate because of the present offensive," James Stauffer wrote to his mother. "This will only make things worse. Everyone cries out against the indiscriminate firing of rockets into the cities of Vietnam. . . . This is awful and we deplore it. But not very many are objecting to the B-52 raids that have been dumping thousands of tons of bombs on South Vietnam. . . . It's a sad, sad, situation and there seems to be no end in sight.

Tran Xuan Quang was ordained pastor of the church at the Gia Dinh community center on Sunday, March 16. One hundred and fifty friends and family members packed the upstairs meeting room. Both his father and his wife's father—highly regarded pastoral leaders in the Evangelical Church—took part in the service. With James Stauffer officiating, Nguyen Huu Phien preached the sermon and Tran Xuan Hi led the ordination prayer.

Jim Bowman and Quang monitor material aid assistance.

Tran Xuan Quang ordained pastor of the Mennonite Church.

Pastor Quang continued to work part-time with VNCS. He and James Bowman, who had earlier worked in Nha Trang, made an excellent team in administering the limited material aid distribution program.

In my letter home in mid-March, I recalled that Lancaster Mennonite Conference Assembly met that week in tandem with the annual EMBMC board meeting and wondered how Conference activities were developing after significant parts of many congregations had formally seceded from the Conference the previous year to form Eastern Pennsylvania Mennonite Church. The turbulent sixties dominated by the Vietnam conflict had introduced many changes into American life—including our Mennonite communities—that many people could not tolerate. This church schism was executed with a minimum of rancor, with the dominant group blessing the dissidents as they parted. This new group was still committed to mission activity but their church and community life would be guided by a rigid discipline and a earlier confession of faith expressed as Christian Fundamentals adopted by the Mennonite Church in 1921.

I wrote about Le Van Thao who had come to faith in Jesus a few years before. The church tried to keep in touch with him after he was drafted. Thao still expressed a warm personal faith when visiting us on home leave. He told how many of his friends were injured or killed when on a reconnaissance patrol near the Cambodian border.

I told about Pham Van Luc who had also come to Saigon on leave. After being drafted into officers' training school, he was now an infantry lieutenant in Chuong Thien province in southern Ca Mau peninsula.

While Luc was on home leave, Mary and I invited him and his wife, Qui, to our home for a Saturday evening dinner. In the next letter home, Mary described the dilemma that he lived with:

He is deeply disturbed about the work he is involved in, but to this point hasn't seemed to feel that he has any alternative. He's deputy commander of his company and they are now at the scene of some of the heaviest fighting currently going on. He is just sick of fighting and killing—VC, civilians, and his own men. In one battle one-third of his company were killed. Sometimes they're on operations for seven days at a time, with no time to bathe and hardly eat. Pray for him. He still seems to feel that he must do what he is doing for the sake of his men and his own life. We only hope he won't lose hold of himself by continuing to go against his conscience. He's considering paying a bribe in order to get a desk job where he at least wouldn't be personally involved in killing. That's the only way out. There's absolutely no chance of getting away. He considers deserting, but then when he's caught, he'd be given a year of hard labor, which is worse than terrible.

He says no one understands what they're fighting for. The fellows will spend the day on operations sometimes, then spend the night gambling and drinking. Tomorrow they'll likely die. They are looked down upon by their own people. When they come to Saigon they can't go into the nicer theaters or even find any girls who are interested in them. They (the girls) want only foreigners or rich fellows. Army boys are poor. Sons of rich families are often stationed in Saigon, thanks to their parents paying the price. They have a saying that they're fighting to make the fat people of Saigon fatter. If they survive, they'll later have the privilege of becoming chauffeurs to haul around the children of these rich families. These boys out on the front are just delighted to hear of rocket attacks on Saigon by the VC. The more the better. All this just goes to show how far the Saigon government is from the people, and also how senseless this war is.

. . . Luc says he still has faith in God, although sometimes it is rather dim because of the intensity of his experiences. But if he didn't have faith, he'd be like all the other fellows, gambling and drinking away his time. So we can give thanks that at least he's still bothered and cares about what he's doing. How we wish he could be spared the soul torture.

There was conflict of a different level at the community center around this time. A church member who had moved away—and now recently returned—came to the center threatening to beat the school principal and another teacher with a stick because of rumors they were not giving a good Christian witness! He was not easily dissuaded from his intentions and was unrepentant for a time. Fortunately, reason prevailed and the relationships were eventually restored.

In our stateside Mennonite communities we were taught that when Christians experienced conflict, it was essential to follow the teaching of Jesus—go to the one whom you had offended, or the one who had offended you and offer or seek forgiveness in order to restore the relationship. Perhaps a concern for "saving face" made it difficult within Vietnamese culture to acknowledge error and seek forgiveness. However, on several occasions we observed and experienced an appropriate cultural equivalent. Persons who were once estranged paid a friendly visit, perhaps bringing a gift of fruit which profoundly symbolized a desire to forgive, seek forgiveness and experience a restored relationship.

Passion Week came in early April. I was invited to speak at the Good Friday service at the International Protestant Church—along with six other persons—on the seven words of Jesus on the cross. I reflected on the agonizing cry of Jesus, "My God, my God, why hast thou forsaken me?" On Easter Sunday the Baptist congregation at Go Vap joined the Mennonites in celebrating the resurrection of Jesus at a sunrise service at the community center. Their youth choir sang and Pastor Do Vinh Thanh spoke. Around 180 people were present for the service and breakfast.

Our Overseas Mission Secretary Paul N. Kraybill arrived in Vietnam Saturday, April 12 for an eleven-day visit. He attended the Sunday worship service of the Gia Dinh church and met with the Mission Council on Monday. That evening Paul announced to the missionary team that Everett and Margaret Metzler agreed to transfer with their family to Hong Kong. On Tuesday Everett and I accompanied Kraybill to Da Nang, Tam Ky and Quang Ngai for three days. Robert Miller, the VNCS director, was also with us. Mortar rounds fell on Quang Ngai during our night there and the next morning we watched as jet planes conducted bombing strikes outside the town.

James Metzler accompanied Kraybill to Can Tho for two days. Alliance missionary James Lewis hosted them, introducing them to church and community leaders. They viewed the Mekong delta as an "open door" for missionary activities. James had an opportunity to discuss with Kraybill their eventual transfer to the Philippines.

The next Sunday Kraybill and Pastor Quang each gave short sermons at the church, followed by a baptismal service for six persons. These included Nhung, the wife of VNCS interpreter and personnel staff Nguyen Van Ninh; although she confessed faith in Christ when they were married, she had never been baptized. Another was Mrs. Anh, one of Mary's English students, forty years old and mother of nine children; on two occasions she had hesitated getting baptized because her husband's parents strongly opposed her decision to be a Christian, but thanks to the encouragement of Mrs. Cuu Trac and the prayers of many, she was happily baptized. Others were Be Hai, the teen age daughter of Mr. and Mrs. Vo Van Hoa, and Mr. and Mrs. Anh, the parents of Co Chin, our cook. Mr. Anh was the gatekeeper at the VNCS office. The sixth person was an older lady.

Mary was able to cultivate an ongoing relationship with her student Mrs. Anh. Her husband, Mr. Nghiep, was a civil servant who was assigned later that year to the Vietnamese Embassy in Thailand. They were permitted to take with them only three of their children; the other six would stay with a grandmother. We invited the couple to our home for supper before they left. On a later out-of-county leave we visited them in Bangkok.

In Kraybill's administrative report, he noted that in the previous seven months around thirty persons were baptized and additional persons received on confession of faith, bringing the total congregation to around seventy-five members.

Mary and I described the congregation in the *Missionary Messenger*: "The congregation represents quite a cross section. We have in the congregation illiterates and university students. We have folks with good jobs and others who at one time made their living begging. Some live in grass houses; others live in more substantial buildings. There are youth and aged. These various people represent opportunities for the church to be the church, in living, sharing, and witnessing to the transforming power of Christ."

Among his "general observations" Kraybill noted that Vietnam Mennonite Mission relationships with the Christian and Missionary Alliance and the Evangelical Church "continue to be cordial and fruitful." He said Vietnam Christian Service was "doing a significant piece of work," but its image had become "blurred" in the eyes of the Evangelical Church. Kraybill said Mennonite missionaries had "cordial and positive" relationships with VNCS, but shared "some of the same concerns reference the VNCS image and the witness of its personnel." Thus, Paul wrote, "We should encourage MCC to restore a separate identity so that the Mennonite relationship to the Evangelical Church is not further compromised."

Kraybill had come to Vietnam with antenna attuned to VNCS relationships. In early March he met with Dr. Louis L. King, the C&MA administrator in New York, who reported on a two-day meeting he had just attended in Saigon devoted primarily to "problems of relationships between VNCS, WRC, and the Evangelical Church." This meeting involved the executive committee of the Evangelical Church, C&MA Vietnam leadership persons, representatives of World Relief Commission, and Dr. King and Grady Mangham from the C&MA New York office. Misunderstandings between the Church and the World Relief Commission were apparently resolved at this meeting. However, King reported "an undercurrent of concern" regarding VNCS which came primarily from Evangelical Church leaders.

Kraybill said that King reported "rather objectively" that the Tin Lanh Church's concern "seemed to stem from their reaction against VNCS's involvement in political issues." King said that Church leaders were disappointed with VNCS to the extent that they were reluctant to even identify with VNCS any longer and even criticized C&MA for earlier assuring them that they would be able to maintain the same kind of relationship with VNCS that they had previously enjoyed with MCC, especially at Nha Trang.

Their reaction apparently stemmed "from certain documents which supposedly were circulated by VNCS following the Tet 1968 military offensive which were in the eyes of certain government leaders, very objectionable, or perhaps even 'treasonable,'" Kraybill wrote. He continued: "If Dr. King's report is correct, there seems to be a stiffening of the Evangelical Church's reaction against any peace activities, and a strengthening of its support for the Vietnamese government."

These "certain documents" were likely the reports of Atlee Beechy's contacts with National Liberation Front and Democratic Republic of Vietnam diplomats the previous summer which Robert Miller had asked the (Tin Lành) VNCS secretaries to type. Thus the criticism might have more correctly been made against MCC rather than against MCC's partners Church World Service and Lutheran World Relief.

During his visit three months earlier, Orie Miller had met with the Evangelical Church president Doan Van Mieng and reported to Kraybill that "no mention was made of any Evangelical Church reaction against MCC or VNCS contacts" with the NLF and the DRV. However, Mieng had apparently communicated to Miller that the Church saw in the MCC workers "a kind of understanding and sympathetic concern which they did not find now in the VNCS non-Mennonite people. Such matters of smoking, drinking, miniskirts and general lack of respect for the church's convictions affected the Evangelical Church's relationship to VNCS," Miller had reported. Criticism of VNCS personnel by Evangelical Church leaders tended to be over lifestyle issues. However, it is unlikely that most Evangelical Church leaders would have known which personnel were recruited by MCC, CWS or LWR.

President Mieng told Miller that he was trying to help the Church understand that VNCS was bringing new resources to the Church but then, as an afterthought, suggested that perhaps "quality is more important than quantity." Orie reported to Kraybill that he told his son Bob that he had fifteen months "to correct the situation." If this was not possible, he said he felt that the Mennonite Mission would need to "withdraw from close identification with MCC and VNCS."

William T. Snyder, the MCC Executive Secretary, also suggested that an administrative change was warranted. In an April 9 memo on "Post-Hostilities Planning, Vietnam" which Snyder prepared for a meeting of the VNCS Consultative Committee the following day, he said that "MCC as the administering agency could not have asked for better backing than we have experienced from the very beginning of this arrangement." But, he wrote,

> It is becoming more difficult for the Mennonite Central Committee as the administering agency of Vietnam Christian Service to retain the close cooperative tie that we have had with the national Protestant church and the Christian and Missionary Alliance. Our difficulties stem somewhat from the fact that the Mennonite Central Committee, in pursuing its basic stance as a historic peace church, believes deeply in a ministry of reconciliation which would include attempting to serve people on both sides of the conflict.

Snyder suggested that, in keeping with discussions a year earlier, possibly one of the other VNCS partners should become the primary administering agency. MCC would still want to be part of VNCS, Snyder wrote, but possibly being "more directly responsible for those projects that are close to the Vietnamese church" which MCC would want to assist for a time following any post-hostilities period. Snyder had in mind the medical programs in Nha Trang and Pleiku.

Snyder said that MCC, "with a somewhat closer tie to the [Evangelical] Church," might be in a better position "to assist the [Church] and other Christian agencies toward better understanding" if MCC assumed a secondary role in VNCS. If not leading VNCS, MCC would also have greater freedom "working with both sides of the conflict," Snyder wrote.

Some Tin Lanh congregations were located within Viet Cong-controlled territory. Many of these local pastors could identify with the VC struggle for national independence. Church leaders who knew Mennonites' interest in working with "the other side" understood that this was motivated by a desire to follow the way of Jesus, not by political views.

Discussions within the VNCS Consultative Committee eventually led to the decision that Church World Service would administer Vietnam Christian Service, effective January 1, 1970.

With the rapid development of the Mennonite Church and the ordination of a pastor, Kraybill noted that it was now urgent for the Mission to develop new patterns of partnership with the church in congregational life and in expansion into new areas. This would include the legal registration of the church in order to hold property. It would also include leadership training "in line with appropriate goals for leadership patterns" and deliberate plans to expand ministries in the Saigon area and elsewhere—most likely in the Mekong delta area.

Kraybill also recommended appointing Vietnamese for our ministries whenever possible. Instead of assigning missionaries to specific locations, he asked that mission personnel be assigned to specialized ministries such as church relationships, social services, administration, leadership training, and literature preparation. Kraybill hoped to maintain a personnel level of five long-term couples, with any transferring persons to be replaced promptly. Besides the older Metzler family transferring mid-year to Hong Kong, he anticipated James and Rachel leaving in October 1970 for an assignment in the Philippines.

In Kraybill's conversation with King before coming to Vietnam, King described a recent meeting with Evangelist Billy Graham in Bangkok, attended by representatives of Alliance churches and mission teams from many countries, where Tin Lanh President Mieng shared a moving experience. Here is the story as Kraybill recorded it:

> When President Johnson announced that the bombing of the North would be halted [on March 31, 1968], Pastor Mieng was deeply disturbed and crushed by what appeared to him to be the beginning of the end for the people of Vietnam. This to him signaled a clear sellout to the communists and he saw the country being taken over and the church destroyed. On several occasions he had been approached by folks who were asking whether there was any plan for the church to migrate bodily to another area. On both occasions he replied negatively. Following the announcement of President Johnson, Pastor Mieng sank to his knees in prayer and could only weep at the anguish that seized him because of this announcement. However, as he prayed and meditated, he became increasingly impressed with the image of Abraham and the promises that God made to him. As a result of this very intense personal experience, he came to the conviction that God was also giving him three promises. First, that he would give them this land or, in other words, would not make it necessary for them to be removed from Vietnam. Second, he would increase their members, and he saw this as a promise for a great spiritual ingathering. Third, he would make them a blessing to other nations around them.

Shortly before this time the Evangelical Church and the C&MA Mission embarked on an evangelistic program called Evangelism Deep and Wide, a model adapted from Evangelism in Depth used effectively in Latin America. As a result of his experience, Pastor Mieng envisioned ten million persons coming to faith in Jesus Christ within ten years. Even though the war and organizational deficiencies handicapped full implementation of the program, some people were led to faith in Christ.

The Mennonite Church was invited to become part of Evangelism Deep and Wide. One element of the plan was to eventually bring Evangelist Billy Graham to Vietnam for a series of meetings. Everett observed that their projections "were based on a rosier solution to the war than we envision," but praised them "for a vision and a goal." Our missionary team acknowledged opportunities for evangelism, but had reservations about employing a large American-style evangelistic campaign.

Graham, in his autobiography, *Just as I am* (New York: Harper Collins, 1997), reports that he was in Bangkok in March 1969 speaking with missionaries about how to end the Vietnam War. According to a Graham memo to President Nixon dated April 15, 1969, which was declassified in 1989, some missionaries who met Graham in Bangkok allegedly suggested that if the peace talks in Paris failed, the President should step up the war and bomb the dikes in North Vietnam.

With the development of the Gia Dinh church in 1965, the Vietnam Mennonite Mission considered how best to develop biblical, theological and leadership training for the church. We were aware that the Baptist Mission was developing a seminary for a few students. We settled on developing a congregational-based Bible school that would offer core courses and grant certificates. I was asked to coordinate this program, so early in the year made plans for two courses to run simultaneously in a sixteen-week term.

Since Everett was preparing to transfer to Hong Kong and James Metzler to the Philippines the following year, I asked them to teach the first courses which were offered at the community center, one course on Saturdays and the other on Sundays—each two hours long. The Bible School opened on May 3. Everett taught the Gospel of Matthew and James Old Testament Survey. James taught in English with Nguyen Van Ninh as interpreter. More than twenty persons from the congregation began one or both of these courses. We were pleased—at the end of May—that sixteen students were attending regularly and ten of these expressed interest in receiving credit for their studies.

James enjoyed the opportunity to teach this course in spite of his already heavy load of English language classes. I picked up the classes when the teachers were unable to teach certain days; I finished Everett's class as he and his family prepared to leave. Certificates were given to eight students at the Sunday morning worship service on August 24.

In order to finish before Christmas, we immediately began a second term. James Metzler taught New Testament Survey and Don Sensenig a class on Christian Living. When James came down with hepatitis, I outlined the class and taught the first few weeks. Like the first term, some students studied both courses, some only one. Seven students received certificates. James mentioned six who completed his course—Nguyen Quang Trung, Ngo Thi Bích, Phan Van Khai, Vo Thi Be Hai, Dang Thi Thu Huong, and Nguyen Dinh Tin. Trung became the key leader of the church after 1975 and eventually president of Vietnam Mennonite Church into the twenty-first century; Bich, Trung's wife, was active in social ministries. Khai successfully dodged the draft, actively supporting the educational work of the church. Years later Be Hai married an Australian who pastors a church in his country. Tin became the youth leader of the Gia Dinh church, and after the Revolution became an active leader in the Evangelical Church of Vietnam. Two more courses, Church History and Evangelism & Church Planting, were offered in the third term which began in January 1970.

On May 11 and 12, 1971, the Viet Cong forces shelled more than one hundred and fifty cities, towns, and military bases throughout South Vietnam including Saigon. Prior to that there were a number of small skirmishes and explosions in Saigon. The Gia Dinh post office was blown up and an explosive charge detonated in the Saigon post office. On Sunday night, May 11, some VC infiltrated into a large elementary school across the street from Luke and Dorothy's house two blocks from the Saigon student center. Government soldiers set up machine guns in Beidlers' yard to attack them, killing several VC soldiers in the action.

Our family took a short restful vacation in Nha Trang in late May, staying in the MCC unit house near the sea. Elisabeth Roggli, the Swiss operating room nurse, showed us the much-enlarged facilities. The hospital staff included doctors Harold Kraybill and Marvin Piburn, surgeon-ophthalmologist. Other nurses were Carolyn Piburn, Katherine Peters and Jane Collins. Nurse Tharon McConnell was the nursing school director. Devadoss Maddimadugu from India was lab technician, Joe Sprunger the hospital logistics coordinator, and Esther Kraybill hostess. Besides the ten international staff members were many Vietnamese staff.

Toward the end of our stay, the Tin Lành Church held its annual conference at the nearby Bible Institute and I was able to attend several sessions. In his "state of the church" presentation, President Mieng noted that the Church had grown in the previous twenty years in the midst of great suffering. He paid tribute to MCC and VNCS that were contributing to God's work in Vietnam. Many C&MA missionaries were in attendance, including Thomas Stebbins, who was replacing Franklin Irvin as Alliance field chairman.

A visitor to Nha Trang during our stay was Dr. Marjorie Nelson, a doctor working in the Quaker rehabilitation center in Quang Ngai. In the January 1968 Tet offensive, when visiting Hue with her IVS friend, Sandra Johnson, the two were captured by the Viet Cong and held about two months before being released. Her story was fascinating. They lived very simply but were never mistreated. Most of their nights were spent in underground bomb shelters since air strikes and bombings were quite frequent. Mary wrote home: "Dr. Nelson spoke of her captivity as a spiritual experience. She was not afraid to die and wasn't fighting or rebelling against her captors or her plight. She became much more keenly aware of beauty all around her. She frequently found herself surrounded by such intense beauty in nature, and noticed sounds and fragrances." After being released she went to the States briefly, then returned to Quang Ngai to continue her work fitting civilian war amputees with prosthetic limbs.

In May 1969 there were statements from both sides at the Paris peace talks. Fearing the United States would force the Republic of Vietnam to compete politically with the communist side, President Nguyen Van Thieu forged a coalition of several political groups into the National Social Democratic Front—committed to continue the military struggle.

Communist and non-communist opposition leaders met secretly in the jungle in South Vietnam on June 6 to 8 to form the Provisional Revolutionary Government (PRG) to better challenge the Thieu government. Announced by the National Liberation Front in Paris a few days later, its stated platform was little different from that of the NLF—withdrawal of US military forces, establishment of a coalition government, free elections and eventual reunification of the country.

On June 17 the Stauffer family went for the day to the beach at Vung Tau—one hundred and thirty kilometers east of Saigon—with Jean Miller, her son Jimmy and several of Everett and Margaret's younger children. They left Vung Tau in Stauffer's 1951 Citroen sedan around 3:00 p.m. so they could arrive home before dark. Ten kilometers from Vung Tau they came upon a long American military convoy parked along the highway. American GIs stopped all traffic saying there was trouble ahead but allowed civilian traffic to travel through. Thirty kilometers further the high-way was dug up at two places one hundred meters apart. James remembered crossing those areas in the morning and noticed that one of those spots now seemed to have fresh soil on it. Three Australian armored personnel carriers (APCs) passed by them going the other direction. Just as their car crossed the last of the two spots they heard a huge explosion behind them, followed by heavy small arms fire. They sped away from the scene.

It was not known whether the mine explosion was triggered by pressure, a change in the magnetic field, or by remote control. It was too scary to think how it would have impacted our missionary team had the mine exploded as the mission's car passed by seconds earlier! Our mis-sionary team had been considering going to Vung Tau for a short conference when the Sensenig family returned in July—before the Beidler and Everett Metzler families left. But now Stauffer, thankful to God for protection, wrote to his "loved ones" at home: "I don't think we will go to Vung Tau for a while."

Phan Ba Phuoc, who had just begun working as an interpreter for the Australians in that area, later explained that an anti-tank mine was apparently planted by a North Vietnam unit that had infiltrated into the area. One of the Australian APCs was destroyed by the explosion which killed eleven soldiers. Later that evening Australian forces attacked the northern unit, claiming to have killed forty men while capturing two. There had been other attacks on Vietnamese govern-ment bases east of Saigon in the preceding weeks.

Violence came to our home on Saturday evening, July 5, when an armed man terrorized Mary and me for forty-five minutes. We were in our large office-bedroom upstairs when an armed man suddenly appeared at the head of the steps around 8:00 p.m. and came into the room, point-ing a revolver at me and forcing us to sit on our bed. He sat down at the desk and said he was part of a Viet Cong unit planning that evening to attack the Gia Dinh police station—less than a kilo-meter away. He said he would not harm us if we cooperated with him. To emphasize his demand, he pulled a hand grenade from his pocket and threatened to pull the pin. With Steven and Becky playing in the room we chose to cooperate. Steven had not seen the gun, yet said to Mary: "I don't think this man should be in our house." Mary calmly agreed and he went back to his play.

The robber asked for our money; he took out 55,000 piasters ($466) but returned the rest to the drawer "because we are good people!" Before leaving he locked me in the bathroom, threaten-ing to return and harm me if I notified the police. He then ordered Mary to go with him down-stairs and forced her to sit on the rear seat of his motorbike. Pastor Quang's assistant Nguyen Huu Lam, who lived upstairs and was conversing with the sewing teacher Ms. Van who lived downstairs, saw them go out and asked Mary whether he could help in any way; he had no idea what was transpiring. Mary, terrorized, weakly said "Thank you." The two drove away; at the end of the alley, he left Mary return home.

At church the next morning, we gave thanks to God for his protection. We were extremely grateful that four year-old Steven and Becky had not understood the drama that unfolded as they played. They suffered no nightmares and soon forgot about the incident. We reported the robbery to the Gia Dinh city police. We did not recognize any suspect when called to the police station a few weeks later. We told Lam and Van to keep the gate and the doorway to our house closed.

Who was this man? He most certainly was not a Viet Cong cadre. Perhaps he was an ARVN soldier angry with the violence within Vietnamese society.

A few days later I wrote home: "Praise the Lord, we were robbed the other evening by an armed man, but nobody was harmed! This is the way our Christian friends would have described it. An unpleasant experience is a cause for rejoicing when one can see God's protecting hand in it."

Mary and I were aware of God's protection in this incident. More than a year later, when the Stauffer family was on furlough, a young woman asked Arlene whether there had been some crisis among the missionary families. She prayed regularly for the Vietnam missionaries but on a particular day sensed a need for more urgent prayer. Checking dates, Arlene recognized that this was the day when we were terrorized! No one could convince us that there were not active unseen spiritual forces guiding our lives.

I had substantial money at home because I was assisting community people improve their housing. Eight hundred houses in the area had been destroyed in the fighting a year earlier, and we had helped many families rebuild their houses. Now we were helping to improve the houses of families recently accepted into the sponsorship programs. Assistance was usually in the form of lumber and sheets of aluminum roofing.

After the May 1968 fighting, material aid supplies were given to families enrolled in the family child sponsorship programs. The center staff usually gave a brief meditation from the gospels before the monthly distribution to family representatives. Each family received fifteen pounds of bulgur—parboiled wheat, two quarts of vegetable oil, a kilo of soap and two cans of MCC beef. Now a year later the center was scaling back this program. Some of the teenagers who had completed their studies in trades were getting good jobs.

At mid-year, William Snyder and Boyd Lowry from Church World Service came to Vietnam. I accompanied them to Nha Trang where they met with all the up-country personnel. On his return to New York, Lowry informed James MacCracken, chairman of VNCS Consultative Committee, that he had to counteract rumors that MCC was withdrawing from Vietnam Christian Service. He said that the MCC concern for peace and for strong relations with the Evangelical Church was important. He wrote: "This emphasis is not to preclude CWS and LWR pursuing the same objectives." Lowry also noted the importance of VNCS keeping in communication with Mennonite Mission personnel.

In his long memo to MacCracken, Lowry wrote:

> On VNCS staff there are approximately ten or fifteen young people who are prepared to go all out for identification with Vietnamese in such matters as housing, additional Vietnamese Language training, and fulfillment of their understanding of PEACE objectives. The VNCS top administration must make special efforts for communicating effectively with all these staff members who represent six or seven denominations. Their idealism is strong and the PEACE implications for VNCS of some of their considered actions are not always clear to them. During the next eighteen to twenty-four months recruitment of staff for VNCS must include as a high priority such qualifications as obvious Christian dedication, needed skills and emotional stability.

While Lowry stressed that "the Peace Church emphasis of the Mennonite Central Committee is not to be diminished," he appeared to be questioning the contribution of idealistic young volunteers and calling for greater emphasis on recruiting trained professionals. "Communication among the partners of VNCS on this essential subject will eliminate unnecessary strains," he wrote.

On July 29, Everett and Margaret Metzler left for Hong Kong with their five children—Eric, Gretchen, Malcolm, Andre and Jennifer. We were sorry to see them go, but understood the contribution they could make to a broader Asian ministry. On a visit to Phnom Penh before they left for Hong Kong, Everett met with the Second Secretary and Press Attaché at the embassy of the Provisional Revolutionary Government and described the work of the Mennonite Mission and of Vietnam Christian Service. The diplomat indicated familiarity with Mennonites and said he had spoken with Japanese Mennonites. Everett was shown pictures of the PRG Organizing Congress two weeks earlier which included photos of Mr. Trinh Dinh Thao, the PRG Chairman.

Completing their three-year mission associate term, Luke and Dorothy Beidler and one-year-old Marta left the same day as Everett and Margaret's family. We were pleased that Luke and Dorothy expressed their willingness to return to Vietnam for another term of service. James and Rachel Metzler moved to the Saigon student center property after the other Metzler family left. Donald and Doris Sensenig returned for their second term a few days later.

Shortly before leaving, Everett wrote to Kraybill and Longacre: "Pulling up roots is a bit painful. I am sure many of our friends think we are doing what some of them would like to do! We still feel it is the Lord's leading, but wish that we had more to show for the years we have spent here."

Having "more to show" for one's efforts is a normal longing. What would Everett have liked to see? A strong Christian congregation meeting at the Saigon youth center? A pastoral training center preparing leaders for an ongoing Christian ministry? Jesus said the Spirit of God, like the wind, "blows where it wills." Why a thriving congregation developed at the Gia Dinh community center and not at the Saigon student center was due to many factors. Thousands of students were influenced by the service-inspired Christian witness of the Saigon student center, and dozens came to faith. Some affiliated with Tin Lanh congregations. Students at the Saigon center came from all over the city. A vital congregation of young people did take shape there in the year following the Revolution.

Our missionary team felt the loss of one of our two senior missionary couples who had nurtured us and modeled a consistent Jesus lifestyle. Everett and Margaret gave serious thought to the way we presented the gospel of Jesus Christ. In an article written for *Missionary Messenger* a few years later, Everett reflected with great insight on the different "Christs" preached by Christian missionaries, suggesting that a Christ calling for an individualistic salvation; a Christ responding to a deep, personal sense of sin; or a Christ expressed by colonial rulers was not very attractive to people. Instead, a Christ "who showed by his life and teachings the 'đạo,' the way men are to live," was more welcome.

"To Asians who are very conscious of community and responsibility to one's family," Everett wrote, "Jesus Christ comes as the ultimate ancestor, the heavenly elder brother, harmonizer, reconciler, and perpetuator of the family leading to a wider understanding of community and family beyond blood relationships." Or to Asians wanting to be liberated from their colonial past, "Christ the revolutionary holds more appeal."

The Gia Dinh church planned a farewell service before the Metzler and Beidler families left. Just after this special gathering, Arlene Stauffer wrote to James' home: "How I wish you could meet all these dear people—saints in the Lord. . . . They are learning to accept each other in Christ as brothers and sisters. Everyone looks forward to the Sunday worship service, which is always different. Sometimes there are spontaneous testimonies and always a lot of singing." Their testimonies, Arlene wrote, tell of "victories in daily life, practical answers to prayer—like the book of Acts come alive."

Arlene then told how she and Mrs. Nga, the principal of Rang Dong School, were visiting all 120 families enrolled in the Educational Assistance Program to determine which families still qualify for assistance. "We meet with so many difficult situations—some still do not have adequate housing now that the rains have begun," Arlene wrote. "Others have little to eat, are sick, out of work, school dropouts, so many women and children alone and in need. The husbands are soldiers—and many have deserted their first wives and taken younger women—common law marriage is almost the rule rather than the exception. It would be most discouraging if it were not for the miracles observed in the changed lives of those who have found the Lord. There are more than a dozen of these families now in our church."

Mary also wrote of the dynamism experienced within the young congregation: "Oh, last night at prayer meeting, Mrs. Thom got up and shared her thrilling experiences reading in the book of Job—for the first time, of course. She wanted to encourage the new Christians to be firm in their faith even when they face difficulties."

Nguyen Van Ninh, the longtime MCC interpreter and administrative assistant, now part of the VNCS administrative team, was invited to England for YMCA orientation. After spending some time in continental Europe he also traveled widely in the United States, meeting former Vietnam MCC workers and missionaries. Visiting Hong Kong and Japan, he accompanied a Japanese YMCA staff person who was coming to Vietnam on assignment. Ninh was gone from early July to early October.

While in the United States, Ninh visited the MCC and EMBMC offices. Speaking during the Sunday school hours at Akron Mennonite Church, Paul Longacre said he gave "a strong statement in support of the Saigon government" which elicited quite a reaction.

Ninh had worked closely with Mennonites for more than a decade and understood their commitment to peace and peacemaking. Why would he—and others—express strong support for the Saigon government—unwilling to negotiate with the other side and committed to continue the military fight against its determined opponents? There were certainly good reasons for not embracing the rigid Marxist policies that brought suffering to many people in the North. The Viet Cong tactics led to many deaths in the South. What assurance did the people have that the revolutionary fervor had already burned through its excesses so that the Saigon government could form a workable coalition with the other side? To embrace a policy of neutralism was only a step away from being out-maneuvered by an untrustworthy opponent, they claimed.

It was clear to us that, while most people were calling for an end to the war, they were not wanting to embrace the same form of governance as the Democratic Republic of Vietnam in Hanoi. Was there another realistic option? The government of Nguyen Van Thieu refused to consider any alternative to continued war.

Due to the shortage of middle schools, the Education Ministry authorized elementary schools to add junior high school classes with no further permissions needed. With Mrs. Nga, the principal, eager to do this, the Mission gave permission to open one grade on the condition that it would be self-supporting from tuition. A month later there were only half enough students enrolled so that the class was eventually dropped. The fall term of Rang Dong School opened with over 500 pupils. During the summer, the enrollment was even higher as public school students wanted an opportunity to continue their studies.

Instead of going to Phoenix Study Group this school year, the four missionary kids of our Mission plus four children from other Saigon missionary families were tutored in Calvert courses by Mrs. Virginia Cook, the wife of VNCS personnel director Douglas Cook.

The Gia Dinh clinic expanded throughout the year. Rachel was kept busy managing the clinic which was open several afternoons with the VNCS doctor, Joanne Smith T. They saw as many as 150 to 200 patients in an afternoon. Rachel had additional home responsibilities when she and James received three month-old Karen Rae for adoption in January. In July, Rachel discontinued her clinic work in order to manage the medical supplies room at the VNCS office when MCCer Ann Falk terminated; here she filled orders for the various VNCS medical programs. The VNCS office was now next door to the student center where James and Rachel lived.

Ruth Yoder returned for a second MCC assignment with VNCS in July. She would have preferred returning to Nha Trang to work with the one-year nurses training program. However, her assistant, Miss Cuc, was doing a fine job and VNCS wanted her to continue. So Ruth accepted the Gia Dinh clinic opportunity and expanded it into a five-day clinic. News of the clinic kept spreading by word of mouth; patients came from up to fifty kilometers away. Some patients were referred to the US Army Third Field Hospital.

Pham Quang Tam was teaching some of the English language classes at the Gia Dinh community center. Fluent in English, he had studied the English language in high school and university and understood the peculiarities of English grammar better than we who had grown up with English as our mother tongue. At the end of June, he became director of the English language program. Being an instructor in helicopter maintenance, he occasionally came to classes in military fatigues.

Tam's wife, Tran Thi Thuan, was one of the teachers in the Rang Dong School. They attended the worship services of the congregation. A thoughtful person, Tam spent time with James Metzler discussing theological understandings of the church. When the youth group was formed in mid-year, Tam was chosen to lead the group.

About this time we rented another house on Nguyen Thien Thuat Street for English classes and other activities, giving up the house on noisy Bach Dang Street. Over eighty students were present at the Bach Dang closing program; Pastor Quang gave a short message on "The Lost Coin" and Mr. Tran Phuong, a Christian layman who served as Vietnam representative of Gideons International, presented a Vietnamese New Testament to each student.

Mary gave an inspirational talk to the young women in the sewing class one afternoon each week. Writing home about it she said: "I enjoy these girls. They're teenagers and nice to work with. Many of them come from mixed-up family situations. . . . Last week one of the girls attempted suicide by taking an overdose of some kind of medicine. She's about fifteen. Her father shaved one-half of her head, so I guess it'll be a long time before she'll come to class again. . . . It's really sad and I feel so much the need to find every means possible to teach them of the worth of their own lives and personalities in God's sight."

Later in the year, we bought sixteen sewing machines and resold them to good students at the wholesale price. These young women were thrilled to have their own machines and earn an income through their skills. Some of the young men who studied mechanics, electrical wiring and other trades in various schools received diplomas and got jobs which augmented their families' incomes.

In mid-August, we received two visitors from Indonesia, Rev. Soesanto Harsosoedirdjo from the Javanese Mennonite Church and Rev. Theophilus M. Hadiprasetya from the Muria Christian Church of Indonesia, who were returning home after attending the Mennonite work camp in Japan. They met with the church council, and the church had a special service to welcome them. Harsosoedirdjo spoke on "God's Children of Light," emphasizing three areas of Christian living: communion with God, bearing witness and service. Hadiprasetya brought greetings from the places they visited—Taiwan, Japan and Hong Kong.

In August, we hired a new "old" staff member, Dinh Van Nam, whom we formerly knew as Chau Hong Luc, the first Vietnamese language teacher that James and I had when we arrived in Vietnam seven years earlier. He would be doing miscellaneous jobs—running errands to town and some secretarial work. "Nam" had worked in our bookroom for a time and then was inducted into the army. After brief military training and assignment, he went absent without leave. Caught and re-inducted into the army, this slight, thin man was forced to work at hard labor. He managed to skip out again and returned to his home area of Mo Cay district of Ben Tre province. This area was mostly under the control of the National Liberation Front and he was asked to teach primary school. He had to grow his own food. He told of his fright one day when an American helicopter suddenly flew over when he was working in the field. Instinct told him to run to hide though he knew that pilots generally considered farmers who run as Viet Cong partisans and blast them with machine gun fire. Shaking with fright and praying fervently, he managed to keep hoeing until the "angry bird" flew away!

Chau Hong Luc (aka Dinh Van Nam) with his family.

After some months, he decided to pick up a "safe pass" leaflet of the Chieu Hoi program that American and South Vietnamese planes scattered, encouraging VC cadres to return to the Republic of Vietnam side; this program was lauded as quite successful. He registered at the Chieu Hoi center in his area under an alias, Dinh Van Nam, was brought to Saigon and underwent training for another livelihood. Although he never was a VC, he was now an ex-VC!

Mary wrote home about his story: "When we first heard his story it was so utterly incredible. . . . This is one way to avoid military service. Just another one of the absurdities of this crazy war. He is a man with average ability, willing to do any kind of a job. He will be staying at our place, upstairs with Mr. Lắm."

On September 3, 1969, Ho Chi Minh died of a heart attack at the age of seventy-nine years. Only a few days earlier he had written to President Nixon whose July 15 letter called for a "just peace." At the same time, the United States proposed secret talks between Henry Kissinger, Nixon's assistant for national security affairs, and Xuan Thuy, North Vietnam's chief negotiator at Paris. Hanoi did accept this proposal. But Ho Chi Minh's August 25 response to Nixon was clear. He accused the United States of a "war of aggression" against the Vietnamese people. The longer the war continued, he wrote, "the more it accumulates the mourning and burdens of the American people." He declared that the plan put forward by the National Liberation Front was the way to solve the conflict. The Americans had to leave and allow for Vietnamese political self-determination. Several days after the President's death, Hanoi announced that leaders had formed a collective team to succeed Ho Chi Minh—Le Duan, first secretary of the Communist party; Truong Chinh, chairman of the National Assembly; Vo Nguyen Giap, defense minister; and Pham Van Dong, prime minister.

In my next letter home, I reflected on Ho Chi Minh's legacy:

> Ho Chi Minh is dead. But I am sure that his dream did not die with his death. For many people even in South Vietnam, Ho was the father of his country, compared to George Washington. To others, he was considered a tool of the world communist movement. I have the feeling history will be on the side of Uncle Ho. I personally am opposed to the use of military force as an instrument of national policy. I also believe that due to the international climate which has prevailed since World War II, Vietnam could have successfully gained independence in a more peaceful fashion. While I must reject Ho's policies and especially his methods, I am sympathetic of his objectives.

I continued: "It is tragic that while the United States has been able to live with communism in Europe, it decided that it could not do this in far-away Asia. This failure has caused the death of hundreds of thousands of Vietnamese and 40,000 Americans. And I am not yet convinced that Nixon is committed to ending the war on terms which both sides can accept."

In late August, President Nixon announced that 25,000 US troops had already been withdrawn and in mid-September announced that a further 35,000 men would soon return home.

Two days before Ho Chi Minh died, South Vietnamese President Nguyen Van Thieu sacked Prime Minister Tran Van Huong, replacing him with Tran Thien Khiem. Although Saigon and Washington were both taking a tougher line of action, Khiem's cabinet lacked strong political leaders.

In early September, Lt. William Calley was formally charged with several counts of premeditated murder for his role in the My Lai massacre in the spring of 1968. There was growing American grass roots opposition to the war, culminating in nation-wide rallies and prayer vigils on Wednesday, October 15.

A number of Americans working with relief agencies in Vietnam, frustrated at the continuing war, began to gather in Saigon. On September 25, James Metzler noted cryptically in his diary: "This eve Don and I attended a meeting of American peaceniks." On October 12, James wrote that they were "being asked to join a group of doves" taking a statement to the American Embassy on Wednesday, October 15, billed as Moratorium Day in the United States.

On Monday, James and Don attended the "International Peace Ring" to discuss plans for the group to go to the Embassy to present a letter to the Ambassador. Assuming that the entire group would not be invited inside the remainder planned a "silent vigil" outside. On Tuesday, James and Don were still deliberating whether to go to the Embassy the following day. James indicated he had "made a half-hearted decision" to go, sensing that doing something was "better than nothing."

James Metzler went with a group of twenty to the Embassy on the fifteenth. He and others kept a silent vigil in front of the Embassy as five persons were invited inside to meet with Ambassador Ellsworth Bunker. They presented a brief statement addressed to "Mr. President." It read: "As millions of Americans today express their opposition to the war in Vietnam, we who work here wish to add our voices to theirs. We know the suffering of the Vietnamese people. We say this war must stop. We call for the immediate withdrawal of all American troops." The statement was signed by thirty-two persons, including James and seven Americans who worked with Vietnam Christian Service.

The vigil attracted the attention of the local and international press. Some Vietnamese papers reported on the October 15 statement as well as a September "Letter from Vietnam" addressed to "friends" which was also sent to President Nixon. It described the ongoing suffering of the people, calling on others to join them in demanding that the American government end the war. That letter declared: "This war must be stopped!"

While none of us missionaries had a hand in drafting this September letter, we supported the basic thrust of the letter so four of us missionaries were among the forty-nine persons who signed the statement. We identified ourselves as missionaries, but not the agency. Fifteen VNCS-ers also signed the statement. Some of these names appeared in several Vietnamese newspapers. The following week Don happened to be at the Joint United States Public Affairs Office center when newsreels from the United States were shown to the local press. Included was a close-up shot of James Metzler at the Embassy. A few days later, James Stauffer met a prominent Tin Lanh lay leader who—having seen the articles in the local Vietnamese newspapers—expressed appreciation for our attempts to speak for peace. He said that more American missionaries should have signed the letter. He claimed that the majority in the church were behind us.

This represented another "escalation" in our actions to work to end the war. We had spoken out in messages to the American people, calling for the United States to change their policy that was bringing devastation on a people. Now our position was being expressed publicly in Vietnam. How would the Saigon government, we wondered, propped up by the United States and committed to continuing the military struggle respond to this public action? Not any of us was ever questioned by security personnel.

Writing in late October to Harold Stauffer, the EMBMC associate overseas secretary, I observed that James and Rachel were experiencing satisfaction in their work and were quite willing to stay in Vietnam until the end of their term in August 1971. Working with students at the Saigon student center and teaching in the Bible school in the Gia Dinh church was rewarding. There was good interest shown in the two English Bible classes each Sunday morning at the Saigon student center. Mr. Minh, an Evangelical Church Christian who taught a beginners' English class, also taught one of these Bible classes. Although suffering the agony of the continuing war, James—along with the rest of us—was finding opportunities to express concerns about the peoples' suffering to both American and Vietnamese audiences.

In my letter home explaining political developments, I wrote:

> Vietnamese want peace. Many of our friends are convinced that the war is senseless and must be stopped. Yet many of the folks we have learned to know in Saigon are afraid of peace. They have lived so well the last few years due to the military and economic support of the US. Now

when U.S. commitment here will lessen, many are afraid of what will happen. Some of these people see only two alternatives: either continuing to fight until they can militarily defeat the other side, or a capitulation to the other side and the acceptance of communism.

I would say that we missionaries are opposed to communism, but we believe that the half million American troops have done much more harm than good. . . . When U.S. troops leave, the Vietnamese will be able to resolve their problems in line with the political realities in Vietnam.

In late October, the government announced new austerity measures to cope with the runaway inflation. Prices of luxury goods and basic commodities skyrocketed; gas prices doubled. The black market rate of exchange was double the official rate of currency exchange which our Mission received. While the new measures were aimed at the wealthy, the pain was felt more acutely by the poor. At the Thursday evening prayer meeting of the Mennonite church, Pastor Quang, speaking to the concerns of the people, shared the passage from Romans 8 affirming the members that nothing could separate them from God's love. He read God's promise in Isaiah 41:10: "Fear not, for I am with you, be not dismayed, for I am your God; I will strengthen you, I will help you, I will uphold you with my victorious right hand."

On November 3, President Nixon delivered a nationwide television speech outlining his view of the situation in Vietnam and the options to follow toward peace. Explaining his policy, he said:

In the previous administration, we Americanized the war in Vietnam. In this administration, we are Vietnamizing the search for peace. . . . We have adopted a plan which we have worked out in cooperation with the South Vietnamese for the complete withdrawal of all US combat ground forces, and their replacement by South Vietnamese forces on an orderly scheduled timetable. . . . The rate of withdrawal will depend on developments on three fronts. One of these is the progress which can be or might be made in the Paris talks. . . . The other two factors . . . are the level of enemy activity and the progress of the training programs of the South Vietnamese forces.

A Gallup Poll the following day showed that seventy-seven percent of Americans backed the President with only seven percent opposed.

James Metzler invited his advanced English class to discuss Nixon's speech. "All sides and views expressed," James said. But in Washington on November 15, more than 250,000 persons gathered in a massive protest against the war.

Additional details of the March 1968 killing of several hundred unarmed civilians in the My Lai villages had been seeping out in the American press for months. The November 20 publication of the graphic photos of the massacre stunned the world; Americans could not believe that their soldiers would do anything like this! The release of these photos belied the claim of South Vietnamese President Nguyen Van Thieu that no massacre had occurred in this Quang Ngai village.

Coupled with dissatisfaction of the government's increased taxation to balance its budget, retired generals Duong Van Minh and Tran Van Don challenged Thieu's leadership. Thieu sharply attacked them. In a letter to Paul Kraybill, I noted that Thieu could weather this opposition: "'Big Minh' may have the people on his side, but Thieu has Nixon!"

In mid-October, the Associated Press religion writer wrote an article published in many American newspapers reporting that "many church relief agencies in Vietnam depend strongly on U.S. military presence and don't want to see an American troop pullout."

The writer, Bennet Bolton, attributed this view to Dr. Atlee Beechy who was the first VNCS director in 1966, whom Bolton identified as a "veteran Protestant missionary leader." He quoted Beechy saying that "the use of periodic or frequent military protection by some relief workers and missionaries makes the church's work appear dependent on military power." Many missionaries, Beechy was quoted, "favor the U.S. military presence and oppose US military withdrawal."

This was true. We knew that personnel of many agencies strongly supported the American military presence and activity in Vietnam. The problem with the article was that it appeared that Beechy advocated the US military presence in order to accomplish agency objectives! Boyd Nelson of Mennonite Board of Missions was one who wrote to the editor of an Iowa paper asking that they clarify that "Dr. Beechy's basic point states that . . . the identification of American Christian mission and relief goals with American political and/or military aims there stand to damage the Christian cause in Vietnam." Nelson wrote that the Mennonite agencies in Vietnam had long "been deeply concerned with the effects of American military presence and operations in Vietnam" and articulated these concerns to their churches, the U.S. government and the U.S. public long before the war became a major public issue in the United States.

In consideration of some possible VNCS-Mennonite Mission collaborative project in the Mekong River delta, in October Robert Miller, Dean Hancock, James Stauffer and I spent two days in Can Tho, the third largest city of South Vietnam located 160 kilometers southwest of Saigon. Meeting with local church leaders and representatives of international agencies, we surveyed areas of need and considered opportunities for ministries. Noting that war-displaced peoples were scattered throughout the city rather than in refugee camps as in Central Vietnam, Stauffer observed: "There is no end to the vast needs of a war-weary people."

Paul Longacre, MCC Director for Asia, visited Vietnam for a week in mid-November. In this his third visit since leaving Vietnam in 1967, Paul was again "impressed with the broad scope of effective Christian service being given by the fifty-nine VNCS foreign workers and approximately twice as many national staff." He noted "excellent prospects of securing a number of Asians and Europeans to replace departing North Americans." With the coming change of overall VNCS administration from MCC to CWS, beginning January 1970, Longacre suggested a review of the guidelines drawn up in 1966. Longacre met with the Mennonite missionary team and encouraged the Mission to take the initiative in any new work in Can Tho.

By year's end, there were 64,000 fewer American troops in Vietnam than at their maximum number but there were still 479,000 American soldiers there. Over 9,400 had been killed in 1969.

In a November newsletter to friends, James and Arlene Stauffer wrote: "American troops are beginning to leave but not their war machinery! Vietnamization of the war means only a continuation of bloodshed and heartache for the Vietnamese. They are caught as victims in a war the Americans escalated and are now afraid of being abandoned. Don't grow weary praying for peace in Viet Nam!"

VIETNAMIZATION TESTED

Chapter 31

On New Year's Day, 1970, Mary journaled: The past year "has brought to me a deeper involvement in the life of the church here than I ever experienced before."

Pastor Quang had been ordained the year before. His leadership in the church was greatly appreciated and highly respected. His sermons were clear and easily understood. He invited us missionaries to preach also; sometimes we missionaries heard him preach sermons similar to what we had preached a few months before—but now more clearly communicated and much more easily understood by the congregation! Thanks to Quang working in the VNCS office and learning to know their staff, several local and international VNCS personnel regularly attended the worship services of the church at the Gia Dinh community center. They even shared in the foot washing ritual which sometimes followed the first-Sunday-of-the-month communion service. There were around eighty-five baptized members of the church.

Mary taught the adult women's Sunday school class, one of six classes each Sunday morning. Quang had asked Mary and me to help improve the Sunday school program, so we met with the teachers. Surprised when Quang asked her to teach the adult women's class, Mary argued that having native Vietnamese speakers would be more effective. Quang replied, "There are no foreigners in this church!"

In mid-February, the community center hosted a four-day Wednesday through Saturday seminar on educational principles for the Rang Dong elementary school teachers and Sunday school teachers with Co Bay, a staff member of World Vision who had earned a bachelor's degree in Christian Education. Mary was pleased that Bay knew her subject matter well and presented it attractively.

The third term of the congregational Bible school began early January with James Metzler teaching Church History and James Stauffer coordinating a course on Evangelism. Evangelical pastor Nguyen Nam Hai, Metzler's language teacher and the secretary of the Evangelism Deep and Wide program of the Evangelical Church, gave one presentation. Don led one period on "evangelism and social work." Ten or twelve students were enrolled in these classes.

Thirteen students were enrolled in the fourth term from June to August. James Metzler taught Doctrines of the Bible and Donald Sensenig Church History. Beginning in late October, I taught the fifth term, offering only one class, "The Church, the People of God."

The 1970 lunar New Year, Tet, came on Friday, February 6. We said goodbye to the Year of the Rooster and welcomed the Year of the Dog. Many people, especially the older people, did not know what date—even the year—they were born. But they knew the animal of their birth year. Since the animal cycle repeated every twelve years, when people mentioned the animal under which they were born, others would recognize whether they were twenty-four, thirty-six, forty-eight or sixty years old. Since the twelve animals were paired with the ten elements, a complete cycle would be completed at sixty years of age—a full life.

There are religious elements to *Tết Nguyên Đán*, the Lunar New Year. Those who practice the cult of ancestor veneration welcome the spirits of their ancestors home for the holiday. Tet for the

Mennonite congregation in Gia Dinh became a time for members to give thanks for God's guidance the previous year. On this first day of Tet, seventeen persons gave testimonies at the church. It was a *vui* time—a happy occasion. On the second day, members of the Congregational Council visited the homes of persons associated with the church—visiting seventy-three homes. James Stauffer said he drank several liters of tea!

There were several deaths around Tet this year. The father of Nguyen Van Ninh died at the age of seventy-five. Mary helped the family sew loose-fitting white cotton mourning clothes which family members wore to the funeral held at the French Protestant Church on Thong Nhut Street, Saigon, which was the first funeral service Pastor Quang officiated.

After Tet, our family spent a few pleasant days at the beach town of Vung Tau with James and Rachel's family. We arrived home to receive the sad news that Oanh-Oanh, the vigorous, always smiling one-year-old daughter of VNCSer Doug Beane and his wife Mai, had died early that morning. A concern of all parents whose child is ill with diarrhea, she apparently had suffered dehydration and died in the Third Field Hospital. Doug and Mai had worked together in Quang Ngai. Doug and Pastor Quang now worked together in the VNCS material aid department. Pastor and Mrs. Quang accompanied Mai and Doug to Mai's home area just outside Saigon where Oanh's body was laid to rest.

Around the same time, the grandmother of Phan Ba Phuoc died. Since Phuoc happened to be in the city at the time, he was expected—as the family's oldest son—to participate in the traditional rites of ancestral veneration. This was difficult for Phuoc since it required votive offerings and prayers for his grandmother's safe arrival in the nether world. The Evangelical Church in Vietnam forbade participation in these rituals; the Mennonite Church had not adopted any official position on this, but generally followed the same understanding. This was the issue of the Chinese Rites controversy which engaged the Catholic Church over several centuries until 1939 when the pope affirmed that Christians can take part in these ceremonies honoring parents. Evangelical theologians continue to debate whether this is worshipping parents as gods.

It was a tradition for friends to give cash gifts when a family experienced death; these helped cover funeral costs. We missionaries followed this practice, though it was a challenge for us since we had relationships with so many families through the service programs of the community center. We often observed that it seemed so easy to die in Vietnam. Death from illnesses struck people at all ages. And the war continued to rob people of life.

But there was also new life. On January 23, Donald and Doris Sensenig welcomed the birth of their son, Kent Allen, who joined their family of three daughters, Anne, Lynne and Jean. Living in a culture where having a son is important, friends congratulated Don and Doris. Writing to Mission headquarters, I said that, while Don always appeared to be happy, for several days after his son was born, Don's smile "never left his face!"

Don had recently written an article for *Missionary Messenger* telling of an older, respected Vietnamese friend who asked him to use his influence to persuade the American authorities to establish brothels for the American soldiers in Vietnam, a system the French had set up earlier as a method of controlling prostitution and related problems. Having just returned to Vietnam from a furlough in the United States, Don observed that a significant number of Mennonites were in favor of the Vietnam war, or at least tolerated it, in an attempt "to stop communism," provided they did not need to be involved. Yet he assumed that these same people would strongly oppose prostitution.

"If we inwardly accept war as a necessary evil," Don wrote,

> We must logically accept its accompanying evils. My Vietnamese friend has no "split moral-
> ity" but is ready to be involved in the other evils too. In this sense he is facing his responsibility
> more honestly than those who would declaim against prostitution, etc., while tolerating or even
> "blessing" war. . . .
>
> I am compelled to cry out in anguish when I hear a gospel that proclaims inner peace with
> God, while washing its hands of the messy struggle for peace among nations and races and classes.
> Redemption dare not mean withdrawing from the life of the world in a corner where saved
> people create a little world of their own concerns.

Asking the readers to come up with their own formula for involvement, Don wrote: "For me
just now it means actively working to get U.S. troops out of Vietnam" and developing a Christian
witness "that includes some peace-hungry soldiers and some war-approving civilians!"

Don's mother and step-father, Elta and Orie Miller, visited for several days at the end of the
month to meet their grandson. Miller also wanted to review the MEDA poultry project which at
this time was still doing alright.

Paul Erb's book, *Orie O. Miller: The Story of a Man and an Era*, had just been published in
1969 (Herald Press), and Mary and I enjoyed reading it before the Millers arrived. Writing home,
Mary noted that, while he had physically aged, Orie was "still able to think clearly and with vision
for the future. . . . One cannot imagine what the Mennonite Church would be like today if there
had been no Orie Miller," she wrote. "We likely wouldn't be here either." She commented on "his
humility, and his ability to reconcile people who mistrusted each other—this because of his own
reliance on the Lord."

Although retired from an executive role, Miller continued to think strategically. Meeting
with the Mission Council, he encouraged us to "enter a new work . . . when the door is open—
not try to beat it down after it is closed!" He questioned whether the Mission should retain the
Saigon student center property at 336 Phan Thanh Gian unless it would become a meeting site
for an inner-city congregation. In a memo to Paul Kraybill February 5, he proposed that this
property might eventually be sold and used to finance the acquisition and development of a
permanent church and school site in Gia Dinh. He concluded by saying: "I encouraged missionaries to look and plan ahead—to eliminate 'Post War Vietnam' and 'Peace' from vocabulary
and wait-thinking, and promised more Travail praying at home and for Far East new workers,
and including Vietnam as already blueprinted." While Miller's typical language is a bit cryptic,
we understood he wanted us to preach and live the gospel and work at establishing the Church
without excessive regard to political and military happenings around us—something we had
little power to change. In the 1969 Annual Report prepared February 5, I closed with the comment: "Opportunities for a Christian witness continue unlimited in Vietnam if the church can
be sensitive to the needs."

Just before Tet, our bookroom monitor, Dinh Van Nam, received word that his two older
sisters tripped a grenade booby trap as they walked along a path near their country home. One
was killed; the other taken to the province hospital with severe injuries. It was not clear—nor did
it matter—who set the booby trap, the Viet Cong or the ARVN forces. This contested area was
frequently bombed and his father had earlier been injured. Plant life in their area was destroyed by

chemical sprays. Reporting this in the February *News and Concerns*, Mary and I wrote: "At the beginning of 1969, many Vietnamese were hopeful that peace would soon come to their land. It has not. Americans may now be under the illusion that peace is returning to Vietnam. People here see the conflict dragging on indefinitely." In *News and Concerns* a month later, James Stauffer wrote: "Peace? Sorry, no sign of it yet! If the present situation continues, peace is still a long way off—some of the most hopeful would say three or four years—many predict ten—some twenty!"

A former friend of President Nguyen Van Thieu and his political critic, Tran Ngoc Chau was arrested and sentenced to ten years at hard labor for criticizing corruption and advocating political accommodation with the Provisional Revolutionary Government.

While many American officials were expressing optimism about the American policy of Vietnamization, others saw it differently. Le Duan, First Secretary of the Communist Party, told a gathering in Hanoi that the people "must be prepared to fight for many more years" to force the withdrawal of American forces from Vietnam. Listening to the radio, I heard President Thieu on January 8 make the doubtful claim that his government controlled 97 percent of the people in the territory of the Republic of Vietnam. Although he predicted more years of fighting, he spoke about victory over the communists.

On February 21, the U.S. presidential assistant Henry Kissinger met with Le Duc Tho in their first secret talks. After the third meeting in April, these talks were discontinued for lack of progress. In February, it became known that U.S. bombers had been carrying out raids over Laos. In March the premier of Cambodia, Lieutenant General Lon Nol, seized control of the government from Prince Norodom Sihanouk. Pursuing neutralist policies, Sihanouk had managed to keep his people out of the war devastating their neighbor. The following month, U.S. forces invaded Cambodia to attack Viet Cong bases there.

Thursday, March 26, was a national holiday—the day President Thieu promulgated the Land to the Tiller law, a program providing landless peasants with up to four acres of land instead of giving one-third of their produce to landholders. Large landholders could retain no more than thirty acres. The United States provided the funds to pay for the land appropriation. Earlier land reform programs in the South promulgated under President Diem had been ineffective. The 1970 law was more effective in eliciting support for the Republic of Vietnam but as a political influence in the conflict it appeared to be too little too late.

In mid-March, a fire destroyed 162 houses in Hang Xanh, three kilometers from the community center. On March 25, with VNCS supplies, staff from the community center distributed to each victim family a blanket, two towels, a can of pork, three cans of soup, noodles, nails, a bundle of new and used clothing, and five cakes of soap. Thirteen families who lost their homes to another fire at Lo Voi near the community center were also given assistance.

Community center staff conducted a review of seventy-six families terminated from the Family Child Assistance program in 1969—in most cases because a child had completed the study of a trade and the family's economic situation had improved. By April, twenty-five additional families were terminated. This freed us to accept new families, some from the Hang Xanh area. We continued giving small amounts of material aid—vegetable oil, soap and canned beef—to families enrolled in the sponsorship programs. With the Stauffer family planning to go on home leave, Mrs. Quang (Nguyen Thi Tam) replaced Arlene as caseworker for the Educational Assistance Program which provided tuition and other assistance to poor families of children in Rang

Dong School. Miss Luan ended a year of service in the clinic and Miss Tien, a recent graduate of the Nha Trang nursing program, became assistant to the VNCS doctor Joanne Smith T. Since James Stauffer was leaving for furlough, Dinh Ngoc Chau, a man with administrative experience, was invited to become assistant director of the community center. A member of the Tin Lanh Church, he was currently worshipping with the Mennonite congregation.

Easter came on March 29. After the 6:00 a.m. sunrise service and simple breakfast, the church had a baptism service for four persons: two older women, one man and a young woman of twenty years. The man and one woman were spouses of previously-baptized believers.

Around this time, the staff from the community center published the first issue of *Sống Mới* (*New Life*), a "quarterly" magazine of the *Hội Thánh Tin Lành Mennonite-Việt Nam* (Mennonite Evangelical Church-Vietnam) edited by Pham Quang Tam and his team. This first issue—twenty-eight pages which included news of the church and center and many inspirational articles from other sources—was produced by our mimeograph printer. A few more issues were prepared, but the publication was soon discontinued.

The Viet Cong launched attacks on several targets throughout the South in early April. On Sunday afternoon, April 5, a week after Easter, I attended the funeral service at the large central Saigon Tin Lanh Church on Tran Hung Dao Boulevard for three chaplains who were killed in an attack on the Psychological War College in Da Lat a few days earlier.

Fifty Buddhist, Catholic and Evangelical chaplains were together for a routine training course when at 2:00 a.m. the center was directly hit by a mortar or rocket. The survivors ran from the building, one group running into a Viet Cong sapper squad. Though they called out, "Don't shoot! We're chaplains!" they were cut down by AK-47 bullets. Seventeen chaplains died—eleven Buddhist, three Catholics and three Evangelicals pastors, Sinh, Son and Ton. These seventeen who died represented nine percent of the total chaplains in an armed force of over one million men. I had once met Pastor Ton. A few months before Christmas the previous year, his wife and unborn child were killed when a rocket or mortar struck their parsonage. Leaving his three young children with their grandparents, Ton joined the chaplaincy corps.

There was a military honor guard and band at the funeral, and banners declared that these men had died for God and Country. Even though the government always sought opportunities to direct propaganda against the other side, I was thankful that the ministers in charge of the service did not condemn the communists nor vow revenge.

Effective January 1, 1970, the administration of Vietnam Christian Service changed from Mennonite Central Committee to Church World Service. Robert W. Miller, the Vietnam director, now reported to Boyd B. Lowry in New York rather than to Paul Longacre in Akron.

Lowry came to Vietnam April 4 for a three-week visit. MCC Executive Secretary William Snyder was also there April 14-21. Lowry visited all the VNCS units in the country and met all the VNCS personnel. By this time VNCS had added additional agriculture and community development programs at Ban Me Thuot and Dak To in the central highlands and at Dong Ha—north of Quang Tri near the so-called Demilitarized Zone. Lowry and Snyder also met with the Mennonite missionary team. We missionaries were impressed with Lowry's sensitivities in relating to the Evangelical Church and to the Mennonite programs. Given Vietnam's uncertainties, no one could predict how long the current VNCS cooperative arrangement would continue. Snyder was clear that MCC wanted to relate closely to the medical programs with the Evangelical Church and to the Mennonite

Mission even after Vietnam Christian Service phased out—whenever that might be. MCC was currently contributing around $200,000 annually to the VNCS program and Snyder saw this soon dropping to half that amount, of which $75,000 would be for program expenses.

Henry Dick, a Mennonite Brethren pastor from California, accompanied Snyder to Vietnam with the purpose of contacting Mennonite men serving with U.S. military forces. Dick had served in the Canadian Air Force during WW II and became a conscientious objector to war.

Already in 1966, Dick, Robert Miller and William Snyder had discussed a possible pastoral visit to Mennonite men in the armed forces. There was additional conversation with the MCC Peace Section in 1967 and MCC offered to co-sponsor this visit with the Mennonite Brethren Church. After the 1968 Tet attacks scuttled these plans, the MCC Executive Committee agreed to fund this April visit. Contacts were made with the Executive Director of the Armed Forces Chaplains' Board in Washington and with Chief of Chaplains Colonel William Fitzgerald, MAC-V Joint Command at Tan San Nhut air base in Saigon. Before leaving the States, Dick had secured fifty-two names of an estimated two hundred Mennonite men in the armed forces in Vietnam. Snyder and Dick were met at the airport by a very accommodating Catholic Chaplain Col. Fitzgerald when they arrived. In his week in Vietnam, Dick traveled to Nha Trang and Cam Ranh Bay, Da Nang, Pleiku and Long Binh as well as Saigon. Some men about whom he inquired were out of the country on rest and relaxation. One had been medically evacuated. Dick met personally with thirteen Mennonite men, spending significant time with them. All of the men expressed appreciation for his visit. One man said: "I can't believe that our church has sent a visitor. I didn't know the church was really that interested in us." Another GI who had come from a jungle fire base, soaked with perspiration, said: "Man, I'm glad to see you! I have travelled all morning by helicopter, walking and by bus. I sure think it is great that the church cares enough to visit us."

At most places, Dick also had "peace seminars" with three to five chaplains that lasted an hour and a half. He said "it was possible to state our position against war and yet retain a non-judgmental attitude toward those with different convictions." One chaplain asked him to speak with a young Church of God man who had declared himself a conscientious objector to war a few weeks earlier.

When Henry Dick met with the Mennonite missionary group, he commented that Mennonites love everybody "except people in military uniform!" We recognized the irony of our commitment to sharing the gospel in Vietnam while hesitant to relate to U.S. military personnel. Given the complex military and political issues in Vietnam, we tried to minimize our association with Americans—not only military personnel but also official civilian Americans or those working for private contractors. Mary and I had hoped that we would be able to meet GIs who had some relationship with our congregations in the States; we earlier had received visits from my cousin who was in the U.S. Air Force. Many Alliance and Baptist missionaries related closely to military personnel. MCC people in units away from Saigon—like Nha Trang and Pleiku—had more interaction with American GIs than we missionaries in Saigon.

The Mennonite Mission at this time had two matters to process with government agencies. One had to do with permission for the growing church to legally hold property. The other had to do with securing an automobile without paying exorbitant import taxes.

The Mennonite Mission could not import an automobile tax-free. MCC's agreement with the Ministry of Social Welfare December 1959—now covering Vietnam Christian Service—gave them permission to import vehicles tax free. We spoke with Ministry of Social Welfare officials about seeking similar authorization. They found our conversation confusing. As far as they were concerned, MCC's contract permitted MCC to provide the resources needed for any Mennonite welfare project; why were we inquiring? With this interpretation, VNCS agreed to help the Mission import a car to be used in our cooperative projects. We would purchase, import, license and insure the car. The Mission sold its 1951 Citroen sedan and ordered a new Datsun Bluebird station wagon. The vehicle arrived and was cleared through customs in late October.

On a family weekend trip to the sea at Vung Tau, the Sensenig family had a scare. When driving home, Don shifted this new car to neutral, then pulled the key so Doris could open the locked glove compartment—not realizing that the steering wheel locked when the ignition key was pulled. The car coasted ahead into the path of an oncoming convoy of Vietnamese army trucks. The ten trucks roared by on the ditch side, while Don frantically tried to back out of the way, ears ringing with the curses and speeding engines. Doris and the children were not at all amused. Providentially, they suffered no casualties.

The Mennonite Mission had not yet purchased property in the Gia Dinh area and some members of the congregation interpreted this as our reluctance or inability to help them secure a permanent church center. The congregation had already raised or pledged around 300,000 piasters ($2,500 U.S.) for this purpose, a small fraction of what would be needed. The Mission asked the church to adopt a constitution as a prelude to officially registering, but congregational leaders were too busy with other duties to devote much time to this. Kraybill indicated that the Mission Board would be willing to budget $50,000 to $60,000 in grants and loans over a five-year period.

The congregation asked Nguyen Van Ninh and me to secure legal recognition to purchase property. A Ministry of Interior official said that—with the "temporary permission" granted to the Vietnam Mennonite Mission in 1964—we should now submit a letter to the Ministry requesting permanent status with legal rights to hold property. We needed a board to represent the church to the government. When we tried to explain that the church and Mission were separate, the official did not make a distinction. We were told the board could have all Americans, none, or both Vietnamese and Americans. Kraybill was concerned that should the Mission ever be forced to leave, the property would still be in the hands of a legally-recognized body. (When the country was united under the Socialist Republic of Vietnam, all Mennonite properties were confiscated. The process of property registration was likely irrelevant.)

In late May, the church selected a seven-member Administrative Council which submitted documentation to the Interior Ministry. Designated vice chairman, I was the only non-Vietnamese member. Pastor Quang was chair, Ninh secretary and Mrs. Hoang (Ty) treasurer. Trung was minister of evangelism, school principal Mrs. Nga minister of education and culture, and Mrs. Ngoc Anh minister of medical and social work.

In July, the congregation also chose two deacons and two deaconesses with practical assignments to visit the Christians, to welcome visitors to the church and to perform other services for the congregation. Experimenting with various forms of leadership and service in the congregation helped the church to find appropriate patterns.

An unrealistic currency exchange also plagued the Mennonite Mission, VNCS and other service agencies—only 118 piasters to the U.S. dollar. The weak piaster continued falling after the government instituted new taxes in late 1969. When an expected devaluation early 1970 did not occur, it was frustrating to transfer funds at the official rate when the Hong Kong market rate and the local black market rate was three or four times more. *Newsweek* magazine reported that the resistance to devaluation was coming from government officials who profited from the black market. Larry Roth, the VNCS treasurer, noted the irony of Mennonites "heavily subsidizing the government's policy of continuing the war."

After conversations with our home offices, both VNCS and the Mennonite Mission decided to borrow piasters from a bank as a hedge against devaluation. We benefitted even though we had to pay the prime interest rate of 18 percent. We repaid the loans after the new 275 piasters to the dollar rate of exchange was announced on October 3. Thirteen months later, in mid-November 1971, the currency was further devalued to 410 piasters to the dollar.

The Phu Tho project that James and Rachel Metzler initiated was abandoned after the 1968 Tet offensive. In May 1969, VNCS and the Mennonite Mission discussed developing a joint ministry in the Xom Gia area also in the western area of the city and I agreed to work with Margaret and Dean Hancock, the VNCS program director, in shaping the program. The Mission envisioned a combined evangelism and a social ministry program, similar to what we had done in Gia Dinh. We anticipated that Don Sensenig would give significant time there when his family returned to Vietnam.

However, with little input from us, VNCS personnel in mid-1969 rapidly developed a full service program at Xom Gia with daycare and housing assistance programs, calling it the Saigon Social Service Center No. 4. By the end of the year, activities included a kindergarten, embroidery classes, English classes, an occasional clinic, and a loan program. When Sensenig was prepared in September to work at the center, there was already a staff of six persons with plans to hire more persons. Don saw opportunities for Bible teaching and presenting the gospel—even though the center director was not enthusiastic about having religious activities there. In early 1970, Don was teaching two English classes there. He learned to know five Tin Lanh families from that area and with their support organized the first Sunday afternoon service of singing and Bible study on April 26. With weak support from the director and Don's primary commitment at the student center, the spiritual ministry at Xom Gia never developed as we had anticipated.

Elmer Kennel preached at the community center the last Sunday in April. A minister from near Lancaster, Pennsylvania, Kennel and his wife Edith had come to Vietnam to visit their son Paul who was now back in central Vietnam working directly with World Relief Commission. The Kennels arrived several days before their suitcases caught up with them! Author and Professor David Augsburger also visited briefly for two days and spoke to nearly one hundred persons at both the Saigon student center and the International Protestant Church.

In early April, Cambodia withdrew its military forces from the eastern part of their country as North Vietnamese military forces infiltrated the area. ARVN troops then invaded Cambodia to attack these North Vietnamese units. This Vietnamese incursion into Cambodia stirred up centuries-old latent hostility of the Cambodians against the people who had annexed some of their territory. Vietnamese civilians living in Cambodia were massacred; this, in turn, sparked student demonstrations in Saigon against the government for not protecting ethnic Vietnamese living in Cambodia! When President Thieu ordered all the schools closed, we used this three-week break to repaint the interior walls of the student center.

On May 1, the U.S. and ARVN soldiers launched a joint military offensive against North Vietnamese military units in Cambodia including the "Parrot's Beak," a salient of Cambodian ter-

380 A Vietnam Presence

ritory located only sixty-five kilometers northwest of Saigon. In a speech delivered to the American people April 30, President Nixon defended this action as necessary to protect the lives of American troops and to "guarantee the continued success of our withdrawal and Vietnamization programs." Nixon said this action was informing the leaders of North Vietnam "that we will be patient in working for peace; we will be conciliatory at the conference table, but we will not be humiliated. We will not be defeated." Not to take this action, Nixon said, would demonstrate that "the world's most powerful nation" was acting "like a pitiful, helpless giant."

This invasion into Cambodia reignited domestic opposition to the war in the United States. Just two weeks earlier, the Vietnam Moratorium Committee had announced that it was disbanding due to lack of funds, acknowledging that Nixon's policy of withdrawing American troops had weakened Americans' opposition to the war. Although the American secret bombing of Cambodia had begun more than a year earlier in mid-March 1969, the announcement of ground troops being sent into Cambodia triggered a groundswell of reaction in the United States, particularly on university campuses. The National Guard shooting of four students May 4 at Kent State University provoked more demonstrations and many universities were closed.

Writing in the May *News and Concerns*, James and Rachel Metzler recognized "the military rationale for our government's action," but were "grieved" that Cambodia and Laos were now further involved in this war. They noted that unrest in Saigon was growing as students, wounded veterans and others demonstrated against the government because of its "indifference to the oppression of Vietnamese by Cambodia." The real objective of the students, however, was to bring an end to the war. The riot police broke up demonstrations using tear gas; students who sang peace songs were arrested and tortured. During this time, high school and university students continued to use the study facilities at our student center.

The military foray into Cambodia caused the death of many North Vietnamese soldiers. Many ARVN soldiers also lost their lives, including men who had lived near the Gia Dinh community center. Thousands of Vietnamese civilians living in Cambodia fled across the border into Vietnam. In mid-May, Pastor Quang, Trung, and Lam accompanied James Stauffer to Tay Ninh to visit a camp where 10,000 refugees had fled. The Mennonite congregation solicited relief goods which they distributed at the refugee camp.

Living in Saigon, we rubbed shoulders with many people. Mary and I were invited to the VNCS house for dinner late May where we met CWS Executive Director James McCracken and Dwight Swartzendruber, a Mennonite from Iowa who had served in several countries with MCC and CWS and now worked in the CWS New York office. A few days later, James, Rachel, Mary and I were invited to the home of Rev. Pierre Medard, pastor of the French Protestant Church in Saigon for eleven years; his family was moving to France. In mid-June, Mary's cousin, Ruth Kennel, a nurse who had earlier worked with MCC in Indonesia, stopped in for three days. It was quite special for our family when Mary's sister Martha Kauffman came for a ten-day visit the end of June.

In late June, James Metzler and James Stauffer met with ten congressmen from the U.S. House of Representatives who came to Vietnam on a "fact-finding mission." This delegation wanted to receive more than the standard official American political and military briefings. Stauffer observed that "several seemed somewhat receptive to our viewpoint but others were rather hawkish." One of the congressional aides asked to meet with him privately and Stauffer introduced the aide to persons critical of the Saigon government's policies.

Part of the delegation's mandate was to visit a prison in South Vietnam which might pave the way for a visit to a U.S. prisoner of war camp in North Vietnam. Tom Harkin, a congressional aide, convinced two of the congressmen to investigate stories of torture in the 'tiger cages" in the prisons on Con Son Island, the place Paul Leatherman and I had visited four years earlier and where VNCS had placed a doctor for more than a year. Don Luce, former IVS team leader in Vietnam and now in Saigon working for the World Council of Churches, accompanied them as interpreter. On the flight to the island, Frank Walton, the director of USAID Office of Public Safety described this "largest prison in the Free World" as like "a boy scout recreational camp." They were met by Colonel Nguyen Van Ve, the commander of the island, and were shown the prison complex. Using a map drawn by a former prisoner, Luce diverted from the planned tour and found the tiny door to the "tiger cages." A guard inside opened the door and they walked inside the stench-filled area where they viewed the sick emaciated prisoners who called for water. Harkin took photos that were printed in *Life Magazine*. This precipitated an international protest which led to the transfer of the prisoners from the cages. Some were sent to other prisons and others to mental institutions. This did not necessarily change the treatment of prisoners in Vietnam, however, since torture was routinely part of prisoner interrogation.

A Fellowship of Reconciliation (FOR) delegation visiting Vietnam at the same time included Rabbi Belfour Brickner, one of the founders of Clergy and Laymen Concerned, and Ron Young, FOR National Youth Secretary who had earlier coordinated the marches on Washington. Two VNCS persons, Bill Herod and Judy Danielson, interpreted for them. Student unrest and opposition to the policies of the Saigon government continued. On Saturday morning, July 11, Judy was present as a one thousand-strong student rally led by the FOR delegation members marched toward the American Embassy. Dispersed by police tear gas, Judy had her shoulder bag torn away by police when she tried to get the names of students being arrested. Describing his and Judy's involvement, Herod said: "While I think the purpose of the [FOR] Delegation's visit is subject to question, and the result open to criticism, nevertheless I am proud that VNCS continues to recognize its obligation to make available our experience and our observations on the situation here to any who will listen—church officials, congressmen, or pacifists." This incident was reported in Saigon's newspapers, so I discussed the article with students in my English language classes. Some of the students felt that the participation of the Americans and other foreign students was helpful in expressing their grievances. Other students declined to comment.

VNCS doctor Grace Kleinbach, in her July termination report, expressed criticism about "an oversensitivity (almost phobia)" within Vietnam Christian Service "regarding words or actions by members which might result in a reprimand" by Vietnamese government or US military officials. While reasoning that it was inappropriate for non-citizens to physically demonstrate, she said that VNCS personnel with Vietnamese language facility who were aware of injustices and public sentiments were in a good position "to offer verbal protests to US officials and citizens both in Vietnam and in the United States." Kleinbach also criticized the inordinate control of the Tin Lanh hospital board in Pleiku while contributing only one percent of the operating costs.

Kevin Byrne, an MCC volunteer in Dong Ha, below the DMZ, wrote home late July about a VC attack at the Ha Thanh Refugee Camp the night before that killed nine people. Among them was a man who had recently defected from the Viet Cong and rallied to the government; he was tied up and beaten to death. Others killed were selected government officials, an ARVN soldier, and civilians caught in the crossfire.

On his way back to Dong Ha with others, they came upon another tragedy that had just occurred. A young man and woman riding a small Honda motorcycle struck a mine. Both were instantly killed, his body lying on one side of the road, hers on the other side. The road had been "swept" of mines that morning, but missed this one off the side of the road.

Is it any wonder that American service personnel called for the war to end? Kevin concluded his letter home, "We are daily involved in a hideous way in the suffering . . . that is being wrought in this land. We are not the whole cause of it, certainly, but we are very significantly involved. This is what is wrong. . . . This awful suffering of the people must stop. And it must stop now."

On June 24, 1970, the U.S. Senate voted to repeal the Tonkin Gulf Resolution which President Johnson used in August 1964 as justification for the massive military involvement in Vietnam. President Nixon did not object to this Senate action, saying that his administration justifies its current military activity primarily on the constitutional authority of the President as commander-in-chief to protect the lives of U.S. military forces. A rather illogical argument—send troops to another country, then use the pretext of protecting them to engage in military activities!

In July, Atlee Beechy began a nine-month-long peacemaking odyssey which included visits to emissaries of the Democratic Republic of Vietnam and the Provisional Revolutionary Government in Europe and Asia—Paris, Prague, Berlin, Oslo, Stockholm, New Delhi and Vientiane.

The VC attacked several district towns and polling places during the August 30 election when an estimated six million people in South Vietnam cast votes for thirty Senate seats in the National Assembly. Even though ten anti-government candidates won, the Senate remained in control of the pro-government bloc, further strengthening President Thieu's tough uncompromising stance—totally opposed to any accommodation with the pro-communist forces.

That night a bomb exploded at the primary school in the Go Jong refugee camp near Di Linh where VNCS gave assistance, blowing the front from one of the rooms. It was not clear whether the attack was related to the election. Scrawled on the blackboard were the words in Vietnamese: "We have bombed this building because it belongs to Americans." The children came to school the next day, not afraid to study. So the classes were rearranged for the remaining classrooms. VNCSer Terry Bonnette arranged for a carpenter to repair the damage.

Bonnette reflected on the meaning and significance of this incident. "I do not think this was an expression of hostility against VNCS, but against Americans in general," he wrote. "VNCS has worked in Di Linh for three-and-a-half years now and I am sure that the VC know us, know what we do, and know what we stand for." He noted that VNCS worked closely with Father Khoa, the Catholic priest who occasionally spoke with VC personnel. Father Khoa had told Bonnette that the VC support the literacy training that VNCS was providing for the people. While the VC might not have "a special liking for us," Bonnette indicated that they both understood and tolerated the VNCS contribution in the area.

In late August, Russel Kleinbach, who had earlier worked in Pleiku, wrote from his home in the States to Boyd Lowry suggesting that VNCS needed to "immediately evaluate its policy and program" in up-country Vietnam units. Referring to an ambush in the spring near Dak To when Ron Ackerman and Bill Rose narrowly escaped injury or death, Kleinbach said VNCS had to "establish a relationship with the revolutionary government . . . either at the organizational or unit level."

James and Arlene Stauffer and their three children left in July for a year's furlough in the States. There were now only six missionaries at our weekly Bible study, prayer and fellowship

Martin Rock.

meeting, although Ruth Yoder usually attended, and Martin Rock, the MCC volunteer serving as VNCS office assistant, often joined us. Within a few months, James and Rachel Metzler would terminate; this would leave only Don and Doris Sensenig and Mary and me. However, Beidlers would soon be returning and the Mission Board was sending four new mission associates. With Stauffers gone, I had additional responsibilities at the community center. Pastor and Mrs. Quang and Mary and I were on the board of the center; I was director. Pastor Quang asked whether Earl and Pat Martin could be recruited to return to Vietnam with the Mennonite Mission.

The ordained missionaries made up the Vietnam Mennonite Mission Council that reviewed and planned ministry programs and procedures. With all these personnel changes, I asked Kraybill whether the Council should be comprised only of long-term male ordained missionaries! I noted that half the members of the church's Congregational Council were women. Kraybill suggested that one of the women and a mission associate might also become Council members.

Paul and Esther Bucher arrived on August 20 as new mission associates. Both were Pennsylvania natives—Paul from a York County farm and Esther from Pottsville, Schuylkill County, a minister's daughter. They both had graduated from Eastern Mennonite College, and had just married in January. Titus Peachey and Maynard Shirk arrived early September. Both were also graduates of Eastern Mennonite College; Maynard was from eastern Lancaster County, Pennsylvania, and Peachey from Ohio, the son of a minister.

Luke and Dorothy Beidler arrived back on September 20 with Marta and Ken, who was born in Pittsburgh where Luke was in graduate study. James Metzler left the following day for a short visit to Hong Kong and the Philippines before heading home. Rachel left three days later with Karen for Manila where James and Brian joined them for the flight to the U.S. Mary wrote home: "It's unbelievable that Luke and I will be the 'oldest' missionaries around here. We always thought we were 'juniors.'"

In his first letter home to his parents on Sunday, August 23, Paul Bucher wrote:

In Vietnam there are Hondas, cars, military trucks, bikes, and people crowding the streets. Driving is a real art, twisting, pushing, stopping, etc. Everyone drives with an inch to spare and although there are traffic lights, intersections look more like two herds of cattle crossing than a flow of orderly traffic. . . .

There are many men dressed in various military garb, there are many planes at the airport in concrete hangars, there are helicopters overhead every hour but still we do not get the impression that this country is in war until we talk to the people. They ask us in church to pray for a son who has lost his papers and is in danger of being drafted, other members are in the Army, other sons have been wounded. The people here are tired of war, of a war that is slowly affecting everyone.

The Buchers had just attended the worship service of the Gia Dinh congregation and Don interpreted the gist of the service for them. I had been invited to preach that morning. The Buchers moved into the Gia Dinh house that the Stauffer family had vacated.

Bishop P. J. Malagar of the Mennonite Church in India—on his return from a work camp in Hong Kong—spent a week in Vietnam the end of August. Pastor Quang, Ninh and Trung—all of whom had deferments from the draft—had applied for passports to attend the work camp; the passports were never issued. Later we learned that the Prime Minister had to personally approve these requests—and he was on an Asian tour for ten days. Malagar spoke on the theme of "joy" to the youth of the church at their Saturday evening meeting. On Sunday morning he preached on being peacemakers and in the evening on the need to be a missionary church. He described the Hong Kong work camp and said plans had been made to hold the First Asia Mennonite Conference in India the following year. The church really appreciated this visit. Soehadiweko Djojodihardjo from Indonesia had also planned to visit Vietnam on his way home from the work camp, but was unable to obtain a visa.

We had to deal with other passport problems. Ms. Ly Tuyet Nga, a staff member of the community center who had worked as interpreter in the clinic, then as school secretary and part-time teacher, had been accepted—along with Ms. Huong from Nha Trang—into the MCC "trainee" program to spend a year in North America working in a home or church institution. They were scheduled to begin their orientation in the U.S. by mid-August, but by early September had not yet been issued visas. Due to the compulsory conscription laws, we knew not to try to secure passports for young men. The Ministry finally approved their leaving on three conditions: the sponsoring agency must purchase the air tickets, no foreign exchange would be available, and a tourist tax of $850 would need to be paid! VNCS was unable to get the last condition waived. It was unfortunate that the two young women were unable to go. Ms. Nga had applied to study in the nurse training program a year earlier but was not accepted because her school records were lost! Her family had had a good life in North Vietnam before migrating to the South in 1954. She gave most of her income to help her siblings go to school. She was a committed member of the church and taught in the Sunday school.

In early September, Trung was involved in a serious traffic accident. He and I had just picked up some lumber in the old Willys Jeep to assist a community family in repairing a house. Trung had limited experience driving the Jeep, and when he turned onto the street he struck a group of four schoolgirls walking home from school. They were all hurriedly taken to the nearby Nguyen Van Hoc Hospital for treatment and were released. One girl suffered a fractured collarbone; another girl suffered head lacerations. We indicated our responsibility to care for them and I reported the incident promptly to the police. The police officer said it was only Providence that prevented more serious injuries and nobody disagreed!

We told the families that we were liable and immediately informed our insurance provider. We were then surprised when one father filed a suit against Trung. Knowing that an American agency was involved, we thought he saw an opportunity to seek a large financial settlement. When we met with the father, however, he claimed that he was only asking for money to pay his daughter's medical expenses. I felt somewhat chastised that we had not personally offered any cash assistance immediately—prior to the family receiving help from the insurance company. Nurse Ruth Yoder visited the families and took the child to the Children's Hospital where a British doctor found no indication of any serious injury. She soon returned to school.

After the suit was filed, Trung was held at the police station until he made bail. After I was informed, I spent time running to the police station, insurance office, and court. Several days after the accident Pastor and Mrs. Quang, Trung and his wife, and Mary and I visited all the families involved. Although the father said he would withdraw the suit, the case was scheduled to come before the court in late November.

The four newly-arrived mission associates began two months of formal language study mid-September—along with three VNCSers and three Quakers—at Em Dem, the VNCS unit house. Titus and Maynard lived at Em Dem; later they moved into a second floor room of the Saigon student center where the Sensenig family now lived. It seemed that the Sensenig family moved nearly every year. In contrast, Mary and I had only lived in our third house since arriving in Vietnam eight years before.

Among the new VNCS volunteers in language school was Teruko Yano, an MCC nurse from Japan assigned to the Nha Trang clinic-hospital. After standard training, she had done an extra year in midwifery. Teruko was from the Hyuga Christ Mennonite Church and a member of Japan Christian Medical Association.

While in language study, Paul and Esther each taught an English language class three evenings each week at the community center. This made a full schedule, especially with the Tuesday evening missionary fellowship gatherings. Paul also taught a conversational English class later at the (Buddhist) Van Hanh University—a class he enjoyed very much. Titus taught English at the Saigon student center. Maynard's forte was not teaching English, and we arranged for him to work with VNCS half-time in vehicle maintenance. Esther and Titus also signed up to teach English at the Vietnamese American Association under professional supervision.

Don, Trung, and I went to Can Tho in the Mission's old Citroen in late June for three days to make concrete plans for our Mission to begin a Christian witness, following through on Paul Kraybill's recommendation a year earlier to develop a "witness-service project in the [Mekong] Delta area." Dorothy and Luke Beidler indicated their readiness to locate there.

We men met with Le Van Thao, a young man from our church who was stationed in Vinh Long. We also visited Vu Thi Quy and her husband, Pham Van Luc, a junior officer who was stationed in a military unit in Chuong Thien province, further south. On the way back to Can Tho, we stopped briefly at Trung's boyhood home at Long My and met his widowed father.

In Can Tho we met with several Tin Lanh pastors and with missionaries Herman and Dottie Hayes (Baptist) and James Lewis (Alliance). We talked with several Evangelical Christian young men affiliated with the Christian Youth for Social Service (*Thanh Niên Cơ Đốc Xã Hội*) including Le Ngoc Can, who had briefly assisted us at the Saigon student center.

I again went to Can Tho with Luke soon after the Beidler family returned to Vietnam. Paul Bucher assisted them on their move to Can Tho in mid-October.

Death claimed a VNCS volunteer on October 21. Nurse Gloria Redlin, from Oshkosh, Wisconsin, was assisting in "Pat Smith's Hospital" in Kontum. One week earlier while taking an American military advisor back to base late one night on a small Honda motorcycle, she drove by an ARVN checkpoint without stopping. The guards opened fire. The man was instantly killed and a bullet struck her spine. She was airlifted to the American military hospital at Cam Ranh Bay south of Nha Trang. Doctors said she would recover, though perhaps with paralyzed legs. Ruth, the nurse at our community center clinic, said Gloria had the motivation to push herself to the limit and might walk again. But she suffered a cardiac arrest and died—three months before she was scheduled to terminate. Mary and I had known Gloria fairly well; she had sung with Mary in the Saigon Choral Society choir, and bought handicrafts from some of the women in the Gia Dinh community for her mother to sell in the church bazaars. Friends attended the memorial service for Gloria on Friday, October 30.

In late October, Hans De Boer, the German author of *The Bridge is Love,* who lived in South Africa, spent several days in Vietnam. Meeting with us missionaries he said one cannot be a real Christian without being jailed at least once every three years! Describing his visit, Mary wrote home: "He believes that if a Christian takes his faith seriously, he will speak out against injustices he sees, even to the government, or without fear of offending the government. It was a very stimulating visit [but] I'm not sure we're ready to implement all his ideas here. We feel that—as guests in a country—we have a certain responsibility to conduct ourselves according to the wishes of the government under which we live and work, but he doesn't sympathize with this idea."

In a speech on October 31, President Nguyen Van Thieu said the communists viewed negotiations as a way to gain time and "achieve victory gradually." Declaring that his government controls over 99 percent of the people in South Vietnam, Thieu said his government would never agree to a coalition government with the Communists. He predicted a military victory soon, saying, "We are seeing the light at the end of the tunnel."

A U.S. Special Forces covert team on November 21 raided the Son Tay prison camp west of Hanoi, but found no American prisoners of war. Immediately after the raid, U.S. warplanes carried out the most sustained bombing raids in the North in over two years. In a letter home November 27, Mary wrote about "the U.S. foolishness" of the previous week. She referred to a *Newsweek* article suggesting that the war would continue ten more years. By pursuing "Vietnamization," President Nixon had managed to quiet much of the American protest of the war.

Two days after writing this, Mary gave birth to Jonathan Daniel Martin in the Adventist Hospital. I had promised Pastor Quang that I would preach at the worship service that Sunday. Eleven persons were baptized that morning: a husband and wife, six young women, two young men and an older woman. Assured by the mid-wife that there was plenty of time, I left the hospital with Mary in labor—Ruth Yoder stayed with her—preached the sermon and hurried back in plenty of time before the baby arrived! This event serves as an example in conversations decades later about whether I put my family or "the work of the Lord" first!

A week later when I was teaching the Sunday afternoon Bible school class, Esther stayed with Mary. Esther was amazed at the generosity of friends who came to see Mary and the baby: "Mary's been home only a week but lots of people have stopped in to see both of them. They bring fruits and eggs . . . , a specialty because of their high price of about 25 piasters (nine cents U.S.) an egg. They have so many eggs they don't know what to do with them all. It's really interesting how the poor people may buy a dozen oranges to give. Right now good oranges cost about 280 piasters ($1.00 U.S.) for ten—the fruit dozen here."

With Jonathan born so close to Christmas, Steven and Becky were able to play the roles of Joseph and Mary watching the baby in a cradle as we celebrated Christmas at home. Mary and I were grateful that our son Steven was again the picture of health. After many weeks of chronic diarrhea, in mid-August he was treated at the US Army's Third Field Hospital for tropical sprue; a month later he began regaining the weight he had lost.

In late November, Doug Hostetter came to Vietnam for ten days. The National Student Association (NSA)—representing more than five hundred colleges and universities in the United States—had been invited by student unions in both Saigon and Hanoi to come to Vietnam to discuss Vietnamese perspectives on bringing peace to their country. The American team was composed of student body presidents and editors of student newspapers. Doug was invited to join the team because of previous Vietnam experience and his facility in the language. The original plan was to have half the group go to Saigon while the others go to Hanoi. After working on statements they were all planning to meet in Hanoi to work out the draft of a "peace treaty." All those planning to go to Saigon were denied visas by the Vietnamese Embassy. Since Doug was invited late and was not on this list, he came alone as a tourist and met informally with students and leaders of student unions. He also visited Tam Ky, the town he had left a year and a half earlier, where he spoke "with teachers, students, monks, pastors, country peasants, refugees and old friends." In Saigon he met with Mennonite missionaries and MCC personnel, and also with the leaders of the Mennonite church who asked him to carry greetings to the Evangelical Christians in the North.

Doug flew from Saigon to Vientiane, then to Hanoi on December 11 where he joined the other fourteen members of the NSA delegation. His contribution was unique in that he spoke the Vietnamese language. The draft treaties of both North and South were similar, calling for the total withdrawal of all foreign military forces, cessation of bombing in both North and South, and for the people to determine their political future without outside interference. Describing the happening, Hostetter said he "had to struggle with the meaning of being a Christian in a situation of international conflict."

John A. Lapp, representing the MCC Peace Section, spent a week in Vietnam mid-December. Don Sensenig accompanied him on a visit to up-country VNCS units. On Saturday evening, December 19, Lapp spoke on Christian pacifism at the International Protestant Church. Paul Bucher commented that the forty persons gathered were evenly split "between the convinced and the not-convinced." After "all the hard questions" were asked and answered, there were "no converts!" he observed.

At the end of 1970, forty-eight expatriates signed an open letter to U Thant, the Secretary General of the United Nations, detailing North and South Vietnamese and American non-compliance with the Geneva Convention regarding warfare, specifically mentioning military attacks against hospitals, saturation bombing in populated areas, assassinations and treatment of prisoners of war. Included among the signatories were missionaries Donald Sensenig, Paul and Esther Bucher, as well as ten VNCS personnel.

This letter accompanied a letter to President Nixon deploring the ongoing war: "We do not see peace any closer . . . today than it was when you took office in January 1969," it read. It assailed the bombing which maimed and killed, chemicals which defoliated the land, and involvement in the Phoenix Program which was assassinating community leaders. "Mr. President," the letter said, "We urge you to stop sending young Americans . . . to kill people of Indochina and to stop sending more and more weapons and chemicals of destruction for the Indochinese to use to kill each other and destroy their own land."

The use of the term "Indochina" underscored the expansion of the war into Cambodia and Laos. The letter urged the President to take positive steps to bring peace to the region.

BOOK THREE

TRANSITION
1971-1975

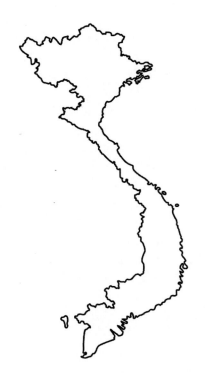

ELUSIVE PEACE

Chapter 32

"An exotic little land somewhere in Asia has become a symbol of so many things which are wrong today, a word to describe an era when so many good intentions turned out so wrong. An American history of Vietnam is being written, but the last chapters have not yet been acted out. As statesmen, historians, and people from all ways of life deal with the question of American involvement in Indochina, Christians, too, will continue to ask, 'What was the Church doing in Vietnam?' which is really many questions depending on the emphasis or inflection you use."

This I wrote in mid-1971 to church friends in the *Missionary Messenger*. I explained that we missionaries continued to go about our work with some normality—and with too little difficulty. I then told about a young American I met who, before coming to Vietnam, was involved with issues of racial injustice in southern United States. Here in Vietnam, he witnessed much injustice, suffering and death. "It is very difficult to live in Vietnam," he said to me, "unless one lives at a very superficial level."

The young American was twenty-six year-old Alexander Shimkin who came to our home on several occasions just to talk. He had come to Vietnam with International Voluntary Service (IVS). Appalled that the Army of the Republic of Vietnam (ARVN) forces and their American advisors forced civilians at gunpoint to use hand tools to remove mines resulting in many injuries and deaths, Shimkin and another IVS volunteer reported this to an American journalist. Both men were dismissed from IVS in early 1971 for violating procedures in speaking to the press without authorization. Shimkin then became a stringer for *Newsweek* magazine and documented the deliberate killing of thousands of civilians by American forces. Accompanying another journalist in Quang Tri province a year later, he was caught in an ambush and killed.

I then described recent opportunities to ponder the meaning of life and death with friends. I had recently been asked by a new Christian believer to help conduct a funeral service for his soldier son killed in the Mekong River delta. The war also claimed a friend whom we first knew as a thirteen-year-old schoolboy when we arrived in Vietnam. And shortly after Easter 1971, VNCS worker Ted Studebaker was killed in an attack in Di Linh where he served as agriculturalist. His commitment to the Jesus way of peace and love was an inspiration to us all.

I concluded the letter: "You know the temptation to superficiality. . . . Pray for us and with us that Christians in Vietnam might be true examples of a compassionate Christ."

I wrote this letter just after *Washington Post* and the *New York Times* printed excerpts from *The Pentagon Papers*, a "top secret" study of the origins and development of the Vietnam War which was commissioned by former Secretary of Defense Robert McNamara four years earlier. By the summer of 1967, McNamara was convinced that the U.S. policies in Vietnam had failed. He wanted to know why the United States had not succeeded, whether this failure could have been prevented, and what lessons could be drawn to prevent similar misguided adventures. This study, *The History of US Decision-Making in Vietnam, 1945-1968*, was completed in January 1969.

Daniel Ellsberg, an employee of RAND, a think tank financed largely by the U.S. Air Force, was involved in the study. Initially a strong supporter of the war, Ellsberg eventually came to believe that the United States had no justification for going to war in Vietnam and needed to fully disengage as soon as possible. Realizing after Nixon delivered his November 3, 1969, speech that the President was not planning to withdraw from Vietnam, but rather continue the war by relying on South Vietnamese ground troops, Ellsberg decided that the document had to be released. Having a set of the reports in the RAND office and access to a copy machine, he began copying the 7,000-page top-secret documents at night. The publication of the Pentagon Papers did not change President Nixon's policies, but it contributed to the American public's growing cynicism of U.S. intentions in Vietnam. To us missionaries, these documents confirmed what we had been saying for many years.

The April 26 death of Ted Studebaker stunned the VNCS team. When rockets or mortar shells exploded near the VNCS unit house after midnight on Sunday, April 25, everyone in the house ran toward the bunker. An explosive charge then blasted open the back door and several armed men entered. They encountered Ted and shot him. Ted's wife of just over a week, Ven Pak Lee, Phyllis Cribby, and Daisy Banares managed to crawl into the bunker. One of the guerrillas opened the door to the bunker, saw Phyllis and closed the door. After the armed men left the house, the women waited until daybreak when they found Ted's body and immediately informed Alliance missionary, George Irwin, who lived nearby. There were simultaneous attacks on other nearby sites including the government's Ethnic Minorities office, a government primary school, and the national police station—where many were injured.

VNCS had begun working in the district town of Di Linh in September 1966 with rather successful agricultural, public health, and literacy programs. It was known that the NLF cadre and the NVN soldiers operating in the area were not from the local community. They did not like health and educational programs which benefitted the displaced Koho people, concerned that it would weaken any influence they might have with the ethnic minority. No one believed that Ted was specifically targeted, only that the VC action was likely directed against Americans in general. A few community people believed that the VC were not responsible for Studebaker's death and have postulated other theories. However, the circumstances of the attack and Ted's death were carefully investigated and reviewed.

In 1967, Lee Brumbeck, one of the first VNCSers in Di Linh, learned to know Father Tran Van Khoa, a Vietnamese Catholic priest who worked in a village six kilometers from Di Linh, and provided him with some material aid supplies to give to all those in need, including medical supplies. Brumbeck understood that the priest would be giving these medical supplies to the NLF, along with a Vietnamese language brochure describing the work of VNCS. A few weeks after the priest was able to give these supplies, the NLF cadres returned the medicines along with a letter saying that the medicines should be used by the Americans who need them "for their GIs who are attacking the Vietnamese people." The letter read, "Although we have many needs, we have enough strength to fight them for ten years, twenty years or more until we defeat them. Please let the Americans know about this." The VNCS Saigon administration first learned this information just before Brumbeck terminated in 1968.

Ted's body was brought to Saigon. Phyllis Cribby accompanied Ven Pak to Ohio for the funeral service. Ted was the seventh child of a farm family active in the West Milton Church of the Brethren near Dayton, Ohio. A graduate of Manchester College and Florida State, he came to Vietnam at the age of twenty-three. After Vietnamese language study, he was assigned to agricultural development work in Di Linh area where he learned to speak the Koho language. At the end of his two-year term, he married Ven Pak Lee on April 17 in Di Linh, officiated by a Koho pastor. Ven Pak, a native of Guangdong province in China and resident of Hong Kong, was a volunteer with Asia Christian Service.

Ted's death came six months after the death of Gloria Redlin. A memorial service for Studebaker, led by missionary Don Sensenig, was held at the International Protestant Church in Saigon on May 7. The "love chapter," I Corinthians 13, was read in unison. Fr. Khoa read Psalm 90. Short meditations were given by Don and Mennonite pastor Tran Xuan Quang. Robert Miller, VNCS director, shared remembrances. Special music was given by Lynn and Betty Vogel. Doan Van Mieng, the president of the Evangelical Church, led in the closing prayer.

Shortly before his death, Ted had written: "I believe strongly in trying to follow the example of Jesus Christ as best I know how. Above all, Christ taught me to love all people, including enemies, and to return good for evil, and that all men are brothers in Christ. I condemn all war and conscientiously refuse to take part in it in any active or violent way. I believe love is a stronger and more enduring power than hatred for my fellow men, regardless of who they are or what they believe."

Terry Bonnette, the Di Linh unit leader, said he would likely have also been killed had he been there at the time of the attack. Both Phyllis and Terry believed strongly that it was important to continue their work in Di Linh. Terry asked: "How can a 'Christian presence' be taken seriously if we desert these who have come to trust and respect us? How can we witness to the love of God through Jesus Christ if we cannot forgive and love those who have wronged us? . . . I feel it is important and vital enough for us to remain and even important enough for us to risk our lives. . . . We have decided we . . . must take the risk. Our families in the United States understand this."

The Vietnam Mennonite Mission and the Gia Dinh Mennonite congregation reviewed their programs in early 1971 during the February 4-11 visit of Mission Board secretary Paul Kraybill, who was accompanied by Lancaster Mennonite Conference bishop overseer, Donald Lauver. Paul Longacre had told Kraybill that the large child sponsorship programs at the Gia Dinh community center "should be given a hard look."

Lynn Vogel was now VNCS program director for projects in the Saigon area; as a conscientious objector to war, he was performing alternative service. In January 1971, he prepared a confidential memo, Comments on the Status of Saigon Area Projects. A trained social worker, Vogel critiqued both social service centers where VNCS worked with the Mennonite Mission. Vogel wrote that the Mennonite community center in Gia Dinh, designated by VNCS as Social Service Center #3,

> . . . under the direction of Luke Martin, has been a rather difficult center to understand and thus to supervise because of the sensitivities involved in working with a joint project of the Vietnam Mennonite Mission and VNCS. With the FCA [Family Child Assistance] program in particular, a program unique to the Mission effort, I have serious doubts about the advisability of conducting a "public welfare" program for a limited number of families. The addition of a

FCA young people on a day's outing.   *EAP students visit a park.*

trained social worker to the staff of the center has tempered my questions somewhat. But in terms of community development and self-help, the selection of the poorest families for constant and continuous infusions of money and material aid (at least for a period of two years) is detrimental to the encouraging of a sense of unity and self-support on the part of the entire population. The initiation of a day care center project may do much to involve the entire community, rich and poor, in a unified effort. Also, the granting of assistance to non-FCA-EAP families on an emergency or loan basis may provide additional balance in the center program.

Vogel indicated that "a consistent problem" at the community center was "a lack of strong Vietnamese direction" and "a surprising amount of paternalism in the decision-making process at the center." Vogel was hopeful that the VNCS social worker who worked with the center staff, Margriet Lap, would be a good catalyst to improve the programs.

Teenagers were enrolled in the Family Child Assistance program with the goal to help them to learn trades to support themselves and their families. Besides tuition, some of the funds were used for uniforms, other clothing and tools. Inasmuch as some of these children were already working to support the family, some supplemental assistance was given the family while the child was in training. Some material aid was given monthly; the May 1968 fighting devastated the area which also led to more general material aid distributions. The total FCA enrollment was 150 youth. A review the previous year indicated that the young people were enrolled in the program an average of eighteen months before termination and new families enrolled. Assistance was not necessarily given to the poorest families in the community; there had to be a young person with an initiative to learn a trade.

The Educational Assistance Program (EAP) was, likewise, a sponsorship program with the sponsors making a smaller monthly contribution than to the FCA program. The children enrolled in the program received tuition to study in the Rang Dong Elementary School. They were provided with uniforms and received limited material aid monthly. Instead of all the resources going to the children enrolled in the EAP program, some of the money was used to cover the tuition cost of other students. Of the 500 to 600 students at Rang Dong, around one-half the students were enrolled tuition-free. Thus, the resources from 150 sponsored children provided tuition assistance to nearly twice as many children.

Activities for children—(l to r), Mrs. Bich, Pastor and Mrs. Quang, Muong, Lam and Khai.

(For decades sponsorship programs operated by international voluntary associations have generated pro and con criticism. A large-scale, scientific research study by Bruce Wydick and others in 2013 reported that the sponsorship programs of Compassion International had "statistically significant impacts on years of schooling; primary, secondary, and tertiary school completion; and the probability and quality of employment" in the communities served.)

It was appropriate for MCC to raise questions about the total financial resources going to this one community center. When the currency was devalued in October 1970, the center received significantly more piasters. When the currency was again devalued in November 1971, the piaster amount remained about the same while the additional piasters generated were used in other programs.

Vogel reported "a surprising amount of paternalism in the decision-making process at the center" with the staff unable to freely make suggestions for improving the programs! I had served as director of the community center from January 1965 to mid-year 1967, and again in mid-1970—a few months before Vogel reviewed the program. I was involved on the board when James Stauffer and Arlene Stauffer directed the program and the Sensenigs worked with me while I served as director. I was also in charge of the FCA program most of the time, working closely with Co Bich, the leading FCA staff person. She was given guidance by Marta Brenden and later by Margriet Lap—VNCS social workers. I reviewed the cases with Co Bich which helped protect her from being charged with favoritism.

Was my—was our—decision-making paternalistic? Perhaps so. James Stauffer and I both learned by experience that the community center staff did not function well with an egalitarian administrative style. The Stauffers had regular staff meetings and so did I. When Arlene left in mid-1970, we invited one of the school teachers to become the lead EAP caseworker. When she soon resigned, the pastor's wife, Nguyen Thi Tam, became the primary EAP worker. In May

1970, Dinh Ngoc Chau became assistant director. Chau was a member of the Tin Lanh Church who had some administrative experience. He was the son of Mrs. Cuu Trac who regularly visited families in the community. When the Stauffers left in July 1970, Pastor and Mrs. Quang became members of the board of directors. In an October letter I had written: "I am just back from a visit to Quang's house. . . . They are serving with us on the 'Board of Directors.' I am the director, but I usually like to check most things out with them before I do something. I discussed the hiring of a new social worker, some problems the staff at the clinic are experiencing, and plans for the staff meeting of all the center personnel on Thursday morning." Tran Xuan Quang became director in 1972. Inasmuch as he was also pastor of the church, he faced other specific challenges.

Glenn Noteboom (CWS) was also thinking about paternalism. In his termination report in early 1972, he wrote there is a danger that a foreign agency like VNCS will have a "paternalistic colonialist" mentality expressed "as a rich, all-knowing messiah coming to save the poor, disadvantaged Vietnamese." While the intentions are good, "a subtle feeling of superiority" is unconsciously communicated to the recipients of the assistance. Noteboom said that American agencies could learn much from the experience in U.S. ghettos "where the paternalism of the white middle class and of the churches is being rejected and power and control is being demanded by the people themselves." He insisted that the Vietnamese needed to be seen "as equals" and more power and control given to them.

Vogel's review also included the Social Service Center #4 in Xom Gia, a community in the western part of Saigon which was intended from the beginning to be a joint Mennonite Mission-VNCS project. He said this center "has consistently been our weakest center program, and still suffers from a lack of strong Vietnamese leadership."

The Mission had envisioned this as a combined evangelistic and service center—not that the Mission would "use" (or misuse) services as a direct evangelistic tool, but that the service programs and an evangelistic ministry would be launched simultaneously—like the community center in Gia Dinh had been. When VNCS developed the service program without active Mission involvement, it became difficult for the Mission to later integrate its interests into the programs, especially when these were not shared by the assistant director of the center. Don Sensenig began relating to the center in late 1969 and was named director in 1970. In September 1970, the Sensenig family moved into the Saigon student center property where Don assumed responsibility for directing that program as well. Here he spent significant time interacting with students, teaching English classes and Bible classes, and organizing a student social-work club—all with the help of the newly-arrived mission associates. Consequently he gave limited time to the Xom Gia center.

In the review, Vogel mentioned the challenges the assistant director faced with two "strong personalities" among the center staff. Although relationships within Vietnamese society generally run harmoniously, sharp disagreements frequently occur. Vietnamese would often quote the proverb, "Ten people—eleven different ideas!"

In January 1971, Marcy Weber described life at the Pleiku Evangelical Clinic and Hospital. Other staff members were Dr. Margaret Fast and Ursula Horn, a VNCS nurse, and Akiie Ninomiya, the hospital coordinator—an Asian Christian Service volunteer from Japan who Marcy would later marry. The average census in the hospital was thirty-two; staff examined 130 outpatients daily. Marcy was quite pleased with the conscientious staff of the hospital, most of them ethnic Jarai. Yong, a young Jarai man with some nursing training, was doing cataract surgeries with a doctor

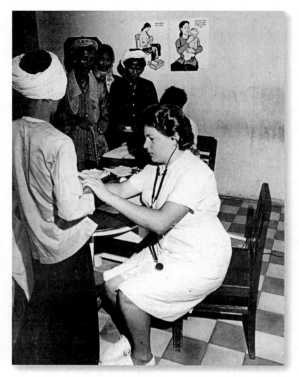

Marcy Weber with patient.

supervising. Marcy said they had a good relationship with the hospital administrator, Tin Lanh Pastor Truong Van Sang. He expected to be consulted on every matter even though he spent little time there.

If things were going well at the Pleiku clinic, there was a speed bump at the Nha Trang clinic and hospital. The hospital administrator had been informed about the availability of a doctor and another staff person. Although he had earlier indicated interest, he now said he was sorry that these two could not work there because of their Catholic faith! They were viewed as having a different religion. To have them at the clinic would not be "in keeping with the spirit of the Church's common organization," the administrator said. He did allow the one volunteer to work in the drug room, but the doctor was not invited to come. At the beginning of the Evangelical Church movement in Vietnam, Catholic priests and their faithful in some areas had strongly opposed the Evangelical Church, so it was not surprising that some Tin Lanh leaders would not welcome Catholic staff.

The chair of the Social Relief Committee of the Tin Lanh Church, Nguyen Van Van, thanked VNCS—among other agencies—for the assistance given to victims of floods caused by super typhoon Kate in late October in Quang Nam province around Da Nang. Doan Van Mieng, the president of the Church, was always gracious and thankful for the support VNCS was giving to the Church. Expressing gratitude to MCC-VNCS for cooperation in the health programs with the Church since 1960, as well as relief for victims of war and natural disasters, he wrote: "Thus the Lord's name has been honored inside as well as outside the Church."

Robert Miller's administrative team was made up of Director of Business Affairs, Leif Dahl; Doug Beane, office manager; Director of Personnel and Community Relations, Nguyen Van Ninh; and Director of Program, R. Dean Hancock. There were three assistant directors: Lynn Vogel for Saigon Projects, William Herod for Province Projects and Tran Xuan Quang for Special Projects. VNCS was committed to finding, training and placing Vietnamese in most of these positions. In June Quang resigned from his position in order to give more time to the Mennonite church and Doug Beane became director for special projects.

Kurt and Frieda Sawatzky were working in community development in Ban Me Thuot since late 1969. In February 1971, Kurt wrote to the chief of Darlac Province, Colonel Chau Van Tien, about the appalling plight of thousands of relocated ethnic minority people who were not provided with adequate food, water and shelter. Kurt had visited a resettlement village in late December and early January and heard shocking stories of the people being rounded up by ARVN soldiers who then stole and destroyed their ceremonial jars and other belongings, forcibly removing them from their hamlets, making them leave their rice, water buffaloes and other animals behind. Sawatzky drafted a letter to the province chief earlier, but did not send it because Colonel Wayne Smith, the senior U.S. military advisor to the province, said he was aware of the problems and the people's grievances were being rectified. "There can be no excuse for treating the Montagnard people in such a manner in a country that claims to be a democracy," Sawatzky now wrote to Col. Tien. "I appeal to you to use your authority as province chief to correct the wrongs that have been done to the people."

Sawatzky initiated a protest that—over a period of a few months—resulted in changes in the way the government treated the ethnic minorities. Sawatzky reported the problem to Gerald C. Hickey, an American anthropologist researcher who had spent several years researching ethnic minority people. Visiting the village with a young Rhade leader the following day, Hickey confirmed Sawatzky's reports. The people had earlier requested that the government provide better security because the Viet Cong entered their villages regularly to propagandize and demand rice as taxation, forcing them to buy rice they did not have in order to pay the tax. Instead, the government forcibly removed them with only a few days' notice and burned two of their villages to the ground.

Hickey wrote to Hoang Duc Nha, Minister of Information and advisor to President Thieu, his cousin. The President asked Major General Ngo Dzu, the commander of II Corps, to discuss the matter with Hickey. Maj. Gen. Dzu would not be convinced, and by April had relocated an estimated 40,000 people from over one hundred villages. The general was unable to provide security to the villages and wanted to deprive the Viet Cong of rice and other commodities by removing the people and destroying their villages, much like the Americans did by bombing country villages in central Vietnam a few years earlier, forcing the people to come to the towns for survival.

Ursula Horn, the VNCS nurse from Germany who came through Lutheran World Relief, worked fulltime in the Plei Ko Tu resettlement camp from mid-December, visiting nearly every day. By mid-April more than three hundred people had died, mostly children from six months to five years old—due to malnutrition, intestinal infections and malaria. Writing to the province chief on April 13, she urged the government to dig wells for clean water and provide nutritional food until the people become self-sufficient. Hugh Manke, the IVS chief of party, flew to Washington to testify at the U.S. Senate hearing on refugees chaired by Senator Edward Kennedy, chair of the Subcommittee on Refugees, taking with him copies of Ursula's letter and a January 6 letter of Kurt Sawatzky to Dr. Hickey. VNCS director Robert Miller and Bill Herod visited Pleiku in mid-April and were interviewed "off the record" by *Newsweek* and *New York Times* reporters. Atlee Beechy, now home in Goshen, Indiana, also sent Kennedy a letter, describing the unsanitary condition of the camp he visited in February.

Hickey's views were reported in articles in *New York Times* and the *Washington Post*. Hickey also spoke with William Colby, the head of CORDS, and with John Paul Vann, who would soon become senior American military advisor in II Corps. By May, Colby and Vann tried to stop the relocations. There is evidence that military tactics were forced to change. In early June, Maj. Gen. Dzu said that he wanted to resettle ten thousand additional ethnic minority people but "American sensitivity prevented it."

Paul Kraybill came to Vietnam on an administrative visit in early February 1971, one week after Tet, the lunar New Year, accompanied by Lancaster Mennonite overseer bishop Donald Lauver. We missionaries appreciated Lauver's sensitivity to Vietnamese culture. Kraybill and Lauver met with Evangelical Church president Pastor Mieng and with Thomas Stebbins, chair of the C&MA mission. They conversed with VNCS administrators. During their week's visit, they spent significant time with the leadership team of the growing Mennonite church and traveled to Can Tho with Don and me.

In his administrative report, Kraybill observed that there was "evidence that the war in Vietnam [was] receding" and that life in many parts of South Vietnam was "getting closer to normalcy" than it had been for many years. The fact that we had driven to Can Tho by car seemed evidence of this. Yet on the drive from Vinh Long to Can Tho we saw two bodies lying along the road; apparently government soldiers had killed these young men and carried their bodies to the road to remind the passers-by of the fate of those who supported the other side.

Kraybill noted the good relationship the Mennonite Mission had with the Evangelical Church and that we were "one with them in spirit, in evangelism, and in evangelical faith." He believed the Mennonite church could be a witness to the Tin Lanh Church in "the Biblical concept of peace, discipleship, social concern, and quality of Christian fellowship that should characterize a Biblical church." If those aspirations appear somewhat pretentious, the Alliance mission and the Evangelical Church leaders would likely have admitted that they emphasized "saving souls," hoping that persons would then be baptized and become part of a local congregation. Mennonites emphasized a stronger communal Christian fellowship.

Kraybill wrote:

> The Mennonite congregation at Gia Dinh is growing and now numbers about 112 members. It is becoming more Vietnamese and consequently more attractive to the Vietnamese people. The congregation is similar to the Evangelical church of Vietnam in many ways, yet consciously Mennonite. In defining the distinctions, the members refer to flexibility in worship and fellowship patterns, feet-washing, stronger social concern and a growing conviction regarding war. Admittedly the peace conviction is still rather nebulous and has not been implemented, but it is clear that there is recognition of this concept. There is deep appreciation for the style of missionary service and the close identification of missionaries with people and their suffering. The congregation feels a relationship to the larger worldwide Mennonite fellowship and also made a significant gesture in sending a verbal message of greeting to the Christians in North Vietnam via Doug Hostetter several months ago.

The Mission Secretary was projecting a transition in the relationship of the Mennonite Mission to the developing Mennonite church. The church had already organized a Church Council (*Ban Quản Trị*) distinct from the Congregational Council (*Ban Đại Diện*). This Church Council was now seeking legal status to hold property and in the future would relate to other Mennonite congregations that would be formed. Beyond this, Kraybill envisioned a Mission-church partnership quite distinct from the relationship of the Alliance Mission to the Tin Lanh Church where each had an autonomous status. He wanted to see a temporary merging of the Mission and church leading eventually to the dissolving of the Mission.

Kraybill wrote:

It seems evident that an American organization will be able to continue, but in order to assure that the church can develop authentically, it is important that the American mission organization be phased out as soon as possible. Vietnamese responsibility and initiative are important to a growing church which will relate to the Vietnamese people effectively and withstand the political storms that certainly lie ahead. This does not assume any major reduction of personnel or assistance for the immediate period ahead. Rather, missionaries move into a new relationship of identity with the church and assignment and administration by the church instead of the mission.

Kraybill observed that the church "was open to the concept of mission-church partnership and welcomes such a relationship even though it is not the traditional pattern of missions in Vietnam where church and missions have been kept quite separate and distinct." To implement this strategy, Kraybill recommended that the Mission Council and the Church Council form a Joint Administrative Council (JAC) by August 1 for a two-year period; this new council would "be responsible for administration of all mission program activities, missionary assignments, program policy and budget."

This recommendation was implemented through basically combining the Church Council (*Ban Quản Trị*) with the Mission Council. Three missionaries were on the council, James Stauffer, Don Sensenig and I. Six members—three men and three women—were from the church: Tran Xuan Quang, Tran Thi Ngoc Anh, Phan Tuyet Nga, Nguyen Quang Trung, Nguyen Thi Hoang and Nguyen Van Ninh. There was some surprise expressed that the missionaries would be outnumbered on the committee, and appreciation for the confidence the Mission had in the church. James Stauffer called the first meeting August 28. He and Pastor Quang prepared the agenda.

Kraybill said the Mission Council would still—for a time—continue to deal with missionary business such as allowances, benefits, housing, transportation, and children's education. The Mission Council was also responsible to plan for quarterly gatherings of the entire missionary group. Kraybill appointed as the Mission Council chair James Stauffer, soon to return to Vietnam from furlough; Paul Bucher, treasurer; and Donald Sensenig. I was secretary.

Kraybill recommended a continued "Christian witness to the Gospel of Christ through proclamation of the Word and the deed of love and service." There would be a gradual phase-out of Mission Board subsidy, with a minimum of material aid assistance and more emphasis on self-help. VNCS was also cutting back on support to the Gia Dinh community center. Given that the funds to the community center were generated by MCC's two sponsorship programs, a substantial part of the total VNCS program budget was going to the community center—the piaster equivalent of $27,200 US and a quarter of VNCS program budget! Fifty-nine percent of this was going to the Family Child Assistance program, 25 percent to the Educational Assistance Program, 14 percent to the clinic and health program, and 2 percent to the day care.

A top issue for the church was the matter of a new church facility. Considerable time was spent discussing with the Congregational Council the kind of facility to be erected, the cost, and in what way the Mission could best help. By this time the church was no longer meeting upstairs in the main community center building—the former Martin apartment—and was meeting at the rented student center property on Nguyen Thien Thuat Street, a much more satisfactory meeting space, but still not large enough. On Sunday with Kraybill present, Pastor Quang announced that by Christmas they would have new church facilities! It was estimated that $34,000 would be needed for property purchase and construction. The church would contribute $4,000. The Mission would provide $16,000 from current balances and the 1971 budget. The Mission Board would loan the balance of $14,000, one-half of which was to be forgiven in future budgets.

On this visit, Kraybill was not interested in discussing specific ministry programs or missionary assignments; this was the task of the joint council. He reminded us missionaries to identify with and be an integral part of the local church, even to accepting guidance and discipline from the church.

Donald Lauver spent significant time encouraging Pastor Quang in his leadership ministry. Lauver found Quang to be "a very humble man," committed to leading a well-ordered church—"one that disciplines in love and not in judgment."

After Kraybill left, it was decided that Esther and Paul Bucher would move to Can Tho to support Luke and Dorothy Beidler. Don and Doris Sensenig would stay at the Saigon student center; in addition to directing the center, Don would prepare literature for publication and distribution. James Stauffer would work in the Xom Gia community center after they returned. Titus would work in student ministries in Saigon. We were still considering various assignments for Maynard—one related to MEDA. Lloyd Fisher, MEDA's executive director, had visited Vietnam briefly in January. But the MEDA program was never revived.

In addition to teaching English at the Gia Dinh community center, Paul Bucher also taught an English conversational composition class at the (Buddhist) Van Hanh University. In January, Esther also began teaching a class there. This gave them the chance to interact with Buddhist devotees. Esther and a Quaker friend went to a Buddhist pagoda during a holiday in early March to attend

Church choir.

Congregation after worship.

a women's meeting. One of the women told Esther: "We are both women, so you can understand how we don't care about fighting, but only want peace for the safety of our children, husbands, and brothers. We are sad and in fear of their death where there is war. We want the Americans to go home and stop making war." Esther also spoke with a school teacher whose teacher husband had written a letter to the government requesting improvement of the school system; for this he was arrested, tried and sentenced to twenty years in prison—on Con Son Island.

VNCS organized a conference for all their personnel February 19 to 22 at the International Protestant Church in Saigon. There were eighty participants, one-half from the Saigon area and the others from up-country. Forty-four expatriates attended. Winifred and Atlee Beechy participated. Atlee reviewed the initial VNCS goals. He had been on assignment since the previous summer to contact diplomatic personnel of the Democratic Republic of Vietnam and the Provisional Revolutionary Government.

In Beechy's two weeks in Vietnam, he traveled to Pleiku, Da Nang and Tam Ky, and spoke with dozens of people, Vietnamese and international, representing a wide variety of professions. He and Robert Miller had a good exchange with Doan Van Mieng, the Evangelical Church president. Pastor Mieng indicated that the total Evangelical community then numbered 100,000 people, including children. He expressed appreciation for past help received from MCC and VNCS, and voiced no complaints about VNCS. In a letter to Akron, Beechy said it is imperative that MCC personnel keep in communication with Tin Lanh leaders because he sensed a "growing criticalness of the Evangelical Church by a number of VNCS workers." Beechy and Miller also spoke with a few Alliance missionaries; Tom Stebbins expressed a sympathetic understanding and support for the MCC interest and concern for North Vietnam, saying he would very much like to visit the North.

A local newspaper, *Gió Nam*, was printing comments from Vietnam's religious leaders about the ongoing peace talks. In mid-February it published their interview with Pastor Mieng who said the greatest aspiration of the people—both in the North and the South—was for peace. After more than twenty years of war, the people had suffered almost more than they could take.

"Yet if only one side has the will and works for peace, while the other side does not, then we have only a comedy and we may never meet each other," Mieng said. Referring to the manner of solving this cruel never-ending war, he continued: "Whenever the two regions are ready to come together in a spirit of harmony, recognizing that this fratricidal killing will gradually lead to annihilation, peace can immediately be restored to this dear land. Though the representatives of the two regions have met in Paris many years already, they have only met but not yet come to a meeting of hearts; though they have sat together in the same room, their hearts are still thousands of miles apart."

Asked about the chances of attaining peace, Mieng only said, "The Evangelical believers in Vietnam and in the entire world are praying for peace in Vietnam, asking God to grant that the hearts of the authorities in the North as well as the South may come to agreement so that our dear land from Nam Quan to Ca Mau will have peace and prosperity."

In Beechy's report from Vietnam, he wrote: "The war in Vietnam is like a contagious infection which has failed to respond to massive medication. The patient remains critical and the infection has spread to epidemic proportions" with no end in sight. "The basic . . . human tragedies, the repressive measures of the Saigon government, the disruption, the fear and despair of the masses lie firmly embedded below the artificial calm of Saigon."

Beechy noted that the Saigon government and the Americans were describing as successful the South Vietnamese invasion into Laos—Lam Son 719, begun in early February—despite the heavy losses the ARVN soldiers sustained. When we missionaries asked friends about the fighting in Laos, they simply replied, *"Chết nhiều qúa!"* (So many dead!).

Beechy observed that the US administration was deluding the American people, talking of disengaging through "Vietnamization," but really committed indefinitely to large scale military and economic assistance "to keep a corrupt and repressive government in power and enable it to continue the war." Beechy's conversations with Vietnamese emphasized "the urgency for stopping the war." For the responsible Christian, Beechy wrote, this meant a "vigorous protest" of the war and a corresponding "compassionate ministry" among the hundreds of thousands of victims.

Vietnam Christian Service "belongs in this agonizing place in this moment of history," Beechy wrote. He encouraged greater Vietnamese involvement in VNCS planning and administration. He said VNCS should expand its relationships with Buddhist groups. He asked: "In what ways, if any, may VNCS use its influence in trying to stop the war?"

Beechy commented on his peace mission since the previous summer, including more than five months spent in Asia—India, Indonesia, Vietnam, Laos and Japan. He observed that, in Vietnam "both the Catholic and the Protestant Churches have identified themselves quite closely with U.S. political and military goals [which] has further blurred the image of the church. The church here, as in other areas, has shown an ambivalent attitude toward war and violence. On occasion it has declared itself against violence but mostly it has accepted it as inevitable."

Beechy said that addressing the root causes of war and structural violence was increasingly being seen as an integral part of the Anabaptist-Mennonite peace witness. Yet in Vietnam, he said, "there appears to be an understandable reluctance to come to grips fully with the question of non-participation in war. Our first task is to understand our brethren if we are to move into meaningful exchanges with them on these matters."

Commenting on his visits to embassies and consulates of the Democratic Republic of Vietnam (DRV) and the Provisional Revolutionary Government (PRG), Beechy said he was respectfully received at all places. Everyone expressed appreciation for the Mennonites' concern and expressed hope that peace might soon come. However, they indicated "no intention of giving up their struggle [for] independence and freedom from all foreign domination" which had been at the heart of their struggle for thirty years. They expressed appreciation to MCC for medical supplies they had received.

In March 1971, shortly after the Beechys left Vietnam, MCC's executive secretary William Snyder made a week's visit to Vietnam. Church World Service's Boyd Lowry was also there at the time.

MCC's Asia Director Paul Longacre, in a working paper prepared for Snyder, stated that VNCS should "drastically reduce and phase out much of the direct service programs" and devote more attention to "enabling" ministries relying more on local personnel. Support for institutional programs like the clinic hospitals would continue, but should focus on helping these programs become self-sufficient. He proposed that the child sponsorship program like we had at the Gia Dinh community center should be cut by one-third.

"How long should we stay with VNCS?" Paul asked. "By remaining in VNCS we can hope to have some influence on the direction of their program. By moving out in a separate direction, we may have a bit more latitude in working with the Tin Lanh church, the C&MA and Mennonite Mission. Moving out of VNCS would give us greater flexibility in relating to the church but the type of program the church wants us to expand is almost totally institutionally related. We cannot be very creative [in the clinics and hospitals] at Nha Trang and Pleiku."

Longacre concluded by suggesting that MCC should become independent while continuing a cooperative relationship with VNCS. With Robert Miller soon terminating, MCC would no longer have an administrative person to relate to the two hospital boards, so Longacre proposed that MCC recruit someone who could have a minimum of six months language study before assuming the duties of MCC representative for Vietnam.

Snyder noted that MCC's experience within Vietnam Christian Service "had been significant and our relationships cordial" during the five years the agencies have worked together. However, Snyder said that MCC and the other partners have divergent priorities, such as the degree of commitment to Vietnam programming, relationships with the Evangelical Church and the developing Mennonite church, mission interests of denominations within Church World Service, and "a more active 'peacemaking interest' on the part of MCC."

Snyder noted that Mennonite Central Committee "did not envision VNCS as a long term-relationship for MCC at the time [they] entered into it, and there are MCC members who are expecting us to return to something similar to the period before the emergency." He recommended that in the spring of 1973 "a review of MCC participation in VNCS be made with the possibility of planning a different basis for cooperation." He anticipated that after the 1972 US presidential election, the direction of a political resolution to the conflict might be clearer. MCC's withdrawal from VNCS was actually implemented January 1, 1973.

In March 1972, James MacCracken, the executive director of Church World Service, understanding MCC's interest in again working independently, expressed deep appreciation for the cooperation of MCC and CWS in "this holy ministry of service in Vietnam." Having designed the "concept of Vietnam Christian Service," MacCracken said that…

> The fact that the Mennonite Central Committee was already present in Vietnam and the fact that the Mennonite Churches are traditional peace churches were both important components of the planning strategy. . . . We in Church World Service had been very explicit that as a major priority we did not wish to tamper with the integrity, the peace concerns, and the uniqueness of the Mennonite Central Committee operation or philosophy. I have rejoiced repetitively since the beginning of this fellowship at the sensitive and loving care we have had for each other as individuals and as organizations. The Vietnam Christian Service is unique throughout the annals of Church World Service.

Allen and Jeanie Stuckey came to Vietnam with their family in August 1969, with Allen picking up the medical work at the Nha Trang clinic/hospital from Harold Kraybill. Dr. Stuckey did a brief stint at the Pleiku clinic in early April 1971. After dinner on Good Friday evening when he was relaxing with the other members of the VNCS unit, a man dressed in the uniform of an ARVN colonel pushed open the door demanding, "Where is Dr. Stuckey?" The officer was invited to sit down for a cup of tea. They had a fairly pleasant half-hour conversation, the officer telling of his rather unpleasant training experience in the United States. Suddenly the officer stared at Stuckey and said: "You're like all the other Americans. You think Americans are intelligent, and Vietnamese are dumb."

When Stuckey declined an invitation to go to the man's home for dinner, the colonel stood up and drew his pistol, yelling for two young men who came in with M-16 automatic rifles. One of the men grabbed Allen by the nape of his neck and the officer hit him over the head with his pistol. He was led outside and thrown into a jeep, then taken to a cemetery outside the city.

When this confrontation began, neither Allen nor the others knew whether this was a prelude to an attack on a military base or Viet Cong in ARVN uniforms kidnapping the doctor to assist them. At the cemetery Allen was beaten and told he was being killed because he had insulted the commander of the base near the clinic. That afternoon while examining an ethnic minority boy at the clinic, the commander had entered, demanding that the doctor immediately examine his two sick sons. Allen did not know him but promised to examine the boys later that afternoon. The officer left and did not return.

After haranguing Allen and putting a gun to his forehead, the colonel kicked him and again threatened him. The men then sped away in the jeep, leaving Allen alone. Allen had a sense of peace, knowing that he was loved by God. He learned later that his father in Ohio had been prompted—at that exact time—to pray for his son. Allen then walked in the light of the moon to a village where he was treated kindly at the home of the village elder who arranged for Allen to be taken back to the clinic. Easter Sunday was a special day for Allen.

In April 1971, Beidlers came from Can Tho to Saigon for the first of the projected quarterly "conferences" involving all the Mennonite Mission personnel. Meeting half days, we asked the questions: "What is God doing within us?" "What is God doing in Vietnam?" "What do we see happening around us?" In a meditation Friday afternoon, Pastor Quang expressed some of his concerns for the church. On Saturday, we had a picnic meal together at a Catholic retreat center by the Saigon River.

Following the conference, Paul and Esther Bucher moved to Can Tho with the returning Beidler family. They rented two upstairs rooms from a family who lived downstairs. The cost: 8000 piasters per month—$30 U.S., plus sixty-five cents for electricity! At first they used bicycles to get around—seemingly the only Americans in Can Tho who still relied on such primitive transportation! Paul was now serving as treasurer for the mission, so this meant monthly travel by bus to Saigon to prepare the financial report.

Although Mary and I were now in Vietnam nearly a decade, we continued to be amused by interesting dynamics of Vietnamese life. Soon after the young evangelist at our church purchased a small Honda motorbike, it was stolen. Through an intermediary, Lam managed to contact the thief who offered to return it for 20,000 piasters! Lam bargained on the price, and by evening had it back for 13,000 ($47 U.S.)!

The rising cost of living was forcing families to earn extra piasters wherever they could. Early in the year some families in Saigon began raising quail in their home for the eggs which restaurants used in soups and other menus. Promoters showed that with the rising demand for breeding stock, one could quickly clear a profit, and inflated prices seemed to confirm this. One woman from our congregation begged to borrow 40,000 ($145 U.S.) from us to buy *two pairs* of breeding stock! We said, "Sorry, but..." By evening that same day, the speculation bubble burst and the price tumbled. One friend had bought fertile hatching eggs for $2.50 U.S. apiece! They were now worth only 13 U.S. cents! A few people became piaster millionaires overnight while others lost their life savings.

Pastor and Mrs. Quang vacationed in Nha Trang for a few weeks in March. Quang was torn between the demands of his VNCS job as director of special projects and the equally demanding responsibilities as pastor of the Mennonite congregation. We had already discussed how the Mission might provide some salary by his becoming involved in leadership training and literature production. However, he liked the freedom of not being dependent on the church or Mission for his livelihood. Several weeks later, Quang resigned from his VNCS position because he wanted to "give priority to his work as pastor." He did arrange, however, to work three days weekly with the VNCS material aid program, a job in which he already had experience.

This was also a difficult time for Trung and Bich who were both staff members of the community center. Bich's father died in central Vietnam in mid-March and Trung and Bich with their three children flew to Qui Nhon for the funeral. A few days after he returned home from the funeral, Trung was to appear in court concerning the Jeep accident seven months earlier. Trung failed to show up, thinking the court date was the following day, and was sentenced two months imprisonment. This he appealed.

Trung's father was also ill and died a few weeks later. I went with others to wash and wrap the body and place it in a coffin, and I was asked to lead in a prayer there. The coffin was then taken to Trung's home where Quang led the funeral service on Good Friday morning.

The church was filled for the Good Friday evening worship service; the Easter sunrise service was held outdoors. Don's Sunday morning English Bible class at the Saigon student center was growing and several students accompanied him to the worship services at the Gia Dinh church. A third-year medical student had recently expressed faith in Jesus Christ and was eager to join Quang's catechism class in preparation for baptism. A group of students meeting at the Saigon student center were also doing volunteer work at an orphanage—along with Don and Titus. Pham Quang Tam, the coordinator of the English classes at the community center, was now appointed to also direct the entire English language program at the Saigon student center.

With Dr. Joanne Smith T and nurse Ruth Yoder gone in mid-1971, we had to decide what to do with the community center clinic. Some advised closing it and I would have argued for this. But with the Mission and the church moving toward joint program planning, I did not want to close a program the church felt should be continued. Miss Tien, who graduated from the one-year nursing program in Nha Trang, had done good work the previous year. Mrs. Connie Chase—whose husband worked for the RMK-BRJ construction consortium—volunteered to work a few mornings each week; she had once worked with Dr. Smith T and Rachel Metzler at a Baptist clinic. A Tin Lanh friend of Pastor Quang recommended Dr. Nguyen Nhu Nguyen, who worked in the large Quang Trung military hospital. He agreed to work two hours at our clinic three afternoons each week.

In July we completed the first ten classes of Gia Dinh congregation adult Bible training school. This included Old Testament and New Testament surveys; doctrinal studies on God, Man and the Church; Evangelism, Church History, the Christian Life and book studies on Matthew and John.

On July 15 U.S. President Richard M. Nixon dramatically announced that his security advisor Henry Kissinger had visited Peking (Beijing), and that he himself would be going to the People's Republic of China seeking normalization of relationships. Preparing the monthly *News and Concerns*, Luke Beidler asked: "When will peace come?" He wrote:

"Today we visited the home of our household helper. Co Oanh's brother was lying in a closed coffin. Yesterday, along with three other soldiers, Thanh touched off a mine which blew the four of them out of this life. This tragedy came near to us and again raised the question, when will peace come? The youth of Viet-Nam are dying by the thousands, enthusiasm and budding love cut short before blooming. I put myself in Thanh's place and tried to imagine how my wife, children, brothers and sisters, and parents would feel. Thanh was no more evil than I. He had no more desire to kill or be killed than I. This war is no more his war than mine. It is foolish to say that Asian boys should die instead of American boys. In my mind it is tragically unnecessary for this war to continue except for corrupt and powerful elders who have more pride than wisdom, more concern for self and position than for the lives and futures of the powerless. Insistently pray and beg the powers-that-be to end these tragedies."

Thanh was twenty-seven years old and the third child in his family killed in three years.

Now living in Can Tho nearly a year, Luke and Dorothy taught English at the Can Tho University while continuing their Vietnamese language study. Paul and Esther were teaching English to teachers in the agricultural college. In June the two couples opened a student center and reading room near the College of Sciences. Our Mennonite missionary team had just completed studying *The Christian Way*, a study of the Sermon on the Mount written by John W. Miller, and Beidlers and Buchers considered using this material for a Bible study class for students who had not yet made a commitment to follow the way of Christ. Paul wrote to his parents: "Here in Vietnam the idea of making [a] decision for Christ seems to run so counter to the culture. I think there may be something to emphasizing each little response to the spirit of God—if it be a reading of the Word of God, or attending a class to find more out about him or a taking of a personal inventory of one's life to see how it compares to God's."

Following through on a proposal for a modest Family Child Assistance program of twenty to thirty families to be developed in Can Tho, with a corresponding decline in the number of cases at the Gia Dinh center, a social worker from the Gia Dinh community center spent a few weeks in Can Tho studying specific community and family needs.

In mid-July, Paul and Esther Bucher had an unexpected encounter with a former classmate from Lancaster Mennonite High School. As they rode their bicycles home, this American GI in a passing army truck recognized them and stopped to talk. The guy was bored with army life and anxious to get home—"there's nothing to do over here," he complained.

The Beidlers and Buchers were asking themselves how much they wanted to associate with other Americans in

Luke and Dorothy Beidler family in Can Tho.

Can Tho. Besides the military and official civilian personnel were the many American civilians working for large American construction consortia. The biggest conglomerate, Raymond International, Morrison Knudson, Brown & Root, and J. A. Jones Construction (RMK-BRJ), spent nearly one billion US dollars from 1962 to 1973 in unaudited construction of military bases, airports, and harbor facilities. In early July the Beidlers were invited to a big party at a neighbor's home for twenty-five Vietnamese families with around twenty-five American men—all but one with a Vietnamese "wife" even though half of them also had wives and families back in the States. These women begged Luke and Dorothy to teach them English so they could survive when they followed the men to the United States.

Luke commented on the Vietnamese presidential elections set for October 3. General Duong Van Minh, Vice President Nguyen Cao Ky, and a few others had announced their intention to challenge President Thieu. Luke asked a friend to record a speech of one of the presidential candidates—printed in a newspaper—so he could listen and practice the language. After finishing the recording, his friend had second thoughts and asked that it be erased. Embarrassed, he said that if someone heard him reading the speech and reported it to the police, they would confiscate the tape, and he would lose his job and position as a civil servant. "Go ahead and study the speech; it's very interesting and I like it," he told Luke. "But I'm afraid to have my voice on the tape." Beidler asked a rhetorical question, "Do you think the elections will be honest?" In late August, Minh and Ky dropped out of the race, accusing Thieu of rigging the election; he was the sole candidate in the October 3 election.

The Stauffer family returned to Vietnam in early August 1971 for their fourth term of service; this would become their last term! They rented a house in the Phu Tho area—near where James and Rachel were trapped in the 1968 fighting. The twelve members of the Mennonite Missions team gathered two days the first weekend in August: James and Arlene Stauffer, Donald and Doris Sensenig, Luke and Dorothy Beidler, Paul and Esther Bucher, Maynard Shirk, Titus Peachey, and Mary and me. On Sunday we discussed church growth after a picnic-type lunch on the roof-top patio of the Saigon center.

On Monday after our gathering, Pastor Quang met with the Mission Council to discuss personnel assignments. The Stauffers would work at Xom Gia, hoping to develop a church there. The Sensenigs would continue at the Saigon student center. Martins would help support Pastor and Mrs. Quang at the Gia Dinh center and church. Beidlers would continue in Can Tho with Buchers supporting them until the following summer. Peachey would teach English classes at both the Saigon and Gia Dinh centers. Shirk would continue to work with VNCS as an up-country maintenance specialist and give some support at the Gia Dinh center.

We also agreed that "if someone feels moved to write another 'Letter to American Christians'" as we had done in 1967, "he or she should proceed to do so with the backing of the group." We had long concluded that President Nixon was "not planning to end the war but only 'change the color of the corpses.'" With the upcoming October presidential election, the United States might have encouraged the running of a more conciliatory candidate than President Thieu. None of us took the time to draft a letter.

International Voluntary Service terminated its programs in August. The agency continued working in Vietnam after the July 1967 resignation of several key leaders. Their primary contract was with the Ministry of Agriculture but their program funds and much of their personal support came from USAID. They worked mostly in rural community development but also provided English language training in colleges and universities.

Now, however, the United States was not only withdrawing the military forces, it was also cutting back USAID programs. Fewer funds were going to the Agricultural Ministry, so the Ministry ended its IVS contract in June, though granted a two-month extension. A few IVSers found other assignments and stayed beyond that date. Mennonite volunteer Johanna Gehman continued to work at a Catholic orphanage in Sa Dec until October when she left with her adopted daughter, Bo Cau.

Election for members of the Lower House in the National Assembly were held August 29. The President stressed his "Four Noes": no coalition government, no neutralism, no partitioning of the country, and no freedom for the communists to operate openly in South Vietnam. It was common belief that all province chiefs, who owed their appointments to President Thieu and the payment of designated bribes, were ordered to produce the votes for the pro-Thieu candidates. One of my friends, a provincial councilor, filed complaints against the provincial authorities. Some opposition candidates won in the cities, but pro-Thieu candidates from the Mekong River delta gave him a strong majority in the 159-member lower house.

In mid-year Robert W. Miller completed his three-year term as VNCS director and returned to the States with his family. In his termination report, he noted that the Saigon office was now making more decisions locally based on program guidelines developed with the New York CWS office. Local VNCS volunteers were also able to more easily submit project proposals.

Vietnam Christian Service in June had projects or personnel at thirteen locations, working with educational, medical, social work, construction, agricultural and community development, and material aid projects. The agricultural and community development projects appeared to be less effective; people in the countryside were more concerned about survival than in long-term development. VNCS was utilizing more indigenous staff, but still recruited expatriate doctors, nurses, physical therapists, and agriculturists.

Miller observed how the death of Ted Studebaker starkly led to a heightened security awareness for volunteers. The dangers could not be entirely avoided, however, since some of the areas of greatest needs were precisely in less secure areas. Miller sensed that VNCS had good relationships with the Evangelical Church, Christian and Missionary Alliance, Mennonite Mission and Asian Christian Service. ACS had been able to provide needed medical personnel for the programs in Nha Trang and Pleiku.

Miller predicted that "the war would continue on a reduced scale for several more years." As long as the Saigon government continued to receive substantial U.S. support it would refuse major concessions to the other side. North Vietnam and the NLF had time to wait, he noted. It also appeared that the Saigon government was becoming more restrictive of the activities and personnel of the voluntary agencies, perhaps in part due to the recent criticism by IVS personnel. In spite of this development, Miller said that "VNCS and other voluntary agencies should continue to speak to the Saigon government regarding injustices they may see."

Lynn Vogel, the director of Saigon programs, terminated about the same time. He affirmed the VNCS contribution of Christian "presence" by providing persons with technical skills and competent Vietnamese language facility. "In a time of increasing unpredictability for westerners (particularly Americans) working in Vietnam," he wrote, "our language ability remains our most ready witness to our Christian concern for and dedication to the people of Vietnam."

Roger W. Getz, the new VNCS director, had served as an agricultural missionary with the American Baptist Church in Burma, in the Philippines, and among Native Americans in Oklahoma.

With Miller's leaving, there were no longer any North American Mennonites in the VNCS administrative office. Anticipating that MCC would soon again be working independently, the Akron, Pennsylvania, office assigned Max Ediger to a three-year term to Vietnam, beginning in July 1971. From Corn, Oklahoma, a graduate of Bethel College, Newton, Kansas, MCC wanted Max to receive a thorough orientation to Vietnam which would include several months of language study. Max did his basic language study in Quang Ngai. In mid-October he completed two months of study and was anxious to become involved in some projects while continuing study halftime.

Ediger wrote a letter November 19 that was published in Bethel College's newspaper early December. Already familiar with the displaced people in the several refugee camps around Quang Ngai, he wrote:

> These refugees do not want to be given food and clothing, they want to be able to grow their own food and buy their own clothing. They do not want to be moved from place to place in search of security, they rather want to be able to go back to their homes and farms and re-establish their family life. They do not want a foreigner coming into their camp telling them how sorry he is that they have been treated so badly and giving them clothing and food to help ease his and this nation's conscience, they want to be left alone to live their own life in their own way. The war must end, the people must be allowed to live. . . . If we really want to help these people, we must end the war.

At the first meeting of the Joint Administrative Council of the church and Mission on August 28, missionaries stressed that the Mission Board commitment to "partnership" was the pattern the Mission had followed in Tanzania, Ethiopia and Honduras, and was not inspired by the American government's current policy of "Vietnamization." The Council would be responsible for administration of all mission program activities, missionary assignments, program policy and budget for a two-year transition period. At the recommendation of Pastor Quang, James Stauffer was elected chair. Quang was named vice chair and Ninh secretary. At the next meeting, September 18 and 19, the various programs of the Gia Dinh community center were reviewed. There was support for continuing the primary school, clinic, Family Child Assistance program and English language program, noting that Mission subsidies would be eventually terminated. There was support for a self-supporting day care program. The joint council also discussed the need for trained cadre and leaders to serve the church in evangelistic, pastoral and service ministries.

In September, our family was stunned by the death of the young daughter of our household helper, Co Chin. Tuyet, nearly three years old, had lived with her mother at our home since she was a few months old. Chin's fourteen year-old brother on an errand had taken her on his bicycle; when a dump truck turned up the street, he was not able to move away and she fell under the truck. We all learned much about life and death as Mary helped prepare the body for burial and we attended the funeral the following day, the service conducted by Pastor Quang. Chin's parents were both members of the church, her father Anh serving as a deacon. Quang used the occasion to preach a sermon on death on Sunday, and the following Sunday preached on "What is Life?" In her journal two days after the tragedy, Mary wrote: "We'll never be the same again. We've seen and felt death. Friday, September 17, was the longest day I can remember." Tuyet was a wonderful playmate to Becky and

Steven, and we fondly remembered Tuyet's delight in carrying a lighted lantern during the autumn children's festival
a week before her death. Nine days after Tuyet's death, her
twenty-three year-old mother gave birth to a son.

Friends urged Mr. Anh to file charges against the
truck driver in order to receive financial payment. Anh
declined and instead invited the driver to come to the
church.

A few years earlier, one of Mary's English language
students was critically injured when the wheels of a large
American truck knocked her down and ran over her. The
expanding war brought not only large convoys of military
vehicles, but also many American tractor trailer trucks
onto the already-filled narrow streets of South Vietnam's
capital. One afternoon when returning home from class,
Luong Thi Luong became another victim of an exhaust-
emitting behemoth on the streets of Saigon. Mary visited
her in the hospital. Her condition gradually improved
and she recovered, albeit with lifetime effects from her
internal injuries. Given the ongoing military conflict, un-

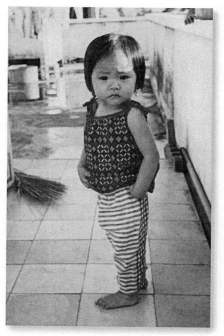

Tuyet.

sanitary conditions aggravated by the war, limited medical care, and congested roadways, we often
observed that it was very easy to die in Vietnam.

In early September, five more persons were baptized. Manh, the man married to our household helper, was planning to be baptized but had been picked up as a draft dodger and was now in
the military prison. Two young women, Mai and Loan, Mr. Ngoc and Mr. Thuong, husband of
one of the school teachers, were baptized. We were especially delighted that Mrs. Le Thi Hai was
baptized. Now in her fifties, she was one of the first people in the community to express faith in
Jesus when we moved to the area and opened the community center in late 1964, but she delayed
baptism to avoid offending her husband's parents. Now she was prepared to take this step—with
her husband's blessing.

Prior to the presidential election of October 3, there were demonstrations in Saigon and
other urban centers against the "one-slate election" with only President Nguyen Van Thieu's name
on the ballots. We all had managed to stay away from the demonstrators. In late September, the
students at Phoenix Study Group where our children studied—John, Rose and Carl Stauffer,
Anne and Jean Sensenig, and our son Steven who was in first grade—were asked to bring emergency rations to school in case the demonstrations blocked the streets around the school. Police
broke up the gatherings with massive doses of tear gas. Schools were closed for a week. In Can
Tho, military police in flak jackets were also stationed at the university.

President Thieu "won" the election with nearly 95 percent of the votes cast. Many people
were angry that Nixon fully backed Thieu. One newspaper editorialized that the United States
was now the main enemy of the Vietnamese people. Two weeks later, James Stauffer wrote home:
"The opposition to the government and the U.S. is continuing. The students have resorted to
guerrilla tactics in the streets. . . . Perhaps one newspaper editorial sums up the feeling of most

people: 'US Remains, Thieu Remains, The War Will Continue!' Once again we have denied the people here the peace they long for."

The National Assembly validated the election and President Thieu was inaugurated at a ceremony in the square in front of city hall under the most stringent security precautions that Saigon had ever seen. Hundreds of soldiers with automatic rifles and fixed bayonets and rolls and rolls of concertina barbed wire surrounded the square.

Although previously unable to obtain exit visas, the Vietnam Church was able to send representatives to the Reconciliation Work Camp in India early October 1971. Nguyen Van Ninh, who two years earlier had traveled to Europe and the United States, went to Calcutta (Kolkata) as the representative from the church in Vietnam. He flew from Saigon late September with Titus Peachey and Maynard Shirk. Yoshihiro Ichikawa and Teruko Yano, the two Mennonite volunteers from Japan working with Vietnam Christian Service, also went.

The First Asian Mennonite Conference was scheduled October 12 to 18 in Dhamtari, India. Pastor Quang and I flew from Saigon to Bangkok, then to Calcutta the following day. We visited the work camp site twenty miles north of Calcutta at the Shaymnagar Christian Hospital, then traveled by train to the conference site. This was a significant occasion for Quang to meet church leaders from other countries. Paul Kraybill also attended the gathering. Following the conference, Everett Metzler, Hong Kong representative, traveled with Ninh, Quang and me to visit the inter-church Union Biblical Seminary where Mennonite missionary Kenneth Bauman was then serving as president. We visited a village established by Mahatma Gandhi, then traveled to Bihar state where Mennonite missionaries Paul and Esther Kniss operated a bookstore in Ranchi. We visited Gaya and Bodh Gaya, the place where Gautama Buddha is said to have obtained Enlightenment. Ninh and Quang traveled on to New Delhi while Everett and I returned to our homes via Burma.

Mary had taken us to the airport on Wednesday, October 6. When she arrived home she learned that a Rang Dong School teacher, Ms. Bich Lien, had taken her own life. It was later

Students in Phoenix Study Group.

learned that her parents, followers of the Cao Dai religion, had repeatedly refused to allow their oldest child to marry the young man with whom she was in love because he was Catholic. She was a baptized member of the Mennonite church, but was not active in the church since she traveled to her home each weekend. The next day friends from the church went to her country home to attend the funeral.

The three Japanese pastors who attended the Asia Mennonite Conference visited Vietnam on their way home—Takashi Yamada, Horoshi Yanada, and a Brother Mori. Stauffer flew with them to Nha Trang on Air

Pastor Quang addresses the Asian Mennonite Conference.

Vietnam's new Boeing 727 plane—only forty-five minutes. There they saw leaders of the Evangelical Church and visited with Teruko Yano who worked at the hospital. The three pastors met with the Gia Dinh congregation at the Thursday evening prayer meeting, the Saturday evening youth meeting, the Sunday morning worship service, and the afternoon training class.

When I returned home from India, there was a letter from an attorney stating that if the Mission did not vacate the Gia Dinh community center property by November 16, the owner would initiate court proceedings against me! We learned that she took this step to speed the negotiation process for the church to purchase this property; she knew the court would not immediately evict us. She had accepted the church's offer of six million piasters ($22,000 U.S.) the church had offered, but did not agree to the terms. She requested substantial payment in dollars to support her children studying in North America. The other problem was that the Ministry of the Interior had not yet approved the Church Council that was to hold the property. Kraybill reluctantly authorized the church to proceed with the purchase in the name of an individual if recommended by the Joint Administrative Council. The church unanimously chose Pastor Quang to represent the church in this purchase.

Anticipating currency devaluation, we borrowed funds from the bank to purchase the property. However, it was fortuitous for us that on Monday, November 15, after President Thieu addressed the National Assembly on economic matters, the national bank announced another currency devaluation. We could now receive 410 piasters to the dollar—almost 50 percent more than before, and two-and-a-half times more than early October 1970! What would have cost nearly $22,000 now cost around $14,600 U.S. But this revaluation, taken to attract private capital from Vietnam and abroad, soon caused prices to rise by up to 50 percent on staples like rice, milk and other basic foods. We missionaries received our support allowances in local currency. Because of the earlier unrealistic rate of exchange, we missionaries had been receiving 170 percent of the EMBMC allowance index. We could now have gone to 100%, but chose to receive less than that. At a time when the Vietnamese people had to tighten their belts, we felt that we should also do some of the same.

On December 27, the title of the Gia Dinh center property—fourteen meters frontage with a depth of fifty-five meters—was transferred to the Vietnam Mennonite Mission, Tran Xuan Quang and Nguyen Van Ninh serving as representatives. A friend of Pastor and Mrs. Quang helped get the necessary documents from the Ministry of Interior. Binh Hoa village of Gia Dinh province—where our property was located—agreed that the property could be sold to the *Hôi Truyên Giáo Tin Lành Mennonite* (Vietnam Mennonite Mission). When the Interior Ministry issued their document, a copy would be placed with the title, together with a letter from the Joint Administrative Council giving authorization to Quang and Ninh to purchase the property.

The Joint Administrative Council took other significant action at their meeting mid-December—that the Gia Dinh congregation assume responsibility for the operation of the community center, with recommendation that Pastor Quang serve temporarily as director of the center. Some of us earlier were reluctant, in principle, to see him become director, concerned that the dual role as director of the community center and pastor of the congregations might not be compatible; some church members might demand favors or community persons might affiliate with the church in hopes of receiving special services. There was no question that he was qualified; he and his wife had also served with the Stauffer and Martin couples on the center's board of directors.

The missionaries met in Saigon for a fellowship conference the last weekend in November. Planned by Esther and Paul, we sensed that we were brought into a closer relationship with God and with one another. On Sunday noon we had a short Thanksgiving praise service and a Thanksgiving meal with tablecloth, candles, name cards and plenty of good food—but no turkey! Paul and Esther were delighted to be Uncle and Aunt with twelve nieces and nephews, giving "a touch of home" to the gathering. Luke Beidler preached at the Gia Dinh church that Sunday morning and our missionary group sang, in Vietnamese, "Revive Us Again." This was an opportunity to make the congregation aware of the Christian witness being given in Can Tho.

The four missionaries in Can Tho—Dorothy, Luke, Esther and Paul—were all teaching English classes in several different colleges of the 5,000-student Can Tho University. Paul and Esther were also teaching staff and war victims at the National Rehabilitation Institute and at the Christian high school related to the Tin Lanh church. Luke developed relationships with a group of university students who organized special English classes to help eleventh-grade high school students pass their exams. Over 350 students signed up in five days. Twenty to thirty students daily used the reading room at the Beidler home, and came evenings to play ping pong. Luke and Paul taught two Sunday morning English Bible classes.

Paul and Esther, especially, were developing friendships with

Luke Beidler leading an English Bible study.

some of their fellow teachers. In their letters home, they described what was happening around them. One weekend in July, after Paul played ping pong with one of the teachers Saturday evening at the Beidler residence, he and Esther accepted an invitation from the teacher and his wife—also a student of theirs—to go out Sunday morning for a bowl of Chinese noodle soup. Buchers invited them back to their upstairs apartment. Esther noted that their conversation was different from that of many of their neighbors who shared the latest gossip and repeated common superstitions. This woman majored in psychology, and they talked about beliefs and religions. The woman wondered why they, as Christians, tolerated the ancestral altar of their landlady in their upstairs room.

Esther explained: "I said I respect another's belief even though I don't believe that way. So right away she said, 'Yes, I think any religion is okay, too.' I said, 'No I think there's only one way but I respect another's.' Then we got talking about how what one believes affects the way they live. All in all Paul and I felt very glad about the beginning of a friendship with them and others."

In early September, Esther wrote:

> Lately I've been thinking a lot more about how I can share Christ with Chi Hai (downstairs) and the real reason for living. Can I ever share with her without letting the factor of privileged background and materialism come up?
>
> . . . When I speak of Christ she often compares it all to Buddhism and says that she loves others, lives right and all just so she can be blessed when she dies. I am trying to learn some more vocabulary so that I can speak of salvation and sins and the spirit of God that lives within us when this miracle of forgiveness happens which is not like the Buddhist belief. However, I still think God's power and love have to be felt by her and although once she has this knowledge of salvation, etc., she has to feel the need of God.
>
> I feel that she does have a need in her life and she often is very worried and bemoaning her financial situation to me. But how, as I said in the beginning, will my God be separated from my wealth and all that she may be able to receive from me? I know it's possible and I really have to be open to God's power working through me.

Paul wrote home in mid-September, five months after moving to Can Tho:

> The other day I was talking with my tutor, a Protestant, about war. For him, fighting the communists is a sacred duty and it is hard for him to see how a person could still be a Christian and not go to war. He felt that our [pacifistic] stand was unrealistic and I told him it would be for a Vietnamese unless he had a God of Power. . . . For a person who wouldn't fight or join the army, Vietnam could be the worst place of all. Sometimes punishment for bad behavior is being forced to go to the front lines and run errands for the soldiers without a personal gun.

The Stauffers were now involved in ministries at the Xom Gia community center in the Phu Tho area of Saigon. Each morning James took their three children by Lambretta scooter to Phoenix Study Group, the private school where our children studied. He then checked in at the Xom Gia center—three kilometers from their home—where Miss Anh supervised five teachers and social workers in community welfare projects which included sewing and literacy classes, kindergarten, a loan program, recreational activities and a bookroom. James was working to develop a spiritual dimension to this center.

When people at the outdoor market near their home asked to study English, Arlene formed English classes at their home; Arlene was also involved in the newly-formed women's fellowship in the Gia Dinh congregation and attended the women's prayer meetings there. James responded to other opportunities. A group of Tin Lanh teachers in public high schools who organized monthly lectures invited Stauffer to speak on "The Hippie Revolution in America" at My Tho, seventy kilometers south of Saigon. James told this group of two hundred high school students how many hippies were coming to faith in Jesus.

On the morning of the American Thanksgiving Day some of us decided it would be better to fast than to feast. So we went to the military cemetery beyond Go Vap that I had visited before. The main morgue had been moved to the Bien Hoa area since this cemetery was now full—with 17,000 graves! We did meet a grief-stricken mother who begged Don and me to help her find air transportation to take the body of her son to central Vietnam. She thought the Americans should help—she had been waiting six days already. But the U.S. Army had long stopped worrying about dead Vietnamese! Before we left, I was stunned to discover the grave of a friend, Nguyen Thanh Hoa—the freshly-built grave marker included his photograph! As an affable thirteen year-old middle school Catholic student in 1962, Hoa was strongly anti-communist, even declaring that he would kill a brother if he embraced this ideology. Later we met occasionally. He was drafted into officers' school and later commissioned a tank commander in the mountain areas of Vietnam. I had heard that he was killed in March 1971—apparently in Pleiku by a sniper's bullet.

In 1971, fifteen ARVN soldiers were dying for every American killed. Several hundred Vietnamese soldiers were dying each week. In a letter to his brother, James Stauffer wrote: "The moral fiber of this nation has been ruined by the war. Bribery is the rule for almost all public service. Soldiers are almost forced to steal and loot because of their extremely low wage. Our government has created a mass army of 1,100,000 men—but fails to provide their basic needs—food! Bullets, bombs, weapons—yes!! The Vietnamization of the war is America's second greatest immorality. The first was her participation in it which is still continuing—in the air instead of on the ground."

After Christmas, the United States carried out several days of sustained bombing over North Vietnam, the heaviest since the saturation bombing of 1968. There appeared to be little progress at the Paris peace talks.

Grave of student friend Nguyen Thanh Hoa.

TRANSITIONS

Chapter 33

In a letter early in 1972 to his "Dear Brother," James Stauffer wrote: "Thank you for your brotherly advice. I guess I need it sometimes. Some of your statements concern me, however. 'To simply be anti-war even as a Christian falls short of the Christian calling,' you said. But isn't it part of our calling as followers of Christ? I'm sure you are not pro-war but you almost seem indifferent to it. I thought, as Anabaptists, we have had over 400 years of history as a non-resistant, peace-promoting brotherhood. Menno S[imons] wrote some scathing letters to the authorities of his day denouncing their wars. War is SIN and hell; I'm against both!"

Stauffer continued:

> I'm sorry that you are disturbed by my anti-American feeling. I feel that America has made a terrible mistake by intervening in Indo-China. If you could only witness the death and devastation that she had brought to the thirty million people of North and South Vietnam, the three million in Laos, and the seven million in Cambodia, maybe you would understand. All the democratic principles on which our nation stands have been violated in this war. We have aligned ourselves with those forces that are resisting aspirations for national independence. The UN has condemned our actions. So have the 500 million people of India and the 100 million of Japan. Our European allies have not given one bit of military aid to our effort. Our Asian "allies," Korea, Thailand, etc. have been "bought" and are in it for the money.

Stauffer's letter to a family member illustrates the difficulty of changing a person's viewpoint. "My country, right or wrong!" was a familiar refrain of many "patriotic" Americans during the sixties and seventies. As for Mennonites schooled in a two-kingdom theology, what the government did was none of our business; we were to pay our taxes, pray for government leaders, and keep our mouths shut!

A few days later, Stauffer wrote to his mother: "Many people here . . . were very anxious during the days that Nixon escalated the bombing of the North. A local . . . editorial asked, 'What does Nixon hope to gain by it? What does it mean?' They continued: 'It means one thing for sure, *Nixon wants war—not peace!*' His talk of 'winding down the war' has a hollow ring over here!"

Since taking office three years earlier, American President Richard M. Nixon had withdrawn more than 400,000 GIs, leaving 139,000 military personnel still in Vietnam. At the same time he was increasing aerial bombing. After a month's recess the official peace talks resumed in Paris January 6. At the end of January, Nixon announced that Henry Kissinger had been conducting secret negotiations with North Vietnam, but both sides were far from a settlement.

In March 1972, MCC doctors Norman Blair, Allen Stuckey, and Margaret Fast joined some twenty other international medical doctors working in Vietnam in sending a letter to President Nixon and to the American Medical Association: "Although we are now quickly and completely removing American military personnel from Vietnam, we still hope that the American government and people will not forget the victims in Indochina who are still suffering because of the tragic errors of the American government. We think that the humanitarian medical programs should be withdrawn last of all."

Appearing in a Vietnamese newspaper, the letter noted that, although American military hospitals earlier treated only a small number of civilian war victims, they were now no longer accepting any. The writers also expressed the need for medical care to political prisoners. The letter concluded:

> "In keeping with humanitarian objectives, we urgently request the support of the American people so that—whatever government emerges when these struggles in Indochina end—these emergency medical programs will continue as long as needed. People will be injured and killed due to unexploded ordnance, buried mines and artillery shells for a long time. The rehabilitation of war victims must continue for many generations."

In December 1971, the Mennonite Church in Gia Dinh completed the purchase of the property occupied by the community center since late 1964, and anticipated rebuilding the facilities in 1972. There was hope that Vietnam Christian Service might provide much of the capital to build and equip the Rang Dong School.

The Joint Administrative Council had recommended that the local congregation assume responsibility for the administration of the school and community center. On January 1, 1972, the Congregational Council accepted this recommendation and the Mission promptly worked with Pastor Quang to effect this transfer. It seemed most appropriate for Pastor Quang to assume the role of director of the community center. It was understood that there would be some personnel changes. At her own initiative, Mrs. Phan Tuyet Nga, the principal who had effectively developed Rang Dong School, submitted her resignation.

In a letter home, Mary noted that the community center was "a pretty big animal." She wrote: "We've made a lot of mistakes, but the Lord has used the witness of the Center to help many understand his love. Pray that it will continue to serve the church and the community and not be a burden to the church."

Foot washing service—Paul Bucher with Khai.

Quang became director of the center March 1. He and his wife were very familiar with the activities of the school and center activities, having served on the board of directors. The ministries developed well under his leadership. With Vietnam Christian Service now committed to supporting indigenous programs, VNCS administrators were happy to continue relationship with the Gia Dinh community center. Quang would be overwhelmed with work since he still gave a few days weekly to

VNCS. Eventually he resigned from VNCS work to give full-time to the church and community center. Nguyen Quang Trung served as his assistant. Phan Van Khai, a soft-spoken man who managed to dodge the draft during the whole war, replaced Trung as monitor of the bookroom. In mid-January, Pastor and Mrs. Quang traveled to Can Tho with Maynard Shirk to visit the Beidler and Bucher couples and observe their ministry. Aware that the Martin family would be going on home-leave midyear, Quang invited Esther and Paul to return to the Saigon area to work with them in supporting the ministries of the Gia Dinh community center and church. In a letter home, Paul wrote: "Quangs would like us to come to Gia Dinh, but only want us to come if we want to go. We're not at that point yet! I think the church feels very reluctant to exercise its power in regard to missionary placements."

Pastor and Mrs. Tran Xuan Quang.

Paul and Esther liked living in Can Tho, a city of 100,000 people with a university of around five thousand students. They were teaching English—Paul fourteen hours weekly and Esther six. On Sunday morning, Paul led a discussion group at eight and an English Bible class later. But they had little interest in relating with the undisciplined American soldiers around them. Paul wrote home of the incident in their alleyway where a drunken GI threatened to kill the landlord's whole family because $1,500 was stolen from his Vietnamese "wife." In another incident, Luke Beidler had seen an American riding in a truck reach down and shove a young man driving a Honda motorcycle, causing the man to lose his balance and nearly fall under another moving truck. "These are the kinds of things we hear students and adults alike tell—only it isn't every day that we see them with our own eyes," Paul wrote.

The Beidlers and Buchers met with other missionary families for fellowship and prayer every Thursday afternoon. These families did not have the same innate hesitation of relating to U.S. military personnel. One week the Baptist family invited the Mennonite couples to go swimming in the beautiful military swimming pool—nearly empty all afternoon. It was so relaxing they thought they might use it again since they got so little recreation. Esther wrote home: "We usually don't bother too much with something connected with the military but when we've been sick, we've been terribly grateful for their medical help at the hospital."

The Joint Administrative Council in mid-March recommended that the Buchers be assigned to the Saigon-Gia Dinh area in July. With Martins leaving for furlough and the church beginning a building project, it seemed wise for the mission bookkeeper and treasurer to be in Saigon. The Beidlers would not be without colleagues with whom to associate—the Alliance and Baptists each had a family in Can Tho, and VNCS was placing a former Methodist missionary to Korea, Lela Johnston, to a physical therapy assignment there.

On January 24, the Interior Ministry approved the "Board of Directors of the Vietnam Mennonite Mission" which enabled the church to hold property. The Board consisted of Tran Xuan Quang, president; Nguyen Van Ninh, secretary; and members Nguyen Quang Trung, Nguyen Thi Hoang, and Tran Thi Ngoc Anh; as vice-president, I was the only missionary on the board. A friend of the Quangs, a Mrs. Mai, had volunteered to help secure this permission. In contacting officials over a period of several weeks, she was reminded that the Ministry could leave the papers lie on their desks for a few years. She thought it appropriate to give the officials a small gift of around $25 U.S. to help them celebrate the Tet New Year! Our Vietnamese colleagues had less hesitation to "grease palms" than we had. What is remarkable is that the gift was so small. Yet it hardly would have been good taste to demand hundreds of dollars from a non-profit religious organization.

With this legal status, the Joint Administrative Council decided to also transfer the Saigon student center property from a private individual to this legal board. The Council appointed Pastor Quang to serve as a delegate to the July Mennonite World Conference in Curitiba, Brazil; the Interior Ministry failed to authorize an exit visa in time.

In early February, James Stauffer, now working in the Xom Gia area on the western outskirts of Saigon, wrote to his mother: "Praise the Lord, revival has broken out in Vietnam."

A year earlier, a few Alliance missionaries recognized that they were performing their service ministries without a sense of the presence and power of the Holy Spirit. After months of fasting and praying, they experienced a renewal of spirit. This influenced their annual missionary conference in May 1971, and led to closer fellowship among the missionary staff at the Nha Trang Bible Institute. Students of Professor Orrel Steinkamp in the fall term were studying the history of Christian revivals. When a student in December reported on a church revival in Indonesia, another student asked, "Why couldn't that happen here?" A student instantly confessed sin, followed by many others. For several days, a spirit of revival moved over the entire campus. Students, filled with the Spirit, "experienced miracles and witnessed with unusual grace." Over the Christmas vacation, students spread this revival movement within their congregations.

I spent most mornings in the office at the Saigon center, and Stauffer invited all missionary men—Don, Titus, Maynard and me—to join him at noon in Bible study and prayer for revival. He wrote home: "We have had some good discussions but I still long for a greater prayer burden and seeking after God. We had a warm, joyful fellowship last evening [in our weekly missionary gathering] for which I praise the Lord."

Just before Tet, this year on Tuesday, February 15, I observed in a letter home that people were not buying as many things as usual. The cost of basic consumer goods had

Maynard, Don, James and Titus.

risen sharply and many people who worked on American military bases, with U.S. construction firms, or for the U.S. Agency for International Development were being laid off.

Early in the year, I suffered humiliation at the Saigon Post Office where I had gone to purchase a first-day postage stamp cover. As I stood in line I had a sudden urge to check my hip pocket; my wallet was gone! Instantly I confronted the guy next to me who held out two empty hands. Although I assumed it was one of the three fellows near me, I knew that I could not accuse an innocent person. Even the policeman nearby could do nothing since there was no evidence. While I lost money and my driver's license which would involve a hassle to get replaced, the loss of pride hurt most. I had been in Vietnam for over nine years and had never been pick-pocketed!

With intelligence reports indicating large People's Army of Vietnam (PAVN) troop movements down the "Ho Chi Minh Trail" which ferried military supplies from the north to the south, the United States in February began heavily bombing this supply line and the area around the Demilitarized Zone. Bui Thi's brother Thanh, who was staying with us for a month, told us that NLF cadre had come back to the villages in Quang Ngai province after the American troops had evacuated the area. There were also numerous sightings of the "enemy" in Di Linh district where Ted Studebaker was killed the year before. International personnel working in Kontum and other towns in the central highlands were evacuated due to fears of attacks.

Maynard Shirk had many opportunities to travel around South Vietnam repairing vehicles and doing other maintenance work. In early 1972 he went with Tom Spicher and Gunnar Barnes to visit a refugee camp just south of the Demilitarized Zone where Tom was giving assistance to an elementary school for camp children. Afterwards the three drove up to the military base on the south edge of the DMZ where they met two U.S. Army sergeants who welcomed them, then took them up a high observation post to show a powerful telescope using laser rays, equally effective day or night. An attached radar unit measured the distance to the accuracy of one meter which enabled them to call in shells from an artillery base located twenty kilometers south of them.

"We observed the whole process," Shirk wrote. "The whole ghastly process was executed by laughing, joking soldiers, none of whom came closer than three miles to the killing they were doing. . . . And that is the demonic genius of the technologized American military. The military no longer needs a draft. They just need our money to develop machines and hire operators—cheerful, laughing, joking operators."

In early February I accompanied VNCS director Roger Getz to Nha Trang to attend a meeting of the Tin Lanh hospital board. While there I met Dr. and Mrs. John Schmidt—the founders of the MCC Kilometer 81 Paraguay Mission to Lepers. On a four-month assignment to Vietnam through the American Medical Association with Volunteer Physicians for Vietnam, they had been evacuated from Ban Me Thuot. MCC had arranged a short-term VNCS assignment for Schmidt's wife, Clara, so she could accompany her husband.

The Mennonite Church at the community center gathered for praise and storytelling the first day of Tet on Tuesday, February 15. There was good participation and it was hard to close the meeting—even after going overtime by 30 minutes.

Mr. Thanh was a carpenter who had come to faith in Jesus. Though he still struggled with some issues, he would often express his faith poetically, sometimes singing a song that he composed during the worship service. Trong had been a gambler with a notorious anger which he vented

Some men of the church: Thanh, Muong, Xuan, Anh and Trong.

Bay, Hai and Van with Mary.

on those who failed to pay their gambling debts. Now he had a quiet but equally forceful testimony of victory over his gambling habit and fierce anger. Xuan was a quiet man whose wife was chosen to be a deaconess. Mr. Anh was chosen to serve as a deacon. Mr. Muong had been a member of the Tin Lanh Church, and expressed a firm faith in God. Mrs. Bay was illiterate, but expressed a profound faith in God's love and care. Van was a caring person and also chosen as a deaconess. Mrs. Hai was our neighbor.

Mary wrote home: "Tet has passed peacefully. . . . I don't know of any time quite like Tet when time actually seems to stop. Suddenly no one asks whether it's the fifteenth or sixteenth or what according to the solar calendar, but everything is reckoned according to the lunar calendar. That continues up until maybe the fifth or sixth day of the New Year then gradually everyone shifts back to the solar dates again. So it seems sort of like a parenthesis in the middle of the month. I'm hardly aware of the passing of the middle of February because everything was Tet then."

The Mennonite Mission was invited to take over a thriving Bible correspondence program. An American missionary in Hong Kong began the Living Word program in 1965 with a basic English six-lesson course—God, Man, Jesus Christ, repentance, assurance, and the Christian life. Translated into Chinese and Vietnamese, thousands of students had taken these lessons and there were several hundred students currently enrolled. When the funding support ended, a local Chinese pastor and brother-in-law of Pastor Quang, Luong Bao Thai (Timothy Thai), asked whether the Mission would be able to continue the Vietnamese and English courses. The Joint Administrative Council saw this as a great opportunity and agreed to sponsor this program, effective April 1. Although the Mission had not budgeted for the $150 to $200 monthly costs, we were able to use funds sent by an Old Order Mennonite mission supporter from the Weaverland Mennonite Conference.

We anticipated preparing new lessons to offer students. Don was appointed to head the program, and Pastor Quang—who had earlier worked with the Navigator's Bible correspondence course—to serve as advisor. Mr. Do was asked to continue reviewing the students' lessons and responding. Titus and Maynard vacated their upstairs room at the Saigon student center to give Do an office, and moved into a rooftop room in the Martins' house in Gia Dinh.

In July, Don Sensenig reported that 1,200 lessons in the Vietnamese language were sent and received each month, and 150 in English. He quoted a student who said: "The lessons brought me a real benefit in the work of creating a new person. . . . I have received Christ to be my Saviour. I hope with a strong faith in Him, I will be able to avoid a life of selfishness and sin."

A young woman, however, was at a different place. She wrote: "I am greatly surprised by the statement, 'There is no salvation in any other, for there is no other name . . . whereby we can be saved.' Why no others? Why only Jesus? Does this mean that other religions, such as Buddhism, for example, that include the foundations of our Asian philosophy, are superfluous?"

In March, William T. Snyder, MCC's Executive Secretary, informed Eastern Mennonite Board of Missions that MCC was considering discontinuing its involvement with VNCS. When formed in 1966, MCC viewed their participation in this joint agency as a temporary arrangement during an emergency period. MCC had administered the VNCS program three years and CWS had already also led the joint program for three years. An ad hoc Ecumenical Meeting on Indochina which convened in early March in Geneva anticipated forming an "ecumenical fund" of several million dollars contributed by European and American churches to give assistance to post-war Vietnam. Although MCC's relationship with all these agencies was good, working with a large umbrella program was not MCC's normal pattern of operation.

MCC was now anticipating a much smaller program, staffed by personnel recruited by MCC and administered directly from the Akron, Pennsylvania, office. Snyder said a major MCC programming interest would be "in the area of reconciliation," and wanted to cooperate as much as possible with the Mennonite Mission and church in Vietnam as well as with the Evangelical Church in Vietnam. It would emphasize good Vietnamese language facility for its personnel.

Roger Getz had met Snyder at the Geneva meeting, so I had already reported to Paul Kraybill that MCC's relationship to VNCS would likely change by the end of the year. Kraybill supported this so that MCC's interests would "not be swallowed up" in a larger program. We missionaries felt quite positive about our relationship with VNCS but understood MCC's rationale for administering its own programs. We wanted MCC's disengagement to be done carefully to prevent lowering VNCS morale or harming its image within the Evangelical Church.

Carl Beck, Mennonite missionary from Japan and director of Reconciliation Work Camps, visited Vietnam in early April to plan for a summer work camp. He joined in the April 2 Easter Sunrise worship service at Gia Dinh attended by one hundred and fifty persons; five persons were baptized. At the evangelistic service on Saturday evening when the influential Tin Lanh lay leader Huynh Minh Y preached, six persons expressed their desire to accept Jesus Christ as Savior and Lord.

The Asia Mennonite Conference in October supported Beck's proposal to organize the eighth work camp in Vietnam in 1972 and asked that both a woman and man aged eighteen to thirty be invited from each country having a Mennonite church. The Joint Administrative Committee appointed Nguyen Van Ninh, Titus Peachey and Maynard Shirk to plan for the camp. Ninh proposed that Nha Trang had good potential for the camp. The facilities of the Evangelical

Church's Bible Institute would be available in July and a possible project would be building a sea wall in front of the clinic and hospital. By locating the work camp in Nha Trang, they hoped that youth from the Tin Lanh Church would also be involved. And no place in Vietnam was quite as idyllic as the Hon Chong rocks by the sea!

The Gia Dinh congregation began working seriously in March to determine how to rebuild the church facilities on the newly-purchased property. Quang had blueprints and cost estimates prepared; in early April a request was submitted to Vietnam Christian Service for assistance in building the school and community center, costing around $35,000 U.S. A copy of the blueprints was sent to Kraybill, along with a sketch for the remodeling of the main building for the church auditorium and a pastor's residence upstairs which would be implemented with Mission and church funds. The decision was eventually made to raze all the buildings and build the church facilities attached to the classrooms.

On April 6 and 7, the missionaries, together with the Quang family, met in Saigon for our quarterly fellowship conference. The theme of our Bible study was "Our living hope" (I Peter). We then spent an extra day at the Vung Tau beach. During this time, the plight of the country was never far from our minds.

On March 30, North Vietnam had launched a massive strike across the DMZ, following up with thousands of troops supported by tanks and heavy artillery. Within days they controlled much of Quang Tri province. They then attacked in Binh Long province, capturing the district town of Loc Ninh, 125 kilometers north of Saigon, and the central highlands between Pleiku and Kontum. Ron Ackerman worked in Dak To, but on April 13 was in Saigon. Tom Spicher, MCCer working with VNCS at Dong Ha just below the DMZ, survived a withering rocket and mortar attack before fleeing south with thousands of others. The Nixon administration responded to these attacks by ordering B-52 strikes above the DMZ—the first since November 1967—and by the middle of April were bombing even the areas around Hanoi and Hai Phong.

After being evacuated to Hue, Spicher returned briefly to Dong Ha where he was very up-set by what he saw. Old men whom he knew, were sitting around weeping—for separated families and widespread destruction from artillery and aerial bombing. They did not want to leave their land and homes. They were glad to see Tom, but he soon left because he felt an American presence was a liability to them. Tom told about a Christian pastor—riding his motorbike out in the countryside—who had found a small child all alone, crying, separated from his family.

Bill Rose (r) speaking with Dean Hancock, a Vietnamese pastor, and Ron Ackerman.

The renewed military activity by both sides triggered renewed American public demonstrations against the war. The Eastern Mennonite Board Overseas Ministries office drafted an April 7 letter to President Nixon. Signed by Mission Board President H. Raymond Charles and Overseas Secretary Harold Stauffer, it expressed concern about the renewed warfare. After briefly describing EMBMC work in Vietnam, the letter reads: "We have been increasingly concerned about military operations in Indo-China in which the United States government has played a major role. To us, this course appears counterproductive to the best interest of all persons concerned. We believe the United States bears heavy responsibility for the extreme suffering, loss of hope and death experienced by many innocent victims. This continuing destruction undermines the intentions and integrity of groups such as our own who seek to serve constructive purposes there."

Since Mennonites have often been known as the "quiet in the land," the letter said "that characteristic may have unintentionally identified us with the 'silent majority'" in the United States. The letter referred to the December 1967 statement the missionaries had prepared, calling for a change in policy that would recognize the concerns of the Vietnamese people. The two Republican senators from Pennsylvania, Hugh Scott and Richard Schweiker, acknowledged this letter. Schweiker said he was calling the Senate to set a specific date when U.S. involvement in Indochina would permanently end.

Harold S. Stauffer, now secretary in the EMBMC Overseas Office, invited me to assume the responsibility for the Asia programs during the year we planned to be on leave. Before Paul Kraybill terminated his position with the Mission Board on June 30, an Asia Consultation was being planned in late June. To prepare for this interim assignment, I spent ten days in late April traveling to Bangkok, Thailand; Vientiane, Laos; and Hong Kong. We made plans to visit the Philippines on our way to the States.

There was evidence of renewed life within the Gia Dinh congregation. In a letter to *Missionary Messenger,* Mary noted that Pastor and Mrs. Quang were spending two evenings a week visiting church families to guide them in establishing a family devotional hour. They found many homes where Bible reading and prayer were already shared together. Twenty to thirty people were coming to the weekly Thursday evening prayer meetings, sharing the scripture that they had read at home, often beginning with "I read this book for the first time!" Even in our house, where our cook and her husband had been fighting each other, for a few months now they were living peaceably and reading the Bible and praying together each night.

Mary also wrote home about my barber whom I invited to church. Sunday was his busiest day so he came Thursday evening with his wife. She had been reading the Bible for several years and said they worship Christ in their home. When someone from church asked if she believed in Jesus, she did not know quite how to answer; she was not familiar with church terminology.

Mrs. De (Chanh), a secretary working in the Family Child Assistance office, was part of the church but had not yet been baptized. She was a faithful student of the Sunday afternoon classes. At home she looked for opportunities, when her husband was in the room, to tell her children what she was learning. He had accompanied her and their children to the Easter sunrise service. We prayed for these families.

In a letter home in mid-April, James Stauffer said "the big talk in Saigon now is the escalation of the war." Writing that things were "normal" in Saigon, he said they were "rudely awakened" at

3:50 a.m. on April 13 when a VC sapper unit succeeded in blowing up thousands of tons of ammunition at the American base in Long Binh—thirty kilometers away.

And the Viet Cong had sent several rockets into the outlying areas of Saigon, killing fifteen people. The same day, VC forces attacked An Loc, the capital of Binh Long province only one hundred kilometers north of Saigon, sending thousands of civilians fleeing south to the large Binh Duong province town of Thu Dau Mot, situated along the Saigon River only twenty kilometers from downtown Saigon.

Writing home, Mary told about a friend—the mother of a teenager who had received assistance through the Family Child Assistance program, who had gone to Binh Duong province north of Saigon to buy produce to resell. There at the bus station, she met persons who had fled the fighting. People had fled through fields trying to avoid the fighting all around them. Fields were littered with dead bodies. People then walked for several days without food and water. Some sold their rings on the way to buy rice. Babies died on the way and were abandoned without burying. In desperation, some mothers gave their babies urine to drink.

This woman returned home and went to the women with whom she peddled on the street, collecting money to purchase pre-cooked rice on the black market which she took to the people. Mary went through her drawers, picking out baby clothes to give to the woman for the homeless children. In the letter home, she wrote:

> I was deeply moved by this woman's compassion. She's about my age, the mother of six children. Her husband's out of a job. She used to sell black market things and did quite well. But because of his having no work, they used up all the capital. . . . Now she runs about each day trying to find a little something to buy and resell for a small profit to feed her family. Often they don't have enough to eat. But she was moved by the needs of these people so much worse off than she and spent her energy, time, and resources to help them. She's not a Christian, but knows what it means to give of herself in Christ-like compassion.

In Mary's long letter home, she wrote:

> I guess there's no need to go into detail about the present situation. You're watching the news and maybe know more than we do. . . . I'm wondering whether it's right for me to pray for peace because I must confess I have no faith that this will ever end. We are told to pray in faith. There will never be a solution until ALL American military men leave. We pretend to be withdrawing, but are dropping seven million dollars' worth of bombs a day. The Vietnamese are responsible for the ground fighting and are dying by the hundreds.

Don Sensenig, Maynard Shirk, and Pastor and Mrs. Quang went to Binh Duong to assess the situation and made plans to give assistance.

The Buchers, still living in the Mekong River delta where military activity tended to be lighter, also wrote home about the increased fighting. "The present escalation of the war by both sides upsets us." Paul wrote home. "We listen to incomplete radio broadcasts a couple of times a day. . . . Last week the ammunition dump at the main air field about ten miles from us was hit by a VC rocket or shell. It continued exploding for over a day injuring people long after with the flying pieces of shell."

Stauffer wrote to his mother at the end of April:

> The future of South Viet Nam is rather dark! The daily news reports defeat after defeat. It could be that the reckoning day has come. The US has been able to keep things covered up and to hide her real impact on this country for about fifteen years, but now the fallacy of it all is being shattered. Nixon's policy in Vietnam has not been based on the facts of the situation here. He is still following the path of the French from 1945 to 1954. He has underestimated the desire for national independence. . . .
>
> The war is beginning to affect our friends. Our caretaker at the Gia Dinh Center, Mr. Bat [Muong], has three of his four sons in the army. The unit that his son, Phuoc, belonged to was overrun and only fifteen out of one hundred have reported back to their headquarters. They don't know if he is dead, wounded, captured or still to show up. Another son is at Bong Son which is also surrounded by NVA. No report yet on him.

James, Arlene, and their three children had recently sung at the International Protestant Church. Donald Bubna, the current pastor, and his wife invited the Stauffer family out to dinner after the Sunday evening vespers a few weeks later. Bubna wanted to discuss pacifism with Stauffer—after having heard Mennonite evangelist Myron Augsburger speaking at an Alliance conference in the States. Stauffer wrote: "Some of his sermons sound like he agrees with the nonresistant view, but he still has some problems with it."

No one had all the answers to the Vietnam tragedy.

Stauffer finished his letter on May Day, a national holiday. He wrote: "There are reports that Saigon will be hit today or tonight. . . . Everything still seems 'normal' except for the many funerals of army officers and the constant [identification] checking of young men and soldiers. Almost every block is a checkpoint with a truck or two to carry off the fellows they pick up. It makes one sad to see all these young men forced to go out and fight and probably lose their lives."

Doan Van Mieng, the president of the Evangelical Church, called on all congregations to observe a day of fasting and prayer on Sunday, May 7, for the country and people of Vietnam. Four days later, Vietnam's President Thieu declared martial law—the first time since the 1968 Tet offensive—and lowered the draft age to seventeen years.

In response to the "intensification of the conflict in Indochina," the Mennonite Church in North America also issued a call to each congregation to set aside May 28 or 29 "as a special day of prayer and fasting."

President Nixon, in a speech April 26, said his Vietnamization policy "has proved itself sufficiently." He would continue to withdraw U.S. ground forces, but keep on bombing, he said, "ensuring South Vietnam's survival as a separate country." The U.S. Navy, in fact, had doubled the number of warships off the Vietnam coast. In response to the DRV and PRG request to resume the Paris Peace Talks, Nixon said he was asking Ambassador William Porter to immediately return to the Paris Peace Talks. This meeting was later described as "fruitless."

A week after Nixon's speech, the Mennonite missionaries and a few MCC personnel wrote to the President, "compelled to share another viewpoint." Compared to the 1967 "Letter to American Christians" that we prepared over several months, this May 3 letter spoke much more explicitly to the historical political issues underlying of the Vietnam conflict. Identifying ourselves as "church workers and missionaries" serving in Vietnam with the Mennonite Church, the letter critiqued the American attempt from 1954 to legitimize a political alternative to the Communist Viet Minh nationalist movement, and called on his Administration to withdraw all its forces and set a date for the "cessation of hostile action by all U.S. military forces" which might be "the catalyst that begins the long, painful way toward change and compromise."

It was signed by all the missionaries in Saigon and by Tom Spicher, Max Ediger, and Ron Ackerman, MCC personnel serving with VNCS at Dong Ha, Quang Ngai and Dak To. Don Sensenig sent it to the EMBMC publicity office, suggesting that it be published in *Missionary Messenger* and sent to other Christian magazines.

In the accompanying letter, Sensenig said the letter "might not contain 'the whole gospel,' but we believe the gospel underlies its appeal . . . to government leaders and to the public at large to recognize sin and unrighteousness and judgment at work in our government's actions," and to "take certain politically feasible steps toward change in the direction of protecting the innocent and restraining evil."

Sensenig asked several questions:

> Should we not spend time and effort in proposing and supporting policies that can alleviate some of the suffering of the poor and powerless? Can we not uphold "the things that make for peace," even in the political areas of contending factions and less-than-ideal compromises?
>
> A significant part of our task is calling Christians themselves to deeper commitment to peacemaking. For example, too many Christians view the Viet Nam conflict as the good guys ('free world') against (using the weapons of carnal warfare) the bad guys (atheistic Communists). This letter calls attention to the distortions underlying that viewpoint. [It] is only one small attempt to allow justice, mercy and faith to contend with violence in our national life. What can we do that will move our nation away from its suicidal reliance on violence?

It was printed in *Gospel Herald*, the periodical of the Mennonite Church. Delton Franz, the director of MCC Peace Section's Washington office that had opened only four years earlier, commented on the use of this letter: "I am very glad for the wide circulation your recent letter to the President received in the Mennonite press. I think our Mennonite constituency has received considerable insight from the perspective of EMBMC mission personnel on the scene. We were able to share copies of the letter with government officials on June 13 and 14 when an inter-Mennonite delegation spent those two days here in Washington out of concern for the escalated bombing in Vietnam."

This delegation, in addition to meeting with White House staff advisors, also met with Senators William Saxbe (Ohio), James Pearson, (Kansas), William Spong (Virginia), Richard Schweiker (Pennsylvania) and several Representatives. Led by Peace Section chairman William Keeney and Paul Longacre, the delegation included John E. Lapp (Mennonite Church), Elmer Neufeld (General Conference Mennonite Church), Vernon Wiebe (Mennonite Brethren), John Stoner (Brethren in Christ), and Myron Augsburger of Eastern Mennonite College. Times had indeed changed within a few years. Five years earlier when James Metzler had spoken on campus against American policies in Vietnam, Augsburger was critical of Metzler's stance.

Yet there were still critics. *Guidelines for Today*, a newsletter published by a group of conservative Mennonite leaders, wrote:

The recent letter by Mennonite missionaries in Vietnam to President Nixon on the Vietnamese situation is an example of the naiveté persons can have on political affairs, the kind of misreading of history that is being done today. While Christians certainly cannot support any bloody and devastating war such as that in which the US is now engaged in Vietnam, neither can they make judgments against one nation without taking into account the total picture. Nothing is ever said . . . to the Chinese and Russian leaders that are as deeply involved as America in supporting the conflict. Nothing is ever said as to what would take place in South Vietnam were the North to take over.

Sunday, May 7, Mary noted in her journal that the day had been set aside for prayer and fasting for Vietnam. "As we worshipped and prayed together this morning," she wrote, "there was weeping. But there was also praise. Mr. Bat's [Muong's] son, returned from the dead, was present to tell of his experiences as a soldier."

When the staff of the community center had planned a farewell party for Mary and me ten days earlier, Nguyen Muong, the caretaker, was asked to lead in the closing prayer. He prayed for his son Phuoc at Dau Tien and for his oldest son Thong—just married—at Bong Son. There was severe fighting in both areas. The next day we were told that Phuoc was probably killed. His company was surrounded and the company commander killed. The survivors decided to break out through the Viet Cong forces. A few days later Mr. Bat got word that Phuoc managed to reach another

Mr. Muong with son Thong.

company with a minor head wound. On his way to our house to tell us the good news, Titus Peachey handed Mr. Bat a telegram which read, "Thong safe in Qui Nhon." This was seen as an answer to the prayers of many.

Mary and I sent a letter to the congregations that supported us. "In the five weeks since the new offensive began," we wrote,

> The toll of human suffering has been overwhelming. Thousands of soldiers and civilians on both sides have been killed. . . . Thousands more have been injured, hospitals so full that they cannot accept all the wounded; small hospital beds now have three patients. Over 450,000 people have fled their homes to become refugee statistics. . . .
>
> Deserters in military prisons have been "pardoned" by President Thieu to be sent out to fight! Men are picked off the street and sent into army training camps. Teen-age boys and grandfathers alike are impressed into service.
>
> It is not necessary now to discuss the origins of the Vietnam conflict which began thirty years ago, nor the direct US involvement which began in 1954. It is important to note, however, that

the present US policy is not to end the war, but rather to continue the war by equipping the South Vietnamese to fight as US ground troops are withdrawn. Many Vietnamese are fearful of tomorrow, but all desperately long for peace.

In early May, Mennonite missionaries joined with missionaries of other agencies in praying for peace. James Stauffer wrote home: "It is interesting to hear missionaries pray now. Some think that God is on the U.S.-SVN side and that their military force will keep Vietnam open for the preaching of the Gospel. Some are losing confidence in the U.S. Army's ability to defeat the 'satanic forces' and are calling on God to intervene and save the country. Others are calling on God [to] carry out His will in the whole situation."

VNCS personnel at Dak To in the central highlands and at Dong Ha below the DMZ evacuated. Doug Beane spent several days in late April with Max Ediger and Stewart Herman in Quang Ngai evaluating the situation, concluding that although Quang Ngai town was relatively secure, VNCS personnel should not travel to the district towns. Dennis Metzger and Yoshihiro Ichikawa wanted to stay in Tam Ky. Metzger wrote: "Hiro and I believe that our relationship with the people would be severely damaged should we evacuate before they do." Since Tom Spicher was unable to return to Dong Ha, he requested an early termination. In his termination report, he wrote: "Upon leaving Dong Ha with refugees from the area, I finally understood why there had been so little enthusiasm for development work. . . . The future is uncertain as long as there is war."

With some international personnel evacuating from areas of heavy fighting, the EMBMC home office reassured us of their prayers and of our freedom to evacuate should this seem necessary.

With my plans to leave Vietnam, Don Sensenig was appointed to serve as Vietnam Mennonite Mission secretary. Don responded to Harold Stauffer, who had succeeded Paul Kraybill as overseas secretary, noting that our missionary team discussed factors relevant to any evacuation: "Our usefulness if we stay, our influence on the safety or danger of those with whom we work, decisions of other missions such as the C&MA, personal decisions or needs of individuals and individual families, need to protect our children from danger, and possible emotional strain." He referred to the position of Pastor Quang: "If the time comes when our presence endangers the church or our Vietnamese friends and co-workers, then we should go; but we should stay as long as possible (implying even under dangerous conditions) to back up our professions of commitment to the church and willingness to suffer with them."

Don reported that Saigon was "quite quiet and normal in almost every way, except for a 10:00 p.m. to 6:00 a.m. curfew." University classes were suspended and some students were to report for guard duty. With men up to age forty-three subject to the draft, there was the possibility that Pastor Quang—who had been deferred—would be drafted. Sensenig wrote: "He told me recently he will go to jail rather than return to the Army; I'm not sure if it's because he's an ordained pastor now or if he's come personally to a nonresistant point of view. I heard him tell two students who asked his opinion the other day that this is a matter for individual conscience to decide."

The church was being taught that commitment to the way of Jesus Christ came above the responsibilities to any government. However, there was no common agreement within the church about each individual's duties to the government. "We appreciate the prayers and concern of all of you in the church," Don wrote. "We hope and pray this crisis will be a decisive one, one way or the other, that will end the war soon, perhaps within a few months. We've had such hopes before, of course."

There was much agonized reflection and prayer during these weeks in April and May. Mary wrote home in mid-May: "During the past weeks our hearts were often very heavy because of the situation in Vietnam. I felt heavy because so much of the suffering was caused by America's involvement in this war. If communism is going to be ruling eventually, it could have done so with much less bloodshed in 1954 when the Geneva Accords called for free elections all over the country."

In a cynical frame of mind, she wrote: "Of course, America loved the Vietnamese people too much to let that happen. Now look how they love them!"

In Can Tho, Paul Bucher also wrote about changes there. University classes were suspended and professors were forced to do guard duty. Paul was encouraged by a "kind sort" of a teacher friend who said, "I'm scared; I don't think I could kill anything. I don't even know how to shoot a gun." Student reactions varied—some supported the massive U.S. bombing of North Vietnam while others were against it. Some friends who had once talked about joining the Liberation Front now criticized the military invasion by the North. Some said that the U.S. should bomb the dikes along the Red River and the civilians in the North. Others said the bombing and the mining of the harbors in the North would only escalate the conflict. Some said all Americans should leave Southeast Asia.

Yet in Can Tho, a new program planned by the Mennonite Church took shape. After weeks of planning, Ms. Vo Hong Lieu began teaching a home economics class for twenty-four young women from poorer families in Can Tho in early May. This was a structured three-month course teaching the skills of sewing, cooking, and child care. Funding came from the MCC Family Child Assistance sponsorship program. Ms. Hong Lieu was active in the large Tin Lanh church in Can Tho and had worked several years as a caseworker with Christian Children's Fund.

The Joint Administrative Council met on Saturday, May 20 with a full agenda. We had significant discussion about training programs for the church. Don was currently teaching the book of Genesis in the Sunday afternoon program within the Gia Dinh congregation. This was the twelfth class in the first cycle of classes that we had originally anticipated. Previous courses included Surveys of Old and New Testaments, doctrinal studies on God, Man and the Church; Christian Living, Evangelism, Christian Education, Church History, and book studies on Matthew and John. Seven or eight church members registered for each of these classes.

Ms. Lieu demonstrating homemaking skills.

The Council decided to continue another cycle teaching additional subjects. Where possible we would utilize materials used by the Tin Lanh and Baptist churches.

These courses had been taught by missionaries. It was now recommended that Eastern Board recruit new personnel to replace Peachey, Shirk, and the Buchers who would soon terminate, among them someone to give primary attention to theological and leadership training.

The war was never far from our thoughts; James Stauffer wrote home:

> The renewed fighting is heartbreaking, to say the least. I am sorry that the NVN chose to make this all-out assault on SVN. I condemn them for their resort to violence and their many inhumane actions. But Nixon's policy drove them to it. And our reaction to their violence is absolutely unbelievable and indescribable. It is just sheer madness. It doesn't make sense for Nixon to be seeking peace with China and Russia and at the same time be waging an all-out war on these small nations of Indo-China. He is dropping two tons of bombs every minute—spending seven million daily on bombs alone—something Johnson tried for four years without results. May God have mercy.

On May 26, around ten days before our family left Vietnam, James Stauffer, Donald Sensenig, Tom Spicher and I met with US Ambassador Ellsworth Bunker at the fortress-like Embassy on Thong Nhut Boulevard. Some of us had been discussing this possibility for a few weeks and sent him copies of our May 3 letter to President Nixon and our 1967 statement. We were given an appointment several days after I called in. When we were welcomed late afternoon, with the Ambassador were his special assistant and his Minister for Political Affairs, Josiah W. Bennett.

We introduced ourselves and briefly described the work of the Mennonite Mission and our relationship with Vietnam Christian Service. The Ambassador had read the materials we had sent him and shared his views on these items for perhaps twenty minutes—agreeing with some of our statements, disagreeing with others. We responded with some of our objections and concerns in a frank exchange of views. While acknowledging that we were pacifists, we assumed that he held to a traditional just war theory and stated our views that the U.S. military force and violence were far out of proportion to any good that could be accomplished.

The Ambassador declared that the United States, as a world power, has the responsibility to use this power for the benefit of other nations besides Vietnam. He acknowledged the U.S. did not know very well how to fight in Vietnam. He stated that fighting a limited war with limited objectives and limited means permitted the other side to withdraw and resupply in sanctuaries.

Bunker said substantial progress was made in recent years in bettering the lives of the rural people. The Vietnamese people had their own land; they owned Honda motorcycles, tractors and outboard motors. He declared that President Thieu had significant and growing support, and pointed to the strong opposition in the upper and lower houses of the Assembly as evidence of its democratic ways. He believed that the People's Revolutionary Government would win only fifteen percent of the votes in South Vietnam under an internationally supervised election. The Ambassador said that President Thieu believes that Ho Chi Minh made a mistake in not calling a ceasefire in 1965 before President Johnson introduced US ground troops. If the North Vietnamese President had done this, the communists would now control the whole country, Bunker said. He predicted that the current military activity would end in another stalemate and that North

Vietnam would be willing to negotiate seriously sometime after the U.S. fall elections. But the war would continue for now.

We challenged many of the assumptions and views of the ambassador. As we left, Mr. Bunker said we were doing good work and should keep it up! We left his office with appreciation that he had given fifty minutes of his time, but with some reservation about the effectiveness of this attempt to speak "truth" to power. Yet we knew that many American officials in Saigon believed that the Saigon government was not viable and that it was only a matter of time until the communists controlled the government—some even thinking that this might be preferable.

Don Sensenig recalled that as we were leaving the Embassy, one of Bunker's aides asked if our Mennonite supporters in the States knew we were making this presentation to U.S. officials, and whether they would approve, since he understood that Mennonites did not get politically involved!

Martin family.

Our family left Vietnam on June 6. We spent a week with the James and Rachel Metzler family in the Philippines to become acquainted with their ministry. Mary and I with our three children arrived in Philadelphia on June 20.

I was interviewed by *Intelligencer Journal,* the local Lancaster, Pennsylvania newspaper. I was quoted as saying: "I've been critical of U.S. policy in Vietnam since I first went there. . . . My position has changed very little over nine years of working with the Vietnamese people and seeing their problems first hand. . . . The U.S. should never have become involved, but having become involved, they should make a greater effort to become disengaged." By providing unlimited support to President Thieu, I said, the U.S. has "made it difficult for the South Vietnamese to come to terms with the other side." While acknowledging that President Nixon's policy of Vietnamization may have "made some progress," I said "the war could drag on for another four, eight or ten years."

It was not easy for Paul and Esther Bucher to complete their term of English classes at Can Tho University. Students begged them for passing grades. Without good grades they would be drafted into the armed forces. Students who passed would only have to do local guard duty. The students asked: "Will you fail someone, which would be the same as killing them?" So Esther asked herself: "According to the ethics of being a responsible teacher, to pass someone who is not qualified is not fair to him particularly since in my case the students will be teaching next year; but to fail them and send them into the war machine (when they could be teaching small children a little something) doesn't seem right either."

The Buchers moved from Can Tho to the Martin's house in Gia Dinh where Titus and Maynard lived. On their journey to Saigon they passed areas pocked with craters from B-52 carpet bombing—many of them fifteen feet deep.

Soon after our return to the United States, Mary and I took part in the special Asia interest conference as well as the orientation program of Eastern Mennonite Board of Missions. Without our involvement, the missionaries in the orientation sessions wrote a letter to President Nixon on June 23 asking him "to find an alternative to the present destructive military involvement." Published in the *Gospel Herald* under the caption, "Missionaries Speak Out," it was signed by thirty-six persons.

This letter was sent to the White House and a spokesman at the State Department acknowledged it in a letter which read: "President Nixon has asked me to reply to your letter signed by Mennonite missionaries expressing their concern about the war in Viet-Nam. We appreciate knowing your views on this matter of great concern to us."

The letter stated that the President was "seeking to end the Indochina conflict in a genuine peace," noting that on May 8 he "put forth a generous new offer for peace. He proposed that American prisoners of war be released and an internationally supervised ceasefire throughout Indochina be put into effect." In return the U.S. "would stop all acts of force throughout Indochina and would withdraw all American forces from Viet Nam within four months." This "would allow negotiations on a political settlement among the Vietnamese themselves."

Truong Nhu Tang, Minister of Justice in the People's Revolutionary Government, later described Nixon's May 8 speech as "ambiguous." It was significant in that it did not call for the People's Liberation Army to leave the South.

Several months later, Walton Hackman, executive secretary of MCC Peace Section, thanked Harold Stauffer, the Mission overseas ministries secretary, for copies of letters Stauffer had sent him. "Your missionaries," Hackman wrote, "are certainly to be commended for the forthright way in which they have spoken their convictions. While I am sure you have gotten some criticism for this, it has also been a great inspiration to many who also speak."

By mid-year, plans were well underway for a change in the VNCS structure. On June 15, 1972, Boyd B. Lowry, the Church World Service administrator serving as Operations Director of Vietnam Christian Service, sent a memo to all the VNCS personnel describing the coming administrative changes. MCC, which had viewed the cooperative arrangement within Vietnam Christian Service in 1965 as temporary, was now interested in returning to "its normal pattern of organization and cooperation." He referred to the "Mennonite point of view" articulated by MCC Executive Secretary William T. Snyder:

> We would like to move toward an arrangement that would provide MCC with greater flexibility and mobility in relating more closely to the national church, the Mennonite Mission and Church, and the Christian & Missionary Alliance. . . . The longer term interest of the Mennonite Central Committee in Vietnam is, in our judgment, not the same as CWS and LWR, although we have shared common interest during the past six years. We have appreciated this period of working together. . . . It is our hope and full expectation that MCC may be able to cooperate with CWS and LWR on the local level under whatever new arrangement is established.

In early, July Paul Longacre, now serving as assistant MCC executive secretary, reflected on the future of MCC-Vietnam. He had recently met with officials of the Democratic Republic of Vietnam and the Provisional Revolutionary Government in Paris, and attended the meeting of the Commission on Inter-Church Aid, Refugee and World Service of the World Council of

Churches in Geneva. Longacre said that MCC's planned separation from VNCS in January 1973 "will provide opportunities for new directions on the part of MCC as well as for CWS-LWR." He sensed that…

> CWS-LWR may even be welcoming this opportunity. Of necessity and desire they want to cooperate with the new ecumenical thrust. If they would have to be sensitive to the MCC concerns on this issue they would . . . need to hold off a bit. Also all partners have been frustrated somewhat during the past few years in feeling our programs in Vietnam have not really been cutting at the real issues and needs there. The agencies have been realistic enough to know that programming for the real needs and issues is difficult if not impossible at the present state. Yet the frustration persists. The change in relationships provides MCC with new opportunities to pursue some more creative programming [and] should provide more opportunity for responsible influence and greater cooperation with the Tin Lanh Church and C&MA mission.

One of MCC's strengths, Paul indicated, was "placing volunteers at the grass roots level and letting them listen and respond to needs as they hear them." The larger VNCS structure made it more difficult to do that. Longacre said that MCC must find a way to give at least some token assistance to people living in areas controlled by the PRG. He also recommended that MCC plan to make "a rather significant contribution to North Vietnam," possibly $30,000 to $50,000 in medical supplies, either directly or through the American Friends Service Committee.

There were eleven persons recruited by MCC serving with VNCS at this time: Margaret Fast, Pleiku; Kurt and Frieda Sawatzky, Ban Me Thuot; Ron Ackerman, Dak To; Max Ediger, Quang Ngai; Norman and Joy Blair, Jean Hershey, Lowell Jantzi, and Teruko Yano, Nha Trang; and Yoshihiro Ichikawa, Tam Ky. Longacre informed these persons about the coming administrative changes. He said that the Akron, Pennsylvania, office would solicit the counsel of the MCC field personnel to help formulate creative and solid programming. Max Ediger was being asked to be MCC's "temporary representative" until the end of 1972, and Longacre encouraged the MCC personnel to communicate their ideas and concerns to him or directly to Robert Miller, MCC's Asia director.

"MCC's interest since 1954 has been to serve as a resource and stimulator to the Tin Lanh church on the concern for Christian social service," Longacre wrote. "When MCC returns to its normal longer term role, we hope it will allow us to be more effective in that mission." Significantly, Longacre wrote that MCC was interested "in carrying out its concern for peace and reconciliation."

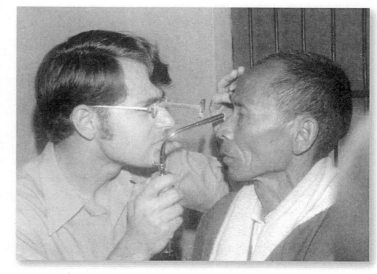

Dr. Blair at the Nha Trang Hospital.

Max, in late July, wrote to Akron: "Most of the MCC volunteers seem to be looking forward to MCC operating independently." Admitting there would be downsides to leaving VNCS, they would also "be given more responsibility and more freedom to develop their personal Christian witness." As a smaller Mennonite group, Max wrote, "we feel . . . we can be more unified and create a closer fellowship than was possible with VNCS."

This was not a unanimous viewpoint. Ron Ackerman, "a concerned Mennonite with an ecumenical viewpoint," told Longacre that any benefits of a break in MCC from VNCS do not "have enough merit to make the change worthwhile" for the Vietnamese and ethnic minority people among whom he worked. He said that VNCS "has been recognized as a compassionate force" in caring for people and noted that good relationships with the Tin Lanh Church were determined by the personalities of the volunteers; not all Mennonites had good relationships with Tin Lanh pastors and churches. Conversely, some CWS and LWR volunteers had good relations with the Church. He noted the difficult challenges that MCC personnel often had in relating to Tin Lanh medical programs in Nha Trang and Pleiku. A recent example of this was the experience of Margaret Fast in Pleiku who was terminating early because the hospital administrator asked her to leave.

Writing to Robert Miller, Fast said that, as far as church leaders were concerned, "the quality of care is quite secondary to appearance and levels of spirituality. . . . If you intend to continue a close relationship with the Tin Lanh Church it will probably be wise to find a doctor who is more devout than I have been."

Before leaving Vietnam, Tom Spicher had expressed similar views. "Participants and recipients have benefitted from VNCS cooperation. MCC personnel have lived in close contact with other Protestants, developing life-long friendships," Tom wrote. "The Protestant church in Vietnam has found some non-MCCers more accommodating than MCCers. Friendship with the Tin Lanh church in VNCS does not always follow denominational lines."

Planning for the two-week Sunday-to-Sunday Mennonite Reconciliation Work Camp August 6 to 20 continued throughout the spring and summer. Although youth were expected from Japan, Korea, India, Indonesia, Hong Kong and Taiwan, many had difficulty securing visas. One camper came from Hong Kong, three from Japan, one from the Philippines and three from Taiwan. On Saturday before the camp, Esther and Paul took Carl Beck, camp director, and four of the campers to My Tho where they met the Coconut Monk, the eccentric man committed to peace. The campers met with the Mennonite church in Gia Dinh on Sunday. By Sunday evening

Jean Hershey with Mrs. Thuoc, director of the nursing school.

many of the young people from the congregation had also signed up for the camp. Around thirty campers flew to Nha Trang on Monday morning in an Air America plane VNCS had requested.

Besides the eight international youth who arrived, MCC nurse Teruko Yano from Nha Trang and Quang Ngai volunteer Yoshihiro Ichikawa joined the group. A number of American volunteers participated, making an average of thirty or thirty-five campers daily. The work project consisted of building a seawall near the Evangelical Hospital designed to keep the road from washing into the sea. Work began at six o'clock in the morning consisting of digging a ditch sixty meters long, one and a half meters wide, and about two meters deep, lugging large rocks for six masons who built the wall foundation. Breakfast was served at 8:00 when James Stauffer led in a study of the Seven Beatitudes from the Sermon on the Mount. Then another stretch of hard work until 11:00 when the tools were cleaned and campers enjoyed a swim in the bay. After lunch at 1:00, campers relaxed with siestas and swimming until 4:00. Afternoons and evenings were filled with discussions, singing, introduction of different countries, talks on Anabaptism, and visits to places of interest around Nha Trang. Arlene Stauffer had volunteered to oversee the kitchen, and Co Bay, their cook, managed the meals. The kitchen crew put in long hours—sometimes from 6:00 a.m. to 10:00 p.m. Camp director Beck declared that the excellent food was the best of eight years of camps! On Saturday, the nineteenth, the group traveled by bus to the cool mountain city of Da Lat and returned to Saigon on Sunday. Their final gathering was Sunday evening with the Gia Dinh congregation, concluding with a communion service. For the campers, it was an unforgettable two weeks.

The contractor on August 21 began demolishing the buildings at the Gia Dinh Community Center to construct the new facilities on the lot—fourteen meters frontage with a depth of fifty-five meters. The worship center with office (14 x 8 meter structure) was built behind the front courtyard with the apartment for the pastor's family upstairs. Behind the church building was the three-story school building with six large classrooms, accessible from the right side of the church building. On the right rear side of the property were other rooms for clinic, sewing room and several offices. The construction costs for the church building with parsonage were around $12,000, with the Mission providing $7,000 as a grant and lending up to $7,000 additional funds to be repaid over three years.

The church was also interested in opening a satellite witness and service program with a day care nursery in the vicinity of Cau Bong, named after the bridge over the canal separating Saigon's District 1 and Gia Dinh city. Since all the available funds would not be used in constructing the church facilities, the church proposed buying a small property for the day care center.

The congregation submitted a request to Vietnam Chris-

Reconciliation work camp at Nha Trang.

tian Service for a grant from the Fund for Reconciliation to build the school and additional facilities for the community center. The Gia Dinh church, with very limited financial means, pledged the equivalent of $1,000 U.S. The Saigon VNCS office in early September—partly due to additional piasters generated through a more favorable exchange rate—approved a large grant. However, some of the administrators of the Fund were asking, "If the Mennonites are pulling out of VNCS, why give them some $30,000 for this project?" There was also a feeling that the Mennonites were not putting anything into this project! At a meeting of CWS Southeast Asia Working Group in late September in New York, I spoke with Harry Haines, director of the United Methodist Committee on Relief, to clear up these questions and learned that the grant would be approved. The much-appreciated service Pastor Quang had given to VNCS and his close association with Doug Beane and other VNCS administrators helped secure that commitment. The total complex was completed in December.

Coupled with on-and-off sessions of the Paris peace talks in August was major military activity as both sides tried to seize territory prior to a possible cease-fire. Highways north and east of Saigon were cut. In early August there was an attack against ARVN forces in a rubber plantation at Long Thanh, only twenty-five kilometers east of Saigon. Viet Cong guerrillas blew up several thousand tons of ammunition at the large Long Binh army base thirty-three kilometers away. Viet Cong forces took control of Que Son district of Quang Nam province located between Da Nang and Tam Ky. The battle for Que Son district capital resulted not only in heavy ARVN casualties but in hundreds of civilian deaths.

Pastor Quang heard these stories when he went to the nearby town of Hoi An to see how VNCS could help the 20,000 refugees. When fighting erupted, many members of the Que Son Tin Lanh congregation went to the church house for protection. Thinking that the Viet Cong fighters had gone into the church, a military official requested it be bombed. U.S. planes bombed it, killing twenty-nine persons; several others died later. The church deacon and his wife were killed. Two of the pastor's children were killed; one of these was a young woman engaged to be married to a student at the Nha Trang Bible Institute. The pastor's wife was seriously injured. Several weeks later, Maynard Shirk helped the Tin Lanh Relief Committee to distribute blankets and cans of MCC-donated beef to the survivors. He noted that not only did the blankets and beef come from the United States, but the bombs as well!

Shirk wrote from Pleiku in late October where he was coordinating clinic activities for a few months, noting that road travel was quite dicey. "The boys in black" had mined or ambushed several civilian buses on the highway between Ban Me Thuot, Pleiku and Kontum, causing many civilian casualities. There were military attacks in the district towns of Quang Ngai province. There was heavy fighting deep in the Mekong Delta province of Chuong Thien, and west and east of My Tho city—one place only forty-six kilometers south of Saigon. Don Sensenig wrote: "Let's pray for peace; is there more we can do? God help us."

Esther wrote home in mid-September after she and Paul had gone to the Vietnamese military cemetery where they saw 200 coffins waiting to be claimed by family members of the victims. Each coffin was identified with the name of the man, date of death and unit or division. Some coffins had been there three weeks.

"Did you ever smell the smell of death?" Esther asked. "I could still smell it when I came home. That odor is ghastly. We just went to see, visit and perhaps in some small way understand a smattering of the suffering that people are going through in this country."

Don Sensenig walked into the Binh Dan Hospital across the street from the student center, filled with civilian and military wounded spilling out into the aisles.

Robert Miller and William Snyder went to Vietnam late September to work out details for MCC's changed administrative pattern. At the two-day conference in Saigon with MCC personnel, Ediger was appointed director of Vietnam MCC programs beginning January 1973.

On September 28, the Stauffers, Sensenigs, Buchers, Shirk and Peachey—along with Mrs. Quang—flew to Can Tho in an Air Vietnam DC-3 where they joined Dorothy and Luke Beidler for a three-day missionary conference to review and project plans and programs. Some lodged in the homes of Baptist and Alliance missionaries. Luke gave a meditation on Messiah as a Servant. In one session, the group compared American and Vietnamese cultural expressions with the gospel teachings, with Mrs. Quang giving helpful perspectives, even sharing the criticism that Vietnamese have of American missionaries! Pastor Quang did not attend; he was still recuperating from influenza. She related some of the challenges they faced at the Gia Dinh Community Center and Church—which precipitated group confession and prayer. After returning home Saturday evening, Stauffer visited the Quang home; they were all reassured that God's Spirit was working things out.

In early October, James Stauffer wrote home: "Saigon is still quiet as far as the war is concerned. The death toll in the continued fighting is still very high. Almost every day someone we know of has a friend or relative who is killed. Our helper lost her 42 year-old brother the other week. He left a wife and seven children. He was a captain in the army. Peace looks as far away as ever!" Two weeks later he wrote: "Saigon is still expecting an attack before the [November 7 American] election. The fighting has come within six miles and the B-52s are dropping their deadly thirty tons each only fifteen miles away. The road to Dalat was out for three full days stopping Saigon's main source of vegetables. Prices continue to rise and yet life goes on as normal in so many ways. The fortitude of these people never ceases to amaze us."

With missionaries living so close to the Binh Dan Hospital, discharged patients sometimes came to the Center requesting bus fare home. In mid-October a young man asked Don for help so he and his ten-year-old brother could return home more than a hundred kilometers away. The boy had been riding a water buffalo that stepped on unexploded ordnance, the resulting explosion killing the animal and seriously injuring the boy who lost an eye. A month earlier a neighbor of the caretaker lost an eye when his hoe struck a grenade or an unexploded shell.

All of us frequently received requests from strangers for transportation money for special needs. Often we gave a bit of assistance—usually not the total amount they requested. On one occasion, a young man asked Don for money to transport the body of his mother to their home area after she had died in a local hospital. A few years later, when Sensenigs were living in another part of the city, the same young man came asking for assistance. Yes, his mother had died and he needed to take her body home!

Ediger wanted to close the service unit in Quang Ngai but the heavy fighting throughout the province did not make this feasible. There were over 140,000 new refugees, most from the district towns of Duc Pho, Mo Duc, and especially Ba To. He worked with a local citizens' relief committee to provide rice for the people. American B-52 bombers had leveled Ba To town, "leaving nothing but huge craters."

The B-52s were America's monstrous killing machines. Designed for nuclear warfare, they were outfitted to carry conventional bombs. They were first used in Vietnam in June 1965 to carpet bomb an area northwest of Saigon, flying from Guam. Most of the thirty planes carried fifty-one 750 pound bombs each. Later some of the B52s flew from U Tapao base in Thailand.

North Vietnam proposed a military ceasefire at the Paris peace talks in early October to include a "National Council of Reconciliation" that would settle the political issues of the two sides. After Henry Kissinger implicitly agreed to allow North Vietnamese troops to remain in the South, North Vietnam's Premier Pham Van Dong on October 21 announced acceptance of a cease-fire as the first step in a peace process—the U.S. would withdraw all forces, prisoners of war would be released, and the two warring sides would form a coalition government to hold general elections within six months.

Already in 1968, President Johnson conceded there would need to be a political settlement and negotiations began in Paris. Though Nixon's Vietnamization policy for a time appeared to reach for a military victory, Henry Kissinger realized a political settlement was needed. Conceding that the communist forces would continue to exert political influence in the country, some form of coalition government would allow the two sides to compete politically.

Kissinger flew to Saigon to meet President Nguyen Van Thieu on October 22, ostensibly to convince South Vietnam's President to accept this offer, but Thieu was adamantly opposed to permitting the North to retain its military forces in the South or accepting any form of coalition government. The war would go on.

Sensenig wrote to me about Thieu's "very hard line" two-hour speech October 24:

> The crunch is coming for someone, it seems. Unless President Nixon figures he can scrape by the elections without a ceasefire, after which the war can continue. . . . But the problems are still almost intractable, it seems to me. Hard-line Catholics and hard-line Communists seem incapable of producing *"con lai."* . . . A coalition government seems like a crippled, artificial creation in this situation with its backroom power plays, violently opposed factions, suicidal polarization, strongman traditions, etc. My vision of the future is as muddy and/or bloody as ever. I see more war until a collapse. [*Con lai* was the term describing the offspring of American male liaisons with Vietnam women].

The government of President Nguyen Van Thieu was unbending. On October 29, all citizens were ordered to display the yellow flag with three red bars of the Republic of Vietnam or face arrest. To possess and display the NLF flag was punishable by death! The next morning a combat policeman in brown khaki uniform came into the Saigon student center, pistol in holster, and told Sensenig that they needed to fly a flag. Don told him there was already a small flag painted on the front post. That was fine, the policeman said, but they also needed to be flying one by the next day, suggested size 1.2 meters by 80 centimeters.

"What does a real live Anabaptist do in such a case?" Don asked, answering the question in his next breath: "Well, this one is going to give Ong Hai the money to go buy one and display it!"

A few days later Bucher observed that "recent events had "brought a 'threat of peace' for Vietnam. That is the way it was first viewed here. The red and yellow signs are everywhere! And the flags!! It hurts my eyes to see so much emphasis put on nationalism when peace demands brotherhood. Even the Saigon center is flying a big flag, on orders of course. . . . Slowly people are allowing their hopes to be raised, and their expectations increased. Some people are beginning to think peace. May it come soon and last long."

Titus Peachey noted during this critical time in South Vietnam that the attendance of the Sunday morning Bible classes at the student center was increasing with up to forty students. They were planning to use materials Don was developing for the correspondence courses based on the Gospel of Luke. Near the end of the year around sixty students expressed interest in pursuing this correspondence course.

In late October, Don and Quang flew to Can Tho where they and Luke Beidler met with representatives of Christian Youth for Social Service who proposed opening a student hostel. The Mission, subject to approval of the Joint Administrative Council, expressed willingness to provide the rental costs for one year for a fifteen-student facility. Given the uncertain political situation, with the university still closed, Sensenig suggested that they rent a property by the month rather than pay a year in advance.

After the US elections when Nixon was reelected, Stauffer wrote in the *News and Concerns* newsletter: "Some people are optimistic, some are pessimistic. Most are hopeful with a certain amount of apprehension. They're tired of war but afraid of some points of the peace plan. Then, too, both sides are building up their military strength which seems to point to more war—not peace! May God have mercy!"

Stauffer also reported news about the Evangelical Church in North Vietnam, cut off from the churches in the South for eighteen years. A Chinese pastor, formerly from Hanoi but now living in Singapore, had recently sent an encouraging telegram to Tom Stebbins, C&MA chairman in Vietnam, reporting "a new moving of God's Spirit among the remaining Evangelical Christians in the North," with many youth expressing faith and groups of believers planning to rebuild dilapidated or destroyed church buildings." This was great encouragement to Stebbins and several of his friends who had been praying daily "for peace, revival and reunification of North and South Vietnam."

Titus and Don lead Sunday morning Bible class.

In mid-November, Stauffer described another "first" in Saigon. U.S. military chaplains organized a fellowship hour and lunch for all the pastors and missionaries in the Saigon area. Participants included Catholics and at least one Jewish person. This kind of ecumenicity would have been unimaginable years earlier. Stauffer decided not to attend the next gathering. It "really tears me around," he wrote. "They feel that all U.S. soldiers and especially the chaplains are ministers of God. Since U.S. military force is helping to keep this land 'open for the Gospel,' the soldiers are a necessary part of 'God's team.' They seem to overlook the moral character or even the religious beliefs of a U.S. soldier so that even an immoral, atheistic U.S. soldier 'deserves our support and prayers for the good job he's doing over here.'"

On Sunday, December 10, the Gia Dinh congregation first met in the newly-built facilities. The worship space accommodated 150 comfortably and could hold up to 200 persons. Already some thought the auditorium was too small! The next day, Pastor and Mrs. Quang moved into the upstairs parsonage with their three daughters—Hang, Hong and Huong—and their son Dat. Believers felt that having permanent facilities increased the reputation and witness of the church. Having only rented properties suggested that the church was temporary and could easily move away.

At year's end, Stauffer wrote that 1972 had become "the worst year yet for death, destruction, despair and uncertainty. . . . The war is a roaring success. Thousands die each week. Cities are being leveled. Hospitals are crowded. Graveyards overflow. Men curse, women weep, babies cry but no one seems to care enough to try to stop it." He observed that the ultimate irony was expressed in a newspaper headline, "Typhoon Threatens War!" Natural phenomena were interfering with fighting the war.

On December 16, Henry Kissinger announced that the peace talks had failed to achieve what Nixon considered a "just and fair agreement to end the war." Within two days, the U.S. launched the most concentrated bombing of North Vietnam, primarily in the densely-populated area between Hanoi and the port city of Hai Phong. This "Christmas bombing," called "barbaric" by North Vietnam, dropped 40,000 tons of bombs. Bach Mai Hospital, Hanoi's largest hospital, was bombed. When the bombing ended December 31, fifteen B-52s and eleven other U.S. aircraft were lost, mostly from surface-to-air missiles. Still the U.S. military considered the bombing a "success" because 97 percent of the planes made it through Hanoi's bomber defense system!

In her Journal of December 22, Esther wrote: "Dear God, this killing just goes on and on and we wonder if you allow it for some reason. Are we supposed to stand up and start doing something? Are we supposed to write letters to U.S. officials, or what is our role that we should play? It's easy to get depressed when you feel like it just goes on and on. (And now somewhere faraway someone is getting bombed because the curtains are shaking but there is no noise.); it is worse, too, when you're not doing anything about it because you don't know *what* to do."

NEW DIRECTION 1973

On January 3, 1973, Robert W. Miller, now MCC Asia Director, sent out "An Expression of Concern Regarding Peace in Vietnam." Noting that 388 persons were working with Mennonite Central Committee in thirty-six countries, he declared:

> In no place has MCC involvement been more agonizing than in Vietnam where volunteers have served since 1954. Each new year marks a time of renewed hope for peace among the people of Vietnam, but every year there has only been more bloodshed. War for the Vietnamese is measured not in tonnage of ordnance or numbers of sorties, but in the inconsolable anguish of a mother who has lost her only son or in the immeasurable scars of the orphan ripped from his ancestral family. . . . We appeal to members of the US Congress to take the initiative in bringing the Vietnam war to an end.

On January 27, the United States and the Democratic Republic of Vietnam signed the Paris Accords—the Agreement on Ending the War and Restoring Peace in Vietnam. The ceasefire agreement worked out between the four parties in Paris went into effect the following day, Sunday. Late Saturday night, the missionaries in Saigon felt and heard the closest carpet bombing by American B-52 planes they had experienced in months.

On Sunday morning, Paul and Esther Bucher were prepared at eight o'clock to record "the jubilance of people and bells," but there was no dancing in the streets of Saigon. As on other days, the same noises of bombing, artillery and other explosions were heard.

The ceasefire agreement was welcomed by the members of the Gia Dinh Mennonite Church, giving hope that their relatives and friends in the army might soon be able to return to their families and join in the work of the church. Yet others in Saigon viewed peace as "dangerous," afraid that it would give the Viet Cong an opportunity to strengthen militarily and politically.

The parties around the peace table were unable to find common ground to resolve the basic political issues over which the war was fought—who governs the population in South Vietnam and reunification of the country. Neither the North nor the South was defeated and both declared victory. The war would go on; ceasefire violations began immediately. Yet at least the cease fire agreement provided a way for the United States to fully remove its military forces. But the American forces did not all leave. Many GIs were rotated back into Vietnam in civilian clothes to give support to the Vietnamese armed forces. By early February there was a 1,200-man Defense Attaché under the U.S. Embassy and twenty-three U.S. civilian agencies employing thousands of technicians to supply and provide maintenance for the South Vietnam's air force.

January 1, 1973, saw the return of Mennonite Central Committee to its earlier status as an independent service agency. VNCS and MCC directors agreed that they would consult regularly and coordinate their programs. MCC personnel working with VNCS projects—and vice-versa— would continue their assignments if willing to do so. There was currently a fairly small MCC team. Norman and Joy Blair, Jean Hershey, Teruko Yano and Lowell Jantzi were at the Evangelical hospital in Nha Trang. (Nurse Ann Noel Ewert arrived in January). Max Ediger served as the country representative. James Klassen was in language school. Yoshihiro Ichikawa was working with VNCS in Tam Ky.

Paul Longacre went to Vietnam mid-February for a twelve-day visit to "obtain firsthand information on the political situation as it relates to MCC's present and future program activity," and to "encourage MCC Director Max Ediger along with MCC staff to plan for and engage in programs of reconstruction in addition to their present activities." Longacre said that "both optimism and pessimism" were expressed regarding political and military developments. In conversation with persons from the Summer Institute of Linguistics, Christian & Missionary Alliance, Baptist Mission, World Relief Commission and World Vision, Longacre learned that all these agencies had recently increased their staff members and seemed to have a greater readiness to cooperate with one another.

Except for "a few notable exceptions," Longacre observed that leaders of the Tin Lanh Church seemed to be more closely aligned to the existing Saigon government than ever before. This, he surmised, could cause future problems for the church in the event of greater political accommodation with the other side.

The Asia director of American Friends Service Committee programs described to Longacre a project they were hoping to implement in an area controlled by the Provisional Revolutionary Government. At some point they planned to report this to the Saigon government. Longacre noted that the AFSC director did not fear government retaliation because they had developed a significant program providing prostheses for war amputees in Quang Ngai.

Longacre observed that MCC had made a smooth transition from Vietnam Christian Service into a separate agency again. The medical program at Nha Trang was doing well with only one doctor, Norman Blair, who was performing many ophthalmologic procedures. The one-year nursing school was also functioning quite well. Maynard Shirk was coordinating the work at the Pleiku clinic. Dr. Pradham, an Indian doctor loaned by Asian Christian Service, planned to spend several more months at the Pleiku clinic hospital, but the board chairman's "rigid and sometimes arbitrary policies and actions" negatively affected the general staff morale so the medical program was not operating effectively.

The Peace Accords provided for an International Commission of Control and Supervision (ICCS) to monitor the implementation of the accords. Representatives came from Canada, Hungary, Poland, and Indonesia. The Canadians documented thousands of ceasefire violations by both sides. President Nixon on March 15 threatened that the US might re-enter Vietnam militarily to prevent ceasefire violations! It was not long before people began referring to these military skirmishes as the beginning of the third Indochina war. On June 13, the signers of the Paris Accords signed another agreement to end the cease-fire violations! But this proved little more effective than the earlier agreement. After helping monitor the withdrawal of American military forces and the exchange of prisoners, Canada withdrew from the ICCS on July 31 and was replaced by Iran.

In mid-February, Atlee Beechy and Doug Hostetter met representatives of the Democratic Republic and the Provisional Revolutionary Government in Europe. MCC expressed interest in working in PRG-controlled zones but did not receive any specific proposals. Should this occur, Beechy said it would likely require some compromise with MCC's normal manner of operation. He cautioned against becoming "excessively naïve—or too self-righteous."

MCC staff identified a need to clear unexploded ordnance from farmlands, confirmed by persons from an American Explosive Ordnance Disposal (EOD) team. Other needs considered included helping local agencies to resettle the still 650,000 internally-displaced people and to assist war prisoners being released. MCC Akron was recruiting eight more persons for Vietnam assignments.

Mennonite Mission personnel and MCC workers expressed the need for educational materials in the area of peace and reconciliation. Pastor Le Hoang Phu, professor and dean of the Tin Lanh Bible Institute in Nha Trang, welcomed books and other materials on peace and reconciliation.

In early January, furniture was moved into the classrooms of the new Rang Dong School and community service center in Gia Dinh. The clinic, the sewing class, and the family and educational assistance staff moved into their new rooms on the first floor of the social service center.

As usual, the Mennonite congregation in Gia Dinh planned a praise and testimony meeting on the first day of *Têt*, Saturday, February 3. One woman testified with joy that she had overcome the addictive habit of chewing betel nut! James Stauffer joined other church leaders in visiting families on Sunday afternoon and on Monday. Most people said *Têt* was not happy. The ceasefire announced a week earlier was not being observed by either side. Prices of consumer goods again increased drastically—gas and sugar increased fifty percent—which would boost prices on everything else. The poor would suffer the most.

The Gia Dinh Church celebrated their new church auditorium, parsonage and community center with a dedication service on Sunday afternoon, February 18. The church was filled with over two hundred persons including many friends from other churches. The program included singing, Bible reading, a recounting of the history of the church and social service center, special songs by the youth group, and reading of congratulatory letters and telegrams. Tran Xuan Hi, Pastor Quang's father, preached a sermon emphasizing that our bodies are the temple of God—more important than buildings. Total financial expenditures for property purchase and construction was around $60,000 U.S.; $32,665 had come from the Fund for Reconciliation through Vietnam Christian Service to construct and furnish the social service center and school.

In January, the 124-member church elected a board of elders, four deacons, and committees for a ladies' group and the youth group. All those holding leadership roles in the congregation were to be members of the congregation. Pastor Quang believed that this would strengthen lines of accountability and would accentuate the caring relationships within the congregation. The three lay evangelists—Ninh, Trung and Lam—were responsible to give counsel to the Sunday

New church and Community Center.

Dedication of new church facilities.

Left: Nguyen Quang Trung leading dedication service. Right: Overflow crowd. Rang Dong School classrooms are on the left with social service center on ground floor in the rear.

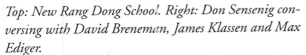

Top: New Rang Dong School. Right: Don Sensenig conversing with David Breneman, James Klassen and Max Ediger.

school, church prayer meeting, witnessing band and the youth groups. Nguyen Dinh Tin was chosen leader of the youth group.

The church rejoiced in the public commitment Mr. and Mrs. Tran Cong Chanh made to follow the way of Jesus. Mrs. Chanh (Nguyen Thi De), a staff member of the Family Child Assistance program, was a believer for some time and would share her understanding of the biblical message with her family. She waited to publically declare her faith and request baptism until he was prepared to join her. She became a strong leader in the church and community.

There was dynamism in the interaction between members of the congregation. Each Thursday evening a group of thirty-five or more adults gathered at the church to talk about living the Christian life and to pray for one another. Seated in a large circle, various lay men and women led the discussions. Paul Bucher described one of the meetings in mid-January. A man read—with help from another—the story of Achan's deceit described in Joshua 7. Soon the group was involved in a lively discussion of good and evil, evil spirits, and free will. Even though Don, James, Esther, and Paul were present in the meeting, they were merely spectators to the discussion. At the end, the discussion leader said he chose that passage because he had a sin in his life—smoking. Now he was promising God and the group that he was going to quit smoking—gradually! Paul observed that this was a bit different from our idea that one had to immediately break off bad habits, but very realistic. Bucher asked his parents to pray for these members, and for the nations that were involved in the Vietnam conflict—"if they aren't going to stop the war completely, that they might quickly end it gradually!"

One of the members, Thanh, a carpenter and father of twelve children, was poetic and often wrote poems and songs. At the end of the Good Friday communion service, he sang a song he was inspired to compose during the service. Nearly two hundred people gathered on the rooftop of the school building for the 6:00 a.m. Easter sunrise service.

Esther usually attended the Tuesday women's meetings in homes. Late February they gathered in a house still bearing scars from the 1968 bombings. It had no electricity; light came through the door. Although the small house had no ceiling, it was better than most homes. Before prayer they shared their own needs. A widow with one child and no employment was selling eggs, making only five cents profit per dozen. The women were brought to tears with the story of one of the men in the church who had only rice and salt to eat—not even the ubiquitous fish sauce. A few months later, the ladies cut out patches and sewed quilts for needy persons. It was a first for the group and reflected Pastor Quang's concern for practical and relevant Christian living.

In March, Pastor Quang had to deal with a trusted member of the church who was stealing the offering money. Quang immediately asked the member to resign from all responsibilities in the church for three years and denied communion for six months. The member made a written confession and promised to pay back the stolen money. When the resignation was announced, a "family situation" was given as the reason for the resignation. Some church leaders felt this discipline was too severe so Quang agreed to review it each year. Others, including some of the missionaries, felt that the details should have been reported to the whole congregation, but Quang said this would bring greater harm to the congregation. Quang said the money was already given to the Lord, so the sin was against the Lord and not against the congregation. Stauffer was impressed with the "forgiving attitude" of the church leaders.

Paul and Esther developed a close friendship with Pastor and Mrs. Quang, praying with them and lending a hand with the heavy administrative load of the community center and the challenges of leading the congregation. They were also ears to hear issues and concerns which they could communicate to the senior missionaries.

The missionaries were all together in Saigon for several days in early February for fellowship and planning. Titus shared a meditation, *The Release of the Spirit*, by Watchman Nee, the well-known Chinese Christian evangelist and author who had died in prison a year earlier.

Paul and Esther also had a modern day horse-rustling story to tell. In early January when visiting the Beidler family in Can Tho, they went to the university to meet friends. As they were leaving the university campus on Luke Beidler's old Lambretta scooter, a student ran out and called for someone to help him recover his Honda motorcycle that he saw two young guys steal while he was sitting in class. Esther hopped off the scooter and the student hopped on. Paul could not drive fast because the scooter had poor brakes. Esther assumed it would be a wild goose chase because there were multiple streets the thieves could take. But Paul soon returned—smiling. Paul and the student came upon the two guys waiting to cross a one-way bridge, unaware that someone was following them. Paul pulled alongside the stolen vehicle and the student jumped off and grabbed the handlebars of his Honda, knocking it over and throwing the two thieves off balance. They ran like mad and disappeared!

When Harold Stauffer asked me to draw up five-year plans for Eastern Mennonite Board of Mission involvement in Asia, I solicited proposals from personnel in Hong Kong, Vietnam and the Philippines. The Vietnam missionary team identified four goals with suggested strategies for reaching these goals.

The first stated objective was to "grow in understanding and absorbing God's love and salvation and the style of life to which He calls us." The missionaries said this required personal and group disciplines of prayer, worship, Bible study and repentance.

A second objective was to "express God's salvation and the gospel life style in local Christian communities." This required living among the people, sharing with all members of the community in prayer, worship, and fellowship, encouraging all members to express their spiritual gifts, develop simple catechetical-type lessons based on the Sermon on the Mount, sharing Anabaptist biblical insights, and supporting practical lay training through existing groups—prayer meetings, women's and youth meetings, and lay leadership classes.

The missionaries said a third objective was to "proclaim and interpret God's love and the gospel way, calling all [persons] to choose life over death, and participate in Christian community." Suggestions for implementing this included literature production and distribution—especially peace literature, Bible correspondence courses, Bible classes in Vietnamese and English at our student centers, and reaching out beyond the existing Gia Dinh congregation. They also brainstormed about ways to engage other missions and churches, particularly the Tin Lanh church, in implementing strategies of peacemaking in situations of conflict.

The last objective stated was to "contribute to the physical-economic, social-intellectual development of society at large." Strategies included self-supporting roles like teaching English, providing study facilities, continuing family and educational assistance programs for school-age children, and supporting voluntary agencies, especially MCC and VNCS.

In a return letter to a church that had written to them, Don and Doris in late February wrote:

> We appreciate the concern and prayers of many Christians for Vietnam. They are needed! The basic conflicts are still present and unresolved, and it remains to be seen if the "third Indochina war" is ahead, or if steps can be made to keep the conflict at a less violent level. The church needs prayer and assistance to find its peacemaking role in this situation. The fear of communism has taken such a large part of the church's energies that the Gospel of love for all men has tended to become the gospel of "fight the communists to the death so the church can live." And that is surely not a whole gospel.

I visited the Indiana campuses of Goshen College and Associated Mennonite Biblical Seminaries in early February, attempting to recruit persons for Vietnamese Mennonite Mission assignments. I was told that the best person to serve as Bible teacher and leadership trainer was already in Vietnam—James Klassen. During Longacre's visit to Vietnam in late February, the suggestion was made that Klassen might give half-time to teaching in the lay leadership training program at the Gia Dinh congregation and half-time to the MCC office.

On my visit to the AMBS campus, I met Tin Lanh pastor Phan Xuan Tin, a long-time friend of MCC personnel, who was spending a year there. Having once been a missionary to Vietnam's ethnic minority people, he had served on the board of the joint MCC-Evangelical Church hospital in Nha Trang, and was a teacher at the Church's Bible Institute.

In early March, the missionary men, together with Quang, Ninh, Trung and Lam, gathered for morning Bible study and prayer. The second week, James Klassen led a discussion on the passage in I Peter 2:13-17 "Be subject for the Lord's sake to every human institution . . ." Ninh appreciated Klassen's explanation of "subjection"—to obey governmental authorities when this does not violate God's will, and to accept the consequences without resistance or bitterness when one is unable to obey the government's orders.

The last U.S. ground troops left Vietnam March 29 as Hanoi released the last of 587 U.S. prisoners of war. The U.S. continued a Defense Attaché Office with fifty officers. More than 8,500 U.S. civilians stayed on. In a letter home in early April, James Stauffer wrote: "Saigon looks different with all the American soldiers gone. However, we see more Americans in civilian clothes—many of them riding around in military jeeps, etc.! I don't know! Nothing has really changed much. And now the B-52s are doing some of the most savage bombing of the war around Phnom Penh in a desperate effort to keep it from falling. But in the process, they are killing thousands of civilians."

Vietnamese prisoners of war were also being exchanged. Peter Downs, who worked with VNCS in Da Nang, witnessed one prisoner exchange in Quang Tri, the city that had been obliterated in the fighting a year earlier when five thousand civilians were killed as they attempted to flee south on National Route 1. This "Avenue of Terror" was still lined with wrecked military vehicles and mountains of artillery shell casings when Downs traveled to Quang Tri. Downs described to Buchers the exchange of 400 prisoners from the South for 200 prisoners held in North Vietnam. Those who returned to the North were received with little fanfare. South Vietnamese officials, however, made their returnees strip to their shorts and throw their clothing into the river! They were each given a small flag of the South and a band playing stirring music welcomed them into the reception center.

Although the Saigon government refused to admit it held "political" prisoners, the ceasefire agreement also set the stage for the Saigon government to release some persons held without formal charges. Leaders of the An Quang Buddhist temple had submitted a list of several hundred persons they wanted released. Don Sensenig learned from the newspaper that the government was releasing sixty-seven prisoners and would later release more. Max Ediger had approval from Akron headquarters to work in this sensitive area, so Don accompanied Max to the temple to talk with leaders about ways MCC might assist these persons as they returned home.

Esther Bucher assumed a new role in April. Aware that VNCS therapist Anne Scahill, who also served as hostess at the VNCS guesthouse, would soon be terminating, Esther expressed interest in being hostess. Although the Buchers would complete their three-year term that summer, the home office approved their request to extend their term one year. Even though she was not recruited by Church World Service, VNCS director Roger Getz was pleased to employ Esther.

She and Paul moved into the guesthouse early April. Her Vietnamese language facility enabled her to serve well. The Vietnam Christian Service office was adjacent to the Mennonite student center and the VNCS guesthouse down the street a few houses—replacing Em Dem in the Gia Dinh area.

In extending their terms, Paul also looked for additional employment besides the financial accounting he was doing for the Mennonite Mission and for MCC. In March, he learned that Phoenix Study Group, the small school the missionary children attended, needed a math teacher for the seventh and eighth grades because the teacher was suddenly leaving. Although apprehensive about facing American kids again, he enjoyed teaching math two hours daily.

Esther and Paul had just begun an exciting new role as foster parents to an orphaned infant. In mid-January, they visited the Halfway House, a World Vision infant hospital in Saigon under the direction of Elsie Weaver. Elsie's husband, Steve Weaver of Harrisonburg, Virginia, was the assistant director of World Vision in Vietnam. The Buchers expressed interest in caring for one of the infants. A week later they brought home healthy five-week-old Helene fathered by a black American GI. Both Esther and Paul delighted in caring for her.

Helene fell victim to the Vietnamese preference for light-skinned complexions. Esther became upset with the comments made by people at the Mennonite church—expressing prejudice against the baby's black skin! But Helene's charm soon won over Esther's babysitter and a few weeks later the church people were also saying, "She's pretty and cute" instead of "It's too bad she's black." Helene became Alix Pia when Elsie reported that the baby's adoptive parents in the United States had chosen a new name. Alix stayed with the Buchers until May; she left Vietnam the middle of June. Paul and Esther later cared for another infant for several months.

Devadoss Maddimadugu from India returned to Vietnam on March 31, now with his wife Doris and seven-month-old Esther, staying two weeks at the VNCS guesthouse. Just before they left for language school in Da Lat, there was a Sunday morning electrical fire in their bedroom closet that burned some of their clothes. The cook, Chi Nam, was in the kitchen at the rear of the property. When alerted by a passerby, she yelled for help. Neighbors called the police and fire trucks and pulled other suitcases from the room. One neighbor brought a chemical fire extinguisher which controlled the blaze until firemen arrived.

Still working part-time in the Mission Board office in Salunga, Pennsylvania, I informed the missionary team in mid-March that

Doris and Devadoss Maddimadugu with Esther.

MCC administrators were discussing inviting one of the missionaries to serve as director of Vietnam programs. Max Ediger wanted to be released of this responsibility in order to work at grassroots programs. "In terms of our priorities, I would be reluctant to see one of us give too much time to this assignment if we are needed for evangelism and church building roles," I wrote. However, I noted that there would be opportunities for a peace ministry by relating to church and government leaders at various levels. I asked for their views. Sensenig replied, suggesting that I might be able to serve as the "peace man" MCC and EMM talked about recruiting, but questioned whether I should assume the MCC administrative role "as that is too big or too detailed a job to handle while being of some use to the Gia Dinh church, evangelism [and] lay training."

In mid-May, Robert Miller proposed that I accept a half-time assignment as the MCC Vietnam director for two years. The director, the memo read, "would be responsible for the administration of MCC personnel, projects, material resources and finances. He would also be responsible for the MCC peace and reconciliation work. He would handle relationships with the Evangelical Church, Christian & Missionary Alliance, Vietnam Christian Service, Mennonite Mission and Church, Vietnamese government and other organizations as necessary. He would represent MCC on the hospital boards at Nhatrang and Pleiku." In an official proposal to the Mission Board that I assume this role, Miller said this would "help strengthen the close ties between MCC and Mennonite Mission and Church."

The Vietnam Mission Council on May 30 recommended that I serve again as secretary of the Mission when we returned to Vietnam in July. The Council members agreed that my chief assignment would be to help develop a new Christian witness in the Cau Bong area—a high-density residency area located between Saigon city and the Gia Dinh community center. After hearing about the invitation that I become the MCC representative, Sensenig wrote to me: "I'm still wondering where you will get the time to be a good MCC director and also be Mission secretary and also contribute to the development of Cau Bong as a new witness and service center. Perhaps you could serve MCC as a consultant with definite scheduled times to work on MCC matters monthly or even weekly."

In a memo to the EMBMC executive committee, I noted that I would have less time for church development and leadership training. James Klassen, however, would be able to do some Bible teaching. I recognized that I could combine some Mission and MCC administrative tasks. I also welcomed an opportunity for more association with Evangelical Church leaders and saw opportunities for an informal peace ministry.

I asked that Vietnamese Mennonite church leaders discuss my assignment. I saw my role in developing a ministry in the Cau Bong area to be more a consultative role; I did not want to be viewed there as "Mr. Director" as I had been at the Gia Dinh community center. I indicated that Harold Stauffer, the EMBMC secretary, saw positive elements in a joint MCC-Mennonite Church assignment outweighing any negative aspects. In mid-June the Joint Administrative Council in Vietnam approved the proposal that I accept the MCC role.

A joint Mennonite Central Committee-Vietnam Mennonite Mission conference was planned for early June in Da Lat. All ten missionary personnel attended, along with nine of the eleven MCC volunteers, plus Ninh and Pastor Quang from Mennonite Church. Eleven children were there. Although most were Americans, there were now the Indian couple, two Japanese volunteers, and a Canadian. One of the MCC cooks from Nha Trang prepared all the meals.

One conference session was given to a discussion of relationships—MCC and Mennonite Mission, the Mennonites and the Evangelical Church, and the Mennonites and those of other religions. Another session focused on "how to overcome frustration, tension and depression." There was much time given to singing and recreation. This conference coincided with the conclusion of the week-long C&MA missionary conference, and Saturday evening the Mennonites played the Alliance basketball team, winning the first game but losing the second.

The group had a Quaker-style worship service Sunday morning after which many also attended services at the local Vietnamese or Koho ethnic minority churches. Sunday afternoon was focused on the peacemaking task in Vietnam. Ninh described that discussion as the best he had ever heard, touching on all aspects of peacemaking—not just on the war. In the evening, the Mennonite group again joined the Alliance missionary team for a "Singspiration" and communion service. James Stauffer said the conference brought a new sense of unity between MCC and the Mennonite Mission. With an increased sense of security in the countryside, the people from Saigon traveled the 308 km to Da Lat in two VNCS Volkswagen vans.

The following Sunday morning, Quang preached on peace at the Gia Dinh congregation, building into his sermon many of the ideas shared at the Da Lat conference, emphasizing the personal aspect of peacemaking in families and neighborhoods.

The six-member Sensenig family left Vietnam for furlough on June 11; Maynard Shirk and Titus Peachey left the following day after completing their terms of service. MCC Akron had already approved a recommendation for a one-year half-time State-side assignment for Don to prepare materials on peace and reconciliation in Vietnam.

The Sensenig family requested more than a normal furlough. Already in October, Don had written that he and Doris were seriously thinking of not returning after a year's furlough. There were several reasons. Anne would be going into ninth grade, and there was no American high school program currently in Vietnam. Doris felt handicapped in the language; she cared for two small children during her language study period when Don osmotically learned the language. After being apart from family for most of ten years, they wanted their children to be able to spend time with aging grandparents. Added to this, Don said, was the challenge—along with the other missionaries—of living "in a culture so different from our own," especially the "Viet Nam syndrome" of Americans overrunning the country. While not closing the door to further Vietnam service, they wanted to, at least, be on leave longer than a year.

I urged them to discuss their concerns with church leaders, assured that the church would give them a sympathetic hearing. I indicated that EMBMC would accommodate their need to visit children should they study at an international school in a neighboring country.

Don discussed this with the Council in late January and church leaders expressed their hope that they would not "lose" the Sensenig family. "How does one make decisions that affect many people?" Don asked. He said his and Doris's primary concern is that they had "not really been 'Vietnamized' enough" to make the most significant contribution to the gospel witness. Now considering a two- or three-year leave, Don wrote, "An extended furlough does not mean a permanent withdrawal from the ambiguities of trying to be useful disciples in Viet Nam!" I acknowledged these challenges and expressed the hope that they might be prepared to return after two or three years' leave. (In early 1975 they were making plans to return to Vietnam, but the dramatic collapse of the Republic of Vietnam ruled this out.)

Paul Kennel, an MCCer who earlier worked with WRC in Central Vietnam, returned to Vietnam in June to serve as administrator of the Hoa Khanh children's hospital in Da Nang, a facility that developed from a medical clinic established by U.S. Marines. At Kennel's request, he was appointed by Eastern Mennonite Board of Missions to this assignment. He was unable to meet frequently with the other missionaries. Kennel was accompanied to Vietnam by Gerry Keener, recruited directly by WRC who, after language study in Da Lat, served as personnel director at the hospital. (Gerry and his wife Donna accepted an Eastern Mennonite Mission assignment in Vietnam in 1997.)

On our July 1973 return to Vietnam, we visited EMBMC personnel in the Philippines and in Hong Kong. In Hong Kong we met Mennonite evangelist Myron Augsburger who had just spent two days with the missionaries in Saigon—his third brief visit to Vietnam—so we asked him about his impressions. Augsburger, in his eighth year as president of Eastern Mennonite College, knew most of the missionary personnel. He said the Mennonite Church in Vietnam was intimidated and afraid to witness. The missionaries had too much guilt about the American involvement in Vietnam, he said, and reacted against the kind of missionary work done in Vietnam without developing an adequate alternative strategy. He urged the strategy of building brotherly relationships of love and caring.

Mary and I understood the concern Augsburger expressed but did not fully accept his critique. We missionaries were committed to sharing the reconciling message of Jesus Christ and did pursue a strategy of love and caring. Yet being Americans did influence the way we shared the Gospel message. I challenged Augsburger to train the kind of missionaries needed in Vietnam! He said younger churches around the world welcomed teachers who could help equip them in evangelism and Christian discipleship and said that Eastern Mennonite Seminary was prepared to lend Bible teachers to spend terms of several weeks in Vietnam and elsewhere. (The following January, after a visit to the Evangelical Bible Institute at Nha Trang, I informed Augsburger that the Institute was excited about the possibility of a visiting professor teaching in the areas of theology or New Testament.)

Our family arrived back in Saigon on July 22. Duane Bishop, a new mission associate, arrived the following day. Duane grew up in Vermont where his parents had gone from Pennsylvania to plant churches. He recently graduated from Eastern Mennonite College. Soon after arriving, Duane took part in a work camp for university students which Max Ediger had organized in Bao Loc near Da Lat. He enrolled in the September Vietnamese language study term in Da Lat.

It was "good to be back in Vietnam," I observed in a report to Salunga. We stayed with Paul and Esther at the VNCS guest house for ten days until we rented a house off Bach Dang Street near the center of Gia Dinh, only a block from where we had lived before. It had four bedrooms. Luke Beidler said it was good our house was not a dog—we could not afford to feed it! The rent was lower than for many smaller houses and the extra rooms were used by missionary and MCC personnel visiting Saigon.

We quickly noticed that food costs had increased sharply, making life difficult for those with the lowest incomes. At an August meeting of the Mission Council, there was agreement that we missionaries needed a larger piaster allowance. The missionary team had earlier chosen to accept the lowest allowance by which we "could squeeze by." We decided now to increase the piaster allowance. While it would benefit us, it also allowed us to share more with others.

We rejoiced that the church in Gia Dinh was continuing to grow. And at the Saigon student centers, up to forty people came to the Sunday morning English Bible classes—mostly students, but also adults from various walks of life. They studied lessons prepared by Don Sensenig on the background, the life, and the teachings of Jesus, including the call to follow Jesus—based on the Gospel of Luke. Many then stayed for the Vietnamese language worship service.

Several years earlier, the C&MA Mission had established a student program in Saigon. After finding that it did not lead to many conversions to the Christian faith and the establishment of congregations they closed the program, believing that their financial resources were best used in other programs. In spite of few persons making a public commitment of faith, the Mennonite Mission and church believed that our student program continued to reach a strategic segment of the population with the gospel of Jesus Christ. In a November newsletter to friends, James and Arlene Stauffer again summarized the ministry: "And so we patiently sow the seed, pray and wait for a spiritual harvest."

The Saigon student center property had been purchased in 1960 under the name of a lay member of the Evangelical Church. Now the Joint Administrative Council wanted the property transferred to a properly-constituted church body. This process was pursued throughout the year; on December 26, the property was transferred to the Mission with Pastor Quang serving as representative. The total cost was around $13,500 U.S.

Wedding of Minh and Fred Kauffman.

The summer of 1973 was filled with significant passages for Pastor Quang's family. Mrs. Quang's sixty-three-year-old mother, the wife of Tin Lanh pastor Nguyen Huu Phien, suffered several strokes. Mrs. Quang's sister Minh, a junior at Goshen College in Goshen, Indiana, returned to visit her mother. In late July, Minh's fiancé, Fred Kauffman, came to meet the family and to celebrate their formal engagement ceremony on Wednesday evening, August 1.

After the engagement ceremony, Pastor Phien, mindful of the cultural traditions discouraging a wedding within two or three years of a parent's death, urged the couple to get married right away. Wedding dresses were sewn and all the arrangements made. Since Fred's Nebraska farmer parents were unable to come on such short notice, Mary and I were asked to stand in for his parents on Sunday, August 5, when James Stauffer performed the wedding ceremony at the Gia Dinh church. Mrs. Phien died in late September. The family and church arranged a traditional Christian funeral service at the Gia Dinh church.

I began my role as MCC Vietnam representative September 1—a two-year half-time assignment to be reviewed after a year. James Klassen, who had arrived the previous October, also accepted a half-time assignment with the Mennonite Mission teaching in the Gia Dinh congregation Bible school. One Sunday in March, he preached at the church.

Don and Joyce Wyse and their three children arrived in June and went to Nha Trang where Don became the second physician working alongside Norman Blair.

Four additional MCC personnel arrived on July 25, Wallace and Claire Ewert, and Murray and Linda Hiebert—all Canadians except Linda who was from the US. Klassen flew with them to Da Lat to enroll in the language school August 17. The following day Klassen took the newcomers to Bao Loc where they visited refugee camps of the minority people and where they interacted with students at a work camp. On Sunday morning, returning to Da Lat on a wet highway, the Land Rover skidded and overturned. Those injured received first aid at the Di Linh government hospital and were flown to the Tin Lanh hospital in Nha Trang on a Vietnamese air force helicopter where they were treated by Doctors Blair and Wyse. Claire had suffered a concussion and fractured clavicle. Linda suffered a leg injury. Jim's neck was sprained requiring a neck collar for several months. But by mid-September, the four were engrossed in language study. Their good recovery was confirmation to Klassen that they all still had "a living contribution" to make.

In late September, Max and I flew to Pleiku. Pastor Nguyen Hau Nhuong, who earlier had been a missionary in Laos, was recently named the new hospital administrator and we were now trying to reopen the clinic and hospital; for a few months it was only staffed by a local nurse with limited training. Alliance missionaries told us the city was now "quiet," but the day we arrived heavy artillery was supporting a military operation attempting to retake the ARVN Le Minh camp at Plei Djereng—west of Pleiku—which Saigon forces had abandoned with heavy casualties after an attack several days earlier.

The next day, Max and I flew to Nha Trang to meet with the hospital personnel to plan the 1974 budget. We were pleased with the development of the one-year nurse training program with around fifteen students—now directed by Mrs. Thuoc.

On October 10, Max and I again flew to Nha Trang for a hospital board meeting. Instead of flying home we took a public bus on Route 1 leaving Nha Trang at 7:00 a.m. It took us over nine hours to cover the 450 km because of the many police checkpoints. At Phan Thiet, the military police inspected baggage and confiscated canned goods; the government was trying to deprive the Provisionary Revolutionary Government of rice, salt, gas, sugar and other important commodities. We were amazed that we did not see any Americans at any time on the road.

We planned an MCC conference at the VNCS guesthouse in Saigon the first weekend of November 1973. We gave significant time to considering the relationship between MCC and the Tin Lanh Church, a perennial subject of conversation when MCC personnel gathered. While some volunteers felt a warm friendship with the Church, others were very critical, even asking whether the Evangelical Church was an authentic expression of the Christian faith. In a short paper I presented, I suggested that our association with Tin Lanh—like husband-wife relationships or the interaction of persons who share close unit life—causes us to experience feelings of both love and hate, unity and disunity, respect and contempt. I noted that MCC ever since 1954 was committed to working closely with the Tin Lanh Church.

I characterized the Evangelical Church as holding "generally to Calvinistic doctrines" in a "mildly fundamentalist tradition." Most American Mennonite churches, I said, saw themselves "in neither the evangelical/fundamentalist camp nor in the so-called 'ecumenical' grouping." Instead, we viewed ourselves "as a kind of bridge between those two positions. . . . The strong Mennonite ethical concern, the stress on Christ as Lord, our concern for brotherhood and non-participation in military activity—these were areas where we viewed the Christian life and faith from a different perspective."

I quoted from the 1936 constitution of the Tin Lanh Church, revised in the fifties: "The purpose of the Church is to unite Vietnamese from the whole country who sincerely worship God, trust in and propagate Jesus Christ's Gospel of salvation according to the doctrines revealed in the Old and New Testaments of the Scriptures." The draft of the Church's current proposed revised constitution added a statement: "The Vietnam Evangelical Church also serves the people in the area of education and social welfare." It seemed evident that MCC had helped the Tin Lanh church to a wider understanding of the Church's mission. I also referred to the Christian Youth for Social Service (CYSS), an association of young Evangelical Church professionals; their national head, Pastor Nguyen Van Do, had told us that MCC provided the inspiration for the formation of their agency.

A key rationale for MCC to work independently from Vietnam Christian Service was to maintain a special relationship with the Evangelical Church, I said. Even as MCC helped the Tin Lanh Church to see its responsibilities in social welfare, I suggested that we can now "emphasize the Gospel ministry of love, peace and reconciliation."

I quoted from a study C&MA missionary Reginald Reimer had done the previous year about the evangelical church movements in Vietnam. Referring to the Mennonite missionaries, he said they "were carrying on an exemplary ministry of social service. Their peace witness provided a much needed dimension to the total impact of foreign Christians in a war-torn country. [They] were better identified with the Vietnamese people than many missionaries of other societies."

Reimer, however, concluded that the Mennonites' "motivation to win Vietnamese to Christ seemed crippled by a touch of 'presence theology.'" Reimer used missiologist Peter Wagner's definition of "presence theology" which emphasizes "being" Christians in the world and doing good works, but "hesitates at the point of gospel proclamation, and eschews 'persuading' men to become Christians."

I suggested that we had "much to learn" from the Tin Lanh Church—their commitment to sharing their faith in Jesus with all people. We wanted to continue to support them in medical ministries in Nha Trang and Pleiku. One of the three summer work camps that Max had coordinated was largely under CYSS leadership. I expressed the hope that this relationship would continue.

There were clear reasons, however, for MCC volunteers to express frustration in relationships with many Tin Lanh persons. One was the Evangelical Christians' sense of entitlement. A few weeks after the conference, Joy Blair of Nha Trang articulated for others the exasperation in working with the Evangelical Christian community at Nha Trang. Members of the Church were treated in the clinic free of charge while others had to pay fees. If they needed to be admitted to the hospital, members of the Church paid less for private rooms than others who stayed in large open wards. This might have been overlooked if the local congregations contributed generously to the operating expenses of the hospital and clinic, but they gave nothing. And the hospital administrator was limiting or refusing rice to needy patients. I made plans to address these issues with the hospital board.

MCC Asia Director Robert Miller arrived for a five-day visit during our November gathering in Saigon. Immediately after the weekend conference, Wally and Claire moved to Pleiku to work with agricultural development and support the reopening of the hospital. Klassen spent three weeks helping to get them settled in. We were hoping that C&MA doctor Robert Green, planning to transfer from Ban Me Thuot to Pleiku to work with leprosy patients, could also become chief medical officer of the Pleiku Evangelical clinic and hospital.

The Hieberts returned to Nha Trang, with Murray replacing Lowell Jantzi as hospital coordinator; Linda joined nurses Ann Ewert and Jean Hershey. Teruko Yano had recently terminated. Jean would transfer to Pleiku at the end of the year.

During Miller's visit, the new MCC two-year contract with the Ministry of Social Welfare was signed. The agreement referred to MCC's goals: "MCC aims to help to serve the social welfare needs of the people of Vietnam in the areas of community development, educational assistance, and health without regard to race, religion or political belief. MCC seeks to realize the will and intention of those who make these resources available to reach the goals stated above."

Vietnam Christian Service had signed their contract with the Ministry a few weeks earlier. The Ministry was concerned that the MCC contract be sufficiently different from that of VNCS to justify our having a separate contract. MCC's specific services included supporting the two medical programs with the Evangelical Church and the nurse training program. Without mentioning the Gia Dinh community center, it referred to supporting social welfare programs, child care, public health services, and assistance to needy children to attend primary and secondary schools. The Ministry official found unique MCC's support to the Evangelical Church, our proposals to organize work camps, promote agricultural and community development, and help families reclaim land abandoned during the war. We anticipated a yearly budget of $80,000.

The day before Miller left, he, Max and I had an audience with U.S. Ambassador Graham Martin who had replaced Ellsworth Bunker four months earlier. When Miller described MCC's programs, Martin said that he knows more about Mennonites than we might be led to believe! He said his father was Baptist, and he admitted having pacifist leanings during his youth. The Ambassador claimed that the United States was carefully adhering to the Paris Accords while the other side was constantly violating them, moving men, tanks and guns into the South.

The issue of large numbers of political prisoners being held by the Saigon government had recently received international attention. Ambassador Martin had assured the U.S. Congress that there were no political prisoners in South Vietnam. When we expressed this concern, the Ambassador challenged us to give him the facts about the existence of even one political prisoner being held in the South! His definition of a political prisoner was anyone who was arrested and imprisoned for criticizing the Saigon government when similar criticism of the American government would be tolerated in the United States. Miller told the Ambassador that the Embassy in the past had not expressed much interest in the facts; Martin said that there was now a change!

Ambassador Martin asked whether MCC works in areas controlled by the Provisional Revolutionary Government. We said we would like to, but had not yet been able. He said he hopes we can work in such areas, but is unable to help us. He suggested that Max work in a PRG area for two years and then report to us on their political prisoners!

The Ambassador gave us more time than we expected, undoubtedly recognizing that we had a significant constituency in the United States. (Martin retained his post in Saigon until the collapse of the Saigon government on April 30, 1975, when in humiliation he was evacuated by helicopter from the roof of the embassy.)

On the second November weekend, the missionaries were all together in Saigon where we reflected on the theme "God's Salvation Today." Duane Bishop came from the Da Lat language school. Beidlers came from Can Tho in the Mekong Delta. It was good to talk, share, pray and play together. Duane was assigned to move to Can Tho to support the Beidlers in their ministries.

A significant project in Can Tho was a cooperative student hostel program with Christian Youth for Social Service (CYSS). Mr. Yukio Miyazaki of YMCA International also expressed interest in a partnership. In early December, the three agencies signed an agreement: YMCA and the Mission shared the rental cost; CYSS directed the student hostel, now enlarged to thirty students. YMCA was in charge of student activities, leadership training and recreation. The Mission was responsible for a reading room downstairs.

Two typhoons swept across the South China Sea into central Vietnam in mid-November 1973, the first inundating Quang Ngai and two neighboring provinces, the second striking further south, even inflicting some damage to the Nha Trang hospital facilities. We did not have many material aid supplies in the warehouse but we released some canned beef chunks, eighteen bales of children's clothing, and a bale of towels for CYSS to distribute in the Quang Ngai area.

Max had hoped to take the Air Vietnam flight to Quang Ngai on Saturday morning, November 17. Not able to get on that flight, he bought a ticket for the afternoon flight. This afternoon flight was cancelled because the morning plane disappeared and failed to arrive. Several days later, the wreckage of the C-47, the military transport version of the familiar DC-3, was found strewn over a mountain west of the provincial city—apparently a victim of the storms. Among the twenty-seven persons who died was Rich Thompson, one of the Quaker volunteers serving with the American Friends rehabilitation and prosthesis center in Quang Ngai. We all knew him as a pleasant young man who frequently stopped by our office to talk with Phan Phuong Hang, the MCC secretary with whom he had a growing friendship.

Ms. Phuong Hang had worked in the MCC office since the beginning of the year. She had attended a Christian school in her youth; her father affiliated with the Evangelical Church a decade earlier, partly to avoid being arrested by the government of President Ngo Dinh Diem. Phuong Hang read books on philosophy and religions, and become interested in the Bible through her relationship with Mennonites. She had not identified as a Christian. However, one night in late October when she was troubled and sad, unable to sleep, she suddenly found herself praying to God for the first time in her life!

Max managed to get to Quang Ngai a few days later to investigate flood damage. He was at the morgue when Rich's body was being prepared and he helped wash the bodies of other crash victims. While he was there, ten or more bodies of soldiers were brought in. Some of the bodies were blindfolded and gagged—apparently prisoners. Max said it appeared as if they were killed by an explosion rather than by gun fire because their bodies were crushed and broken "like some giant had stamped on them." In a memo Max wrote, "It would perhaps be very constructive if all those involved in the manufacture of war materials would spend a week in a morgue like this one, working with the results of their labors."

Max was pleased with the CYSS material aid distribution in Quang Ngai province. Some money was also given to the local Red Cross to buy rice for a few hundred families. Max arranged for MCC employee Mr. Hau to give school supplies to ninety families that had suffered some severe loss.

In spite of the fact that he helped expedite limited relief supplies, Max was upset by the short-term benefits of giving material aid benefits:

> I do not like relief distributions. I have constantly told myself I will never again get involved in such activities. I come away from them frustrated and angry. Yet, when the situation arises I feel I want to get involved. I always wrestle with the issue of getting involved and feeding a few people despite my dislike for the work, or not getting involved and knowing that I could have helped at least a few people. I am glad I went to Quang Ngai at this time. I had to see what the situation was like and how much the people really were suffering. But I do not like putting band-aids over the problems. The people we gave rice to had something to eat for several days, but now they are probably hungry again. That gives me no feelings of satisfaction. Again I will say, 'I will not get involved in relief distribution again!' at least not until the next emergency!

Our letters home continued to talk about the war. The two chief negotiators of the Paris Peace Accords, Henry Kissinger and Le Duc Tho, in October were awarded the Nobel Peace Prize, surprising us and our Vietnamese friends. After all, the war was continuing. Kissinger accepted the award—Tho never did.

We invited the fourth son of Mr. and Mrs. Nguyen Muong, Nguyen Dinh Tin, youth leader of the Gia Dinh congregation, to serve as the MCC office assistant. Although exempt from military service to care for his parents because his three brothers were in the armed forces, he was still called for a month of basic training.

Around this time the twenty-year-old son of an Evangelical family attending the Mennonite congregation was killed; three or four soldiers walking together were all killed when one stepped on a mine. Neither Mary nor I could forget the deep sobs of the 83-year-old grandmother when we went to console the family. The young man's mother said they believed the Lord would protect him since he was preparing to train for pastoral ministry.

Paul and Esther Bucher invited all the VNCS, MCC and Mission personnel in Saigon—twenty-five in all, including children—to a dinner of roast turkey and all the fixings at the VNCS guest house two days before the U.S. Thanksgiving Day, November 22.

In September, Paul returned to Phoenix Study Group in Saigon to teach math to seventh and eighth graders; around 135 students were enrolled in kindergarten through eighth grade. James Stauffer, serving as chairman of the school committee, learned that the U.S. Embassy anticipated "normalizing" their Saigon post, and supported having the Study Group merge into an American Community School. Aware that other Asia schools had problems with drugs and other discipline problems, not all parents were enthusiastic about the prospect of a large American Community School. Summer Institute of Linguistics personnel working in Nha Trang had organized their own school for their children there. In fact, Joy Blair and Joyce Wyse were both teaching in this program. As military action continued, it soon became clear that the U.S. Embassy would not be opening a school in Saigon.

Bucher interacted with a broad spectrum of Americans at the Phoenix Study Group. In a letter to Paul's home church, Paul and Esther wrote: "The fighting is still very much present in

Vietnam despite an official 'ceasefire' and 'American withdrawal.' The other night at a school party we met some American wolves in sheep's clothing. Nice people we've known for a while, their business is war and killing people. Pray with us that the work of such men on both sides might be confounded and that the glory and the Peace of the Lord, our true King, might shine through."

In October, U.S. intelligence reported that the North Vietnamese had infiltrated 70,000 additional military personnel since the cease-fire, along with 400 tanks, artillery and anti-aircraft guns, and had built an all-weather road through the mountainous jungle to Tay Ninh province, northwest of Saigon. Americans referred to this artery as the Ho Chi Minh Trail.

On Monday morning, December 3, Saigon awoke with a huge dark cloud hanging over the city. In early morning the Viet Cong attacked the Shell and Esso fuel storage area at Nha Be, just south of Saigon. The fires burned all week, consuming millions of gallons of fuel, forty to fifty percent of the civilian supply. The armed forces still had all they needed! The government immediately closed all gas stations on Monday; the rest of the week there was a run on all the gas stations that received the rationed fuel. It seemed senseless to wait for an hour to buy ten liters of gas, so we purchased a couple of bikes. The time it took to travel from our Gia Dinh home to the Saigon office was about the same by bicycle or scooter—twelve or thirteen minutes.

Earl and Pat Hostetter Martin returned to Vietnam with their daughter Lara Mai in early October for their second MCC assignment. While it was assumed that they most likely would return to Quang Ngai, they were encouraged to check out the Mekong River delta and spent some time visiting in the Can Tho area. Pat might have been able to work as a therapist at the rehabilitation hospital; it was less clear what work Earl would find. However, with their prior experience in Quang Ngai, it seemed they might work more effectively there. They stayed in Saigon, however, until the birth of their second child in January 1974.

While in Can Tho, they visited the provincial hospital where they spoke with farmers who had lost limbs to mines while working in the fields. They were also able to learn something about the prison system. After speaking with a Lieutenant Oanh—who worked in a military court—Earl was invited to visit a military prison. Most of the prisoners were deserters, absent without leave for more than sixteen days. Major Ba, the officer in charge of the prison, said that the prison camp held between two and four thousand prisoners. The men got nothing more than a little rice and tea every day—no meat, vegetables or fish sauce. There were no beds; the men lay close together on concrete slabs in little sheds. Knowing Earl was a Protestant, Maj. Be said he would be happy to have more visits from Protestant chaplains because a strong religious faith would increase the men's determination to fight the communists! Lt. Oanh said that many of the prisoners—when released—would be sent out unarmed to the front lines for six months to carry ammunition and clear minefields. They would wear shirts marked "Laborer, Deserter."

At the An Quang Buddhist temple in Saigon, Earl and Max met with the Venerable Thich Phap Lan who was working with the "Committee Campaigning for the Release of Prisoners," and spoke to prisoners just released from the notorious Con Son Island prison. Max gave a small monetary gift to buy materials for distribution in the prisons, support for prisoners when they were released, and a travel allowance to enable them to return home after they got their ID papers.

Akron supported these initial efforts to reach out to prisoners. After reading our reports, Robert Miller wrote: "We continue to encourage you to assist prisoners and their families in any way that you can. We recognize that large amounts of funds are likely not needed for this purpose but encourage you to do what is possible. . . . I would also encourage you to submit a few documented cases [of political prisoners] to the ambassador."

We were soon able to document the story of Dang Thi Hien. Pat Lewis, VNCS therapist who worked in the Binh Dan Hospital across the street from the Saigon student center, told the Buchers about a young paralyzed woman handcuffed to a stretcher in a ward with a police guard. Paul suggested that Earl and Pat Martin visit her. Pat learned that Hien had been arrested at the Phu Nhuan Market in the northern part of the city after talking with an alleged communist sympathizer. After first being taken to a police station, she was then transferred by Jeep to Hau Nghia, 110 km northwest of Saigon, where she was interrogated and tortured in an effort to induce a confession. (The Vietnamese term for interrogation also means torture!) She refused to admit to any charges and was subjected to horrible torture causing her to become paralyzed from the waist down. She was then taken to the Binh Dan Hospital for therapy which Pat Lewis could not give since she was handcuffed! When Pat Martin later took a *New York Times* reporter in to hear Hien's story, the secret police asked them both to go with him to the police station. The police guard expressed surprise that they did not know that civilians were not allowed to talk to "political" prisoners! Officially, such a category did not exist.

Shortly after Hien was returned to the Hau Nghia interrogation center, Earl went with Hien's mother to inquire about her. After repeated refusals, they were allowed into the prison and met her. Although Hien's mother was not particularly upset that her daughter was in prison, she was concerned about her well-being. An official admitted to Earl that they had no evidence that she was involved with the communist network.

Given the current procedures of the government, we knew that Hien might be held indefinitely without trial. We wondered what we should do. Perhaps she was a security threat to the government, though we had no indication that this was so. We knew of some students who had been imprisoned merely because they sang songs or translated articles calling for peace. How might the Republic of Vietnam interpret our advocacy on behalf of prisoners?

PEACE AND RECONCILIATION

Chapter 35

With a fifty-year history at the beginning of the seventies, Mennonite Central Committee commissioned Robert Kreider to lead an MCC self-study. Former dean of Bluffton College, he had served on MCC's board of directors for fourteen years. He and his wife Lois arrived in Vietnam late April 1974 for a two-week visit. The entire MCC team met with them in Nha Trang from May 2 to 4.

Kreider's visit was helpful in defining "peace and reconciliation" as MCC's main objective in Vietnam at this time. The MCC Vietnam team was committed to this.

This was already expressed in the MCC Vietnam Annual Report I prepared six months earlier which read: "The goal of MCC is not so much to develop programs as it is to meet and share with the Vietnamese people. The emphasis is placed on people rather than programs, and MCC volunteers are encouraged to develop language skills and receive cultural orientation which will enable them to communicate with the people. Volunteers are encouraged to find ways to express Christian love and concern to help bring about real reconciliation and peace. We are reminded of many areas where we can learn from our Vietnamese brothers and sisters."

The MCC relationship with the Democratic Republic of Vietnam developed further when Atlee Beechy made a ten-day visit to Hanoi in January 1974.

Although there was earlier talk about the need for "post-war" reconstruction, the continuing war made all such planning quite tentative. In the year following the January 1973 "cease-fire," it was estimated that 60,000 people had been killed. This prompted Republic of Vietnam President Thieu to declare that the war had "restarted." Each side accused the other of carrying out illegal military activity.

The lunar New Year came on January 23. The day before Tet, three members of the Quaker team in Quang Ngai, Paul and Sophie Quinn-Judge and Diane Jones, were captured by PRG units when they were returning home from visiting a refugee village in an area considered safe. Twelve days later they were released on a Sunday morning and walked into the Quaker unit house. Earl Martin was there at the time, having gone to Quang Ngai on an exploratory visit. They reported how they were moved around, by day or by night, and treated as prisoners rather than as guests, though they were given more freedom after they were clearly identified. They were often asked why they—as Americans—were still in Vietnam after the cease-fire, and asked why the United States was still sending weapons to the Saigon forces.

In early February, Paul and Esther Bucher met twelve members of the Church Women United group from the United States who "descended" on the VNCS guest house, seeking first-hand impressions of what was happening in Vietnam. One evening, Doan Thanh Liem, a forty year-old Catholic lawyer working with the World Council of Churches Commission on Inter-Church Aid, Refugee and World Service, spoke to the group. Having grown up in a very anti-communistic Catholic family, he told how he had learned that one can neither hate nor love governments, but live openly and truthfully. A few days later, Esther accompanied the twelve women to a Buddhist temple where they shared a meal with Mrs. Ngo Ba Thanh—a persistent critic of the government who chaired a women's Action for the Right to Live organization. It was a unique experience for Esther to meet mothers of political prisoners, including the mother of Saigon Student Union president Huynh Tan Mam. Some of these women begged Esther to petition the U.S. President for the release of their family members.

The delegation of Church Women United followed soon after a ten-day visit mid-January of several prominent Americans who visited prisons and met newly-released political prisoners. We did not arrange their schedules, but some of us served as interpreters. We learned from three persons who met with Ambassador Martin that he said his "Mennonite and Quaker friends" had not been able to find any evidence to substantiate reports of political prisoners! This stirred us in our task of gathering materials.

Max prepared a small booklet of twenty-some pages containing facts and stories of political prisoners entitled "Release Us from Bondage" which was sent to the MCC Peace Section for distribution to churches in the United States. This booklet containing poetry written by prisoners and illustrated by them, prepared prior to Easter, April 14, suggested various action responses. One suggestion was for a group "to covenant together for a one-week fast and meditation." Participants were asked to eat only one bowl of rice each day and "share this 'prison meal' together as a way of empathizing with political prisoners." This booklet was distributed widely beyond Mennonite churches.

Executive secretary of the MCC Peace Section Walton Hackman expressed appreciation for this Passion Week project. "As you are no doubt aware," he wrote, "the American public has tried to put Vietnam out of its consciousness. The kind of Easter emphasis which you and your colleagues have proposed will certainly help to prick the consciousnesses of many who would like to forget about Vietnam. Blessings as you continue to work for peace that has not yet been achieved in Vietnam."

Addressing the issue of physical torture of persons who did not support the political agenda of the Saigon government, we wanted to publicize the prevalence of these practices without highlighting our role in reporting this. When *The Mennonite* published material that James Klassen had sent to his pastor, Robert Miller asked that letters and reports of a sensitive nature be first cleared with the Akron office, saying that otherwise persons might use them quoting "an MCC volunteer in Vietnam." Miller, however, supported our engaging the issue of political prisoners. He thanked us for the material we had sent about Dang Thi Hien and urged us to gather information on additional cases and submit them to Ambassador Martin, pointing out "inconsistencies in other aspects of US policy." Miller also wanted to send copies of these materials to Senator Edward Kennedy's office. He asked that we not publicize our meetings with the ambassador.

We, in Saigon, were very careful in releasing personal information about prisoners and even specific officials who worked inside the prisons. On April 25, we submitted an extensive report to Ambassador Martin. Referring to the meeting, Robert Miller, Max and I had with the Ambassador several months earlier, I wrote: "You expressed the view that we might unwittingly be tools of communist propaganda against the government of the Republic of Vietnam. You challenged us to present information which would substantiate charges that political prisoners are being held in South Vietnam."

Noting the public awareness that many people were arrested and severely interrogated for expressing political views in opposition to the government, the letter read: "It seemed rather difficult to present any documentation which you would accept. When we learned that you have, on occasion, told visitors that the Mennonites have not presented any evidence to indicate that there are political prisoners being held in South Vietnam, it seemed imperative that we respond to your request."

We presented the ambassador a detailed story of the imprisonment and torture of Dang Thi Hien. Among the other documents submitted was a photocopy of the release papers of a prisoner released late 1973, clearly identified as a "political operative." We also submitted a list of 264 political prisoners currently in Saigon's Chi Hoa Prison, many of them arrested after the January 1973 Paris Agreement, some as recently as November. A number of them were identified as belonging to a political front, with others designated as political trainers.

I described attending a military field court in Saigon with a Vietnamese lawyer a few months earlier where five persons were charged with "disturbing public order," a catch-all charge against anyone who did not demonstrate support for the government. I noted that we knew students who were arrested and imprisoned for singing songs of peace and that we knew the man who spent more than a year in Chi Hoa Prison for the "crime" of translating *The Indochina Story*, a book published by the Committee of Concerned Asian Scholars in 1970. This man, who assisted Max Ediger in translating many documents, was charged with "threatening national security." We asked the Ambassador that the United States should use its influence to urge the government to change its prison system.

We received no acknowledgement from the Ambassador's office after submitting these materials. Nor did we return to speak with the Ambassador.

In assisting prisoners, we worked with others like the Buddhist Venerable Thich Phap Lan and Father Chan Tin, the Redemptorist Catholic priest. They were generally not lacking for funds. MCC's prisoner assistance was a low budget program. Max was providing vitamins and around $200 monthly to purchase food for prisoners. Earlier he had given a grant of nearly $1,000 to a Buddhist organization that assisted prisoners, but gave no more because they failed to give a detailed report about how these funds were used. A small gift was given to a lawyer who was helping a prisoner of conscience appeal his case.

Mary went with Hien's mother on occasion to visit her daughter in prison. After Hien was released from prison—walking with crutches—Earl and Pat, now living in Quang Ngai, in early July arranged for her to get physical therapy at the Quaker Rehabilitation Center there. Paul Bucher and Max went to the Ministry of the Interior to inquire about her identification cards which were given two days later. She was not given discharge papers. "After all, she was never arrested!" the men were told.

The MCC medical programs at Nha Trang and Pleiku commanded

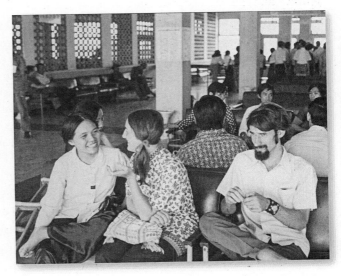

Esther and Paul Bucher assist Hien to fly to Quang Ngai for therapy.

much of my attention. The two doctors at Nha Trang, Norman Blair and Don Wyse, were terminating mid-year, and MCC was uncertain whether replacement doctors could be recruited. In early February, I received a call from Dr. Wyse, informing me that the Nha Trang hospital administrator was offered a large grant from USAID ($60,000 U.S.) to develop a pediatric program at the hospital—part of a comprehensive child welfare program funded to the tune of $7.2 million. In conversation with Akron, Miller agreed with Don and me that we would not become involved with this, even if the hospital board might consider it. We suggested that any new focus of the hospital board or the MCC staff such as public health work or a pediatric program should be done within the current resources of the hospital. Later conversations with USAID administrator Hugh O'Neil indicated that they had a much more modest program in mind for the Nha Trang clinic—adding a few pediatric beds, building a kitchen and hiring additional nurses to provide care for malnourished children—some of whom would be placed for adoption overseas. We did not support this and the hospital board chose not to pursue it.

Norman Blair in November 1973 had prepared a comprehensive report of MCC's medical programs. The ophthalmology program was meeting a real need, he wrote, but the general clinic and hospital were duplicating services found elsewhere in Nha Trang. Blair cited the need to provide clinics in the rural areas around the city but noted that the hospital administration seemed uninterested. The nursing school, so urgent when it began five years earlier, was now less relevant because of new government training programs. To continue, Blair suggested, students might be recruited from ethnic minorities. But currently there were too few patients in the general clinic and hospital to offer sufficient training opportunities for nursing students. Thus an argument could be made to relocate the nurse training program to Pleiku. There were medical needs in the Pleiku area, but administrative problems and the lack of a medical doctor at the clinic had to be resolved before a training program could be considered.

Given the difficulty in recruiting overseas medical personnel, Blair suggested that "equivalently qualified Vietnamese" should be recruited. He called attention to a perennial problem—the unwillingness of Evangelical Christians from the Nha Trang area to contribute financially to the hospital, not even paying for personal clinic services. Blair wrote:

> Over one-third of the work we do is not paid for. In the hospital this is partly made up of people too poor to pay. In the clinic, it is mostly because Tin Lanh people and people in Tin Lanh organizations do not pay. If all pay who could, the hospital would almost be self-supporting with no price increase and no MCC subsidy except for the support of MCC personnel. . . . In 14 years of work in Nhatrang, the Tin Lanh church has yet to demonstrate good faith that it intends to contribute financially to the operation of the hospital.

Prior to the MCC conference the end of February, I prepared a Review and Proposals for the Nha Trang clinic. We expected the Evangelical Church to finance the clinic and hospital, while MCC would support training programs, including scholarships for medical staff to get more specialized training. The review noted that MCC promised to recruit a replacement doctor and asked the Evangelical Church to recruit a second doctor. Doan Van Mieng, the president of the Church, told us about a Tin Lanh doctor working in the provincial hospital in Nha Trang who might be able to transition to the Tin Lanh clinic and hospital.

We anticipated holding a conference for all MCC and Mission personnel in Da Lat the end of February. However, with insufficient space there, we reserved twenty-two rooms in the Hay Hoang Hotel in the coastal town of Long Hai, just north of Vung Tau. This was not a luxurious hotel; in fact, some rooms had dirt swept under the bed! One of the MCC couples who had briefly vacationed in this same hotel after arriving in the country said the amenities of the hotel were much improved compared to several months earlier—meaning, of course, they were now much more used to this kind of facilities in war-torn Vietnam!

Others invited to the conference were Pastor and Mrs. Quang; Nguyen Van Ninh, now working with Asia Christian Service; Catholic lawyer Doan Thanh Liem; and Nguyen Hau Nhuong, the new administrator of the Pleiku Evangelical Clinic. Mission Associates Mark and Ruth Ann Mininger had just arrived in mid-January and were studying Vietnamese in Da Lat; this was their first opportunity to interact with the Mennonite team. Fifty-eight persons, including children, participated.

Our mornings were spent in Bible study and discussions, based on the theme of "jubilee" from the first chapters of John Howard Yoder's *The Politics of Jesus* (Herald Press, 1973), released a year earlier. Afternoons were given to swimming and other recreation and the evenings to singing and group activities.

Mr. Liem spoke on the theme, "Ideas for creative involvement in Vietnam." He proposed that there be a moratorium on foreign aid with the purpose of giving the Vietnamese people a chance to regain some dignity and arrive at their own solutions to their country's problems. Foreigners could give moral support to the people. He stressed that Vietnam would not starve if funds were cut off and said that other countries had more desperate need for that aid. "Brothers and sisters" were needed more than specialists or benefactors, Liem said; persons willing to immerse themselves totally in Vietnamese life, in the language, culture, and institutions of Vietnam, who were sensitive to the differences in life style, and who could give moral support to the people. Most of us appreciated Liem's comments. Pastor Quang preached the Sunday morning communion sermon, using the story of Jesus feeding the five thousand.

Back in Saigon, we missionaries continued talking about lifestyles, discussing relevant sections of Art Gish's book, *Beyond the Rat Race* (Herald Press, 1973), at our Tuesday night fellowship meetings. Children's education was one of the aspects discussed. Our children were not studying in Vietnamese schools beyond the kindergarten level. While saying we wanted to identify with our Vietnamese friends, we still chose the better of two worlds. However, Max Ediger wrote to William Snyder, asking that his support be reduced considerably so he could live on the same level as several Vietnamese young men with whom he lived. Snyder affirmed Max's decision, although both he and Max knew that MCC would be there to assist Max for health care or other unexpected needs.

On January 8, 1974, an article appeared in the local English daily, *The Saigon Post*, entitled, "MCC Promotes Clearance of Dangerous Areas in QN." Datelined Saigon, it read:

An American couple of the Mennonite Central Committee (MCC) recently arrived in Saigon for a first hand study of the situation of unexploded ammunitions lying underground at rural areas in Quang Ngai province. This social organization planned the work with the hope of helping local inhabitants clear dangerous regions so as to thoroughly exploit land in the cultivation.

Mentioning no names, the article described other MCC projects. It noted MCC's earlier cooperation with Vietnam Christian Service, then reported that there were seventeen foreigners and fifty Vietnamese personnel working with two Mennonite agencies—MCC and the missionary agency.

The article concluded with this paragraph: "MCC voluntary foreign personnel have been encouraged to learn Vietnamese and uphold the Christian love in all circumstances to contribute to the restoration of a genuine peace in this part of the world."

We had not anticipated this publicity. Our secretary, Phuong-Hang, had shown a copy of our annual report to her sister who worked for Vietnam Press Agency. It is not clear whether the story was picked up by Vietnamese language newspapers. We were pleased that the article identified the problem of unexploded ordnance lying in agricultural land. A few people asked us about our idealistic couple who were planning to pick explosives from the fields!

Phuong Hang, along with Tran Thi Ly, a nurse at the Nha Trang clinic and a member of the local Vinh Phuoc Tin Lanh congregation, had just been accepted into the MCC North American exchange program. Hang and Ly were to have left for the United States in early August but the Interior Ministry did not process their requests for exit visas. When the visas were granted in November, rather than wait until the following August with no assurance they could leave then, arrangements were made for them to go just before Christmas. Hang was assigned to work in a day care nursery in Lansdale, Pennsylvania, and Ly to work in a Colorado hospital.

Earl and Pat moved to Quang Ngai in mid-February, a month after Pat gave birth to their son Minh. A few days earlier, Robert Miller had written: "Earl's main assignment is to investigate the munitions problem in the whole context of refugees moving back to their land."

It was not long before Earl was compiling reports of casualties from incidents where people were injured or killed by the 5 percent to 10 percent of the expended munitions that failed to explode. A week after their move, an older sister of their friend Nhuan was killed while gathering firewood since kerosene and charcoal were very expensive. The Martins wrote: "As she was gathering the wood, she struck an M-79 grenade that was shot from some grenade launcher—perhaps several years ago. . . . But when Nhuan's sister hit the egg-sized object accidently, the thing exploded and sent steel pellets through her head."

A few weeks later, Mrs. Pham Thi Luan, the forty-five year-old wife of Nguyen Quynh and mother of six children, was killed when the heavy hoe she was using to loosen the soil struck a buried M-79 grenade. A small hole in the rice field, a broken hoe handle, and a tattered hat marked the spot.

While unexploded artillery shells and mines were more powerful, the M-79 grenade was a particular threat to the lives of the country people. They were particularly prevalent around former American military bases. The grenade was armed by a spin-activation when fired from the launcher. Farmers would find them in their fields, perhaps striking them with their hoes, and children would be attracted to these shiny "toys." Farmers who found them often gingerly picked them up and dropped them into abandoned wells.

Earl suggested several possible responses to the problem of unexploded ordnance (UXO). Publicizing the problem was crucial. It was also important to prompt ARVN forces to clear the land for the farmers; but they were still fighting a war and had few UXO experts. One could let the farmers solve the problem themselves—though it meant that some would be killed or injured.

Earl proposed that MCC secure a tractor—outfitted with shields—that would plow the fields for farmers for a fair charge. He wanted to begin as soon as possible. In July, Earl gave money to a family to rent a tractor to plow their field that had not been tilled for several years. Later he learned the money was not used as intended—the family was hungry and purchased food.

M-79 grenades were not the only explosive Martin was concerned about. In Duc Pho district, thirty kilometers south of Quang Ngai town, the ARVN forces were trying to clear an area that had been held by the NLF for a long time. Booby traps and mines had been placed in brush along the fence rows. The ARVN conscripted local civilians, including teenagers, to cut down the brush and clumps of bamboo with machetes and hoes. Many persons were injured and some killed by exploding mines. An ARVN officer explained: "We don't have a lot of bulldozers to clear the mines. We rely mostly on manpower!"

Miller suggested that a used tractor be purchased in Quang Ngai so the program could begin right away. There was conversation about partnering with some local organization. Earl spoke with a local representative of Youth for Social Service (YSS), a Buddhist organization that had placed two tractors in Quang Ngai province to help farmers plow up fallow fields. I also spoke with the person in Saigon who headed up the YSS national office.

Le Duyen, chairman of the local Buddhist Social Welfare Committee, also expressed interest in working with MCC. Duyen offered to arrange for persons to run the program. Earl wrote: "Of all the groups or agencies that could possibly run a program as we envisioned it in Quang Ngai province, this group seems to be the most likely candidate. Politically in Quang Ngai, the Buddhists seem to have attempted to steer a course of being open to both sides and some of their clinics are in contested areas."

Miller authorized us to purchase a tractor whenever a satisfactory plan was worked out with a local group. In a program requiring multiple personnel—a manager, someone to schedule plowing, various drivers, and a person to collect fees—Earl was warned by friends to avoid the misappropriation of funds. Further delay in securing a tractor, however, would damage any credibility MCC had earned in the community. An agreement was signed with Duyen in late January.

Place where Mrs. Luan was killed on March 28, 1974.

We purchased a new tractor in Saigon. When the fast-moving events of early 1975 led to the whole Quang Ngai province coming under the control of the "liberating" army in March, the tractor was still in Saigon! The Quaker rehabilitation center in Quang Ngai continued to function after the change in government and Earl arranged for staff members of the center to take the tractor to Quang Ngai in June 1975.

Pastor and Mrs. Quang continued to guide the ministries of the Gia Dinh community center and church through 1974. A year after the new facilities were opened, attendance at the Rang Dong primary school morning and afternoon classes topped 500 students. In early 1974, James Klassen began teaching a new course on evangelism in the congregation's Bible school with more than thirty students enrolled, the highest group ever.

Rather than expand the overflowing facilities at the Gia Dinh community center, the Joint Administrative Council chose to open a satellite ministry nearby. After a long search in the Cau Bong area two kilometers away, a small building was found in Van Kiep alley off Chi Lang Street; it seemed more expedient to purchase than to rent the property. Mrs. Nguyen Thi Hoang, the treasurer of the Gia Dinh congregation, was invited to direct the program. Mary and I were asked to give guidance to the director. Mrs. Hoang had no trouble recruiting 30 three-to-five-year-old children of working mothers for a day care program. The Gia Dinh congregation had a short praise service at Van Kiep Sunday afternoon, March 17. The next morning forty-four children showed up! The church made plans to open a small bookroom staffed by volunteers from the church youth group and hoped eventually to organize Gospel preaching meetings.

James and Arlene, now living at the Saigon student center and headquarters building, were pleased at growing student interest in the two Sunday Bible classes and discussion hour—around fifty persons. The first Sunday in April, Arlene spoke on "The Greatest Ransom Ever!" with Ms. Phuong Hang, the MCC secretary, interpreting. Some students were staying after the meeting to ask questions. James wrote home: "Some are really seeking and we need to pray that they will turn themselves over to God. Some people with psychological training feel that it is very hard for the Vietnamese to commit themselves to anything after all these years of having foreigners dominate their lives."

James coordinated the literature and Bible correspondence program. Nguyen Quang Trung, the pastoral assistant, corresponded with students, assisted by Anh Do. Trung ordered 100,000 reprints of a tract we had printed six years earlier, *Tình Thương Là Gì?* (What is Love?). The Evangelical Church requested 70,000 copies. Others went to the Church of Christ and to the Baptists. In February and March, Do had sent out 3,069 Bible correspondence lessons. One response came from a young ethnic Cham from Phan Rang in central Vietnam. Most Cham people adhered to Hindu or Islamic faiths. Bich described his coming to faith:

> From the time I enrolled in this correspondence course until now a great change has taken place in my life, affecting my speech and actions.
>
> One day I was reading the Word and meditating. Suddenly as if an invisible hand was strongly pushing me, I was compelled to go to the nearby church. It was Sunday and a service was in progress. My normal apprehensiveness and bashfulness disappeared, and the moving force within me brought me directly to the pastor, who was greatly surprised at my boldness. Nevertheless, he prayed and helped me believe in the Lord. He has promised to baptize me by the end of the month. I praise the Lord, and extol the living Father that He has saved me! This is my testimony since studying your correspondence course.

The piaster was devalued in late March, the second time in a month—now 605 piasters to the US dollar. In her letter home, Mary reflected on its implication for us: "The economic situation keeps getting worse. We ask ourselves and each other often what it means to be Christian brothers in this time and place. In the U.S. we live fairly simply, we think, but here living the same way, we are rich. We go to church and pray with people who hardly have enough to eat." James also was concerned about the high living costs. In a letter home, he wrote: "It bothers me that we spend almost ten times as much as our Vietnamese brothers each month just to live."

We did not want to make people feel indebted to us by our giving monetary gifts, but tried to be alert to opportunities to help in times of family emergencies like illness and death. At such times families could accept gifts without embarrassment or expectations of reciprocity.

Arlene and Mary were quite involved with the women's ministries at the Gia Dinh congregation. In a letter home, Mary wrote:

> Yesterday the committee of the women's fellowship went visiting. We stopped at fourteen homes! One woman wept as she told of how sick she has been, yet she has to stand and sell all day in front of her house if there is to be anything for the family to eat. She has a daughter in the States who hasn't written or sent any money for a long time. This woman has TB and has been at death's door a number of times. . . . Pray for her. Her husband does very little to support the family. They are both church members.

Paul and Esther joined Doan Thanh Liem and others in an outing by the Saigon River the first Sunday morning in April when they discussed the pedagogical views of Paulo Freire and liberation theology. Among the group were two young men who had been prisoners of the Viet Cong. Ky was working with the Buddhist Youth for Social Service when he was captured while visiting a village in 1972. He was a prisoner for nineteen months until released after the Paris Agreement. Held in a room with many others, he was not allowed to talk. He described conditions as hard—many times having only rice with salt to eat—the same food his captors had. He feared that he might never be released to see his family again.

Binh, trained as a Catholic priest, had a different experience. After being captured, he was taken to the North and to Hanoi. Being sympathetic to some of the goals of the other side and seeing both good and bad points of each side, he was treated better than many prisoners—in effect being placed on his honor in a village under the control of the PRG and allowed to continue his work. Paul wrote home:

> It was really exciting to see his enthusiasm for living the Christian life every day—like Jesus would live in every situation twenty-four hours a day, and his religion was relative—he had little interest in all the ceremonies, pomp, etc. associated with the Catholic Church. A modern day Vietnamese Anabaptist. During the past year since he returned to this side he's been reading all he can about Christianity and liberation, preparing himself for the future possibility that South Vietnam would be under the rule of the PRG or some other such government. A person like him shares our Mennonite vision of the church better than many Vietnamese Mennonites do.

The next week, Paul and Esther spent several days in Can Tho where they earlier worked with the Beidlers. Duane Bishop had joined Luke and Dorothy in teaching English. Ms. Lieu just opened a new economics and sewing class across the Mekong River in a Hoa Hao Buddhist community. In late April, James went to Can Tho to meet with several students enrolled in the Bible correspondence courses. By then Duane and Luke had stopped using motor scooters to get around, relying on bicycles or walking. The pace of life in Can Tho was definitely slower than in Saigon. Esther observed that Luke had "changed from the workhorse he used to be, to a more relaxed slower person."

Highway travel was more secure at this time. At the end of March, I took a regular bus to Da Lat, the first I had ever traveled on highway #20. The road was fairly good; at one place it was broken up, apparently by a mine explosion. At a village, we were delayed two hours; Catholic farmers were demanding free land from the government. In Da Lat, I visited Ruth Ann and Mark Mininger who were studying in language school. The next day I took a cross-country taxi—with passengers packed like sardines—to Nha Trang to attend the hospital board meeting. The two MCC doctors were leaving in the summer and MCC had not yet been able to recruit replacements. We had asked the Evangelical Church to appoint a doctor and it now appeared that Dr. Tran Thi Quang Hanh might be available.

Since Paul and Esther were leaving Vietnam the end of July, we hired Vu Huu Si, a young graduate of Dalat University in accounting and bookkeeping, on a part-time basis to take over Paul's bookkeeping job. Si did an excellent job of keeping the books. We could have hired a local person for this job much sooner.

Robert and Lois Kreider came to Vietnam Sunday, April 28, for a two-week stay. The next day we received a cablegram reporting that Mary's mother had died on Sunday evening. After phoning home and then joining our missionary group at the Stauffer home in our weekly Bible study and prayer, Mary made the decision not to return to the States to attend the funeral.

I flew with the Kreiders to Quang Ngai for a short visit. Paul and Esther were vacationing in Quang Ngai at this time. Paul described the area: "We had always heard so much about war, destruction, hunger . . . , and the insecurity of the countryside. . . . The countryside was so beautiful. . . . It was the time for transplanting the rice—which means people were plowing, harrowing the fields, getting them ready to plant. Others were planting the small rice seedlings in the flooded fields amidst other already planted seedlings."

But there were reminders of the war. Earl told stories of farmers who

Quang Ngai farmers.

Unexploded M-79 grenades.

had picked up more than thirty M-79 grenades from their fields and dropped them into old wells. At least six farmers were killed and others injured around just one former military base in the previous year. Still they farmed because the alternative was to go hungry. Earl told of one farmer tilling his field with a plow share made from bomb shrapnel with other parts from a napalm canister.

After spirited conversation among the group gathered in Quang Ngai—Esther and Paul, Max, Yoshihiro, Robert and Lois Kreider, Pat, Earl, and me—Earl drafted a letter addressed to members of the United States Congress, questioning the appropriateness of the Nixon Administration's request for a large military subsidy to the Saigon government. This draft was discussed further among the MCC personnel at our meeting in Nha Trang.

After returning to Saigon, we prepared to fly to Nha Trang on Thursday, May 2, to meet with the entire MCC team—the funeral date for Mary's mother. Mary and three-year-old Jonathan had already made plans to accompany me while Steven and Becky stayed with the Stauffer family. Mary expressed her thoughts in a letter home:

> The [MCC] group met for discussion on Thursday evening and at the close joined us in special prayer for you at the time you were preparing to go to the funeral. Luke and I then spent those hours (10:30 to 11:45 p.m.) on the beach. There was a fairly bright moon. It was very quiet except for the gentle lapping of the waves against the shore. I can think of no place where I would rather have spent that time since I couldn't be with you all. The lapping of the waves spoke of the coming and going of life and, as always at the ocean, I was moved by the greatness of God's power and our smallness. Yet, for all our smallness in comparison to the size of His creation, of the brief space of time we fill in all the centuries, He still takes note of all our needs and loves us.

Mary reflected on "weighing the decision" about whether to travel home for the funeral service. We had always assumed that we would not return to the States should there be a family death. Had she gone, she would have had to secure an exit visa and plane ticket. She was also reluctant to go without the children and me. And yet,

> To stay meant missing out on a very significant family occasion. I wanted to be there. I was not able to share this sorrow in person with you or to be of any help or comfort in this time of need. But we felt the decision to stay was the best. I had assumed I'd make the decision, then be at peace about it. Still, at many times I was overcome with the intense longing to be there. As Luke says, some decisions don't have a right and a wrong side to them. I have no guilty feelings and still believe this was best, but will always be sorry I had to miss it.
>
> We tried to consider, too, what would be best in relation to the Christians here. Many of them are appalled at the money it takes to travel from here to there, so it seemed they would understand if I didn't go. On the other hand, most Vietnamese will go to whatever means necessary in order to get home for such an occasion if it is at all possible. It's part of their whole understanding of respect for parents.

Closing her letter, Mary wrote: "We hope sometime when you feel ready to travel that you'll make plans to stay with us for a month or two." Three months later her father and sister came for a two and one-half week visit.

Observing, probing and listening to MCC personnel gathered at Nha Trang, the Kreiders understood what MCC personnel were saying. Mennonite Central Committee in Vietnam would "need to be flexible, Spirit-led, with an accent on being a friendly presence, listening, talking, and judicious reporting." MCC would "continue a diversified program sensitive to the changing political climate" of Vietnam and would include "advocacy for those who suffer in silence—the political prisoners." MCC would attempt special programs such as removal of unexploded ordnance. We would continue some of our medical services while seeking to "extricate MCC from the heavy staffing commitments at the Nha Trang hospital." We would gather stories from Vietnamese and minority people—and of war suffering. Through literature and dialogue, we would "continue to seek ways of sharing the gospel of peace and reconciliation."

In early May, an older brother of MCC assistant Nguyen Dinh Tin was seriously injured by grenade shrapnel while on a Sunday patrol near Can Tho. Several hours later he was evacuated by helicopter to the military hospital where he was bandaged and x-rayed. When Mr. Muong, his father, heard of the incident, he and another son immediately took the bus, arriving at the hospital after visiting hours, so were denied entrance. After persistent insistence, they entered and found Phuoc—still bloodied and hungry—who had not been given anything to eat for two days! That Thursday evening at the Gia Dinh church, Mr. Muong gave thanks for God's mercy in sparing his son who had just been engaged to be married. Dorothy and Luke visited Phuoc before he was released to recuperate at home; his family hoped their son would be given a medical discharge from the armed forces.

No one in Vietnam was untouched by the war. Ann Noel told of her relationship with Ms. Phuc, a staff member of the Nha Trang clinic:

> One day last week I went home after work with Phuc, one of my friends and co-workers. As we rode our bikes by the Non-Commissioned Officer (NCO) Academy, she talked about her sixteen-year-old brother. "Next month he will be drafted into the army. He'll have to come to this place and learn how to fight." She then paused and sadly added: "He's still so young."
>
> She talked about the futile-angry-tragic feeling she gets every few weeks when she learns that another friend or relative has been killed or injured in the war. She said that some of the soldiers are so young that they react to the war like the children they are; and not like the men they—all too soon—are expected to be. They get homesick, cry for their mothers and families, and have to be comforted by their commanding officers. Phuc said, "They sometimes have to give the boys chè* to make them happy, just like babies."
>
> As we rode past a rifle range, Phuc said, "Sometimes when several soldiers . . . are together, and they are scared they will die, they all throw away their guns and crowd together in one place, because it's better to die together with friends than alone with a gun!" *[sweet drink or pudding]

There were signs on the horizon that the United States was becoming more hesitant to continue providing unlimited weaponry for the Vietnam conflict. In early April, the House of Representatives rejected the White House request for increased military aid to South Vietnam. The following month, the House opened impeachment hearings against President Nixon for his role in the Watergate scandal. On August 9, 1974, the beleaguered President resigned, leaving Vietnamese President Nguyen Van Thieu without his ally in the White House.

Sixteen MCC personnel and six Mennonite missionaries signed the letter that was sent May 28 to three key United States Senate and two House of Representative leaders asking them "to do all within [their] power to drastically reduce the armaments flowing into this country." Stating

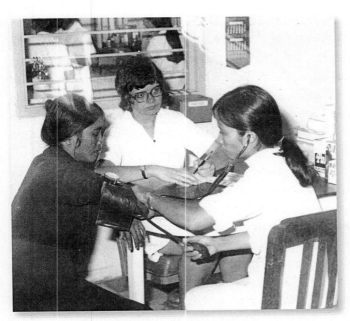

Ann Ewert at the Nha Trang Hospital.

that "violence committed by both sides must be condemned," the letter argued that a steady flow of armaments only assured the continuation of the fighting and prevented a political resolution to the conflict.

Mailed to the MCC Akron and the EMBMC Salunga offices, the letter was forwarded jointly by MCC Assistant Executive Secretary Paul Longacre and Harold S. Stauffer, EMBMC Overseas Ministries Secretary, on June 12 to Senator J. W. Fulbright, chair of the Foreign Relations Committee; Senator Edward F. Kennedy, chair of the Subcommittee on Refugees; Senator John L. McClellan, chair of the Senate Appropriations Committee; Representative George H. Mahon, chair of the House Appropriations Committee; and Representative Thomas E. Morgan, chair of the House Foreign Affairs Committee.

In an inter-office memo, Robert Miller affirmed this letter from the MCC personnel and Mennonite missionaries. "This task of presenting the facts about what is happening in Vietnam is increasingly important as people try to forget Vietnam," he wrote, "and the effort should be continued."

In a letter home, I wrote: "It is sad how the war just keeps going. It is rather impossible to blame one side or the other. There are times when it seems that one side is more irresponsible than the other. But neither side is committed to a peaceful resolution of the conflict. But they both claim to want peace! We would say: 'Peace is the way to peace.'"

I then related a recent conversation with a young woman at the MCC office. Having observed that some persons appeared to favor the NLF more than the Saigon government, she told her father that the Mennonites do not support the policies of the Saigon government. "Then they must support the policies of the other side," he said. She tried to explain to her father that MCCers did not support either side, but her father could not understand this! Such was the thinking among many in Saigon. Any form of neutralism—any thought of accommodation with the other side was illegal; the thought could not be entertained.

Newspapers reported a Viet Cong shelling attack on Bien Hoa—twenty-seven kilometers north-east of Saigon—early morning June 3 killing many civilians. One rocket landed in the Tan Hiep prison where many political prisoners and suspected pro-communist persons were held, killing seventeen women and injuring many more. We wondered whether Ms. Hien was among them.

I visited Phnom Penh, Cambodia, five days in late May at the request of Robert Miller to ascertain relief needs there. Nearly one-third of the Cambodians had fled their homes due to warfare. Although not prepared to field a medical team, MCC offered to send food and other material aid supplies to the pediatric hospital World Vision was building for the Alliance mission and contribute a small cash grant to the Khmer Evangelical Church to use for in emergency relief.

As part of a working vacation, our whole family went with me to Nha Trang in late June to attend the hospital board meeting. The board organized a farewell next day for the departing administrator, Rev. Le Khac Tuyen, and a welcome for the incoming administrator, Rev. Nguyen Linh.

Dr. Don Wyse and his family left in early June and soon Dr. Tran Thi Quang Hanh and her husband, Dr. Tran Minh Canh, moved into the vacated house. Both were active members of the Evangelical Church. Drafted into the military ranks, Dr. Canh worked in the Vietnamese military hospital in Nha Trang. Dr. Quang Hanh had worked in the city's civilian provincial hospital. She was born in Quang Ngai but had most of her schooling in Saigon and graduated from the medical college of Saigon University six years earlier with a specialty in obstetrics. She had performed surgeries at Saigon's Binh Dan Hospital—located across the street from the Mennonite Mission office and student center. She worked a year as the sole doctor in the government community clinic at Thu Thiem, the community across the river from downtown Saigon. She also helped the Saigon's Nguyen Tri Phuong Tin Lanh congregation open a clinic a few years earlier.

Already in April, I had informed the hospital board that we wanted to discuss long-term plans. Pastor Tuyen, the administrator, said this would mean reviewing our joint agreement.

To Robert Miller, I wrote:

> There are many Vietnam MCCers (in Nha Trang and elsewhere) who feel that our objectives are not compatible with Tin Lanh objectives, so we should make plans to terminate this relationship. This is not my feeling. I feel that, even with all the problems of Tin Lanh, the Evangelical Church Christians are brothers and sisters to us. Not all MCC's projects should be with the Tin Lanh church, but we should maximize our relationship at places like Nha Trang and Pleiku. With good relationships at Nha Trang, we will have opportunities to share our understanding of the gospel of love and peace with the hospital staff and with students and staff [at the Bible Institute].

I suggested, however, that perhaps we should terminate our joint relationship with the Church now becoming the sole administrator. The Church could then yearly request MCC personnel and funds. We might then be in a stronger position to suggest changes as conditions for our support—like having a professional hospital administrator, more funds contributed locally, laymen on the hospital board, or higher medical standards. This could mean that MCC might not be officially represented on the board, except that an MCC doctor could meet with the board.

"We are ready to consider a change in the nature of our relationship at Nhatrang," Miller replied. "We would be open to the idea of the church relating to a number of organizations in connection with the hospital and not just MCC. . . . This would give them a broader basis of support for personnel, funds and supplies. . . . In the future we would not necessarily need to be represented on the board except through staff representation. . . . You can begin discussing these ideas with the hospital board and with [the Church President] Pastor Mieng."

We were pleased that the Evangelical Church had managed to recruit a doctor. The Board agreed to a minimum term of three years for Dr. Hanh and anticipated a long tenure. MCC agreed to pay her monthly salary of 70,000 piasters ($115 U.S.) plus their house rent for 1974 and perhaps longer. Although this was twice her previous salary, she gave up a private practice she had in addition to her position at the provincial hospital.

I sensed this husband-wife doctor team had a long-term interest in supporting the Tin Lanh clinic and hospital. Both of them had a great deal of respect for Don Wyse and Norman Blair. They were especially impressed at the high quality professional care and personal interest Norm gave to each of his patients.

Dr. Blair and his wife Joy, along with Joy's sister Jean Hershey, completed their terms and returned to the States the end of June. After Norman left, the patient load at the clinic and hospital dropped significantly and many of the MCC clinic staff said there were not sufficient patients to warrant having a second doctor. However, since we had promised the Evangelical Church that we would provide one doctor, I hoped we might recruit a doctor who could support and affirm Dr. Quang Hanh and continue the eye program of previous doctors. In mid-July we received a confirmation from Akron that Dr. John Willms had accepted an invitation to come to Vietnam.

Rev. Linh, the new hospital administrator, called a special meeting of the board July 10. Among the actions taken were plans to raise some of the fees and a requirement that patients with money pay a ten-day deposit before being admitted into the hospital ward; this would be waived for poor patients. The board supported the clinic that Ann Noel and Sinh were holding for the ethnic minority people at Phuoc Luong on Tuesdays and Fridays. They reported MCC's willingness to sponsor Le Thi Y's nursing studies at the Saigon Adventist hospital. Ms. Y, a member of the Gia Dinh Mennonite Church, would be required to work at the Adventist hospital for at least three years after graduation. The board also invited Dr. Quang Hanh's husband, Dr. Canh, to work at the clinic in his off-time without remuneration. Dr. Hanh, as medical director, was reshaping the medical programs of the clinic and hospital. She proposed a pre-natal clinic on Saturdays and a weekly dental clinic. She also proposed doing away with the residential program for tuberculosis patients.

After our family's vacation stay in Nha Trang, we flew to Da Nang where we took a small bus on a three-hours-plus journey to Quang Ngai, staying with Earl and Pat. We then spent a few days in Da Lat where we visited Mark and Ruth Ann Mininger who were nearing the end of their language studies. We attended a bilingual English and Vietnamese Sunday afternoon vesper service. It was moving to hear two young women singing a duet—one Vietnamese and the other an ethnic Koho. In many settings, the ethnic minorities were viewed as inferior.

The last week in July we missionaries met in Saigon—Stauffers, Martins, Beidlers, Buchers and Miningers. (Duane Bishop had left in mid-June for his wedding and returned with his wife Pat in early August.) Pastor and Mrs. Quang were there, as well as MCCers Devadoss and Doris Maddimadugu. The sessions were coordinated by Luke and Dorothy Beidler. Everyone was invited to report what they had been doing the past months and their feelings about it. A special characteristic of this conference was Pastor and Mrs. Quangs' openness to express their heart concerns. Quang and Tam had earlier shared with Esther and Paul their feelings of frustration about the church and lack of affirmation from the missionaries.

Esther journaled about this just two days before she and Paul left Vietnam: "For the first time since I've been here, Mr. and Mrs. Quang shared freely what they feel and think. What wonders me is why now? It's interesting that this never happened before. . . . I feel so much more at peace and ease about [leaving] if I feel that Quangs will receive spiritual and personal encouragement from the other missionaries here."

Paul also wrote about Quang's frustration as pastor of the Mennonite congregation. People's lives were not being changed as he hoped. Some Christian men had problems with alcohol and might even give a verbal testimony at church while intoxicated. Other men would argue with their wives. As a result people from the community could scoff saying, "What do we need Christ for? We live better lives than those Christians."

> Quang always takes a patient view of sin and refrains from setting himself up as a judge. Still the other Sunday night he had seen too much and so told the members who were gathered together for Prayer Meeting at a member's home that he was quitting if there weren't some changes in people's lives. The following Thursday evening at Men's Prayer meeting he had to be even more blunt say[ing] what it was about various people's lives that troubled him. The Spirit must have been at work, for rather than getting mad at Quang and the church, these individuals said, "You're right! And if you hadn't said something to me now about it, I would have gotten so deep into this thing that I would have been lost to the church." And from these men the revival spread to their wives. And Quang, too, was reading Timothy where Paul exhorted Timothy to keep preaching the message even if no one was listening. And he, too, realized his error. This is the beautiful part of the Gia Dinh church. The Spirit is at work changing it continually and giving us victory in our daily lives.

In a letter home, I commented that Pastor and Mrs. Quang expressed the view that missionaries should make a "life or death" commitment to serve in Vietnam. They sometimes feel that the Mission may not have a full commitment to help the church in Vietnam develop to maturity. As an example, Everett and Margaret were transferred to Hong Kong even though they had the greatest understanding of the Vietnamese language, culture and people.

Participants of Pleiku work camp—Ursula Horn (center), Wallace Ewert and Max Ediger.

I flew to Pleiku to attend a meeting of the hospital board on August 10. This came at the end of a good two-week summer work camp for university students which Max Ediger coordinated, emphasizing service to others and reconciliation—speaking to others and listening.

The resignation of Richard M. Nixon as President of the United States on August 8 was a significant event affecting the Vietnam conflict. In compelling South Vietnam's President Nguyen Van Thieu to agree to the Paris Peace Accords in January 1973, Nixon had given Thieu personal assurance of a massive retaliation if the Viet Cong threatened the survival of the regime. Now with Nixon gone, there were questions whether his successor would honor those promises. James wrote home a few days after Nixon's resignation:

> Most Vietnamese that we have met lately are worried about Vietnam now that Nixon has stepped down. On the other hand, they are aware of the fact that his policy only means more war. They are hoping that Ford will make greater efforts for peace. One man in my class this [Sunday] morning hopes that the US can prevail on the USSR and China to stop military aid to the North and that Ford will stop war aid to the South. If all outside intervention was cut off, the war would soon stop and the South and North would get together. Many are hoping for this.

The U.S. Congress did indeed substantially cut military aid to the Republic of Vietnam, on August 5 setting a ceiling of one billion dollars for military aid to South Vietnam for fiscal 1974; this was reduced to $700 million a few days later. In 1975, it would be $300 million—compared to $2.8 billion in 1973.

While many people pondered the political future of Vietnam, we missionaries and leaders of the Mennonite Church on August 28 discussed "The Church in the Future." Meeting as a consultative council were Mission personnel; the Joint Administrative Council; the Committee of Representatives of the Gia Dinh congregation; youth, Sunday school and witness band leaders; and a representative from Can Tho—twenty-five persons. The relationship of the Mennonite Mission to the local church was a sensitive matter. At the August 28 meeting, the local autonomy of the church was affirmed and a decision was made to dissolve the Joint Administrative Council that had functioned for three years, effective September 30. A new Church Administrative Committee responsible for all program planning would take its place, effective October 1. Church leaders requested that missionaries continue to serve by virtue of their involvement in the local ministries. James was chosen chairman, Tran Xuan Quang vice-chairman, Nguyen Van Ninh secretary, and Do Van Thuong and I members. A clarification that all decisions for the church were now to be made by church leaders *in* Vietnam provided helpful guidance during the difficult months and years following the April 1975 revolution.

Mary's father and sister, John and Martha Kauffman, visited us for three weeks in August. Martha set up a quilt frame and taught quilting to women of the Gia Dinh church. The Kauffmans' visit coincided with severe illness of our son Steven and Rose Stauffer. Both were stricken with dengue hemorrhagic fever transmitted by mosquitoes. High fever and diarrhea led to dehydration. Fortunately, they received intravenous fluids at the Adventist hospital where they were nurtured back to health. The hospital had moved to the former U.S. Army Third Field Hospital when American forces withdrew; it had earlier been the campus of the American Community School.

Luke Beidler also spoke of the demanding task of nurturing the Gia Dinh congregation. In the October *News and Concerns*, Luke Beidler wrote:

Pray especially for Pastor and Mrs. Tran Xuan Quang. They bear the brunt of the day-to-day leadership at the Gia Dinh Center and Church. A steady stream of discouraged, hungry, unemployed, spiritually needy people find their way to the Pastor's door. By sharing in prayer we believe you will actually be sharing his burden and doing something to support the Work of God in this country.

Pray for many, many of your Brothers in Christ who are right now in offices, in hospitals, in outposts of the massive military machine in this country. Many of them are struggling with consciences which tell them that killing and violence are counterproductive and contrary to the teaching of their Lord. . . . I believe that the Holy Spirit understands our longings in prayer and through our prayers will do something constructive for our Brothers.

In the midst of the struggles, there was evidence that the Gospel was changing lives. Five additional persons were baptized at the Gia Dinh church in November, bringing the total baptized members to more than 140. There was also new life at the Saigon student center. There were over seventy persons attending the Sunday morning Bible classes—growing eventually to one hundred students. James Stauffer had begun an instruction class for two persons who had accepted faith in Jesus Christ. Mark and Ruth Mininger had now completed six months of language studies in Da Lat and moved to Saigon. Mark was teaching English at the student center and also taught an English Bible class Thursday evenings with fifteen students.

In the year after the January 1973 signing of the Paris Peace Accords, the Saigon government seized many areas under Viet Cong control, but now the VC was regaining control over many of these regions. The country's economy was hurting badly; the cost of living had increased one hundred percent since the Accords were signed and the currency devalued by forty-four percent. In June 1974, more than three hundred Catholic priests released a statement attacking government corruption, believing that this weakened the ability of the government to compete with the other side. In September, this Movement to Oppose Corruption led by Father Tranh Huu Thanh denounced President Thieu himself. Catholics took to the streets, calling on Thieu to resign and demanding more press freedom. Around the same time, the United Buddhist Church under the leadership of Thich Tri Quang formed the Force for National Reconciliation, calling for full implementation of the Paris Accords and the release of all political prisoners. This Force called for an end of the fratricidal war that was still—more than a year after the Paris agreement—killing thousands monthly. It also called for the end to dictatorship and the establishment of genuine democracy, a respect for basic human rights, and for the normalization of relations between the South and North leading to reunification.

It was clear that North Vietnam and the Provisional Revolutionary Government wanted reunification of Vietnam on their terms. President Thieu refused to change policies; he and many others maintained that accommodation with them would eventually lead to full control by the communist government. In a two-hour television speech to the country on October 1, President Thieu blamed most of South Vietnam's troubles on the communists. No one was convinced that Thieu would make good his pledge to deal firmly with corruption. Without a political settlement, people with whom we spoke generally assumed that the conflict would continue until one side won a decisive military victory over the other, or whenever Saigon was prepared to share significant political power with the PRG. Some said cynically that there would be peace only when the North took over the whole country.

In my October 16 letter to Robert Miller, I wrote: "I think there will likely be significantly new military activity in the next six months. Many believe the PRG/DRV is stronger militarily than in 1972. ARVN morale is dropping in many areas because of decreased military supplies." At that time a clear military victory appeared unlikely—neither side possessed the power to defeat the other side militarily. Yet with poor morale among Saigon's armed forces personnel and decreased US support coupled with a military buildup of the other side, the stage was being set for changes in the year ahead.

We missionaries were pleased that our Mission Board overseas secretary Harold Stauffer and his wife, Connie, spent a week with us in late October. Harold had not visited Vietnam for several years and it was Connie's first visit. Since the Mission team and the local church now assumed the task of long-term planning, visits by the EMBMC administrators were no longer a high priority. The Stauffers' visit, however, was quite useful as they observed and reflected with us the dynamics of our missionary team relationships. Harold commented on the "political pressures [that] continue on the current government of South Vietnam," and opined that these "pressures and realities . . . tend to distract from priority ministry involvement by religious groups such as EMBMC missionary personnel."

We missionaries understood Harold's critique, yet we were not prepared to blithely go about our work without thought to the political and military developments which affected the lives of the people.

On Saturday and Sunday, October 25 and 26, the Gia Dinh congregation celebrated the tenth anniversary of the founding of the community center. In a letter home two days later, Mary recalled our association with the center. We had lived and worked there at the beginning and continued a relationship with the center and church during our second term. Now Pastor and Mrs. Quang were fully in charge. Mary wrote: "We enjoyed our work there and made many friends and had a staff of good workers, but we also had many difficulties, especially in the area of ironing out difficulties between staff members. So, in some ways, we're glad those days are past. We realized that often because of our way of administration, we were even the cause of some of those misunderstandings. But we still have many happy memories."

In early November, James and Arlene Stauffer, Duane and Pat Bishop, and Mary and I attended an anthropology seminar in Da Lat at the Alliance conference center, formerly the Dalat School. Mary and I and our children traveled by car with Reginald and Donna Reimer, Alliance missionaries. Attended by ninety missionaries and service workers, papers were presented on the topics of Vietnamese ancestor worship, leadership training, and church organization. Ms. Yen, a professor of Da Lat University, spoke on "Inter-relationships between Vietnamese and Foreigners." Walter Routh, Jr., former Southern Baptist missionary now working independently in Quang Ngai province, described starting house churches without any reliance on foreign financial help; some of these twenty-eight groups were located in VC-controlled or contested areas.

We had a good hospital board meeting at Nha Trang in August. The new administrator, Pastor Nguyen Linh, asked all the current board members to stay on. When he expressed his opinion that the hospital and clinic hire only Evangelical Christians, Pastor Ong Van Huyen, the oldest board member who had earlier served as dean of the Bible School, said the primary conditions for hiring personnel should be professional qualifications, experience, and their attitudes. He, of course, would prefer Christians, but he noted that others often have better qualifications.

The board expressed appreciation for Ann Noel and Ms. Sinh making visits to the Phuoc Luong resettlement area. Dr. Quang Hanh supported their going to Tri Nguyen Island once a month to dispense medicines.

Not appreciative of the South Vietnamese government policies, Murray Hiebert—at one of the board meetings—proposed that the hospital no longer fly the three-striped flag of the Republic of Vietnam and instead, fly no flag at all. Everyone knew that the local government officials would soon show up if they did not display a flag. After brief discussion, Pastor Huyen had the last word: "We will fly the flag. And when (*khi nào*) the other side takes over, we will fly their flag!"

For months we had been trying to chart a clear direction for MCC's medical program in Nha Trang. At our quarterly gathering of all MCC's personnel held in Nha Trang September 5-7, we reviewed a document prepared for the occasion—"Philosophy, Objectives and Guidelines." Reporting to Akron headquarters, I noted that we—the twelve MCC personnel, VNCS Indonesian nurse Geysje Marentak who worked at Nha Trang, and I—needed to clarify our mission in Vietnam and communicate this to our home office.

An aversion to working in institutional settings was expressed at our gathering. I had good relationships with many persons in the Evangelical Church. But many MCCers working in the two Evangelical clinics and hospitals had to put up with procedures they found intolerable.

"The MCC community in Vietnam is concerned with *peace and reconciliation*," I wrote to Robert Miller. "This may sound idealistic. But we came to realize that, unless we stress this, we may not do it at all." I said that we were more interested in changing the attitudes of people than in dispensing medicines to them.

While most MCC personnel did not feel comfortable with a "missionary" label, and some might have even pondered whether Christians should even attempt to convert to the Christian faith Buddhists or those who worshiped ancestors, yet they were committed to expressing and living out the teachings and life of Jesus Christ.

Following our Nha Trang meeting in early September, we invited MCC personnel to send comments about the medical programs to our Saigon office. Max summed it up this way: "I think our medical work has been rather successful as medical work, but as a peace witness it has been a failure." Others made similar comments.

A specific action of the Conference was a request that Max, Jim and I sharpen the statement on MCC Vietnam Philosophy, Objectives and Guidelines. This document, dated September 1974, was sent out with a cover letter noting an expressed problem "of running a medical institution which is no longer fulfilling its original purposes." MCC personnel were saying that priority must "be given to dealing with the source of Vietnam's ills—the continuing war." Noting that MCC in many countries addressed problems of over-population, food shortages, illiteracy and disease, the document stated that "in Vietnam the problem is the war itself, hence the emphasis on peace and reconciliation."

The draft statement said that "MCC volunteers in Vietnam are an international Christian community of pacifists committed to the urgent tasks of peace and reconciliation." We wanted to invest resources "to become involved with people or in projects seeking to end conflict and bring about reconciliation between people," working with "those oppressed without regard to ethnic background, religion or political beliefs in a way that affirms persons and enhances human dignity." We also wanted to communicate "Vietnamese concerns to the international community."

In a September 13 letter to Robert Miller, to which I attached our proposals for a new direction for the joint MCC-Tin Lanh medical programs, I said that initially it seemed like "a revolution was in progress" at our Nha Trang conference. However, we believed our proposals were "the logical steps" we needed to take.

We proposed that the Evangelical Church assume full responsibility for administering the Nha Trang medical program at the earliest possible date. MCC's difficulties in recruiting key medical personnel was a factor. Already having a Tin Lanh doctor, Dr. Quang Hanh, serving as medical director was also an incentive. Additionally, there was the sense that—if the Church wanted a medical program—it was time for them to manage it rather than continue a joint administration.

There was also our concern for peace and reconciliation. Our statement read:

> In the past several years there has been in the Evangelical Church a movement away from a strong apolitical stance to one of pro-Saigon, often strongly anti-communist, pro-American. This has made it difficult for many MCCers to work happily with the Church in a society that has become militaristic. MCCers have slowly been drawn into a difficult situation. Military personnel come to the hospital, military doctors work at the hospitals, military personnel (chaplains) serve on the hospital boards, nursing students practice in the military hospital. This is not a criticism of the Evangelical Church alone, for US military doctors also came to the hospitals when American MCC doctors were serving there.
>
> MCCers feel that their peace concerns are severely compromised. There is also the feeling of most MCCers that the close association we have with Tin Lanh compromises our position to all the people of Vietnam. We recognize that we cannot "reform" the Evangelical Church. We believe we would have more and greater opportunities for a witness to the Gospel of peace if we were not so closely involved with this organization.
>
> *Our goal should be to turn over the medical institutions completely to the Tin Lanh Church in a manner that they can continue these institutions if they choose.* We will provide support over the next few years on a decreasing scale which will enable the Church to raise its own support or find alternative means of support. (Italics original).

Though proposing that MCC cease to be an administrative partner by the end of 1974, we were aware that our agreement with the Church obliged us to give a year's notice prior to terminating our agreement. We suggested that the MCC director would still make periodic visits and might meet with the hospital board at the request of the board or director, and some MCC personnel working there could serve as regular or ex officio members of the board. MCC would provide a doctor for another year or two; we had already reported to the Board that Dr. John Willms would be coming in November.

We also proposed that Ann Noel continue as a clinic nurse to the end of her term, recommending that she move toward greater involvement in preventive medicine and public health programs. Geysje Marentak was completing her assignment in November. Devadoss, the lab technician, was transferring to the Pleiku Clinic, and Murray would continue turning over coordinating responsibilities to others.

While the Evangelical Clinic at Pleiku had a growing number of patients, we likewise proposed that we also cease being an administrative partner to that program. We proposed continuing the financial level of support to the Nha Trang and Plieku programs through 1975, with a readiness to consider further personnel or funding requests "if the program fits within MCC objectives and guidelines."

We had no clear recommendation regarding the nursing school. In early October, twelve students graduated—three ethnic minority persons. Linda Hiebert, who directed the nursing education, was asked to visit other nursing schools, speak with government officials, and prepare a proposal. She noted that—since 1966—the school had graduated six classes totaling fifty-five nurses. Her early November report concluded:

> On the grounds that the government seemed quite capable of handling nursing education in south Vietnam, that the surplus of one-year nurses was making it difficult for our graduates to find jobs, that [the Evangelical Hospital] seems to be able to find trained nurses elsewhere, that our school is having difficulty providing adequate nursing experience for its students, that there is little support for the idea of starting another Montagnard nursing school, and that other private medical institutions do have other educational options for their staff, I would suggest that there is no longer a need for MCC to participate in the operation of the nursing school.

Since the patient load at the Nha Trang clinic and hospital was so low that Dr. Quang Hanh could easily manage, the MCC staff at Nha Trang also recommended that Dr. John Willms not come to Nha Trang. However, I believed that we should keep our commitment to the church and to the local hospital board. Acknowledging that work would be slow at first, I informed Dr. Willms that this would allow for some language and cultural orientation. We also anticipated that he would receive training for ophthalmologic surgery. Robert Miller supported having the Willms family come. John and Frances Willms with sons Peter (sixth grade) and Michael (ninth grade) arrived just before Christmas. Their older daughter was in twelfth grade in British Columbia.

Miller indicated that our proposals were "the direction which we here feel MCC should take in connection with the medical programs, that is, planning for the Vietnamese church to take primary responsibility for the projects with the MCC contribution declining step by step." He asked me to communicate with the church president our need to review the medical programs.

In early October, Ann Noel related an incident which did nothing to endear the clinic staff to the hospital administrator nor to the institution. The administrator's aged father came to the clinic, expecting preferential treatment, and kept moving to the front of the line. Ms. Sinh, the nurse, asked him to get back in turn. Although she did not know the patient and had not been asked to treat him early, she received a forty-five minute tongue-lashing and was told the clinic had no need of persons like her—the clinic would get along fine if the entire staff were Evangelical Christians!

I met with Pastor Mieng late October and followed up with a letter, expressing appreciation for the privilege of working with the Church on these projects since 1960, but noting that "the changing medical needs in Vietnam and MCC's difficulty in recruiting sufficient professional medical personnel now make it imperative that we clarify the changing nature of our relationship in the medical projects."

I observed that from the beginning, the church was responsible for the administration of the clinic and hospital, while MCC was "primarily responsible for the medical aspects of the programs." Now that the church had recruited Dr. Tran Thi Quang Hanh to serve at Nhatrang and was attempting to get other doctors released from military obligations to serve in the Church's medical programs, a change was warranted. We would continue to support the programs as much as we could, but we were asking them to seek support from other organizations as well.

In the annual Vietnam report prepared in September, it was stated this way:

> While MCC is still able to attract volunteers, it has become increasingly difficult to recruit specialized personnel. It is extremely hard to administer institutional programs when continuity is not secured. It is also doubtful whether MCC should attempt to administer any institutional programs in Vietnam. We want to receive only highly motivated persons who are willing to develop language skills for effective communication. Volunteers must have the ability to engage in a work assignment which is appreciated by the people, but of primary importance is the ability to articulate the way of love and peace.

We expressed a rather ambitious objective: "We believe that we can help create situations where progress can be made toward national reconciliation."

After serving as MCC Vietnam director for nearly a year, I indicated to Miller that I would be willing to continue for another year but did not see continuing beyond mid-1975. James Stauffer would then be on home leave and I would need to pick up more responsibilities with the Mission and the church. I was satisfied with the relationship I had with the Evangelical Church on the hospital boards at Nha Trang and Pleiku and hoped that there would be more opportunities to share Mennonite biblical and theological concerns with the Church in places like the Nha Trang Bible Institute. I also told Miller that I wanted to "maintain the necessary liaison with government agencies while trying to keep an appropriate distance."

I had assumed that Max would work more with personnel administration, but it soon became apparent that since most of the MCC personnel worked with the Tin Lanh medical programs, I needed to give attention to personnel matters in Nha Trang and Pleiku. Even though I spent more time with the MCC assignment than I had anticipated, I was pleased with the good support team in Saigon. In addition to his work camp activities, Max served as administrative assistant. Jim Klassen spent time procuring medicines and assisted the Mennonite Church in leadership education. We also had a good Vietnamese staff. Nguyen Dinh Tin worked with official papers. Vu Huu Si was working halftime as bookkeeper and Ms. Tan Nhat Tieu was replacing Phuong Hang as secretary-receptionist.

Miller wanted me to continue. In an internal memo, he indicated that my serving as MCC director had "strengthened the already good relationship between Eastern Board and MCC efforts in Vietnam. Our efforts there are compatible and mutually supportive." Harold Stauffer, following his October visit, also stated that there was "real value in one person symbolizing at top administrative levels the relationship between MCC and EMBMC programs." However, he encouraged MCC to recruit another director or provide stronger administrative support for me.

At year's end, Ann Noel Ewert and Linda and Murray Hiebert were the only MCC personnel in Nha Trang, except for the newly-arrived Willms family. Geysje Marentak had returned home to Indonesia in late November. Nurse Jean Hershey returned for a new term to work at the clinic and hospital in Pleiku, together with Devadoss and Doris Maddimadugu. Claire and Wallace Ewert were working in Pleiku with agriculture and community development. Earl and Pat Martin were in Quang Ngai; Yoshihiro Ichikawa would join them after his short home leave. Max was away for three months leave.

Mary and four-year-old Jonathan accompanied me on a visit to Pleiku in late November. In mid-December, Norman and Ruth Kraus came to Vietnam for two weeks. James and Arlene Stauffer accompanied them to Nha Trang where Norman gave two evening lectures at the Evangelical Church Bible School—even though it was exam week. Kraus had just published *The Community of the Spirit* (Eerdmans, 1974) which emphasized that salvation is not just persons being reconciled to God but also involves the formation of an apostolic community with a mandate to witness to the world that Jesus is Lord.

During the Kraus's visit, MCC and Mennonite Mission personnel met in Saigon for a weekend conference December 13 to 15. As usual, our gatherings included lots of singing and recreation. On Saturday we met at a Catholic retreat center by the Saigon River where Kraus shared the essence of his book.

We arranged for prominent Buddhists to meet with us Saturday evening to discuss the theme of "peace and reconciliation." The Venerable Thich Quang Do, Secretary General of the *Viện Hóa Đạo* (Institute for the Dissemination of the Dharma) and advocate for peace between the two sides in Vietnam, had been active in the 1963 protest movement. He emphasized the foundational need to "think peace." Positive thoughts for peace would find expression in positive actions. Thich Giam Duc emphasized the need to recognize the aspirations of the people for peace and work together with them toward that objective.

We were thankful that these men were willing to meet with us. This was our first experience of interacting with Buddhist leaders who advocated peaceful accommodation between the warring factions in Vietnam. We were reminded that we, as foreigners, had a unique role in Vietnam.

(After the revolution Thich Quang Do refused to become part of the government-sponsored Buddhist association and continued to give leadership to the United Buddhist Church well into the twenty-first century—arrested frequently and isolated by the government.)

The following week, Kraus taught a class at the Gia Dinh congregation on evangelism. Even though Christmas time was the busiest time of the year at the Gia Dinh center and church, support was good. Forty-five persons attended at least one session of classes and fourteen were there for all five sessions. He emphasized that the Christian community—the church—is central to the gospel and the preaching of the gospel. The gospel is the announcement of Good News which includes not only Christ's ministry and passion but also Pentecost which saw the formation of the community of the Spirit that is governed by love.

In a December newsletter to friends, Mary and I were "praising God . . . for signs of new life and interest in the gospel, both in Can Tho and at the Saigon Center." At each place able and committed young people were leading others to faith in Christ. More soberly, we also wrote: "Pray for peace here. It is almost two years since the cease-fire. Since January 27, 1973, around 300,000 have been killed, injured or missing."

Christmas was a memorable time at the Gia Dinh center. The congregation planned several programs using the theme, "God becoming Man." Mary directed the youth choir and led the combined primary, intermediate and youth choirs—eighty strong—in the closing songs. We were thrilled to see the enthusiasm expressed and thanked the Lord "for the privilege of seeing his Spirit working."

Dang Thi Hien went with us to the Christmas Eve service at the Gia Dinh church. A year earlier she was handcuffed to a hospital bed, with legs paralyzed due to beatings and other torture in prison, accused by the security police of having association with the Provisional Revolutionary Government, something which was permitted by the January 27, 1973 Paris Agreements—but not tolerated by the Saigon government. She had regained the use of her legs through therapy at the Quaker center in Quang Ngai and returned to her Saigon home. Now she was concerned that security police might again be following her and asked to stay with us for a few days. As the youth presented the Christmas story through skits, she was struck by the hostility of King Herod toward the coming of another king. Walking home together in the silent night, Hien observed that our world was not much different from the world the Christ-child entered.

THE REVOLUTION SUCCEEDS

Chapter 36

After the Christmas celebration at the Gia Dinh church, our family went to Can Tho for several days, welcoming 1975 with Duane and Pat Bishop and the Beidler family. Both Duane and Luke were teaching English eight hours weekly at Can Tho University. Luke was also teaching English in a Catholic seminary in Vinh Long, some thirty kilometers north of Can Tho.

Duane was also enjoying the challenge of teaching English language Bible stories in their home on Sunday mornings and Thursday evenings. Though many students were more motivated to learn English than to understand the way of Jesus, Duane was encouraged by his students' growing knowledge of Jesus the Christ. He was also learning more about the perspectives of his students. Following his Bible class on the first Sunday of the year, he wrote:

> Today one of my friends said, "There are many religions because there are many peoples. If a person in the West does something good we call him a Christian. If a person in Vietnam does something good, we call him a Buddhist. All religions have the same purpose—to teach people the right way to live." That's the framework in which he and many other students come to the Bible. So I pray that God will free him and others from this bond and allow them to see the uniqueness of Christ.

Church leaders meet with Pastor Quang: Nhung, Nguyet, Hoang, Trung, Khai, Lam, Tam and Hoa.

486

That Sunday the Gia Dinh Mennonite Church had its annual congregational meeting. With five persons having been baptized the previous year, the official membership of the congregation was now 143. Twelve persons were enrolled in a catechism class. Eighty students were enrolled in six Sunday school classes with an average attendance of sixty. Phan Van Khai, a soft-spoken man in his thirties who continued to successfully evade the draft, was Sunday school superintendent. Twenty-five women were involved in the weekly ladies' fellowship led by Mrs. Nguyen Thi Hoang (Mrs. Ty). Their activities included reading through the Bible, studying the lives of Bible women (which Mary taught), sewing for needy people, and visitation. Their witness group had visited more than one hundred homes the previous year and two persons had confessed faith in Jesus. Mr. Vo Van Hoa, one of the deacons, chaired the mutual aid committee that assisted members at times of death or other family crises.

Nguyen Dinh Tin, an MCC staff employee, was the newly-chosen leader of the youth group with Mr. Do Van Thuong, a public school teacher, serving as advisor. An average of twenty-five youth participated in their activities. On occasion, they planned activities with the sixty community young people who were studying trades through the Family Child Assistance program. Over four hundred students were enrolled in the Rang Dong elementary school, some studying in the morning, the others in the afternoon. Two hundred of these students received free tuition through the MCC Educational Assistance Program. The community center, directed by Pastor Quang with the support of his wife, employed thirty-three staff members, most of them teachers in the school.

An event in early 1975 proved to be an omen of things to come; the People's Army of Vietnam on January 6 seized the capital of Phuoc Long province 120 kilometers north of Saigon after a series of attacks over three weeks, inflicting high casualties to the ARVN forces.

This was hardly a surprise to American authorities in Washington. Nine months earlier, a secret joint report by several U.S. intelligence agencies noted that, while both sides in the conflict had "improved their military capabilities" after the Paris Accords of January 1973, in the event of a country-wide offensive by the communist forces, there was "doubt" that the ARVN forces would be able to stop the communist offense without the US providing "large-scale logistical assistance." It suggested that the communist forces might be easily able to seize areas of the northern and mountainous areas of South Vietnam. If this were to happen, the report predicted that "the adverse psychological impact might be more significant than the actual impact on the military balance. As a result, a situation could develop in which the GVN would be unable to regain the initiative without the reintroduction of US combat air and naval support."

The capture of Phuoc Long enabled the Viet Cong forces to anchor their supply line into the heart of South Vietnam through the so-called "Ho Chi Minh Trail" along the Lao border. President Thieu's response was to call for three days of national mourning for the victims of these battles. A prayer service was held at the International Protestant Church Thursday afternoon, January 9. In a letter home, Stauffer noted how this defeat affected the morale of the ARVN forces. "I'm afraid President Ford is going to get sucked into this thing again," he wrote. "And, yet, he can hardly act without the consent of Congress." In reality the US Congress was no longer generous in providing additional funds and war materiel.

An Alliance missionary asked MCC to provide relief supplies for refugees who had fled Phuoc Long, adding to the 1.4 million persons who fled their homes in the two years following the January 1973 Peace Accords. But MCC was no longer warehousing large amounts of material aid supplies. At a meeting of voluntary agency representatives, Phan Quang Dan, Vice Premier and Minister of Social Welfare, predicted that the level of fighting would increase and the government would lose control of more villages and districts.

While Thieu's government hoped that the U.S. would still come to the rescue, Hanoi's leaders interpreted Saigon's lack of a military response as their opportunity to go on the offensive. Gen. Van Tien Dung, commander-in-chief of the People's Army of Vietnam, secretly went south to direct communist forces.

In mid-February, I wrote to the Akron MCC office that the "loss of Phuoc Long is at least a short-range psychological defeat for the Republic of Vietnam. The people in many parts of the country are saying, 'If the other side can capture Phuoc Long, the government cannot protect us either.' I would not rule out the possibility that the government was prepared to sacrifice Phuoc Long in order to call attention to the 'desperate situation' so that they might receive additional military aid."

We did not know what the U.S. response might have been had Nixon still been in the White House. President Ford requested Congress for $522 million additional military aid in late January, but this was not granted. Henry Kissinger, whom Ford retained as Secretary of State, had privately indicated three years earlier that "if we can live with a communist government in China, we ought to be able to accept it in Indochina."

There was also heavy military action in Quang Ngai province. In January, Earl Martin reported that the government forces suffered heavy casualties attempting unsuccessfully to push the Viet Cong forces back, bringing the morale of the ARVN troops to a new low. A local school teacher told Earl and Pat, "We really don't like the communists, but we must admit they have a righteous cause, and that's something we just do not have."

Earl said that the morale of most people supporting the Saigon government "is pretty pessimistic." A recent USAID survey indicated that more than ten thousand persons in the Quang Ngai area were not getting more than one rice meal per day. People wanted to go back to their land to produce rice, even though those who tried to go back were accused by the government as being Viet Cong supporters.

There was significant military activity elsewhere. Can, the son of the caretaker at the Saigon student center, was listed as missing after his outpost at Ca Mau was overrun. And Thong, an older brother of the MCC staff member Nguyen Dinh Tin, was critically injured by a mine explosion and lay unconscious in the huge armed forces military hospital at Go Vap, just a few kilometers from the Mennonite community center. The oldest son of seventy-year-old Mr. Muong, Thong was part of a squad sent on a road-clearing operation. The "other side" had built earthen mounds across the road to cut off traffic. After removing the obstruction, as they were leaving, Thong saw a small wire sticking from the ground and stooped to pick it up. This triggered a mine explosion which threw him to the ground. Though not struck by flying shrapnel, the blast concussion caused internal injuries and paralyzed him from the waist down. In early February, another youth from the church, Tam, son of deacon Vo Van Hoa, was injured and lay in the same military hospital.

Khuc Kim Ben's brother was killed in December. Ms. Ben, a well-educated young woman from the Evangelical Church who participated in the life of the Mennonite congregation, told

Mary that her brother and four cousins—all from Christian families—were killed in the war within ten months' time. Some of their non-Christian relatives heartlessly attributed their deaths to the families' forsaking the cult of the ancestors when they embraced the Christian faith.

Vietnam hosted a ten-day International Conference on Children and National Development in January at the new Polytechnic College in Thu Duc—near Saigon. Sponsored by several government ministries, it involved more than 1,200 participants, including 300 persons who came from thirty countries. Dr. Phan Quang Dan, the Minister of Social Welfare, gave the keynote address. A staff member of the Ministry invited me to be on the child welfare subcommittee. Other committees focused on juvenile delinquency, child nutrition, pediatrics, and formal and non-formal education. The Vietnamese press was generally critical of the conference, arguing that organizing funds could have been used in better ways. Jean Hershey and I attended the conference—along with a caseworker from the Gia Dinh community center.

The conference reported that more than one million Vietnamese children were orphans—defined as children under the age of fifteen who had lost one or both parents. Nearly half of South Vietnam's twenty million people were under the age of fifteen. Vietnamese officials estimated that half of the country's population had been refugees in the previous decade—many of them displaced two or three times.

Jean heard a few people note that the war was the real problem, but it was generally accepted that there was no end to this war. In one discussion group, a Vietnamese social worker—apparently Prof. Ms. Nguyen Thi Oanh—proposed that Vietnam no longer accept foreign aid. This proposal did not appear in the final resolutions! Jean and I agreed that the objective of the conference was to plead with other countries and agencies for assistance so the government could get on with the war!

International voluntary agencies were invited to prepare displays. Rather than describe the projects in which we were involved, MCC decided to sermonize a bit by entering a large poster with verse that Jim Klassen had written:

"We are concerned about…
The children of Vietnam / All children of Vietnam / Not just of the rich
Not just of the poor / Not just of one side / Not just of the other."

On the other side of the poster we wrote the text of a recent Vietnamese song where a child is asked who she loves. The child expresses love for parents, the people and the country. Lastly the child is asked what she likes and answers, "I would like PEACE!" Several people expressed appreciation for this poster.

In late January, I met with the Executive Committee of the Evangelical Church to give our rationale for a new relationship in the Nha Trang and Pleiku medical programs. I noted that the medical situation and needs in Nha Trang had changed since 1960 with new medical facilities in the area. I emphasized MCC's difficulty in recruiting medical personnel which raised questions about whether MCC should be administering any medical programs. I also said that MCC had redefined its primary task to work with ministries directly contributing to reconciliation and peace. I suggested it was now time for the Church to assume full responsibility for the medical programs. MCC would continue to provide personnel and funds within MCC's guidelines and resources, but would no longer need to be represented on the local hospital boards. I also encouraged the Church to seek resources from other organizations.

President Mieng expressed thanks for MCC's cooperation the previous fifteen years. He said that "during this time of economic crisis and military demands on the people, the Church still requests that MCC continue to assist with medical personnel and finances." Others expressed appreciation for the kind of service MCC gave, praise for the nursing school, and hope that these programs would continue. I indicated support for training hospital personnel.

Writing to Akron, I said that "the stage has been set now for working out some new understanding which we might find more appropriate for today. There are some Vietnam MCCers inclined to terminate all relationships with the Evangelical Church, but I cannot accept this. Hopefully we can be a more positive influence if we do not need to be directly involved in the hassles of administrative matters."

John Willms was feeling at home in Nha Trang. He and Frances had no idea that Nha Trang would be so lovely. Ophthalmologist Randall Clark, on a short-term assignment, was providing training in eye surgery to Dr. Willms, and the hospital board even invited Dr. Clark to consider staying. Dr. Quang Hanh, the medical director, was authorized by the board to develop a maternity program and to recruit a trained and experienced midwife to serve as the head ward nurse.

Quang, the pastor of the Gia Dinh Mennonite church, was making plans to attend the annual March meeting of Eastern Mennonite Board of Missions and Charities. On the first Sunday of February he preached on the need for revival using the text in II Chronicles 7:14: "If my people who are called by my name humble themselves, and pray and seek my face, and turn from their wicked ways, then I will hear from heaven." Two days later Quang's oldest daughter, Hang, went with Mary to visit Quang's parents, Pastor and Mrs. Tran Xuan Hi, who were in declining health. Mrs. Hi described how she had taken a bus down to Ca Mau, at the southern-most tip of South Vietnam, to visit her youngest son, Phuoc, who was wounded more than a month earlier. She wanted to bring him home, but had to wait until his leg could be placed in a cast. It had been broken by shrapnel. She described how the military hospital there specialized in amputations—limbs were left lying around and dogs carried them away. Food was provided but her son was unable to walk to get it. He would give a food ticket to a child to bring the food; the people who prepared the tray ate some of the food and the child ate the rest. Phuoc had no one to bring him water. Seeing all the suffering in the hospital, Mrs. Hi said she was unable to eat.

Writing home about this, Mary said that often Christians in Vietnam, just like in the States, have simple answers to everything. "I thought perhaps Quang's parents would say they have no worries or fears and this was the will of God," she wrote. "But they said they are burdened and worried. They are hurting very much." They did, however, find comfort and strength in their faith in the Lord. Mary also wondered what dreams and hopes fifteen-year-old Hang had for the future: "Get married and have her husband killed, or does she dream of going to another country to live?"

The lunar New Year fell on Tuesday, February 11. Normally civil servants had three days of vacation, but this year the government decreed that workers return to work on the second day since soldiers on the battlefields were not able to have much of a holiday.

On February 17, I flew from Saigon to Bangkok en route to Bangladesh to attend a gathering of Asia MCC representatives. I had been reluctant to take the time off but found the interaction with other MCC Asia representatives invigorating. I returned to Saigon nine days later.

Aware in mid-January that the White House was preparing to make a request to the Congress for substantially increased military aid to South Vietnam, Jim Klassen sent a letter to President Ford. "If you are truly interested in the welfare of the people of Vietnam and in the restoration of peace in Vietnam," Jim wrote, more weapons were not the answer. If both sides continued to "fight to the finish," he observed, there was little chance for the current Saigon government to survive. Yet the United States could still play a significant role in urging the Saigon government to broker a political settlement.

In mid-February, Earl wrote to Senator Mike Mansfield, the Senate Majority Leader, who had long opposed the American war policies, describing the plight of the farmers who in contravention to the Paris agreements were not being allowed free movement back to their lands. "We appeal to you," Earl wrote, "in the name of the refugees of Viet Nam, in the name of peace for this country, in the name of human decency, stop the flow of swords into this land."

In early February, Earl had sent me in draft form "An Appeal for Peace to the Congress of the United States." The one-page statement briefly recited the ongoing warfare since the peace agreement had been signed two years earlier and insisted that increased American military aid would lead to "a new round of military escalation [that would] only increase the suffering of the Vietnamese people and preclude any chance for a negotiated political settlement." It called on Congress "to pursue more positive and constructive alternatives" which included calling for a reconvening of the parties involved in the Paris agreement to reduce the military aid to Vietnam's warring parties, and for the United States to actively encourage all parties in South Vietnam "to settle their differences politically." It enjoined the United States "to bind the wounds of war" in Vietnam, Cambodia and Laos.

I showed this Appeal to Ernest (Ernie) Campbell, who had followed Getz as the executive director of Vietnam Christian Service. He said he would be willing—with brief editing—to sign the statement. I received permission from the chairman of the Council of Voluntary Agencies (CVA), Gene Tunnell of Baptist Social Services, to present the appeal at the scheduled February 4 Council meeting.

I distributed the statement at the meeting, stating that our primary concern was not whether the U.S. Congress grants more military aid, but whether this was the most effective way to attain the common objective of peace. I asked agency representatives whether they would support sending a letter like this to Congress or whether the Council might take other steps to urge the warring parties in Vietnam to find a political resolution to their struggle.

VNCS Director Ernie Campbell suggested that the Council should do something, and this statement might be good. Both Gene Tunnel and Gene Evans of CAMA expressed some interest in a statement that might be addressed to all parties providing military supplies to the belligerents. Tunnel suggested that the Republic of Vietnam should not object to a statement sent to all parties. CAMA was the new C&MA social service organization.

Representatives of several agencies said they could not support any statements at all. Comments made were: "Our agency is non-religious and apolitical;" "We cannot speak for our agency; we just carry out their policy which is not made in Vietnam;" "Our supporting constituency would not support this;" "Our agency would need to withdraw from CVA if CVA supported such a statement." One representative made a motion that it was "inappropriate" to discuss such a matter in the Council. After a few more pleas for consideration, a vote on the motion was supported by half of the members present. After the meeting adjourned several persons expressed dismay that the Council held a position that it was "inappropriate" to show concern about peace.

There was no further action by the Council. The "Appeal for Peace" statement was, however, signed by thirty persons—fourteen MCC personnel, seven Mennonite missionaries, two VNCS workers, and six from the American Friends Service Committee. It was presented to several members of a visiting American congressional delegation and sent to Delton Franz of the MCC Washington office to distribute to congressional persons. Franz indicated that it would be sent to targeted congressional persons.

At the request of President Ford, a bipartisan congressional delegation traveled to Vietnam in late February. Gene Stoltzfus, who had resigned from IVS a few years earlier, accompanied one of the representatives to assist in scheduling meetings with opposition persons. Paul Longacre also asked Earl to help arrange contacts. However, with the delegation visit managed by U.S. Embassy staff, few members had any significant contact with persons other than pro-government persons. When the delegation met with the President in early March, most urged limited financial assistance to the Saigon government. Representative Paul "Pete" McClosky, however, clearly stated: "The North Vietnamese are going to win."

The group of believers meeting at the Saigon student center was "growing in numbers and maturity." Five new believers were baptized at the Sunday morning worship service on February 9: two young women—Ly and Quyen—and three young men—Cam, Hoang, and Thong. One was twenty-seven years old. They each gave verbal expressions of their faith in Jesus Christ and how their lives were transformed. More than twenty persons from the worship group celebrated a New Year's dinner up on the roof patio the day before. The group studied a new Bible correspondence course Don Sensenig prepared on the life and times of Jesus from the Gospel of Luke.

James Stauffer had gone with Pastor Quang to Can Tho a few weeks earlier to conclude the purchase of the property used as a hostel for male university students. Working with Christian Youth for Social Service, the Mennonite Church agreed to purchase the property for five million piasters ($8,300) rather than continue renting it for several years. (In light of the political transitions which occurred a few months later, this purchase could be likened to the prophet Jeremiah's purchase of land [Jeremiah 32] shortly before the people's exile to Babylon.)

Robert Miller and Joyce Bratton, his administrative assistant, came to Vietnam for a short administrative visit on March 5. All MCCers were invited to Saigon for a conference with Miller on Friday and Saturday, March 7 and 8. Yoshihiro Ichikawa and Max Ediger had just returned from home leaves—Max to resume working at programs from the Saigon office alongside James Klassen. During Miller's visit, the Hieberts returned from Manila where Murray had gone for medical treatments. The entire Pleiku team came down: Jean with her daughter Vui, Wally and Claire Ewert with their son Matthew, and Devadoss (Doss) and Doris Maddimadugu with Esther. Wally was doing agricultural work with Kpa Dai, an ethnic minority man who had earned an agricultural degree from the University of Hawaii. Doss was appreciated as a lab technician in the clinic and hospital. Earl and Pat with their two children were down from Quang Ngai. The Willms family and Ann Noel Ewert came from Nha Trang. Ann enjoyed interacting with the Willms family; she now even liked working with the hospital administrator.

Miller met with Evangelical Church president Pastor Mieng and the directors of both the Nha Trang and Pleiku medical programs. He noted that under our proposal, "MCC would no longer be represented on the local hospital boards but would relate to the programs through an Evangelical Church contact at the Saigon level. We would continue to provide personnel and funds for the hospital programs on a reduced basis but would encourage the church to also find other sources of support." Miller said that Pastor Mieng "recognized the need to review our relationships from time to time . . . , seemed open to the changes we were proposing, [and] gave MCC a warm welcome to continue involvement in the medical work and to help in other Evangelical Church efforts."

Miller spent considerable time with MCC personnel "discussing assumptions, objectives and plans regarding MCC work in Vietnam." It was clear that much of the program initiative was now coming from MCC personnel on assignment. He wrote: "Vietnam workers want to give primary emphasis to the problem of achieving peace through reconciliation and healing. They recently prepared and signed a letter to the Congress of the United States appealing for peace. Assistance to political prisoners and their families will continue. A small agricultural program is developing at Pleiku. . . . Plans call for MCC to make a tractor available to a Buddhist service organization in Quang Ngai to be used in clearing fields of unexploded grenades. We are also considering the possibility of assigning personnel to Quang Nam Province just south of Danang where the needs are great."

Miller and Bratton also met with the Church Administrative Committee of the Mennonite church. Committee members expressed support for my continuing role to "provide a tie between MCC and Mennonite church work." Max would serve as assistant director managing the Saigon office until MCC recruited a new assistant. This would allow me to give more time to training programs in the Mennonite church. Before leaving, Miller and Bratton met with Ernest Campbell and concluded that "MCC-VNCS relationships appear to be in good shape."

The Nha Trang personnel returned to their work after the Saigon conference, and the Earl and Pat Martin returned to Quang Ngai March 11. Jean was planning to return to Pleiku on March 11, but delayed her leaving because she had sprained her foot. The Maddimadugus and the Ewerts were taking a few days of vacation.

After small attacks in early March, on March 10 the People's Army of Vietnam (PAVN) launched a major assault on the central highlands town of Ban Me Thuot. By March 13, the entire province was in their hands. Now Pleiku, nearly 200 kms north of Ban Me Thuot, the headquarters of the ARVN Military Region II (II Corps), came under rocket attacks.

Knowing Pleiku was not defensible, President Thieu ordered all ARVN forces to withdraw from the central highlands on March 14 and transferred the regional military headquarters from Pleiku to Nha Trang. Officers and civilians with resources rushed out of town. As the ARVN soldiers, their families and many civilians fled toward the coast, they were ambushed by the PAVN forces, causing enormous casualties. Some of the Tin Lanh clinic staff barely escaped with their lives. The ethnic minority people in the city, however, returned to their villages outside Pleiku.

Several missionary families were caught in Ban Me Thuot, raising concerns that they might suffer the same fate as six missionary personnel who were killed there during the Tet offensive more than seven years earlier. Eventually it was confirmed that they were captured, along with a USAID man and a few other foreigners. This included Alliance missionaries Norman and Joan Johnson, Dick and Lillian Phillips, Betty Mitchell—whose husband Archie had been captured along with Daniel Gerber in 1962—and SIL linguists John and Carolyn Miller and daughter

LuAnne. Most of us knew the Millers well since they had lived near the Evangelical clinic and hospital in Nha Trang. (Carolyn tells their story in *Captured* [Chappaqua, NY: Christian Herald Books, 1977].)

Earl sent a letter to Robert Miller on March 17 citing examples of growing PRG activity in Quang Ngai province. Many people were worried. The wealthy were leaving town. Friends dropped by their house, surprised to see that their family was still there. "So after a while one wonders if one is being heroic, committed, stubborn, or stupid," Earl wrote. "Pat commented this afternoon that it's kind of like the Second Coming. It could be today or it could be a long time from now, but in the meantime you have to go on living."

After discussing various evacuation options, Earl wrote: "But for now, we are here. . . . We hesitate to write a letter like this lest it appear we are pushing panic buttons. Be assured that we are sleeping well and no one has bitten off his fingernails. We just thought we'd like to let you in on the mood here in the revolutionary heart of Viet Nam!"

The next morning, in pen, Earl scribbled: "For the record, Bob. If this morning's news reports are true that Saigon is turning Pleiku and Kontum over to the other side without a fight, and if that should happen in Quang Ngai, we would welcome the chance to stay."

We in Saigon had heard that when the ARVN forces had evacuated the highland, a doctor from the US and one from New Zealand had stayed at Minh Quy Hospital in Kontum, fifty kilometers north of Pleiku. I wrote home: "I know some of the MCCers are prepared to stay if the areas they are working in are in danger of being taken over by the other side—if there is some indication that they might be able to continue to help the people. But we are not making any plans to send people back to Pleiku!"

I also wrote to Miller the same day: "We need to assume that it will be several weeks until our personnel return [to Pleiku], and they might not return at all. . . . You should also give some consideration to long-range planning if the people cannot go back. Reassignment to some other area in Vietnam, reassignment to some other country, or early termination might be considered."

Writing to the Mission Board secretary, I suggested the war would continue for a long time. "If the Saigon government changes its policies, likely with another leader, there might be a political settlement reached," I wrote. "Many people who do not want to live with the communists are reaching the conclusion that some accommodation must be made with them. We have spoken with some people who wonder why the United States is deserting them. Others are asking why the United States is still giving military assistance to continuing the war."

On March 19, Earl wrote to his parents: "Just a note to say that we probably will be leaving Q. Ngai in the next day or two. There's no imminent threat on Q. Ngai but many of our Vietnamese friends (and the American official people) think it would be wise to leave now when we can make a relaxed exit. Hopefully, we'll be gone for only a short time and can come back again."

Over the next few days, Pat and Earl discussed the options—all leave, all stay, or Pat and the children leave while Earl stays? On Thursday, March 20, Robert Miller learned from the American Friends office in Philadelphia that the Quaker prosthetic team in Quang Ngai was planning to evacuate to Saigon. Somehow they got word that, although the PRG appreciated their work, they would be a liability during a time of transition.

In light of the fast-moving changes in the military landscape, it seemed somewhat incredible to Miller that, at the recent MCC workers' conference, "the question of security and what workers should do or should not do in the event of takeover by the other side" had not even been discussed. "We were so busy talking about assumptions, objectives and plans for MCC work, we just did not get to it," Miller observed. However, before Miller left Saigon he had asked me to discuss with MCC persons what they would plan "in case of takeover by the other side."

What Akron did not know and what we in Saigon did not know—on Thursday morning, Pat and the two children had already left Quang Ngai on a C-47 bound for Da Nang, the last Air America evacuation plane from Quang Ngai. We later learned from Pat that both Earl and Pat had planned to leave Quang Ngai by road the previous day, but National Road #1 was closed.

In response to Akron's telegraphed request for information, I wrote: "We do not know what is happening. We suspect that you know more than we do. We hear many rumors." Thinking that the Quaker team was still in Quang Ngai, I wrote: "I suspect that Earl and Pat may have decided to stay in Quang Ngai." Before sending the letter the next morning, I penned: "Pat and the children with all the Quakers came to Saigon last night. Earl may follow later. Hiro flies to Danang today. Hopes to eventually join Earl."

On Friday morning, March 21, after communication with the Philadelphia AFSC office, Joyce Bratton sent a memo to Miller: "Earl has chosen to stay in Quang Ngai. The situation is bloodless, very, very, little violence. ARVN soldiers are simply walking away. The situation is not violent. AFSC is cabling [their personnel] today it is acceptable that the six of them return to Quang Ngai. . . . AFSC finds compelling reasons for all of them to go back."

I informed Miller that Earl, Pat, Yoshihiro (Hiro), Max and I discussed Hiro's assignment a few days after Joyce and he left Vietnam. There was agreement that he would go to Quang Ngai rather than returning to Tam Ky where he had earlier worked with VNCS. We had also discussed our response should it appear that the PRG would attempt to take over the area. I wrote: "Everyone indicated some interest, and there was a common understanding that we would support anyone who felt that he should stay."

I told Miller that Hiro and I talked about the wisdom of his going to Quang Ngai at a time when others were leaving; he had no hesitation about going. I noted that Earl sent five telegrams to our Saigon office Friday through Sunday. He said he was prepared to leave if there seemed to be the prospect of heavy fighting. Earl also described the mood of the people—"fearful on Thursday, more relaxed on Friday, again afraid on Saturday."

On Tuesday, March 25, before I knew what was happening in Quang Ngai, I wrote to Earl—a letter he never received. "I appreciate your willingness to stay at a time when the U.S. guys say go," I wrote. "I do not know what decisions you have made now. It seems clear to me that if the PRG takes Quang Ngai, the government will make an effort to take it back, and this means heavy fighting." How wrong I was!

That morning I sent a letter to Akron and Salunga after learning that Saigon military command lost contact with their Quang Ngai military garrison. "We do not wish to join the rest of the population in panic," I wrote. "As far as we know, Earl and Yoshihiro are still in Quang Ngai. They felt that their staying could help reassure the people who stayed."

Earl had long suspected that Chi Mai—a staff member of the Quaker center, a double amputee who lost her both legs to a mine explosion—might be able to assist him in contacting some PRG official. On Friday evening—the day after Pat left town—Earl spoke to Mai and was immediately introduced to another person who would assist him. On Saturday afternoon Earl was surprised when Yoshihiro Ichikawa walked into the house unannounced. After flying to Da Nang and finding no more flights out, he had taken a public bus to Quang Ngai, likely the last bus into town.

On Sunday, March 23, Earl followed—at a distance—the guide into the countryside and met a PRG official who welcomed him. Though invited to stay in camp that evening, Earl thought it best to return to Quang Ngai. On his return, however, he was detained by ARVN soldiers and taken the next morning to the government interrogation center in Quang Ngai. Later that day the soldiers deserted their posts, melting away from Quang Ngai, enabling Earl to walk back home. At 2:15 a.m. Tuesday morning, March 25, the PRG military forces entered Quang Ngai encountering no opposition.

In this fast-changing scene most of the Alliance missionaries had already left Da Nang, Tuy Hoa, Nha Trang and Da Lat. Frances Willms and the boys were reserving a flight from Nha Trang to Saigon. Max had already left for Nha Trang for further discussions with John and the Hieberts.

On March 25 I informed the EMBMC and MCC offices that "the most optimistic voices at the U.S. Embassy predict the Republic of Vietnam will not last more than one year. Some suggest that it will be only a matter of weeks. . . . There does not seem to be any immediate threat on Saigon. . . . I do not think that we missionaries will be leaving Saigon soon. Pressure seems to have eased in the Delta, and the Beidlers and Bishops traveled by road back to Can Tho yesterday." I noted that the Stauffer and Beidler families were due for home leave within a few months; Luke and Dorothy had already extended their term by one year. Mark and Ruth Ann Mininger already had tickets to depart April 3. Duane and Pat Bishop and Mary and I would be the only ones left with the Mennonite Mission until Don and Doris Sensenig returned in the summer.

Over the next few days, I frequently contacted the Japanese Embassy to learn any news about Yoshihiro and Earl. The Embassy picked up a broadcast reporting that liberation forces "safely protected from fierce fighting" around ten foreigners in Quang Ngai, including one American and several Japanese. On March 27, I also sent a letter of inquiry to Major Phuong Nam, PRG military representative of the International Commission of Control and Supervision at the Tan Son Nhat airport. I did not contact the U.S. Embassy; had I contacted Embassy personnel, they likely would have probed me about whether the men had stayed voluntarily. (In early April Ambassador Martin sent a message to the U.S. State Department regarding a few Americans who were in areas controlled by the People's Army. Referring to Earl, the message said that he "could have decided to remain" in Quang Ngai, and suggested consultation with families and agencies before taking any action.)

The Beidler and Bishop families had come to Saigon for a missionary retreat the weekend of March 21 to 23 with our family and the Stauffers. We had planned to discuss the topic of small-group evangelism, led by Duane and Pat. There were some suggestions that perhaps the crisis engulfing the entire country called for another focus but in the end we stayed with the planned theme. In retrospect it seemed that we might have been fiddling while Rome was burning!

On Monday, March 24, Deputy Prime Minister Doctor Phan Quang Dan met with representatives of voluntary agencies, reporting that there were 600,000 new refugees in Military Region I around Da Nang and 200,000 new refugees in Region II, now headquartered in Nha Trang. Dr. Dan hoped that agencies might organize medical teams to help these people.

The *New York Times* of Monday, March 24, carried an article stating that the Provisional Revolutionary Government was requesting food assistance for the many people who had fled their homes. With the MCC Akron administrators sensing an opportunity to engage "the other side," on Wednesday Robert Miller cabled Mr. Nguyen Van Tien, the PRG liaison in Hanoi, offering to help. Miller had written to Mr. Tien on March 18, proposing an MCC delegation spring visit to Hanoi and to "the Provisional Revolutionary Government area of South Vietnam."

On April 1, the PRG responded to Miller's cable, requesting condensed milk, canned pork and sodium glutamate.

With the communist forces now controlling Quang Ngai province Tuesday, March 25, South Vietnam was effectively cut in two with the larger population areas of Da Nang and Hue now isolated from the south. After growing military pressure against Hue, the government later that day ordered the evacuation of ARVN forces from the imperial city to the sea. Many civilians joined other military personnel and their families fleeing eighty kilometers south to Da Nang, the largest city in central Vietnam. A planned strong military defense of the city never happened because pandemonium broke out in the city. Tens of thousands of civilians and military personnel converged on the airport and the seaport attempting to flee by plane or boat. Many died. By Easter Sunday, March 30, Da Nang was under the control of the People's Army of Vietnam.

While we were now frequently phoning the Akron office, we still wrote letters, usually delivered within three days—mail service was remarkably good. This was a chaotic time. On March 27, Miller expressed concern that I "might not be aware of the rapidly deteriorating security situation!" It was a valid concern. On March 29, however, I wrote: "Chaos rules much of Vietnam now. The military thrust of the other side has penetrated more quickly and successfully than anyone could have anticipated even a few days ago." I noted that the "near-anarchy" of the ARVN soldiers was more dangerous than the military threat from the People's Army.

In a letter to me on March 31, Miller said Akron would assist Nguyen Van Ninh if he wanted to leave Vietnam with his family. We were aware that he would choose to leave if it appeared that the PRG was coming to power. Since he had worked with MCC for nearly twenty years, Akron administrators believed they had some responsibility to assist him.

Months earlier, Pastor and Mrs. Quang had been invited to attend the annual meeting of the Eastern Mennonite Board of Missions meeting in March. They both requested passports, even though the Ministry of Interior rarely allowed both husband and wife to leave the country. Quang did not want to go if his wife was not permitted to accompany him, but we encouraged him to go anyhow. The day after securing his documents, Quang left Vietnam on March 13, the day the PAVN succeeded in taking Ban Me Thuot. He flew first to Taiwan where the Mennonite church was concluding its twentieth anniversary celebration. A few days later he flew on to the United States, arriving in Philadelphia on Tuesday, March 18, where he was met by Don Sensenig and Paul and Esther Bucher. Don said Quang was "in very good spirits." His U.S. visa allowed him to stay until April 20 but he talked of leaving earlier.

On Thursday morning, Don took Quang to visit my parents, then went to the Weaverland Mennonite Church in eastern Lancaster County to attend the biannual meeting of the Lancaster Mennonite Conference. The Mission Board meetings followed—Friday through Sunday. At the Friday business session, Quang presented a short but comprehensive report of the work of the Mennonite church in Vietnam, articulating its organization, priorities and opportunities. He also gave two addresses on Saturday and Sunday—"We love because [God] loved us first" and "Then we should love one another."

"Pastor Quang won our hearts" is the way one board member described his presentations. The *Missionary Messenger* editor, Nathan Hege, wrote:

> Seldom have we met anyone who has come through so positively as a man burdened for his people, with little comment on the political situation, although he has known war for 30 years of his life. . . . Repeatedly the pastor lost his voice, choked with emotion, when he spoke of the great spiritual needs of his people and his concern for children and young people who may not be well enough grounded in the faith in the event of a communist takeover in Vietnam. . . At one point Pastor Quang said that he would not want to make it a request, but he hoped that if possible, at least one missionary would be willing to stay on in Vietnam, regardless of the outcome of the war, to symbolize that we stand together in times of crisis. However, he did make one strong request—that the church in America spend a day in prayer for the people of Vietnam.

The editor wrote that Quang believed that his trip at this time "was the planning of God. He said he no longer feels alone after meeting a church in America who cares."

Passion Week followed the EMBMC annual meeting. In a phone call to Akron on March 24, I said that Pastor Quang's family was well. "There is some shakiness in the city. . . . The night guards are more trigger-happy than usual. . . , but things are fairly calm," I reported. "The Mennonite church is preparing for their Good Friday service and Easter Sunday service."

I had promised Pastor Quang that I would preach at the church on Good Friday and on Easter Sunday, March 30. This was an intense time. Frances Willms and their two sons flew from Nha Trang to Saigon on Good Friday. On Saturday we received a mailgram from Miller, "Appears Situation Deteriorating Rapidly," suggesting that we arrange for most MCC personnel to travel to Bangkok and wait there.

More than two hundred persons packed into the Gia Dinh Mennonite church meeting house that was dedicated only two years earlier. It was an emotional but also an inspiring Easter worship service. It was also special for me, knowing that twelve hours later, Pastor Quang would be preaching the Easter sermon in my home congregation in New Holland.

By now reports were coming in about the fate of the people in Ban Me Thuot and elsewhere. On Easter Sunday, Mrs. Quang learned—confirmed four weeks later—that Quang's sister, her husband and children were massacred in Ban Me Thuot. And hearing the frantic attempts of many people to leave Da Nang with tragic results, we began to wonder what it might be like if and when a military showdown came to Saigon.

There was also an Easter Sunday morning service at the Saigon student center where the youth choir from the Gia Dinh congregation sang. Around ninety persons were present when three young women were baptized: Nguyet, Lan, and Luong.

The wife of Phan Ba Phuoc, the first baptized believer in 1960, also stopped in at the Saigon center to visit James and Arlene. Sang and her four children just arrived from Da Lat, carrying a letter from Phuoc, who was asking Stauffers and Mary and me to each take one of their children! Although Sang did not want to give up any of her children—she was expecting their fifth child—Phuoc was afraid that they would be killed "when the other side takes over." Sang said Phuoc, who by now had been inducted into the armed forces, had to stay in Da Lat to prepare to defend it from an expected attack; he was being trained how to shoot enemy tanks!

On Easter Sunday evening, I wrote home. On the Vietnam map under glass on my desk at home I daily redrew the lines of government control as ARVN soldiers abandoned each city, province or district—Ban Me Thuot, Pleiku, Kontum, Quang Ngai, Hue, Da Nang. The PRG flag was now flying over the former US Consulate building in Da Nang where only four days previously an American spokesman said there was no immediate danger! And Nha Trang was also under pressure. Some people were already leaving the country. Akron was recommending that most MCC personnel temporarily leave the country.

If I had not been associated with the church, I would not have been too concerned about people's reactions. But we had the means to leave while others did not. "I would be very hesitant to leave unless the church supported this," I wrote. I noted that at the time of the 1968 Tet offensive, James Stauffer said that some members of the church encouraged them to go while others suggested they stay. It seemed strange for MCC personnel—particularly medical staff—to leave if they had skills and training to assist people at a time of great need.

Early that morning we had taken Mark and Ruth Ann to the airport, a departure that was planned several weeks earlier. Our children enjoyed watching the flight activity. Ten year-old Steven, who had read in the morning paper that U.S. ships with helicopters were coming toward Cambodia and Vietnam for possible evacuation of people, said: "I wish we can be here. It's so interesting here. I was born here, and this is my home!"

"It is encouraging that many are still optimistic about some kind of political settlement soon," I wrote. "I was listening to the PRG radio broadcast this evening and they were calling for the formation of a government in Saigon which is prepared to implement the Paris Accords. . . . [But] the idea of a coalition government is still a dirty thought to the rulers in Saigon. The only real alternative seems to be continued bloodshed, and the end result perhaps more undesirable."

We were not immune to the escalating panic that gripped many in the capital city that next week. On Monday morning, March 31, we discussed booking flights for some of the MCC "refugees" from central Vietnam. We did book tickets for the Beidler family to leave for furlough April 17. The Stauffer family was also planning to leave when the children's classes closed. James observed: "Some of the Christians here don't want to see us leave. We're glad that they love us and we have felt a lot of oneness with them. Please pray that this can be worked out, because we don't feel that our staying would help them that much."

In another letter to his brother, Stauffer wrote: "I'm sure you're following the news here. Please be assured at this moment that Saigon is still 'normal.' . . . Of course, we realize that panic, and all the other things that possess people here, could break loose at any moment."

A few days earlier, Max had gone to Nha Trang to attend a board meeting of the hospital. One morning he and Murray visited an old Korean military camp which was receiving large numbers of persons who had fled Ban Me Thuot. They heard horrible stories of how "hundreds and hundreds" of people died fleeing toward the coast—children separated from their parents, husbands and wives separated. Why did the people flee? They feared a battle. ARVN soldiers also forced them to leave and torched their houses! And panic precipitated increased panic.

With the arrival of rogue ARVN forces in Nha Trang, there was robbery and looting. When Murray drove into Nha Trang city one day, an ARVN soldier shot at a motorcycle driving ahead of Murray. On Sunday, March 30, it was quiet at the Tin Lanh hospital. Dr. Willms, Linda and Murray Hiebert, and Max decided to stay; they visited friends and went swimming. They would not have known of the panic had they not gone into town.

Then one of the cooks said they should leave quickly, and the American consular officials kept phoning them. Murray wanted to stay in Nha Trang; yet he was still recuperating from a January surgery and wondered whether he would survive if the incoming PRG made them march to the mountains. Although Frances and their two sons were already in Saigon, John Willms firmly believed he should stay—a position shaped by his commitment to serve in the way of Jesus. Max and others argued that it would be imprudent for the doctor to stay alone; after all, he had just arrived a few months earlier and did not speak the Vietnamese language. After exhausting marathon deliberations about what they should do, they all went to the airport Monday morning, March 31, and by evening were in Saigon. The next day the Liberation Army entered Nha Trang city without a fight.

We were very surprised that our children in Saigon returned to Phoenix School after the Easter holiday. School officials received no recommendation from the American Embassy. The evacuation of American personnel from other cities had accelerated the flight of ARVN soldiers and some civilians and we suspected that Ambassador Martin did not want to spark a mad rush of desperate Vietnamese from their country by ordering American family dependents to leave. However, on Good Friday, President Ford had already ordered naval ships with helicopters in the South China Sea to steam to an area near Vietnam's coastline.

On Tuesday, April 1, Mary and Pat went downtown to get inoculations which would be required for international travel. Mary wrote home:

> The whole country is in a panic and maybe the first panic button has been pushed for Saigon with this morning's BBC announcement that Saigon may topple in a matter of weeks. If the prediction is as correct as some others that have been made around here lately, it may be a matter of days! . . . At the rate, unbelievable things have been happening here, nothing could surprise us anymore. . . . Many Saigonese are desperate to get out of here if the Communists take over. They'll go by ship and drown if necessary, but they won't live under Communism.

Not only were the communist forces now controlling central Vietnam as far south as Nha Trang, there were reports that the Viet Cong were pushing into Long An province southwest of Saigon. Panic was now the new "normal" for many people in Saigon.

Max, Jim, and I did not need much encouragement to follow Akron's recommendation that the upcountry MCC personnel now in Saigon temporarily transfer to Bangkok. Although we had arranged for their lodging in Saigon, they frequently came by the office to check things out. With the office overflowing with people, it was difficult to get any work done. Miller said we should respond to local social needs if we could, but observed that this might be difficult in the "rapidly changing situation."

We made plans for the displaced MCC personnel to fly to Bangkok on Sunday, April 6, and stay at the YMCA hotel. We suggested that Akron send some administrator to help reassign them.

We reported that we had given $4,600 to the Evangelical Church relief committee for emergency feeding planned at Vung Tau and other places.

The Beidlers and Bishops came to Saigon from Can Tho on Thursday. We did not want anyone to have to leave on government evacuation flights, so made airline reservations for Beidlers to go to the States and for Stauffers to go to Manila until the end of their son John's school term when they would return to the States for furlough. It was decided that Pat and Duane Bishop and Mary with our children would also leave Vietnam temporarily. I had indicated by phone to Harold Stauffer that I would stay "with travel documents in order," hoping there would be some political settlement arranged before a military attack on Saigon.

On Friday, April 4, Mary wrote home: "Talk about opportunities to trust the Lord, we're blessed with many! We're learning something of the human response to stress situations. A week ago I said one day I was up, the next day down. Now it's one hour I'm up, the next one down. And sometimes the feelings change even faster than that."

From press reports, we heard mixed signals from the Provisional Revolutionary Government—from suggestions that all Americans should leave to promises that all foreigners would be protected. Paul and Mary Contento, who worked with Inter-Varsity Christian Fellowship and had stayed for months in China after Mao Zedong came to power, said people could stay; but they were not staying. Mary and I reasoned that should Saigon capitulate like Da Nang, Nha Trang and other cities, we would prefer staying. If, however, it appeared that there might be an all-out military assault on Saigon, we would not want to subject our children to the unnecessary terror of rocket and artillery attacks. Mrs. Bay, the older illiterate woman who had come to faith a few years earlier, came to see us: "Trust the Lord and stay with us," she urged.

We asked other friends at church. Deacon Hoa displayed the logic of people who had lived through many years of conflict. Yes, some people might be killed in an attack on Saigon, he said, but added: "And when the fighting is over, we who remain will go on living!" He and others admitted that if a battle seemed imminent, they would take their families to relatives outside Saigon. Such an option was not possible for us. We did not think the Viet Cong forces would deliberately harm us. But what if angry ARVN troops created mayhem in the city—as they had done elsewhere? In the end, we decided that it was appropriate for Mary and the children to leave for Bangkok—at least for a short time.

On Thursday evening, April 3, Mary and I went to the Gia Dinh church where Scripture was read and we prayed together, but the impending unknown still weighed heavily on us. The next day Mary wrote home:

> Our heaviest burden is for the church. We've talked often about preparing the church to live under a C[ommunist] govt. We never felt escaping was the answer. That society needs salt, too. Yet we can pick up and leave. As someone in the church said, "I feel angry and rejected if you leave, yet I understand why you would want to leave." In a sense it seems all our teaching about love is going down the drain. Luke feels he should stay on longer if at all possible. We all know, of course, that if the other side takes over, our presence can quickly change from an encouragement to the Church to being a threat to the physical safety of any who associate with us. There may be Christians with special skills who may be able to work under such a govt, but we're not sure they'd have any use for missionaries since they have no "need" for religion. So, if in fact the other side takes over, we have very little hope of ever living in Vietnam again. This breaks our hearts.

. . . If and when we get out of this situation, we're going to need a long time to sort things out and find healing.

A strange plan was hatched in Saigon that week. With several voluntary agencies already processing orphans for international adoptions, on Wednesday the Welfare Minister Dr. Phan Quang Dan submitted a request to Prime Minister Tran Thien Khiem for permission to airlift 1,400 children to the States and other destinations. He said this would "create world-wide sympathy, especially in the United States, which will bring benefits to the Republic of Vietnam." He said that the American Ambassador also believed that the sight of these children fleeing communism would help reverse a negative public opinion. This was quickly approved and plans were underway the following day for what became known as the "Babylift."

The adoption agencies scurried to find caretakers to accompany these children. One of the first planes to leave—a C-5A Galaxy plane—crashed on takeoff on Friday, killing seventy-eight children and twenty-five US Defense Attaché Office personnel who had agreed to care for the children on the flight. Mary was on the rooftop patio with niece Lara Mai and observed the stricken plane go down.

The Babylift children were indeed welcomed on arrival in the United States; President and Mrs. Ford met the first plane. Vietnamese newspapers were critical of the Babylift, however, seeing this as a foreign nation robbing Vietnam of its most precious resource.

A reputable adoption agency contacted our office, looking for escorts, and on Saturday Luke and Dorothy Beidler, Duane and Pat Bishop, and Devadoss and Doris Maddimadugu were among sixty persons assigned their charges—four hundred children, to fly from Saigon to Seattle and New York. By Sunday they were in the United States—exhausted by the demanding 24-hour care of babies and small children. Reflecting later on their willingness to help out in a crisis, some wondered whether they had actually contributed to the long-range wellbeing of these children. In one week 1,700 children had left the country for the United States, Canada, Australia and Britain.

After the MCC persons left for Bangkok on Sunday, April 6, Jim Klassen wrote a long letter home: "At this point," he penned, "Luke Martin and Max and I do not plan to evacuate from or to be evacuated from Vietnam in the near future." He noted that Mary and the children were planning to leave on Tuesday.

So here we are. Luke. And Max. And myself. Three Mennonites—foreigners, Americans—in Saigon. Right now. Presenting planning to stick it out through thick and thin. Why? Okay, here goes. . . .

I think all three of us see our staying as part of our commitment to Christ and to His kingdom of peace and reconciliation. In some sense, the integrity of our years of witness is tied to our staying with our Vietnamese brothers and sisters through these days. The foreign Mennonites in Vietnam have always stood for peace and reconciliation (sometimes more explicitly than other times), and I have pushed the Vietnamese Mennonite Church as hard as I could to take these central issues of the Good News seriously in war-torn Vietnam. And now that Mennonite Church told the Mennonite missionaries that if all the missionaries leave now because of the political-military situation, the church will be angry, sad, and lonely. Although recently I haven't participated in a lot of activities out at the Gia Dinh Mennonite Church, they still remember me. They know who I am. They know where I am.

I have been investing quite a bit of time with some new believers at our student center here on Phan Thanh Gian [Street]. They, too, know my stance. I've preached my understanding of the implications of Christ's life-style very bluntly. I've diagrammed the dichotomy between following Christ and following Caesar very clearly. I've let them know that our commitment to Christ does not depend on what kind of political system is in power. Yes, I need to stay for their sakes. And outside the Mennonite community, there's a wide variety of Christians and non-Christians with whom I've shared my feelings about peace as opportunities presented themselves.

Explaining that MCC personnel who left were "refugees" from Nha Trang, Quang Ngai or Pleiku and many were near the end of their terms, Klassen wrote:

We have had such a unity of purpose that I could feel with them as they left. They left. I say that simply and uncritically. I do not think less of them for leaving. Maybe in the near future or in the distant future some of them will return.

Maybe a second reason would be that we feel MCC should make its personnel and resources available for Vietnam after any changes that may take place, and now it seems that the best way to do that is to retain a physical presence here in Vietnam throughout any changes. . . . Our staying should help make the seriousness of our commitment evident, and should be one way of trying to make clear that MCC is truly "a Christian resource for meeting human need" regardless of what kind of government is in power. . . .

Maybe a third reason, suggested to us by one of our Vietnamese friends, would be simply to record the truth as we see it and experience it. . . . I must say that I'm at peace with God and with myself in the decision to stay. And I probably should add that it currently has the approval of MCC Akron, the blessing of the Mennonite missionaries, and the support of the MCCers.

"What will I be doing during the days ahead?" Clean off my desk. Grading the final tests of the Bible class last summer. Teaching a Bible class for new believers. Teaching a Sunday morning English Bible class. Serve as temporary head of the English teaching program.

Then, too, I would like to start participating more regularly in some of the activities of the Gia Dinh Mennonite Church to try to lend them some support through these difficult days.

So that's the way it looks right now. Luke and Max and I plan to stay in the Mennonite Center on Phan Thanh Gian. And if there is a breakdown of public order in Saigon we would keep a very low profile and not go out on the streets at all. . . . In the meantime we are working with several Vietnamese organizations in order to help displaced people and refugees in a variety of ways.

On Tuesday, April 8, Mary and the children flew to Bangkok on an Air Vietnam Caravelle. The Stauffer family left that evening for Manila. Just after Mary, Steven, Becky, and Jonathan boarded the plane, an order came to halt all air traffic because an unknown plane had just bombed the Presidential Palace downtown where President Thieu lived. First Lieutenant Nguyen Thanh Trung, a Vietnam Air Force pilot secretly working for the other side, flew an American F-5E fighter bomber from the Bien Hoa Air Base—just east of Saigon—bombed the palace, causing little damage, then flew off to a PRG-controlled area in central Vietnam. Mary was actually elated when the order came to disembark the plane, since she did not really want to leave. But when the order was rescinded, she and the children soon flew off. In Bangkok, they joined the MCC personnel who were staying at the YMCA facilities on Sathorn Tai Road.

Lt. Trung was not the only pilot to make unauthorized flights. A few days earlier Pham Quang Tam, a member of the Evangelical Church who was in charge of the English classes at the Mennonite centers, under the ruse of delivering relief supplies to refugees, took an unguarded C-130 Hercules transport plane from the Long Thanh air base, also east of Saigon, and flew it to Singapore with several families, including his pastor father. The ploy was discovered when two air force personnel on the plane refused to go with them, forcing them to land. When the plane took off again it was shot at, but not hit. After landing in Singapore, all were arrested and imprisoned. Singapore promised to return the plane as well as Tam and the other pilots, but they implored the Vietnamese Embassy there not to send them back, claiming that they would be executed. They were all declared refugees after the Saigon government surrendered.

In mid-April, Max answered a friend of MCC in the States who was critical of MCC personnel leaving Pleiku and Nha Trang—and finally Saigon. "It is impossible to put into writing what took place during the days prior to their departure," Max wrote. "It was not just a simple decision of staying or going. I spent three agonizing days in Nhatrang with our staff trying to decide whether or not to leave the hospital. We finally decided to leave. . . . I still am not comfortable with that decision, but . . . it worked out that way."

There were many factors discussed: Were people emotionally prepared to deal with whatever might happen? Was it important to have good language skills and understand the local situation? Was it important to stay if there was nothing to do? Even if one had skills to help the displaced people, was it appropriate to become involved if the government already had sufficient funds and supplies to help?

"Our present plan," Max wrote to his friend,

> . . . is for the three MCC staff in Saigon to stay put and to be prepared to work with the PRG once they take over. At that time, should the PRG be interested in our working in Nhatrang and Pleiku again, we will recall our staff and go to work. . . . Jim Klassen and [I] have no plans to leave Saigon. . . . Our most sincere prayer is that in the very near future peace will finally come and all of the thousands of refugees will be able to return to their homes and the work of rebuilding Vietnam can finally begin.

Robert Miller had earlier informed us that Pastor Quang was planning to stay in the United States until about April 18. However, if he was needed by his family and the church, he would return earlier. He expected to receive some advice from us. I did not write to Quang, but his wife had written to him. Later on the day Mary left, I talked with Mrs. Quang at the home of her older sister, the wife of Pastor Timothy Thai. After several attempts we were able to phone Pastor Quang who had gone to Goshen, Indiana, and was staying with Mrs. Quang's sister, Minh Kauffman. Both she and I spoke with Quang. He was non-committal; he would return to Vietnam if she wanted him to, or wait longer in Goshen if this is what she advised. When she told him that all the missionaries had left but me, he told her to "take hold of" me! I was not to leave unless she and the family were in tow. Quang told us that all the congregations in Lancaster Mennonite Conferences were asked to spend time in prayer for Vietnam on Wednesday, April 9.

After the phone call, Quang wrote, thanking me for helping his wife phone him, which was very comforting to him. He said that night they prayed "that the church in Vietnam and we here might know what to do in these sad days." Anticipating difficulties from a future government, he asked me to call a meeting of the congregational council of the Gia Dinh church to divide the believers into small groups so they could arrange to worship in their homes. Concerned that the time might come when there would be a scarcity of Bibles, he requested that Bibles and New Testaments were to be carefully stored and strategically placed. He expressed the hope that the situation would become clearer so that he could soon return home. "I hope I can return to Vietnam, but if not at this time, I will wait and seek some other opportunity," he wrote.

After the children were in bed at the Bangkok YMCA that first evening, Mary wrote to our parents, reflecting on what was happening. Although the whole city of Saigon "was tense and afraid" the previous week, she noted this heaviness had lifted. "Some people," she wrote, "said they decided to not let any reports—good or bad—influence their feelings." The Gia Dinh church was feeling sad, she said, with Pastor Quang gone and now seeing the missionaries leave also. People were glad that I was staying. Mary had told friends that she hoped to return within a few weeks.

"We have never considered ourselves ready to run at the first sign of danger," Mary wrote. "I would certainly still be in Saigon if I didn't have children. The [children] had mixed feelings about going. If indeed we cannot continue to live in Vietnam they will be very sad. . . . Luke and I both felt right about our decision for now."

I wrote to Robert Miller that day, noting that I was now the only Mennonite missionary remaining. "For the past years we have been trying in informal ways and through teaching to suggest that the church can live under any kind of a government," I wrote; "things have been happening so fast that we have not really had time to think through the issues carefully. We have all experienced panic along with the rest of the population. I should not say, 'the rest of the population,' for some people are hopeful that everything will soon be over when everyone can again live a peaceful life."

I reported on the American Embassy evacuation plans, using ships going down the Saigon River and planes from Tan Son Nhat airport, possibly involving Marine ground troops and fighter bomber support. Some Vietnamese persons who had worked closely with the Americans would be helped to leave. I told Miller that the Ninh and Quang families had indicated they wished to leave the country.

That day, April 8, the armies marching south first engaged the ARVN in what would be the last major battle of the war at Xuan Loc, sixty kilometers northeast of Saigon.

With others gone, it was now easier for Max, Jim and me to focus on things at the office. But people kept coming and going all day, some persons hanging around for hours. On Wednesday morning a student walked into the office, asking, *"Tại sao các bạn Cơ Đốc đi hết?"* ("Why did all my Christian friends leave?") He had gone to see a friend of another mission organization and found the entire staff gone. It was difficult to answer him. Preparing a long letter to Harold Stauffer and Robert Miller, I wrote: "It is unfortunate that we all left so soon. This has been particularly difficult for the Christian community." I acknowledged that Murray and John had wanted to stay, but we encouraged them to leave. And on Sunday before she left, Mrs. Bay and others at church were saying to Mary, "Trust the Lord and stay here with us!"

It was unfortunate that Pastor Quang was not in Saigon while these tremendous changes were taking place. But neither I, nor the church leadership team—while hoping and praying that he would return—was requesting that he return at this time. Everyone recognized that each person had to decide what to do. Mrs. Quang and her siblings had lived with her pastor father and mother in North Vietnam before 1954 and she did not want to live under that political system again. Even if Quang had been willing to live with a PRG-installed government, I understood their fear of possible arrest if they stayed for they had heard a few community voices accusing them of living off the Americans!

The church and the community center were functioning—though the Rang Dong School was closed as were all schools—and persons were appointed to take care of all activities. We gave the April wages plus three additional months salaries to all staff persons—a procedure other foreign voluntary agencies were doing. They understood that they were to continue working as long as possible. If the programs were to end, this would become their severance pay.

In addition to the money already given to the Tin Lanh relief committee, we gave $2,600 and several bales of blankets and clothing to Christian Youth for Social Service. CYSS took a boat to the coastal city of Vung Tau to distribute food and other relief supplies to disheveled refugees arriving by boat from central Vietnam. Max was working with groups of students from Quang Ngai, Quang Tri and Ban Me Thuot living in Saigon who had been cut off from their families' support for several weeks, buying rice and helping them find a place to stay.

Pastor Nguyen Hau Nhuong, the administrator of the Pleiku Clinic, left Pleiku the day before the government abandoned Pleiku and managed to get to Saigon. An ARVN Tin Lanh chaplain took the MCC Toyota station wagon. Somehow he managed to get the Toyota down to Nha Trang, then south to Phan Rang or Phan Thiet and left it at the Tin Lanh church. Another pastor got the vehicle on a boat to Vung Tau and then drove it to Saigon! He asked whether MCC could reimburse some of the expenses. I hesitated; after all, we had not asked anyone to bring the car! I did give him the piaster equivalent of $500 U.S.—though later I questioned my judgment. Pastor Nhuong got permission from the Health Minister and head of Public Health to organize a medical team to work in a refugee camp. He asked to use the Toyota and was upset that the other pastor was using the car and that I had given him money. Nhuong also headed a group to give assistance to Tin Lanh pastors and other Christians who were now homeless. We gave $500 to buy rice for thirty to forty families.

In a post script of a letter to Akron and Salunga, intended for Atlee Beechy, I wrote: "I pray that you can help Quang think through some of the issues these days. I do not think you can recommend anything. It is strange that we Mennonites, who have had a history of wandering, and even recently have hailed Peter Dyck's exploits in getting people out of Berlin—now have very little interest in helping Vietnamese Christians leave Vietnam."

On April 9, MCC was informed by the Friends Committee on National Legislation that the PRG in Paris confirmed Earl Martin and Yoshihiro Ichikawa were alive and well and that the AFSC doctor, Tom Hoskins, was safe; he had flown to Da Nang on March 27 and worked in a downtown hospital for a time after the change in government.

MCC was the only agency that responded to the PRG request for food. In a telephone conference call on April 9, the MCC Executive Committee authorized $100,000 from MCC funds plus a similar amount contributed by Church World Service "for the purchase of condensed milk and canned pork for needy civilians in the PRG areas." Everett Metzler, the MCC and EMBMC representative in Hong Kong, was asked to purchase and ship these commodities. Two weeks later, the milk and pork was shipped from Hong Kong to Hai Phong on the ship *SS/20 Thang*.

On April 10, President Ford addressed a joint session of Congress, requesting $722 million in supplemental military aid for Vietnam and Cambodia plus $250 million in economic and refugee assistance. The Congress took no action on this.

In a letter to Pastor Quang on April 11, I portrayed something of the ambivalence of those days. "Yesterday," I wrote, "I talked with your wife [who] would like you to return soon." At the same time, I respected his wife's wishes that he not return "at this time." I told of meeting with the Church Administrative Committee one noon: "The church wanted you to be with them during this time of crisis, but everyone was willing to assume more responsibilities."

Although the Gia Dinh church wanted Quang to return, I told Mrs. Quang that there was no need for him to return immediately if it was their intention as a family to leave Vietnam. Writing to Don Sensenig on April 12, I said there was "no reason for [Quang] to come and give responsibility to others who might also leave. Better for those who are ready to stick it out—come what may—to assume responsibility now."

In a letter to the Mission Board secretary, I described the response of many Evangelical Christians to the military offensive:

> Perhaps there is nothing that strikes horror in the minds of many Christians [more than the fear of living under "Godless Communism." For the past twenty years I have tried to learn by study, reading, and visits [to] communist countries about the experiences and the responses of religious people, especially Christians, to communist society. I think a very clear argument can be made that a proletarian dictatorship clashes head on with the personal freedom of every man under God which we value so highly. . . . I think it is very normal that they do not welcome the PRG 'liberators' with open arms. It seems that those people in Vietnamese society who have once lived with the Viet Minh are the most eager to escape.

I noted that many Tin Lanh Christians were trying to leave Vietnam. Some had gone to the seaports of Vung Tau and Rach Gia, others to the island of Phu Quoc, hoping to leave by boat if or when the Saigon government collapses. Some Catholic priests were leaving areas of conflict with their people. However, many Catholic priests, especially of the Redemptorist order, stayed in areas when the ARVN troops left. The April 11 issue of the *Chính Luận* daily newspaper carried a statement released by Saigon Archbishop Nguyen Van Binh of Saigon, calling on all Catholics to remain calm and to work for peace:

> In every situation, Catholics should be masters of the situation and remain calm—thanks to their faith—so they can clearly realize these times. Panic will only make the situation worse and will lead to personal disaster.
>
> The Catholic Church sincerely wishes that the situation will quickly stabilize and that security for the people will be assured. However, under no circumstances will the Church lead or approve a Catholic military unit. The Church also has never advocated an exodus to other countries as reported by groundless rumors.
>
> Catholics will, together with all other people, try harder to play a role in bringing peace and

reconciliation to the people of Vietnam. This is essential at the current time and is also a demand of the Gospel of Christianity.

Everything is from God, who has reconciled us to himself, thanks to Christ, and has given to us the ministry of reconciliation. II Corinthians 5:18.

The statement then expressed the Church's hope that the implementation of the Paris Accords would bring an end to the conflict and guarantee the personal rights of the people.

Pastor Tran Xuan Hi, the father of Pastor Quang, preached at the Gia Dinh church on Sunday, April 13. He criticized pastors of the Evangelical Church who were leaving their flocks. After the worship service, the high school student who lived with us, Bui Quang, and I ate a simple rice meal in a small restaurant. We then rode east a few kilometers to Thu Duc where we visited a refugee reception center set up at the agricultural university. There were four thousand people there—from Pleiku, Quang Tri, Da Nang, Da Lat, Qui Nhon, and from nearby Dinh Quan. It was painful to speak with people who had fled their homes for the nth time. In the afternoon the youth of the Gia Dinh church went to help in an area near Ba Chieu Market where hundreds of houses were destroyed by fire only two days earlier.

In Bangkok that Sunday Pat Hostetter Martin left with Lara and Minh for Nigeria where her parents were on a mission assignment. She would wait there until Earl's status became clear. It appeared that Jean Hershey and her daughter Vui would soon fly to the States, and Ann Ewert would head for Canada; Wally and Claire had already flown to Canada. That would leave only Linda and Murray Hiebert and the Willms family; MCC suggested a possible medical assignment for John in Nepal. In a letter home, Mary said there was good communication between Saigon and Bangkok. Voluntary agency people were traveling back and forth, hand-carrying mail. While waiting, the children were learning to swim in the Y pool and Mary had them concentrate on school lessons for a short time each day.

Mary and I were writing to each other nearly every day. On April 15, she wrote:

> Steve and Becky both talk about returning to Saigon. Suddenly today I was overwhelmed, too, with the desire to return. . . . I feel like I was involved in real living the past weeks in Vietnam and now I'm suddenly set aside, in a vacuum. . . . It's hard to believe all that our Vietnamese friends are going through. . . . I mentioned to you that I've been talking to [the children] lots since we're here. Steve reads the newspaper and asks a lot of questions. This eve he said it seems more scary here than when we're there. Maybe we're talking too much. . . . I told Alfie [Campbell] how I was feeling like going back. She advised against it. . . . I know another reason I want to go back is because I'm not yet ready to face the possible reality of not being able to live there much longer.

The afternoon of Wednesday, April 16, I talked again with Mrs. Quang. She had learned that Quang's sister's family, confirmed killed weeks earlier, were alive and well in Ban Me Thuot! There were no mass killings as had been rumored. I already had learned to question any wild stories! Mrs. Quang also heard that the Christians in Da Nang were continuing to meet to worship as before. The Liberation Army soldiers were now well-entrenched in Nha Trang, and were billeted in a Catholic seminary near the Tin Lanh Bible Institute. Pastor and Mrs. Ong Van Huyen, Bible professor and member of the clinic board, were forced to call on local PRG authorities for protection from looters.

We had secured some medicines, and that afternoon a nurse from the Gia Dinh Mennonite congregation who had studied in Nha Trang, Truong Thi Ngoc Sa, and other young people from the church and the Saigon student center distributed these medications to some of the 70,000 refugees at the An Loi refugee camp near Long Thanh. It seemed that the needs of the people were cared for relatively well. A week earlier Kpa Dai, an MCC staff person who had come from Pleiku, assisted persons in the camp to construct temporary shelters, and requested blankets and mosquito nets, medicines, food and kitchen utensils. He reported that there were around 16,000 minority persons there from Stieng, Cham, Nung, Thai, Rhade and Jarai ethnic groups.

People were coming to our office from morning until night. That day Max, Jim and I decided that we are taking everything too seriously and that it was time to celebrate with *Foremost* ice cream that we had bought. But we had too many visitors to eat it! Having stayed several days at the office, I went to our home in Gia Dinh that evening after attending prayer meeting at the church. Manh, an army deserter and husband of our household helper, Co Chin, read from Mark 13:10 and following verses—the warning of the great tribulation that Jesus spoke about. This sounded much like what was happening around us.

In a phone call to Akron on Wednesday, April 16, I requested another remittance of $8,000; I had earlier requested $20,000. We were using these funds for small aid assistance. We did not give any monies to assist people to leave. I told Paul Longacre and Don Sensenig that Mrs. Quang had learned that it might be possible for her family to leave the country if affidavits were submitted to the U.S. Immigration Service. I also asked them to submit an affidavit for her youngest sister, Van, and for her father, retired Pastor Nguyen Huu Phien. I reported that I was also preparing a list of names to submit to the American Embassy in Saigon. I learned that the MCC Executive Committee had asked Atlee Beechy to travel to Bangkok to assist in reassigning MCC personnel, and that he was now planning to arrive in Bangkok on April 25.

I was disappointed that Beechy would not arrive sooner, as Mary and I anticipated meeting to discuss our own family plans. Now most of the MCC personnel had already left Bangkok. In a letter to me that day, April 16, Mary wrote that some of the remaining MCCers were "antsy," and would have liked to have some conversation with persons from Saigon or Akron. She also wondered why we had not been communicating by telephone.

On that same day in nearby Cambodia, the Lon Nol government surrendered. The following day the Khmer Rouge entered Phnom Penh, driving the people out of the city—the beginning of a reign of terror that led to the deaths of nearly two million people.

On Friday, April 18, Mary wrote me: "We're eager to see you if you can come next week, but I feel as you do, it would be hard for you to take off if things were falling apart by then. So please use your own judgment and don't feel you must come because of us." Aware that I was hoping they could return to Saigon, she wrote: "We're still very eager to come back and I know that you, in the situation, know how it feels better than we at a distance. Nevertheless, if we jumped out of the frying pan before it was even hot, do we want now to jump into the fire?

Also enclosed was a letter that Steven wrote at his own initiative:

Dear Daddy,

I want to go back to Vietnam very badly. I don't feel that we have to be traped here in Bankock if Saigon ain't going to be attacked soon.

I am learning to swim & I already know how to float. I am also practicing to dive.

We went to the Central Dept. Store. . . .

We need a daddy around here.

Steven

That day, April 18, I wrote to the Eastern Board Overseas Ministries secretary, proposing possible arrangements for our family. I thought that Mary and the children might be able to return to Saigon in early May. Then if the situation "would deteriorate further," they might go to Manila where they could join John Stauffer in school. Or our family might consider staying in Saigon regardless of political or military developments. I hoped to meet Atlee Beechy in Bangkok April 25 or 26. In a postscript on a copy to Mary, I said I likely would return to Saigon on Sunday, April 27. I said that Mrs. Quang was at home "but *definitely* wants to leave. And she is counting on *me* to get their family out. I will find it hard to come to Bangkok next weekend if things are falling apart here."

In a letter to Duane and Pat Bishop, I wrote that "Indian summer" aptly described the current climate in Saigon, a term that Ernie Campbell had used. "The panic of a few weeks ago subsided, but concern about the future remains. . . . The mood of the people at this point is that, sooner or later, the other side will be controlling the country. 'Sooner' would be within a few weeks. 'Later' would be within one or two years."

I told of Pham Quang Minh, the CYSS leader in Can Tho who stopped by the Mennonite office that morning. Minh said that the CYSS leaders had just met and they all signed a statement of commitment to stay and serve the people in the Spirit of Christ regardless of what happened. When I reported this CYSS stance to Do Van Thuong, the secretary of the Gia Dinh congregation, he was greatly encouraged.

Mary's letter the next day from Bangkok recorded some stress. Becky was not feeling well and pouted. Four-year-old Jonathan sang "I ain't gonna study war no more" before falling off to sleep. My letter to Mary that day expressed a range of feelings—from peacefulness to frustration and anger. People were coming to the office requesting introductions to the U.S. Embassy for help in leaving the country.

I knew that I would have to find a way to help Mrs. Quang and her family leave. I had also just learned from Pham Van Luc that he and Qui would likely soon leave; she was working as an interpreter for some American intelligence agency and believed it unwise to stay.

I also told of meeting Pastor Nguyen Linh, the administrator of the Nha Trang Tin Lanh hospital, who had come to Saigon the previous day in the pickup truck with their ten children. He reported that looters had broken into the hospital buildings and Pastor Pham Xuan Tin was shot at when he tried to stop the looting. He said it would have been impossible for Dr. Willms to have done anything.

I closed the letter with a touch of realism: "I have tried to sound a fairly optimistic note about coming back, but this might not be realistic. I suppose you are really getting more information than we are here. On the American station at noon there was not one word about Vietnam. . . . Not any longer in the news!"

I had been staying at the Saigon office but on Sunday morning, April 20, drove the scooter out to our house near the Ba Chieu Market. Bui Quang, the high school student who resided with us, prepared a wonderful breakfast of rice and peanut soup. We then went to the church where Mrs. Quang's father, retired Pastor Nguyen Huu Phien, preached a relevant sermon based on a text from Habakkuk 3:17-18: "Though the fig tree does not blossom. . . , yet I will rejoice in the Lord, I will joy in the God of my salvation." MCC staff member and youth leader Nguyen Dinh Tin read from the first chapter of Habakkuk—a reference from the seventh century before Christ which seemed to fit Vietnam during March and April. After the service the Congregational Council met to consider Pastor Quang's request to form house groups. Leaders were appointed for five different areas: Nguyen Quang Trung, Nguyen Bat, Vo Van Hoa, Do Van Thuong and Pham Van Luc.

On Sunday afternoon, Jim Klassen and I took the Datsun out to the An Loi refugee camp near Long Thanh—along the way to the coastal city of Vung Tau. While we had provided some limited medical resources, we did not want to be directly involved in the relief work. It seemed clear to us that the people had to resolve matters themselves. We met people who asked whether the U.S. was going to give additional military aid and whether the American soldiers would be coming back. It seemed that they did not realize that the Paris Agreement two years earlier had enabled U.S. forces to leave and given a period of time for the Vietnamese parties to come to some political settlement. And now that opportunity was gone.

I managed to place a phone call to my parents and that night wrote them, describing the activities of the day. "I cannot justify the military offensive of the other side," I wrote, "but it seems to me that it has been clear to everyone for several years which direction things would ultimately go. Still Saigon refused to make the political accommodations they needed to make to work out a satisfactory adjustment with the other side. . . . The thought of a communist takeover of the whole of Vietnam is not very attractive to me and to many of the people. The alternative of continuous struggle is not very attractive either."

On Monday, April 21, Mary wrote to family and friends, noting how difficult it was to leave Saigon two weeks earlier:

> We had always said a Christian can live under any political system. We talked of preparing the church to live under Communism. Suddenly in a few weeks' time, it seemed that Communism was about to take over the country. We were talking of leaving and many Christians were panicking along with others, or maybe more so, and we wondered what all the nice things we said about love and peace meant. They can live under Communism, but we can't? They can suffer, but we can't?
>
> There were times that we took some of our clues from other missions and planning to leave seemed right. But at other times all our reasons for leaving sounded like a bunch of baloney. Pastor Quang's being in the States has certainly made everything much more difficult for us and very, very difficult for his wife and family. With him gone and for us to all leave, the church would be on quite a limb. There are some who can give some leadership, but no strong person to rally everyone around the church for strength and fellowship so badly needed in these days…This whole decision to go or stay is extremely difficult and is still not resolved. Some Vietnamese friends say we should go. Others appreciate if we stay. But all of them, if they had a choice, would not stay and keep children in such a situation.

President Nguyen Van Thieu resigned the evening of April 21, blaming the United States for betraying him and his people. This followed the PAVN capture of Xuan Loc after battling for nearly two weeks. The People's Army now had no major obstacles on its way to Saigon. Seventy-three year-old Tran Van Huong, who had served as vice-president under Thieu, became president.

Atlee Beechy was in Akron on April 21, preparing to leave the following day with Don Sensenig for Paris to meet with PRG and DRV diplomatic representatives. Beechy was authorized to negotiate $250,000 in additional aid to the Provisional Revolutionary Government and would seek a similar amount from the Canadian International Development Agency (CIDA) if there was interest. Beechy also hoped to arrange to meet Earl Martin and Yoshihiro Ichikawa somewhere in Vietnam.

On Tuesday morning, April 22, Nguyen Dinh Tin and Jim Klassen went to a meeting called to discuss relief needs. There some persons shared a *Declaration Concerning Evacuation to Foreign Countries* which had been drafted and signed on April 19 by more than one hundred persons, most of whom were representatives of Catholic social agencies. Aware that the United States was facilitating the evacuation of certain persons from Vietnam, the statement expressed support for the April 8 announcement of Archbishop Binh and called on the Catholic faithful to "do their utmost to contribute to returning peace and reconciliation to and among the people of Vietnam." Every Vietnamese, "without distinction of religion, viewpoint or locality, has the duty and the ability to contribute to the solving of the vital problems of our nation," the statement said. The signatories affirmed that no matter what happened, "we shall remain in our native land to make our small contribution to the work of reconciliation in our nation."

Returning to the office, Tin set about writing a statement entitled, *A Declaration by Mennonite Christians Regarding Evacuation from Vietnam*. Referring to many reports of evacuations, the statement said that they, "a group of Mennonite believers, feel that we have a responsibility to challenge the spirit of our people." Therefore, they declared that they would "not leave the country under any circumstance." Guided by the

Nguyen Dinh Tin (l) with other youth.

Word of God, they would serve their fellow countrymen, accepting hardship and sacrifice, and "accept life or death because of their overwhelming faith in the living God." Urging "Christians and all fellow-citizens to have the fortitude and courage to remain . . . to rebuild [their] homeland in both spiritual and material ways," they promised to stay. Tin and several others signed this statement.

That morning I had breakfast with Ninh, the long-term MCC administrative assistant and now executive director of Asia Christian Service, who was making plans to leave the country.

I had gone to the Defense Attaché Office at Tan Son Nhat airport the previous afternoon and learned that under the evacuation procedures then being implemented—code named Frequent Wind—the processing procedure for leaving had been simplified for Vietnamese family members of American citizens. Ninh had an American friend who was prepared to "adopt" his family, and he suggested that I could take Mrs. Quang and her family in tow. At breakfast Ninh showed me three forms that I would need to fill out, but I was not prepared to sign an affidavit that Mrs. Quang was my wife and that we had lost the marriage certificate! Yet I suggested to Ninh that if he wanted to leave, he should initiate procedures that afternoon. I then visited the American Embassy and learned that the Embassy had no specific plans to evacuate personnel who worked for American voluntary agencies.

I ate lunch at the office with Tin and Jim after they returned from their meeting. Just as we finished lunch the phone rang. Ninh said they were going to the airport and suggested I come along. I told him to call Mrs. Quang—and the clandestine operation was under way. I was concerned about getting through the entrance gate but had no trouble. I filled out an affidavit of support listing the Quang family as my dependents and guaranteeing travel expenses and resettlement support. They no longer required the form swearing the person was his spouse and the marriage certificate lost! I indicated they were family members, however, and the American officials understood the fiction. I briefly left to pack an overnight bag, then rejoined the long waiting line. By 8:00 p.m. we got our names on the manifest for a C-130 flight leaving for Clark Air Force Base in the Philippines. Here I learned that I did not need to accompany the group. By this time the city was under curfew, so I decided to spend the night at the airport.

That night I sat on bleachers by a tennis court with the Ninh and Quang families nearby. Naked light bulbs softly illuminated the humid air that enveloped all of us. No one slept. I began writing a letter to Mary. I asked fifteen year-old Hang, Quang's oldest daughter, how she was feeling. "*Buồn,*" she simply replied—Sad!

At the staging area, Ninh met a friend who had come from Hai Phong to the South on the same ship as he after the Geneva Accords of 1954. Just before 1:30 a.m. Ninh and several other men joined me on the bleachers. We were strangely relaxed, having made it through the stress of the previous weeks and now the official hurdles at the airport. A few planes were taking off, but there were no distant sounds of artillery.

Ninh's emotional voice was subdued as he described leaving Hanoi and Hai Phong twenty years before. Some of his family had stayed in the North until near the end of the population exchange deadline when his father in Saigon sent a telegram saying he was very sick. Ninh knew what that meant; he had to go south to join his father. Now—with his family—he was again leaving everything behind. Though sad, he was not upset. "I feel light," he said, "light enough to fly." I observed that this was like the Jewish Year of Jubilee when debts were forgiven and land returned.

I stayed with the families until around 7:00 a.m. when they boarded the bus for the tarmac. They were now scheduled to fly a C-141 jet directly to Guam. Disregarding cultural expectations, I had ignored Mrs. Quang's request that her father and younger sister accompany them. Instead of boarding the bus, I ducked out, hurried home, rested a bit, and headed for the office and cabled the States that the two families had left. By noon Wednesday, April 23, the church learned that Mrs. Quang was gone, and I was asked to confirm it. The church secretary, Mr. Do Van

514 A Vietnam Presence

Thuong, called a meeting of the Congregational Committee for 5:00 p.m. to discuss the needs of the shepherdless flock. Others who attended were Phan Van Khai, Nguyen Huu Lam, Nguyen Thi Hoang (Mrs. Ty), Nguyen Dinh Tin and me. Some expressed disappointment that Quang had not returned home and Thuong agreed to write Pastor Quang asking whether he planned to return. Lam was asked to temporarily continue to serve as acting pastor. Someone suggested that I do this but I said that this was not the time for a foreign pastor—to which they all agreed. Trung was asked to give leadership to the Saigon student center.

Tin presented the statement declaring a commitment to remain in the country; Mrs. Ty liked it and immediately signed it. Mr. Thuong also agreed with this view but as a civil servant, a teacher, did not want to sign it. Because of the government-decreed early curfew, it was decided to have prayer meeting at 6:30 to 7:15. Since the government prohibited groups of more than three persons to meet together, we decided it best to all gather at the church.

I slept at home on Wednesday night. I stayed up until 2:00 a.m., going through some items and packing a bag to take with me to Bangkok on Friday. I awoke Thursday morning, April 24, to discover the watch by my pillow was gone. The bedroom door was open, a sign that "visitors" had been there. They had broken the steel frame on the front window, crawled in and unlocked the front door and apparently carried things up over the fence. The attractive new locally-made red bicycle we gave to Steven on his tenth birthday two months earlier—brand name *Martin*—was gone. So was the radio we had just bought, and lots of piasters and $100 U.S. which I planned to use for my plane ticket, taken from my wallet which I had placed under my pillow! So the next day I decided to move out and asked Bui Quang and Chin, our cook of several years, to help clean things out. I took many of the things to the Gia Dinh center and told Chin to give the things away. I left my books there, planning to get them in the next week or two.

The week of April 20 to 26 was very tiring. People would call us at 6:30 a.m., come at 7:30 a.m. and stay until 7:30 p.m. They would crowd the office asking information and about help to leave the country. Jim took a couple of people to the American Consulate to check for papers. A friend of Arlene's asked for help. I was tied up, so she asked Max. Not wanting to go, but not wanting to be unhelpful, he consented to go with her to the American Embassy. Crowds prevented them from entering so she suggested a side door. At that point, a foreign TV newsman moved toward them to record this couple seeking permission to leave! The Marine guard was letting no one enter. Max pulled himself away when people mobbed him—asking for help—and headed back to the office, vowing never to return to the Embassy! We MCC persons intended to stay; why should we help others leave? I did check at the Consulate for an affidavit on behalf of our friend Nguyen Thi Hong and her four children, but it apparently had not been filed in time. People with affidavits of support who received a telegrammed approval from Henry Kissinger in the State Department were granted permission to leave for the United States.

Three members of the Congregational Council—Thuong, Trung and Tin—came to the office Friday afternoon, April 25, asking whether our Mission had any plans to help people leave the country. I said I knew of no church group with plans to evacuate their members. They had heard reports of a church arranging for a boat to leave from Vung Tau. Tin said nothing. Mr. Thuong said that one of the members of the church, Mr. Tinh, reportedly bought poison he planned to take if the communists came to Saigon.

During that last week of April, I prepared "To whom it may concern" introduction letters for a few staff members of the Mennonite centers, as well as for a few staff members of the Nha Trang and Pleiku medical programs who asked about leaving. These letters might have helped anyone who left; most of these people did not leave Vietnam.

I spoke by phone with Evangelical Church President Doan Van Mieng a few times that week. He welcomed me to come to his office, but I did not get there. He apparently was ambivalent about evacuation; since most Evangelical Christians were staying he was determined to stay. Around April 24, the *Chính Luận* newspaper published a statement calling on Evangelical Christians not to leave Vietnam, indicating that the Tin Lanh Church had no plan to evacuate Christians. A similar statement was published in *Trắng Đen* newspaper April 26. The announcement was not signed by the church president, but rather by three district superintendents from the southern area, Nguyen Van Quan, Nguyen Van Xuyen, and Dang Van Luc.

I sometimes wrote letters on the run—while I was waiting. On Friday afternoon, April 25, I wrote to Mary: "I had planned to be winging my way to Bangkok by now, having had a reservation on a Thai International flight this morning for several days already. I learned only this morning that the flight was cancelled. I wasn't too upset, but it still seemed right to go if I could. . . . If I can come, fine, if not, fine too. I do really want to talk with you."

I discussed with Jim and Max whether to skip going to Bangkok since the flight was cancelled. Should I just plan to stay in Saigon? Was it important to make a short trip there? We agreed that we wanted to know what Atlee Beechy had learned in his conversation with the PRG delegation in Paris. Did the PRG affirm having MCC personnel stay and work? Had they given information concerning the whereabouts of Earl and Hiro? We also believed that it would be useful to secure U.S. dollars in case the Vietnamese currency would be changed. And personally, since Mary and I had not been together since she had left two and a half weeks earlier, I wanted to talk with her about planning if we would be separated for a period of time. They supported my going.

On Friday night at the Saigon center, I went up on the roof patio—alone. The moon was shining. Since curfew began at 8:00 p.m., everything was quiet. I knew that "the other side" had artillery and rockets within range of the city. Still it was peaceful. I wondered whether I would be staying or whether I would be able to go to Bangkok on Saturday. Later Max came up on the roof. That afternoon he had met an Associated Press reporter who was trying to find out which foreigners were planning to stay. The journalist told Max that Saturday would be the last day for the evacuation of Vietnamese civilians, and Saturday or Sunday the last day for the evacuation of American personnel. On Monday, the last day of the lift, senior Vietnamese government officials would leave. He assumed that when all senior officials are gone, order would break down and wealthy residential areas would be looted.

I cabled MCC Akron on Saturday morning, April 26, reporting that public order was still good in Saigon but many people were requesting assistance to leave the country. I indicated that I was unable to go to Bangkok since many commercial flights were cancelled and said I would try Air Vietnam on Sunday. We were no longer able to phone. I asked them to cable the substance of Beechy's findings in Paris. "We are at peace," the cable concluded.

That morning I listened to President Huong's speech—not very conciliatory. I knew that China Airlines had a flight scheduled to leave for Bangkok at 1:00 p.m., so I scootered to the airport to see what the conditions were and how the flights coordinated by the U.S. Defense

Attaché Office were moving. I learned that there would be a special Air Vietnam Bangkok flight late afternoon. I also learned that China Airlines had many no-show passengers—apparently the people had already left on special evacuation flights. So I hurried back to the office, conversed with Max and Jim, grabbed my bags and hurried back to the airport. The Boeing 707 flight left shortly behind schedule with several vacant seats. By mid-afternoon I was at the Bangkok YMCA. Atlee Beechy had already arrived.

Mary and I had been living in two different worlds and now found ourselves "on different pages." We needed to talk. I needed to spend some time with the three children. I needed to talk with Atlee Beechy. The Willms family was leaving for Nepal April 30 and Linda and Murray Hiebert would likely go to Laos. I talked of returning to Saigon Monday and Beechy expressed interest in returning with me. But there were no flights Monday afternoon or evening. By noon Monday we heard that the PAVN forces were at the large bridge on the Bien Hoa highway, only two kilometers from our Saigon house!

The communist forces would not negotiate with President Huong. On Monday, April 28, he resigned and General Duong Van Minh assumed the presidency. But it was too late to negotiate. On Wednesday, April 30, communist forces entered Saigon with little resistance. North Vietnamese tanks rolled down Thong Nhut (Unity) Boulevard past the now-deserted American Embassy and crashed through the gates of the Presidential Palace. North Vietnamese Colonel Bui Tin accepted the surrender from General Minh. The colonel reportedly told Minh, "You have nothing to fear. Between Vietnamese there are no victors and no vanquished. Only the Americans have been beaten. If you are patriots, consider this a moment of joy. The war for our country is over!"

A NEW DAY

Chapter 37

Vietnam's long struggle for independence was over!

"The events of the past few weeks have been among the most demanding of my life," I wrote on April 30—right after I learned that the Saigon government had capitulated. "I am just beginning to try to comprehend the significance of all of this, not only for Vietnam and my friends there, but for our personal lives."

I could not fully explain why I happened to be in Bangkok with my family. I had hoped to be in Saigon, but had not taken care of business and returned to Saigon in time. Within hours of the dramatic announcement Mary and I were already discussing with Atlee Beechy what might be next for us.

"First in priority is our interest in continuing our relationship to Vietnam," I wrote. "While it is doubtful that we could enter Vietnam as missionaries, MCC will want to continue its ministries." We instinctively knew that it was highly unlikely that we could return to Vietnam, and discussed other possibilities.

"Saigon surrendered. . . . Thank the Lord for that!" Don Sensenig wrote the same day. "I really feel relieved and happy, because it could hardly have ended any other way, and now it has happened without further suffering needed. . . . It seems symbolic to me that the place collapsed within hours of the American pullout. It has been an American effort from beginning to end, and that is very clear by the way it ended. And we richly deserve to be stuck with caring for those who went with us, some in good conscience, many or most for the benefits to be gained."

Don continued:

> [President] Ford has asked Congress to stop action on the humanitarian aid bill. Apparently now that Vietnam is Communist, he wants to discontinue aid. That remains to be seen. I am depressed constantly by the lack of understanding of the Vietnam situation here in the US. Not only right now but for years. . . . The common reaction heard these days goes something like this: what a shame that these cowardly Vietnamese didn't come through for us after we've invested so much blood and money in them. They weren't worth it. There seems almost no realization that the past two decades, or fifteen years especially, have been a basically American show, an American project, and these Vietnamese who've "betrayed" us are really our own creation. It's such a tragically one-sided view of things, and will plague us into the future. I don't think our country has really learned the right lessons from it all. At least we will be more cautious before entering an Asian land war again, one would hope; and that's something.

A few days later, I wrote a ten-page "Thoughts on Vietnam," recalling the unforgettable days and weeks in Saigon.

> Max and Jim supported my leaving. But we were getting the feeling that the end was near in Saigon, and we all felt that I should be there. . . . I have a strong desire to be in Saigon. At the same time I sense a responsibility to be with the family. I am glad that Max and Jim felt right

517

about staying. . . . I long to return to Saigon. I clearly intended to be back. I came out with one pair of trousers, three shirts, and a few changes of underclothing. . . . I realize that I could not psychologically pack more. To do this would have been to admit the possibility of not returning, something I could not do.

I recalled the opportunity I had to speak to the church on Good Friday and Easter, and the strength I received by taking part in the Thursday night meetings at the church in the weeks before I left—especially the evening Mrs. Bay prayed for me since I was separated from my family. It was this illiterate woman of faith who had come to see Mary and me in early April with the plea: "Trust the Lord and stay with us."

In his report to Akron, Atlee Beechy described the "emotional trauma" of the Willms, Hiebert and Martin couples; the other MCC personnel had already left for their homes. He wrote:

> The Martins' personal and spiritual investment obviously was deepest coming out of thirteen years of sensitive and intense involvement. Christians, particularly the emerging Mennonite church, had been for them of central concern over the years. The church's future now seemed threatened. Luke was caught between a sense of responsibility for those he had left in Saigon and the needs of his family. Those first days were days of listening, clarifying and responding. Movement from deeply-etched memories of the past to a shifting present toward finally an unknown future was difficult and painful. Our people appear to have made good progress in this journey.

Needing to leave Thailand because of limited tourist visas, Linda and Murray left for Vientiane, Laos on May 3, and our family followed with Beechy a few days later. There we were able to observe a slower "revolution" taking place with daily demonstrations against American voluntary agencies. The Lao coalition government—made up of communist Pathet Lao, neutralists and rightists—was weakening; the Pathet Lao, supported by the now-victorious Communist government in Vietnam, would soon take over the reins of government. Beechy proposed, and Akron agreed, for the Hieberts to stay in Vientiane for a time to aid in communication with our persons in Vietnam and to develop limited assistance to Laos. Our family would remain in Bangkok to gather news about Vietnam developments and to support the Hieberts. We stayed at the YMCA for a few more weeks, moving in late June to a rented apartment nearby. With help from Ernest Fogg, the Bangkok representative of the WCC Fund for Reconciliation and Reconstruction in Indochina, we arranged a relationship with the Church of Christ in Thailand so we might be able to secure visas to stay in Thailand.

I had left Saigon on Saturday, April 26. Rockets were fired into Saigon that night and again on Sunday night. On Monday, Tran Van Huong resigned the presidency and Duong Van Minh assumed the position. As stipulated by the Paris Agreement two years earlier, President Minh immediately released the political prisoners, declared press freedom and ordered the US Defense Attaché Office and its employees to leave Vietnam within twenty-four hours.

The government of General Minh ordered a twenty-four hour curfew Monday evening, April 28. Jim spent a relaxed Tuesday morning at home reading a book on The Lord's Prayer. In spite of the curfew, at noon a new Christian came to visit him at the student center. "She had thought that I had left," Jim wrote, "and consequently could hardly contain her joy that I was still here—barefoot, blue-jeans, and shirt-tail flying. . . . I explained that President Minh had only asked U.S. military personnel to leave Vietnam . . . , and that I was still planning to stay."

On Wednesday, April 30, one "didn't need a sixth sense to know that there was fighting close to Saigon—uncomfortably close," Jim wrote. Occasional rockets were landing in Saigon; after one exploded near the Saigon student center where they were living, he, Max and a few friends cleaned out a small storage space in the house which might offer some protection from incoming rockets. At 10:15 the radio announced that there would soon be an important announcement. Jim describes it: "At 10:30 it happened: there was to be a cease-fire, and the government of the Republic of Vietnam would turn its power over to the Provisional Revolutionary Government. The rocketing stopped immediately."

After lunch there was much shooting on the street. ARVN soldiers who were asked to turn in their weapons simply abandoned them on the streets where children picked them up and fired into the air until the ammunition clips were empty! By mid-afternoon the streets were carnival-like. People were looting furniture and other items from the nearby Vietnam Christian Service guesthouse! Occasionally a truck-load of PRG soldiers went by. Quaker friends who had come from Quang Ngai stopped in to visit. Other friends brought permits for Jim and Max issued by the new PRG government. By evening, James related, "I felt very tired. And so I went to bed, not yet able to comprehend the changes that had taken place, yet grateful that the many long years of fighting were over and hoping that the new government would truly be a good one."

Reflecting on the preceding days, Klassen recognized that he lived with stress, because he would be exhausted each evening. Having made the decision to stay in Vietnam, it was "like coasting along in God's grace," he said. "It almost felt as if I was sleeping through the revolution."

Ten days later from Bangkok I wrote to the parents of James Klassen and Max Ediger. I said: "The revolution has finally come to Saigon, and this will mean a changed life for everybody. Max and Jim knew the issues that were at stake. They recognized the injustice and corruption and many other problems of the old society, but they were not under any illusions that the new masters would turn out a perfect society. In fact, they were concerned that the new society might not be any better than the old. And many people—among them many Christians—were afraid about loss of personal freedom."

Max's parents replied, saying that they were in touch with Klassen's parents; both families supported their sons in their decision to stay in Vietnam. They said that many people had contacted them, impressed that their sons had "put their trust in the Lord and [did] not yield to fear."

After the Provisional Revolutionary Government took over Quang Ngai on March 25, Earl and Yoshihiro were given official identification papers which allowed them to travel outside the town. They accompanied some of their friends returning to their country homes which the conflict forced them to abandon years earlier. Yoshihiro was also asked to interpret for some Japanese technicians who worked in a sugar cane refinery. On Sunday, April 6, Earl worshiped with the believers at Quang Ngai's Tin Lanh church.

Two weeks after the PRG came into Quang Ngai, the two men were ordered to immediately leave for Saigon. They left Quang Ngai on Wednesday, April 9, traveling to Qui Nhon by jeep, motorcycle taxi, and on the roof of a mini-bus. Here in Qui Nhon they were mysteriously detained for two weeks. Leaving for Nha Trang on April 25, they spent a night at the Tin Lanh clinic where they met a doctor who had come south with the advancing army. They talked with the doctor long into the night. The two men learned that the hospital had been looted by ARVN deserters and drug addicts who had broken out of prison, gotten guns and terrorized the people.

The next day they walked the hospital grounds where they met Ong Van Huyen, dean and a professor at the Bible Institute, who appeared to take the political changes in stride; several decades earlier Huyen had been pastor in a zone controlled by the Viet Minh.

Earl and Hiro continued south to Phan Rang, then on to Phan Thiet and Binh Tuy. On the morning of April 30, they heard on Far Eastern Broadcasting Company (FEBC), the Christian radio station in Manila, that U.S. Ambassador Graham Martin had left Vietnam. The report noted that journalists and a few relief workers were staying, among them Max Ediger of Mennonite Central Committee! "We have talked about this for years," Max was quoted as saying, "and now we realize that having talked of love for our Vietnamese friends, and told them not to yield to fear or ignorance, we cannot leave them in this hour of need." After lunch Earl managed to pull in Radio Australia from a set they bought in Phan Thiet, and heard the news that at 11:30 a.m. the North Vietnamese tanks had rolled through the gates of the Presidential Palace to victory.

With that announcement, Earl and Hiro immediately set out on the 150-kilometer journey to Saigon. No buses were running so they hopped lumber trucks and all sorts of conveyances. From Bien Hoa, they got a ride with a Catholic priest. Near Saigon, four young people from a privileged family out on a joy ride with the family's car took them a distance where they caught a bus to within a few blocks of the Mennonite office. Then they sprinted, reaching their destination at 4:00 p.m. on May 1. With a chain locking the gate, they wondered whether anyone was there. They rang the bell—several times. The door then opened and Max Ediger appeared: "Hiro! Earl! I don't believe it!" Max and Jim Klassen welcomed them in. That evening—and late into the night—the foursome shared their stories.

It was some time before the men could send telegrams or letters from Saigon. First were telegrams to Vientiane which the Hieberts passed on. In a May 16 letter to Robert Miller, which he sent with exiting journalists, Max said they had "experienced no serious problems during the past weeks and feel very positive about the change in government." The Gia Dinh community center and the Saigon student center had survived the revolution in excellent shape, and most of the personnel were back at work and in excellent spirits. All the Vietnamese MCC staff members had come back, although there was not really much work to do.

"The revolution came off very quickly and smoothly," Max wrote.

> We were much impressed with how little life was interrupted by it. On the day of liberation, most everything shut down, but on the next day the market was going, some busses were running and the garbage truck even came around. . . . North Vietnamese troops have shown themselves to be extremely polite and friendly. . . . We have had much informal and exciting contact with local PRG cadre and North Vietnamese troops. . . . The panic gave way to feelings of relief that the war was finally over, and excitement that finally Vietnam was united. It was a truly great experience for us to see this take place.

With the exception of the missionaries who were trapped in Ban Me Thuot, Ediger said that all the missionaries had left before April 30. The flight of the missionaries created a "suction" that pulled many Vietnamese pastors along, he wrote. "The effect this is having on the local church is both disastrous and liberating." he observed. For many Christians who felt deserted it was a crisis of faith in the Christian message. The reality that most of the missionaries were American tended to reinforce a general view that Evangelical or Protestant Christianity was an American religion. On the positive side, however, "the exodus was like a liberation for the church," Ediger wrote. Churches which lost their pastor turned to capable lay leaders.

In a May 11 letter to Harold Stauffer and Robert Miller, I admitted that we missionaries "contributed to the evacuation mentality." I wanted to return to Vietnam—if it might be possible. In another letter to the two administrators, I suggested that returning to Vietnam would indicate a willingness to live under a different political system and would enable us to identify with Christians as they adapt to a new regime. We might help implement some MCC programs. A foreign presence also "might temper any revolutionary harshness and affirm a policy of humanization," I wrote. In June, Miller wrote a letter to the Embassy of the Republic of South Vietnam in Paris, requesting that I and the family be authorized to return to Vietnam. There was no response to this request.

In late May, I met Yukio Miyazaki, Executive Director of YMCA Vietnam, in Bangkok after he left Saigon. He had flown from Japan to Saigon when the collapse of the Saigon government seemed imminent. Writing to Robert Miller after my conversation with Miyazaki, I rhetorically asked why, when we spoke on the phone on April 28 in Bangkok, Atlee Beechy and I had not been encouraged to go to Saigon as quickly as possible, rather than advised to wait a few days. How would one know what was the best option? It likely would have made no difference since, to my knowledge, there were no more commercial flights into Saigon.

Max also commented on the fear which led many to evacuate. "Since liberation," he wrote, "we have been unable to find one verifiable story of an execution." People who had been "executed" suddenly showed up in excellent health.

Earl wrote in mid-May to Pat, hoping to send the letter with exiting journalists: "For the first time in my life, I think I understand what revolution really means," he wrote.

> In the past two months . . . I've experienced such extremes of hope, fear, exhilaration, horror, and optimism, it's difficult to imagine it was a mere fifty-seven days. There were times fearing I might not live through the fighting; there were several arrests. . . .
>
> I often wondered if it was wise for me to have stayed, although with few exceptions I concluded it was very, very important that I did stay. For example, I think we . . . perhaps communicated the message we've been talking about for years more effectively in those two weeks than in many months preceding. Friends seemed very glad we stayed. It seemed to validate so much. . . . The events of the past months have been so terrible and so wonderful! A revolution in process. It is not going to be easy for many people to make the changes which will be necessary over the coming years. But then it wasn't easy for the refugees and the political prisoners over the past years either. What is on everyone's lips—revolutionary and non-revolutionary alike—is the tremendous relief that the war is over. Viet Nam will be unified and peaceful.

The four MCC men in Saigon did not yet know what they might be able to do. "What is clearest of all is that we are definitely not in charge of things around here," Earl wrote. "They are really in charge of their own affairs at this point. May it always be so."

Earl was sorry that Pat could not have been there, yet thought it best that she had gone with the children. "I'm really sorry Luke was not able to get back from Bangkok on time," he wrote.

His presence would have been valuable, not only for the encouragement he could have been to friends here, but for the witness he would have been able to make to the home churches about what happened here.

There have been some pretty strong words said about some of the Vietnamese church leaders who fled, leaving their "flocks" abandoned. I hope I will be able to find the needed grace not to criticize too harshly those Vietnamese leaders who left. I only hope they will not be made some kind of heroes by the church in the States when the real heroes are those who resolved to stay and serve God here and contribute toward rebuilding their broken land.

Americans were trying to come to terms with what was happening in Vietnam. At the May bimonthly meeting of the Eastern Mennonite Board of Missions & Charities, Don Sensenig declared: "Praise the Lord the war is over!" Nathan Hege, the editor of *Missionary Messenger,* noted that . . .

> Sensenig sees the dawn of a new day in a country torn by war for 30 years. . . . Don tells us now that two opposing ideologies were battling out their differences on the soil of a neutral people. He said most Vietnamese have longed for peace . . . and have wanted only the chance to get back to their farms to lead a normal existence. Our missionaries have been telling us this for the past ten years. Will they now be proven right?
>
> It is hard for us to admit that any satisfactory peace will result. We have our ears tuned for words like "bloodbaths," "executions," "loss of freedom."

Would the church in Vietnam be able to exist and continue its work? the editor asked. "Don believes it will continue and that Christians will be able to adjust to the new government's requirements without compromise of conscience.

By early June we began getting more news from Vietnam, some via Vientiane, some from hand-carried letters to Bangkok.

Max, Jim, Hiro and Earl lived together at the student center and MCC office in the living quarters vacated by the Stauffer family early April. Living together was good for morale. Bui Quang, who had lived with us, was also there even though his family had gone to the countryside. Chi Do, Stauffer's former cook, also stayed and cooked. After repeated insistence, they finally were able to get her to eat with them at the same table— quite unlike Vietnamese custom. MCC staff members, Chi Tieu and Anh

Max with Manh Tuong and Le Van Nghia, former political prisoners.

Tin still came often to the office, although there was little to do, and joined the men for lunch. Tin was also involved in a revolutionary social welfare committee near his home in Gia Dinh.

James Klassen had more work opportunities than any of the other three. He had been involved in teaching for the church, and now in the absence of Pastor Quang and the missionaries, church people came to him for advice. On Monday, May 5, church leaders asked him to meet with them. Decisions were made about paying May salaries, terminating the persons working with the Bible correspondence programs, distributing household items from Martins' house, and removing the barbwire from the wall around the Gia Dinh community center! Do Van Thuong, the secretary of the Church Administrative Committee, was the only CAC member remaining in Vietnam. There were tasks to do: foreigners had to register with the new government and MCC had to be introduced, a chairman had to be chosen for the Vietnam Mennonite Church, the activities of the Gia Dinh and Saigon centers had to be registered, and someone needed to be designated to lead the believers at the Saigon center.

The Sunday morning activities at the Saigon student center continued as before: Nguyen Quang Trung led a Vietnamese Bible study, Jim led an English Bible study on the Gospel of John, and Max led a period of singing. Jim enjoyed these activities. Since the Thursday evening Bible study on I Peter was taught in the Vietnamese language, preparation consumed two days of Jim's time. Bui Quang, who expressed faith in Jesus Christ to Mary's father in August, asked Jim for baptism. Jim demurred but Quang persisted, so Jim agreed to do this with Nguyen Quang Trung assisting. In preparation for catechism, Jim handed out Vietnamese translations of *The Anabaptist Vision, The Portrait of a Peacemaker*, and *Who are the Anabaptists?*

In late May, persons from the local Revolutionary office paid a friendly visit to the Saigon center, asking about the activities and who owned the house; the men had no indication about the reason for the visit. Next door, the VNCS office was sealed after Chi Yen, the director, asked the Revolutionary Committee to take over Vietnam Christian Service. It was now under the authority of the Ministry of Health, Welfare and Disabled Veterans. It eventually became a rice distribution center and the nearby guesthouse a billet for *bộ đội*, the army troops.

We learned that the Gia Dinh community center was confiscated on Friday, May 23, on the grounds that the "owner" had fled the country. The congregation immediately protested the loss of the facility. By Sunday, they learned that they could use the church building for worship, but permission was given too late to meet that day. On Sunday, June 1, forty people met for worship. Youth activities for fifteen persons followed. Then church members met with members of the district Military Management Committee and ward representatives of the Provisional Revolutionary Government. Nguyen Huu Lam, the pastoral assistant, was charged to make sure nothing was lost from the property. Church members were told that the government would be responsible for the school. After the discussions, the church members and local PRG cadre ate a meal together in the parsonage.

Max related uncomplimentary stories having to do with Tin Lanh leaders. "As you can imagine," Max wrote, "some of our previous questions concerning working together with Tin Lanh are accentuated right now." It appeared that some of the younger pastors had a different orientation than many of the older pastors who had lived with—and even respected—the earlier communist Viet Minh.

Max was "quite certain" that the new government would not want foreigners administering any programs. "It will be impossible for MCC to operate programs as we have done in the past," he wrote. Aware that MCC was planning to request permission for Pat and the children and for our family to return to Vietnam, he was sure that this would not happen. "In fact," he wrote, "we expect to be asked to leave at any time."

In early June, the Prime Minister of the Democratic Republic of Vietnam, Pham Van Dong, called for the normalization of relations with the United States, conditioned on American economic aid and a pledge to observe the 1973 Paris cease-fire agreement. The U.S. Congress was unwilling to give economic aid. (Diplomatic recognition would not come for twenty years.)

Max, Yoshihiro and Earl were pleased with their first contact with the new officials—a cordial visit at the PRG Foreign Ministry with Dr. Le Van Loc on June 11. Having met Doug Hostetter and Atlee Beechy two years earlier in Paris, Loc seemed to be familiar with MCC. He expressed interest in knowing what kind of assistance MCC might want to give to Vietnam.

Around 125,000 Vietnamese citizens fled their country with the collapse of the Saigon government in the spring of 1975. Many were first funneled through Guam and then went to facilities like Camp Pendleton, California; Fort Chaffee, Arkansas; and later at Fort Indiantown Gap, Pennsylvania. Mennonite congregations sponsored the Nguyen Van Ninh and Tran Xuan Quang families. The MCC men in Saigon discouraged Akron from helping to resettle those who fled Vietnam, arguing that it was more important to assist those who stayed, or to assist those who fled in fear to be able to return to their country. This latter hope proved to be illusory; Vietnam had too many other demanding issues to deal with.

In early June, Mary and I received a letter from Pastor and Mrs. Quang. Quang indicated that his years with the Gia Dinh center and church were the best experiences of his life. He felt that the Lord had opened the way for his early March departure from Vietnam to attend the Mission Board meeting, and he was not asking to return to Vietnam now. Tam, his wife, wrote: "Although the Mission or you may blame us for not staying and caring for the Church and center, we are happy to accept the blame—the Church and the brothers and sisters in Vietnam will certainly

MCC transfers the tractor to PRG representatives from Quang Ngai.

blame us for deserting them, but certainly they will blame the missionaries for deserting us first."
Very well stated, I thought.

All military and police personnel, as well as civil servants of the former Republic of Vietnam, were required to register with the new authorities. After common soldiers did their three days of "reeducation" in May, in mid-June military officers and government workers were told to report for their reeducation and to bring provisions for ten days or a month. Prepared to complete this requirement so they could get on with their lives, hundreds of thousands of men reported and were taken to work camps where they were then detained for months or years—most of them at least three years, others seven, eight or ten or more years. Persons who had engaged in intelligence or psychological warfare activities were detained the longest. Tin Lanh pastors who became armed forces' chaplains fell into this category. Political indoctrination, confession of "errors," and hard and dangerous work with limited food and medical care made up the regimen in these camps. Many died of disease. Some Buddhist bonzes, Catholic priests and Evangelical pastors were also forced into reeducation camps. None of the staff members of MCC or of the Vietnam Mennonite Mission were required to go away to reeducation camps. However, along with other citizens, most were expected to go to short classes in their communities to learn the ways of the new government.

At the end of June, the MCC men had a more substantive meeting with Dr. Le Van Loc of the PRG Foreign Ministry, spending more than one and a half hours with him. Noting that MCC was a relatively small organization, they said MCC wanted to continue symbolic assistance to the people of Vietnam and reported Robert Miller's offer of $25,000 immediate assistance with considerably more likely available.

Loc recognized MCC had limited resources, but said that they were "especially appreciative of the three organizations, Medical Aid for Indochina, American Friends Service Committee, and the Mennonite Central Committee for expressing support in the years even before the liberation of all of South Vietnam." He quoted the adage—the way a gift is given is more important than the gift itself! He said Vietnam needed gasoline, fertilizer, two-wheeled hand tractors and replacement parts. They discussed how long the four men should stay in Vietnam, and Dr. Loc indicated that the consular section would help them when they were ready to leave.

Sensing that Dr. Loc was urging the men to soon return to their homes to communicate the essence of the revolution they were observing, Earl was now ready to leave to rejoin his family. The other three men would stay longer. Robert Miller was in agreement. "Our interpretation work here will be greatly enhanced by our having representatives still in Vietnam who are in a position to continue providing us with information on developments," he wrote them. "If all Mennonite workers leave Vietnam, what we have to say to people here about the situation there will be much less credible."

Akron ordered thirty Japanese Yanmar rototillers valued at $75,000 which they hoped to ship from Hong Kong, and was also shipping fifty tons of milk powder worth $65,000 from Canada.

AFSC field directors Keith Brinton and Claudia Krich flew from Vietnam to Vientiane on a United Nations flight July 4. When Mary and I met them in Bangkok, they said the morale of the MCC men was high, citing their relationship with the church and student community.

Our family went to Vientiane on July 18 to apply for non-immigration visas for Thailand. There I spoke with an official in a United Nations office who said that all foreigners would soon be leaving Vietnam since their entry visas had been authorized by the previous government.

Earl flew from Saigon to Vientiane with Quakers Paul and Sophie Quinn-Judge on July 28, then on to Bangkok where he spent a few days with us before leaving August 3 to unite with his family.

Mary and I listened to Earl's stories of the revolution, often talking long into the night. Writing home, Mary described Earl's intense emotions observing people experience "the fulfillment of some of their highest hopes, the crushing of some of their greatest dreams, overflowing joy at meeting family members not heard from for twenty years, overwhelming sadness at having lost family members and not knowing of their fate or if their whereabouts would ever be known." We were reminded that friends would have welcomed our staying. Yet had we stayed, we too would likely be making plans to leave.

Earl reported that Doan Van Mieng, president of the Evangelical Church, had stopped by the Mennonite office—most recently two weeks before Earl left Saigon. Pastors reported that many people were moving out of Saigon, resulting in smaller attendance in some congregations, while some congregations in the countryside had greater attendance. All of the many churches in Saigon were still active. Mieng told the MCC men that the annual Evangelical Church Conference held in Saigon June 15 to 17 was uneventful. However, the men learned from others that the Church adopted a new constitution and removed from office church leaders who left the country; it was reported that twenty-nine pastors, evangelists and theological students had left.

Earl learned from another pastor that two Evangelical Christians associated with the Provisional Revolutionary Government gave greetings to the conference. One of these had earlier served as an evangelist. He brought with him a letter from the general secretary of the Tin Lanh Church in the North, Pastor Bui Hoanh Thu, expressing hope for the unification of the Church.

When visiting Redemptorist priest Chan Tin, a critic of the Thieu government who also became a critic of the new regime, Earl asked how many Catholic priests left the country. "Very few!" replied Fr. Tin. Earl asked Catholic Professor Nguyen Ngoc Lan, Chan Tin's friend and collaborator, the same question. Thinking of many priests who opposed the revolution, Lan answered: "Not enough priests left!"

Earl recounted a fascinating story about a member of the Mennonite Fellowship, Dinh Van Nam (Chau Hong Luc) that occurred a few days after liberation. Among the *bộ đội* (infantry men) he saw in downtown Saigon was one who had a cross painted on his canteen. Intrigued, Nam asked him whether he was Tin Lanh. Receiving an affirmative answer, they embraced!

The Mennonite church in Gia Dinh experienced more difficulties. Under the new government, many of the former Civil Defense Corps (*Nhân Dân Tự Vệ*) personnel were allowed to become new "revolutionary" guards—signified by tying a red ribbon on their arms. Several of these were stationed at the community center to make sure that none of the assets were removed. During an argument among the guards in early June, one of these guards was murdered; the perpetrator was arrested. At the request of Nguyen Huu Lam, the ward chief and his family moved into the apartment with Lam. Consequently many church members were reluctant to meet there for worship. Mr. Nguyen Thanh Long, a deacon in a Tin Lanh congregation and dentist by profession, was now a member of a local district People's Revolutionary Government committee and offered to help resolve the matter. He was an advocate for a United Evangelical Church.

On Sunday, June 15, the Gia Dinh Mennonite congregation called a meeting to plan for the future, attended by twenty-seven official members. Attitudes toward Pastor Quang were now more conciliatory. The youth leader, Nguyen Dinh Tin, said: "He who is without sin, throw the first stone." The members elected a new Church Administrative Committee of Do Van Thuong, secretary, Nguyen Quang Trung, Phan Van Khai, Nguyen Huu Lam and Nguyen Thi Hoang. Thuong, Khai, Lam, Hoang and Tin made up the local Congregational Committee. Mrs. Hoang (Ty) was given charge of the community center, even though there was doubt that they would be able to continue providing services. Soon after this meeting, Mr. Thuong, a school teacher, had to report for reeducation. He did not return home until two and one-half years later!

Nguyen Quang Trung was appointed to take charge of the activities of the Saigon student center. On June 29, four persons were baptized at the Saigon student center—Bui Quang, Hang, Thang, and Tan. Trung led the service; Klassen was responsible for the baptism ceremony. "Certainly that is one of the highlights of my entire stay in Vietnam," Jim wrote. "The candidates shared their personal pilgrimages straight from the heart without any notes prior to the ceremony itself."

When authorities announced that permission was needed for any kind of meeting, Trung quickly got permission from the ward, district and the city security committees for the Christian group to meet on Sundays, on Tuesday mornings, and Thursday afternoons, and for the student center and bookroom to be operated. Trung also was called to Can Tho to help resolve a matter related to the January purchase of the property for the student hostel. The government was asking for payment of real estate taxes. This appears ludicrous in light of the eventual confiscation of the property!

There was little for Tin to do at the MCC office. For a time he worked for a health and hygiene committee near his home; he was impressed with the positive spirit of the cadre. Tin believed the church should be more revolutionary and "should set an example with joyful revolutionary living." Later he joined a group of other Christian young people farming near Ho Nai, a rural area east of Saigon.

The MCC office now looked different with a picture of Ho Chi Minh adorning the wall. The flag of the People's Revolutionary Government and the national flag were displayed outside— at the request of the Vietnamese staff.

In late June, our family of five moved from the Bangkok YMCA to a nearby apartment. A few days later, the Everett and Margaret Metzler family came from Hong Kong; we spent several days vacationing with them at Hua Hin beach—a special time for reminiscing and renewal.

I made frequent visits to the news bureaus in Bangkok and filed reports of Vietnam developments to the Akron MCC office. When Quakers Keith Brinton and Claudia Krich looked over these notes on their visit, they said they accurately reflected what was happening on the ground in Saigon. After Earl left Bangkok, I prepared an article about the church in Vietnam, concluding with this statement,

> What does the future hold for the church? One can only speculate. The PRG has a clearly-defined policy of religious freedom. It is certain that South Vietnam will choose reunification with the North. Both the Catholic and Evangelical churches are active in the North, and both have given strong support to the policies of the government. We pray that Christians in the South will sense a new calling to serve the people, and support the new government while giving a prophetic witness to the State when necessary. This was difficult under the old regime, and it will not likely be easier under the new.

Three months after liberation, we were receiving some international mail from Saigon, although we were also receiving mail hand-carried from people exiting Saigon. The same irregularity applied to mail going to the men. For months mail from the Akron office was sent directly, with copies sent to Duane and Pat Bishop in Hong Kong and Murray and Linda Hiebert in Vientiane to forward to Saigon. It was not until November 20 that the men in Saigon received a letter from us in Bangkok. The sea might have carried a letter more quickly by bottle! That week in November, they received more than a dozen letters. "This house goes into an uproar every time we get a letter of some kind," Max wrote. "News is becoming more precious to us than *nước mắm*," the ubiquitous fish sauce.

In an August 8 letter to James Stauffer and me, Jim Klassen said he felt no urgency to leave Vietnam—he was prepared to stay or to leave. Klassen reported that the ward chief had moved out of the Gia Dinh church property. The Christian group meeting at the Saigon student center had chosen a group of four persons to meet with Nguyen Quang Trung to guide program activities. Trung had also secured permission to offer English language classes. Teachers would receive five kilos of rice every ten days to supplement the low salaries. The MCC men were excited that they would be able to assist the Vietnamese teachers. These anticipated classes never materialized.

Earl and Pat and their children arrived in Pennsylvania August 20. A visit to MCC in Akron followed soon afterward. On September 9, Earl went with Robert Miller to Washington, DC, to testify before a Subcommittee on International Trade and Commerce of the House Committee on International Relations, requesting that the Administration remove Vietnam from the Trading With the Enemy Act and asked that the trade embargo be lifted. MCC sent copies of Miller's testimony to each congressional person.

Bills were introduced in both the House and Senate to amend the Trading with the Enemy Act to repeal the embargo on U.S. trade with North and South Vietnam, but the bills never reached the floor. (The U.S. trade embargo was not lifted until February 1994.)

In a letter early September, Klassen thanked us for our telegrammed greeting of love and peace we had sent for the Gia Dinh congregation. The church had just asked him to send greetings to Pastor and Mrs. Quang, asking whether they were yet reunited—a clear indication that warm feelings for the pastor's family were again evident. Jim also reported that the executive director of the American Friends Service Committee, Lou Schneider, had been invited to visit Vietnam for the big national celebration on September 2, and was then able to travel to Saigon. He met briefly with AFSC workers Tom Hoskins and Julie Forsythe. The three MCC men hoped that it might be possible for MCC representatives to travel to Vietnam and meet them.

MCC began a limited refugee resettlement program in the summer of 1975. Don Sensenig, assisted for a time by Pastor Quang, facilitated many Mennonite congregations throughout the United States in sponsoring refugees through Church World Service, one of several agencies accredited by the U.S. government. Canadian churches also sponsored refugees who came to Canada. This program broadened to assist refugees from Laos and Cambodia as well. MCC's resettlement program eventually included people from other areas of the world and continued for fifteen years.

In October, Donald Jacobs, slated to succeed Harold Stauffer as EMBMC overseas secretary, visited Mary and me in Bangkok. We arranged a lunch meeting with Koson Srisang, the general secretary of the Church of Christ in Thailand, and worked out an agreement to have CCT sponsor us for visa purposes. Mary would give volunteer time to assist the church in Vietnam refugee resettlement programs, while I would continue to gather information on Indochina developments and write.

Linda and Murray Hiebert occasionally came from Vientiane to Bangkok. In September, we purchased several tons of vegetable seeds in Bangkok which we sent to Vientiane for distribution to refugees who were returning to the countryside. Now we were arranging another shipment of seeds to be distributed to the people of Vientiane who were planting gardens to help them become more self-sufficient.

When I accompanied Jacobs to the Don Muang airport, I met Tom Hoskins and Julie Forsythe, the last AFSC personnel in Vietnam who had just arrived from Saigon. They affirmed the good morale of the MCC men in Saigon.

At the airport, I also met Alexander Kowles, an independent missionary who left Saigon on the same plane. A former Alliance missionary in China, he stayed in Da Nang where he had been teaching English for several years and continued teaching. A few months after the revolution some of his students said he should get written permission to teach. He received no response to his request. On August 30, he was ordered expelled from the country for violating the laws by teaching English without permission!

Kowles said that the Tin Lanh district superintendent in Da Nang was able to freely travel around to visit his churches. In Saigon, before leaving the country, Kowles stayed at the Chinese Alliance Church in the Cholon area, eating simple meals of rice, a bit of fish, and *rau muống*, the poor man's vegetable now called *rau giải phóng* (liberation vegetable)! This local church functioned well, led my Miss Dorcas Sue. Kowles had met the three MCC men and met twice with Tin Lanh President Mieng. From Mieng, he learned that one of the Tin Lanh pastors in the country was held by the authorities; two others were restricted to their home areas.

Fr. John Tabor also left Vietnam about the same time. A former U.S. Navy builder, Tabor studied at St. Joseph's Seminary on Cuong De Street, Saigon, and was ordained in 1974 and assigned to a parish twelve kilometers northwest of Da Nang city. Accused of traveling to certain places without prior position, he was ordered to leave the country. He was told that Vietnam did not need foreign priests. Catholics continued to attend Sunday mass, but fewer people went to weekday masses because people were required to attend late evening government reeducation sessions in their local communities and go to work early.

Tom and Julie brought mail from the three MCC men in Saigon. In late September, the Provisional Revolutionary Government had introduced the new *liberation đồng*, worth 500 of the previous currency. Like all residents, the men turned in all their old currency to a bank and were issued some of the new currency; they could request the balance as needed. Assuming that they might be staying awhile longer, Max asked Akron to send $2,000 more. A few weeks later, Vern Prehiem, who succeeded Robert Miller as MCC Asia Director, notified the men that the U.S. State Department gave permission to send this money. However, the American government denied a license to purchase small Japanese tractors to export to Vietnam; MCC would have those funds sent from Canada.

On October 22, the MCC men in Saigon had their third visit with Dr. Loc from the Ministry of Foreign Affairs. On this occasion, they presented four hand-held mine detectors that MCC had imported early in the year for use in Quang Ngai. Dr. Loc said they would be used by the General Office of Agriculture. There was some question about their effectiveness since so much shrapnel was in the ground from exploded munitions.

Dr. Loc affirmed the simple life the men were living. They understood his comments about the importance of telling stories about the revolution to people in the States as a gentle reminder that they should soon plan to leave. "MCC is small, but small relationships are very important," Dr. Loc said. "MCC is playing a very important part in building a bridge of understanding between the peoples of America and Vietnam."

In late October, Mary, Jonathan and I had to leave the country to pick up new Thai non-immigrant visas. Since Steven and Becky were in school, they had been granted student visas! On October 30, the day after we arrived in Vientiane, Mary and I had the unexpected opportunity of welcoming from Hanoi the missionaries detained in Ban Me Thuot nearly seven months earlier. We walked out on the tarmac to greet SIL members John and Carolyn Miller with six-year-old LuAnne, and C&MA missionaries Betty Mitchell, Lillian and Richard Phillips, and Joan and Norman Johnson.

Back in Bangkok, we invited the Millers to our home and heard their stories around the dinner table. Nearly all the group had experienced severe illnesses. Just before leaving Hanoi, valuable papers were taken from them—Dick Phillips's doctoral thesis and Bible translations in Mnong and Bru prepared by the Phillips and Miller couples. During the entire ordeal, the missionaries were able to have regular periods of Bible study together. Summing up the whole experience, John said: "In one way, it was a waste of time; but, boy, we learned so much."

In response to MCC's request to visit, Vietnamese authorities proposed a July 1975 date, then cancelled it. Robert Miller expressed the urgency for a visit in a letter to the Vietnam Committee for Solidarity with the American People:

> Our supporting groups here in North America are very interested in continuing to provide assistance and to maintain relationships with the people in both North and South Vietnam. But they have questions regarding what kinds of aid are needed, how assistance is being used and how the people of Vietnam are progressing in their post-war reconstruction activities. It is essential for us to be able to discuss with you and other appropriate officials plans for aid in the coming year so that we can interpret needs and possibilities to our supporting organizations. . . . Earlier this year we sent [food] for the PRG. . . . We want to talk to the PRG about additional assistance.

Another date was set for October and then cancelled. The visit finally took place in November. Miller led the MCC team which included Dan Zehr from the Winnipeg MCC office, Linda Hiebert and me. We flew from Vientiane to Hanoi on Wednesday, November 12, on an Aeroflot flight—along with American Friends Service Committee Laos personnel Louis and Eryl Kubicka and their young daughter. After checking into the new Cuban-built *Thắng Lợi* (Victory) Hotel and lunch, we met our hosts of the *Việt Mỹ* (Vietnamese American) Committee at their headquarters. Mr. Do Xuan Oanh, general secretary of this committee, spoke of their desire to normalize relations with the United States and to heal the wounds of war. We also discussed possible assistance projects with Xuan Oanh and with Mr. Pham Van Thinh, Viet-My's technical expert. That evening we met with Mr. Hoang Quang Tung, editor of the government's *Nhân Dân* (Peoples) daily newspaper.

On Sunday, November 16, the following news item in *Giải Phóng* (Liberation) and other newspapers brought cheer to the three MCC men in Saigon:

AMERICAN FRIENDS VISIT VIETNAM

Liberation News Service--- Responding to the invitation from the Vietnamese-American Solidarity Committee, a group of representatives from the Mennonite organization (an Evangelical denomination) consisting of Robert Miller, Daniel Zehr, Luke Martin and Linda Hiebert, together with representatives of the American Friends Service Committee (Quaker denomination) consisting of Lou Kubicka and Eryl Kubicka, arrived in Hanoi November 12, 1975, on a visit to Vietnam.

These two organizations have actively participated in activities opposing the American war of aggression in Vietnam, and continue many creative activities to assist the Vietnamese people to bind the wounds of war and rebuild the country.

During our days in Hanoi, we were kept busy. We visited the Bach Mai Hospital—where twenty-eight doctors and nurses were killed in the infamous 1972 "Christmas" bombing by the U.S. Air Force—and the memorial on Kham Thien Street where hundreds of civilians died. We

Tin Lanh church in Hanoi.

observed a day care center, a secondary school, and an orphanage that had received some Quaker aid. We visited factories and areas where new housing was being constructed.

We were taken to the Ho Chi Minh mausoleum. We visited the Temple of Literature, the ancient university. We were taken to see the Hanoi Circus and to hear a symphony performance. We had dinner with the vice-mayor of Hanoi. We met with medical doctors. We met representatives of the United Nations High Commissioner for Refugees (UNHCR) and of UNICEF (United Nations International Children's Emergency Fund). We talked with persons representing the Christian Conference of Asia and a person from CIMADE, the French Protestant relief and developmental organization.

At the Hanoi congregation of the Vietnam Evangeli-

Meeting Evangelical Church leaders—Bui Hoanh Thu, Daniel Zehr, Robert Miller, Hoang Kim Phuc, Luke Martin and Linda Hiebert.

cal Church, we conversed with Pastors Hoang Kim Phuc, the Church president; Bui Hoanh Thu, the vice president and general secretary; and Mrs. Nguyen Thi Loan, a member of the Church council.

We visited a vegetable cooperative near Hanoi and a collective farm outside the city, and traveled forty-five kilometers north to Bac Giang province where we visited a bombed school that had received MCC building supplies to enable them to rebuild.

In our initial meeting with the Viet-My Committee, the Kubickas asked to meet the Prime Minister, Pham Van Dong. To our surprise, several days later we were told that we would meet with him on Tuesday, November 18. When we were driven to the Presidential Palace, formerly the palace of the governor of French Indochina, the smiling Prime Minister came down the outside steps and welcomed each member of the joint MCC-AFSC delegation. He talked about the need for assistance in rebuilding.

This visit was reported in the Vietnamese press: "On November 18, Premier Pham Van Dong met with representatives of the Mennonite organization (belonging to Evangelical denomi-nation) and representatives of the 'American Friends Service Committee' (belonging to Quaker denomination) delegation who are visiting Vietnam. Premier Pham Van Dong conversed cordially with the American and Canadian friends of the two delegations."

Later that day, the AFSC office in Philadelphia relayed the text of a cable sent from Hanoi:

> Quaker Mennonite Delegation met 18 November with Premier Pham Van Dong who shared following message: "I send to the American people our greetings of peace and friendship. Now there is peace. If we want to have real peace we must have friendship." He asked us to urge the American people to contribute to healing the wounds of war. The premier sees urgently needed help in reconstruction to be humanitarian not political. . . . He sees our efforts for normalization to be work of great significance which requires strong conviction. "You are religious and adhere to religious ideals. Your faith will strengthen you." Please share Akron Winnipeg suggest news release. - Quaker Mennonite Delegations

On Saturday, November 22, we flew to Saigon with a short layover at the now-silent Da Nang airport which once sent American planes around the clock to bomb both North and South Vietnam. In Saigon, we were met by a delegation headed by Mr. Nguyen Van Cung, vice-president of the NLF committee of Ho Chi Minh City. Among several others who met us were Mr. Nguyen Chau An of Saigon's Truong Minh Giang Tin Lanh congregation, Mr. Nguyen Kim Thinh of the Gia Dinh Chi Lang Tin Lanh congregation, and Mr. Nguyen Thanh Long. An was identified as a Protestant and representative of the Foreign Affairs Section of Ho Chi Minh City Military Management Committee. (Saigon officially became Ho Chi Minh City when Vietnam was formally unified on July 2, 1976.) Thinh was introduced as a "patriotic Protestant" and cadre of the NLF Committee, and Long a Protestant and member of the pre-sidium of the NLF Committee of Ho Chi Minh City. I recognized An and Thinh, having seen them at Tin Lanh church activities previously, but knew neither of them well. Thinh was an uncle to Nguyen Quang Trung of the Mennonite congregation. Although I had never known Long, I recognized him from Klassen's letters as the head of the United Evangelical Church (*Hội Thánh Tin Lành Thống Nhứt*).

After checking in at the Ben Nghe (formerly Embassy) Hotel near Saigon's central market, we met with Mr. Nguyen Van Hieu, Minister of State and member of the Administrative Council.

Robert Miller with Nguyen Thanh Long.

Hieu outlined problems South Vietnam was now facing: the economy heavily dependent on raw materials from abroad, lack of machine and animal power, excessive manpower in the cities and the old army, resettlement needs, and social problems—prostitutes and drug addicts. He said South Vietnam wanted good relationships with all people, including the United States. He indicated the status of the three MCC men in Saigon was problematic because the South did not yet have diplomatic missions. They were only prepared to do "business" with delegations such as ours.

That evening, we phoned the MCC office and spoke with Max. We invited them to meet us at the hotel. Miller met them in the lobby, but was told by a committee member that they could not meet us. It was clear that Americans were no longer in charge of things in Saigon!

On Sunday, November 23, we asked to attend a worship service in one of the Tin Lanh churches but were told that plans had already been made for us to go to the seaside town of Vung Tau. While most in the party went swimming, Mr. Long and I lounged together on beach chairs, talking about developments in the churches.

During the struggle of the Viet Minh against the French, Long said he came to see the cause of Christ and of the Revolution to be similar. He said many Evangelical Christians supported the revolution and saw no problem with Christians participating with Marxists in the revolution. "Some of us begin with Christian assumptions," he said; "others begin with a materialistic ideology." Long's vision was for all the Evangelical churches in the South to join the United Evangelicals. When this occurred, he said, they would seek union with the church in the North to form *the* Evangelical Church of Vietnam. The Baptists, Mennonites, Assemblies of God, and Church of Christ had joined the united church, Long said, and many individual congregations of the Evangelical Church, but not yet the ECVN as a body. Long said that unity was crucial because Jesus taught it in the Gospel of John, chapter 17. He said that Ho Chi Minh also stressed that there was strength in unity. Long seemed to imply that the survival and growth of the church required this kind of unity.

Mr. Long reported that eighty students were studying at the Tin Lanh Bible Institute in Nha Trang. Among the professors were pastors Ong Van Huyen, Vu Van Cu, Pham Xuan Tin, Kieu Toan and Nguyen Huu Cuong, he said.

Mr. Long said around forty to fifty persons met for worship each Sunday at the Gia Dinh Mennonite congregation—now related to the United Evangelical church. Nguyen Quang Trung was serving as the leader of the church, assisted by Phan Van Khai. Sometimes they had guest speakers.

Jim Klassen informed us later by letter that the Gia Dinh church and center buildings were not available to the church throughout September. At the end of September, Nguyen Quang Trung showed Jim a statement signed by the church members acknowledging Trung as Chairman of the Church and expressing their willingness to join the United Evangelical Church—of which Mr. Long was the chairman. Jim affirmed Trung that church leaders needed to make their own decisions. The Gia Dinh Mennonite leaders hoped that, by joining the union, Mr. Long would help return the church and community center buildings. However, it was not until the church's executive committee agreed to make Rang Dong School a public elementary and junior high school that the government allowed the church to again use the church's meeting space for religious activities. They quickly prepared the classrooms, registered students for levels I and II (grades 1-5, 6-12), and the school formally opened on October 19 like the rest of the schools throughout the South. Trung initially served as principal; former teachers and other school staff who had completed short re-education sessions staffed the new Rang Dong School. Mr. Long told me that the enrollment was around 700 children in two half-day shifts, and would probably rise to 1,000 the following year.

(The Rang Dong School continues to serve the area into the twenty-first century. The alley of Phan Van Tri Street was named Ngo Duc Ke Street. Area maps available on Internet show the Rang Dong School.)

It was not clear to us whether the United Evangelical Church was only a vision of Mr. Long or whether it also had the support of the new government. Mr. Long died in September 1976. And the movement apparently died with him as the government took a more confrontational stance toward religious groups.

Among the several social welfare institutions we visited on Monday, the day after our Vung Tau trip, was the experimental curative center for male drug addicts just opened at the Fatima Center on the Saigon River at the Binh Loi Bridge. Officials said there were around 50,000 young drug addicts in the Saigon area alone. Eighty young men were already there and they anticipated up to two hundred men coming for six to eight weeks' treatment, utilizing traditional and Western medicines, acupuncture and psychotherapy. Four doctors and twelve nurses were on the staff. One of the doctors recognized me as a missionary. I asked if he was Dr. Son, and he nodded.

I had first met Tran Thanh Son two years earlier when he volunteered to assist at the Evangelical Clinic and Hospital in Pleiku. Active in the Inter-Varsity Christian Fellowship, he was drafted into the medical corps after graduation and assigned to work in the large military hospital in Pleiku. In Bangkok in October, I had read a United Press International release about a Dr. Tran Thanh Son completing a re-education program. Now he was here at the drug treat-

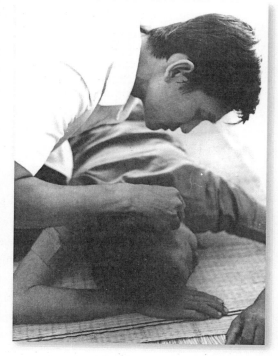

Dr. Son treating addict with acupuncture.

ment center, using acupuncture to control the pain during the addicts' difficult withdrawal period.

On November 25, we visited additional medical treatment centers—a facility making prostheses for amputees, a center treating patients with venereal diseases, and the psychiatric hospital at Bien Hoa where treatment was given to persons suffering psychosis from war trauma or adverse development caused by toxic chemicals.

Since our hosts had not yet promised that we would meet the three MCC men, Miller reminded them that our North American supporters would not understand nor appreciate any failure to meet them. Late that afternoon, we finally met with James Klassen, Max Ediger and Yoshihiro Ichikawa for one and a half hours at our hotel. Although carefully staged with others present, we told them about our visit. Max told about his feelings on reconciliation in Vietnam, and Jim reported on his work with the church.

The next day we returned to Hanoi where we reflected on our trip and discussed with our hosts the visit to the South and our meeting with the MCC men. Mr. Xuan Oanh expressed appreciation that the men stayed in Vietnam, but made it clear that it was now important that they leave. He said it was difficult to assure their safety during these unsettled times. It was clear that the authorities did not consider them MCC representatives; the government wanted to work directly with the headquarters supplemented by periodic delegation visits. After conferring with the others, Miller informed Xuan Oanh and Nguyen Van Tien, the PRG special representative in Hanoi, that he would recommend that the men soon leave. The next day we discussed possible aid projects and on November 29 flew to Vientiane and Bangkok.

In Vientiane, Miller cabled the men in Saigon:

> It was good to see you in Ho Chi Minh City although our time together was too short. We have been thinking about you much since then. . . . We were hoping you could serve as liaison for MCC on project arrangements. You have had good contacts with Dr. Loc but have not been able to talk with other ministries. It is clear to us from our visit that the PRG [does] not consider you as our representatives but just as Mennonites staying on in Vietnam. It seems clear that they want to work on assistance plans through visits like ours rather than having agency representatives at this point.

Miller also wrote to them, noting that there was little for them to do except attend cultural events and write, suggesting that they should "leave within the next three to six weeks when [they] are ready." In closing, he wrote, "When you leave please tell friends there that we are planning to continue assistance to Vietnam and hope to make periodic visits and keep in touch with them. . . . We appreciate all you have done and are doing and pray for God's guidance for all of us."

A summary report of the visit identified possible assistance projects—condensed milk, vegetable seeds, medical equipment, and acrylic yarn—then stated: "Now is the right time for a major emphasis on assistance to Vietnam. The post-war needs are great. The Vietnamese are eager for assistance. In a few years from now they will hopefully get their economy going again and will be able to meet their basic needs, but at the present time we have a real opportunity and responsibility to help."

I was home in Bangkok only a few minutes when a newsman called to ask about the Vietnam visit. Since I had regularly gathered information about Vietnam developments to send to Akron, I was acquainted with several press offices. The Associated Press released an article commenting on our meeting with Prime Minister Dong expressing Vietnam's desire for friendship with the United States, normalization of relations, and desire for economic aid.

After returning home, Miller went to the capital where MCC's Washington office scheduled a news conference on December 3. Only one reporter came—from *The Washington Post*. In his two days in Washington, Miller met with congressional persons and State Department personnel. Dan Zehr held a press conference in Canada that received good coverage.

The three men stayed in Saigon for Christmas. On Sunday, December 21, the second floor of the student center was packed out for the Christmas service which included the choir from the Gia Dinh congregation as well as the choir from the student center. Klassen attended the Christmas Eve service at the Gia Dinh church and then joined the crowd at the Tin Lanh church on Tran Cao Van Street until 1:00 a.m. This edifice was formerly the International Protestant Church. On Christmas day there was another service of baptism at the student center when five persons affirmed the Christian faith.

With the lunar New Year coming on January 31, 1976, Max, Hiro and Jim wanted to celebrate the big holiday in a Vietnam no longer at war. Anticipating leaving the country soon, the men moved from the large student center to a small apartment on Dong Khoi Street. We had known this as Tu Do Street; during the French era it was Catinat Street.

Trung and Mr. Long of the United Evangelicals assumed control of the student center property. The growing believer group was looking forward to meeting there on Sunday, February 1, the second day of Tet, and they invited other friends and relatives. Whether by accident or by Mr. Long's design, the group was locked out that Sunday! Consequently many of the group gathered informally that afternoon at the Tin Lanh Church on Tran Cao Van Street.

On February 6, 1976, the three men submitted applications for exit visas. During Jim's final weeks, the fellowship group from the student center met with other groups—at Tran Cao Van Street and with the Tin Lanh church at Su Van Hanh Street. Jim gave parting greetings to the Gia Dinh Mennonite Church on February 15.

On April 3, the Ministry of Foreign Affairs issued Jim's exit visa and the Ministry honored the three men with a farewell luncheon on April 6. Klassen paid a visit to Doan Van Mieng, the Tin Lanh Church president. Pastor Mieng was well. He said his son, Tin, was attending the Nha Trang Bible Institute. Enrollment was good, but the school lacked finances. He asked Jim to convey greetings to the Alliance missionaries and to thank them for their ministry—"The church in Vietnam exists because of them."

On Wednesday, April 7, Klassen flew to Bangkok. By then our family had already left Bangkok. We had anticipated a home leave in June. However, after Mary's eighty-two year-old father suffered injuries in a December traffic crash, we were urged to return to the States sooner. Since it was no longer so crucial to monitor Vietnam news from the Bangkok base, we left Thailand in February.

Jim arrived at his Kansas home on April 21. Max arrived home on May 7, just over two weeks later. It was not long before the duo was crisscrossing the States, speaking in churches and colleges, accepting TV interviews, facing sympathetic audiences and hostile groups which considered their observations about the revolution as communist propaganda. Yoshihiro Ichikawa left Vietnam on October 22, 1976—nearly eighteen months after liberation.

MCC's pattern of operation called for a resident presence to oversee projects and report program developments. Vietnam found this unacceptable. Committed to finding a way to assist the Vietnamese people who had suffered so much, the MCC Executive Committee accepted this limitation. "The weight of the present opportunity for MCC to bear tangible witness to the love of Christ and the integrity of the church in relating to various economic/political systems [and] the strategic timing of assistance as a ministry toward reconciliation between Vietnam and America" argued for this exception.

The Executive Committee adopted a 1976 Vietnam budget of "$500,000 cash and approximately $500,000 worth for contributed material aid supplies." In addition, MCC would apply to the Canadian International Development Agency (CIDA) for grants totaling one-half million to one million dollars. MCC was also willing to channel postwar aid from other agencies that had not developed contacts in Vietnam. After much discussion, this was approved unanimously by MCC board members at the January annual meeting.

Vietnam reported the receipt of material aid, using it as intended, and welcomed periodic visits by MCC representatives. Already by late May 1976, another four-member MCC delegation visited Vietnam for seventeen days to view assistance programs and confirm new projects. MCC continued this pattern of delegation visits, later posting a Vietnam director in Bangkok who made frequent visits to observe programs. In 1990 MCC opened a resident office in Hanoi.

On July 2, 1976, the National Assembly proclaimed the official reunification of Vietnam as the Socialist Republic of Vietnam. Gia Dinh province and other areas surrounding Saigon were annexed into metropolitan Ho Chi Minh City. The government slowly implemented central political control over all aspects of society, weakening the economy. Religious freedom was curtailed. The Gia Dinh Mennonite church property was confiscated in June 1978 along with properties of other religious organizations. The student center property was also confiscated. After the Binh Dan Hospital used this facility for a few decades, in 2007 an advanced medical center was built on this and adjoining properties.

The "dark decade" which brought hardships to many people only began to end with the adoption of the socialist-oriented market economy *đổi mới* reforms in 1986. During this era committed church members participated in the life of other churches that remained open. It would be years before the Mennonite church would clearly emerge, phoenix-like, to continue an open Christian witness in Vietnam.

AFTERWORD

There are various criteria for evaluating Christian ministry and witness. One might seek to determine effectiveness—based on communities or lives of people positively affected by the gospel of Christ. Mennonites have emphasized the discipline of faithfulness to the teaching and example of Jesus Christ.

Catholic missionary work in the sixteenth century led to the development of a vital indigenous Christian Church in Vietnam. There was limited witness by French Protestants in the late nineteenth century. Beginning in 1911, missionaries of the Christian and Missionary Alliance passionately proclaimed the Gospel of Jesus Christ, inviting persons to turn from their old ways to following and worshiping the living God. Through this witness, many people came to faith; these Vietnamese believers in turn shared in a witness which led to the establishment of the Evangelical Church of Vietnam.

Born through persecution in sixteenth century Europe, Anabaptist Mennonites in many places became the quiet of the land. This was especially true of those who fled to America, the new world. This stance began changing in the late nineteenth century when the church moved out of isolation into mission and service in other communities and countries. This work expanded in the twentieth century with the formation of the Mennonite Central Committee. By the decade of the fifties, MCC and many Mennonite mission agencies were actively witnessing and serving in dozens of countries around the world. In most places they worked alongside other international mission agencies or with the local Christian churches.

This then was the way Mennonites worked in Vietnam—alongside the Christian and Missionary Alliance, and alongside the Evangelical Church of Vietnam. Mennonites learned much from other Christians but also shared with others their understanding of the gospel of Jesus. Some Evangelical Church pastors agreed with Mennonites that the Good News of Jesus is the gospel of peace.

It is perhaps not coincidental that North American Mennonites went to Vietnam at the same time that America's political and military machine replaced the departing French colonial power. However, one could make a case that MCC personnel and missionaries would have gone to Vietnam in the nineteen-fifties even if the United States had not become involved in Vietnam. MCC and a Mennonite mission agency were active in Algeria during that same era when that North African country was also seeking independence from its French colonial past. But Vietnam played out much differently than Algeria.

In mid-century, the United States, now the most powerful country in the world, became obsessed with an urgency to restrain and eradicate what it viewed as a pernicious ideology which held political sway in the Soviet Union, had recently triumphed in China, and continued in parts of Korea where an open conflict with terrible death and destruction had just ended in a stalemate. It was not viewed politically expedient for America to see another territory in Southeast Asia come under the control of a communist government. Thus the United States made its fateful commitment to South Vietnam.

During the early years of their involvement in Vietnam, beginning in 1954, Mennonites did not sense incompatibility with the American ideal of a free and open political system in

South Vietnam, seeing it as eminently preferable to a classic, rigid, communist-controlled order. Even when the government of the Republic of Vietnam became more oppressive, as guests in the country, Mennonites sought to minister and witness without much regard to the political realities. These sentiments changed during the stormy era of 1963 to 1965 when the United States determined to use its military might to defeat the Vietnamese revolutionary forces committed to uniting their country by military power when not permitted to do so politically through general elections.

With the evangelical Protestant Christian faith already identified with the United States in the Vietnamese minds, the overwhelming American political and military engagement only magnified this perception. Some Mennonite mission leaders did not fully comprehend this reality. They encouraged us, in essence saying: "Don't confuse the faith in Jesus with the policies of the United States. After all, America is not a Christian nation. You are called to proclaim the gospel; do not concern yourselves with political issues." Mennonite missionaries and service workers certainly recognized unique opportunities for proclaiming the gospel. But we missionaries could not ignore the escalation of destruction and death brought about by the American military policies.

In the midst of the overpowering American military occupation of South Vietnam, we Mennonite missionaries sought a more quiet presence, preaching and teaching, offering needed services to people within the communities in which we lived and worked. In 1972, a researcher of the evangelical Christian movement within Vietnam praised the Mennonite missionaries who "were carrying on an exemplary ministry of social service [with] their peace witness [providing] a much-needed dimension to the total impact of foreign Christians in a war-torn country." Yet he concluded that "their motivation to win Vietnamese to Christ seemed crippled by a touch of 'presence theology'," defined as *being* in the world and engaging in good ministries without persuading others to become followers of Jesus Christ. We understood this critique, while protesting that we were inviting people to accept Jesus Christ as Savior and encouraging them to follow the way of Jesus.

As the military conflict intensified, there was a perceptible growing divide between Mennonite missionaries and most of the missionary personnel of other agencies. Many of them welcomed the American military presence and publically prayed for success in their attempts to rid the country of those identified with the Viet Cong. Eventually, we sensed that many leaders of the Evangelical Church—but not all—shared this stance, even though they continued to maintain they were apolitical. Perhaps we Mennonites would have remained on the sidelines if military leaders would have followed so-called just-war principles. But we could not remain silent when the military strategies pursued and tactics used by the United States and allied forces brought injury and death to hundreds of thousands of innocent people in the countryside, and body counts became the measure determining a successful pursuit of the war.

We had to speak out against the American War, not primarily to support the growing swell of opposition in the United States, in Asia and around the world. We spoke because we could not be true to our understanding of the gospel if we remained silent. Some heard us. Many did not. Some Mennonites in North America tended to support the U.S. military policies. Many of those who confessed faith in Christ and were baptized into the fellowship of the Mennonite church in Vietnam also found it too difficult to stand up against monstrous political and military forces.

Those of us who worked in Vietnam were in dialogue with our agency administrators and other Mennonite church leaders. We challenged them, and they inspired and supported us. We cautiously spoke out. MCC amplified its prophetic voice in 1968 by opening an office in Washington, DC. It is for others to judge the validity of our witness and service.

In the face of massive American political and military involvement, James Metzler made a strong argument that there was no way that Vietnamese people could correctly hear and observe the true Gospel of Jesus Christ from Americans. Our missionaries could identify with the words attributed to Francis of Assisi, "Preach the gospel, and if necessary, use words!" In the communities where we worked, we were viewed by many people either as agents of the US Central Intelligence Agency or as do-gooders who were there to save our own souls by doing what we believed would bring us rewards in the next life!

In his book *Reaching the Other Side*, Earl Martin describes how he was told in early 1975 that many educated people in Quang Ngai believed that he and his wife, Pat, worked for the CIA. Some people likely changed their minds when Earl stayed after the Saigon government forces fled on March 25. But not everyone was convinced. Take the case of Nguyen Van Muc from Quang Ngai. From a Catholic family, he became a member of the Evangelical Church and married a young woman who worked with Vietnam Christian Service as a sewing teacher in a refugee camp. He and his wife knew Earl Martin and Pat Hostetter well. In the mid-nineties, Muc and his family immigrated to the United States and settled near our family. When Earl was speaking at a nearby church, I invited Muc to go along. After the evening, Muc said to me, "I am now convinced that Earl was not working for the CIA in Vietnam!"

Some persons will make the argument that most people in South Vietnam did not want to live within a communist society and were prepared to sacrifice much to live within a more free society. Many of these viewed American involvement as an altruistic attempt to come alongside the people to defend themselves from the Democratic Republic of Vietnam that wished to impose its rigid rule over the whole country by military force. Some will point to draconian policies implemented following the 1975 communist victory that led to suffering for so many people as evidence that the United States should have continued the military struggle—even if it had ignited another world war—perhaps even a nuclear war. A simplistic slogan "Better dead than Red" expressed that view. Even if a people accept that position, few would support the validity of foreigners imposing that policy onto another people.

Shortly after we left Vietnam, we reflected on several questions: To what extent could we as foreigners legitimately involve ourselves in the political issues of another nation? Could we missionaries exercise a "moral authority" in speaking to local injustices? Should the Mennonite witness against the military policies of the Saigon and Hanoi forces have led to a greater identification with and support of a "third force" alternative? Was there a viable third way? To what degree could missionaries identify with the victims of injustice? Did our concern about injustices perpetrated by the Saigon government seriously consider the downsides of the only pragmatic alternative—the communist one?

In the history of human affairs, there are so many variables. One cannot say what would have happened if peoples and governments would have chosen different courses at crucial times. We sought to follow the way of Jesus Christ and the leading of God's Spirit in our relationships with all people.

When we missionaries left, did we leave a Mennonite church in Vietnam like we might have desired? Four years earlier Donald Sensenig had written a short article "On Being a Missionary in Vietnam." He noted that "our missionary opinion" on crucial issues in Vietnamese life would likely not be considered too seriously since we were aliens, Americans appearing to have limitless opportunities, yet handicapped in sharing "at a deep level" with our Vietnamese friends. He wrote:

> So we are driven toward simply sharing "the gospel," giving our opinions on what it means and how it applies, and trusting the Holy Spirit to make it meaningful and applicable, because our applications may not be taken too seriously. Indeed, the impact of the words and deeds of Jesus and His early followers carries its own weight, without our poor power "to add or detract." And hopefully within the church the Spirit has gathered over the years, our views and contributions may carry more weight. Although on second thought, I'm not sure how much more. In both cases we receive a respectful hearing. There are those who will actually listen to us! But because we are to some degree foreign to Vietnam's ideas and ways of thinking, and to some degree immune to its peculiar problems and agencies, we are definitely limited.
>
> Another answer suggests itself, of course. Become less foreign, more vulnerable, more understanding, more deeply part of Vietnam. Of course! And we do try. Thank God for the efforts to attain just these sensitivities that our missionaries in Vietnam work at daily. There is doubtful value in rating missionary groups on a scale of such attitudes, the differences will generally be of degree only, rarely a completely qualitative difference. Still, I am grateful for the many honest efforts to tear down walls and reach over the more resistant ones. Which is simply to express again the limitations of our role as overseas (foreign) missionaries.

Mennonite Central Committee and the Eastern Mennonite Board of Missions and Charities had different—but partially overlapping—objectives. MCC was committed to helping relieve human suffering by providing material assistance, particularly food and medical care "In the name of Christ." MCC believed this goal could be achieved by working closely with the Evangelical Church. The objective of Eastern Mennonite Board of Missions and Charities was to introduce the gospel of Jesus Christ as the way to God, and invite people to accept Christ by faith, and welcome them into a Christian community—the church. EMBMC also established educational and social programs. The two Mennonite organizations worked in harmony with each other and related closely to the Evangelical Church.

Embracing the life and teachings of Jesus Christ for Mennonites has meant service to others and a mission of inviting others to this faith. Living among and working with persons who practiced Buddhism, Caodaism, ancestor veneration, Catholic or Evangelical Christianity or no faith, North American Mennonites tried to respect the integrity of each person.

Missionaries sustained a vision of friendship evangelism that would see persons come to faith in Jesus Christ and live out that faith in the church. The escalating war changed the context and manner in which the gospel of Jesus was presented. MCC concern for the material wellbeing of the people changed its focus from providing food, clothing and medical care to a commitment to work for peace and reconciliation. Both missionaries and MCC personnel recognized that our very presence in Vietnam had all sorts of political implications. Ethical issues in the highly complicated political and military context were tainted with ambiguity. Church leaders involved in international ministries are compelled to recognize that these issues—writ large in Vietnam—

also exist to some degree whenever the church becomes involved in another community, another culture, another country.

The merger of Mennonite Central Committee with other agencies in 1966 was generally a positive experience for MCC, Church World Service, Lutheran World Relief, and for the Tin Lanh Church—even with all the issues this entailed. When MCC again became independent in 1973, MCC sought to relate more closely with Mennonite missionaries and to the Vietnam Mennonite Church.

In *From Saigon to Shalom,* * James Metzler helpfully considers important missiological issues the Christian Church faces when it becomes involved in mission and service. Aside from the ethical and missiological issues, the Christian Church needs to reflect more theologically on the Vietnam experience. Jonathan Tran, born in the late sixties, who came to the United States with his family as a young child in 1975, reflects on the American War philosophically and theologically in his book, *The Vietnam War and Theologies of Memory**. Acknowledging the factors that preceded direct American military involvement in Vietnam, he argues that the United States, lacking a view of eternity, was impatient and sought to impose its time on another people. Frustrated in their assignments, military personnel perpetrated a pattern of atrocities against the Vietnamese people.

> Americans went to Vietnam because they feared time. The reported pandemic spread of communism threatened the fall of American interests around the globe. Killing became the only sure way to keep the dominos from falling. America committed itself to 25 years of killing because its temporality doomed it to making sure history came out right. To do so was to view time shorn of eternity, to grasp creation as if there were no Creator, Reconciler, and Redeemer, and to conceptualize the culmination of God's self-giving in something like America's manifest destiny.

More than 58,000 American soldiers died in Vietnam. We Mennonite missionaries have come to view all American soldiers who served in Vietnam—even those who returned home—as victims of the war. Stanley Karnow in *Vietnam** calls the war in Vietnam "a war that nobody won—a struggle between victims. Its origins were complex, its lessons disputed, its legacy still to be assessed by future generations. But whether a valid venture or a misguided endeavor, it was a tragedy of epic dimensions."

That Americans are unable to agree on how to remember Vietnam, and will probably never come to terms with it, places an intolerable burden on those who killed in Vietnam. Within the Church, Tran reminds us that "in the ritual enactment of Christ's life, death, and resurrection," in remembering and confessing, persons can receive forgiveness and restoration.

American Mennonites in the twenty-first century are doing critical work in the area of conflict transformation, restorative justice, and conciliation. Understanding Vietnam theologically enables collaborative ministries among veterans as well as with refugees and programs in Vietnam such as assisting families affected by Agent Orange and removing unexploded ordnance which continue to maim and kill persons born decades after the war.

The two-decade North American Mennonite involvement in Vietnam experienced a drastic change in 1975. What has been the ongoing—the lasting—effect of those ministries?

The Gia Dinh Mennonite congregation's facilities were permanently confiscated, and the church was not even permitted to meet in homes for many years. Members of the church attended local Tin Lanh or Baptist congregations that continued meeting. There was little correspondence from members of the church for several years after the Revolution. By the early eighties, believers were meeting occasionally in homes, and a church leader identified more than thirty families totaling more than two hundred people who were related to the Mennonite Church. Pastor and Mrs. Tran Xuan Quang returned to visit family and friends in the early nineties and were welcomed by the Mennonite church group.

The Mennonite Central Committee continued an uninterrupted program with Vietnam, providing relief aid and technical assistance in the areas of agriculture, medicine and education. After being administered from Bangkok for many years, MCC opened an administrative office in Hanoi in 1990. In 2004, MCC celebrated fifty years of Vietnam ministries.

The exodus of persons from Vietnam spawned refugee communities in many areas of North America, leading to the formation of many Catholic and Protestant Vietnamese churches. Among them are Mennonite congregations in Canada and the United States. In 1997, pastors representing Vietnamese Mennonite churches in North America visited Ho Chi Minh City, establishing a relationship with an independent house church movement. Another group in central Vietnam identified as Mennonites, and in 2003 these three entities formed an all-Vietnam Mennonite Church. Testing came to the church the following year, and the union did not hold. One group went on to seek official status for the church, which was granted in 2007. Eastern Mennonite Missions became officially supportive in the area of theological education. This story is told in "The Mennonite Church in Vietnam," *Churches Engage Asian Traditions.** Today there are dynamic ministries with thousands of believers in dozens of faith communities.

The development of the Vietnam Mennonite Church, indeed the growth of the entire evangelical Christian church in Vietnam since 1975, is remarkable. Christians are committed to serving God and their communities. May God's grace and blessing enable the entire Church of Christ in Vietnam to serve and witness to their people and to the entire world.

* See listing in Annotated Bibliography

BRIEF VIETNAM TIME LINE

1954	Jul 21	Geneva Accords signed ending French Indochina War, 1946-1954
	Aug 13	Orie Miller arrives in Saigon, welcomes first MCC worker on Aug. 16
1955	Oct 23	Ngo Dinh Diem proclaims Republic of Vietnam with himself as President
1956	Apr 5	MCC signs agreement with C&MA to work at Ban Me Thuot Leprosarium
1957	May 30	James and Arlene Stauffer arrive as first EMBMC missionaries
1959	Jan	Refused elections to unite, Hanoi changes "political struggle" to "armed struggle"
1960	Mar 1	MCC signs agreement with Evangelical Church to begin Nha Trang medical program
1961	May 28	First Mennonite baptism
1962	Feb 8	U.S. forms Military Assistance Command, Vietnam to direct conduct of war
	May 30	Daniel Gerber, Archie Mitchell and Ardel Vietti kidnapped
1963	Nov 1	President Ngo Dinh Diem ousted in military coup and is assassinated
1964	Jul 22	Mennonite Mission rents Gia Dinh property and opens Community Center
	Aug 2	Tonkin Gulf "incident" leads to U.S. bombing North Vietnam
1965	Mar 8	First U.S. combat troops arrive at Da Nang
	Apr 19	Nine persons baptized at Community Center; congregation forms
	Dec 8	Mennonite missionaries release "Statement of Concern" about U.S. fighting a war
1966	Jan 6	CWS, LWR and MCC sign agreement forming Vietnam Christian Service
	Dec 21	VNCS group meets with Billy Graham
1967	May 15	CORDS formed, placing all official U.S. activities under military direction
	Nov/Dec	Mennonite missionaries send "Letter from Vietnam to American Christians"
1968	Jan 30	Tet Offensive brings war to the cities
	Mar 31	President Lyndon Johnson limits bombing, proposes negotiations
	May 13	Paris Peace Talks begin
	May 25-Jun 7	Warfare in area near Mennonite Community Center
1969	Jan 18	Paris Peace Talks resume with four parties
	Jan 20	President Richard Nixon inaugurated, develops strategy of Vietnamization of war
	Mar 16	Tran Xuan Quang ordained pastor of Mennonite Church
1970	Oct 17	Luke and Dorothy Beidler begin ministry in Can Tho
1971	Apr 26	VNCSer Ted Studebaker killed in Di Linh attack
1972	Mar 30	North Vietnam launches major offensive across Demilitarized Zone
1973	Jan 1	MCC resumes ministries independent of VNCS
	Jan 27	Paris Peace Accords signed
	Feb 18	Dedication of new Mennonite Church and Community Center
1974	Aug 8	Richard Nixon resigns U.S. presidency following Watergate scandal
1975	Mar 10	North Vietnam forces attack Ban Me Thuot, beginning ARVN rout
	Apr 30	Saigon government surrenders; four MCC persons voluntarily remain

GLOSSARY OF VIETNAMESE WORDS

Vietnamese diacritics are provided here for the names, places and other terms listed in the text according to Vietnamese alphabetical listings. The initial consonants *D/d* and *Gi/gi* are pronounced as *Z/z* in the northern dialect and *Y/y* in the southern dialect. The *Đ/đ* is similar to the English *D/d*. The *S/s* is similar to the English *Sh/sh*. The *X/x* is similar to the English *S/s*. The *Th/th* is similar to the English *T/t*. The *Ng/ng* is like the *ng* in si**ng**ing. The *Nh/nh* is like the Spanish *ñ*.

An Khê	Cái Sắn	Dương Cầm Chương
An Lộc	Cam Ranh	Dương Văn Minh
An Lợi	Cần Thơ	Đa Nhim
Ấp Bắc	Cao Đài	Đà Hoa
Ba Tơ	Cao Thắng	Đà Nẵng
Bà Chiểu	Cao Văn Viên	Đà Lạt
Ban Quản Trị	Cần Đước	Đakao
Bàn Cờ	Cầu Bông	Đào Vân Diệu
Bạc Liêu	Cây Quéo	Đào Văn Hoa
Bạch Đằng	Chánh Hưng	Đạo Dừa
Ban Đại Diện	Chân Tín	Đắc Tô, Đắk Tô
Ban Mê Thuột	Chẩn Y Viện	Đặng Thị Hiền
Bảo Đại	Châu Hồng Lực	Đặng Thái Hùng
Bảo Lộc	Châu Văn Tiên	Đặng Thị Thu Hương
Báp-tít	Chi Lăng	Đặng Văn Lực
Bắc Giang	Chí Hòa	Đặng Ngọc Phúc
Bàu Giang	Chị Bảy	Điện Biên Phủ
Bến Hải	Chiêu Hồi	Đinh Văn Nam
Bến Tre	Chính Luận	Đình Ngọc Châu
Bệnh Viện Bình Dân	Chợ Lớn	Định
Bích Liên	Chợ Quán	Định Quán
Biên Hòa	Chúa	Đoàn Thanh Liêm
Bình Dương	Chùa Ấn Quang	Đoàn Văn Miêng
Bình Hòa	Chương Thiện	Đông Hà
Bình Lợi	Cô Chín	Đỗ Đức Trí
Bình Long	Cô Do	Đỗ Hữu Nghiêm
Bình Phước	Cô Hai	Đỗ Xuân Oanh
Bình Thuận	Cô Khuyên	Đỗ Vĩnh Thành
Bình Xuyên	Cô Ký	Đỗ Văn Thương
Bông Sơn	Cô Năm	Đông Hà
Bùi Chu	Côn Sơn	Đồng Ông Cộ
Bùi Đình Đạm	Công Lý	Đồng Khởi
Bùi Công Đồng	Cường Để	Đồng Nai
Bùi Quang	Cựu Trắc	Đồng Xoài
Bùi Thi	Dân Chủ	Đức Phổ
Bùi Hoành Thử	Dầu Tiếng	Đức Trí
Bùi Thị Xuân	Di Linh	Đức Chúa Trời
Cà Mau	Diên Khánh	Êm Đềm
Cam Phú	Duy Cách Lâm	Gia Định
Cai Lậy	Dương Thành Châu	Gia Long

Giải Phóng	Lăng Ông	Ngô Tùng Châu
Gió Nam	Lê Văn Ái	Ngô Đình Diệm
Gò Vấp	Lê Ngọc Cẩn	Ngô Đình Thị Hiệp
Hà Nội	Lê Du/Đu ?	Ngô Đình Nhu
Hai Bà Trưng	Lê Duẫn	Ngô Bá Thành
Hải Dương	Lê Duyên	Ngô Đình Thục
Hải Phòng	Lê Văn Duyệt	Nguyễn Thị Bảy
Hàm Nghi	Lê Quang Định	Nguyễn Văn Anh
Hàng Xanh	Lê Thị Hai	Nguyễn Châu Ân
Hậu Giang	Lê Ngọc Hương	Nguyên Văn Bình
Hậu Nghĩa	Lê Văn Lộc	Nguyễn Văn Bông
Hiền Vương	Lê Lợi	Nguyễn Đam Cúc
Hiếu	Lê Hoàng Phu	Nguyễn Hữu Cương
Hòa Hảo	Lê Đình Sung	Nguyễn Thị Đệ
Hòa Hưng	Lê Vĩnh Thạch	Nguyễn Văn Độ
Hòa Khánh	Lê Văn Thái	Nguyễn Văn Hai
Hoàng Đức Nhã	Lê Văn Thảo	Nguyễn Nam Hải
Hoàng Kim Phúc	Lê Đức Thọ	Nguyễn Văn Hiếu
Hoàng Quang Tùng	Lê Khắc Tuyển	Nguyễn Thanh Hòa
Hòn Chồng	Lê Thị Vân	Nguyễn Thị Hoàng
Hồ Huệ Bá	Lê Thị Ý	Nguyễn Văn Học
Hồ Thu Cúc	Lịch	Nguyễn Thị Hồng
Hồ Chí Minh	Liên Khương	Nguyễn Huệ
Hồ Trung Tý	Lò Voi	Nguyễn Văn Hương
Hội An	Long An	Nguyễn Phi Khanh
Hội Dục Anh	Long Bình	Nguyễn Khánh
Hội Thánh Tin Lành	Long Hải	Nguyễn Cao Kỳ
Huế (city)	Long Kiến	Nguyễn Ngọc Lan
Huệ (name)	Long Mỹ	Nguyễn Hữu Lắm
Hùng	Long Thành	Nguyễn Linh
Hưng	Long Xuyên	Nguyễn Tấn Lộc
Huỳnh Thị Dung	Lộc Ninh	Nguyễn Thành Long
Huỳnh Kim Luyện	Lương Thị Luồng	Nguyễn Thị Loan
Huỳnh Tấn Mầm	Lương Bảo Thái	Nguyễn Thanh Mạc
Huỳnh Tấn Phát	Lý Trà	Nguyễn Văn Mục
Huỳnh Minh Ý	Lý Tuyết Nga	Nguyễn Muông (Bật)
Hứa Hớn Long	Mạnh Tường	Nguyễn Văn Mỹ
Hương	Minh Quý	Nguyễn Thành Nam
Khàm Thiên	Mỏ Cày	Nguyễn Tuyết Nga
Khánh Hòa	Mộ Đức	Nguyễn Văn Ngay
Khánh Hội	Mục-sư	Nguyễn Như Nguyên
Khe Sanh	Mỹ Lai	Nguyễn Thúy Nguyệt
Khúc Kim Bên	Mỹ Tho	Nguyễn Hậu Nhương
Kiều Công Thảo	Nam Quan	Nguyễn Văn Ninh
Kiều Toản	Nghĩa Hành	Nguyễn Thị Oanh
Kim Ngân	Nghiệp	Nguyễn Xuân Oanh
Kinh Đô	Ngọc	Nguyễn Hữu Phiên
Kính	Ngô Thị Bích	Nguyễn Thanh Phong
Lái Thiêu	Ngô Du (Dzu)	Nguyễn Đình Phước
Lao Bảo	Ngô Công Đức	Nguyễn Tri Phương
Lăm Lễ Trình	Ngô Đình Cẩn	Nguyễn Văn Quan

Nguyễn Phúc Quế
Nguyễn Phú Sanh
Nguyễn Thị Sen
Nguyễn Kim Sơn
Nguyễn Thiện Sỹ
Nguyễn Thị Tâm
Nguyễn Chánh Thi
Nguyễn Văn Thiệu
Nguyễn Kim Thịnh
Nguyễn Hữu Thọ
Nguyễn Ngọc Thơ
Nguyễn Thiện Thuật
Nguyễn Vân Tiến
Nguyễn Đình Tín
Nguyễn Văn Tốt
Nguyễn Văn Trỗi
Nguyễn Quang Trung
Nguyễn Thành Trung
Nguyễn Văn Tự
Nguyễn Văn Vạn
Nguyễn Văn Vệ
Nguyễn Lưu Viên
Nguyễn Xuân Vọng
Nguyễn Văn Xuyến
Nha Trang
Nhà Bè
Nhung
Nội Bài
Ông Văn Huyền
Phạm Xuân Ẩn
Phạm Văn Đồng
Phạm Thị Luận
Phạm Văn Lục
Phạm Quang Minh
Phạm Văn Năm
Phạm Văn Thiện
Phạm Quang Tâm
Phạm Văn Thịnh
Phạm Thị Xuân Hương
Phạm Xuân Tín
Phan Quang Đán
Phan Tư Dung
Phan Thanh Giản
Phan Thị Phương Hằng
Phan Văn Khai
Phan Thị Tuyết Nga
Phan Đình Phùng
Phan Bá Phước
Phan Huy Quát
Phan Rang
Phan Khắc Sửu
Phan Thiết

Phan Văn Tranh
Phan Văn Trị
Phan Văn Xuyến
Phát Diệm
Phật Giáo
Phú Bài
Phú Nhơn
Phú Nhuận
Phú Thọ
Phước Long
Phước Lương
Phương Nam
Plêiku
Quan Âm Tự
Quang Trung
Quảng Nam
Quảng Ngãi
Quảng Trị
Quế Sơn
Qui Nhơn
Quốc Hận
Rạch Giá
Rạng Đông
Rừng Lăng
Sa Đéc
Sài Gòn
Sóc Trăng
Sông Vệ
Sư Vạn Hạnh
Tam Kỳ
Tâm Giáo
Tân Định
Tân Hiệp
Tân Sơn Nhất (Nhứt)
Tân Nhất Tiều
Tân Trạch
Tây Ninh
Tết Nguyên Đán
Tết Trung Thu
Thái Văn Nghĩa
Tháng Bình
Thái Vị Thủy
Thanh Niên Cơ Đốc Xã Hội
Thạnh Lộc Thuật
Thầy
Thị Nghè
Thích Quảng Độ
Thích Giám Đức
Thích Quảng Đức
Thích Pháp Lan
Thích Nữ Nhất Chi Mai
Thích Trí Quang

Thiên Mụ
Thông
Thông Nhứt
Thới Lập
Thu Bồn
Thủ Đức
Thủ Dầu Một
Thủ Thiêm
Thủy Phương
Thừa Thiên
Tiền Giang
Tin Lành
Tổ Chức Xã Hội Tin Lành
Tôn Thất Thiện
Trà Vinh
Trắng Đen
Trần Thị Ngọc Ánh
Trần Minh Cảnh
Trần Công Chánh
Trần Ngọc Châu
Trần Như Chương
Trần Văn Chương
Trần Hưng Đạo
Trần Văn Đệ
Trần Văn Đổ
Trần Văn Đôn
Trần Xuân Hi
Trần Văn Hương
Trần Văn Khoa
Trần Thiện Khiêm
Trần Thị Lý
Trần Văn Mỹ
Trần Thượng Nhơn
Trần Phương
Trần Thự Quang
Trần Xuân Quang
Trần Thị Quang Hạnh
Trần Thanh Sơn
Trần Hữu Thanh
Trần Quốc Toản
Trần Quang Thuận
Trần Thị Thuận
Trần Đình Tụ
Trần Cao Vân
Trần Văn Văn
Trần Lệ Xuân
Trí Nguyên
Trịnh Đình Thảo
Trung Tín
Truyền đạo
Trương Minh Giảng
Trương Thị Kính

Tương Thị Ngọc Sa
Trương Văn Sáng
Trương Như Tảng
Trường Chinh
Tuy Hòa
Tự Do
Tự Đức
Tươi
Vạn Kiếp
Văn Tiến Dũng
Viện Hóa Đạo
Việt Cộng

Việt Minh
Việt Mỹ
Việt Nam
Việt Nam Cộng Hòa
ViệtNam Dân Chủ Cộng Hòa
Vĩnh Bình
Vĩnh Long
Vĩnh Phước
Võ Thị Bé Hai
Võ Văn Hoa
Võ Nguyên Giáp
Võ Hồng Liễu

Vũ Văn Cự
Vũ Thị Quí
Vũ Hữu Sĩ
Vũng Tàu
Vườn Chuối
Vườn Lài
Xá Lợi
Xóm Chiếu
Xóm Gía
Xuân Lộc
Xuân Thủy

PERSONS WHO SERVED WITH
MENNONITE CENTRAL COMMITTEE

Ackerman, Ronald	8/69-9/72	Agriculturalist	Dak To
Beechy, Atlee	2/66-8/66	VNCS Director	Saigon
Beechy, Winifred	5/66-8/66	Volunteer	Saigon
Blair, Joy	11/71-6/74	Teacher	Nha Trang
Blair, Norman	11 /71-6/74	Physician	Nha Trang
Bowman, James	4/66-4/69	Material Aid Administration	Nha Trang, Saigon
Brenneman, Fred	2/66-4/66	Physician	Nha Trang
Byrne, Kevin	3/69-3/71	Community Development	Dong Ha
Byrne, Maurice	8/68-11/70	Refugee Assistance	Tam Ky
Cressman, Lois	7/58-8/59	Nutritionist	Saigon
DeWarle, Gary	9/65-9/67	Material Aid Administration	Saigon
Dick, Hildegard	8/59-6/62	Hostess	Ban Me Thuot, Nha Trang
Dick, John B.	8/59-6/62	Physician, Director	Ban Me Thuot, Nha Trang
Eby, Roy	11/54-2/56	Material Aid Administration	Saigon, Da Lat
Ediger, N. Max	7/71-4/76	Director, Community Dev.	Quang Ngai, Saigon
Ewert, Adam	11/54-1/57	Material Aid Administration	Saigon, Da Lat
Ewert, Ann Noel	1/73-4/75	Nurse	Nha Trang
Ewert, Anna	11/58-10/60	Hostess	Ban Me Thuot
Ewert, Claire	7/73-4/75	Nutritionist	Pleiku
Ewert, Wallace	7/73-4/75	Agriculturalist	Pleiku
Falk, Anne	8/66-8/69	Nurse	Tam Ky, Saigon
Fast, Margaret	7/70-11/72	Physician	Pleiku
Gehman, Linford	4/65-9/68	Physician	Nha Trang
Gerber, Daniel	8/61-5/62	Hospital Maintenance	Ban Me Thuot
Gingerich, Jessie	6/66-4/68	Home Economist	Pleiku
Goering, Donald	8/57-8/58	Physician	Ban Me Thuot
Goering, Loua	8/57-8/58	Lab Technician	Ban Me Thuot
Good, Leland	8/58-9/61	Mechanic, Maintenance	Ban Me Thuot
Gregory, Fredric	8/66-11/68	Refugee Assistance	Quang Ngai, Di Linh, Saigon
Harshbarger, Eva	11/54-9/56	Hostess	Da Lat, Saigon
Hasselblad, Marva	2/62-7/65	Nurse	Nha Trang
Hershey, Jean	2/71-4/75	Nurse	Nha Trang, Pleiku
Hiebert, Linda	7/73-4/75	Nurse	Nha Trang
Hiebert, Murray	7/73-4/75	Hospital Coordinator	Nha Trang
Hochstetler, Alan	7/58-1/61	Construction Supervisor	Ban Me Thuot, Nha Trang
Hochstetler, Harlan	9/67-3/68	Agriculturalist	Hue
Hochstetler, Pauline	9/67-3/68	Home Economist	Hue
Hostetter, Douglas	6/66-6/69	Refugee Assistance	Tam Ky

Hostetter, Patricia	6/66-5/69	Refugee Assistance	Quang Ngai
	10/73-4/75		Quang Ngai
Hurst, Carl	2/57-8/58	Material Aid Adm.	Saigon
Ichikawa, Yoshihiro	6/69-10/76	Refugee Assistance	Tam Ky, Quang Ngai
Jantzi, Lowell	10/70-11/73	Hospital Coordinator	Nha Trang
Janzen, Margaret	4/56-6/59	Nurse	Ban Me Thuot
Kaufman, Carl	8/ 65-9/67	Hospital Maintenance	Nha Trang
Keefer, Kenneth	4/66-4/69	Mechanics Teacher	Hue
Keim, Wayne	9/67-9/70	Hosp. Coordinator, Com. Dev.	Pleiku, Dong Ha
Kennel, Paul	2/66-4/69	Community Development	Hue
Kimmel, Chris	11/65-11/67	Agriculturalist	Hue
Klassen, James	10/72-4/76	Admin., Teacher	Saigon
Kooker, Harley	7/66-8/69	Agriculturalist	Hue
Krabill, Grace	9/55-7/58	Hostess	Ban Me Thuot
Krabill, Willard	9/55-7/58	Physician, Director	Ban Me Thuot
Kraybill, Esther	7/66-8/69	Hostess	Nha Trang
Kraybill, Harold	7/66-8/69	Physician	Nha Trang
Leatherman, Loretta	7/66-7/68	Teacher	Saigon
Leatherman, Paul	7/66-7/68	VNCS Director	Saigon
Lefever, Esther	8/56-8/59	Hostess	Ban Me Thuot, Saigon
Lefever, Harry	8/56-8/59	Material Aid, Youth	Ban Me Thuot, Saigon
Lenzmann, Emma	9/65-9/68	Nurse	Nha Trang, Pleiku
Lichti, Elda	8/61-8/64	Hostess	Saigon
Lichti, Rudolph	8/61-8/64	Director	Saigon
Lind, Jonathan	9/67-9/68	Material Aid Administration	Saigon
Lind, Ruby	4/69-10/69	Secretary	Saigon
Longacre, Doris	8/64-6/67	Hostess	Saigon
Longacre, Paul	8/64-6/67	Director	Saigon
Luez, Christopher	8/65-4/68	Physician	Pleiku
Luez, Lois	8/65-4/68	Nurse	Pleiku
Maddimadugu,	2/68-2/70	Lab Technician	Nha Trang
Devadoss	3/73-4/75	Lab Technician	Nha Trang, Pleiku
Maddimadugu, Doris	3/73-4/75	Hostess	Nha Trang, Pleiku
Martin, Earl	2/66-5/69	Refugee Assistance	Quang Ngai
	10/73-7/75	UXO	Quang Ngai
Miller, Jean	8/68-6/71	Volunteer	Saigon
Miller, Robert W.	8/68-6/71	VNCS Director	Saigon
Neufeld, David	2/66-3/68	Social Worker	Quang Ngai, Saigon
Neufeld, Sue	2/66-3/68	Nurse	Quang Ngai, Saigon
Neufeld, Elfrieda	10/58-8/61	Nurse	Ban Me Thuot
Newkirk, Jonathan	8/66-4/68	Community Development	Dak To
Nyce, Carolyn	6/66-4/68	Nurse	Saigon
Pauls, Mary	2/66-2/69	Nurse	Pleiku

Peters, Katherine	9/67-9/70	Nurse	Nha Trang
Preheim, Gayle	8/66-8/69	Community Development	Dong Ha, Saigon, Di Linh
Rock, Martin	12/69-6/72	Administration	Saigon
Roggli, Elisabeth	6/68-10/71	Nurse	Nha Trang
Rutt, Clarence	8/58-10/58	Physician	Ban Me Thuot
Rutt, Helen	8/58-10/58	Nurse	Ban Me Thuot
Sandoz, Jerry	8/66-7/68	Refugee Assistance	Hue, Da Nang
Sauder, June	8/66-4/68	Home Economist	Tam Ky, Hue
Sawatzky, Frieda	8/69-8/72	Community Development	Ban Me Thuot
Sawatzky, Kurt	8/69-8/72	Community Development	Ban Me Thuot
Schmidt, Clara	1/72-4/72	Volunteer	Ban Me Thuot, Nha Trang
Sebus, Juliette	4/56-10/58	Nurse	Nha Trang
Snavely, Helen	8/66-8/68	Nurse	Saigon
Spicher, Thomas	8/69-5/72	Adminis.; Community Dev.	Nha Trang, Dong Ha
Sprunger, Joseph	7/68-9/70	Adminis.; Community Dev.	Nha Trang, Tung Nghia
Stauffer, Sanford	4/66-4/69	Community Dev.; Logistics	Quang Ngai, BMT, Saigon
Steiner, Mary Ellen	6/59-1/60	Volunteer	Ban Me Thuot
Steiner, James	6/59-1/60	Physician	Ban Me Thuot
Strayer, Marilyn	11/66-7/68	Physician	Saigon
Strayer, Martin	11/66-7/68	Architect	Saigon
Stoltzfus, Geneva	8/57-4/60	Hostess	Saigon
Stoltzfus, Glenn	8/57-4/60	Director	Saigon
Stuckey, Allen	8/69-6/72	Physician	Nha Trang, Pleiku
Stuckey, Jeannie	8/69-6/72	Hostess	Nha Trang
Swartzendruber, Duane	2/57-8/59	Construction Supervisor	Ban Me Thuot
Tiessen, Elizabeth	8/66-2/68	Nurse	Di Linh
Troyer, Dana	2/67-5/67	Physician	Nha Trang
Voth, Donald	8/58-8/61	Administration	Ban Me Thuot, Saigon
Weaver, Elnora	3/59-3/62	Nurse	Ban Me Thuot, Nha Trang
Weber, Marcie	1/69-8/71	Nurse	Nha Trang, Q. Ngai, Pleiku
Weidner, Mark	11/66-5/68	Teacher	Hue
Weidner, Susan	11/66-5/68	Volunteer	Hue
Wiens, Delbert	08/54-8/57	Director	Saigon
Willms, J. Frances	12/74-4/75	Nurse	Nha Trang
Willms, John	12/74-4/75	Physician	Nha Trang
Wyse, Donald	6/73-6/74	Physician	Nha Trang
Wyse, Joyce	6/73-6/74	Teacher	Nha Trang
Yano, Teruko	9/70-9/73	Nurse	Nha Trang
Yoder, John E.	10/67-4/68	Administration	Saigon
Yoder, Carl	7/62-8/65	Physician	Nha Trang
Yoder, Phyllis	7/62-8/65	Nurse	Nha Trang
Yoder, Ruth	2/66-7/72	Nurse, Instructor	Nha Trang, Saigon

(Dates are within one month—may refer to total term or only time present in Vietnam).

PERSONS WHO SERVED WITH
EASTERN MENNONITE BOARD
OF MISSIONS & CHARITIES

Beidler, Luke and Dorothy	8/66-7/69	Teaching, student work	Saigon
	9/70-4/75		Can Tho
Bishop, Duane	7/73-4/75	Teaching, student work	Can Tho
Bishop, Duane and Pat	8/74-4/75		Can Tho
Bucher, Paul and Esther	8/70-3/73	Teaching, student work,	Saigon/Can Tho
	4/73-7/74	administration; VNCS hostess	Saigon
Kennel, Paul	6/73-4/75	WRC administration	Da Nang
Martin, Luke and Mary	9/62-7/67	Evangelistic work, teaching,	Saigon
	9/68-6/72	administration; women's	
	7/73-4/75	ministry	
Metzler, Everett & Margaret	11/57-9/62	Evangelistic work, teaching,	Saigon
	3/63-8/66	student work, administration	
	8/67-7/69		
Metzler, James and Rachel	9/62-8/66	Evangelistic work, teaching,	Saigon
	8/67-9/70	student work, literature; nurse	
Mininger, Mark & Ruth Ann	1/74-3/75	Teaching, student work; nurse	Saigon
Peachey, Titus	9/70-6/73	Teaching, student work	Saigon
Sensenig, Donald and Doris	8/63-6/68	Evangelistic work, teaching,	Saigon
	8/69-6/73	student and community work	
Shirk, Maynard	9/70-7/73	Maintenance work	Saigon
Stauffer, James and Arlene	5/57-3/62	Evangelistic and pastoral	Saigon
	9/62-1/65	work, teaching, student and	
	8/66-7/70	community work; administration;	
	8/71-4/75	women's ministries	

VNCS EXPATRIATE PERSONNEL 1966-1975

More than two hundred persons served with Vietnam Christian Service, including seventy-one MCC personnel. Others were recruited through Church World Service (CWS) and Lutheran World Relief (LWR). MCC personnel 1966 through 1972, part of the VNCS contingent, are listed elsewhere.

Aaker, Gerald & Judy - LWR
Allan, Mona E. S. - CWS
Allyn, Margaret - CWS
Armstrong, Jeanne – CWS
Barnes, Gunnar - LWR
Batalden, Abner & Martha – LWR
Batoon, Ireneo - LWR
Beane, Douglas - CWS
Bonnette, Terry - CWS
Brenden, Neil & Marta - LWR
Brumbeck, Lee - LWR
Burgess, John
Cabbage, Lynn - CWS
Callahan, Virginia - CWS
Campbell, Ernest & Alfie – CWS
Carlson, Barbara - CWS
Carpenter, Anne - CWS
Casebolt, Ralph - CWS
Castet, Michel & Dominique - CWS
Channon, Carl & Hazel - CWS
Chaperon, Sue - CWS
Clark, Katherine - CWS
Collins, Jane - CWS
Cook, Douglas & Virginia - CWS
Cribby, Phyllis - CWS
Dahl, Leif & Carol - CWS
Dangers, Skip - CWS
Danielson, Judy - LWR
Dewitt, Helen - CWS
Dickason, Jean - CWS
Dodge, William & Marge - CWS
Dove, Doris - CSW
Downs, Cynthia - CWS
Downs, Peter - CWS

Dybing, Aase - LWR
Elwood, Margaret - CWS
Faulkner, Margaret - CWS
Foster, Wayne - CWS
Getz, Roger & Genevieve - CWS
Gould, Rebecca - CWS
Gribler, Susan - CWS
Gross, Marcie
Gutshall, Jeanne - LWR
Hale, Douglas - LWR
Hall, Wayne - CWS
Hancock, R. Dean & Margaret - CWS
Helstern, Mary Sue - CWS
Hendersen, Martha - LWR
Herman, Stewart - LWR
Herod, William - CWS
Hope, Sam & Nancy - CWS
Horn, Ursula - LWR
Johnston, Lela - CWS
Jones, Brennon - CWS
Jones, Douglas - CWS
Keltie, Patricia - CWS
Kimberly, Salli - CWS
Kimmel, Christopher - CWS
Kleinbach, Grace - CWS
Kleinbach, Russel - CWS
Knepp, Joan - CWS
Landhuis, Jesse - CWS
Lap, Margriet - CWS
Lewis, Patricia - CWS
Lewis, Zelma - CWS
Luken, William - CWS
Marentek, Geysje
McConnell, Tharon - CWS

Matern, Richard & Wilhelmina - LWR
Maw. Thelma - CWS
McCoard, Douglas - CWS
Metzger, Dennis - CWS
Milk, Richard & Juliet - CWS
Miller, Robert L. - CWS
Moomaw, Ira & Mabel - CWS
Neal, Thomas & Mei Hwa - LWR
Newlon, Camille - CWS
Niska, Patricia - LWR
Noteboom, Glen - CWS
Orr, Ross - CWS
Petre, Rufus - CWS
Pilburn, Marvin & Carolyn - CWS
Reardon, Dorothy
Redlin, Gloria - LWR
Richison, George -CWS
Rose, William - CWS

Roth, Larry & Clarice - LWR
Scahill, Anne - CWS
Schmidt, R. John & Clara - CWS
Schulze, Linda - CWS
Selnes, Levie - LWR
Smith, Perry E. H. - CWS
Smith T, Joanne - CWS
Stallwood, Barbara - CWS
Stivers, Willard - CWS
Stoffel, Alfred - CWS
Studebaker, Ted - CWS
Thompson, Everett & Zora - CWS
Verduin, Jan - CWS
Vogel, Betty - CWS
Vogel, Lynn - CWS
Williams, Dwaine & Becky Williams - CWS
Woodruff, Lance - CWS
Workman, David & Dorothy - CWS

ANNOTATED BIBLIOGRAPHY
OF FURTHER READINGS

The primary materials for this book came from archival materials and private collections of personal letters. The MCC Archives are located at Mennonite Central Committee, Akron, PA. The EMBMC materials are at Eastern Mennonite Missions, Salunga, PA. Vietnam materials and archival notes used in preparation of this book will be deposited at the Lancaster Mennonite Historical Society, 2215 Millstream Rd, Lancaster, PA 17602 as "Luke S. Martin, 1933- , Personal Papers." The personal letters and journals of James Stauffer, James Metzler, Margaret Metzler, Mary and Luke Martin, Paul Longacre, Esther and Paul Bucher were invaluable; these are privately held. An early fully-footnoted manuscript may be made available to serious researchers.

The following materials are suggested for readers interested in further understanding the Vietnam experience.

Vietnam History

Bowman, John S., General Editor. *The World Almanac of the Vietnam War*. New York: Pharos Books, 1985.

Hickey, Gerald C. *Window on a War: An Anthropologist in the Vietnam Conflict*. Lubbock, TX: Texas Tech University Press, 2002.

Karnow, Stanley. *Vietnam: A History*. New York: The Viking Press, 1983.

Logevall, Fredrik. *Choosing War: The Lost Chance for Peace and the Escalation of War in Vietnam*. Berkeley: University of California Press, 1999.

_____. *Embers of War: The Fall of an Empire and the Making of America's Vietnam*. New York: Random House, 2012.

Topmiller, Robert. *The Lotus Unleashed: The Buddhist Peace Movement in South Vietnam, 1964-1966*. Lexington, KY: The University of Kentucky Press, 2002.

Turse, Nick. *Kill Anything that Moves: The Real American War in Vietnam*. New York: Henry Holt and Company, 2013.

Bowman's *Almanac of the Vietnam War* is very helpful in locating the various political and military developments from 1932 to 1984.

Fredrik Logevall's *Embers of War*, for which he won the Pulitzer Prize, and his earlier work, *Choosing War*, are carefully researched and documented. Stanley Karnow's *Vietnam* was published to accompany the acclaimed PBS Television Series.

Topmiller's book provides helpful insights into the little understood Buddhist opposition to the war. Nick Turse documents the savage ferocity of the war.

Gerald Hickey's book helps readers understand the experiences of the many ethnic minorities of Vietnam's central highlands.

Vietnam Christianity

Đoàn Văn Miêng. *Ân Điển Diệu Kỳ: Tự Truyện Mục Sư Đoàn Văn Miêng [Amazing Grace: Autobiography of Pastor Doan Van Mieng]*. Hà Nội: Nhà Xuất Bản Tôn Giáo, 2011.

Gheddo, Piero. *The Cross and the Bo-Tree: Catholics and Buddhists in Vietnam*. New York: Sheed and Wade, 1970.

Lê Hoàng Phu. *A Short History of the Evangelical Church of Vietnam* (1911-1965). PhD thesis, New York University, 1972.

Lê Văn Thái. *Bốn Mươi Sáu Nam Chức Vụ [Forty Years in Ministry]*. Self-published, 1970.

Nguyễn, Kimson. "Mission History of Vietnamese Evangelicals in the Pioneering Stage: A Vietnamese Perspective," *Journal of Asian Missions,* 16:2, 2015.

Reimer, Reginald E. *The Protestant Movement in Vietnam: Church Growth in Peace and War among the Ethnic Vietnamese*. MA thesis, Fuller Theological Seminary, 1972.

_____.*Vietnam's Christians: A Century of Growth in Adversity.* William Carey Library, 2011.

Piero Gheddo's *The Cross and the Bo-Tree* is a classic. The other books listed relate to the Evangelical Protestant activities.

Le Hoang Phu's *A Short History* and Reimer's *The Protestant Movement* gives sweeping developments of the Evangelical Church of Vietnam from 1911. Kimson Nguyen's short piece gives more emphasis to earlier French Protestant ministries. The two autobiographic works by Le Van Thai and Doan Van Mieng, who both served as Church president, give helpful insights. Reimer's 2011 centennial book documents the growth that took place in the difficult post-war period.

Mennonites in Vietnam

Beechy, Atlee. *Seeking Peace, My Journey.* Goshen, IN: Pinchpenny Press, 2001.

Eby, Omar. *A House in Hue.* Scottdale, PA: Herald Press, 1968.

Ediger, Max. *A Vietnamese Pilgrimage.* Newton, Kansas: Faith and Life Press, 1978.

Hasselblad, Marva and Dorothy Brandon. *Lucky-Lucky.* New York: M. Evans and Company, 1966.

Klassen, James S. *Jimshoes in Vietnam.* Scottdale, PA: Herald Press, 1986.

_____. "Walking with Vietnamese Christians," *Mission Focus Current Issues*, Wilbert R. Shenk, ed., Scottdale, PA, 1980.

Leatherman, Paul. *A Full and Rewarding Life: A Memoir.* Limited self-publication, 2006.

Martin, Earl S. *Reaching the Other Side: The Journal of an American Who Stayed to Witness Vietnam's Postwar Transition.* New York: Crown Publishers, 1978.

Martin, Luke S., Nguyen Quang Trung, Nguyen Thanh Tam and Nguyen Thi Tam, "The Mennonite Church in Vietnam," 315-336, in *Churches Engage Asian Traditions*, Asia Global Mennonite History, C. Arnold Snyder & John A. Lapp, editors. Intercourse, PA: Good Books, 2011.

Metzler, James E. *From Saigon to Shalom: The pilgrimage of a missionary in search of a more authentic mission.* Scottdale, PA: Herald Press, 1985.

_____. "Vietnam: I Wouldn't Do It Again." *Mission Focus Current Issues.* Wilbert R. Shenk, ed., Scottdale, PA: Herald Press, 1980.

Hasselblad describes her MCC service before the war. Eby, who was not in Vietnam, tells the story of the persons trapped in Hue during the 1968 Tet Offensive. Klassen in *Jimshoes* writes about the early seventies leading up to the April 1975 revolution and its aftermath. Earl Martin describes engaging "the other side" during that same period. Beechy and Leatherman, both MCC personnel who served as directors of Vietnam Christian Service, describe specific Vietnam incidents in their memoirs. Ediger's book has verse, prose, and ink drawings.

Metzler describes the climate in which missionaries sought to share the gospel of Jesus and emphasizes the importance of a valid orientation for ministry.

My piece in *Churches Engage Asian Traditions* describes the development of the Vietnam Mennonite Church from the sixties into the twenty-first century.

GENERAL

Bush, Perry. "The Political Education of Vietnam Christian Service, 1954-1975." *Peace and Change,* Vol. 27, April 2002.

_____. "Vietnam and the Burden of Mennonite History" *The Conrad Grebel Review*, Spring, Vol. 17, No. 2, 1999.

Flipse, Scott Eric. *Bearing the Cross of Vietnam: Humanitarianism, Religion and American Commitment to South Vietnam, 1952-1975.* PhD dissertation, University of Notre Dame, 2003.

James, B. Violet. *American Protestant Missions and the Vietnam War.* PhD thesis, University of Aberdeen, 1989.

Luce, Don and John Sommer. *Vietnam: the Unheard Voices,* Ithaca: Cornell University Press, 1969.

Meinertz, Midge Austin, editor. *Vietnam Christian Service: Witness in Anguish.* New York: Church World Service, 1975.

Nguyen, Viet Thanh. *Nothing Ever Dies: Vietnam and the Memory of War,* Cambridge: Harvard University Press, 2016.

Tran, Jonathan. *The Vietnam War and Theologies of Memory: Time and Eternity in the Far Country,* Challenges in Contemporary Theology. Malden, MA: Wiley-Blackwell, 2010.

Vietnam Christian Service: Witness in Anguish is an evaluation of the ten years of VNCS. Bush and Flipse describe the issues that MCC/VNCS had to deal with in the unpredictable political and military setting. Luce and Sommer describe the work of International Voluntary Service during the war.

Violet James shows how Alliance missionaries viewed the war differently than Mennonite missionaries and MCC persons.

Nguyen, a Pulitzer Prize author, writes about how the ethical questions of the war should be remembered. Tran, also a young Vietnamese scholar, engages the war theologically in thought-provoking conversations.

PHOTO CREDITS

13	Delbert Wiens waits for ferry to cross a river
35	Grace Krabill with children of leprous parents
38	Willard Krabill with interpreter Y'Dun Ksor
43	Dr. Donald Guering and Margaret Janzen make a house call
44	Esther Lefever and Dr. Willard Krabill welcome Orie Miller to Ban Me Thuot
46	Leprosarium-Hospital at Ban Me Thuot
48a	Elnora Weaver treating child at Leprosarium
48b	Don Voth gives Lee Good a haircut
52	Saigon support staff Carl Hurst, Geneva and Glenn Stoltzfus
54	Harry Lefever gives a Christmas bundle to child at Duc Anh Orphanage
62a	Saigon's central Ben Thanh Market
62b	Inside Ben Thanh Market
63a	Cyclo taxi stand
62b	Saigon street scene
63c	Saigon fast food
64a	The kitchen
64b	"Mr. Cook"
70	*SS Cambodge* in Saigon port
71	Margaret Metzler studying language with Teacher Hoa
73a	Sowing rice seed bed
73b	Transplanting rice
75	Celebrating Tet at Le Van Duyet Temple
76	James Stauffer preaches at the Truong Minh Giang chapel
82	Saigon Notre Dame Cathedral
98	Arlene and James Stauffer at Dakao home
100	Everett Metzler teaching English class in home
107a	Nha Trang Hospital Board members
107b	Man from Phuoc Luong
109	Alliance Dr. Ardel Vietti with Don Voth and Dr. J. B. Dick
117	Marva Hasselblad examines patient with interpreter
119	Rudy Lichti with interpreter Ninh, D. I. Jeffrey, and Nguyen Thien Si
123a	Rachel Metzler with Teacher Ky
123b	James Metzler with Teacher Luc
126a	Daniel Gerber with Ruth Wilting
126b	Daniel Gerber on tractor
128	The First Lady Madame Nhu with Ambassador and Mrs. Nolting
131	Burial of missionary linguist Elwood Jacobs
133a	Xa Loi Pagoda
133b	Buddha statue at Xa Loi Pagoda

135	Mennonite Mission Headquarters and Saigon Student Center
139	James Stauffer leading Bible study at the Saigon Student Center
148	Children's activities at Dakao house
151	Buddhist bonzes
152	Margaret Metzler with neighbor children in vacation Bible school
154	Gia Dinh Mennonite Community Center
156a	Phuoc as bookroom monitor
156b	Students in the reading room
158a	Ms. Dung guiding children
158b	Mrs. Bay preparing sandwiches for children
159	American military advisor with Vietnamese unit
162a	Dr. Carl Yoder examining patient
162b	Phyllis Yoder with Susan
173	Don and Doris Sensenig family on scooter
174	Mary Martin and Hong with Steven and Bobi
175a	B-52 bombers carpet bombing
175b	Bomb crater
176	Don Sensenig teaching English
180	Everett Metzler leading a Bible study
184	Bui Thi
186a	Christmas program at Community Center
186b	Don Sensenig leads singing at community Christmas program
186c	Community church choir sings
187a	Carl Yoder at the dedication with interpreter Pastor Le Hoang Phu
187b	Evangelical Clinic-Hospital at Nha Trang
192	Carl Kaufman with village boys
194	Gate to VNCS unit house Em Dem
207a	Atlee Beechy and Paul Longacre with language teachers at Em Dem
207b	Paul Kennel at language study
209	Bake oven at Duc Anh Orphanage shown to Bill Luken and Atlee Beechy
210	Pastor Doan Van Mieng meeting Daniel and Elizabeth Martin
211	US fighter bomber returns from bombing mission
215	Street demonstrations
218	Christopher Leuz observing progress in building Pleiku clinic
223	Atlee Beechy introduces Paul Leatherman to Pastor Doan Van Mieng
225a	Happy school children
225b	Mrs. Nga begins Rang Dong School
226	Ms. Qui with family at Tet
229a	James Metzler preaches at Easter service with Pham Quang Tam interpreting
229b	Students telling story in English
229c	Jacqueline Thimm speaks at Community Center
233a	105 mm canon
233b	Security perimeter at airfield

234	The ubiquitous Huey chopper
239	Funeral for Dinh
246a	Refugee Commissioner Dr. Nguyen Phuc Que
246b	Robert Miller and Paul Longacre make field inspection
249	Billy Graham meets Tin Lanh Church President Doan Van Mieng
254	Anne Falk at Binh Loi Orphanage
256	Dr. Dana Troyer providing training for Drs. Linford Gehman and Harold Kraybill
257	Jessie Gingerich teaching sewing
258a	Tharon McConnell treating child
258b	Pat Hostetter relating to older persons
258c	Earl Martin with school boys
259	Mother with children at Nghia Hanh camp
260	Fred Gregory in refugee camp
262a	Doug Hostetter with Luu of literacy class
262b	Dave Neufeld in the air
267	Chris Kimmel at Hue agricultural training school
268	Gayle Preheim with K'Roh
281	Paul Kraybill visiting Lam at Bible Institute with Donald Lauver and David Thomas
286	Ethnic minority village in Dalat area
288a	Mother consoles son injured in a bombing raid
288b	Child victims of village bombings
291a	Mrs. Bich in FCA office
291b	Ms. Van organized a sewing school
292	Paul and Doris Longacre with Cara Sue
296	Dorothy Beidler teaching elementary school students
305	ARVN soldiers
316	Pastor Tran Xuan Hi surveys damage to Thu Duc Tin Lanh church near Saigon
321	Devadoss Maddimadugu in Nha Trang Clinic lab
329a	Victims of fighting come to Community Center for mosquito nets
329b	Bread for distribution
331a	The Buddha statue survives the destruction in the Dong Ong Co area
331b	Months later vegetation returns
333	Ruth Yoder with student nurses
342	Joanne Smith T at Community Center
343a	Building houses in Dong Ong Co area
343b	James Metzler with a family at their new house
344	Robert and Jean Miller family arrive
345	Newly baptized group
352a	Thoi Lap family mourns the loss of husband and father
352b	Family raising chickens
354a	Jim Bowman and Quang monitor material aid assistance

354b	Tran Xuan Quang ordained pastor of the Mennonite church
367	Chau Hong Luc with his family
383	Martin Rock
393a	FCA young people on a day's outing
393b	EAP students visit a park
394	Rang Dong School activities for children
396	Marcie Weber with patient
400a	Church choir
400b	Mennonite congregation after worship
406	Luke and Dorothy Beidler family in Can Tho
410	Tuyet
411	Students in Phoenix Study Group
412	Pastor Quang addresses the Asian Mennonite Conference
413	Luke Beidler leading an English Bible study
415	Grave of student friend Nguyen Thanh Hoa
417	Foot washing service – Paul Bucher with Khai
418	Pastor and Mrs. Tran Xuan Quang
419	Maynard Shirk, Don Sensenig, James Stauffer and Titus Peachey meet for prayer
421a	Some men of the church: Thanh, Muong, Xuan, Anh and Trong
421b	Women of the church: Bay, Hai, and Van with Mary Martin
423	Bill Rose speaking with Dean Hancock, a pastor, and Ron Ackerman
428	Mr. Muong with son Thong
430	Ms. Lieu demonstrating homemaking skills
432	Luke and Mary Martin family
434	Dr. Norman Blair at the Nha Trang Hospital
435	Jean Hershey with Mrs. Thuoc, director of the nursing school
436	Reconciliation work camp at Nha Trang
440	Titus Peachey and Don Sensenig lead Sunday morning Bible class
444a	New church and Community Center
444b	Dedication of new church facilities
445a	Nguyen Quang Trung leading dedication service
445b	Overflow crowd by Rang Dong School classrooms
445c	New Rang Dong School
445d	Don Sensenig conversing with David Breneman, James Klassen and Max Ediger
449	Doris and Devadoss Maddimadugu with Esther
453	Wedding of Minh and Fred Kauffman
463	Esther and Paul Bucher assist Hien to fly to Quang Ngai for therapy
467	Place where Mrs. Luan was killed on March 28, 1974
470a	Quang Ngai farmers
470b	Unexploded M-79 grenades
473	Ann Ewert at the Nha Trang Hospital
476	Participants of Pleiku work camp with Ursula Horn, Wallace Ewert and Max Ediger

486	Mennonite Church leaders meet with Pastor Quang
512	Nguyen Dinh Tin with other youth
522	Max with Manh Tuong and Le Van Nghia, former political prisoners
524	MCC transfers the tractor to PRG representatives from Quang Ngai
531	Tin Lanh church in Hanoi
531	Mennonite delegation meeting Evangelical Church leaders in Hanoi
533	Robert Miller with Nguyen Thanh Long
534	Dr. Son treating addict with acupuncture

Courtesy Eastern Mennonite Missions, 64b, 71, 73b, 76, 98, 100, 152, 180, 215, 225b, 296, 343a, 417, 421a, 436, 444a and b, 445, a, b, c, and d, 486, 512; courtesy Norman Gerber, 126a and b; courtesy Mennonite Central Committee, 13, 35, 38, 43, 44, 52, 54, 107, 119, 162a, 207b, 246b, 291b, 321, 383, 394, 449, 473, 531; courtesy MCC by Helen Devitt, 329b, 396; courtesy MCC by Rose Dybing, 354a; credit MCC by Frank Epp, 159, 209, 267, 288a and b; courtesy MCC by Alan Hochstetler, 46; courtesy MCC by Doug Hostetter, 305; courtesy MCC by Jerry Isaac, 210; courtesy MCC by Brennan Jones, 262a, 268, 423; courtesy MCC by Paul Longacre, 187a, 434; courtesy MCC by Earl Martin, 467, 470b, 522, 524; courtesy MCC by Clarice Roth, 333; courtesy MCC by Harold Weaver, 435; courtesy MCC by Norman Wingert, 48a and b, 109; courtesy MCC by Lance Woodruff, 192, 218, 223, 246a, 254, 256, 257, 258b, 2258c, 259, 260, 316; courtesy MCC by Carl Yoder, 117; and courtesy Public Plan for Peace in Vietnam, 175a. The cover and all other photos are by Luke S. Martin.

All scripture quotations in the book are from the Revised Standard Version, copyright by the Division of Christian Education of the National Council of Churches.

INDEX

Numbers in highlighted italics indicates photograph

A

Aaker, Gerald, 220, 243, 255, 261, 264-65
Aaker, Judy, 220, 243, 255
Ackerman, Ron, 382, 423, *423*, 427, 435
Adeney, David, 60
Adventist Church, 33, 61, 157, 101
Adventist Hospital, 168, 477
Advisory Committee on Peace Concerns, 270-71, 301
Agent Orange herbicide, 121, 284, 388, 542
aid to "other side," 307
aid North Vietnam, 215
Air America, 208, 216, 287
Air Vietnam, 208
airports,
    Da Nang, 211
    Lien Khuong (Da Lat), 243
    Tan Son Nhat (Saigon), 205
    Phu Bai (Hue), 285
Alliance Witness, 127
American Community Church. *See* International
    Protestant Church
American Council of Voluntary Agencies, 192-93, 272
American Friends Service Committee, 177, 190, 232
    aid to North Vietnam, 240, 284
    personnel captured, 361, 461
    rehabilitation center, 443
American Leprosy Mission, 21, 36
An Khe, 22-23
An, Nguyen Chau, 532
Anh, Ms. (Xom Gia), 414
Anh, Mr. and Mrs. Nguyen Van, 357, 421, *421*
Anh, Mrs. (believer), 298
Anh, Mrs. (Nghiep, believer), 356-57
anti-American, 252
anti-war demonstrations, 200, 212-13, 282, 296,
    305, 380, 424
Apple, Jr., R. W., 212, 325
Armed Forces Council, 174
Army of the Republic of Vietnam (ARVN), 354
    AWOL, 344, 459
    battles, 128, 185, 402, 437, 505
    casualties, 128, 347, 402, 415
    civilians exploited, 390, 397, 467
    invaded Cambodia, 379
    morale, 355, 472, 479
    treatment of injured, 490

Asian Christian Service, 443
Asian Evangelists Commission, 228
Asian Mennonite Conference, 384, 411-12
Associated Press reports, 115, 187, 322, 370-71, 515
Association of Voluntary Agencies, 56
Augsburger, David, 379
Augsburger, Myron, 426, 427
    critiqued mission work, 452

B

Ba, Maj., 459
Babylift, 502
Bac Lieu, 72
bakery. *See* material aid
Ban Me Thuot, 493,
Ban Me Thuot Clinic and Hospital, 35, *46*, 90
    building, 34, 38, 39, 46
    community development, 350
    difficulties, 35-37
    government approval, 37-38, 40
    mobile clinic, 34, 38, 40
    routine, 44
    staff, 37, 39, 42, 48, 106
    statistics, 37, 39
Ban Me Thuot Leprosarium, 10, 16, 21
    C&MA thanks MCC, 106
    MCC commits to, 22-23
Banares, Daisy, 391
Bang, Mr. (contractor), 181
Bao Dai (emperor), 6, 10, 21
Baptist Mission and church, 96, 125, 181, 356, 491
Barnes, Gunnar, 420
Batalden, Abner, 334, 339
Bates, Bob, 60,
Bay, Mrs. (believer), 421, *421*, 501
Bay, Nguyen Thi, 158, *158*
Be Hai, Vo Thi, 353, 356, 360
Beane, Douglas, 396, 429
    Doug and Mai family, 373
Beck, Carl, 422, 435-36
Beechy, Atlee, 195, 205, *207*, *209*, 223, *223*
    on aid to North Vietnam 215
    articulated vision, 223
    advocate for peace, 208, 214, 283, 402
    contacting DRV/PRG, 340, 382, 443, 461, 512
    observe war horror, 208

sermon, 221-22
  1968 visit, 308, 316, 321-22
  1971 visit, 401-2
  1975 visit to Thailand, 518
Beechy, Winifred, 216, 401
Beidler, Dorothy, 235-36, 241, *296*, 324, 326
  teach elementary school, 296, 346
  teach English at university, 239, 282
Beidler, Luke, 235-36, 317, *413*
  advocate for peace, 406
    Bible studies, 413
Beidler family, 232, 332, 364, 383, *406*, 418, 501
  teach English at university, 239, 282, 346
  Can Tho, 386
  Tet Offensive, 309, 311-12, 317, 326
Ben, Khuc Kim, 488-89
Ben Tre, 131, 322
Betsch, Vernon, 166
Bible correspondence courses, 156, 163, 469
Bich, Ngo Thi, 158, 181, *291*, 296, *394*
  church ministries, 232, 360
  FCA program, 342
  NLF letters, 350-51
Bich Lien, Ms. (teacher), 298, 411-12
Bien Hoa, 82, 159
Binh, Archbishop Nguyen Van, 507-8
Binh Dan Hospital, 353, 438, 460, 474
Binh Xuyen, 12
Bishop, Duane, 452, 457
  Bible class, 486
Bishop, Duane and Pat, 475, 486, 501-2
  Hong Kong, 528
Blair, Joy, 434, 455, 458
Blair, Norman, 416, 434, *434*, 443, 464
Blair, Joy & Norman, 475
Bohn, Stanley, 200
Bolton, Bennet, 371
Bonnette, Terry, 382, 392
Bowman, James, 216, 334, *354*, 355
Brao, Rev., 244
Brash, Alan, 191
Bratton, Joyce, 492
Brenden, Marta, 220, 243, 254, 329, 394
Brenden, Neil, 220, 243, 250, 254
Breneman, David, *445*
Brenneman, Fred, 226
Brickner, Rabbi Belfour, 381
Brinton, Keith, 525
Brown, Elizabeth, 210, 276
Browne, Malcolm, 128
Brot Für die Welt, 160

Brumbeck, Lee, 255, 324, 391
  message from VC, 391
Bryerton, Col., 263-66
Bubna, Donald, 426
Bucher, Esther, 383
  letters/journal, 441
  political prisoners, 462
  visit morgue, 437
  VNCS hostess, 448-49
  women's meetings, 446
Bucher, Paul, 383, *417*, 418
  letters, 384
  on peace, 439
  teach Phoenix Study Group, 449, 458
Bucher couple, 383-84, 418, 432, 458, *463*, 469
  in Can Tho, 404, 413-14
  teach English, 400-1
  foster care, 449
  support pastor's family, 446, 475
Buddhism, 32
  Force for National Reconciliation, 478
  granted recognition, 15
  Hao Hao, 12
  politically neutral, 151
  sparked demonstrations, 151, 155, 212, 215
  United Buddhist Church, 151, 215
Bunker, Ellsworth, 266, 274, 276-77, 284, 323
  missionaries' meet, 431-32
Buon Ea Ana village, 34, 127
Burkholder, J. Lawrence, 9-10
Buttinger, Joseph, 58, 83
Byler, J. N., 8, 10, 11, 16, 51-52
Byrne, Kevin, 381-82

C

Ca Mau, 72
Cai San, 34, 52
Callahan, Virginia, 220,
Calley, Lt. William, 368
Cambodia, 509, 473-74, 509
Campbell, Ernest, 491
Can, Le Ngoc, 386
Can, Ngo Dinh, 150
Can Tho, 289, 356, 371, 385, 418, 469
Can Tho programs, 406
  teaching English classes, 413
  grading students, 432
  Family child assistance, 406
  home skills courses, 430, 469
  personnel, 406, 486
  reading room, 413

student center, 406
student hostel, 440, 457, 492, 527
Canadian Mennonite, 209
Canh, Tran Minh, 474-75
Cao Dai religion, 12, 32
Carlson, Barbara, 191
Carlson, Paul E., 103
Cary, Stephen, 177, 190, 193, 199
Catholic Church, 31
    declaration Apr 1975, 507-8, 512
    Marian Congress, 82
    opposition to neutralism, 151
    on revolution, 507-8, 512
    view of coup against Diem, 139
Catholic Relief Services (CRS), 8, 51
Cathey, Rev. Gordon, 209
Cau Bong, 450, 468. *See also* Van Kiep
cemeteries and morgues, 179, 229, 415, 437
Central Intelligence Agency, 82, 126, 211
    merged into OCO, 245
    report information, 286
Chan Tin, Fr., 463, 526
Chanh, Mrs. Tran Cong, 242, 424, 445
Charles, H. Raymond, 121, 319, 424
Chase, Connie, 405
Chau (believer), 178
Chau, Dinh Ngoc, 376, 395
Chau, Duong Thanh, 178, 232
Chieu Hoi (Open Arms program), 267, 367
Chinh Luan, 507, 515
Chinh, Truong, 368
Cho Quan Hospital, 255
Chrisman, Robert M., 39
Christian & Missionary Alliance (C&MA), 32-33
    appreciate MCC, 49, 102, 106
    Bible Institute, 111
    CAMA services, 491
    Dalat School, 14, 119, 166
    missionary team, 281
    New York administration, 23, 26, 35-39, 54, 85
    personnel detained, 495, 530
    personnel killed, 310
    social ministries, 10, 36, 39, 91, 218, 245, 491
    student activities, 453
    Tribes Mission, 11, 22
    Vietnam Mission, 11, 14
    view of Vietnam conflict, 198, 217, 222, 225, 269-70, 297, 326, 360, 371, 539
    view of VNCS, 271
    visit President Diem, 135-36

Christian pacifism, 204, 219, 235, 270, 301, 316, 402, 480
    feared by some, 270, 357-58, 414
    affirmed by some ECVN leaders, 218, 359
Christian presence, 145-46, 258, 347, 392, 408, 455, 539
Christian Youth for Social Service, 61, 324, 386, 440, 455, 457, 458, 506, 510
    student hostel, 440, 492
Chuong, Dr. Duong Cam, 38
Chuong, Tran Nhu, 133, 174
Chuong, Tran Van, 98
Church of the Brethren, 192
Church Women United, 461
Church World Service, 9-10, 18, 194, 542
    proposed joint MCC program, 188, 190
CIMADE, 337, 531
Civil Operations and Revolutionary Development Support, 258, 270, 272-73, 275-77
Clark, Dr. Randall, 490
Classen, Jacob, 339
Clergy and Laymen Concerned, 200, 282-83, 319, 381
Co Bay (WV staff), 372
Co Chin (helper) 357, 409-10, 509, 514
Co Do (helper), 103, 522
Co Khuyen (helper), 177-78,
Co Ky (language teacher), 123, 225
Co Nam (helper), 129, 137-38, 155, 169
Coconut Monk, 349, 435
Colby, William, 397
Cole, David and Pat, 56, 58
Collins, Gen. J. Lawton, 13, 15
Collins, Jane, 361
Comfer, Bernard, 191, 193
Committee of Responsibility (COR), 288-89
communism, Mennonite view of, 4, 41
Con Son, 237, 245-46, 253-254
    tiger cages, 254, 381
Conference on Children, 489
Contento, Paul & Maida, 61, 501
Cook, Douglas and Virginia, 366
corn-soya-milk, 259, 268, 269
Council of Voluntary Agencies, 209, 246, 491-92
Craig, Maxine, 113
Cressman, Lois, 45
Cribby, Phyllis, 391-92
Cu, Rev. Vu Van, 533
Cuc, Nguyen Dam, 334, 366
Cuong, Rev. Nguyen Huu, 533

D

Da Hoa village, 17-19, 65
Da Lat, 11, 15, 77
    material aid distribution, 15
Da Nang
    relief needs, 237, 244
    WRC programs, 34,
Dak (Dac) To, 429
    military activity, 382, 423
    program, 257
    Tet Offensive, 312
Dahl, Leif, 396
Daily News Record, 283
Dakao house, 98
    children's activities, 103, 125
    English classes, 99
    evangelistic ministries, 99
    Martins and J. Metzlers, 123
Dam, Col. Bui Dinh, 238
Dan, Phan Quang, 240, 488, 502
Danielson, Judy, 381
Davis, Robert & Mildred, 61, 132, 191
De, Nguyen Thi, *See* Chanh, Mrs. Tran Cong
De, Tran Van, 110
De Boer, Hans, 386
De Borchgrave, Arnaud, 218
Deets, Dawn, 113
DeLuze, Rev. Bertrand, 10, 20, 36
Democratic Republic of Vietnam, 6, 337, 339-40
demonstrations, 155, 410
Detweiler, Willis F., 9
Devitt, Helen, 191
Dewarle, Gary, 192, 206, 267
Dharmaraj, M. G., 61
Di Linh, 390-92
    local VC activities, 382, 390-92
    staff and programs, 243, 255
    Tet Offensive, 312, 324, 342
Dick, Henry, 377
Dick, Hildegard, 108
Dick, John B., 106-107, *107, 109*, 116
Dick family, Hildegard & John, 105-6
Dickason, Jean, 191
Diem, Ngo Dinh, 9, 37, 150
    approved MCC program, 18, 38
    attempted coup Nov 1960, 102-3
    became president, 21, 26
    Buddhist opposition, 128-29, 132-34
    coup and assassination, 129, 137-38
        people's response, 137-39

opposed unification, 20, 41
crushed opposition, 18, 26
oppression, 53, 80
palace bombed, 121
pro-Catholic, 73, 128, 139
sought ECVN and C&MA support, 135-36
view of Mennonites, 4, 37, 76
Dien Khanh, 216
Dieu, Dao Van, 101-2
Dinh (neighbor), 238-39
Dinh Quan, 130
displaced persons. *See* refugees
Do, Mr., 422
Do, Nguyen Van
Do, Tran Van, 191
Doi, Mr., 11, 13
Dong, Bui Cong, 245
Dong, Pham Van, 20, 368, 439, 524, 532
Dong Ha, 269, 324, 423, 429
    refugee programs, 269, 381
        Tet Offensive, 313
Dong Ong Co, 298, 330-31
Donner, Fred, 287
Downs, Peter, 448
Drescher, John, 201
Du, Le, 19
Duan, Le, 368, 375
Duc Anh Association Orphanage, 52, 54-55, 83
Dulles, John F., 6
Dung, Huynh Thi, 158, *158*, 176
Dung, Phan Tu, 158, 185
Dung, Gen. Van Tien, 488
Duyen, Le, 467
Dzu, Maj. Gen. Ngo, 397

E

East Asia Christian Conference, 58, 191, 192
Eastern Mennonite Board of Missions & Charities, 3, 23, 28-29, 390
    annual meeting, 169, 355, 490
    after the war, 522
    appeals for peace, 424
    commitment to Vietnam, 204
    evacuate an option, 429
    interest in Vietnam, 25-27
    invited to White House, 240-41
    Hong Kong assignment, 163
    mission philosophy, 94, 124-25, 172, 541
    mission strategy, 68-69, 84, 125
    missionaries speak against war, 433
    recruit personnel, 121-22, 447-48

relationship with ECVN, 29, 169, 538
relations with MCC, 45, 48, 347
Eastern Mennonite College (University), 121-22
Eby, Roy, 8, 13, 19-20, 34
Economic Cooperation Administration, 7
ecumenical relations, 84, 193, 248, 270, 347-48, 455
Ediger, Max, 409, **445**, 456, 465, **476**, 514, **524**, 536
   on ending the war, 409
   Mar-Apr 1975, 504, 519, 520
   on material aid, 458
   peace advocacy, 427
   political prisoners, 462
   in Quang Ngai, 429, 457-58
   Vietnam director, 438
   work camps, 477
   writing, 409, 462
Eisenhower, Dwight D., 6
Ellsberg, Daniel, 391
Em Dem, **194**, 195, 206, 216, 292, 449
English language teaching, 184
   evangelistic opportunities, 226
   students, 184
   teach at university, 239
   using biblical texts, 236
Epp, Dale, 257
Epp, Frank, 209
ethical dilemmas, 118-119, 160-61, 189, 189, 194,
   260-61, 263, 298-300, 307, 419, 432, 541
ethnic minorities, 10, 509
   Cham, 468
   ethnic minority churches, 243-44
   grievances, 46, 80
   Jarai, 243, 256
   Koho, 150, 243, 286, 392
   Rhade, 41-42, 47, 256
Evangelical Church of Vietnam (ECVN), 205
   apolitical, 180, 185, 198, 210, 269, 443, 520, 523
      modified view, 357-58, 481, 507, 539
   attitude toward WCC, 108, 188
   Bible Institute, 181, 281, 419, 533
      revival, 419
      welcomed books/professors, 444, 452, 484
   church life, 178, 363
   churches in NLF zones, 359
   ecumenical relations, 18
   evangelism, 348, 359
   catechism and baptism, 96
   executive committee, 489-90
   formation, 33
   lifestyles, 358
   hospital committee, 42, 90-91

   pastors, 79, 95, 135, 136
      military chaplains, 185, 376, 525
   prayer for peace, 426
   professional persons, 415
   social welfare committee, 16, 51-53, 110, 160,
      188, 396, 437, 501
   relations with MCC and VMM, 45, 455
   relations with WRC and World Vision, 321-22
   after revolution, 526, 529, 536,
   statistics, 33, 43, 86, 124, 361, 401
   theological orientation, 454-55
   view of Catholics, 396
   view of Mennonites, 87-88, 236, 357-58, 369
   view of VNCS, 357-58
   view of the war, 198, 281, 414
      effects of, 230, 281, 292, 327
   youth, 248
Evangelical Church of Vietnam (North), 286-87,
   440, 526, 531-32
Evans, Rev. Theodore, 210, 221
Evans, Gene, 491
Evans, Mr., 160
Ewert, Adam, 8, 13, 20, 34
Ewert, Anna, 45, 48
Ewert, Ann Noel, 443, 472, 480, 481, 508
Ewert, Claire & Wallace, 454, 456, 492-3, 508
Ewert, Wallace, 454, 456, **476**

F

Fairchild, Chap., 250
Falk, Anne, **254**, 255, 261-62, 330, 366
Fast, Margaret, 395, 416, 435
Fellowship of Reconciliation (FOR), 177, 381
Fisher, Lloyd, 400
Fitzstevens, John, 276
floods. *See* typhoons and floods
Fogg, Ernest, 518
Ford, Gerald, 500, 507, 517
Foreign Operations Administration, 8-9
Forsythe, Julie, 528, 529
Frantz, Delton, 492,
French Indochina War, 6-7
French Protestant Church, 59, 373
Frey, Earnest & Mabel, 240, 293
Fund for Reconciliation, 437, 518

G

Gehman, Johanna, 408
Gehman, Linford, 173, 256, **256**, 278-79, 315,
   334, 339
General Conference Mennonite Church, 197

Geneva Accords, 7, 31, 41
Gerber, Daniel, 111, 120, *126*
    capture, 113, 115-16, 126-27
Getz, Roger, 409, 420, 422, 448
Gia Dinh, 154
Gia Dinh Mennonite Community Center, *154*,
    165, 353, 468
    administration, 236, 376, 383, 394-95
    beginning, 145, 154-58, 161-62, 164
    children's activities, 156
    cooperate with Social Welfare Ministry, 351
    evangelistic emphasis, 177, 227, 230, 236
        response, 158, 166, 236
    facilities enlarged/dedicated, 181, 182
        nearby facilities, 294, 345, 366, 399
    letters from NLF, 350-51
    material aid, 317, 363, 375
    programs, 154, 341-42
        clinic, 291, 342, 346, 366, 405
        day care, 158, 181, 288
        EAP & FCA. *See* MCC child sponsorship
        elementary school. *See* Rang Dong
        English classes, 157, 226, 236, 346
        literacy classes, 298
        other programs, 166, 228
        rebuild houses, 343, 363
        sewing classes, 345, 366
    after revolution, 520, 523
    visiting speakers, 177
    staff members, 182, 376
        from ECVN, 156, 236
        staff issues, 162, 236, 356
    student hostel, 59, 294-95
        wild night, 319-20
    volunteer activities, 161
    warfare May 1968, 329-332
Gia Dinh Tin Lanh church, 164
Giai Phong, 530-31
Gingrich, Jesse, 220, 256, *257*
Giam Duc, Thich, 484
Giap, Gen. Vo Nguyen, 368
Gio Nam, 401
Gitelson, David, 308, 338
Go Vap, 181, 236
Goering, Dr. Donald, 39, *43*, 45
Goering, Loua, 39, 42, 45
Goldwater, Barry, 159
Good, Leland, 46, *48*, 111
Goshen College, 144, 242
Gospel Herald, 200, 202, 429
Goss, George, 275-76

Graber, J. D., 25-29, 36
Graham, Dr. Billy, 249-51, *249*, 359-60
Grant, James M., 276, 340
Green, Dr. Robert, 456
Gregory, Fred, 257, 259-61, *260*, 347
guardian angels, 93, 124, 173, 206, 216, 295, 310-
    11, 313-15, 361-62, 362, 378, 384-85,
    403-4, 454, 477
Guidelines for Today, 427-28

H

Habib, Philip, 340
Hackman, Walton, 433, 462
Hai (believer), 171
Hai, Le Thi, 166, 169, 172, 233-34, 410, 421, *421*
Hai, Rev. Nguyen Nam, 172, 372
Hai, Nguyen Van, 290
Haines, Harry, 437
Halstern, Mary Sue, 206
Hancock, R. Dean, 255, 342, 379, 396, *423*
Hancock, Margaret, 255, 379
Hang Xanh, 375
H'Chioh, 37. *See also* Y'Don Ksor
Harding, Vincent, 285, 293-94
Harnett, Mngr. Joseph, 12
Harshbarger, Eva, 8, 13-14, 34
Harkins, Gen. Paul D., 121, 151
Harriman, W. Averell, 205
Hasselblad, Marva, 116-17, 191
Hasselblad, Oliver, 116
Hatch, Col. Burton, 240
Hayes, Herman and Dottie, 125, 385
Hege, Nathan, 498, 522
Helstern, Mary Sue, 256
Herman, Stewart, 429
Herod, William, 206, 261-63, 265-66, 381, 396, 397
Hershey, Jean, 434, *435*, 475, 489, 492-93, 508
Hess, Isaac L., 32
Hess, Mahlon, 203, 319
Hi, Rev. Tran Xuan, 81, 354, 444, 490, 508
Hickey, Gerald C., 397
Hiebert, Linda, 456, 482, 530, *531*
Hiebert, Murray, 456, 480, 481
Hiebert, Linda & Murray, 454, 508, 516
    in Laos, 518, 529
Hien, Dang Thi, 460, 462-63, *463*, 484-85
Hieu (believer), 171
Hieu, Nguyen Van, 532-33
Ho Chi Minh, 6, 367-68
Hoa, Dao Van, 5, 64, *71*, 83
Hoa, Nguyen Thanh, (student) 162, 415

Hoa, Vo Van, 353, *486*, 487, 501, 511
Hoang, Nguyen Thi, 100, 164, 171, 174, *486*
    church ministries, 232, 419, 468, 487
    after revolution, 526
Hochstetler, Alan, 46, 48, 106
Hochstetler, Harlan & Pauline, 268
Holdeman Mennonites, 209
Hong, Nguyen Thi, 133, 174, *174*, 514
Hong Kong, 163, 165, 341
    Stauffer assignment, 165
    E. Metzler assignment, 341
Hope, Nancy, 255
Hope, Sam, 248, 267, 272-74, 323
Horn, Ursula, 395, 397, *476*
Hoskins, Tom, 506, 528, 529
Hostetter, Jr., C. N., 107-8, 211
    advocate for peace, 219-20,
Hostetter, Douglas, 220, 244, 261-66, *262*, 267,
    334, 350
    contact DRV/PRG missions, 443
    eschews US protection, 244-45
    issue of biased aid, 336-38
    relations with OCO/CORDS, 245
    Tet Offensive, 313, 320-21
    visit DRV, 387
    witness for peace, 266
Hostetter, Patricia, 220, 244, 258, *258,* 260, 324.
    See also Pat Hostetter Martin
    biased aid, 335-36
Hostetler, John, 109
Hue, 128, 132
Hue program (WRC), 267-68
    agricultural work, 212
    guerrillas in area, 267-68
    programs and staff, 212-13, 243, 267-68, 314,
    343
    Tet Offensive, 314-15, 324
Hue (believer), 178
humorous bits, 11, 12, 81, 134, 147, 160, 191, 213,
    261, 271, 287, 404, 438, 441, 446-47, 465
Humphrey, Hubert, 205, 240-40
Humphreys, Jr. Gen. James William, 246
Hung (believer), 130, 132, 159, 178
    rejected war, 163
Hung (student), 319-20
Hung, Dang Thai, 136, 144, 170
Hunt, Garth and Betty, 96
Hunting, Pete, 184
Huong, Le Ngoc, 107, *107*
Huong, Tran Van, 159, 368, 512, 515-16
Hutchinson, Frank, 190, 195, 213

Huyen, Ong Van, 107, *107*, 479-80, 508, 520, 533
Hurst, Carl, 4, 41, 51-52, *52*, 56-57

I

Ichikawa, Yoshihiro, 411, *524*, 536
    Quang Ngai, 495-96, 506,
    after revolution, 519-20, 522
illnesses, 20, 21, 85, 154-55, 241, 317, 373, 387, 477
Indochina, 388
Intelligencer Journal, 432
International Protestant Church, 52, 62, 71, 76,
    143, 175-76, 227, 356, 426
International Rescue Committee, 56
International Voluntary Service, 124, 144, 407
    Mennonites with IVS, 144, 257, 408
    protest and resignations, 275-76, 296
    volunteers killed, 184, 308
    Wm. T. Snyder role, 144, 308
Intervarsity Christian Fellowship, 60, 61
Irwin, E. Franklin, 7, 326, 361
Irwin, George and Harriet, 79, 391

J

Jackson, Herbert and Lydia, 15, 174
Jacobs, Donald, 528
Jacobsen, Elwood, 130-31
James, B. Violet, 217
James, Dr. G. D., 228
Janzen, Margaret, 34, 37, *43*, 47-48
Jantzi, Lowell, 434, 456
Jeffrey, Rev. D. Ivory, 4-5, 10, 27, 61, 62, 110, *119*
Jeffrey, Ruth, 5, 66, 245
Johnson, Joan & Norman, 493, 530
Johnson, Lyndon, 104, 108, 142, 159, 325
    assessed war aims, 146-47, 197-98, 212, 228,
    324
    met GVN leaders, 211-12
Johnson, Sandra, 361
Johnston, Lela, 418
Jones, Diane, 461
Josephson, Leroy and Nancy, 132, 237, 268, 292

K

Karnow, Stanley, 542
Kauffman, Carl, 192, *192*
Kauffman, Fred & Minh, 453, *453*
Kauffman, Ivan J., 278, 322-23
Keefer, Kenneth, 216, 267, 343
Keener, Gerry, 452
Keeney, William, 269-71, 427
    evaluate VNCS, 270

"peace commando teams," 271
    unbiased aid, 336-37
Kehler, Larry, 202
Kellerman, Robert, 17-18
Kennedy, Edward, 397
Kennedy, John F., 103, 129, 139
Kennel, Edith & Elmer, 379
Kennel, Paul, 206, *207*, 267, 285, 343, 379, 452
Khai, Phan Van, 360, *394*, *417*, 417, *486*, 487,
    527, 533
Khanh, Nguyen, 142, 147, 167
    authorized Mennonite Mission, 150
    Buddhists granted status, 151
    demonstrations, 155, 162
Khanh Hoi (Xon Chieu) programs, 242-43
    personnel, 254
Khe Sanh, 132, 268
Khiem, Tran Thien, 155, 368, 502
Khoa, Fr. Tran Van, 382, 391-92
Kimmel, Christopher, 213, 267
Kidron News, The, 127
King, Louis L., 21, 36-37, 39, 85, 91, 203, 357
    praise for Longacre, 211
King, Jr., Martin Luther, 284-85
Kingsbury, Olive, *35*, 113, 115
Kinh, Truong Thi, 172
Kissinger, Henry, 375, 439, 458, 488
Klassen, J. M. (Jake), 114
Klassen, James, 443, *445*, 448, 536
    advocate for peace, 489, 491
    Apr 1975, 511, 518-19
    on staying, 502-3
    support believer group, 527
    teaching church leaders, 448, 454, 468
    writing, 462
Klein, Wells, 219, 222, 242
Kleinbach, Grace, 381
Kleinbach, Russel, 382
Komer, Robert, 258
Kontum, 177-78
Kooker, Harley, 267, 343
Kooker, Harold, 184
Koren, Henry, 264, 273
Kowles, Alexander, 529
Kpa Dai, 492, 509
Krabill, Grace, *35*
Krabill, Willard, 19, 20, 21-23, 34-45, *38*, *44*, 48,
    56, 58
    describes Protestant work, 43-44
    1965 visit, 193, 202
Krabill family, Grace & Willard, 21, 79

Kraus, C. Norman and Ruth, 234, 484
Kraybill, Esther, 256, 334
Kraybill, Harold, 248, 256, *256*
    family, 220, 256, 361
Kraybill, Paul N.. 4, 30, 144, *281*, 424
    conversation with ECVN leaders, 86-88
    conversations with J. Metzler, 299-300
    on government, 120
    mission-church partnership, 398-99
    on peace statements, 199, 201, 302-3
    relation of mission and service, 84-85
    1959 visit, 84-89; 1962 visit, 121-22
    1964 visit, 143-146; 1965 visit, 167-69
    1966 visit, 230-32; 1967 visit, 280-82
    1968 visit, 327-28; 1969 visit, 356-59
    1971 visit, 392, 398-400
Kreider, Robert, 461, 470-72
Krich, Claudia, 525
Kubicka, Louis & Eryl, 530
Kuntze, Navy Cap. Archie, 206
Ky, Co, (teacher), 123, *123*
Ky, Nguyen Cao, 155, 167, 174, 212, 215, 232
    on Ho Chi Minh, 212

L

Lam, Duy Cach, 77, 86, 88
Lam, Nguyen Huu, 158, 171, 362, *394*, *486*
    attend Bible school, 171, 181, 281, *281*
    church ministries, 232, 302
    after revolution 514, 527
Lancaster Mennonite Conference, 25, 143, 280, 355
    day of prayer, 319
    dress, 65-66, 130, 173, 183, 280
    foreign missions polity, 183
Lan, Prof. Nguyen Ngoc, 526
Landhuis, Jesse, 254
Landmann, Herbert, 335, 340
Laos, MCC aid to, 20, 111, 518
Lap, Margriet, 393-94
Lap, Thoi, 352, *352*
Lapp, John A., 199, 387
Lapp, John E., 283, 427
Lathrum, L. Wade, 270, 277
Lauver, Donald, 143, 280-82, *281*, 392, 400
Leatherman, Loretta, 242, 332
Leatherman, Paul, 222, *223*, 242, 334, 336, 338-39
    advocate for peace, 250
    attend C&MA conference, 271
    family, 220, 242, 33
    meeting with Bunker, 274-75
    VNCS director, 245-46, 254, 264-66, 275-76

Lee, Ven Pak, 391-92
Lefever, Esther, 39, 41, 42, **44**, 51, 54, 60
Lefever, Harry, 39, 41, 52, **54**, 64, 93
    student activities, 57-58, 60, 61, 181
Lenzmann, Emma, 191, 194, 256, 334
Leonhart, William, 220
Leuz, Christopher, **218**, 256, 350
Leuz, Lois, 256-57
Leuz, Christopher and Lois, 191, 194, 206
Lewis, James, 356, 385
Lewis, Patricia, 460
Lich (believer), 132
Lichti, Elda, 119
Lichti, Rudolph, 111, 113-19, **119**, 126, 132, 140, 145
Lichti family, Elda & Rudolph, 118-19
Liem, Doan Thanh, 461, 465, 469
Lieu, Vo Hong, 430, 469
Life Magazine, 381
Lindholm, Richard, 43
Linh, Nguyen, 474, 479, 510
Loan (believer), 410
Loc, Dr. Le Van, 524, 525, 529-30
Lodge, Henry Cabot, 129, 205, 222
Lon Nol, Gen., 375, 509
Long, Charles, 194
Long Hai, 77, 465
Long, Rev. Hua Hon, 44, 90-91
Long Kien. *See* Nha Be, 254
Long, Nguyen Thanh, 526, 532-34, **533**, 536
Long Thanh, 214
Long Xuyen, 289
Longacre Doris, 207, 209, 216-17
    witness for peace, 219
Longacre, Paul, 155, 188-91, **207**, 243, **246**, 261-62
    advocate for peace, 206, 250, 427
    assistant executive secretary, 433-34
    chair CVA, 209, 246
    critique important, 189, 193-94
    director, MCC Asia, 264, 266, 278-79, 307,
        322-23
    family, 155, 206, 209, **292**, 293
    flood relief, 159-161, 188
    propose independent MCC, 401-2
    strategize,188-91
    unbiased aid, 336-39
    working with Beechy, 205-6
    1968 visit, 327
    1969 visit, 371
    1973 visit, 443
Lowry, Boyd, 188, 363
    administers VNCS, 376-77, 433

Luan, Ms. (nurse), 376
Luan, Pham Thi, 466
Luc, Rev. Dang Van, 515
Luc (Lục), Pham Van, 120, 123, 132, **180**, 224
    as army officer, 344, 355-56, 385
    in church ministries, 148, 511
    family. *See* Vu Thi Qui
Luc (Lực), Chau Hong, 123, **123**, 131, **367**, 526
    army experience, 180
    living in country, 235, 367, 374
Luce, Don, 124, 144, 274-76, 381
Luellen, David, 184
Luken, William, 206, **209**, 216
Lum, Ada, 177
Luong, Luong Thi, 410
Lutheran World Relief (LWR), 192, 542
Luyen, Huynh Kim, 53, 86, 88
Ly, Tran Thi, 466
Lyons, Fr. Daniel, 219

M

MacCracken, James, 194, 274, 307, 380, 403
Madam Nhu (Xuan, Tran Le), 50, 58, 128, **128**, 138
Maddimadugu, Devadoss, 293, **321**, 327, 361, 481
Maddimadugu, Doris, 449, **449**
    family, 492-3, 502
Mai (Believer), 410
Mai, Mrs. (Quangs' friend), 419
Mai, Chi, 495
Mai, Thich Nu Nhat Chi, 290
Makil, Gasper, 130-31
Malagar, P. J., 384
Mangham, Evelyn, 65
Mangham, Jr., T. Grady, 27, 35, 38, 130, 198, 271,
    326
Manh, 509
Manke, Hugh, 397
Mann, Charles, 211, 219
Mansfield, Mike, 131
Marentek, Geysje, 481, 483
Martin, Earl, 195, 206, 222, 258, **258**, 260-61, 281
    biased aid, 336
    contact the "other side," 495-96
    early ECVN perceptions, 247-48
    March-April 1975, 494-96, 506, 519-21, 526-27
    named, 232
    peace advocacy, 306, 471, 491
    political prisoners, 459
    unexploded ordnance (UXO), 466-67
    writing, 542
Martin, Patricia Hostetter. *See also* Pat Hostetter

family, 459, 466, 495, 508, 528
political prisoners, 460,
Martin, Daniel and Elizabeth, *210*
Martin, Graham, 456, 462-63, 496
Martin, John, 164
Martin, Luke, 122, 123, 374, 390, 390, 411, 420
    assist MCC/VNCS, 192, 232, 237, 244, 342
    Bible School, 360
    EMBMC assistant, 424, 447
    Gia Dinh community center, 154
    Hong Kong, 331, 341
    March-April 1975, 494-516, 517-18
    MCC Vietnam director, 450, 453, 483, 490
    mission secretary, 429, 450
    peace advocacy, 131, 305-6, 354
    preaching/teaching, 147, 152, 185, 236, 498
    relate to ECVN, 227
    visit ambassadors, 431, 456, 462-63
    visit Cambodia, 473-74
    visit prisons, 185, 245-46
    visit Vietnam, 530, *531*, 533-36
Martin, Mary, 122, 123, 131, *174*
    appealing for peace, 153, 428-29
    on leaving Vietnam, 503, 505, 511, 515-16
    speaking/teaching, 147, 148, 152, 228
    Sunday school teacher, 372
    women's ministries, 345, 366, 469
Martin family, L/M, 132, 318, 362-63, *432*, 470-71, 477
    children, 168, 174, 233, 386-87, 499, 503, 508-10
    Bangkok, 503, 510, 517-18, 527
        visas, 525, 528, 530
    death of Tuyet, 409-10
    friends, 133, 166, 410, 443,
    furlough 1967-68, 285, 293-94, 299, 302, 304-5, 325
    furlough 1972-73, 432
    go or stay, 501-2, 505
    hosting, 226
    vacations, 136, 162, 287
Martin, Raymond, 157
material aid, 11, 50-55
    aid to churches, 16, 188
    aid as weapon, 160-61
    bakery, 52-53, 111, 209, 292
    Christmas bundles, 50, 55, 161
    MCC canned beef, 20, 50, 55, 160, 191
    need for, 155, 188
    philosophy of, 51
    political aspects of, 50, 189, 339

problems of, 110-11, 194
supplies lost, 322
Mays, Jim, 260
McCarthy, Fr. John, 193
McClosky, Rep. Paul, 492
McConnell, Tharon, 244, 258, *258*, 260, 334, 361
McNamara, Robert, 121, 140, 146-47, 150, 159, 390
Medard, Pierre, 380
medical services, 19, 91-92
Mennonite Board of Missions & Charities, 25, 28-29, 203
    interest in Vietnam missions, 21-22, 28
Mennonite Central Committee, 6, 24, 41, 272, 503, 541
    aid to North Vietnam, 16, 192
    aid after revolution, 497, 506-7, 525, 529, 537
    Akron, PA headquarters, 107, 210
    conversations with DRV and NLF, 251, 382, 443
    constituency relations, 210
    crisis in Korea program, 17
    delegation visits Vietnam, 530-35
    executive committee, 7, 10, 26, 243, 272, 537
    peace advocacy, 219-20
    Peace Section, 98-99, 157, 351, 269-71, 278, 322, 387
        advocate impartial aid, 335, 337
    relate to Menno mission agencies, 84-85, 90, 144
    relief and mission coordinated, 183
    refugee resettlement, 528
    relief assistance messy, 189
    trainee program, 384
    Washington office, 427, 492, 540
    White House meeting, 220
Mennonite Central Committee, Vietnam, 390
    administering VNCS, 210
    child sponsorship programs, 145
        Educational Assistance Program (EAP), 291, 345, 365, 393-94
        Family Child Assistance (FCA), 190, 342, 345, 375, 393
        critique, 392-95
    GOV registration, 37-38, 40, 109, 191
    identity issues, 189
    influence C&MA and ECVN, 34, 51, 86, 188-89, 455
    language learning crucial, 194
    material aid. *See* material aid
    Memo of Understanding, 8
    merge into VNCS, 192
        disengagement, 422
    motivation, 43

personnel, 125
political implications, 8, 43-44, 50, 189-90,
programs, *See* Ban Me Thuot, Nha Trang *and*
     Pleiku
relations with C&MA, 10, 22, 49, 60
relations with ECVN, 79, 538
relations with Mennonite missionaries, 42, 63, 168
     joint coordination committee, 44, 60, 78, 89
staff worship practices, 45, 116
student services, 56-61, 90
scholarships, 61
work camps, 57, 60, 181
Mennonite Central Committee, Vietnam 1973-75, 442
     administration, 443
     changed structure 422
          reactions, 422, 435
     desire ECVN relationship, 434-35
          difficulties, 455, 482
          renegotiate relationship, 490, 492-93
     evacuations, 498, 500, 502, 503, 504
     GOV agreement, 456
     office staff, 457, 458, 470, 483
     objectives, 471, 480, 493
     peace/reconciliation, 422, 461, 471, 483, 493,
          502
     personnel, 434, 442-43, 454, 466, 483, 492
     programs. *See* Nha Trang Clinic/Hospital,
          Nurses school, Pleiku Clinic, Quang Ngai
          unexploded ordnance, political prisoners
     relief assistance, 501, 506, 509
     after revolution
          local staff members, 520
          MCC personnel, 522-23, 535
          high morale, 525
          registered, 523, 527
          met officials, 524, 525, 529
          gave assistance, 529
     staff conferences, 438, 480, 492
          joint MCC-VMM conferences, 450-51,
          465, 484
Mennonite Church (US), 3, 200, 305
     call for prayer and fasting, 426
Mennonite Community Center. *See* Gia Dinh Men-
     nonite Community Center
Mennonite Economic Development Associates
     (MEDA), 308, 352, 374
     poultry project, 352-53
Mennonite missionaries
     Americans in Vietnam, 204
     assignments, 231, 341
     associate with other missionaries, 77, 149, 429

attend ECVN conferences, 68, 79, 95, 227, 361
associate with IVS personnel, 134
associate with MCC personnel, 48, 67, 81, 140
associate with US military, 71, 185, 227, 377,
     406-7
     "wolves in sheep's clothing," 459,
associate with VNCS personnel, 240, 321
attend local congregations, 76
attend seminars, 479
children's schooling, 366. *See also* Phoenix
     Study Group
commitment to Vietnam, 63, 83,476, 498
compatible team, 149
critiqued, 452, 251, 479
cultural misunderstandings, 162-63
domestic helpers, 97, 169, 234, 238
evacuations, 166-67, 320, 429
finances, 237, 239, 452
five-year goals, 447
friends war victims, 238, 438, 458, 488
friendship evangelism, 146, 541
giving gifts, 469
heard real life stories, 133, 135, 136, 142, 175
identity concerns, 230, 297, 298-302, 326
interacted with Catholics, 227
language study, 5, 77, 80, 123, 129
leaving April 1975, 522, 524
lifestyle, 71, 81, 86, 465
     adaptable, 63, 75-76
     dress, 80, 130
     food, 129
     bicycles, 64, 72
     scooters, 80, 181, 240
     cars, 361, 378
March-April 1975, 499-502, 521
music ensembles, 72, 74, 130, 227, 228, 348, 426
meeting with US officials, 431-32
motivation, 236
being named, 124
teaching way of peace, 175, 304, 429
prayer, 390, 419
view of Catholics, 82, 96-97, 469
war anguish, 430, 452, 47
weekly gatherings, 149, 164, 382, 385, 419
Mennonites in US armed forces, 164, 377
Metzger, Dennis, 429
Metzler, Edgar, 157, 200, 213, 214
Metzler, Everett, 5, 70, 78-80, 83, 93, ***100, 180***,
     312, 330
     administration, 78, 137
     assist MCC/VNCS, 154, 192, 207

peace advocacy, 195, 203, 283
teaching/preaching, 100, 360
transfer to Hong Kong, 364, 411, 476
　　assist Vietnam program, 507
　　review ministry, 364
writing, 149, 234, 364
Metzler, Margaret, 5, 70, *71*, *152*, 227
　　Bible classes, 100
　　children's ministries, 54
　　friendship evangelism, 100, 164
Metzler family, 42, 70-72, 74-77, 234, 295, 527
　　children, E/M, 79, 98, 121, 139, 361-62, 364
Metzler, James, 122-23, *123*, 125, 152, *229*, 298-
　　　300, *343*, 369
　　demonstrate against war, 282-83
　　language learning, 129
　　peace advocacy, 198-99, 203, 368-69
　　preaching/teaching, 148, 360
　　questions about Vietnam witness, 298-300, 540
　　　on leaving as witness, 300, 326, 328
　　　to the Philippines, 383
　　relief service, 328-29, 333-34, 342
　　Tet Offensive, 309-10, 317-18
　　writing, 147, 155, 229, 235, 298, 299-300,
　　　333, 540, 542
Metzler, Rachel, 122-23, *123*, 283, 330, 366
Metzler family, J/R, 139, 185, 234, 345-46, 383
　　children, 234, 366,
　　Tet Offensive, 309-11, 317
Michigan State University, 77
Mieng, Doan Van, 60, *210*, *223*, 243, 293, 515
　　chosen ECVN president, 107
　　call to prayer, 426
　　Gió Nam interview, 401
　　after revolution, 526, 536
　　speaks at Mennonite gathering, 134
　　thanks MCC/VNCS, 205, 396, 490
　　visits MCC headquarters, 210
　　view of communism, 359
　　view of war, 210
　　vision, 359
Military Assistance Advisory Group (MAAG), 6, 114
　　introduce Special Forces, 103
　　military advisors, 103, 121, 128, 159
　　offered MCC aid, 109, 119
　　training ARVN forces, 102
Military Assistance Command, Vietnam, 121, 131,
　　　See also US armed forces
　　CORDS under MACV, 258, 263-66
military conscription, 108-9, 238
　　conscientious objection, 149, 157

draft, 148, 170
　　draft deferments, 157, 181, 195, 238
Military Provincial Health Assistance, 208, 243, 289
Milk, Juliet, 267
Milk, Richard, 255, 267
Miller, Ernest E., 6-7, 22
Miller, Chap. Harry, 149, 161
Miller, John and Carolyn, 132, 268, 493-94, 530
Miller, Orie O., 5, 24-30, *44,* 374
　　begin MCC Vietnam program, 7-9, 14, 17-18, 22
　　faith in God's leading, 36
　　mission philosophy, 69
　　witness for peace, 201
　　1956 visit, 27, 35-37; 1958 visit, 44-45, 78
　　1962 visit, 124-25; 1969 visit, 352-53, 358
　　1970 visit with Elta, 374
Miller, Robert L., 260-61, 269
Miller, Robert W., 39, 42, 57, 59, 136, 211, *246*
　　peace advocacy, 408
　　on political prisoners, 459-60, 462, 473
　　testifies in Washington, 528
　　visit to ambassador, 456
　　VNCS director, 343-44, 397
　　1961 visit, 111; 1965 visits, 188, 195
　　1966 visit, 239, 246; 1972 visit, 438
　　1973 visit, 456; 1975 visit, 492-93
　　Nov 75 visit, 530-36, *531, 533*
Miller family, Robert/Jean, 343, *344*, 361-62
Mimmie, Pham, 116-17
Mininger, Mark, 478
Mininger, Mark/Ruth Ann, 465, 470, 475, 478, 499
Minh (teacher), 369
Minh (believer), 172
Minh, Gen. Duong Van, 129, 142, 516, 518
Minh, Pham Quang (CYSS), 510
Minh Quy Hospital, 257, 494
Missionary Messenger, 25, 498, 522
　　articles, 4, 30, 300, 301, 333, 373-74
　　prayer letters, 120, 296-97, 357, 390, 424
Mitchell, Archie, 113, 126-127
Mitchell, Betty, 113, 115, 493, 530
Miyazaki, Yukio, 457, 521
Monro, Gardner, 273, 276
Montagnard. See ethnic minorities
Muc, Nguyen Van, 540
Mumaw, John R., 82-83, 182-83
Muong (Bat), Nguyen, *394*, *421*, 426, 428, *428*, 511
Muste, A. J., 213
My, Nguyen Van, 172
My Tho, 349
Myers, Willie, 134, 173, 275-76, 289

N

Nam, Dinh Van. *See* Luc, Chau Hong, 367, 374
Nam, Nguyen Thanh. *See* Coconut Monk
National Association of Evangelicals, 205
National Council of Churches, 188, 347
National Liberation Front, 108, 289, 325, 349
    letters from, 350-51
Navigators, 172
Nelson, Marjorie, 361
Neufeld, David, 255, 257, 259-60, *262*, 316-17
Neufeld, Susan, 258, 260
Neufeld family, Dave/Sue, 206, 213, 217, 244, 261
Neufeld, Elfrieda, 45, 47, *48*
Neufeld, Elmer, 427
neutralism, 151, 153
New York Times, 15, 170, 275, 390, 397, 460, 497
Newbern, William, 227
Newkirk, Jonathan, 257, 277-78
Newsweek Magazine, 227, 318, 379, 386, 390
Newman, John and Joan, 102, 139, 150, 286
Nga, Ly Tuyet, 348, 384
Nga, Nguyen Tuyet, 182, 327, 342
Nga, Phan Tuyet, 225-26, *225*, 227, 417
Nghia Hanh, 259-61, 336. *See* Quang Ngai
Ngay, Nguyen Van, 352
Ngoc Anh, Tran Thi, 419
Ngoc Sa, Truong Thi, 509
Nguyen, Dr. Nguyen Nhu, 405
Nguyet, Nguyen Thuy, 130, 140, *486*
Nha Be programs, 243, 254
Nha, Hoang Duc, 397
Nha Trang, 65
    Hon Chong, 108, 136
    March 1975, 498-500
Nha Trang Clinic and Hospital, **116,** *187, 256*
    chaplain, 105, 188
    dedication, 111, 187
    development, 105-6
    ECVN support, 107, 189, 464
    hospital board, 105, 112, 218, 420, 454, 479
    joint ECVN-MCC project, 105
    renegotiate, 474, 481, 482-83, 492-93
    nurses training, 189, 218, 334, 454, 464, 482
    patient census, 107, 140, 188, 256
    patient support, 107
    Phuoc Luong, 107, 480
    revolution, 519-20
    specialized in eye surgery, 162, 256, 464
    staff, 112, 117, 187, 256, 334, 361, 456, 481
    Tet Offensive, 312
    USAID offer, 464
    US army doctors assist, 116, 117-18
    Vietnamese doctor, 474-75
Nha Trang Orphanage, 16, 65, 91
Nhu, Ngo Dinh, 83, 94, 129, 132
Nhu, Mrs. Ngo Dinh Nhu. *See* Madam Nhu
Nhung, (Mrs. Nguyen Van Ninh), 356, **486**
Nhuong, Nguyen Hau, 454, 465, 506
Nielsen, Ove E., 195, 327
Ninh, Nguyen Van, 34, *119*, 195, **223**, 365, 373, 411
    with Asia Christian Service, 465, 512
    with MCC, 34, 37
    visits MCC headquarters, 365
    with Mennonite church, 342, 348, 419
    on leaving, 497, 512-13
    with VNCS, 396
    with YMCA, 365
    work camp, 422-23
Ninh, Mrs. Nguyen Van. *See* Nhung
Ninomiya, Akiie, 395
Nixon, Richard, 346, 349, 405
    proposed settlement, 433
    resignation, 472, 477
    troop withdrawals, 368, 370, 386, 426
    war continued, 349, 380, 382, 416
Nolting, Frederick E., 104, *128*, 129, 131, 241
Non-governmental agencies, 241
Noteboom, Glenn, 395
Nyce, Carolyn, 220, 243, 254, 257

O

Oanh, Lt., 459
Oanh, Nguyen Thi, 489
Oanh, Nguyen Xuan, 159-61
Office of Civil Operations, 245, 252, 259, 270
O'Neil, Hugh, 464
Operation Reindeer, 11, 15
orphans, 489
Orr, Ross, 207, 216

P

panic, 499-500, 505, 514
paradoxes, 213, 231, 233, 270, 339, 346, 379, 382, 483, 496, 510
Paris peace talks, 349, 361, 415, 416, 426, 437, 439
Paris Peace Accord, 349, 442
    basic issues unresolved, 442, 511
    fighting continued, 461, 484
    International Commission, 443, 496
paternalism, 393-94, 395
Pauls, Mary, 206, 256-57, 350
Pays Montagnard du Sud (PMS), 10, 11

Pax program, 12, 17
Peachey, Paul E., 98-99, 200
Peachey, Titus, 383, 411, *419*, 440, *440*
    English teaching, 407
    student center activities, 400, 405
    work camp, 422
Pentagon Papers, The, 390
People's Army of Vietnam, 7, 420, 520
    infiltrate, 459
    spring 1972, 423, 425
    spring 1975 offensive, 487-88, 493-94, 497
Peters, Katherine, 361
Petre, Rufus, 206, 256-57
Phap Lan, Thich, 459, 463
Phi (patient), 117
Phien, Rev. Nguyen Huu, 81, 166, 354, 453, 509, 511
Phillips, Lillian and Richard, 493, 530
Phoenix program, 388
Phoenix Study Group, 166, 296, 317, 320, 410,
    411, 414, 458, 500
Phong, Rev. Nguyen Thanh, 163, 178, 185
Phu, Le Hoang, 95-96, 140, *189*, 444
Phu Tho (Saigon), 295, 379
Phuc, Rev. Hoang Kim, *531*, 532
Phuoc, Nguyen Dinh, 472
Phuoc, Phan Ba, 121, *156*, 163, *180*, 373
    in armed forces, 498-99
    church ministries, 148, 304
    faith, 98, 100-2, 104
    wife Sang and family, 163, 185, 498
    work at Gia Dinh Center, 156
    working with MCC and IVS, 123, 134
    working with USOM, 176, 239, 362
Phuoc Luong, 227, 475
Phuong, Tran, 97, 366
Phuong Hang, Phan, 457, 466, 468
Phuong Nam, Maj., 496
Piburn, Carolyn and Marvin, 361
Pierce, Bob, 149, 276
PL-480 commodities, 9, 119, 242
Pleiku, 22, 218
Pleiku programs, 456
    clinic and hospital, 190, 243, 256, 350, 454
        C&MA and ECVN support, 194, 381, 481
        clinic statistics, 256
    farm and training center, 256-57
    staff assignments, 395-96
    Tet Offensive, 312
political prisoners, 245-46, 254, 417, 456
    assist, 448, 459, 462-63
Porter, William, 246, 426

Pradham, Dr., 443
Preheim, Gayle, *268*, 269, 313-14, 317, 342
prisoners of war, 127, 448
Provisional Revolutionary Government, 325-26,
    361, 364, 497, 499, 501, 506
public statements against war, 197-204
    An Appeal for Peace to US Congress, 492
    doctors' letter to Nixon, 416-17
    Letter to American Christians, 301-3, 319, 340
        response, 319, 326
    letters to U Thant and Richard Nixon, 387-8
    missionaries' letter to Nixon, 426-27
        critique, 427-28
    Open Letter to US Congressional persons, 472-73
    Statement of Concern, 181, 197-99, 201-3
    Statement to Vietnamese Community, 297
    01/66 *Gospel Herald* and *The Mennonite* 202-3

Q

Quan, Rev. Nguyen Van, 515
Quang, Bui, 508, 511, 514, 522, 527
Quang, Tran Thu, 86, 88
Quang, Rev. Tran Xuan, 81, *354, 394*, 400, 405,
    412
    Asian Mennonite Conference, 411-12
    assist church, 172-73, 181, 225, 227, 232, 342
    direct community center, 395, 417, 524
    pastor Mennonite church, 333, 354, 372, 476
    preaching, 451, 465, 498
    on military service. 238, 429
    with VNCS, 216, 323, 355, 396
    US visit, 497-98, 504-5
Quang, Mrs. Tran Xuan, 81, 333, *394*
    leaving Vietnam, 504, 507, 513, 524
    social ministries, 375, 394
Quang family, *418*, 441, 475-76, 478
    children, 441, 490
Quang Do, Thich, 484
Quang Duc, Thich, immolation, 128, 132
Quang Hanh, Dr. Tran Thi, 470, 474-75, 490
Quang Ngai, 233, 257, 420, 429, 470, 497
    attacks, 312-13, 356, 488
Quang Ngai programs, 222, 257-61
    feeding programs, 222, 242, 257, 259
    identity issues, 257-61
    Nghia Hanh, 259-61, 336
    recreational program, 222, 244
    refugee services, 258
    team members, 222, 244, 257-58, 287
    Tet Offensive, 312-13, 324
    unexploded ordnance, 444, 466

unit house, 287
work with ECVN and C&MA, 257
Quang Tri, 324. *See also* Dong Ha
Quat, Dr. Phan Huy, 174
Que, Nguyen Phuc, 222, 246, *246*, 316
Qui, Vu Thi, 171, 178, 385. *See also* Pham Van Luc
    church ministries. 180, 232
    English language teacher, 226, 236
Quinn-Judge, Paul & Sophie, 461

R

Rach Gia, 81
Ragsdale, Tom, 268, 314
RAND, 391
Rang Dong School, 182, 225, 288, 292
    enrollment, 225, 230, 291, 292, 332, 468
    after revolution, 534
    middle school experiment, 365-66
    programs, 237-38
    scholarships, *See* MCC Vietnam EAP, 291,
        394
    teacher training, 372
Reconciliation Work Camps, 411
    Nha Trang, 422, 435-36
Redlin, Gloria, 386, 392
reeducation, 525
refugees, 9, 162, 425
    camps, 259, 509, 511
    Catholics, 9, 31
    Commissioner of Refugees, 242
    numbers, 193, 259, 296, 321, 380, 438, 487, 496
    Protestants, 71
    war-generated, 188, 190, 259-61
Reimer, Reginald, 455, 479, 539
Reimer, Vernon, 251
religions in Vietnam, 29-33
    ancestor veneration, 96, 373
    Christianity and colonialism, 146, 185, 198,
        235, 297, 539
    French influence, 32, 150
    people's view of, 74, 227, 235, 422
    Protestant denominations, 238, 520-21
Republic of Vietnam
    elections, 95, 237, 291, 295, 382, 407, 408,
        410-11
    exchange rates, 182, 236, 378-79, 412, 468
    flag, 81, 439, 480
    insurrection Jan 1960, 97-98
    neutralism unacceptable, 473
    pro-Catholic, 73
    surrender, 516

visas, 77, 99, 119-20, 121-22, 353
Revelle, Evelyn, 65
Revelle, Jack, 4, 62, 91
Revolutionary Military Committee, 129, 138, 142
Richardson, Jacqueline, *See* Thimm
Richardson, Paul. *See* Lam, Duy Cach.
Rock, Martin, 383, *383*
Roggli, Elizabeth, 334, 361
Rose, William, 382, *423*
Roth, Larry, 379
Routh, Jr., Walter, 479
rumors, 498, 508
Rusk, Howard A., 192
Rutt, Clarence and Helen, 45

S

Sa Dec, 289,
Saigon, 3-4, 62-64,182, 238, 294, 384
Saigon Student Union, 462
Saigon VNCS programs, 254-55
Saigon Mennonite Student Center/Office, *135*
    Bible studies, 102, 282, 291, 369, 405, 440,
        453, 468, 478
    catechism/baptisms, 130, 498
    children's activities, 152
    church formed, 492
    correspondence course, 22, 422, 468
    English classes, 102, 135, 152, 184
    evangelism, 137, 138, 140, 157-58
    literature, 185, 468
    property, 97-98, 133-34, 453
    reading room, 234
    after revolution, 523, 527
    special programs, 139, 148, 180
    student responses, 139
    volunteer work, 405
    worship, 130, 148, 498
Saigon Post, The, 170, 240, 260, 296, 465
Sanders, J. Oswald, 227
Sandoz, Jerry, 267-68
Sang, Rev. Truong Van, 194, 244, 396
Sanh, Lt. Col. Nguyen Phu, 238
Sauder, James and Rhoda, 99
Sauder, June, 255, 261-62, 268
Sawatzky, Kurt, 396-97
    changed ARVN tactics, 397
Sawatzky family, Kurt & Frieda, 350, 396
Scahill, Anne, 448
Schmidt, Clara & John, 420
Schneider, Lou, 528
Sebus, Juliette, 34, 37, 45

security issues, 19, 108, 119, 143. 164, 179, 184-85, 207-8, 213-14
Sensenig, Don, 134, *176, 186,* 236, 311, 317, *419, 440*
   assist COR, 288-89
   assist MCC Akron, 512
   assist VNCS, 232
   Bible teacher, 360, 430
   meet US official, 431
   mission secretary, 429
   peace advocacy, 230, 237, 374, 427
   preaching, 236
   refugee resettlement, 528
   on the revolution, 517, 522
   at student center, 405, 407
   student hostel, 295, 319-20
   writing, 373-74, 451, 541
   Xom Gia, 379, 395,
   Tet Offensive, 324
Sensenig, Doris, 134, *173,* 311, 317-18
   family, 125, 134, 165, 286, 294-95, 364, 378, 451
   children, 134, 147, 165, *173,* 233, 373
Shenk, Wilbert, 144-45, 188
Shimkin, Alexander, 390
Shirk, Frank, 305-6
Shirk, Maynard, 383, 411, 418, *419,* 422, 443
   assist VNCS, 420, 437
Si, Vu Huu, 470
Sihanouk, Prince Norodom, 375
Shelly, Maynard, 201
Sinh, Ms. (nurse), 480, 482
Smalley, William, 70, 122
Smith, Gordon and Laura, 10, 116
Smith, H. Curwen, 7, 8, 12
Smith, Col. Wayne, 397
Smith T, Joanne, 342, *342*
Snavely, Helen, 254
Snead, Alfred C., 26
Snyder, William T., 7, 12, 17-18, 55, 61
   on MCC leading VNCS, 201-2
   peace advocacy, 197, 201-2, 219-20, 300, 325
   relief aid messy, 189-90
   unbiased aid, 338-40, 347
   view of Mennonite missionaries, 308
   1959 visit, 89-92; 1964 visit, 144-45
   1967 visit, 269-72, 275, 283
   1968 visit, 308-16, 20; 1969 visit, 363
   1970 visit, 376-77; 1971 visit, 402-3
   1972 visit, 438
Son, Dr. Tran Thanh, 534-35, *534*
Souder, Eugene, 282
South Vietnam. *See* Republic of Vietnam

Spellman, Abp. Francis Cardinal, 251
Spraggett, Roy and Daphne, 132
Spicher, Tom, 420, 423, 427, 429, 431, 435
Sprunger, Joseph, 361
Srisang, Koson, 528
Stallwood, Barbara, 191
Stars and Stripes, 152
Stauffer, Arlene, 3-5, 80, 295
   children's ministries, 83, 103
   EAP program, 365
   women's ministries, 415
Stauffer, James, 3-5, *76,* 78-83, 120, *139,* 309, *419*
   assist Truong Minh Giang chapel, 66, 99
   correspondence courses, 469
   furlough, 121, 237, 382
   Gia Dinh community center, 236
   Hong Kong assignment, 165, 182
   invitations to preach, 64, 65, 72
   letter to brother, 416
   meet US official, 431
   preacher/pastor, 98, 236
   peace advocacy, 284
   relations with ECVN pastors, 80, 263, 292
   Saigon student center, 468
   Tet 1975 offensive, 309, 315
   witnessing to Jesus Christ, 67-68, 101
   support Xom Gia, 407, 414
Stauffer family, A/J, 58, 62-69, 70-77, 81-82, 95, *98,* 361-62
   children, 101, 121, 165, 477
Stauffer, Harold, 327-28, 424
Stauffer, Harold and Connie, 479
Stauffer, Sanford, 216, 222, 244, 260, 307, 350
Stebbins, Thomas, 361, 401, 440
Special Technical and Economic Mission, 8, 11, 12, 13
Steiner, James, 105
Steinkamp, Orrel, 160
Stemple, Charlotte and Woody, 208, 248, 257, 287
Stickney, David and Mary, 232
Stoltzfus, Eugene, 134, 173, 275, 283, 492
Stoltzfus, Geneva, 42, *52,* 54
Stoltzfus, Glenn, 42, 46, 52-53, *52,* 55-57, 79, 106
Stoner, John, 427
Strayer, Marilyn, 255, 291, 315, 330
Strayer, Martin, 255, 324
Steinkamp, Orrel, 419
Stoffel, Alfred, 220, 246, 253-54
strategic hamlets, 132
Stuckey, Allen, 403-4, 416
Stuckey family, Allen and Jeannie, 403
Studebacker, Ted, 390-92

student center. *See* Saigon Mennonite Student Center
students. *See* Vietnamese people
Summer Institute of Linguistics (SIL), 4, 458
    personnel killed, 130-31, 310
    personnel detained, 493, 530
Sutherland, Spencer and Barbara, 103
Swartzendruber, Duane, 39, 41, 45, 53
Swartzendruber, Dwight, 380
Sy, Rev. Nguyen Thien, 53, 71, *119*

T

Tabor, Fr. John, 529
Tam Ky, 261, 266, 429
Tam Ky programs, 261-66, 320-21, 334
    attack on town, 262, 313
    programs, 244
    refugee assistance, 263
    relations with OCO/CORDS, 263-66
    student support. 261, 263, 266
    witness for peace, 266
Tam, Nguyen Thi. *See* Quang, Mrs. Tran Xuan
Tam, Pham Quang, *229*, 346, 366, 376, 405, *486*, 504
Tang, Truong Nhu, 433
Taylor, Gen. Maxwell, 120, 152, 191
Tet Offensive 1968, 308-318, 324-25
    May 1968 offensive, 328-32
Thach, Rev. Le Vinh, 177, 225
Thai, Rev. Le Van, 18, 27, 45, 54, 58-61, 78, 86-88,
    · 107, *107*
Thai, Luong Bao (Timothy), 421, 504
Thanh (believer), 420, *421*, 446
Thanh, Rev. Do Vinh, 236, 292, 317, 330, 356
Thanh, Mrs. Ngo Ba, 462
Thanh, Fr. Tranh Huu, 478
Thao, Rev. Kieu Cong, 76, 80, 87, 91
Thao, Le Van, 178-79, 355, 385
Thao, Trinh Dinh, 164, 179, 325, 364
The Mennonite, 202, 462
Thi, Bui, 184, *184*, 224, 283
    Thi's family, 184, 287, 353
Thi, Nguyen Chanh, 212, 215
Thielman, Calvin, 218
Thien, Ton That, 222
Thieu, Nguyen Van, 174, 361, 375, 512
    on neutralism, 179, 365, 386, 408, 439, 478
Thimm, Jacqueline, 77, 229, *229*
Thinh, Nguyen Kim, 532
Tho, Mr. (believer), 298
Tho, Le Duc, 375, 458
Tho, Nguyen Huu, 179
Tho, Nguyen Ngoc, 142

Thomas, David, 280-82, *281*
Thompson, Rich, 457
Thong, Nguyen, 428, *428*, 488
Thu, Rev. Bui Hoanh, 526, *531*, 532
Thu Huong, Dang Thi (believer), 360
Thuan, Tran Thi, 366
Thuat (work camp leader), 181-82
Thuc, Ngo Dinh, 128, 150,
Thuoc, Mrs., *435*, 454
Thuong, Do Van, 410, 477, 487
    church ministries, 510-11, 513-14, 523, 527
Tien (nurse), 376
Tien, Col. Chau Van, 397-97
Tien, Nguyen Van, 497, 535
Tieu, Tan Nhat, 483, 522
Tiessen, Betty, 255
Time Magazine, 101, 147
Times of Vietnam, The, 135
Tin, Col. Bui, 516
Tin, Nguyen Dinh, *512*, 527
    church ministries, 360, 445, 487, 512
    with MCC, 458, 512, 522
Tin, Rev. Pham Xuan, 53, *107*, 107-8, 111, 136,
    448, 510, 533
Tin, U Thuang, 191
Tin Lanh. *See* Evangelical Church of Vietnam
Toan, Rev. Kieu, 533
Ton, Rev., 376,
Tonkin Gulf incident, 153, 382
Tot, Rev. Nguyen Van, 53
Trac, Mrs. Cuu, 345, 395
Tran, Jonathan, 542
Trang Den, 515
Tranh (believer), 179
Tranh, Rev. Phan Van, 87, 236
Tri, Do Duc, 102, 18,
Tri Quang, Thich, 151, 212, 478
Trinh, Lam Le, 94
Trong (believer), 420-21, *421*
Troyer, Dana, 256, *256*
Truman, Harry S., 6
Trung, Nguyen Quang, 176, 360, 385, *486*
    church chairman, 533-34, 511
    church ministries, 180-81, 232, 418, 514, 527
    Gia Dinh Center, 176, 384-85, 405
    Trung and Bich family, 329, 405
Trung, Lt. Nguyen Thanh, 503
Trung Tin, 178
Truong Minh Giang congregation, 66, 99, 348
Tsuchiya, Rev. Kazuomi, 228
Tu, Nguyen Van, 171, 181, 289, 331

Tunnel, Gene, 491
Tung, Hoang Quang, 530
Tuoi, Rev., 259
Turner, Kay, 234
Tuy Hoa, 117
Tuyen, Rev. Le Khac, 474
Tuyet, 409-10, *410*
two-kingdom theology, 198, 305-6, 416
Ty, Ho Trung, 174, 231, 289
Ty, Mrs., *See* Hoang, Nguyen Thi
typhoons and floods, 1957, 51
     1961, 111, 120
     1964, 159-61; 1973, 457

U

U Thant, 387
unexploded ordnance (UXO), 417, 465-67, 542
United Evangelical Church, 526, 533
US Agency for International Development, 8, 136,
     191, 407-8
    aid as a bribe, 268, 269
    infrastructure development, 243
    medical programs, 243
    merged into OCO, 245, 258, 272-73, 275-77
    offer to Nha Trang hospital, 464
    wanted VNCS contract, 260-61, 272
US armed forces
    appearance of occupation, 225, 226
    atrocities, 199, 283, 324, 368, 370
    attempted POW liberation, 386
    B-52 bombing, 174-75, *175*, 213, 282, 438-
     39, 441, 442
    bombing Cambodia, 380
    bombing North Vietnam, 153, 166, 211, 441, 415
     "David vs. Goliath," 153
    casualties, 95, 128, 159, 211, 219, 241, 306,
     347, 349, 371
    chaplains, 149, 218, 441
    combat soldiers introduced, 169
    construction conglomerates, 245, 407
    "creating" refugees, 259-61
    evacuation from Vietnam, 166, 448, 500, 505
    hi-tech warfare, 309, 420
    hospitals
     Eighth Field, 116, 118
     Third Field, 241, 282, 366, 387, 477
    invade Cambodia, 375, 380
    logistical support to MCC/VNCS, 161, 208
    Mennonites in armed forces, 377
    numbers, 128, 152, 179, 187, 211, 241, 306,
     324, 347, 371, 416
    offered commissary privileges, 206
    operations, 259-60, 263, 281
    sometimes bored, 406, 418
    strategy of attrition, 203, 305, 346, 390
    veterans, 542
    volunteer work, 149, 195, 244
    weapons, 309, 311
US Congress, 153, 349, 472, 477, 487
US Congressional visits, 153, 380-81, 492, 528
US Congressional persons, 142, 208, 380, 424, 427,
    472-73
US construction consortium, 245, 407
US contacts with North Vietnam, 251, 284, 346
US Embassy, 277
US Operations Mission, 13, 17-18, 42, 119, 176
    proposed MCC program, 42

V

van Beyma, Ulrich H., 65, 68, 83,
van den Brandeler, Adrian, 83, 108
Van (Bay), Le Thi, *291*, 341, 362, 421, *421*
Van, Nguyen Van, 87, 91, 218, 396
Van, Tran Van, 240
Van Kiep center, 468
Vann, John Paul, 396
Ve, Maj. Nguyen Van, 245, 253, 381
Viet Cong
    assassinated local officials, 128, 184-85, 240, 267
    attack bases, 166
    casualties, 347
    disrupted rail lines, 111
    incidents in Saigon, 143, 164, 170, 175, 239, 284,
     328, 354, 360, 425, *See also* Tet Offensive
    kidnapped missionaries, 113-15
    named, 108
Viet Minh forces, 6, 16
Viet-My Committee, 530
Vietnam Christian Service, 247, 273-74, 542
    administered by CWS, 359, 363, 376
    administered by MCC, 205, 210, 217, 307,
     347, 358
     Consultitive Committee, 210, 359
    administrative team, 307, 322, 327, 334, 396
    advocate for peace, 211, 214, 249-50, 323, 381
    autonomy, need for, 214
    Christian presence, 347, 392, 408
    conferences, 252, 401
    expectations for staff, 220-21, 248, 339-40
     staff orientation, 207, 218, 363
     staff views, 350
    forced change of ARVN tactics, 396-97

honored by GVN, 191, 271
identity issues, 242, 258, 260-61, 273-74, 316
internationalize staff, 220
language learning, 207, 343, 408
local staff, 221, 343-44
MCC transitioning, 402-3, 409
Memo of Understanding, 196, 205
minimize US logistical support, 210, 218, 242
name, 205-6, 269
objectives and philosophy, 210, 339-40
personnel and assignments, 211, 242, 243, 249, 342, 371, 376
personnel recruited, 205-6, 216, 220, 321, 343
post-hostilities planning, 308, 316
programs, 252, 327, 334, 408. *See also* Nha Trang and Pleiku Clinics, and Ban Me Thuot, Con Son, Di Linh, Dong Ha Quang Tri, Na Be, Quang Ngai, Saigon (Khanh Hoi-Xom Chieu, Cho Quan Hospital), Tam Ky programs.
program review, 249
program with WRC, 211-12
relations with C&MA, 208
relations with ECVN, 208, 210-11, 217-18, 247-48, 363
relations with Mennonite Mission, 321
relations with USAID, 211, 242, 260-261, 272-73
relations with US armed forces, 244, 267, 377
offered commissary privileges, 206-7
program reviews, 307
rebuilding program, 342
after revolution, 523
security concerns, 207-8, 213-14, 338-39
staff evacuations, 212
staff fatalities, 386, 392
staff terminations, 350
early terminations, 307, 322
staff travel, 208, 286
working in NLF zones, 240, 382
worship, 213, 221, 287
Vietnam countryside, 41, 72-73
Vietnam Mennonite Church, 170-72, 543
alike/different from ECVN churches, 348, 398
Bible School, 360, 372, 405, 430, 468, 484
catechism, 164, 228
characteristics, 280, 294, 345, 357
children's ministries, 177, 232
contributions, 353, 380, 425, 446
discipline, 446
dynamic church life, 178, 364-65, 424, 445-46, 478

congregational life, 345, 398, 487, 509
evangelism, 340-41, 345, 348
family devotions, 424
form house groups, 511
home Bible studies, 289
greet North Vietnam church, 387
growing pains, 142
international visitors, 61, 384, 412, 435-36, 484
members, 171-72, 225, 231, 298, 340-41, 348, 478
ECVN Christians, 236, 333
missionaries, 172, 372
meet with Baptist church, 292
military service, 149, 280-81, 344
on missionaries leaving, 505, 511,
organization, 165
Congregational Council (Ban Đại Diện), 180-81, 231, 232, 505, 511, 514
Administrative Council (Ban Quản Trị), 378, 398
Joint Administrative Council, 398, 409, 413, 417, 418-19, 430, 450, 477
Church Administrative Committee, 477, 527
Elders/pastoral assistants, 444
deacons, 378, 444,
peace prayers, 428
peace teaching, 168, 175, 364, 398
publication, 376
relate to ECVN, 341, 398
relate to GOV, 297, 378
after revolution, 524-28, 542-43
rituals:
baptisms, 170, 344-45, 348, 356, 410, 478
communion, 143, 225
foot washing, 143, 225, 348
funerals, 373, 405
ordination, 354
weddings, 288, 296
secure church center, 412-13, 417
building dedication, 423, 436, 441, 444
service programs, 328
Sunday school, 372
Tet Offensive, 319, 332
wanted missionaries to stay, 505
welcomed Paris Peace Accord, 442
women's meetings, 469
worship services, 178, 239, 288, 332
Christmas, 348, 484-85, 536,
Easter, 228, 284, 356, 376, 405, 424, 498
Tet, 353, 372-73, 420-21, 444

youth, 445
Vietnam Mennonite Mission,
    assist MCC/VNCS, 192, 195, 232
    board of directors approved, 419
    commitment to Vietnam, 475
    evangelism, 225
    government registration, 93-94, 101, 149-50
    literature, 165
        Bible correspondence courses, 235, 421
    Mission Council, 149, 232, 331, 383
        prepare statements on war, 181, 198, 407.
            See also public statements
        study and prayer, 142
    mission philosophy, 87, 168
        a Vietnam presence, 145-46
    mission strategy, 78, 80, 83, 87-88, 125, 144,
        225, 226
    News and Concerns newsletter, 80
    peace advocacy, 197, 387
    peace witness, 232
    personnel assignments, 98, 154, 231, 235, 359,
        364, 383, 385, 400, 407
    radio program, 235
    relations with ECVN, 84, 121, 135, 157, 281,
        321, 357
        complementary to ECVN, 149, 134, 225,
            398
    relations with MCC, 84
    relations with US forces, 146, 149, 378
    relations with VNCS, 357
    relation to government, 198, 377-78, 386
    team Bible study and prayer meetings, 419
    team conferences, 183, 404, 407, 413, 423,
        438, 446, 457, 475
        joint with MCC, 450, 465, 484
    training program, 232
Vietnamese culture and customs
    death/funerals, 224, 239, 373, 376
    weddings, 225, 453
    festivals
        Christmas, 72, 185-86
        Children's Autumn, 157, 181, 237-38
        Tat Nien, 166
        Tet Nguyen Dan, 74-75, 166, 224, 372, 421
    food, 129-30
    language, 124, 129, 169
    legends, 138
    sayings, 236, 395, 525
Vietnamese people
    characteristics, 293
    education important, 226

family dynamics, 67, 165, 169
fled in 1975, 524
held various views
    about Americans, 209
    of communism, 170, 222, 239, 252, 346,
        365, 488, 494, 540
    of Mennonite missionaries, 185, 236, 237
    of Saigon government, 344, 365
    of US involvement, 146, 182, 297, 301
    of war, 170, 177, 208, 210, 219, 231,
        304, 369-70, 430
resilient, 160
religious views, 96
rural-urban divide, 153
sensitive, 116-17, 176-77
resolving conflict, 356
students, 57, 282, 381, 430
Vietnamization, 349, 370, 371, 415, 426
Vietti, E. Ardel, 39, 45, 49, *109*, 113, 116, 126-127
Vogel, Lynn, 392-96, 408
Vogel, Betty, 392
Vong, Rev. Nguyen Xuan, 188
Voth, Donald, 45, 46-48, *48*, 103, *109*, 109-11,
    332, 334
Vung Tau, 77, 361
Vuong (pastor), 159

W

Walton, Frank, 381
Walton, Maj. Spencer, 117
War, The
    aspects of civil war, 149
    ARVN. *See* Army of Republic of Vietnam
    casualties, 208, 219, 239, 241, 306, 318, 347
    civilian, 208, 224, 238, 268, 288-89, 292
    civilian pawns, 131-32, 164, 179, 234-35, 374-75
    ended, 516
    perpetrated by US, 147, 210, 212, 222, 517
    truces, 224, 241
    war effects, 174, 294, 296
        black markets, 191
        economic difficulties, 140, 180, 404, 419-20
        food, 239, 243
        housing, travel, 183, 226
        inflation, 236, 370
        prostitution, 218, 373
    refugees. *See* refugees
War, Mennonite missionaries' comments, 168. *See
    also* public statements against war
    Beidler, Luke, 406
    Everett Metzler, 183, 234

Don Sensenig, 230, 237, 317-18
James Metzler, 229-30, 293, 298-99
James Stauffer, 238, 301, 415, 431
Margaret Metzler, 180
Luke Martin, 169, 177, 179, 390
Mary Martin, 237, 425
Washington Post, 390, 397, 536
Weaver, Elnora, 48, *48*
Weaver, Elsie and Steve, 449
Weaver, Winston, 296
Weber, Marcella, 191, 334, 395-96, *396*
Webber, Dr. J. M., 20, 36
Westmoreland, William, 151, 191, 243, 308-9
    strategy, 203, 258, 305, 324
Weidner, Mark, 285
Weidner, Mark and Susan, 267
Wheeler, Gen. Earle, 324
Wiebe, Vernon, 427
Wiens, Delbert, 4, 7-8, *13*, 43, 42, 50-51
    begin MCC programs, 7-10, 12, 13, 15-20
    meet President Diem, 17, 37
    work with CWS, 18, 65
Willms family, John and Frances, 496, 508, 516
Willms, Dr. John, 475, 490
Wilting, Ruth, 113, *126*, 126-127, 310,
"winning hearts and minds," 193, 243, 336
Witmer, John, 134
Wiwcharuck, Peter, 286-87
Woodruff, Lance, 250, 264
Workers' Party, 82
World Council of Churches, 60, 90-91, 108, 187,
    347, 518
World Relief Commission, 108, 191, 212, 345
World Student Christian Federation, 59, 60

World Vision, 149, 245, 286, 296
Wycliffe Bible Translators. *See* SIL
Wyse, Don, 464
Wyse, Joyce, 458
Wyse, Don & Joyce, 454, 474

X

Xinh, Mrs. (believer), 298
Xom Chieu (*See* Khanh Hoi)
Xom Gia (Saigon), program, 379, 395
Xuan (believer), 421, *421*
Xuan Oanh, Do, 530, 535
Xuyen, Rev. Nguyen Van, 515

Y

Y, Huynh Minh, 64, 93, 422
Y, Le Thi, 475
Y'Ham (pastor), 47
Yano, Teruko, 385, 411, 412, 456
Y'Dun Ksor, 37, *38*, 50
Y'Don Ksor and H'Chioh, 37
Young, Ron, 381
Young Men's Christian Association, 56, 60, 457
Yoder, Carl, 162, *162*, 187, *187*
Yoder, Phyllis, *162*
Yoder family, Carl & Phyllis, 117, 182, 173
Yoder, John Howard, 16, 202, 335-39, 465
Yoder, Ruth, 206, 216, 256, 337, 366, 383
Yoder, Samuel and Ethel, 61, 132
Yong (medical assistant), 395

Z

Zehr, Daniel, 530, *531*, 536
Zeimer, N. Robert, 48, 319